Date on Database

Writings 2000–2006

C. J. Date

Apress®

ISBN-13 (hc): 978-1-59059-746-0 [*Originally published as a hardcover first edition on November 21, 2006.*]

ISBN-13 (pbk): 978-1-4302-4308-3

ISBN-13 (electronic): 978-1-4302-4309-0

Trademarked names, logos, and images may appear in this book. Rather than use a trademark symbol with every occurrence of a trademarked name, logo, or image we use the names, logos, and images only in an editorial fashion and to the benefit of the trademark owner, with no intention of infringement of the trademark.

The use in this publication of trade names, trademarks, service marks, and similar terms, even if they are not identified as such, is not to be taken as an expression of opinion as to whether or not they are subject to proprietary rights.

While the advice and information in this book are believed to be true and accurate at the date of publication, neither the authors nor the editors nor the publisher can accept any legal responsibility for any errors or omissions that may be made. The publisher makes no warranty, express or implied, with respect to the material contained herein.

President and Publisher: Paul Manning
Lead Editor: Jonathan Gennick
Editorial Board: Steve Anglin, Mark Beckner, Ewan Buckingham, Gary Cornell, Morgan Ertel, Jonathan Gennick, Jonathan Hassell, Robert Hutchinson, Michelle Lowman, James Markham, Matthew Moodie, Jeff Olson, Jeffrey Pepper, Douglas Pundick, Ben Renow-Clarke, Dominic Shakeshaft, Gwenan Spearing, Matt Wade, Tom Welsh
Coordinating Editor: Tracy Brown Collins
Copy Editor: Nicole LeClerc
Compositor: Susan Glinert
Indexer: C. J. Date
Cover Designer: Anna Ishchenko

Distributed to the book trade worldwide by Springer Science+Business Media New York, 233 Spring Street, 6th Floor, New York, NY 10013. Phone 1-800-SPRINGER, fax (201) 348-4505, e-mail orders-ny@springer-sbm.com, or visit www.springeronline.com.

For information on translations, please e-mail rights@apress.com, or visit www.apress.com.

Apress and friends of ED books may be purchased in bulk for academic, corporate, or promotional use. eBook versions and licenses are also available for most titles. For more information, reference our Special Bulk Sales–eBook Licensing web page at www.apress.com/bulk-sales.

Any source code or other supplementary materials referenced by the author in this text is available to readers at www.apress.com. For detailed information about how to locate your book's source code, go to www.apress.com/source-code/.

Dedicated to the memory of John Lennon and George Harrison

Treason doth never prosper, what's the reason?
For if it prosper, none dare call it treason.

—Sir John Harington

Contents at a Glance

Contents

PART 1 ▪▪▪ Some Preliminaries

PART 2 ■■■ And Now for Something Completely Different

PART 3 ▪▪▪ Relational Database Management

CHAPTER 12   Data Redundancy and Database Design 217

**CHAPTER 13   Data Redundancy and Database Design:
Further Thoughts Number One** 255

PART 4 ▪▪▪ SQL Database Management

PART 5 ■■■ Further Relational Misconceptions

PART 6 ▪▪▪ Subtyping and Inheritance

PART 7 ▪▪▪ Relational *vs.* Nonrelational Systems

About the Author

C. J. DATE is an independent author, lecturer, researcher, and consultant, specializing in relational database technology. He is best known for his book *An Introduction to Database Systems* (8th edition, Addison-Wesley, 2004), which has sold over three quarters of a million copies at the time of writing and is used by several hundred colleges and universities worldwide. He is also the author of many other books on database management, including most recently:

- From Morgan Kaufmann: *Temporal Data and the Relational Model* (coauthored with Hugh Darwen and Nikos A. Lorentzos, 2003)

- From Addison-Wesley: *An Introduction to Database Systems* (8th edition, 2004)

- From O'Reilly: *Database in Depth: Relational Theory for Practitioners* (2005)

- From Addison-Wesley: *Databases, Types, and the Relational Model: The Third Manifesto* (3rd edition, coauthored with Hugh Darwen, 2006)

- From O'Reilly: *The Relational Database Dictionary* (2006)

Another book, *Go Faster! The TransRelational^t*™ *Approach to DBMS Implementation*, is due for publication in the near future.

Mr. Date was inducted into the Computing Industry Hall of Fame in 2004. He enjoys a reputation that is second to none for his ability to communicate complex technical subjects in a clear and understandable fashion.

Publishing History

Edgar F. Codd: A Tribute and Personal Memoir

Originally published in *ACM SIGMOD Record 32*, No. 4 (December 2003). Reprinted by permission of ACM.

An Interview with Chris Date

Originally published on the website http://www.oreilly.com (July 2005). Reprinted by permission of O'Reilly Media, Inc. and Tony Williams.

Good Writing Does Matter

Originally published in two parts as *Commentary* in the *Business Rules Journal* on the website http://www.BRCommunity.com (February and April 2002). Reprinted by permission of Business Rule Solutions, Inc.

On the Notion of Logical Difference; On the Logical Difference Between Model and Implementation; On the Logical Differences Between Types, Values, and Variables

Originally published (the last in two parts) on the website `http://www.dbdebunk.com` (July 2004). Reprinted by permission of Fabian Pascal.

Why We Need Type BOOLEAN

Originally published as *Commentary* in the *Business Rules Journal* on the website `http://www.BRCommunity.com` (May 2004). Reprinted by permission of Business Rule Solutions, Inc.

What First Normal Form Really Means

Originally published on the website `http://www.dbdebunk.com` (June 2003). Reprinted by permission of Fabian Pascal.

A Sweet Disorder

Originally published on the website `http://www.dbdebunk.com` (August 2003). Reprinted by permission of Fabian Pascal.

Double Trouble, Double Trouble

Originally published in two parts on the website `http://www.dbdebunk.com` (April 2002). Reprinted by permission of Fabian Pascal.

Multiple Assignment

Originally published on the website `http://www.dbdebunk.com` (February 2004). Reprinted by permission of Hugh Darwen and Fabian Pascal.

Data Redundancy and Database Design

Originally published in two parts on the website `http://www.dbdebunk.com` (March and April 2005). Reprinted by permission of Fabian Pascal.

Data Redundancy and Database Design: Further Thoughts Number One

Originally published on the website `http://www.dbdebunk.com` (July 2005). Reprinted by permission of Fabian Pascal.

Tree-Structured Data

Originally published on the website `http://www.dbdebunk.com` (November 2004). Reprinted by permission of Fabian Pascal.

Twelve Rules for Business Rules

Originally published as a White Paper by Versata Inc. (`http://www.versata.com`, May 1st, 2000). Reprinted by permission of Versata Inc.

Two Remarks on SQL's UNION

Originally published in the *Business Rules Journal* on the website http://www.BRCommunity.com (August 2004). Reprinted by permission of Business Rule Solutions, Inc.

A Cure for Madness

Originally published in two parts on the website http://www.dbdebunk.com (August/September 2004). Reprinted by permission of Fabian Pascal.

Why Three- and Four-Valued Logic Don't Work

Originally published on the website http://www.dbdebunk.com (February 2006). Reprinted by permission of Fabian Pascal.

There's Only One Relational Model

Originally published on the website http://www.dbdebunk.com (February 2001). Reprinted by permission of Fabian Pascal.

The Relational Model Is Very Much Alive!

Originally published on the website http://www.dbdebunk.com (August 2000). Reprinted by permission of Fabian Pascal.

What Do You Mean, "Post-Relational"?

Originally published on the website http://www.dbdebunk.com (June 2000). Reprinted by permission of Fabian Pascal.

A Database Disconnect

Originally published on the website http://www.dbdebunk.com (March 2003). Reprinted by permission of Fabian Pascal.

Is a Circle an Ellipse?

Originally published on the website http://www.dbdebunk.com (July 2001). Reprinted by permission of Fabian Pascal.

What Does Substitutability Really Mean?

Originally published in three parts on the website http://www.dbdebunk.com (July 2002). Reprinted by permission of Fabian Pascal.

Models, Models, Everywhere, Nor Any Time to Think

Originally published on the website http://www.dbdebunk.com (November 2000). Reprinted by permission of Fabian Pascal.

Basic Concepts in UML: A Request for Clarification

Originally published in two parts on the website http://www.dbdebunk.com (December 2000, January 2001). Reprinted by permission of Fabian Pascal.

A Comparison Between ODMG and The Third Manifesto

Originally published in *Foundation for Future Database Systems: The Third Manifesto* (2nd edition, Addison-Wesley, 2000, pp 448–471), by C. J. Date and Hugh Darwen. Reprinted by permission of Pearson Education, Inc., Upper Saddle River, New Jersey, and Hugh Darwen.

An Overview and Analysis of Proposals Based on the TSQL2 Approach

Originally published on the website `http://www.thethirdmanifesto.com` (October 2002, revised September 2003; further revised March 2005). Reprinted by permission of Hugh Darwen.

The Role of the Trade Press in Educating the Professional Community: A Case Study

Originally published on the website `http://www.alternativetech.com` (July 2000). Reprinted by permission of David McGoveran.

Acknowledgments

I'd like to acknowledge the helpful suggestions and comments on earlier drafts of some of the chapters, and other technical assistance received, from various friends and colleagues: Manish Chandra, Hugh Darwen, Mike DeVries, Jonathan Gennick, Val Huber, Jonathan Leffler, David McGoveran, Gary Morgenthaler, Dan Muller, Fabian Pascal, Lauri Pietarinen, Ron Ross, Nick Tindall, Stephen Wilson, and Gene Wong. I'd also like to thank my wife, Lindy, for her support throughout the production of this book and all of its predecessors.

As for my editor, Jonathan Gennick, and all of the other staff at Apress, their assistance has been as friendly, obliging, and professional as I could possibly hope for. It's been a pleasure to work with them.

C. J. Date
Healdsburg, California, 2006

Preface

This book is the seventh in a series. All but one of its predecessors were published by Addison-Wesley (in 1986, 1990, 1992, 1995, and 1998, respectively); the exception was privately published by myself this year (2006). Like those predecessors, it consists of a collection of papers on the general topic of relational database technology—basically all those of my papers from the period 2000 to 2006 that seem to me worth preserving in some more permanent form.

The book is arranged into seven parts, as follows:

Part 1: Some Preliminaries

Part 2: And Now for Something Completely Different

Part 3: Relational Database Management

Part 4: SQL Database Management

Part 5: Further Relational Misconceptions

Part 6: Subtyping and Inheritance

Part 7: Relational *vs.* Nonrelational Systems

Each part has its own introduction, and I'll leave further details of individual papers to those introductions. There's also an appendix, documenting my experience (such as it was) in trying to enlist the help of the trade press in my self-appointed mission to educate the database community on matters to do with relational technology.

A brief note on the book's structure: As with earlier books in this series, most of the chapters were originally intended to stand alone; as a result, each typically contains references and examples—sometimes even appendixes—whose numbering is unique only within the chapter in question. To a very large degree, I've preserved the independence of individual chapters; thus, all references within a given chapter to, say, Example 3 or Appendix A are to be taken as references to the indicated example or appendix within the chapter in question. There is also, I fear, a small amount of overlap among certain of the chapters; I apologize for this fact, but felt it was better, as already indicated, to preserve the independence of each individual chapter as much as possible.

I also need to say a word about SQL. A book of this nature inevitably contains many references to—sometimes detailed discussions regarding—the SQL language. As is well known, however, there are many distinct dialects of that language (at least as many as there are commercial SQL products). Please understand, therefore, that all references to SQL throughout the book refer specifically to the standard form of that language, barring explicit remarks to the contrary; deviations from that standard found in some particular product are generally not discussed.

PART 1

■■■

Some Preliminaries

This first part of the book is a bit of a potpourri. It consists of three chapters. Chapter 1 is a tribute I wrote to mark the occasion of Ted Codd's passing in 2003; Ted was the inventor of the relational model and has a legitimate claim to being the father of our field, and I can't think of a better way to open the book than with such a tribute. Chapter 2 contains the text of an interview I did to mark the publication of my book *Database in Depth: Relational Theory for Practitioners* (O'Reilly Media Inc., 2005); I include that interview here because it contains, among many other things, my best attempt at justifying my strong claim that *theory is practical!* Finally, Chapter 3 explains the concept of deconstruction as a technique for criticizing technical (and other) writing, and illustrates that technique with reference to some SQL writings specifically. All three of these chapters are directly relevant to what follows in later parts of the book.

CHAPTER 1

Edgar F. Codd: A Tribute and Personal Memoir

This is an expanded version of a piece that originally appeared on the SIGMOD website (`http://www.acm.org/sigmod`) in May 2003. Here's the opening paragraph from that earlier piece:

> *By now there cannot be many in the database community who are unaware that, sadly, Dr. E. F. Codd passed away on April 18th, 2003. He was 79. Dr. Codd, known universally to his colleagues and friends—among whom I was proud to count myself—as Ted, was the man who, singlehanded, put the field of database management on a solid scientific footing. The entire relational database industry, now worth many billions of dollars a year, owes the fact of its existence to Ted's original work, and the same is true of all of the huge number of relational database research and teaching programs under way worldwide in universities and similar organizations. Indeed, all of us who work in this field owe our career and livelihood to the giant contributions Ted made during the period from the late 1960s to the early 1980s. We all owe him a huge debt. This tribute to Ted and his achievements is offered in recognition of that debt.*

However, I've discovered I was operating on a false assumption when I wrote this paragraph. To be more specific, I've found—and it's a sad comment on the state of our field that I feel I have to say this—that many database practitioners, and even some researchers, really don't know who Ted was or what he did. In my own day-to-day database activities (for example, on the seminars I teach), I often encounter people who've never even heard of him! So I thought it would be a good idea to amplify and republish my original tribute: in particular, to elaborate briefly on the nature of some of Ted's numerous technical contributions. I'd also like to say a little more about "Ted the man"—i.e., Ted Codd as I personally remember him, and what he meant to me.

Background

Ted Codd was a native of England and a Royal Air Force veteran of World War II. He moved to the United States after the war and became a naturalized U.S. citizen. He held M.A. degrees in mathematics and chemistry from Oxford University and M.S. and Ph.D. degrees in communication sciences from the University of Michigan.

Ted began his computing career in 1949 as a programming mathematician for IBM on the Selective Sequence Electronic Calculator. He subsequently participated in the development of several important IBM products, including the 701, IBM's first commercial electronic computer, and STRETCH, which led to IBM's 7090 mainframe technology. Then, in the late 1960s, he turned his attention to the problem of database management—and over the next several years he created the invention with which his name will forever be associated: **the relational model of data**.

Database Contributions

Ted Codd's relational model is widely recognized as one of the great technical innovations of the 20th century. Ted described it and explored its implications in a series of research papers—staggering in their originality—that he published during the period from 1969 to 1981. The effect of those papers was twofold:

- First, they changed for good the way the IT world perceived the database management problem.

- Second, as already mentioned, they laid the foundation for a whole new industry.

In fact, they provided the basis for a technology that has had, and continues to have, a major impact on the very fabric of our society. It's no exaggeration to say that Ted is the intellectual father of the modern database field.

To give some idea of the scope and extent of Ted's accomplishments, I'd like to highlight in this section what seem to me the most significant of his database contributions. Of course, the biggest of all was, as already mentioned, to make database management into a science (and thereby to introduce a welcome and sorely needed note of clarity and rigor into the field): The relational model provides a theoretical framework within which a variety of important problems can be attacked in a scientific manner. Ted first described his model in 1969 in an IBM Research Report:

"Derivability, Redundancy, and Consistency of Relations Stored in Large Data Banks," IBM Research Report RJ599 (August 19th, 1969)

He also published a revised version of this paper the following year:

"A Relational Model of Data for Large Shared Data Banks," *CACM 13*, No. 6 (June 1970) and elsewhere[1]

(This latter—i.e., the 1970 paper—is usually credited with being the seminal paper in the field, though this characterization is a little unfair to its 1969 predecessor.) Almost all of the novel ideas described in outline in the remainder of this section, as well as numerous subsequent technical developments, were foreshadowed or at least hinted at in these first two papers; in fact, some of those ideas remain less than fully explored to this day. In my opinion, everyone professionally involved in database management should read, and reread, at least one of these papers every year. (It's true they're not all that *easy* to read, being fairly abstract and somewhat mathematical in tone. On the other hand, they stand up extremely well to being read, and

---

1. Many of Ted's papers were published in several places. Here I'll just give the primary sources.

indeed repeatedly reread, over 30 years after they were written! How many technical papers can you say that of?)

Incidentally, it's not as widely known as it should be that Ted not only invented the relational model in particular, he invented the whole concept of a *data model* in general. See his paper:

"Data Models in Database Management," *ACM SIGMOD Record 11*, No. 2 (February 1981)

This was the first of Ted's papers to include a definition of the term *data model*. It also addressed the question: What purposes are data models in general, and the relational model in particular, intended to serve? And it then went on to offer evidence in support of the claim that, contrary to popular belief, the relational model was the first data model to be defined. (The so-called hierarchic and network models, which are often thought to have predated the relational model, were actually defined after the fact by a process of induction—in this context, a polite word for guesswork—from existing implementations.)

In connection with both the relational model in particular and data models in general, the paper also stressed the importance of the distinction, regrettably underappreciated even today, between a data model and its physical implementation.

Ted also saw the potential of using *predicate logic* as a foundation for a database language. He discussed this possibility briefly in his 1969 and 1970 papers, and then, using the predicate logic idea as a basis, went on to describe in detail what was probably the very first relational language to be defined, *Data Sublanguage ALPHA*, in:

"A Data Base Sublanguage Founded on the Relational Calculus," Proc. 1971 ACM SIGFIDET Workshop on Data Description, Access and Control, San Diego, Calif. (November 1971)

ALPHA as such was never implemented, but it was extremely influential on certain other languages that were, including in particular the Ingres language QUEL and (to a much lesser extent) the IBM language SQL as well.

If I might be permitted a personal anecdote at this point, I remember being invited, in 1974, to Anaheim, California, to present the basic ideas of the relational model to the GUIDE Database Language Working Group. (I probably don't have that title quite right, but it was a project within GUIDE, the IBM user group, to examine possible programming language extensions for database access.) Members of the working group had coded five sample applications using various database products of the time (TOTAL, IDS, IMS, etc.), and the meeting began with those various solutions being presented. I distinctly remember the group's reaction (chiefly amazement, mingled with delight) when I was able to show that each of their applications—which I came to stone cold, never having seen them before that afternoon—involved *just one line* of ALPHA code! At that point, the IBM representative to the group took me off to one side and told me "not to come on too strong about this relational stuff." I said: "Why not?" He said: "Because we don't have a product." To which I answered: "Then maybe we should get one." SQL/DS was announced a mere seven years later ...

Back to Ted. Ted subsequently defined the *relational calculus* more formally, as well as the *relational algebra*, in:

"Relational Completeness of Data Base Sublanguages," in Randall J. Rustin (ed.), *Data Base Systems: Courant Computer Science Symposia Series 6* (Prentice-Hall, 1972)

Very loosely speaking, relational calculus provides a notation for *defining* some desired relation (typically the result of some query) in terms of others, while relational algebra provides a set of operators for *computing* some desired relation from others. Clearly, each could be used as a basis on which to define a query language. As I've already indicated, QUEL is an example of a language that's based on the calculus. SQL, by contrast, is a mixture: It includes some elements that are calculus-based, others that are algebra-based, and still others that are neither.

As the title indicates, the paper also introduced the notion of *relational completeness* as a basic measure of the expressive power of a database language. Essentially, a language is said to be relationally complete if it's as powerful as the calculus. To quote: "A query language ... which is claimed to be general purpose should be at least relationally complete in the sense defined in this paper. [Such a language need never resort] to programming loops or any other form of branched execution—an important consideration when interrogating a [database] from a terminal."

The same paper also described an algorithm—*Codd's reduction algorithm*—for transforming an arbitrary expression of the calculus into an equivalent expression in the algebra, thereby (a) proving the algebra is relationally complete and (b) providing a basis for implementing the calculus.

Ted also introduced the concept of *functional dependence* and defined the first three *normal forms* (1NF, 2NF, 3NF). See the papers:

"Normalized Data Base Structure: A Brief Tutorial," Proc. 1971 ACM SIGFIDET Workshop on Data Description, Access, and Control, San Diego, Calif. (November 11th–12th, 1971)

"Further Normalization of the Data Base Relational Model," in Randall J. Rustin (ed.), *Data Base Systems: Courant Computer Science Symposia Series 6* (Prentice-Hall, 1972)

Simplifying considerably, we can say that:

- Given relation R, attribute B of R is functionally dependent on attribute A of R—equivalently, the functional dependence (FD) $A \rightarrow B$ holds in R—if and only if, whenever two tuples of R have the same value for A, they also have the same value for B.

- Relation R is in third normal form, 3NF, if and only if the only FDs that hold in R are of the form $K \rightarrow B$, where K is a key. (In the interests of accuracy, I should say that this is really a definition of what subsequently became known as *Boyce/Codd normal form*, BCNF, not 3NF as such. Part of the confusion arises from the fact that Ted himself referred to BCNF as "third" normal form for some years.)

Between them, Ted's two normalization papers laid the foundations for the entire field of what is now known as *dependency theory*, an important branch of database science in its own right. Among other things, that theory serves as a basis for a truly scientific approach to the problem of logical database design.

As an aside, I note that the first of the two papers, the tutorial one, also includes arguments for excluding pointers from the user's view of the database. The relational model's total ban on pointers is just one of many factors that sharply distinguish it from its competitors. Indeed, any language that exposes pointers to the user, in any shape or form, forfeits all right to be called relational—and the introduction of pointers into the SQL standard in particular can thus only be deplored. But I digress.

There's something else I'd like to say here. Normalization is sometimes criticized on the grounds that "it's all really just common sense"; any competent professional would "naturally" design databases to be fully normalized anyway, without having to know anything about dependency theory at all. In other words, the problems with less than fully normalized designs are "obvious," and common sense is sufficient to tell us that fully normalized designs are better. But what do we mean by "common sense"? What are the *principles* (inside the designer's brain) that the designer is applying when he or she chooses a fully normalized design? The answer is, of course, that they're exactly the principles of normalization. In other words, those principles are indeed just common sense—but (and here comes the point) they're *formalized* common sense. The whole point is to try to identify such principles and formalize them—which isn't an easy thing to do! But if it can be done, then we can *mechanize* them; in other words, we can get the machine to do the work. Critics of normalization usually miss this point; they claim, quite rightly, that the ideas are all basically common sense, but they typically don't realize that it's a significant achievement to state what "common sense" means in a precise and formal way.

Yet another crucial notion introduced by Ted was that of *essentiality*. Ted defined that notion in:

"Interactive Support for Nonprogrammers: The Relational and Network Approaches,"
Proc. ACM SIGMOD Workshop on Data Description, Access, and Control, Vol. II,
Ann Arbor, Michigan (May 1974)

This paper was Ted's principal written contribution to "The Great Debate." The Great Debate—the official title was *Data Models: Data-Structure-Set vs. Relational*—was a special event held at the 1974 SIGMOD Workshop; it was subsequently characterized in *CACM* by Robert L. Ashenhurst as "a milestone event of the kind too seldom witnessed in our field." (I should explain that "the data-structure-set model" is just the CODASYL network model by another name.)

The concept of essentiality, introduced by Ted in this debate, is a great aid to clear thinking in discussions regarding the nature of data and DBMSs. Basically, an "information carrier" (in other words, a construct for the representation of data) is said to be *essential* if and only if its removal would cause a loss of information. Now, the relational model provides just one way to represent data—namely, by means of relations themselves—and the sole essential information carriers in a relational database are thus necessarily relations, *a fortiori*. By contrast, other data models typically provide many distinct ways to represent data (lists, bags, links, sets, arrays, and so on), and all or any of those ways can be used as essential information carriers in a nonrelational database. One way of representing data is both necessary and sufficient; more than one introduces complexity, but no additional power.

As a matter of fact, it's the concept of essentiality that forms the underpinning for the well-known, and important, *Information Principle:*

The entire information content of a relational database is represented in one and only one way: namely, as attribute values within tuples within relations.

I heard Ted refer to this principle on more than one occasion as *the* fundamental principle underlying the relational model. (I remark in passing that a better name for it might be *The Principle of Uniform Representation.*)

It seems appropriate to round out this discussion with a succinct, reasonably formal definition of the relational model. (This definition doesn't come from any of Ted's papers—it's my own attempt to capture the essence of what Ted was talking about in all of the papers I've been discussing, as well as many others.) Briefly, the relational model consists of five components:

1. An open-ended collection of **scalar types** (including in particular the type *boolean* or *truth value*)

2. A **relation type generator** and an intended interpretation for relations of types generated thereby

3. Facilities for defining **relation variables** of such generated relation types

4. A **relational assignment** operation for assigning relation values to such relation variables

5. An open-ended collection of generic **relational operators** ("the relational algebra") for deriving relation values from other relation values

Let me conclude this section by observing that Ted's work on the relational model didn't just set the entire field of database management on a solid scientific footing—it also provided the foundations for the careers of numerous people, myself not least (and doubtless many readers of this tribute could say the same). Not to mention the fact that there is, and continues to be, tremendous intellectual excitement, rigor, and integrity, in those foundations that Ted laid down. (By the way, I don't want to give the impression that all of the foundation-level problems have been solved. They haven't. That's partly why the field is still so rewarding!) So those of us who have continued in Ted's footsteps haven't just had a career and a livelihood, as I said before—we've had work that was, and continues to be, both interesting and useful. We all owe Ted an enormous debt of gratitude.

Other Contributions

Ted Codd's achievements with the relational model shouldn't be allowed to eclipse the fact that he made major research contributions in several other important areas as well, including *cellular automata*, *multiprogramming*, and *natural language processing*, to name just three. Other people are better qualified than I to comment on those contributions; all I'd like to do here is draw attention to some of the key references. First, the work on cellular automata is documented in a monograph by Ted:

Cellular Automata (Academic Press, 1968)

Second, Ted in fact led the team that developed IBM's very first multiprogramming system. He reported on that work in:

"Multiprogramming STRETCH: Feasibility Considerations" (with three coauthors), *CACM 2*, No. 11 (November 1959)

"Multiprogram Scheduling," Parts 1 and 2, *CACM 3*, No. 6 (June 1960); Parts 3 and 4, *CACM 3*, No. 7 (July 1960)

As for his work on natural language processing, see among other writings the paper:

"Seven Steps to Rendezvous with the Casual User," in J. W. Klimbie and K. L. Koffeman (eds.), *Data Base Management*, Proc. IFIP TC-2 Working Conference on Data Base Management (North-Holland, 1974)

Other research areas to which Ted contributed include *online analytical processing* (OLAP) and *business automation.*

In addition to all of his research activities, Ted was professionally active in several other areas as well. In particular, it doesn't seem to be widely known that he was the founder of SIGMOD! (More precisely, he founded the ACM Special Interest Committee on File Description and Translation, SICFIDET, which later became an ACM Special Interest Group, SIGFIDET, and subsequently changed its name to the Special Interest Group on Management of Data, SIGMOD.) He was also tireless in his efforts, both inside and outside IBM, to obtain the level of acceptance for the relational model that he rightly believed it deserved: efforts that were, of course, eventually crowned with success.

Note: I think perhaps I should qualify the foregoing remarks a little. It's true that the relational model is now widely accepted. At the same time ... I don't want to appear churlish, but I feel bound to say how much I regret the fact (as I'm quite sure Ted did too) that the model still hasn't been implemented either faithfully or properly. To elaborate very briefly:

- *Faithful implementation:* Today's products don't implement the model faithfully. Instead, they suffer from sins of both omission and commission: Certain important relational features aren't supported at all, while other nonrelational features are.

- *Proper implementation:* Today's products also fail in all too many ways to deliver on the full promise of the relational model (regarding data independence, for example).

Further discussion of such matters would clearly be inappropriate here, but I think it would be just as inappropriate not to mention them at all.

Personal Memories

I first met Ted in 1971. I'd been doing some database work myself for IBM in England in 1970-71, as a result of which I entered into a correspondence with Ted, and he invited me to the U.S. to present my ideas at various locations within IBM. So I got to meet Ted at the IBM San Jose Research Laboratory, where he was working at the time. I was immediately struck by his energy, and in particular by the care and precision with which he expressed himself. He was always careful never to overclaim. For example, in his paper "Further Normalization of the Data Base Relational Model," he states that one advantage of normalization is that it "[tends] to capture some aspects of the semantics (minor, of course)." I love that parenthetical remark! What a contrast to some of the overblown claims we so often encounter elsewhere in the literature.

Following our meeting in 1971, Ted and I began a collaboration—at first informal, later more formal—that lasted essentially throughout the remainder of his career. The precise nature of that cooperation varied over time, but the essence of it was that Ted continued to do research on his model and I took it on myself to present and explain his ideas at technical conferences, user group meetings, and the like. In this connection, Ted was always encouraging, supportive, and generous to me, as indeed he was to all of his friends and coworkers. For example (this is from a letter to me dated April 7th, 1972): "I am pleased to learn you are contemplating writing a [database book] ... The kind of book you propose is much needed ... I feel confident that you can produce an excellent book. You may make use of any of the material in my papers for this purpose."

Other people who had the opportunity to work with or for Ted over the years have confirmed to me what an inspiration he could be in their own endeavors.

Ted was easily one of the most unforgettable characters I ever met. He was a genius, of course—and like all geniuses he "stood at a slight angle to the rest of the universe." It wasn't just database, either. Something else he displayed his genius in was *losing things* ... When we were working together in Codd and Date Inc. (a consulting company we and Sharon Weinberg, later Sharon Codd, started in the early 1980s), I once personally saw him lose a crucial document as he crossed from one side of our office to the other. I didn't see it go—I just saw him start off with it on one side of the room and arrive at the other side without it. I don't think we ever found it again.

Another way his genius manifested itself was in a somewhat idiosyncratic sense of humor (again I suspect this is a property that is common to many geniuses). Things that most people didn't think were funny at all he would sometimes find incredibly funny; conversely, he would fail, sometimes, to see the funny side of things that other people thought were hilarious. When Sharon, Ted, and I were forming our consulting company, the question of a company logo came up, for use on business cards and the like. I said I thought the logo should incorporate a stylized picture of a table. Sharon agreed. Ted said: "I don't get it—we're not in the furniture business, are we?"

There are many, many Ted Codd stories, but I think one more here has to suffice. (I like this one, though actually I wasn't there when it happened. So it might be apocryphal. But it does have the ring of truth about it.) Apparently, when Ted was made an IBM Fellow—see the next section—he said: "It's the first time I recall someone being made an IBM Fellow for someone else's product."

Concluding Remarks

Ted was a genuine computing pioneer. And he achieved more in his lifetime than most of us ever will or could, if we had ten lifetimes. Look at the honors he was awarded (and this is only a partial list):

- IBM Fellow

- ACM Fellow

- Fellow of the British Computer Society

- Member of the National Academy of Engineering

- Member of the American Academy of Arts and Sciences

- 1981 ACM Turing Award

- Outstanding recognition award from IEEE

- First annual achievement award from IDUG

- 2001 Hall of Fame Lifetime Achievement Award from DAMA

All thoroughly deserved, of course.

Ted was an inspiration and a good friend to all of us who had the privilege, fortune, and honor to know him and work with him. It's a particular pleasure to be able to say that he was always scrupulous in giving credit to other people's contributions. Moreover, as I've already mentioned (and despite his huge achievements), he was also careful never to overclaim; he would never claim, for example, that the relational model could solve all possible problems or that it would last forever. And yet those who truly understand that model do believe that the class of problems it can solve is extraordinarily large and that it will endure for a very long time. Systems will still be being built on the basis of Codd's relational model for as far out as anyone can see.

Ted is survived by his wife Sharon; a daughter, Katherine; three sons, Ronald, Frank, and David; his first wife Libby, mother of his children; and six grandchildren. He also leaves other family members, friends, and colleagues all around the world. He is mourned and sorely missed by all.

■ ■ ■

CHAPTER 2

An Interview with Chris Date

The following interview was conducted by Tony Williams and originally appeared on the O'Reilly website (http://www.oreillynet.com/pub/a/network/2005/07/29/cjdate.html) on July 29th, 2005. Chris Date adds by way of preamble:

> *Another interview I did recently was published in the Northern California Oracle User Group (NoCOUG) Journal, Vol. 19, No. 2 (May 2005), and some of the questions and answers in that interview are inevitably very similar to some of those in what follows. Also, answers to many of the same questions—along with further discussion, in some cases—can be found in my recent book* Database in Depth: Relational Theory for Practitioners *(O'Reilly Media Inc., 2005).*

How did you get started with relational theory?

As with so many things, this was basically just luck—a matter of being in the right place at the right time. I was working at IBM in England, where I had been hired as a programming instructor. I had been doing that job for a while, but IBM had a very enlightened policy according to which you weren't allowed to spend all your time just teaching—from time to time you had to rotate out and get down into the trenches, as it were. So I rotated out and joined a little research group, where I was given the job of figuring out what the PL/I language should do to support this new thing called database management (this was early 1970). So I played with IBM's database product IMS—that was IBM's major product offering at the time—and I studied the CODASYL DBTG database specifications; IMS was hierarchies and CODASYL was networks. Then Ted Codd published his famous paper "A Relational Model of Data for Large Shared Data Banks" (*Communications of the ACM*, Vol. 13, No. 6, June 1970). So I read that paper, and—speaking here as a mathematician!—to me it was obvious that the relational model was the right way to go. Looking back, if I'd realized how long it was going to take to get the world at large to agree with that position, I don't know if I would have been quite so enthusiastic ... Anyway, I began corresponding with Ted at that time, I met him some little while later, and one thing led to another.

In the introduction to your new book (*Database in Depth*) you write that some things needed to be said again. How would you summarize those?

Goodness! Where to begin? There's so much nonsense out there ... so little true understanding, that it seems to me that just about *everything* needs to be said again. Perhaps I can illustrate by quoting a typical document off the Web. The document I have in mind is called "Weaknesses of the Relational Model," and it comes from an academic institution in Germany (so the lack of understanding I'm talking about certainly isn't limited to the U.S., nor is it limited to the commercial world). Here are the alleged "weaknesses," quoted *verbatim*, except that I've numbered them for purposes of subsequent reference:

1. With regard to data modeling, you can't define attributes which are of complex types (arrays, records, tables). Each relation has to be in first normal form. Or in other words: A "simple" natural structure must be divided into many flat structures (= tables/relations). The result is a complex structure of relations.

2. Result of a query is a flat table. Any complex structure, which has been input of the query has got lost.

3. No way to define recursive programme structure (using SQL).

4. The type system of SQL doesn't match with the type system of the embedding language ("type mismatch").

5. Controlling integrity constraints costs a lot of time (need to control the usage of primary/foreign keys).

6. Lack of mechanisms to control the physical level of the database (only simple clustering).

7. Definition of operations detached from data definition.

Considered as "weaknesses of the relational model," every single one of these is just plain wrong. Number 1 displays a lack of understanding of first normal form; ditto number 2 (and by the way, that phrase "flat table" all by itself demonstrates a huge failure to understand what relations truly are; I could write several pages on this issue alone). Number 3 is not only false as a statement of fact, it also makes the mistake of equating the relational model and SQL—as does number 4 also. Number 5 is 180 degrees wrong; I mean, *not* "controlling integrity constraints" is what costs us, and I don't mean costs only with respect to time—there are other costs too, ones that I regard as much worse. Number 6 ignores the fact that the relational model *deliberately* has nothing to say about "the physical level of the database"; one objective for the relational model was always to give implementers a high degree of freedom at the physical level, in order to make possible a high degree of data independence (I discuss this issue at some length in the O'Reilly book, as a matter of fact). And number 7 is just flat wrong again.

In a later question you mention the fact that the O'Reilly book has an epigraph from Leonardo da Vinci, and I'll get to that question in due course. But I think it's pertinent to mention here that the book has a second epigraph also, from Josh Billings: "The trouble with people is not that they don't know but that they know so much that ain't so." The document just quoted illustrates this point only too clearly.

By the way: If you're not familiar with it already, you might like to take a look at Fabian Pascal's website http://www.dbdebunk.com, which contains (among other things) numerous ignorant quotes like the one at hand, together with some analysis and deconstruction of those quotes on Fabian's part. I contribute to that website myself on a fairly regular basis.

Since the first edition of Codd and Date we have seen many trends such as 4GLs through to object-oriented databases. Any that have appealed or do you feel they are a flash in the pan?

First, a small point (or perhaps it's not so small): I don't quite know what you mean by "the first edition of Codd and Date." For some years Ted and I did have a consulting company called Codd and Date; however, your phrasing suggests we might have collaborated on a book. In fact we never did. The history was like this. Ted was a genius; there's no question about that, and he came up with these wonderful ideas. But like so many geniuses, he wasn't too good at communicating his ideas to ordinary mortals. So that was my job: to be that ordinary mortal! Once I'd understood the ideas myself, I was able to explain them to other people ... and that's what I did. In particular, I wrote a book called *An Introduction to Database Systems,* which was a textbook on database management that covered the relational model in particular (though it covered a lot of other things too). The first edition of that book appeared in 1975 (it's in its eighth edition now). But yes, I agree that many things have happened since that first edition, if that's what you meant. So let me turn to your question regarding the "many trends" ... Once again I fear my answer has to be fairly lengthy; please bear with me.

Actually I rather like your use of the word "trends" here. Because the truth is, so many of the things that have arisen over the years have indeed been just that, trends. The relational model is not and never was a mere "trend." The relational model is a solid scientific theory. *Nothing* has appeared on the horizon to replace it, and in my opinion it's extremely unlikely (I don't say impossible, you never know what's around the next corner) that anything ever will. The reason I say this is that the relational model is based on set theory and predicate logic, elements of which go back well over 2000 years. These disciplines in their various forms have been studied, analyzed, used, and extended by huge numbers of very smart people over the past two millenia (I refer here to logicians and mathematicians, of course); thus, it seems to me very unlikely that there's anything seriously wrong with them. By contrast, alleged competitors to the relational model—things like the so-called object "model" or the so-called semistructured "model" (and I set the term "model" in quotes very deliberately here)—simply don't have the same kind of pedigree as the relational model does, nor do they enjoy the same kind of scientific respectability.

So I certainly don't find "appealing" any of the things that (it's been claimed at one time or another) are supposed to replace the relational model. And in this connection I'd like to say explicitly that I reject, as proposed "replacements" for the relational model, both (a) XML and the semistructured "model," which I see as reinventing the old failed hierarchic "model," and (b) objects and the object-oriented "model," which I see as reinventing the old failed network "model."

But the trouble with the relational model is, it's never been implemented!—at least, not in commercial form, not properly, and certainly not fully. So while it's true that there have been a couple of developments in the marketplace over the past few years that I do quite like, I like them primarily because I see them as attempts to implement pieces of the relational model that should have been implemented years ago but weren't. I refer here to (a) "business rules" and (b) "object/relational DBMSs." I'll take them one at a time.

- *Business rules:* Business rule systems are a good idea, but they certainly aren't a new idea. Without going into a lot of detail, business rule systems can be seen as systems that attempt to implement the integrity piece of the relational model (which today's mainstream SQL products still—over 35 years after the model was first described!—so signally fail to do).

- *Object/relational DBMSs:* To a first approximation, "object/relational" just means the domains over which relations are defined can be of arbitrary complexity. As a consequence, we can have attributes of relations—or columns of tables, if you prefer—that contain geometric points, or polygons, or X rays, or XML documents, or fingerprints, or arrays, or lists, or relations, or any other kinds of values you can think of. But this idea too was always part of the relational model! The idea that the relational model could handle only rather simple kinds of data (like numbers and strings and dates and times) is a huge misconception, and always was. In fact, the term object/relational, as such, is just a piece of marketing hype ... As far as I'm concerned, an object/relational system done right would simply be a *relational* system done right, nothing more and nothing less.

That said, I must now add that, as so often, "Between the idea / And the reality / ... Falls the shadow" (T. S. Eliot—one of my favorites). While business rules and object/relational systems are both good ideas in principle, it doesn't follow that today's commercial realizations of those ideas are well done. In particular, today's object/relational systems (and the SQL standard)—in what I regard as a totally misguided attempt to accommodate certain ideas from object systems—have introduced pointers into SQL databases! Ted Codd very deliberately excluded pointers from the relational model, for all kinds of good reasons, and I think the addition of pointers to SQL has to be seen as the final nail in the coffin of any claims SQL might ever have had of being a true relational language.

Enough of this grousing. The next thing I want to say is that, while the relational model is certainly the foundation for "doing databases right," it's *only* the foundation. There are various ways we can build on top of the relational model, and various attempts have been made to do such a thing over the past 25 years or so. Here are a couple of examples:

- *Higher-level interfaces:* It was never the intention that every user should have to wrestle with the complexities of something like SQL (or even the complexities, such as they are, of the relational algebra). I always rather liked the visual interfaces provided by Query-By-Example and the "visual programming" front-ends to Ingres, for instance. And there are many other attractive front-ends that simplify the business of building applications on top of a relational (or at least SQL) DBMS. 4GLs too can be regarded as a higher-level interface—but I was never very impressed by 4GLs as such, in part because they never seemed to be precisely defined anywhere; the idea might have been OK, but without a formal definition of the semantics of the language some very expensive mistakes can be (and were) made. Natural language systems are another example; I still have an open mind about these, but I don't think anyone could claim they've been a huge success as yet.

- *Special-purpose applications:* I think the right way to view things like OLAP and data mining is as special-purpose applications that run on top of the DBMS. I mean, I don't think these things should be part of the core DBMS (I could be wrong). Either way, however, I do want to complain about the CUBE stuff in SQL, which takes one of the worst aspects of SQL—its support for nulls—and "exploits" it to make it even worse. But that's a particular hobbyhorse of mine ... I think I'd better stop right here.

On the dedication page you quote Leonardo da Vinci on theory without practice. Do you feel there is a lack of theory in most practice of database design? Do you feel this is a problem for the industry?

There are several issues here. If by "database design" you really do mean design of databases as such, then (as I explain in the O'Reilly book) there really isn't very much theory available anyway—though it's true that what little theory does exist is ignored far too often (especially in data warehouses, where some truly dreadful designs are not only found in practice but are actually recommended by certain pundits). But even if designers do abide by what design theory we have, there are still far too many decisions that have to be made without any solid theory to help. We need more science!

On the other hand, if by "database design" you really mean "DBMS design"—if not, then forgive me, but use of the term "database" for "DBMS" and/or "DBMS instance" is all too common and is (in my opinion) very confusing and deserves to be thoroughly resisted—then most certainly there are all too many departures from theory to be observed. And yes, it's a huge problem for the industry, and indeed for society at large (since society at large places such reliance on those defective products). This is an issue I do feel very strongly about, but I'm afraid it'll take a few minutes for me to explain why. Again, please bear with me.

First of all, it's a very unfortunate fact that the term "theory" has two quite different meanings. In common parlance it's almost a pejorative term—"oh, that's just your theory." Indeed, in such contexts it's effectively just a synonym for *opinion* (and the adverb *merely*—it's *merely* your opinion—is often implied, too). But the meaning in scientific circles is quite different. To a scientist, a theory is a set of ideas or principles that, taken together, *explain* something: some set of observable phenomena, such as the motion of the planets of the solar system. Of course, when I say I it explains something, I mean it does so *coherently:* It fits the facts, as it were. Moreover (and very importantly), a scientific theory doesn't just explain: It also *makes predictions,* predictions that can be tested and—at least in principle—can be shown to be false. And if any of those predictions do indeed turn out to be false, then scientists move on: Either they modify the theory or they adopt a new one. That's the scientific method, in a nutshell: We observe phenomena; we construct a theory to explain them; we test predictions of that theory; and we iterate. That's how the Copernican system replaced epicycles[1]; how Einstein's cosmology replaced Newton's; how general relativity replaced special relativity; and so on.

As another example, consider the current debate in the U.S. over the theory of evolution versus creationism (also known as "intelligent design"). Evolution is a scientific theory: It makes predictions, predictions that can be tested, and in principle it can be falsified (namely, if those predictions turn out to be incorrect). In particular, evolution predicts that if the environment changes, the inhabitants of that environment will probably change too. And this prediction has been widely confirmed: Bacteria evolve and become resistant to medical treatments, insects evolve and become resistant to pesticides, plants evolve and become resistant to herbicides, animals evolve and become resistant to disease or parasites (in fact, something exactly like this seems to have happened in the U.S. recently with honeybees). There's also the well-documented case of the Peppered Moth (*Biston betularia*) in England, which evolved from a dark form, when the air was full of smoke from the Industrial Revolution, to a light form

---

1. At least in the scientific world. As is well known, there were those who refused to accept the Copernican system for many, many years—but the naysayers were certainly not scientists.

when the air was cleaned up. By contrast, creationism is not a scientific theory; it makes no testable predictions, so far as I know, and as a consequence it can be neither verified nor falsified.

By the way, Carl Sagan has a nice comment in this regard:

> *In science it often happens that scientists say, "You know, that's a really good argument, my position is mistaken," and then they actually change their minds, and you never hear that old view from them again. They really do it. It doesn't happen as often as it should, because scientists are human and change is sometimes painful. But it happens every day. I cannot recall the last time something like that happened in politics or religion.*

Now let's get back to databases. The point is, the relational model is indeed a theory in the scientific sense—it's categorically *not* just a matter of mere opinion (though I strongly suspect that many of those who criticize the model are confusing, deliberately or otherwise, the two meanings of the term "theory"). In fact, of course, the relational model is a *mathematical* theory. Now, mathematical theories are certainly scientific theories, but they're a little special, in a way. First, the observed phenomena they're supposed to explain tend to be rather abstract—not nearly as concrete as the motion of the planets, for example. Second, the predictions they make are essentially the theorems that can be proved within the theory. Thus, those "predictions" can be falsified only if there's something wrong with the premises, or axioms, on which the theorems are based. But even this does happen from time to time! For example, in euclidean geometry, you can prove that every triangle has angles that sum to 180 degrees. So if we ever found a triangle that didn't have this property, we would have to conclude that the premises—the axioms of euclidean geometry—must be wrong. And in a sense exactly that happened: Triangles on the surface of a sphere (for example, on the surface of the Earth) have angles that sum to more than 180 degrees. And the problem turned out to be the euclidean axiom regarding parallel lines. Riemann replaced that axiom by a different one and thereby defined a different (but equally valid) kind of geometry.

In the same kind of way, the theory that's the relational model *might* be falsified in some way—but I think it's pretty unlikely, because (as I said in my answer to the previous question) the premises on which the relational model is based are essentially those of set theory and predicate logic, and those premises have stood up pretty well for a very long time.

So, to get back (finally!) to your question—do I feel the lack of attention to theory is a problem?—well, of course my answer is *yes.* As I said in another recent interview: This is the kind of question I always want to respond to by standing it on its head. Database management is a field in which, in contrast to some other fields within the computing discipline, there is some solid theory. We know the value of that theory; we know the benefits that accrue if we follow that theory. We also know there are costs associated with not following that theory (we might not know exactly what those costs are—I mean, it might be hard to quantify them—but we do know there are going to be costs).

If you're on an airplane, you'd like to be sure that plane has been constructed according to the principles of physics. If you're in a high-rise building, you'd like to be sure that building has been constructed according to architectural principles. In the same kind of way, if I'm using a DBMS, I'd like to be sure it's been constructed according to database principles. If it hasn't, then I know things will go wrong. I might find it hard to say exactly what will go wrong, and I might find it hard to say whether things will go wrong in a major or minor way, but I *know*—it's guaranteed—that things will go wrong.

So I think it's incumbent on people not to say "Tell me the business value of implementing the relational model." I think they should explain what the business value is of *not* implementing it. Those who ask "What's the value of the relational model?" are basically saying "What's the value of theory?" And I want them to tell me what the value is of *not* abiding by the theory.

The Third Manifesto introduced the relational language Tutorial D, and you use it for the examples in the new book. Do you think it has a future as an implementation or do you never intend it to be implemented?

Again I'd like to clarify a couple of things up front. First, I'd like to explain what *The Third Manifesto* is. *The Third Manifesto* is a formal proposal by Hugh Darwen and myself for the future of data and data management systems. It's a fairly short document (maybe 12 pages); it's also pretty terse and, to be frank, not all that easy to understand. So Hugh and I wrote a book of some 500 pages (!) to explain it. The third edition of that book (title *Databases, Types, and the Relational Model: The Third Manifesto*) is due to be published late this year or early next year.[2] And the first confusion factor is that people often refer to that book, loosely, as *The Third Manifesto*—but it really isn't; in fact, the *Manifesto* proper constitutes just one chapter in the book.

Now, in the *Manifesto* proper we—I mean Hugh Darwen and myself—use the name **D** generically to refer to any database language that conforms to the principles laid down in the *Manifesto*. Note that there could be any number of distinct languages that all qualify as a valid **D**. (Perhaps I should say explicitly in passing that SQL is not one of them!) And in the *Manifesto* book we introduce a particular **D**, which we call **Tutorial D,** that's meant to be used as (we hope) a self-explanatory basis for illustrating relational ideas—self-explanatory in the sense that if you're familiar with any conventional programming language, you should have no difficulty in following it. (I should mention in this connection that I've previously used **Tutorial D** in several other books, as well as in live seminars, and my experience does tend to confirm that it's sufficiently self-explanatory for the purpose.)

However, **Tutorial D** is, in a sense, only a "toy" language; it has no I/O and no exception-handling and is incomplete in various other ways as well. It follows that **Tutorial D** *per se* could never serve as a true industrial-strength language. But that doesn't mean we don't want to see it implemented! We believe it could serve as an extremely useful vehicle for teaching and reinforcing relational concepts before students have to get their heads bent out of shape from having to learn SQL. And as a matter of fact some implementations do exist; you can find details (including downloadable code) at the website http://www.thethirdmanifesto.com.

As you might expect, Hugh and I have a long list of follow-on projects to investigate when we get the time—and one of them is to take **Tutorial D** and extend it to become what you might call **Industrial D**. When it's defined, we would certainly like to see **Industrial D** (which by that time will probably be given some fancier name) to be implemented in commercial form. That's definitely one of our goals.

You say some fairly harsh things about SQL. What are the major flaws? Do you think SQL has a future or do you think it will be replaced by something closer to the relational model?

"You say some fairly harsh things about SQL": Well, you're not the first person to make this comment. One correspondent wrote: "As a practitioner, SQL is what I have to work with, and

---

2. It was published by Addison-Wesley in 2006.

while I don't mind some criticism of its shortcomings, [your] criticism starts to look more like a personal vendetta" (though the same correspondent did subsequently say it "finally made sense at the end of the book as to why [you] did this"). This is how I replied to these comments:

> *Oh dear. I tried hard to tone down my rude remarks; obviously I didn't succeed. I could have been much ruder, though! But the fact is that SQL fails in so many ways to support the relational model adequately—it suffers from so many sins of both omission and commission—that any book that both covers the relational model faithfully and discusses SQL as well cannot avoid being negative about SQL to some extent. It was interesting to me to discover (it wasn't explicitly intended on my part) how, almost always, the SQL formulation of any given problem was lengthier and more convoluted than its **Tutorial D** counterpart.*

The same correspondent also felt that **Tutorial D** was a "distraction" and didn't "seem to help in illustrating relational concepts"—implying, I suppose, that if I wanted to use any language for the purpose I should have used SQL. Here I replied as follows:

> *This comment I do find surprising. I have to use some syntax to illustrate the concepts (even Ted Codd did this in his very first papers), and SQL manifestly doesn't do the job. **Tutorial D** not only does do the job but was expressly designed to do so! How would you illustrate the relational EXTEND or SUMMARIZE operators—or even projection— using only SQL, without getting involved in a number of distracting irrelevancies? And how would you illustrate the relational concepts that SQL doesn't support at all (e.g., no left-to-right ordering to attributes, relation-valued attributes, TABLE_DEE, etc.)? I could go on.*

At the same time the correspondent also wanted me not to be so explicit regarding SQL's problems: "I think the book would be better served if [you] limited the discussion to just relational theory and let the reader (one enlightened) make [his or her] own judgments about SQL's inadequacies." Here I replied that I didn't agree, because:

- First, I think [the inclusion of SQL coding examples] is desirable to serve as a bridge between what the reader is supposed to know already (database practice) and what I'm trying to teach (relational theory). A book that covered the theory in a vacuum would be a different book—one that I explicitly suggested at the outset I didn't want to write, and one that would probably turn out to be (or at least look) too theoretical for my intended audience. (Incidentally, that different book would certainly have to use **Tutorial D,** or something equivalent, to illustrate the ideas—so this objection contradicts the previous one, in a sense.)

- Second, it's my experience that readers typically do need to have their hands held, as it were—points made only implicitly have a tendency to escape many people. (I don't mean this remark to be offensive! I include myself among those who often need their hands held in this kind of context.)

So yes, I do think SQL is pretty bad. But you explicitly ask what its major flaws are. Well, here are a few:

- Duplicate rows

- Nulls

- Left-to-right column ordering

- Unnamed columns and duplicate column names

- Failure to support "=" properly

- Pointers

- High redundancy

Do I think SQL has a future? Yes, of course—of a kind. Here I'd like to quote something Hugh Darwen and I say in the *Manifesto* book:

> *We reject SQL as a long-term foundation for the future. However, we are not so naïve as to think that SQL will ever disappear; rather, it is our hope that some **D** will be sufficiently superior to SQL that it will become the database language of choice, by a process of natural selection, and SQL will become "the database language of last resort." In fact, we see a parallel with the world of programming languages, where COBOL has never disappeared (and never will); but COBOL has become "the programming language of last resort" for developing applications, because preferable alternatives exist. We see SQL as a kind of database COBOL, and we would like some **D** to become a preferable alternative to it.*

Given that SQL databases and applications are going to be with us for a long time, however, we do have to pay some attention to the question of what to do about today's "SQL legacy" (I like this phrase). To this end, the *Manifesto* suggests that (a) SQL should be implementable in **D**—not because such implementation is desirable in itself, but so that a painless migration route might be available for current SQL users—and (b) existing SQL databases should be convertible to a form that **D** programs can operate on without error. And we've given enough thought to these objectives to believe they can be achieved without compromising on any of the other goals we have for the language **D**.

Do I think SQL will be replaced by something closer to the relational model? Well, I think I've answered this question by now. Indeed, the hope of performing such a replacement is one of the major reasons we wrote the *Manifesto* in the first place.

So where is the future of database development?

Again I assume that by "database" here you really mean "DBMS" ... Some answers to this question are given in the O'Reilly book (pages 172–176); here I'll just briefly mention a few points.

- The first and overriding one is this: We need DBMSs that (unlike the mainstream products of today) truly and fully support the relational model. Again, that's what *The Third Manifesto* is all about.

- Second, there's a promising (and radically different) implementation technology called *The TransRelational*™ *Model* coming down the road that looks as if it might be very well suited to that task of implementing the relational model properly. This possibility is under active investigation.

- Third, I'd like to see good support for *temporal data*. I think support for the time dimension is important already and due to become much more so. Now, several researchers have proposed approaches to this problem—approaches that are, however, fundamentally flawed for the most part (in my opinion), because they violate fundamental relational principles. By contrast, it's my belief that the relational model already includes what's needed to support the time dimension properly. All that's needed is a set of well chosen and carefully designed shorthands. Along with two coauthors, Hugh Darwen and Nikos Lorentzos, I've written about this topic at some length in another book, *Temporal Data and the Relational Model* (Morgan Kaufmann, 2003).

Perhaps I should say explicitly too that I *don't* think XML and XQuery are going to "take over the world" (despite all of the marketing hype to the contrary). People who think otherwise are simply displaying their lack of understanding of database fundamentals. As I mentioned earlier, I see XML (and the semistructured "model" on which it is allegedly based) as an attempt to reinvent the old failed hierarchic "model." This isn't to say that XML has no role to play—it probably does, but (to repeat) the role in question isn't that of taking over the world. XQuery in particular seems to me to be even worse than SQL! No, let me put a positive spin on that: If you like SQL, you're going to love XQuery. (Coming from me, you can take this remark as damning indeed.)

Finally, I have to ask: When Chris Date wants to build a database, what product does he turn to? Do you have time for consumer level products such as Access? Do you think they have a place?

My lawyer has told me to say "No comment" to this one. Seriously, I do have a policy of never answering this question directly; I'm only too aware of what might happen if I were thought to be endorsing some specific product. (Did you expect anything different?) So all I can do is offer some platitudes: Even though they're all deeply flawed, you do have to use one of the existing DBMSs, because they're all that's out there—they're the only game in town, pretty much (though I'm being a little unfair here to at least one product, Dataphor from Alphora, which does constitute an attempt to implement the ideas of *The Third Manifesto*). Which particular product you choose will naturally depend on your own specific requirements (and yes, it might be one of the "consumer level products such as Access"). But whichever one you do choose, you'll be able to make much better use of it if you're familiar with the underlying theory than you would be able to do otherwise ... which is one of the reasons I wrote the O'Reilly book.

■ ■ ■

CHAPTER 3

Good Writing Does Matter

This chapter started out in life as a report on certain aspects of IBM's "relational"—or SQL, at any rate—product DB2. My own work at the time was heavily involved with integrity constraints, so I thought it might be useful to take a look at the integrity support provided by DB2, since DB2 was and is clearly one of the market leaders in the field of SQL products. However, my investigations quickly led me off in another direction entirely. To be specific, I found that, not only was the DB2 support considerably less extensive than I'd hoped, but it was quite hard to understand just what that support actually consisted of, owing to the truly dreadful quality of the user documentation. This chapter subjects a few extracts from that documentation to a detailed critical analysis, with a view, in part, to (just possibly) getting some improvements in the situation.

Note: I wanted to include this chapter in this book because, as well as being relevant, somewhat, to the theme of relational misconceptions in particular (see Part 6), it also serves as an introduction to the gentle art of **deconstruction**. Deconstruction is a technique of literary criticism and analysis, a technique that I find extremely effective in helping combat some of the nonsense that appears in the trade press and elsewhere on matters that I happen to know something about and think are important. Let me elaborate. First, the useful verb *deconstruct* is defined by the *Oxford English Dictionary* as follows:

> *To undo the construction of, to take to pieces ... to analyze and reinterpret (first appearance 1973)*

It's a back-formation from *deconstruction* (first appearance 1882), which is defined as—among other things—"a strategy of critical analysis associated with the French philosopher Jacques Derrida (b. 1930), directed towards exposing ... internal contradictions in philosophical and literary language." In other words, the technique of deconstruction operates on the premise that you can judge a writer's intent only by what he or she has actually said, not by what you might possibly think he or she might possibly have wanted to have possibly said, but didn't.

Preamble

As noted earlier, this is a report on an investigation I carried out a little while ago into certain aspects of IBM's "flagship" DBMS product DB2. For some time now, my own work has had a lot to do with integrity constraints, so I thought it might be useful—I'm an eternal optimist—to take a look at the integrity constraint support provided by DB2 (since DB2 is clearly one of the major players in the marketplace). As so often happens, however, my investigations quickly led me off in another direction entirely. To be specific, I found that, not only was the DB2 support considerably less extensive than I'd hoped, but it was quite hard to understand exactly what support *was* provided, owing to the truly dreadful quality of the user documentation. In what follows, therefore, I intend to subject a few extracts from that documentation to a detailed critical analysis: partly just to complain,[1] but partly to incite real *users* to complain too, with a view (just possibly) to getting some improvements in the situation.

Exhibit A

By way of illustration, here's one paragraph ("Exhibit A") from the DB2 Version 6 Reference Manual, quoted here in its entirety:

> *A table check constraint is a rule that specifies the values allowed in one or more columns of every row of a table. They are optional and can be defined using the SQL statements CREATE TABLE and ALTER TABLE. The specification of table check constraints is a restricted form of a search condition. One of the restrictions is that a column name in a table check constraint on table T must identify a column of T.*

I propose to examine and comment on—or deconstruct, rather—this paragraph one sentence at a time. I've numbered and repeated the sentences one by one for purposes of future reference.

1. A *table check constraint* is a rule that specifies the values allowed in one or more columns of every row of a table.

First of all, the writing is **dire!** For example, what on earth are we supposed to make of the extraordinary locution "the values allowed in one or more columns of every row of a table"? Phrases like "one or more columns" are always grammatically suspect (though I freely admit I've used such phrases myself); "one or more" must include "one" as a special case, but "one columns" is a syntax error. Well, that's just a quibble, of course; much more to the point, just which columns are we talking about? (Remember this is supposed to be a reference manual!) And "the values allowed in one or more columns" strongly suggests it must be the *same* values in every one of those "one or more columns." And "the values allowed in ... every row" strongly suggests it must be the same values in every one of those rows, too. And since when did rows have columns, anyway ("one or more columns of every row")?

Next, note the tacit assumption that the term *table* means a base table specifically. This mistake—I'm tempted to say this **howler**—is ubiquitous, of course (it's certainly not limited to DB2 documentation); in fact, it's one of my pet peeves, and I've written about it before—see, e.g., the article "It's All Relations!" in my book *Relational Database Writings 1994–1997* (Addison-Wesley, 1998). In case you might not have access to that book, let me spell out the argument one more time here:

---

1. To quote from Lily Tomlin's brilliant one-woman show *The Search for Signs of Intelligent Life in the Universe:* "I personally think we developed language because of our deep inner need to complain." (The script, by Jane Wagner, is available from Harper and Row, copyright © 1986 Jane Wagner Inc.)

- Base tables are **not** the only kinds of tables. In fact, it's precisely one of the major strengths of the relational model that not only base tables but also views, snapshots, query results, intermediate results (etc., etc.) are *all* tables. Base tables aren't really special at all.[2]

- To focus for a moment on views in particular: The WHOLE POINT about a view—actually, the whole point about a derived table of any kind—is precisely that it *is* a table. The fact that a view is a table is important in relational systems for much the same kinds of reasons that the fact that a subset is a set is important in mathematics: Because a subset is a set, we can perform the same kinds of operations on a subset as we can on any other kind of set; likewise, because a view is a table, we can perform the same kinds of operations on a view as we can on any other kind of table. (It's true that today's SQL products aren't very good at doing *update* operations on views, but this state of affairs is simply a deficiency in those products—it doesn't undermine the point I'm trying to make. As a matter of fact, some of those products aren't very good at doing *retrieval* operations on views either, but this fact doesn't undermine the point I'm trying to make, either.)

- Of course, SQL itself is partly to blame for the foregoing confusions, because the keyword TABLE is often—though not always!—used in SQL to mean a base table specifically (think of CREATE TABLE, ALTER TABLE, etc.). What's more, the SQL standard and SQL product documentation make frequent use of the expressions "tables or views" and "tables and views," both of which strongly suggest that views, whatever else they might be, are not tables.

- It's my opinion that people who think *table* means a base table specifically are *not thinking relationally*. It's my further opinion that such people are likely to make a number of serious mistakes as a consequence of their lack of relational thinking. And I might seriously be tempted to level this accusation at the designers of the SQL language itself ...

Precisely because the table to which "table check constraints" apply in DB2 has to be a base table specifically, I propose to refer to those constraints from this point forward as *base* table check constraints specifically.

Onward. Let's take a look at Sentence Number 2:

2. They are optional and can be defined using the SQL statements CREATE TABLE and ALTER TABLE.

Given the sentence that immediately precedes this one (i.e., Sentence Number 1), "They" here apparently means either "values" or "columns." Both interpretations make a nonsense of Sentence Number 2, of course; what the writer really wants is for "They" to mean check constraints, but he or she has already forgotten that Sentence Number 1 referred to such constraints in the singular. (OK, it's an easy mistake to make—maybe—but it's also one that's easy to catch in the editing cycle. If there is one.)

---

2. Hugh Darwen points out (in a private communication) that in SQL specifically—though certainly not in the relational model!—base tables *are* a little bit special after all, because in SQL derived tables in general (though not snapshots or views in particular) are allowed to have two columns with the same name, while base tables of course aren't. Pooh.

"They are optional": It would be more logically correct to say that, conceptually, a given base table always has at least one base table check constraint, defaulting to CHECK(TRUE) if nothing else is specified. A small point, perhaps, but (to say it again) this is supposed to be a reference manual.[3] Moreover, I think the writer should also tell us that the base table check constraints that apply to a given base table are all ANDed together, logically speaking.

"They ... *can* be defined" (my italics): Well, I strongly suspect that CREATE TABLE and ALTER TABLE are the *only* vehicles for defining such constraints, but that's not what "*can* be defined" suggests—especially given the first half of the sentence ("They are optional"); for otherwise, why are the two halves of the sentence joined by "and" into a single thought anyway?

Important question: If I try to add a new constraint via ALTER TABLE, what happens if existing rows in the relevant base table already violate the new constraint? (I believe I know the answer to this question. That's not the point. What is the point is that I would have expected the answer to be provided in the documentation right here, but it isn't.)

3. The specification of table check constraints is a restricted form of a search condition.

First of all, if this sentence doesn't actually confuse singular and plural again, it certainly comes pretty close to doing so. But there are more serious objections to it.

"The specification is ... a search condition": Here the writer is using *specification*, very confusingly, to refer not to what the user actually has to specify when writing a base table check constraint, but rather to *a proper subset of* what the user has to specify: namely, that subset of the specification that appears within parentheses in the CHECK clause. (And that CHECK clause in turn is still only a subset of the specification of the overall base table check constraint!) Thus, I would have said rather—more precisely, and more explicitly—that a base table check constraint consists of an optional CONSTRAINT clause and a mandatory CHECK clause; the optional CONSTRAINT clause provides a name for the constraint (if omitted, then the constraint is unnamed), and the mandatory CHECK clause includes a search condition that rows of the base table in question are required to satisfy.

"The specification is ... a restricted form of a search condition": First, "a search condition" should be just "search condition"; "**a** search condition"—emphasis added—suggests (to this reader, at least) *one specific* search condition (and then I want to ask, which one?). Next, "restricted" is a loaded word in this context!—personally, I would have used "limited" here (and I would have added that the limitations in question will be explained later, and given an appropriate forward reference). Why is it a loaded word? Because (as the writer might or might not be aware) the limitation in question is, precisely, that the search condition must be what is known formally as a **restriction condition**—at least, it ought to be, and in DB2 I think it is. Lacking the simple "restriction condition" concept, however, the writer has had to resort to giving a long and apparently arbitrary list of syntactic limitations (see later), instead of explaining to the poor reader what's really going on.

For purposes of future reference, let me give a definition of the "restriction condition" concept here. Essentially, a restriction condition is a truth-valued expression that can be evaluated for a given row—i.e., its truth value, *true* or *false,* can be determined for that row—by examining just that row in isolation; in other words, the expression must be *quantifier-free* (see

---

3. Of course, the expression CHECK(TRUE) will be syntactically legal only if type BOOLEAN is supported. I'm not sure whether type BOOLEAN is in fact supported in DB2 Version 6, but I suspect it isn't—it didn't make it into the SQL standard until 1999, and I'm told that most vendors still haven't implemented it.

my book *An Introduction to Database Systems,* 8th edition, Addison-Wesley, 2004, for further explanation).

Incidentally, given that the search condition in a base table check constraint does indeed have to be a restriction condition, we can see what a rotten term *table check constraint* really is (even if we extend it to *base table check constraint,* as I've been doing). It's a rotten term because it doesn't just constrain values of the specified base table, it constrains values of *individual rows within* the specified base table. By contrast, a candidate key uniqueness constraint might reasonably be called a *table* constraint—it constrains values of the table taken as a whole, not values of individual rows within the table. (And here I deliberately talk in terms of tables in general, not in terms of base tables specifically.) In other words, even the very *name* the writer has chosen for the construct he or she is trying (feebly) to describe gets in the way of true understanding!

4. One of the restrictions is that a column name in a table check constraint on table *T* must identify a column of *T.*

First, the expression "One of the restrictions" tends to suggest that the one mentioned has been chosen arbitrarily from a long list of such restrictions. In fact, of course, the restriction in question is the *crucial* one! So why not say so? And perhaps explain what it really means?—*viz.,* that we're indeed talking about a restriction condition as defined above? And perhaps explain too *why* this limitation is imposed in the first place? *Note:* This latter suggestion, helpful though it might be to the cause of understanding, is almost certainly a nonstarter, however, because it would make it all too obvious that the level of integrity support being described is quite extraordinarily weak. (So far as I'm aware, the *only* general integrity constraints supported by DB2 are base table check constraints. In particular, DB2 doesn't support the more general "assertions" of the SQL standard; in other words, it doesn't support constraints that involve more than just one row, except for the limited special case of candidate and foreign key constraints.)

"[A] column name … must identify a column of *T*"? No: *Every* column name … must identify a column of *T!* Also, the phrasing ("a column name must identify a column") is not very elegant—surely, column names *always* identify columns. Suggested replacement: "Every column mentioned must be a column of *T."*

Restriction Conditions in DB2

A subsequent passage from the same DB2 manual gives what I referred to earlier as the "long and apparently arbitrary list of syntactic limitations" on base table check constraints (or, rather, on the search-condition portion of such constraints). Here it is:

A *check-condition* is a *search-condition* except as follows:

- A column reference must be to a column of the table being created.

- It cannot contain any of the following:

  ▪ subqueries

  ▪ dereference operations or DEREF functions

- column functions

- variant user-defined functions

- user-defined functions using the EXTERNAL ACTION option

- user-defined functions using the SCRATCHPAD option

- host variables

- parameter markers

- special registers

- an alias

Not a very user-friendly list, I would have thought! Also:

- For "A column reference," read "Every column reference."

- For "the table being created," read "the base table being created or altered."

- For "host variables," read "host variable names" or "references to host variables."

- For "column functions," read "invocations of column functions" or "references to column functions" (and similarly for several other entries in this list).

Yes, I know many of these objections are nits, but (to say it one more time) the document is supposed to be a reference manual.

Regarding that business of "column functions," by the way, there's another point to be made. As I'm sure you know, "column functions" is the SQL term for aggregate operators such as COUNT, SUM, and AVG. And it's well known that SQL's syntax for such operators is unorthodox, in that not all of the arguments to a given invocation are specified within the parentheses that follow the operator name in that invocation. (See, e.g., the article "Aggregate Operators" in my book *Relational Database Writings 1994–1997*, Addison-Wesley, 1998, for further discussion of this issue.) As a direct consequence of this unorthodox syntax, a *formal*—i.e., accurate, rigorous, and complete—definition in SQL terms of the restriction condition concept is necessarily much more complicated than the straightforward one I gave earlier. And that fact in turn makes it harder for technical writers to explain SQL base table check constraints properly!

A Suggested Replacement for Exhibit A

Let's see if we can't come up with some text that says what the DB2 technical writer was presumably trying to say in his or her original paragraph (i.e., what I referred to as "Exhibit A"), but does it better. I would suggest something along the following lines (note the change in nomenclature in particular!):

Let *BT* be a base table. Then a *base table row constraint* on *BT* is a constraint (optionally named) to the effect that each row of *BT* must be such as to cause a specified search condition to evaluate to either *true* or *unknown* when applied to the row in question.[4] However, the search condition in question is subject to certain syntactic limitations (see [*insert text here specifying exactly where*]), the most important of which is that every column it mentions must be a column of *BT*. Base table row constraints, if any, for base table *BT* are specified either when *BT* is first defined, via CREATE TABLE, or when it is subsequently modified, via ALTER TABLE; in the latter case, [*insert text here explaining what happens if existing rows in BT already violate the specified constraint*]. *Note:* By default, every base table *BT* is subject to the base table row constraint CHECK(TRUE); also, the base table row constraints that apply to *BT* are all ANDed together, logically speaking.

Longer, yes (somewhat), but I think it's clearer, and it's more complete, and I know it's more precise.

Exhibit B

Now I want to move on to examine another piece of text ("Exhibit B") that appears a little further along in the same part of the same DB2 manual:

> *The check-condition "IS NOT NULL" can be specified, however it is recommended that nullability be enforced directly using the NOT NULL attribute of a column. For example, CHECK (salary + bonus > 30000) is accepted if salary is set to NULL, because CHECK constraints must be either satisfied or unknown and in this case salary is unknown. However, CHECK (salary IS NOT NULL) would be considered false and a violation of the constraint if salary is set to NULL.*

As with Exhibit A, I propose to examine this paragraph one sentence at a time, and I've numbered the sentences for purposes of future reference.

1. The check-condition "IS NOT NULL" can be specified, however it is recommended that nullability be enforced directly using the NOT NULL attribute of a column.

The check-condition "IS NOT NULL" can be specified: Actually, it can't; rather, the check-condition "*column-name* IS NOT NULL" can be specified. (The check-condition is what goes between the parentheses in a check constraint.) Not a big issue, perhaps, but—to say it yet again—the document is supposed to be a *reference* manual.

[It] is recommended that nullability be enforced directly using the NOT NULL attribute of a column: **Nullability?** I assume the writer means, rather, "notnullability," a fact that points up the sloppiness not just of the writing *per se*, but also of the thinking underlying that writing (on this subject, see the final section of this chapter). With respect to the writing, is *nullability* really a word? Presumably it derives from *nullable*. But *nullable* could surely make sense only if there were a verb "to null."[5] Anyway, there *has* to be a better way to say what the writer wants to say.

---

4. Notice that the original text never mentioned this point!—the point that is the very *raison d'être* for "base table row constraints" in the first place, in fact.
5. Actually there is, but my dictionary marks it as obsolete, and I've certainly never heard it used.

[The] NOT NULL attribute of a column: I don't know if DB2 really refers to NOT NULL as "an attribute of a column," but I certainly hope it doesn't, because *attribute* is the formal relational term corresponding to the SQL term *column* ... How about "[The] optional NOT NULL specification on a column definition"?

2. For example, CHECK (salary + bonus > 30000) is accepted if salary is set to NULL, because CHECK constraints must be either satisfied or unknown and in this case salary is unknown.

Rephrase!—e.g., as follows: "Check constraints are satisfied if the specified search condition evaluates to either *true* or *unknown*. Note the *unknown* case in particular[6]; for example, if (a) *SC* is the search condition SALARY + BONUS > 30000 and (b) SALARY is null, then *SC* evaluates to *unknown* and the check constraint CHECK(*SC*) is satisfied." Points arising:

- My switches from uppercase to lowercase and *vice versa* in this rephrasing are all deliberate!

- *Satisfied* is a much better word than *accepted* in this context. "Accepted" could mean merely that the check constraint is *syntactically* acceptable.

- Observe that Sentence Number 2 as quoted uses the same word *unknown* to mean two very different things: (a) "the third truth value," which is a value, and (b) null, which isn't. See, e.g., the article "Nothing in Excess" in the book mentioned a couple of times already in this chapter, *Relational Database Writings 1994–1997* (Addison-Wesley, 1998), for further discussion of the important logical difference between these two concepts and why they shouldn't be confused. (Of course, SQL *does* confuse them; in fact, the SQL standard BOOLEAN data type actually uses null to represent "the third truth value"! To understand the seriousness of this logical mistake, the reader might care to meditate on the analogy of a numeric type that uses null instead of zero to represent zero.)

3. However, CHECK (salary IS NOT NULL) would be considered false and a violation of the constraint if salary is set to NULL.

I'd rephrase this one too. In particular, I don't understand that initial *however;* according to my dictionary, it ought to mean *despite the foregoing,* but that interpretation doesn't seem to make any sense. In fact, let's try restructuring and rephrasing the entire paragraph from beginning to end:

Let *SC* be a search condition; then the check constraint CHECK(*SC*) is satisfied for a given row if *SC* evaluates to either *true* or *unknown* for the row in question. Note the *unknown* case in particular. For example, suppose SALARY is null; then the check constraint CHECK (SALARY + BONUS > 30000) will be satisfied, whereas the check constraint CHECK (SALARY IS NOT NULL) will not. *Note:* This latter example is logically equivalent to specifying NOT NULL as part of the definition of column SALARY; in fact, this latter specification is preferred, for reasons of performance.[7]

---

6. Yes indeed! The fact that integrity constraints in SQL are regarded as satisfied if the specified search condition evaluates to unknown is a serious weakness, and should by rights be another nail in the nulls coffin. It implies among other things that updates in SQL can succeed when they ought to fail. See C. J. Date and Hugh Darwen, *A Guide to the SQL Standard,* 4th edition (Addison-Wesley, 1997), for further discussion.

7. My assumption. The point is, the reference manual really ought to tell us the reason, whatever it might be, but it doesn't.

(Actually I don't see the point of the reference to BONUS in the foregoing and would prefer to simplify the corresponding search condition to just SALARY > 30000, but let that pass.)

Exhibit C

I have another truly dreadful DB2 quote I'd like to "share with you," as the saying goes. Admittedly this one comes from a technical article, not from a reference manual as such, so it *might* be argued—not by me!—that the quality of the writing is not so important. Be that as it may, the quote in question certainly suffers from some of the same kinds of problems as Exhibits A and B (it also manages to introduce some additional ones of its own). It's taken *verbatim* from "Improving Stage 2 Predicates," by Sharad Pande (*DB2 Magazine 4*, No. 2, Summer 1999). Here it is:

> *View materialization. DB2 for OS/390 v.5 uses materialization to satisfy a view reference when the view defining a subselect indicates aggregates processing (such as GROUP BY, DISTINCT, and Column Function) and a *VIEW participates in a join or a *VIEW referencing a statement indicates aggregate processing. Materialization can also occur in statements that contain multiple outer joins or outer joins combined with inner joins; for example, if a *CREATE VIEW statement uses DISTINCT, a SELECT FROM view statement uses GROUP BY, a CREATE VIEW statement uses GROUP BY (or DISTINCT), or a SELECT FROM statement joins this view with another table.*

Deconstructing this impressively awful piece of writing is left as an exercise for the reader. (Maybe that's not nice. Maybe I should just ask you to rewrite the text so that at least it makes sense and is *precise*.)

Just as an aside: I used to joke in seminars that before they were done, the DB2 folks at IBM would make DB2 just as complicated as IMS ever was. Quotes like the one above—if and when you can ever figure out what they mean—lend weight to my suspicion that IBM has been very successful in this regard.

Concluding Remarks

Of course, I'm well aware that many of the criticisms and complaints I've been making might well be dismissed as mere quibbles, and so indeed they are, in many cases. But it's the cumulative impact of all of those quibbles—as well as the ones that definitely *aren't* quibbles!—that wears you down (the death of a thousand cuts?). No wonder technical writers as a class are held in such low esteem, if the foregoing examples can be taken as typical of their craft (and I think they can).[8] Aren't we entitled to technical writing that's accurate, concise, precise, and a pleasure to read?

Anyway, it occurs to me that the overall theme of this chapter could serve as a subtext, at least, to much of the other material I've published recently[9] (in this connection, see in particular the website http://www.dbdebunk.com). In just about every one of those previous publications, I've had occasion to complain about—among other things—the apparent inability of some writer or other to express his or her thoughts clearly. In fact, I want to go further. As far as I'm concerned,

---

8. Apologies to those of my friends who actually are technical writers!
9. And hence to much of the material collected and republished in the present book.

when writers are so manifestly incapable of expressing their thoughts coherently, I have to begin to think they don't *have* any coherent thoughts ... In which connection, I'd like to draw your attention to a wonderful book, *Less than Words Can Say,* by Richard Mitchell (Little, Brown and Company, 1979). Mitchell is (was?) editor and publisher of a monthly publication called *The Underground Grammarian,* and the thesis of his book is essentially that writing **is** thinking. Here are a few quotes to buttress that thesis:

- *(Page 39)* It is no coincidence that the Greeks who first devised discursive prose also constructed formal logic ... Thinking *is* coherent discourse, and the logic and the prose require one another.

- *(Page 40)* [We] have to suspect that coherent, continuous thought is impossible for those who cannot construct coherent, continuous prose.

- *(Page 45)* The logic of writing is simply logic; it is not some system of arbitrary conventions interesting only to those who write a lot. All logical thought goes on in the form of statements and statements about statements ... If we cannot make those statements and statements about statements logically, clearly, and coherently, then we cannot think and make knowledge. People who cannot put strings of sentences together in good order cannot think.

Yes, good writing does matter.

PART 2

■ ■ ■

And Now for Something Completely Different

This part of the book consists of three chapters on the general subject of logical difference. The maxim "All logical differences are big differences," which is due to Wittgenstein, has served my colleague Hugh Darwen and myself very well as a guiding principle in database investigations over the years. It's also highly relevant to much of the material appearing elsewhere in the present book.

■■■

CHAPTER 4

On the Notion of Logical Difference

This chapter lays the groundwork for an occasional, open-ended series of writings on the general subject of *logical difference*. It also explores the companion notion of *logical sameness*. *Note:* I've discussed the concept of logical difference in several previous writings, but the treatment that follows is at least partly new. Overall, it's meant to serve as a central point of reference for future writings by myself and others on this same general topic.

Preamble

If you're familiar with my contributions to the website http://www.dbdebunk.com or various other writings by myself—especially the book I wrote with Hugh Darwen, *Databases, Types, and the Relational Model: The Third Manifesto*, 3rd edition (Addison-Wesley, 2006), referred to hereinafter as simply the *Manifesto*—you'll be aware that I often appeal in my writings to the notion of **logical difference**. That notion is one I find extraordinarily useful in my own work; it's a great aid to clear and precise thinking (not that my thinking is always as clear and precise as it might be, I'm sorry to say). I also find it helpful when I'm trying to understand, learn, and inwardly digest the contributions of others in the database field. And, last but certainly not least, I find it an extremely useful "mind tool" when I'm trying to pinpoint and analyze some of the confusions that are, unfortunately, all too common in that same field. It's a rock to cling to in what can sometimes seem to be an ocean of muddle.

The intent of what follows, then, is to offer a brief general introduction to the concept of logical difference and thereby to set the scene for an occasional and open-ended series of writings on specific important examples of that concept.

Why Is It Important to Think Precisely?

If it hadn't been for the fact that it doesn't exactly trip off the tongue, the title for this chapter might well have been "Some Logical Differences or Fundamental Distinctions that Lie at the Heart of the Database Field." It's my claim—perhaps better, my thesis—that many of the confusions we encounter in the literature (in object database writings in particular) derive from confusion over one or other of the fundamental logical differences I'll be discussing in this series. And I plan to produce a considerable body of evidence to buttress this thesis, both in the present chapter and in subsequent ones.

This isn't the first time I've addressed this issue. In addition to the coverage already alluded to above in the *Manifesto*, I've at least touched on the concept of logical difference in several other places, and in 1997 I published a four-part piece on the same general subject entitled "Why Is It Important to Think Precisely?" (republished in my book *Relational Database Writings 1994–1997*, Addison-Wesley, 1998). So some of the material in this series—the material of this introductory chapter in particular—won't be entirely new. But much of it *will* be new, and in any case I believe it'll be useful to bring the material together in one place to serve as a central reference.

Let me say a little more about that earlier four-part article. After giving a little background, the article discussed four principal logical differences:

1. Model *vs.* implementation

2. Value *vs.* variable

3. Type *vs.* relation

4. Type *vs.* representation

In each case, the article:

- Explained exactly what the difference in question was

- Gave examples from the literature where writers had apparently failed to understand that difference

- Discussed some of the consequences of such failure

I plan to follow this same general pattern in this new series. I also plan to discuss the same four logical differences in particular (as well as many, many others), but in much more depth than I did in that earlier article.

Let me also briefly explain why that earlier article had the title it did (this explanation is taken from that article). As you might know, I've been teaching seminars on database topics for many years, and by now you might expect me to be a little bored with the whole subject. But I'm not. One reason I'm not is the fact that it doesn't matter how many times you teach a given seminar, you can always get questions you've never heard before ... On one occasion, I was claiming that one of the virtues of the relational model was that it enabled you to **think precisely**—in particular, it helped you to articulate problems in a precise manner. Whereupon one student asked: "Why is it important to think precisely?" This question was right out of left field so far as I was concerned! Certainly it was one I'd never heard before. So I replied: "Well, I don't know exactly." Which I thought was a pretty good response, off the top of my head.

Logical Differences Are Big Differences

Throughout our database work in general, Hugh Darwen and I have always tried very hard to follow certain guiding principles (and, of course, this remark is true of our work on the *Manifesto* in particular). Of those principles, the most important—indeed, it underpins all the rest—is this:

All logical differences are big differences.

This dictum is due to Ludwig Wittgenstein.[1] What does it mean? Well, the subject matter of the *Manifesto* is, essentially, the relational model. And the relational model is at heart **a formal system:** just as a DBMS is, or an operating system, or indeed any computer program, come to that. Formal systems are what computers are (or can be made to be) good at. And, of course, the basis of any formal system is **logic**. It follows that—with respect to formal systems in general, and hence with respect to programming in general, and with respect to database management and the relational model in particular—differences that are logical in nature are very important ones, and we need to pay very careful attention to them. To put it another way:

- Computers are very precise in their operation—they don't have much tolerance for error.

- In the field of computing above all, therefore, clarity, accuracy, and precision are surely paramount.

- These remarks are true of database management in particular.

- Thus, any endeavor having to do with database management, if it's confused over issues as basic as (for example) the difference between a value and a variable, or the difference between a type and a relation, is *doomed to eventual failure.*

We also pointed out in the *Manifesto* (slightly—but only slightly!—tongue in cheek) that Wittgenstein's dictum had an interesting corollary: namely, that **all logical mistakes are big mistakes**. Because, of course, a mistake is a difference; it's a difference between what's right and what's wrong. And it's certainly possible to observe a number of logical mistakes that have been made, and still are being made, in the database industry as a whole ...

We also went on to conjecture that the inverse of Wittgenstein's maxim was true as well: namely, that *all nonlogical differences are small differences*—by which we meant, not that differences that are (e.g.) merely psychological in nature are unimportant in absolute terms, but that they *are* unimportant from the point of view of formal systems in particular. We therefore paid little attention in the *Manifesto* to nonlogical considerations, such as matters of syntax. (Syntax is important from a human factors point of view, of course, and we naturally tried to choose good syntax over bad when we came to design our own language in the *Manifesto*. But we don't regard differences that are mere differences in syntax as logical differences, nor for present purposes as very important ones.)

Some Things Are Much the Same

As already explained, this chapter is meant to serve as a general introduction to a series on logical differences. The basic idea is that we often encounter a situation in which we have to deal with concepts that truly are distinct, and yet *either*

---

1. At this point in the first draft of this chapter, I wrote: "At least, I think it is, though, sadly, Hugh and I have never been able to track it down to its source, and we'd be grateful to anyone who could help us in that connection." Little did I know that help was on its way at that very moment. The complete quote is: "As I once heard Wittgenstein say, all logical differences are big differences; in logic we are not making *subtle* distinctions, as it were between flavours that pass over into one another by delicate gradations" (from a lecture entitled "History of the Corruptions of Logic," by P. T. Geach, published in his book *Logic Matters*, Basil Blackwell, 1972). Thanks to Stephen A. Wilson for passing on this discovery. Though I can't resist pointing out that it really isn't clear how much of the quote is Wittgenstein and how much Geach! Logicians themselves—who really ought to know better—aren't always as precise as they might be.

> **a.** The concepts in question are referred to by the same name,

or

> **b.** The concepts do indeed have distinct names, but those names tend to be used very sloppily—sometimes almost interchangeably.

As an illustration of Case (a), consider the term *data model*, which does refer to two very different concepts.[2] As an illustration of Case (b), consider the terms *argument* and *parameter*, which certainly refer to different concepts but are often used as if they were interchangeable.

As another illustration of Case (a), I note that the SQL language often considers two things to be the same even when they're clearly different. For example, in SQL the character strings 'XYZ' and 'XYZ ' (note the trailing blank in the second of these) are considered to be equal if PAD SPACE applies to the pertinent "collation"; similarly, the character strings 'XYZ' and 'xyz' are considered to be equal if the pertinent collation is case-insensitive. In other words, SQL actually enshrines certain confusions over the notion of logical difference in its very definition! A case of "If you can't fix it, feature it"?

So perhaps this series isn't so much about logical differences *per se* as it is about the confusions that can occur when we fail to recognize and act on such differences. But the opposite phenomenon can occur, too; that is, we can find ourselves in a situation in which we're told, in effect, that there's a logical difference between two concepts, and it turns out later that the concepts are in fact one and the same (or at least overlap considerably, and usually unpleasantly). In other words:

- Problems occur over *logical difference* when somebody fails to recognize that two concepts are in fact distinct.

- Problems occur over *logical sameness* when somebody fails to recognize that two allegedly distinct concepts are in fact the same, or at least have a great deal in common.

Before going any further, I must make it clear that the phenomenon of logical sameness is sometimes unavoidable, especially when we're trying to build a bridge between disciplines that have been constructed on different foundations. For example, the relational model has its roots in the mathematics of relations; when Codd first introduced it, therefore, he used the mathematical term *domain* to refer to the sets over which relations were defined. At the same time, the relational model quite explicitly did *not* have its roots in language theory. As a consequence, it was several years before it was generally recognized and understood that what the database community called *domains* and what the language community called *types* were really one and the same.

Note: Just as an aside, I observe that some people don't understand even yet that domains and types are the same thing. The SQL standard muddies the water, too, because it uses the term *domain* to mean something else—not to mention (a) the fact that its notion of *type* is

---

2. Case (a) is reminiscent of the phenomenon found in many programming languages called overloading. Overloading occurs when the language provides several distinct operators with the same name; for example, the name "+" might refer to three distinct "add" operators—one to add two fixed-point numbers, one to add two floating-point numbers, and one to add a fixed- and a floating-point number. Then again, some writers use the term overloading to refer to something completely different ... in which case the term overloading is itself overloaded, and we have a genuine example of Case (a) on our hands.

much more complicated than it ought to be and (b) the fact that SQL also confuses types and representations (one of the original four logical differences mentioned earlier in this chapter).

As another example of logical sameness, consider the terms *intension* and *extension*, which come from logic and mathematics, and their synonyms (perhaps more commonly encountered in the relational world) *heading* and *body*, respectively. The latter terms were introduced by someone who wasn't as familiar with logic as he might have been: namely, yours truly. I have to admit, however, that I don't know how the term "relation schema"—sometimes "relation *scheme*"—came into (occasional) use, even by logicians, as another synonym for *intension*.

To repeat, then, the logical sameness problem is sometimes unavoidable; nevertheless, we should strive to avoid it as much as we can. The next three subsections briefly illustrates some cases where we should have been able to avoid it, but didn't.

Object Orientation

It sometimes seems to me that *every* term used in the world of object orientation is just a new label for something that's been known for years in other contexts under some more familiar name. Of course, the problem is exacerbated by the fact that there doesn't seem to be consensus on the meanings of terms even *within* the object world; however, I think it's fair to say that the key concepts—regardless of what names they go by—are *class, method, message, encapsulation,* and of course *object* itself. I'll defer discussion of the last of these to a later chapter, Chapter 6 (there's a lot to be said about it!). As for the rest:

- *Class* seems to be indistinguishable from **type,** as that term is classically understood.

- *Method* seems to be indistinguishable from **operator,** as that term is classically understood—except that in some object systems methods are "selfish," meaning they're effectively *a special kind* of operator: namely, one that treats one particular parameter as special (a state of affairs that makes life easier for the system but harder for the user).

- *Message* seems to be indistinguishable from **operator invocation,** as that term is classically understood—unless the method concerned is "selfish," in which case the minor exception noted under the previous point applies essentially unchanged.

- Finally, to say something is *encapsulated* seems to be indistinguishable from saying it's **scalar,** as that term is classically understood.

There is, of course, another concept that's frequently discussed in the object world: *class hierarchy.* Here are some synonyms for *that* term:

type hierarchy

inheritance hierarchy

generalization hierarchy

specialization hierarchy

ISA hierarchy

Note: I make the foregoing claims—i.e., regarding logical sameness in the object world—in full knowledge of the fact that many people will object to them (pun intended). For example, take the case of *class* and *type*. Here's a quote from a textbook on object database systems that discusses this issue:

> *Object-oriented systems can be classified into two main categories—systems supporting the notion of class and those supporting the notion of type* ... [Although] *there are no clear lines of demarcation between them, the two concepts are fundamentally different* [sic!] ... *Often the concepts type and class are used interchangeably.* [But I thought they were "fundamentally different"?]. *However, when both are present in the same language, the type is used to indicate the specification of the interface of a set of objects, while class is an implementational notion.* [So why is the class concept "in the language" at all?]. *Therefore ... a type is a set of objects which share the same behavior ... [and] a class is a set of objects which have exactly the same internal structure and therefore the same attributes and the same methods.* [But if all objects in a class have the same attributes and the same methods, is not that class a type, by the book's own definition?] *The class defines the implementation of a set of objects, while a type describes how such objects can be used.* [Contrast ODMG,[3] which—at least in some contexts if not all—uses the terms type and class in a very different way.]

(This extract is taken from *Object-Oriented Database Systems: Concepts and Architectures*, by Elisa Bertino and Lorenzo Martino, Addison-Wesley, 1993. The annotation is mine, of course.)

A little later in the same book, we also find this:

> *With inheritance, a class called a subclass can be defined on the basis of the definition of another class called a superclass.* [Surely—in accordance with its own earlier definitions—the book should be talking in terms of types here, not classes?] ... *The **specification hierarchy** (often called subtype hierarchy) expresses ... subtyping relationships which mean that an instance of the subtype can be used in every context in which an instance of the supertype can correctly appear (substitutability).* [Observe that it does now speak of types, not classes. Observe too that we now have two more terms for the type hierarchy.]

Note: As an aside, I'd like to quote here a passage from the preface to *A Dictionary of Modern American Usage*, by Bryan A. Garner (Oxford University Press, 1998):

> *I should address a question that many readers will wonder about. Should I really name names? Should I give full citations in the way that I do? Won't it mortify a [writer] to find some badly written sentence [quoted] for all the world to see? ... Well, I hope it isn't mortifying, and for me it's nothing new ... The citations appear for three reasons. First, they show that the examples are real, not fabricated. Second, they show the great variety of evidence on which [my] judgments are based ... And third, ...they reflect how the language is being used in our culture in our time.*

I concur!

---

3. R. G. G. Cattell and Douglas K. Barry (eds.): *The Object Data Standard: ODMG 3.0*. San Francisco, Calif.: Morgan Kaufmann (2000).

The Unified Modeling Language

A particularly rich source of examples of the logical sameness phenomenon is provided by *The Unified Modeling Language User Guide*, by Grady Booch, James Rumbaugh, and Ivar Jacobson (Addison-Wesley, 1999). *Note:* I've written on this topic elsewhere too (see Chapter 26 in the present book), but what follows is mostly new.

For my first exhibit, I simply present, without further comment on my part,[4] a set of definitions surrounding the general concept of *data type:*

- *Datatype:* A type whose values have no identity. Datatypes include primitive built-in types (such as numbers and strings), as well as enumeration types (such as Boolean).

- *Type:* A stereotype of class used to specify a domain of objects, together with the operations (but not methods) applicable to the objects.

- *Stereotype:* An extension of the vocabulary of the UML, which allows you to create new kinds of building blocks that are derived from existing ones but that are specific to your problem.

- *Class:* A description of a set of objects that share the same attributes, operations, relationships, and semantics.

- *Domain:* An area of knowledge or activity characterized by a set of concepts and terminology understood by practitioners in that area.

- *Interface:* A collection of operations that are used to specify a service of a class or a component.

- *Component:* A physical and replaceable part of a system that conforms to and provides the realization of a set of interfaces.

- *Primitive type:* A basic type, such as integer or a string.

- *Value:* An element of a type domain.

My second exhibit involves a similar set of definitions surrounding the general concept of *operator* (a term that doesn't actually seem to be used in UML, though the term *operation* is):

- *Precondition:* A constraint that must be true when an operation is invoked.

- *Postcondition:* A constraint that must be true at the completion of an operation.

- *Operation:* The implementation of a service that can be requested from any object of the class in order to affect behavior.

- *Request:* The specification of a stimulus sent to an object.

---

4. In particular, I don't want to comment further on the lack of precision in the definitions, though it's ubiquitous. I think the overall message—that there are far more terms than concepts—is clear enough without such commentary. Nor do I want to comment further on the truly astounding nature and implications of some of those definitions: for example, the idea that values have no identity (?). Nor do I want to get into the many questions those definitions raise. For example, if "a type whose values have no identity" is called a "datatype," then what's a type whose values do have identity called?

- *Stimulus:* An operation or signal.

- *Activation:* The execution of an operation.

- *Execution:* The running of a dynamic model.

- *Action:* An executable atomic computation that results in a change of state of the system or the return of a value.

- *Method:* The implementation of an operation.

- *Message:* A specification of a communication between objects that conveys information with the expectation that activity will ensue; the receipt of a message instance is normally considered an instance of an event.

- *Send:* The passing of a message instance from a sender object to a receiver object.

And one more exhibit:

- *Parameter:* The specification of a variable that can be changed, passed, or returned.

- *Argument:* A specific value corresponding to a parameter.

- *Formal parameter:* A parameter.

- *Actual parameter:* A function or procedure argument.

Miscellaneous Examples

Sometimes it's tempting to think that people are *actively exploiting* the logical sameness problem. For example, in his original paper on the entity/relationship model,[5] Chen reinvented the concept of domains (among other things), but called them *value sets;* then he went on to analyze the relational model in terms of the constructs of his E/R model and concluded that domains were just value sets (!).

Talking of entities and relationships: Of course, we all know that in many approaches—including but not limited to UML, the E/R model, prerelational systems such as IMS and IDMS, and most object systems—a distinction is made between entities and relationships. Well, there certainly is a distinction to be drawn, but it's not an either/or kind of distinction; to be more specific, all relationships are entities, but some entities aren't relationships. (The distinction is analogous to that between, e.g., ellipses and circles—all circles are ellipses, but some ellipses aren't circles.) So in this case we have two terms and two concepts, but the concepts aren't totally separate.

My last example of the logical sameness problem concerns what has come to be called, especially in XML contexts, **the semistructured data model**. Although this term is comparatively new, I have great difficulty in detecting any difference of substance between the thing it's supposed to refer to and the old-fashioned *hierarchic* data model—or, at least, the structural aspects of that model. But this is clearly a subject that deserves extended discussion, so I won't pursue it any further in the present chapter.

---

5. Peter Pin-Shan Chen: "The Entity-Relationship Model—Toward a Unified View of Data," *ACM TODS 1*, No. 1 (March 1976).

Concluding Remarks

I've been wanting to embark on this series for some time. It's certainly needed! One of Ted Codd's objectives when he introduced the relational model was to bring some clarity of thought and expression into a field, database management, that was in sore need of it at the time—and evidently still is. Confusion is rife; confusion leads to mistakes; and we can't even *discuss* those mistakes sensibly if we're confused over basic concepts!

I'll finish up with another quote that I think is highly relevant to the topic at hand. It's from Bertrand Russell's own preface to *The Bertrand Russell Dictionary of Mind, Matter and Morals* (ed., Lester E. Denonn, Citadel Press, 1993):[6]

> **Clarity, above all, has been my aim.** *I prefer a clear statement subsequently disproved to a misty dictum capable of some profound interpretation which can be welcomed as a "great thought." It is not by "great thoughts," but by careful and detailed analysis, that the kind of technical philosophy which I value can be advanced* [boldface added].

These wonderful remarks need no further elaboration by me.

Acknowledgments

I'd like to thank Hugh Darwen and Fabian Pascal for their comments on earlier drafts of this chapter. And special thanks go to Stephen Wilson for resolving the issue of the Wittgenstein quote—an issue that's been open for at least seven years but is now finally closed (I think).

Appendix A: Some Quotes from the Literature

I'm well aware that the body of this chapter is a little light on technical substance. The same is true of this appendix!—but I thought it might help bolster my argument a little to display a few pertinent quotes from the literature (not just the technical literature), with occasional commentary. My aim is partly to edify, partly just to amuse.

With regard to the technical quotes, by the way, I should say that some of them are quite old (and the same will be true of subsequent chapters in this series). One reason for this state of affairs is that I've more or less stopped reading the trade press over the past few years (I don't think I need say why). Another is that it's impossible to keep up!—the nonsense comes so thick and fast. Indeed, what I do see from time to time (especially in material taken off the Internet) tends to confirm my suspicion that little has changed, except perhaps for the worse. Thus, even when the quotes are old, the attitudes and confusions expressed therein still exist and in fact seem to be widespread, and there's still a need to fight the good fight.

And another remark on those technical quotes: Most of them are *extremely* sloppily phrased. As I've written elsewhere,[7] it's very distressing to find such sloppiness in writings dealing with relational technology of all things, given that (to say it again) it was exactly one of the objectives of the relational model to inject some precision and clarity of thinking into the database field.

---

6. I've used this quote in other places, too—in particular in the preface to my own book *An Introduction to Database Systems*, 8th edition (Addison-Wesley, 2004).

7. In "Relational Database: Further Misconceptions Number Three," in C. J. Date and Hugh Darwen, *Relational Database Writings 1989–1991* (Addison-Wesley, 1992).

Without further ado, let's turn to the quotes. My first is *not* from the trade press; it's from Bertrand Russell again. In comparing mathematics and logic, Russell asserted:

> *It has become wholly impossible to draw a line between the two; in fact, the two are one (quoted in William Dunham,* The Mathematical Universe, *John Wiley and Sons Inc., 1994).*

No logical difference here, then!

Talking of logic, here's another beautiful quote from Wittgenstein:

> *Logic takes care of itself; all we have to do is look and see how it does it (from* Notebooks 1914–1916, *entry for October 13th, 1914, ed. Anscombe, 1961; also in* Tractatus Logico-Philosophicus, *sct. 5:473, 1921; tr. 1922).*

Thanks to Declan Brady for drawing my attention to this one.

Here's another of Wittgenstein's famous dictums (this one is from the preface to *Tractatus Logico-Philosophicus*):

> *Was sich überhaupt sagen lässt, lässt sich klar sagen; und wovon man nicht reden kann, darüber muss man schweigen. (What can be said at all can be said clearly; and whereof one cannot speak, thereof one must be silent.)*

There's a logical difference, then, between that which can be spoken of and that which can't. Which might well be taken, incidentally, as a directive to avoid the use of nulls!—since to say "*x* is null" is to say, in effect, that there's nothing we can say about *x*.

I have a few more nice quotes to do with this business of speaking clearly. The first is due to Descartes:

> *When transcendental questions are under discussion, be transcendentally clear (quoted by Simon Singh in* Fermat's Enigma, *Walker and Co., 1997).*

The second is from Ben Jonson (he's discussing "the shame of speaking [and writing] unskilfully"):

> *Neither can his Mind be thought to be in Tune, whose words do jarre; nor his reason in frame, whose sentence is preposterous; nor his Elocution clear and perfect, whose utterance breaks itself into fragments and uncertainties. Negligent speech doth not onely discredit the person of the Speaker, but it discrediteth the opinion of his reason and judgement; it discrediteth the force and uniformity of the matter and substance. If it be so then in words, which fly and 'scape censure, and where one good Phrase asks pardon for many incongruities and faults, how then shall he be thought wise whose penning is thin and shallow? How shall you look for wit from him whose leasure and head, assisted with the examination of his eyes, yeeld you no life or sharpnesse in his writing?*

These remarks are quoted by Richard Mitchell in an essay entitled "Hopefully, We Could Care Less" in his book *The Leaning Tower of Babel* (The Akadine Press, 2000).

My third and last quote on this issue of speaking clearly is from Dijkstra, and is perhaps more directly relevant to my thesis. He's describing the process by which he believes software products should be designed and built:

I have described this [process] at some length because I remember it so well and because I believe it to be quite typical. Eventually you come up with a very formal and well-defined product, but this eventual birth is preceded by a period of gestation during which new ideas are tried and discarded or developed. That is the only way I know of in which the mind can cope with such conceptual problems. From experience I have learned that in that gestation period, when a new jargon has to be created, an excellent mastery of their native tongue is an absolute requirement for all participants. A programmer that talks sloppily is just a disaster. Excellent mastery of his [sic] native tongue is my first selection criterion for a prospective programmer; good taste in mathematics is the second important criterion. (As luck will have it, they often go hand in hand.)

(From E. W. Dijkstra, EWD 648, "Why Is Software So Expensive? An Explanation to the Hardware Designer," in *Selected Writings on Computing: A Personal Perspective*, Springer-Verlag, 1982.)

Following these beautifully clear remarks on the importance of clarity, what are we to make of extracts like this one (from an article in a trade magazine)?

Database vendors are displacing SQL with Java because SQL isn't portable and because object developers cringe at using legacy procedural code in interchangeable component frameworks.

Or this one (from another magazine article)?

JDO also complements EJB (Enterprise JavaBeans). For example, programmers can use JDO and EJBs together to access data, either using persistent classes in Session Beans, delegate classes in BMP (Bean-Managed Persistence) Entity Beans, or a container implementation alternative to JDBC in CMP (Container-Managed Persistence) Entity Beans. Developers need not modify existing applications that use EJBs, but they may wish to implement JDO with EJBs to simplify data access methods.

I've suppressed attributions on these two quotes in order to protect the guilty; but remember what I said about sloppy writing? Examples like these are so badly expressed that it's not even clear what the writers are trying to say, and I'm sometimes forced to invoke what I've referred to elsewhere as *The Principle of Incoherence* (sometimes known, a trifle unkindly, as *The Incoherent Principle*):

It's hard to criticize something coherently if what you're trying to criticize is itself not very coherent in the first place.

Well, never mind that. Let's take a look at some more quotes from the world of objects. The first is from a textbook:

> *An* entity *is any* thing *that needs to be modeled. The definitions of entities and objects are intertwined. Texts on ER modeling describe an entity as an object, and texts on object modeling describe an object as an entity in the problem domain. Webster's describes both* entity *and* object *as "things" and Roget's treats* entity, object, *and* thing *as synonyms. Novices in object technology often ask, "What is an object?" The answer is to explore the "things" that need to be managed by the application, which often turn out to be the objects that the application must model: people, places, inanimate objects, concepts, events, and so on. Entities are the most common form of object modeled in applications.*

(Taken from David Jordan, *C++ Object Databases: Programming with the ODMG Standard,* Addison-Wesley, 1998.)

The next is from an interview with Peter Chen in the *FOCUS Systems Journal,* May 1988—Chen speaking:

> *What's the difference between an entity and an object? In the database world, people tend to be more type-oriented and to need more semantics. That's why we call them entities. [What, the people?] In the programming environment, people want more freedom, so they call them objects ... [Entities] are objects with more semantic value, classified into types, which give more information. We often define entities as "identifiable objects of interest." Everything is an object. Some are identifiable ones [meaning some aren't?] that we have an interest in, and these are entities.*

Next, here's Hugh Darwen (part of a review he did of an early draft of a text on object databases):

> *[A] brief but awful treatise on OODB ... [It] exhibits all of the usual muddles we find in OO literature, arising from the excess of terminology, conflation of important distinct concepts, and distinction of concepts that aren't really distinct. For example, an object, we're told, is something that has instance variables and methods. An example of an object of class INTEGER is the self-identifying (?) object, 3. I don't know what 3's instance variables are. For another example, we're told that every object is an instance of some class. We aren't told about any instances (of classes) that aren't objects. So it isn't clear why we need both terms, nor is it clear what considerations lead one to choose between these terms, nor is it clear why sometimes both are used simultaneously, in object instance. And then there are messages. Apparently a message is a method invocation that is sent from one object (the sender) to another (the receiver). Not only does the sender not appear to have any effect on anything, but also there are frequent subsequent references to messages being sent, not by objects, but by methods. I could go on.*

Perhaps we have to content ourselves with this thought: "Objects in the real world have only one thing in common—they're all different" (anon.). A logical difference with a vengeance!

Let's get back to the philosophers for a moment. The following is taken from *Beyond the Wall* by Edward Abbey (Henry Holt, 1991):

> *What did the wall-eyed Jean-Paul Sartre say to Albert Camus when they ran into each other in the doorway of the Café Flore? Sartre said, Pourquoi ne regards-tu pas où tu vas, Albert? And what did Albert Camus say? Pourquoi ne vas-tu pas vers ce que tu regards, J.-P?*

(So what's the logical difference here?)

Another nice quote on logic, to remind us that it isn't a closed subject:

> *[In] Boole's time, it was common for writers on logic to equate the entire subject with what Aristotle had done so many centuries earlier. As Boole put it, this was to maintain that "the science of Logic enjoys an immunity from those conditions of imperfection and of progress to which all other sciences are subject"* (Martin Davis, Engines of Logic: Mathematics and the Origins of the Computer, *W. W. Norton and Company, 2000).*

Next, I have a quote—or paraphrase, at any rate—from Ted Codd. This piece first appeared in 1974 in Installment No. 4 of an occasional series by Ted entitled "Understanding Relations" in the ACM SIGMOD bulletin *FDT* (subsequently renamed *SIGMOD Record*), *Vol. 6*, No. 4. It has to do with logical difference (or logical sameness, rather). I've published versions of it in a variety of different writings of my own since that time, so it's far from new, but I still believe it's worth repeating here:

> *Regarding the general question of whether any two concepts A and B are "the same" and can thus be equated, there's a simple general principle that can usefully be applied: Simply ask yourself "Is every example of A an example of B?" and, conversely, "Is every example of B an example of A?" Only if the answer is yes to both of these questions is it true that A and B are identical.*

Back to the matter of clarity. I think we all know some speakers and writers who *deliberately* try not to be clear (they usually succeed, too), because they know the paucity of their thinking would be revealed if they made themselves too easily understood. Here's Plato on this subject:

> *[They] are always in motion; but as for dwelling upon an argument or a question, and quietly asking and answering in turn, they can no more do so than they can fly ... If you ask any of them a question, he will produce, as from a quiver, sayings brief and dark, and shoot them at you; and if you enquire the reason of what he has said, you will be hit with some other new-fangled word, and you will make no way with any of them. Their great care is, not to allow of any settled principle either in their arguments or in their minds ... for they are at war with the stationary, and do what they can to drive it out everywhere.*

(Quoted by Richard Mitchell in his essay "Sayings Brief and Dark" in the book *The Leaning Tower of Babel* already referred to earlier.)

Now a few miscellaneous quotes. I'll leave it to you (mostly) to figure out what the relevance, if any, of the concepts of logical difference and logical sameness might be in each case.

> *In language there are only differences (Ferdinand de Saussure).*

> *Information is any difference that makes a difference (Gregory Bateson).*

> *He is no better, he is much the same (Alfred Austin).*

> *N-ary association: An association among three or more classes (another definition from* The Unified Modeling Language User Guide, *by Grady Booch, James Rumbaugh, and Ivar Jacobson, Addison-Wesley, 1999).*

In no engineering discipline does the successful pursuit of academic ideals pay more material dividends than in software engineering (C. A. R. Hoare; I'm not sure I have the exact wording here, but the sense is right).

All large companies know today that speed and being early to market are often more important than being right (Lou Gerstner, IBM chairman, quoted in Informationweek, *February 9th, 1998).* Well, I certainly agree there's a logical difference between speed to market and being right. Some might say there are a few other logical differences involved here, too.

I'll close with a few quotes taken off the Internet. To my mind, these quotes demonstrate both an extreme lack of clarity of expression and a desperate confusion over concepts (the latter, of course, equating—in most cases if not all—to a lack of appreciation of certain logical differences). Note the frightening implications of some of the things said! ("I am supposed to teach a class in this starting next week" ... ?!?)

I need to make a search option into my website. It needs to display products and the user can use any words. Right now I am using access database with all my products in one table. I need help in connecting my database to the internet. I know nothing about database, just creating queries and tables that's it. I would appreciate if you would e-mail me back.

I have been trying to find the correct way of normalizing tables in Access. From what I understand, it goes from the 1st normal form to 2nd, then 3rd. Usually, that's as far as it goes, but sometimes to the 5th and 6th. Then, there's also the Cobb 3rd. This all makes sense to me. I am supposed to teach a class in this starting next week, and I just got the textbook. It says something entirely different. It says 2nd normal form is only for tables with a multiple-field primary key, 3rd normal form is only for tables with a single-field key. 4th normal form can go from 1st to 4th, where there are no independent one-to-many relationships between primary key and non-key fields. Can someone clear this up for me please?

The third example consists of an exchange:

A: How is data independence implemented?

B: What do you mean by data independence?

A: Data independence is the independence between levels in a DBMS, when you can modify a level without interference in another or in your programs.

C: Can you be more specific? I have not heard of this concept in relation to how you have described it. It sounds more like an application design concept rather than an SQL principle.

D: C's right it is a design approach. There is both physical and logical data independence, but there is no way to add data independence to a SQL statement.

Finally—talking about confusion—how about this one for an example of being "unclear on the concept"?

Ultimately, respect for a free press comes with democratic development and economic growth, in part because only a robust private sector can provide enough advertising to give the media independence (New York Times *editorial, September 5th, 2000*).

CHAPTER 5

■■■

On the Logical Difference Between Model and Implementation

One of the most fundamental and important logical differences of all is that between **model** and **implementation;** several others are either special cases or logical consequences of this one, and so it's a good idea to deal with it first. In principle, of course, the model *vs.* implementation distinction should be familiar to everyone in the database field—certainly ever since 1970, when Ted Codd's classic paper on the relational model was published—but the sad fact is that it's one that many people still get confused over, as we'll see.

Note: "Ted Codd's classic paper" is, of course, "A Relational Model of Data for Large Shared Data Banks," by E. F. Codd, *CACM 13*, No. 6, June 1970 (republished in *Milestones of Research— Selected Papers 1958–1982, CACM 25th Anniversary Issue, CACM 26*, No. 1, January 1983). On reflection, perhaps the real problem is that few people seem actually to have *read* this paper. Certainly people often get its title wrong. In the last few days alone, I've seen it referred to as "A Relational Model for Large Shared Databases" and "A Relational Model for Large Shared Databanks," and I'm sure I've encountered other (mis)titles as well. Of course, as Mark Twain observed, a classic is something that everybody wants to have read and nobody wants to read ...

Portions of the present chapter have previously appeared, in somewhat different form, in one or more of the following:

- "Why Is It Important to Think Precisely?" (republished in my book *Relational Database Writings 1994–1997*, Addison-Wesley, 1998)

- "Models, Models, Everywhere, Nor Any Time to Think" (Chapter 25 in the present book)

- *Databases, Types, and the Relational Model: The Third Manifesto*, 3rd edition, by Hugh Darwen and myself (Addison-Wesley, 2006)

- *WHAT Not HOW: The Business Rules Approach to Application Development* (Addison-Wesley, 2000)

- *An Introduction to Database Systems*, 8th edition (Addison-Wesley, 2004)

However, most of what follows is new.

Terms and Definitions

First of all, please note that I'll be using the term "model" throughout this chapter to mean a *data* model specifically. But there's a potential confusion over this more specific term that I need to head off at the pass. Indeed, it's an unfortunate fact that the term is used in the database world with two very different meanings, and we need to be clear as to which of those meanings we intend in any particular context.

The first of those meanings is the one we have in mind when we talk about (for example) the *relational* model. It can be defined as follows:

Definition: A **data model** *(first sense)* is an abstract, self-contained, logical definition of the objects, operators, and so forth, that together constitute the *abstract machine* with which users interact. The objects allow us to model the *structure* of data. The operators allow us to model its *behavior.*

(Please note that I'm using the term *objects* here in its generic sense, not in the special sense in which it's used in the world of object orientation. Also, I'm using the term *users* to mean both end users and application programmers.)

And then—very important!—we can usefully go on to distinguish the notion of a data model as just defined from the associated notion of an *implementation*, which is defined as follows:

Definition: An **implementation** of a given data model is a physical realization on a real machine of the components of the abstract machine that together constitute that model.

(Please note that I'm using the term *implementation* here to mean implementation of "the system"—i.e., the DBMS—specifically, not implementation of some application that runs on top of the DBMS.)

By way of example, consider the relational model. The concept *relation* itself is, naturally, part of that model: Users have to know what relations are, they have to know they're made up of rows and columns (or, better, tuples and attributes), they have to know what they mean (i.e., how to interpret them), and so on. All that is part of the model. But they don't have to know how relations are physically stored on the disk, or how individual data values are physically encoded, or what indexes or other access paths exist; all that is part of the implementation, not part of the model.

Or consider the concept *join.* The join concept, like the concept of *relation* itself, is part of the relational model: Users have to know what a join is, they have to know how to invoke a join, they have to know what the result of a join looks like, and so on. Again, all that is part of the model. But they don't have to know how joins are physically implemented, or what expression transformations take place, or what indexes or other access paths are used, or what I/O's occur; all that is part of the implementation, not part of the model.

In a nutshell, then:

- The model (in the first sense of the term) is *what the user has to know.*

- The implementation is what the user *doesn't* have to know.

Of course, I'm not saying here that users aren't *allowed* to know about the implementation; I'm just saying they don't have to. In other words, everything to do with implementation should be, at least potentially, **hidden from the user**.

As you can see from the foregoing definitions, then, the distinction between model and implementation is really just a special case—a very important special case—of the familiar distinction between *logical* and *physical*. Sadly, however, many of today's database systems, even those that profess to be relational, don't make those distinctions as clearly as they should. Indeed, there seems to be a fairly widespread lack of understanding of those distinctions and the importance of making them, as we'll see in subsequent sections.

Be that as it may, let's now turn to the second meaning of the term *data model*, which can be defined as follows:

Definition: A **data model** *(second sense)* is a model of the persistent data of some particular enterprise.

In other words, a data model in the second sense is just a (possibly somewhat abstract) *database design*. For example, we might speak of the data model for some bank, or some hospital, or some government department.

Having now explained the two different meanings of the term *data model*, I'd like to mention an analogy that I think nicely illuminates the relationship between them:

- A data model in the first sense is like *a programming language,* whose constructs can be used to solve many specific problems, but in and of themselves have no direct connection with any such specific problem.

- A data model in the second sense is like *a specific program written in that language*— it uses the facilities provided by the model, in the first sense of that term, to solve some specific problem.

For the remainder of this chapter, I'll be using the term *data model* (or just *model* for short) exclusively in its first sense.

What Are Models For?

Now, the previous section explained what a model *is*, but it didn't say what models are *for*. Well, actually I think it did, implicitly, but the point is probably worth spelling out explicitly:

The model specifies the user interface (at least abstractly).

In other words, the model determines the functionality of the system from the user's point of view—it specifies the kinds of objects that are available for the user to use, it specifies the kinds of operations the user can apply to those objects, and it specifies the kinds of effects the user can expect those operations to have. To say it again, the model defines the logical *abstract machine* with which the user interacts (that's why the user needs to understand it, in order to be able to do his or her job). Moreover, it does so, by definition, without any reference whatsoever to how that abstract machine is physically implemented. And it's that fact (the fact, that is, that the model and the implementation are kept rigorously separate) that enables us to achieve **data independence**—and I presume we all understand the importance of *that* objective. Indeed, to the extent we fail to observe that separation, we fail to achieve that objective.

Aside: In the first draft of this chapter, I followed the remark "I presume we all understand the importance of *that* objective" by a reference to a footnote that read as follows:

Maybe not!—see the exchange on this very topic, taken off the Internet, quoted in the appendix to the introductory article in this series ("On the Notion of Logical Difference"). If you're not familiar with the concept of data independence, you should be able to find an explanation in any good database textbook.

Then I had second thoughts, and decided to check the textbooks in my own personal collection ... and discovered, to my great surprise, that a fair proportion of them did *not* include any such explanation. Some didn't even have the term *data independence* in the index! (On the other hand, I did say "any *good* database textbook." If a book fails to cover such a fundamental concept, I don't think it can claim to be good.) *End of aside.*

Definitions from the Literature

Before I get to the issue of confusion over the difference between model and implementation, I must admit that the concepts do seem to be a little difficult to pin down precisely. I've already given my own preferred definitions, of course. Here by contrast are some definitions from the literature ...

First of all, here's what UML has to say (these definitions are taken from *The Unified Modeling Language User Guide,* by Grady Booch, James Rumbaugh, and Ivar Jacobson, Addison-Wesley, 1999):

Model: A simplification of reality, created in order to better understand the system being created; a semantically closed abstraction of a system.

Implementation: A concrete realization of the contract declared by an interface; a definition of how something is constructed or computed.

I'm not sure whether I concur with these definitions or not! They don't seem as crisp as mine, but you might disagree.

I note too that the term *architecture* is sometimes used to mean something like what I mean by *model.* As Fred Brooks says in *The Mythical Man-Month,* 20th anniversary edition, Addison-Wesley, 1995: "[The] architecture of a system [is] the complete and detailed specification of the user interface." Or maybe not ... Here's the UML definition:

Architecture: The set of significant decisions about the organization of a software system, the selection of the structural elements and their interfaces by which the system is composed, together with their behavior as specified in the collaborations among those elements, the composition of these structural and behavioral elements into progressively large subsystems, and the architectural style that guides this organization—these elements and their interfaces, their collaborations, and their composition. Software architecture is not only concerned with structure and behavior, but also with usage, functionality, performance, resilience, reuse, comprehensibility, economic and technology constraints and trade-offs, and aesthetic concerns.

What do *you* think?

Next, I took a look at some of the standard database textbooks. The first thing I discovered was that—as in the case of data independence previously noted—most of them didn't even seem to have either *model* or *data model* in the index! And I couldn't find an explicit discussion of the logical difference between model and implementation in any of them. Here's what I did find (boldface and italics as in the originals):

Raghu Ramakrishnan and Johannes Gehrke, *Database Management Systems,* 3rd edition (McGraw-Hill, 2003): "A **data model** is a collection of high-level data description constructs that hide many low-level storage details."

Patrick O'Neil, *Database Principles, Programming, and Performance,* 2nd edition (Morgan Kaufmann, 2000): "A *database model,* or *data model,* is a set of definitions describing how real-world data is conceptually represented as computerized information."

Ramez Elmasri and Shamkant B. Navathe, *Fundamentals of Database Systems,* 3rd edition (Benjamin Cummings, 2000): "A **data model** [is] a collection of concepts that can be used to describe the structure of a database ... By *structure of a database* we mean the data types, relationships, and constraints that should hold on the data."

Note the focus in these definitions on the structural aspects of data specifically (though Elmasri and Navathe do add that "Most [*sic!*] data models also include a set of **basic operations** for specifying retrievals and updates on the data").

I conclude from all of the foregoing that an article like this one is definitely needed.

Examples of Confusion: Performance Issues

In this section and the next three, I'll give examples of confusion over the model *vs.* implementation distinction, with commentary. The first point that seems to need stressing is this:

Since *model* is a logical concept and *implementation* is a physical one, everything to do with **performance** is purely a matter of implementation and has nothing to do with the model.

This point is surely obvious, and yet many people do seem to be confused about it. Here are some typical quotes:

A mid 1990s advertisement for the object database product GemStone: "Maybe you've ... hit the relational performance barrier because you're doing too many JOINs" [uppercase in the original].

Doug Barry, "When to Use Object DBMSs," Computerworld, *October 26th, 1992: "The relational joins ... now either go away because of the object data model or are replaced with data references. And traversing a data reference is considerably faster than a join."*

Won Kim: "On Marrying Relations and Objects: Relation-Centric and Object-Centric Perspectives," Data Base Newsletter 22, *No. 6 (November/December 1994) and elsewhere: "[A deficiency of the relational model is the] join-based retrieval of a collection of related data (even when the need to retrieve the collection of data is known at the time of database design)."*

Mary Loomis, "ODBMS vs. Relational," Journal of Object-Oriented Programming, *July/ August 1990: "Relational database design is really a process of trying to figure out how to represent real-world objects within the confines of tables in such a way that good performance results and preserving data integrity is possible* [note the confusion over logical vs. physical design here] *... [Many] normalized tables could be required to represent a single real-world object class ... This is exactly the root of the performance difficulties with relational DBMSs ... Users and programs typically want to access and manipulate objects, not tables. To manifest an object from its corresponding tables, an RDBMS must do joins. One of the slowest things that RDBMSs do is joins. The more joins there are, the slower the system is—to the point of unacceptability. An ODBMS has no concept of joining. Such processing simply is not necessary when objects are stored as objects."*

John Taschek, "ODBMSs Take On Relational Models" [note that plural, by the way!], PCWeek, *October 9th, 1995: "Relational database servers also depend on primary and foreign keys to link data from separate tables. This means that database administrators must normalize the tables (an often complex process) so that queries can run efficiently and effectively. Databases that consist of a large number of tables are therefore difficult to manage and may be slower since the database engine must go through the complex process of filtering data from each table."*

The common thread running through these quotes is clearly the assumption—or assertion, rather—that "joins are slow." I've had occasion to address this claim in print before (see, e.g., the article "Objects and Relations: Forty-Seven Points of Light" in my book *Relational Database Writings 1994–1997*, Addison-Wesley, 1998, on which the following response is partly based). The fact is, anyone who advances such a claim is seriously confused over the logical difference between model and implementation. Let me elaborate:

- First of all, joins are a model concept, while performance is an implementation concept. Thus, the claim that "joins are slow," as such, is simply nonsense; it's an apples-and-oranges comparison. Now, we might legitimately claim that the way joins are *implemented* in some particular product isn't very efficient; we might even be correct in making such a claim; but the two claims are logically different things. All logical differences are big differences!

- Second, the "joins are slow" claim usually serves as lead-in to an argument that "pointers are faster" (Doug Barry makes such an argument explicitly, and the other writers quoted do so implicitly). In other words, advocates of the "joins are slow" position usually argue that following a pointer from the referencing table to the referenced table or *vice versa* is a good—i.e., efficient—implementation mechanism. Fine: I'll agree to this point for the sake of the argument (though *only* for the sake of the argument, please note!). *But there's absolutely no reason why joins shouldn't be implemented by following pointers internally.* Of course, I know they typically aren't implemented that way in today's SQL products, but that's a deficiency of those products; it's certainly not a defect in, or valid criticism of, the *model*. In other words, (1) *implementing* joins by pointers is very different from (2) *exposing* such pointers in the model. The fact that (1) might be a good idea doesn't imply that (2) is a good idea, and of course it categorically isn't.

- Third, there's a tacit assumption underlying such claims (i.e., that joins are slow) that tables as seen by the user map one-to-one to chunks of contiguous storage on the disk—with the implication that joining two tables means accessing two separate chunks of storage, and hence I/O overhead. This assumption isn't always valid, even today (witness, e.g., Oracle's hierarchic clustering feature). What's more, much more sophisticated facilities are likely to be available in this connection soon (i.e., DBMSs are likely to offer much more effective data-to-storage mapping capabilities in the near future). I plan to examine this latter possibility in writing very soon.

Here's another quote on performance issues. Obviously it commits the same fundamental error (i.e., of thinking the model has something to do with performance), but it also manages to inject some novel errors of its own:

Robin Bloor, "All in the Name of Progress," DBMS Magazine, *January 1995: "[VMark's product] uniVerse ... is a post-relational database [sic] with multidimensional viewing capabilities. It implements the NF2 data model, which is non-first normal form. That is, it adheres to and implements all of the normalizations advocated by E. F. Codd, except for the first. As far as I know, the NF2 data model was invented by IBM in an attempt to address performance problems that occur with relational databases, and it is exceedingly useful when dealing with multidimensional arrays."*

Points arising:

- To do him credit, Bloor himself later in the same article objects to "the use of the marketing term post-relational." So do I!—see my article "What Do You Mean, 'Post-Relational'?" (Chapter 21 in the present book). However, I also object to Bloor's use of the term "database" to mean *DBMS*—another logical difference here, in fact, and one I'll probably come back to in some future writing.

- I discussed "the NF2 data model"—more usually called the NF^2 data model—in my recent article "What First Normal Form Really Means" (Chapter 8 in the present book). The claims that uniVerse supports that model and that it therefore "adheres to ... all of the normalizations advocated by E. F. Codd, except for the first" betrays a serious lack of understanding on Bloor's part, however. To be specific:

  - If it supports repeating groups as I defined them in "What First Normal Form Really Means"—which is what Bloor *might* mean when he says uniVerse supports the NF^2 model—then its basic data object isn't a relation at all, and the concept of "all normalizations except the first" simply doesn't apply.

  - On the other hand, if it *doesn't* support such repeating groups, then it certainly does support first normal form, in the sense that its basic data objects do represent relations. (I'm ignoring the possibility here that the product might commit some other error, not mentioned by Bloor, that would make the foregoing sentence invalid.)

- More important, perhaps, the very suggestion that a given product "adheres" to *any* level of normalization other than first makes no sense, anyway! Products surely never *prohibit* tables from being in (say) fifth normal form—so does that mean they "adhere" to fifth normal form? What would it mean for a product *not* to "adhere" to fifth normal form?

- I'm pretty sure it wasn't IBM that "invented the NF² model." Even if I'm wrong on this point, it's much more relevant to stress the fact that the NF² model certainly wasn't invented "to address performance problems that occur with relational databases" (to say it again, performance isn't, or shouldn't be, a model issue at all). Rather, it was invented to address what was perceived—incorrectly, please note—as a *logical* short-coming of the relational model.

Just as an aside, I remark that uniVerse is the product that was once described by its vendor in its own marketing as "a relational database management system that *literally redefines the meaning of relational*" (my italics). Indeed.

Examples of Confusion: Many Different Data Structures

Another common model *vs.* implementation confusion has to do with the idea that the model should provide many different ways of representing data (i.e., at the model, or in other words the logical, level). I have several quotes to illustrate this point. They're all due to the same person, Mary Loomis; the first two are from an interview she did in *Data Base Newsletter 22* (No. 6, November/December 1994), the others are from her book *Object Databases: The Essentials* (Addison-Wesley, 1995). Let me immediately say that I don't want what follows to be construed as a personal attack; the first two quotes, at least, are concerned with the ODMG specifications, and my criticisms of them are really directed at ODMG, not at Mary Loomis herself, and they should be understood in that light.

Let me begin by giving a little background on ODMG. The term itself is used to refer, a little loosely, to the proposals of the Object Data Management Group, a consortium of representatives from companies from the object DBMS industry. So far as I know, those proposals have gone through four versions to date, all four of which are documented in books published by Morgan Kaufmann:

1. R. G. G. Cattell (ed.), *The Object Database Standard: ODMG-93*, 1994. This is the version Mary Loomis is referring to in the quotes that follow (she was vice chair of the group at that time).

2. R. G. G. Cattell (ed.), *The Object Database Standard: ODMG-93 Release 1.2*, 1996.

3. R. G. G. Cattell and Douglas K. Barry (eds.), *The Object Database Standard: ODMG 2.0*, 1997.

4. R. G. G. Cattell and Douglas K. Barry (eds.), *The Object Data Standard: ODMG 3.0*, 2000. This is the current version; note the slight name change ("data" instead of "database").

Here now are the quotes:

Interviewer: *The ODMG specification includes not only sets, but also lists, bags, and arrays* [though not relations, observe!]. *Doesn't inclusion of these additional collection types cause any proposed query language to become exceedingly complex?* Response: *Not necessarily ... The ODMG's object query language (OQL), for example, is specified fully in about 17 pages. The current SQL specification, by contrast, is a very thick document.*

The ODMG object model recaptures some of the semantics that was lost in the transition from earlier database models to the relational model. Relationships and sequence, for example, are semantic constructs. The fact that the CODASYL model included some of this information does not mean that ODMG's inclusion of those same constructs is a step backward.

An object DBMS builds these relationships into the object database and can use them directly at run time ... By contrast, a relational DBMS must recreate relationships at run time using joins, based upon instructions from an application.

To run through the rows [of a table] in ... sequence requires the relational DBMS to sort the rows.

Now let me respond to these remarks. It seems to me that the big question we need to ask in the face of claims like the ones illustrated by these quotes is this: What's the *real* reason for giving the user two or more ways of doing the same thing? For example, why should the model support both lists and arrays? And if it does support both, how should the user decide whether to represent a given "collection"—for example, the collection of employees in a given department—by a list or by an array?

It further seems to me that the overriding reason for choosing, say, an array over a list in such a situation is surely that the user is expecting the array representation to display the *performance* characteristics of an array. After all, both representations will surely support, in some shape or form, all of the processing the user wants to carry out on the collection, so there's no *logical* reason to choose one over the other.[1] It follows that those arrays and lists had better be *physically implemented* as arrays and lists, respectively—for otherwise there's not much point in giving the user the choice in the first place! It further follows that we've now lost some data independence—the implementation isn't free to replace (say) an array by a list under the covers, because if it does, then applications will break. In other words, this second model *vs.* implementation confusion is related to the first: **The real reason for offering alternative representations is performance.** And *this* fact demonstrates a failure to understand the logical difference between model and implementation in the first place, or why that difference is there. To spell it out one more time:

The purpose of the model is to provide *logical* data structuring and processing capabilities. *Physical* (implementation) concerns should be rigorously excluded.

And if we take these ideas to heart, it's surely *obvious* that arrays, lists, and the like have no place in the model.

---

1. I concede that there might be psychological reasons as well. But I very much doubt whether any product that actually offers such choices does so for purely psychological reasons.

I'd also like to comment on some of the more detailed points raised in the foregoing quotes. In answer to the question as to whether arrays, lists, and the like complicate the query language, Mary Loomis responds that OQL is fully specified in about 17 pages[2] and takes a side swipe at the SQL standard. There are several points I'd like to make in this connection:

- First, I'm no fan of SQL, but it's only fair to point out that the SQL standard addresses *much* more of "the total database problem" than OQL does, and that's one of the reasons why it's "a very thick document" (much thicker now than it was in 1994, incidentally).

- On the other hand, I suspect that Mary Loomis would claim—and if so I would agree with her—that if we were to cut the SQL standard down to just the portions that address the kinds of issues that OQL does, then it would still be much thicker than the OQL specification. As I've had occasion to note elsewhere, SQL is a poorly designed language by just about any standard (pun intended); thus, I'm quite prepared to accept the notion that OQL, *if we limit our attention to the relational portions of that language,* might be a better language than SQL (perhaps less redundant, and certainly more orthogonal).

- Even conceding the previous point, however, the fact remains that, *pace* Mary Loomis, OQL *is* more complicated than it needs to be: It supports bags, lists, and arrays, and so it clearly needs a set of bag operators, a set of list operators, and a set of array operators. In fact, it is axiomatic that if we have N different ways to represent data, then we need N different sets of operators. And if $N > 1$, then we have more operators to implement, document, teach, learn, remember, and use. But those extra operators add complexity, not power! There's nothing useful that can be done if $N > 1$ that can't be done if $N = 1$.

Onward. The next quote includes the claim that "relationships and sequence are semantic constructs" and the further claim that "the fact that CODASYL included such constructs doesn't mean that ODMG represents a step backward" (both quotes slightly reworded here). Well, it seems to me that we have here more of the same confusions once again. Consider relationships, for example. Of course relationships are a semantic construct—but that's not the issue! The issue, rather, is *how that semantic construct should be represented in the model* (indeed, the distinction between a concept *per se* and how that concept is represented is yet another of the great logical differences). The relational model gives us a uniform way to represent all entities and all relationships,[3] and the advantages of that uniformity of representation are clear and well understood (at least, they *should* be). And then, if pointers turn out to be a good way to *implement* certain relationships, well, fine, go ahead and use them—but in the implementation, not in the model. The trouble with CODASYL and ODMG and other suchlike schemes is that they use pointers in the model (thereby making them user-visible and leading to a pointer-chasing, manual-navigation style of access). In my opinion, therefore (*pace* Mary Loomis again), ODMG's inclusion of such pointers definitely is a step backward.

The arguments of the previous paragraph also serve in part to counter the claims in the third quote (repeated for convenience):

---

2. Those 17 pages became 44 in the most recent version of ODMG. What's more, my copy is scribbled all over with questions that I couldn't find the answer to, so I'm somewhat skeptical as to whether those 44 pages really do "fully specify" the language as claimed.
3. It's relevant to remind you that relationships *are* entities, anyway.

An object DBMS builds these relationships into the object database and can use them directly at run time ... By contrast, a relational DBMS must recreate relationships at run time using joins, based upon instructions from an application.

Note the tacit admission here that the purpose of including "relationships"—meaning user-visible pointers—in the model is indeed *performance* ... To paraphrase: "The system can follow the pointers directly at run time instead of having to do joins." Again, therefore, it seems to me that object advocates complicate their model precisely because they don't understand why the model and the implementation were supposed to be kept rigidly separate in the first place.

I note in passing that the SQL standard also includes such user-visible pointers, thanks to the mechanism it calls "REF types"—further proof, if such were needed, that the people responsible for the design of SQL either don't understand the relational model or don't agree with it. REF types constitute a *huge* departure from the relational model, and I've explained elsewhere some of the problems they cause; see my papers "Don't Mix Pointers and Relations!" and "Don't Mix Pointers and Relations—*Please!*" (both in *Relational Database Writings 1994–1997*, Addison-Wesley, 1998). I've never seen a good justification for the introduction of REF types into SQL (and believe me, it's not for lack of asking); in fact, I think its support for REF types means SQL finally has to abandon any claim it might ever have had to being relational.

Analogous remarks apply to the "semantic construct" *sequence*. It's true that sequence is a semantic construct, but again that's not the issue; rather, the issue is how to *represent* that construct at the model level. Introducing an explicit "sequence" construct into the model is a bad idea for exactly the same kinds of reasons that introducing an explicit "relationship" construct into the model is a bad idea.

The fourth quote betrays some related confusions. To repeat:

To run through the rows [of a table] in ... sequence requires the relational DBMS to sort the rows.

Well, of course the desired *logical* sequence might be *physically* represented by an index, or by a pointer chain, or even by physical contiguity (meaning in every case that there's certainly no need for "the relational DBMS to sort the rows"—at least, not at run time). All of these possibilities are supported in SQL systems today! In fact, the options available for *physically* implementing some *logical* sequence are exactly the same in a relational system as they are in an object system. The difference, of course, is that object systems typically require the user to choose the implementation (by choosing to use, say, a list instead of an array), while relational systems keep the choice where it belongs, in the implementation.

I'll close this section with a Ted Codd quote. This exchange occurred on a conference panel, as I recall. We were discussing this very issue—the issue, that is, of whether the model should include a variety of different data structures—and Ted said this: "If you tell me you have 50 different ways of representing data in your system at the logical level, then I'll tell you that you have 49 too many." Quite right.

Examples of Confusion: Objects

The quotes in the previous section all come from the object world. So do those in the present section, but they're more of a *potpourri:*

> *R. G. G. Cattell,* Object Data Management *(revised edition), Addison-Wesley, 1994: "[Only] an object's methods may examine or update [the private memory of the object]; the methods are public."*

I find this quote confused for the following reason: To say that methods are public means they're part of the *model;* to say they can examine or update private memory means they're part of the *implementation.* Quotes like this one lend weight to my contention that object advocates typically fail to make a clear distinction between model and implementation.

> *Malcolm Atkinson et al., "The Object-Oriented Database System Manifesto," Proc. First International Conference on Deductive and Object-Oriented Databases, Kyoto, Japan, 1989: "We are taking a Darwinian approach: We hope that, out of the set of experimental prototypes being built, a fit model will emerge."*

Perhaps the writers here might legitimately claim not to be confused over model *vs.* implementation, but they certainly don't seem to agree that the model should be defined *first* and implementations should be built *second!* Instead, they seem to be saying that we should write a bunch of code first and see what happens ... In this connection, it's relevant to mention that that's exactly what happened with the old-fashioned hierarchic and network "models": The implementations were built first and the corresponding "models" were then defined, after the fact, by a process of induction from those implementations—in other words, by *guesswork.* And it would be a pity to repeat such a huge *logical mistake;* yet that seems to be exactly what some people want to do. Myself, I think we should have some idea as to what we're trying to do before we actually do it.

And here are two more quotes from that same interview with Mary Loomis (*Data Base Newsletter 22*, No. 6, November/December 1994):

> *Even with immutable objects, however, it still is important to separate the issue of object identity from how that identity is implemented. The pattern that represents a fingerprint is an immutable object, yet the designer probably would not want to use that fingerprint's bit pattern as the OID.*

> Interviewer: *Relational purists claim that object identifiers are just pointers in disguise, and that all pointers and navigational access using them should be avoided. Do you agree?* Response: *If object identifiers were truly pointers, I would agree. Object identifiers, however, are* logical *references, which eventually lead to an address or pointer. Object identifiers used as references represent logical relationships between objects. Because they are logical, [they] must be able to cross database and processor boundaries. Ordinary pointers won't work in that kind of broad environment.*

These quotes demand a lot of responses!—there does seem to be a lot of confusion (not just in these quotes, but out in the database community at large) over object IDs. So here goes:

- As far as I can tell, the term "immutable object" just means a *value*. That value can be a simple or as complex as we please—it might, for example, be an integer, or it might be a fingerprint—but it's still a value. And values are self-identifying, by definition. They don't need any further identification *at the model level*. It's true that in the case of large, complicated values like fingerprints we might choose to assign them separate identifiers internally for performance reasons, but that's an implementation issue; to insist that such identifiers be exposed at the model level is to confuse model and implementation once again.

- Note the wording: "The pattern that represents a fingerprint is an immutable object." I would say, rather, that the fingerprint *per se* is the immutable object; the pattern that represents it is, by definition, a matter of how that object is represented internally. Model *vs.* implementation again.

- The quote continues: "[Yet] the designer probably would not want to use that fingerprint's bit pattern as the OID." The reference to "bit patterns" shows clearly that we're talking about an internal representation issue. So what does "the designer"—who I presume is somebody working at some external level—have to do with the question at all? I think there's yet another model *vs.* implementation confusion here.

- I guess I must be a "relational purist,"[4] because I do claim that object IDs are just pointers in disguise. Well, no I don't: Actually, I claim they're simply pointers *tout court,* and you can forget about the "in disguise" bit. That is, their behavior *as defined at the model level* is pointer behavior. Whether they're physically implemented as pointers is irrelevant! Indeed, I accept that they probably aren't, in part because they do have to "be able to cross database and processor boundaries"—but "database and processor boundaries" aren't part of the model. (At least, I hope they aren't. If they are, then that's something else that's wrong with the model.)

- The real issue here, of course, is one I've already discussed: We need to represent "relationships," and "the object model" chooses to do so by means of object IDs, which, I claim, are logically indistinguishable from pointers as far as the model is concerned. And pointers are contraindicated at the model level for numerous reasons, including but certainly not limited to the one the interviewer suggests (namely, that they imply a navigational style of access to the database).

I have one further quote from the same source:

In the terminology of the ODMG specification, "type" refers to the interface or external view, and "class" refers to its actual implementation. One reason [for the distinction] is to be able to optimize without affecting the external view of the type.

---

4. I don't care for the label, though! We should be pure, not purist.

My responses:

- If it's true that "type" refers to the interface, then I'm very puzzled. According to my reading of the ODMG book, *interface* is a loaded word; in fact, it refers to a rather special kind of type! It corresponds to what Hugh Darwen and I call, in our book on *The Third Manifesto,* a union type (possibly a special kind of union type we call a dummy type, but it's hard to tell from the ODMG book *per se*).

- If it's true that "class" refers to the implementation, then it clearly isn't part of the model, and it shouldn't even be mentioned in the context of the model *per se*. Is it so mentioned in the ODMG book? Yes, it is, ubiquitously! In fact, the ODMG model defines *interfaces*— see the previous paragraph—by means of a construct called *class*. Now, I freely admit that there might be some confusion here on my part; but if there is, I don't think it's entirely my fault.

I feel bound to add that the ODMG book itself seems to disagree with Loomis's explanation of the terms *type* and *class*. Here's a quote from that book:

> *A type has an external* specification *and one or more* implementations ... *A* class *definition is a specification that defines only the abstract behavior and abstract state of an object type.*

In my opinion, both terms are being used here in a somewhat unusual way: *Class* is being used to refer to what's more usually called a *type,* and *type* is being used to refer to the combiation of *class* in this unorthodox sense together with the *implementation* of the class in question.

By the way, I can't resist pointing out that if *type* does refer to "the interface or external view" as claimed, then the phrase "external view of the type" apparently refers to the external view of the external view.

Examples of Confusion: Miscellaneous

A failure to understand the logical difference between model and implementation is almost invariably (albeit unsurprisingly) accompanied by a failure to understand what the relational model in particular is. In fact, I think I need to write another article on the logical difference between what the relational model is and what people think it is ... but that'll have to wait. Meanwhile, here are a few more quotes to illustrate the point:

> *Robert M. Curtice and William Casey, "Database: What's in Store?",* Datamation 31, *No. 23, December 1st, 1985: "We expect the current relational craze to give way to more robust systems that employ the ANSI three-schema architecture to deliver a high level of data independence ... [We] doubt that a pure relational system will achieve a high market penetration. Pure relational systems (i.e., ones whose internal, external, and conceptual schemas are relational) are of interest to academics and managers of moderate to small database applications. Experience with relational systems in large applications has pointed out some intricate, yet significant, problems. The inability to deal with data groups (e.g., date in turn contains day, month, and year) has proved cumbersome. The lack of multiple occurring data items, such as 12 monthly buckets, means more work for the system builders."*

I hope we all understand that a "pure relational system" is categorically *not* a system "whose internal, external, and conceptual schemas are [all] relational"! That much should have been obvious, even back in 1985. Even to suggest such a thing is to betray a serious lack of understanding of the model *vs.* implementation distinction in general and the relational model in particular. As for those "intricate, yet significant, problems" with "relational systems in large applications": Well, here the writers might be forgiven, somewhat, because there was indeed a general failure at the time to understand the true nature of first normal form. Let me just say for the record that there's no logical reason why a "pure relational system" should fail to support either "data groups" or "multiple occurring data items"—though I'd like to add, also for the record, that (a) these are both rotten terms for the concepts involved, and (b) I reject the suggestion that these problems are "intricate," or even very "significant."

The next three are all from the same writer, Frank Sweet. The first is one of my all-time favorites:

> From *"What, if Anything, Is a Relational Database?"*, Datamation 30, *No. 14, July 15th, 1984: "COBOL can no more access a relational database than a circle can have corners. It's simply a contradiction in terms ... There's no such thing as a relational database. When you get right down to it, 'relational database' is as meaningless as 'plaid music' or 'scratchy color.' The adjective describes languages or processes, not data. The database itself, the pool of shared business data, can be neither procedural nor relational [sic]."*

What the writer seems to be saying here is that the *real* database (the "database itself") is simply bits and bytes, and bits and bytes aren't relational. But to argue thus is akin to arguing that human beings are never really *thinking*, because what's *really* happening inside their heads is simply that neurons are firing! In other words, I would say that what we have here is **a total failure to abstract**.

> From *"The Trouble with SQL,"* DBP&D 1, *No. 6, June 1988: "[One] prophet of the relational model claims that a database must avoid ... physical access mechanisms to be relationally pure. The gentleman becomes irate with those of us who make a living writing programs—rather than just talking about it—when we point out that the inescapable consequence of such ideological purity is grinding inefficiency."*

I don't think this one needs any further comment from me.

> From *"Techniques For Physical Data Modeling,"* DBP&D 1, *No. 8, August 1988: "[We're] compelled to choose between supporting Codd's rules with a toy or building a real DBMS that breaks the rules. Such theological purity is pointless, of course. All serious DBMSs employ links ... They must, if they are to work. In practice, they follow Charles Bachman's network model, not Codd's relational model."*

Again, no further comment seems necessary.

My last two quotes are taken from a presentation by Mike Stonebraker entitled "Architectures for Object/Relational Databases" at *The Second Annual Object/Relational Summit* (Boston, Mass., August 3rd–6th, 1997). They're taken directly from a slide, which explains the rather terse style:

> *Relational B-trees use ASCII notion of "<"*

> *Relational sort engine uses ASCII notion of "<"*

My problem with these two quotes is the apparent equation of certain implementation mechanisms with the relational model. Of course, I'm quite sure that Mike Stonebraker knows perfectly well there's no such thing as a "relational B-tree" or a "relational sort engine." I also understand (or, at least, I think I do) that what he was probably trying to say on this slide is that certain implementation mechanisms found in traditional SQL products might not work very well when we introduce more sophisticated data type support. But it's not what he *said!* Readers can't always be relied on to tease out what writers mean from what they actually say. Nor should they have to do so, either.

Consequences of Such Confusions

A general failure to appreciate the model *vs.* implementation distinction has plagued the database industry for years, and remains widespread to this day. Confusion has arisen above all in SQL contexts!—a fact that has led to the following consequences, among others:

- Current SQL products are almost all what I call *direct-image* systems—by which I mean they represent each base table by what might as well be called a *stored* table on the disk. That internal representation uses physical contiguity (a) to combine stored column values to make up stored records and (b) to combine stored records to make up stored tables.

- Those direct-image systems suffer from a huge number of problems, including serious performance and complexity problems. Indeed, it's the fact that most of today's products are direct-image systems that has allowed people to get away with the claim that "joins are slow"!—they often *are* slow, in those products.

- The same systems also suffer from an unfortunate loss of physical data independence. *Note:* The stupid debates—which should never have been necessary in the first place!— over whether to *denormalize for performance* (at the logical level) are a direct consequence of this state of affairs.

Other significant consequences include:

- A general "more heat than light" level of discourse in the industry as a whole, to the detriment of all

- Misleading advertising and marketing claims (for example, "relational can't handle complex information," "relational can't do objects," "relational has a built-in performance barrier," and so on)

- Blaming the relational model for the shortcomings of SQL (I expect to return to this particular issue in a future paper)

- A failure to understand that many newer requirements—for example, complex objects, type inheritance, multi-dimensional data, online analytical processing (OLAP), spatial and temporal data, XML documents, and so on—*can* all perfectly well be handled in a relational framework, at least in principle

- Accordingly, a rash of *ad hoc* solutions to these problems that serve only to increase confusion, don't work together terribly well (owing in part to the lack of a common model), and—in my opinion—will ultimately wind up costing us all a great deal (and I don't just mean financially, either)

Concluding Remarks

I've discussed one of the most crucial logical differences of all: namely, that between model and implementation. Later writings in this occasional series will build on that discussion.

Acknowledgments

I'd like to thank Hugh Darwen and Fabian Pascal for their comments on earlier drafts of this chapter.

CHAPTER 6

■ ■ ■

On the Logical Differences Between Types, Values, and Variables

To be is to be a value of a variable
(or to be some values of some variables)

—George Boolos

I'd like to begin this chapter with a few remarks on *The Third Manifesto* (the *Manifesto* for short). The *Manifesto* is described in detail in the book *Databases, Types, and the Relational Model: The Third Manifesto*, 3rd edition, by Hugh Darwen and myself (Addison-Wesley, 2006). In essence, the *Manifesto* is a detailed, formal, and rigorous proposal for the future direction of databases and DBMSs; it can be seen as an abstract blueprint for the design of a DBMS and the language interface to such a DBMS. It's based on the four classical core concepts **type, value, variable,** and **operator**. In this chapter, I want to examine the various logical differences that exist between those concepts. *Note:* As my title suggests, my primary emphasis is on the first three; as we'll see, there's a great deal of confusion in the database community over those concepts. I don't think there's so much confusion over operators, but even there there's some (again, as we'll see).

Incidentally, I said a moment ago that the *Manifesto* could be seen as "an abstract blueprint for the design of a DBMS and the language interface to such a DBMS." Let me now point out that exactly the same could be said of the relational model as originally defined by Ted Codd! The *Manifesto* is 100 percent in the spirit of Codd's work; it continues along the path he originally laid down and is thus—deliberately, of course—very definitely evolutionary, not revolutionary, in nature.

Turning now to "the four classical core concepts," here's a simple motivating example:

- We might have a *type* called INTEGER.

- The integer 3 might be a *value* of that type.

- N might be a *variable* of that type, whose value at any given time is some integer value (i.e., some value of type INTEGER).

- PLUS ("+") might be an *operator* that takes two integer values (i.e., two values of type INTEGER) and returns another.

If you ever find yourself getting confused over any of the concepts being discussed in what follows, I suggest you refer back to this simple example for guidance. Note in particular that, as the example clearly shows, types are in a sense **the most fundamental concept of all:** Values are typed, variables are typed, and operators apply to typed arguments and (if they return a value) are themselves typed as well. In other words, the value, variable, and operator concepts all rely on the type concept.

Following on from this point, let me now draw your attention to the *Manifesto* book's subtitle: *a detailed study of the impact of type theory on the relational model of data, including a comprehensive model of type inheritance.* Indeed, the *Manifesto* is very heavily concerned with type theory. Part of the reason for this state of affairs is that type theory and the relational model are more or less independent of one another. To be more specific, the relational model does not prescribe support for any particular types (with one exception, type BOOLEAN); it merely says that attributes of relations must be typed, thus implying that *some* (unspecified) types need to be supported.[1] A couple of points of clarification:

- First, please note that I use the term *operator* to include all operations, not just ones like PLUS that happen to be expressed in a certain specialized syntactic style. In particular, I use it to include operators that are invoked using some functional notation, as in the case of, e.g., SQRT(N). What's more, the operator PLUS is a little special in other ways as well: It takes exactly two operands, those operands are of the same type, and the result is of the same type too. In general, of course, an operator can take any number of operands, which don't all have to be of the same type, and its result if any can be of a different type again.

- Second, the term *type* is short for *data type*, of course. Types are also known (especially in relational contexts) as *domains;* personally, I prefer *types*, and I'll use that term in what follows, except when quoting from other writers. Just as an aside, I remark that the very fact that the term *domain* was used instead of *type* in the first place—i.e., in the original relational model—has itself been the source of a certain amount of confusion over the years (I've mentioned this point elsewhere; see, e.g., Chapters 4 and 8 in the present book).

Note finally that some of the material that follows has previously appeared, in somewhat different form, in one or more of the following books and papers as well as in the *Manifesto:*

- "Why Is It Important to Think Precisely?" (republished in my book *Relational Database Writings 1994–1997,* Addison-Wesley, 1998)

- Certain other chapters in this book, including in particular Chapters 23, 24, and 26

- *Temporal Data and the Relational Model,* by Hugh Darwen, Nikos A. Lorentzos, and myself (Morgan Kaufmann, 2003)

- *An Introduction to Database Systems,* 8th edition (Addison-Wesley, 2004)

However, the present chapter does include a good deal of new material.

---

1. I plan to revisit this issue—i.e., the fact that type theory and the relational model are independent of one another—in a future paper.

Types Are Fundamental

I've already said that types are fundamental. So what *is* a type? Among other things, it's **a set of values**. Examples might include type INTEGER (the set of all integers), type CHAR (the set of all character strings),[2] type P# (the set of all part numbers), and so on. Thus, when we say that some relation has an attribute of type INTEGER, for example, what we mean is that values of that attribute are integers, and nothing but integers.

Paragraphs 1–6 below—which are intended to be fairly precise and might not be fully understandable on a first reading—spell out the crucial importance of the type concept in more specific detail:

1. Every **value** v is of exactly one type T. (I'm assuming here that type inheritance isn't supported. Even if it is, however, every value still has exactly one *most specific* type. For simplicity, I'll ignore type inheritance for the rest of this chapter, except just to note that several of the concepts we'll be discussing do need some slight extension to their definitions if type inheritance is supported. I plan to come back to this issue in a future paper.)

2. Every **variable** V is explicitly declared to be of some type T, meaning that every possible value of V is a value of type T.

3. Every **operator** is either a read-only operator or an update operator.[3] To simplify slightly, update operators update at least one of their arguments when they're invoked, but read-only operators don't; conversely, read-only operators return a result when they're invoked, but update operators don't. If operator Op is read-only, then it's explicitly declared to be of some type T, meaning that every possible result that can be returned by an invocation of Op is a value of type T.

4. Every **parameter** P of every operator Op is explicitly declared to be of some type T. If Op is read-only, or if it's an update operator but it doesn't update the argument corresponding to P, then every possible argument that can be substituted for P is a value of type T; otherwise, every possible argument that can be substituted for P is a variable of type T.

5. Every **expression** X is at least implicitly declared to be of type T, where T is the type of the outermost operator in X.

6. Every **attribute** A of every tuple type TT or relation type RT is explicitly declared to be of some type T, meaning that every value of A in a tuple of type TT or a relation of type RT is a value of type T.

Note: The remarks under points 3–5 above concerning operators and parameters need some slight refinement if the operators in question are *polymorphic*. I'll ignore this possibility in this chapter for reasons of simplicity, but I'd like to come back and elaborate on it in another paper soon. Meanwhile, let me illustrate the definitions just given in terms of the simple INTEGER example from the introductory section:

---

2. Not to be confused with type CHAR in SQL, which is the set of all character strings of length one.
3. Another logical difference here, by the way! I'll come back to this one later in this chapter, in the section "Variables Are Updatable, Values Aren't."

1. First of all, integer *values* (or just *integers* for short) are self-explanatory. Note carefully, however, that if some given value is of type INTEGER, then *it isn't of any other type*. For example, the value denoted by the numeral 3 is of type INTEGER, and type INTEGER *only*.

2. Here's a possible definition for an integer variable called N:

```
VAR N INTEGER ;
```

N here has explicitly been declared to be of type INTEGER; at any given time, the current value of N is some integer value. *Note:* Barring explicit statements to the contrary, all coding examples in this chapter are based on a language called **Tutorial D,** which is the language we use for examples in the *Manifesto* book.

3. Here's a possible definition for an operator called DOUBLER that takes an integer and doubles it:

```
OPERATOR DOUBLER ( I INTEGER ) RETURNS INTEGER ;
   RETURN ( I + I ) ;
END OPERATOR ;
```

DOUBLER is a *read-only* operator (it doesn't update anything); it's explicitly declared to be of type INTEGER (see the RETURNS clause), meaning the value it returns when it's invoked is an integer. The sole parameter I is also explicitly declared to be of type INTEGER, meaning the argument that corresponds to that parameter when the operator is invoked must be an integer value.

4. Alternatively, we could make the "doubling" operator an *update* operator instead:

```
OPERATOR DOUBLEU ( I INTEGER ) UPDATES { I } ;
   I := ( I + I ) ;
END OPERATOR ;
```

Operator DOUBLEU has no declared type and returns no value when it's invoked (there's no RETURN statement, and the RETURNS clause has been replaced by an UPDATES clause, showing that arguments corresponding to the parameter I are *subject to update*). The argument that corresponds to the sole parameter I when the operator is invoked must be an integer *variable* specifically. The assignment operation causes that variable to be updated appropriately.

Note: It follows that "DOUBLEU(*V*)," where *V* is an integer variable, doesn't have a type, doesn't have a value, and more generally isn't regarded as an expression. Hence the operator must be invoked by means of an explicit CALL statement—e.g., CALL DOUBLEU(*V*);—or something equivalent.

5. In contrast to the foregoing, "DOUBLER(*v*)," where *v* is an integer value, does have a type (INTEGER), does have a value (an integer), and is regarded as an expression—in fact, it can appear wherever an integer literal is allowed. Here's an example:

```
( 5 * DOUBLER ( J ) ) + DOUBLER ( K - 4 )
```

This expression has a type, too: namely, the type of the outermost operator involved, which happens to be PLUS ("+") in this example.

Note: To avoid some possible confusion, I should explain that simple literals and simple variable names are both legal expressions. The "outermost operator" involved in, e.g., the expression 3 is a *literal reference,* and it's of the obvious type. Likewise, the "outermost operator" involved in, e.g., the expression N is a *variable reference,* and it too is of the obvious type.

6. Finally, consider the following *relation* type:

```
RELATION { P# P#, PNAME NAME, COLOR COLOR, WEIGHT WEIGHT, CITY CHAR }
```

This relation type involves five attributes P#, PNAME, COLOR, WEIGHT, and CITY, of types P#, NAME, COLOR, WEIGHT, and CHAR, respectively. (Don't worry if this example doesn't make too much sense to you yet. I'll have more to say about relation types later in this chapter, in the section "Relation Values and Variables.")

More on Types

There's quite a lot more groundwork I need to lay regarding types as such before I can get to the real substance of this chapter, and that's the purpose of the present section.

First of all, types can be **system-defined** (in other words, built-in) or **user-defined**. In this connection, by the way, I'd like to stress the fact that the relational model *never* said all types had to be system-defined!—it simply said there had to *be* some types, so that we could define relations over them. It's true that, in principle, a DBMS could provide a totally faithful implementation of the relational model while supporting system-defined types only; however, such a DBMS would be of limited usefulness, since implementers could never foresee all of the types that users might ever want to use. Thus, the idea that a means should be available for users to define their own types was always present in the relational model, at least implicitly, right at the very outset. That's why I categorically reject claims to the effect that user-defined types represent an "extension" to the relational model; to repeat, type theory and the relational model are essentially *orthogonal* (i.e., independent of one another).

Next, *any type whatsoever,* regardless of whether it is system- or user-defined, can be used as the basis for defining variables, parameters, attributes, and so on. (I note in passing that SQL violates this precept in numerous ways—indeed, SQL's type support suffers from a serious lack of orthogonality—but I don't want to get into a detailed discussion of that issue here.)

Third, any given type *T* has an associated set of **operators** that can validly be applied to values and variables of type *T;* i.e., values and variables of type *T* can be operated upon *solely* by means of the operators defined for type *T* (where by "defined for type *T*" I mean, precisely, that the operator in question has a parameter of type *T*). For example, assume for definiteness that type INTEGER is system-defined. Then:

- The system will provide operators "=", "<", and so on, for comparing integers.

- It will also provide operators "+", "∗", and so on, for performing arithmetic on integers.

- It will *not* provide operators "‖" (concatenate), SUBSTR (substring), and so on, for performing string operations on integers; in other words, string operations on integers won't be supported.

By contrast, if type P# (part numbers) is user-defined, then the type definer—perhaps the DBA—will certainly define operators for comparing part numbers; however, he or she probably won't define operators for performing arithmetic on them (why would we ever want to add or multiply two part numbers?), and arithmetic on part numbers will thus not be supported.

Next, types can be *scalar* or *nonscalar:*

- A **nonscalar** type has *user-visible components.* In particular, relation types are nonscalar, because such types do have user-visible components: namely, their attributes.

- A **scalar** type has no user-visible components. For example, INTEGER and BOOLEAN are scalar types.

Note carefully, however, that even though scalar types have no user-visible components, they do have what are called **possible representations** ("possreps" for short), and those possreps can have user-visible components, as we'll see in a moment. Don't be confused, however: The components in question are *not* components of the type, they're components of the possrep. For example, suppose we have a user-defined scalar type called QTY ("quantity"). Suppose too that a possrep is declared for this type that says, in effect, that quantities can "possibly be repre-sented" by nonnegative integers. Then that possrep certainly does have user-visible components—in fact, it has exactly one such, of type INTEGER—but quantities *per se* don't.

Here's a slightly more complicated example to illustrate the same point:

```
TYPE POINT   /* geometric points in two-dimensional space */
    POSSREP CARTESIAN { X RATIONAL, Y RATIONAL }
    POSSREP POLAR { R RATIONAL, THETA RATIONAL } ;
```

The definition of type POINT here includes declarations of two distinct possreps, CARTESIAN and POLAR, reflecting the fact that points in two-dimensional space can indeed "possibly be represented" by either Cartesian or polar coordinates. Each of those possreps in turn has two components, both of type RATIONAL. Please understand, however, that (to say it again) type POINT *per se* is still scalar—it has no user-visible components.

Note: Please also understand that the *physical* representation of values of type POINT might be Cartesian coordinates, or polar coordinates, or something else entirely. In other words, possreps (which are, to repeat, user-visible) are indeed only *possible* representations. Physical representations, by contrast, are an implementation matter merely—they're not part of the model, and they should never be user-visible.

Each possrep declaration causes automatic definition of the following more or less self-explanatory operators:

- A **selector** operator, which allows the user to specify or *select* a value of the type in question by supplying a value for each possrep component

- A set of **THE_** operators (one such for each possrep component), which allow the user to access the corresponding possrep components of values of the type in question

(Just as an aside, I remark that most of the literature talks in terms not of THE_ operators as such but of "GET_ and SET_" operators instead: GET_ for retrieval and SET_ for update. We—by which I mean Hugh Darwen and I—prefer our THE_ operators, for reasons explained in the *Manifesto* book.)

Here by way of example are some selector and THE_ operator invocations for type POINT:

```
CARTESIAN ( 5.0, 2.5 )
/* selects the point with x = 5.0, y = 2.5 */
CARTESIAN ( X1, Y1 )
/* selects the point with x = X1, y = Y1, where */
/* X1 and Y1 are variables of type RATIONAL     */
POLAR ( 2.7, 1.0 )
/* selects the point with r = 2.7, theta = 1.0 */
THE_X ( VP )
/* denotes the x coordinate of the point value in VP, */
/* where VP is a variable of type POINT              */
THE_R ( VP )
/* denotes the r coordinate of the point value in VP */
THE_Y ( xp )
/* denotes the y coordinate of the point denoted */
/* by the expression xp (which is of type POINT) */
```

As these examples suggest, selectors—more precisely, selector *invocations*—are a generalization of the more familiar concept of a **literal**. Briefly, all literals are selector invocations, but not all selector invocations are literals; in fact, a selector invocation is a literal if and only if all of its arguments are literals in turn. *Note:* I'll have more to say about literals in the section immediately following this one.

By convention, selectors have the same name as the corresponding possrep. Also, if type *T* has a possrep with no explicitly declared name, then that possrep is named *T* by default. Taken together, these two conventions mean that, e.g., we might legitimately define type P# (part numbers) thus:

```
TYPE P# POSSREP { CHAR } ;
```

and the expression P#('P1') would then be a valid selector invocation for this type (in fact, it would be a valid part number literal).

Every type, then, has at least one associated selector and at least one associated set of THE_ operators.[4] In addition, there are certain other operators that *must* be defined for every type, including the following in particular:

- **Equality** ("="): Given values *v1* and *v2* of the same type, the comparison "*v1* = *v2*" evaluates to TRUE if *v1* and *v2* are in fact the very same value and to FALSE otherwise.

- **Assignment** (":="): Given a variable *V* and a value *v* of the same type, the assignment "*V* := *v*," has the effect of establishing *v* as the current value of *V*.

---

4. Every scalar type, that is. Nonscalar types have selectors too, but no THE_ operators; they don't need THE_ operators as such, because they have operators that allow the user to access the components— which are user-visible, by definition—of values of the nonscalar type in question.

Points arising from the foregoing definitions:

- Observe that the variable reference *V* stands for the variable *V* itself in a "target position" (in particular, on the left side of an assignment) and for the current value of that variable in a "source position" (in particular, on the right side of an assignment). It follows that after the assignment "*V* := *v*," the comparison "*V* = *v*" gives TRUE.[5]

- The operators "=" and ":=" are both *polymorphic*. Again, I hope to discuss this topic in a later paper.

Values and Variables

I've now discussed types at some length (and said quite a bit about operators, too); it's time to turn to the other two "core concepts," values and variables. Here are some definitions:

Definition: A **value** is an "individual constant" (for example, the individual constant 3). Values have **no location in time or space**. However, values can be represented by certain *encodings,* and of course such encodings do have location in time and space (see the definition of *variable* below). Indeed, the very same value can have many distinct encodings (in general), and each of those encodings can appear at many distinct locations in time or space (again in general)—meaning, loosely, that any number of distinct variables can have the same value, at the same time or different times. Note that, by definition, *values can't be updated* (because if they could, then after such an update they wouldn't be the same value any longer, in general).

Definition: A **variable** is a holder or container for an appearance of an encoded representation of a value ("an appearance of a value," or just "an appearance," or even—informally— just "a value," for short). Variables do have location in time and space. If variable *V* currently holds an appearance of value *v, v* is said to be *the current value* of *V* (a variable can't hold more than one value at any given time);[6] equivalently, *V* is said to "have" *v* as its current value. Also, of course, variables, unlike values, can be updated—that is, their current value can be replaced by another value, probably different from the previous one. (Of course, the variable in question is still the same variable after the update.)

These definitions are based on ones given in *An Introduction to Data Types,* by J. Craig Cleaveland (Addison-Wesley, 1986). I hope you agree they're straightforward enough, even if they might seem a little wordy. Yet they have a wealth of implications, not all of which are immediately obvious, at least if the existing literature is anything to go by. Here are a few that are worth mentioning right away:

---

5. The fact that successful assignment of some value *v* to some variable *V* makes the comparison *V* = *v* evaluate to TRUE is known as *The Assignment Principle*. Although it sounds trivial, that principle has far-reaching consequences (unfortunately beyond the scope of the present chapter).
6. It can't hold less than one, either!—so long as it's in existence. In other words (although the point is somewhat tangential to the main purpose of this chapter), I reject the concept of "uninitialized variables."

- It follows from the definition that a value might equally well be called a *constant,* and we do indeed usually take the terms to be equivalent. On occasion, however, it's useful to have a term for a "variable" whose value—by design—never changes, and the term *constant* is sometimes used for this purpose.

- The terms *constant* and *value* are thus (usually) interchangeable. By contrast, the terms *constant* and *literal* aren't! A literal isn't a value, it's a *symbol* that *denotes* some value (yet another logical difference here—namely, that between *notation* and *denotation*). The value in question is determined by the symbol in question (and since every value is of exactly one type, the type of that value is also determined by the symbol in question *a fortiori*). Loosely, we can say that a literal is *self-defining.* Here are some **Tutorial D** examples:

```
FALSE                     /* a literal of type BOOLEAN  */
4                         /* a literal of type INTEGER  */
2.7                       /* a literal of type RATIONAL */
'ABC'                     /* a literal of type CHAR     */
P# ('P1')                 /* a literal of type P#       */
CARTESIAN ( 5.0, 2.5 )    /* a literal of type POINT    */
```

- Following on from the previous point, it's worth noting too that distinct literals can denote the same value. For example, the following are three SQL literals of type TIME WITH TIME ZONE that all denote the same absolute value (*viz.*, 6:00 pm London time, which is the same as 10:00 am San Francisco time and 8:00 pm Helsinki time):

```
TIME '18:00:00-00:00'   /* London        */
TIME '10:00:00-08:00'   /* San Francisco */
TIME '20:00:00+02:00'   /* Helsinki      */
```

This example thus serves to emphasize the fact that (as already stated) there's a logical difference between a literal and a value.

The next five sections are devoted to an in-depth exploration of certain further implications of the value *vs.* variable distinction.

Values and Variables Can Be Arbitrarily Complex

Note carefully that there's nothing in the definitions of the previous section to say that values have to be limited to simple things like the integer 3. On the contrary, values can be as complex as we like. But what does "complex" mean here? There are two possibilities, both valid:

- A value can be **scalar**—meaning it's a value of some scalar type and therefore has no user-visible components—and yet have a "possrep" with user-visible components. For example, values of type POINT (in other words, individual point values, or just points for short) are scalar values, and yet we can talk, loosely, of such points as having Cartesian and/or polar coordinates. Strictly speaking, however, those coordinates are *not* components of the point value as such; rather, they're components of the corresponding possible representation(s) of that point value.

- A value can be **nonscalar,** meaning it's a value of some nonscalar type and does have a set of user-visible components. For our purposes, the obvious example here is a *relation* value, where the user-visible components are the pertinent attributes. Another is a *tuple* value, where again the user-visible components are the pertinent attributes.

To say it again, then, values can be arbitrarily complex, and so, e.g., arrays, stacks, lists, tuples, relations, part numbers, points, polygons, X rays, fingerprints, XML documents (and on and on and on) are all values.

Remarks analogous to the foregoing apply to variables too, of course; thus, variables too can be arbitrarily complex (meaning, more precisely, that they can contain values that are arbitrarily complex). In particular, variables, like values, are considered to be scalar or nonscalar according as their type is scalar or nonscalar. Similarly for read-only operators: Such an operator is considered to be scalar or nonscalar depending on whether its result is scalar or nonscalar.

Variables Are Updatable, Values Aren't

The next point is that there's *obviously* a big logical difference between values and variables: **Variables are updatable, values aren't**. To elaborate:

- Values are nonupdatable by definition, as we've already seen.

- As for variables, to say that something's a variable is **precisely** to say it's updatable, no more and no less! That's what "variable" *means*—the current value changes over time. Furthermore, the way to effect those changes (the *only* way) is by updating the variable in question. *Note:* For simplicity, I'm ignoring here the case of a variable that's never actually updated. This simplification doesn't materially affect the discussion, of course.

Just as an aside, I've always thought the term *variable* as used in mathematics (at least in some contexts) was a little bit of a misnomer. Certainly variables in the sense I have in mind don't have values that vary over time, as variables in the computer science sense do. For example, consider the equation

$x + 3 = 5$

Mathematicians would call x a variable here, but it obviously has the constant value 2. Perhaps *unknown* would be a better term; solving a set of equations is the activity of determining the values the unknowns in those equations stand for. Of course, it's true that the set of equations might not have a unique solution, as in the case of, e.g., the set consisting of the single equation $x + y = 0$. In such a case, referring to the unknowns as variables is perhaps more reasonable. But it's still the case that those variables don't vary over time; rather, they vary over some prescribed range.

Back to values *vs.* variables in the computing sense. The fact that there's a logical difference between these concepts accounts in turn for another logical difference: namely, that between **read-only and update operators**. Read-only operators operate on *values;* in particular, they operate, harmlessly, on those values that happen to be the current values of variables. Update operators, by contrast, operate on *variables*—I'm speaking just a trifle loosely here—and they have the effect of replacing the current values of such variables by other values, probably different ones.

And talking of update operators, let me now point out that, logically speaking, *only one such operator is needed:* namely, the **assignment** operator. All other update operators are really just shorthand for some assignment. (I'll spell this point out in detail in connection with the *relational* update operators in particular in the section "Relation Values and Variables," later.) Since we already know that to say something's a variable is to say it's updatable, no more and no less, it follows that to say something's a variable is to say it's *assignable to,* no more and no less. In other words, to say that *V* is a variable is to say, precisely, that the following assignment is legal:

```
V := v ;
```

(where *v* is a value of the same type as *V*). Of course, *v* can be denoted by an arbitrary expression of the appropriate type; thus, the assignment operation takes the general syntactic form—

```
LHS := RHS ;
```

—where *LHS* is a variable reference, denoting some variable *V* of some type *T*, and *RHS* is an arbitrary expression of that same type *T* denoting a value *v* also of that type *T*.

Note: Actually the syntactic form just shown for the assignment operator is *not* the most general. In *The Third Manifesto*, Hugh Darwen and I require support for a more general form that we call *multiple* assignment, which allows several variables to be updated at the same time (I'm speaking pretty loosely here!). Multiple assignment is discussed in detail in Chapter 11; for the remainder of the present chapter, I'll limit my attention to assignments of the simple (or "single") form already discussed.

Pseudovariables

Consider the following simple example:

```
VAR VC CHAR ;

VC := 'Middle' ;
SUBSTR ( VC, 2, 1 ) := 'u' ;
```

After the first assignment here, the variable VC has the value 'Middle'; after the second, it has the value 'Muddle'—the effect of this latter assignment is to "zap" the second character position within that variable, replacing the *i* by a *u*. Note in particular that the left side of that second assignment does *not* consist of a simple variable reference. So is it really true that assignments always take the specific syntactic form shown in the previous section?

Well, yes, fundamentally it *is* true. The second assignment in the foregoing example is really shorthand for the following longer one:

```
VC := SUBSTR ( VC, 1, 1 ) || 'u' || SUBSTR ( VC, 3, 4 ) ;
```

Now the left side is a simple variable reference, as required. As for the right side, the expression on that side denotes the character string obtained by concatenating, in left-to-right order, the first character of the current value of VC, the character 'u', and the last four characters of the current value of VC. It follows that the overall assignment has exactly the effect previously explained.

Here's another example:

```
VAR VA ARRAY INTEGER ;

VA := ARRAY ( 1, 2, 3, 4, 5 ) ;
VA[4] := 0 ;
```

After the first assignment, the variable VA has as its value an array of five integers, with the *i*th array element equal to *i* (*i* = 1, 2, 3, 4, 5); after the second assignment, the fourth element is 0 instead of 4, while the others remain unchanged. Again, the left side of the latter assignment isn't just a simple variable reference; again, however, the assignment is really just shorthand for another one in which the left side *is* such a variable reference. Here's the expanded version:

```
VA := ARRAY ( VA[1], VA[2], VA[3], 0, VA[5] ) ;
```

Note: The expression on the right side here is an *array selector invocation.* (The same remark applies to the earlier assignment to VA also, of course.)

Another example:

```
VAR VE TUPLE { EMP# EMP#, DEPT# DEPT#, SALARY MONEY } ;

VE := TUPLE { EMP# EMP#('E1'), DEPT# DEPT#('D1'), SALARY MONEY(50000) } ;
VE.DEPT# := DEPT#('D2') ;
```

VE here is a tuple variable (i.e., a variable whose permitted values are tuples); I've used dot qualification to express the operator that gives access to tuple components. The second assignment here is shorthand for:

```
VE := TUPLE { EMP# VE.EMP#, DEPT# DEPT#('D2'), SALARY VE.SALARY } ;
```
And one last example:

```
VAR VP POINT ;

VP := CARTESIAN ( 5.0, 2.5 ) ;
THE_X ( VP ) := 6.0 ;
```

Note the appearance in the second assignment here of a THE_ operator invocation on the left side. The assignment is shorthand for:

```
VP := CARTESIAN ( 6.0, THE_Y ( VP ) ) ;
```

It's time to introduce another term. Here again are the expressions appearing on the left sides of the four "shorthand" assignments in the foregoing examples:

```
SUBSTR ( VC, 2, 1 )
VA[4]
VE.DEPT#
THE_X ( VP )
```

Each of these expressions is a **pseudovariable reference**. A pseudovariable reference is an expression that's not just a simple variable reference but nevertheless appears on the left side of an assignment.[7] Such an expression is said to denote a *pseudovariable*—it isn't really a variable as such, but we can think of it, loosely, as something like a variable, inasmuch as it's assignable to (i.e., updatable). As the foregoing examples show, pseudovariables don't really exist in their own right, but they're a very convenient fiction: They provide a mechanism for simplifying the formulation of certain assignments, and they make it easier to talk about the effects of such assignments, because they allow us to think in terms of "zapping" certain components of the target variables (even in situations where, as in the case of variable VP of type POINT, those target variables don't really *have* any user-visible components!).

Note: The term *pseudovariable* is taken from PL/I, but the PL/I concept differs from ours in at least three respects. First, the PL/I term applies only to *built-in functions* like SUBSTR, not to references of the form VA[4] or VE.DEPT# (though PL/I certainly does allow references such as these latter two to appear on the left side of an assignment). Second, PL/I doesn't allow pseudovariable references to be nested, but we do. Third, assignment to a pseudovariable in PL/I is sometimes not just shorthand. For example, the "completion status" of a PL/I variable E of type EVENT can be set *only* by assigning to COMPLETION(E).

There's one more (important!) issue I want to address in this section. Let me repeat one of the original examples:

```
VAR VA ARRAY INTEGER ;

VA := ARRAY ( 1, 2, 3, 4, 5 ) ;
VA[4] := 0 ;
```

Just to remind you, the second assignment here is shorthand for this one:

```
VA := ARRAY ( VA[1], VA[2], VA[3], 0, VA[5] ) ;
```

Recall now that the two expressions of the form ARRAY(...) in this example are array selector invocations; they "select" or specify certain array values, which are then assigned to the array variable VA. Now, you might possibly have had some difficulty with the idea that the array variable VA is indeed a single variable; many people would say rather that it's a kind of "collection" of several variables, called VA[1], VA[2], and so on. Here's a quote in this connection (it's from "Array Variables," Chapter 11 of *A Discipline of Programming*, by Edsger W. Dijkstra, Prentice Hall, 1976):

> *I have been trained to regard an array* [he means an array variable specifically] ... *as a finite set of elementary, consecutively numbered variables, whose "identifiers" could be "computed."*

However, Dijkstra then goes on to give two good sound reasons (details of which I omit here for reasons of space) for rejecting this point of view. And he concludes:

> *The moral of the story is that we must regard the array in its entirety as a single variable, a so-called "array variable," in contrast to the "scalar variables" discussed so far.*

---

7. Or, more generally, appears as an argument to some update operator, where the argument in question is supposed to be a variable specifically.

It follows that the assignment

```
VA[4] := 0 ;
```

really does have to be considered, not as an assignment to a hypothetical "elementary variable" called VA[4], but as an assignment—one that just happens to be expressed in a certain short-hand syntactic style—to the entire variable VA.

As an aside, I remark that pseudovariables aren't just convenient for the user—they make life easier for the system too, because they're easier to implement efficiently. (I readily admit that I'm no implementer myself, but it seems to me that the implementation would have to do quite a lot of work to recognize that the assignment

```
VA := ARRAY ( VA[1], VA[2], VA[3], 0, VA[5] ) ;
```

"really" involves just assigning to VA[4].) Historically, however, I think we let ourselves be beguiled by such considerations into thinking that the individual elements of an array—VA[4], for example—were variables in their own right. But they aren't.

Remarks analogous to the foregoing apply to variables of all types (all nonscalar types in particular). A variable of type *T* is a variable of type *T!*—it's never a "collection" of variables (no, not of any type). Indeed, the frequently used term "collection" for things like array variables is really quite misleading. In my examples, therefore, the variables VC, VA, VE, and VP must indeed all be regarded as single variables, and the idea that we might be able to "zap" some "component" of them is only (as previously claimed) a convenient fiction—one that in fact isn't wholly accurate.

Variables Have Addresses, Values Don't

This next logical difference is an immediate consequence of the fact that variables have locations in time and space but values don't. Fundamentally, in fact, a variable is *an abstraction of a piece of storage,* while values (or appearances of values, rather) are the things we can put in those "pieces of storage." It follows that **variables have addresses, but values don't**.

Let me immediately explain that (of course) I'm not talking here about physical addresses. I'm not interested in physical addresses. What I mean is that, at least conceptually, any given variable does have a location in space, and that location in space can be identified by some kind of address. We can **point to** variables.

It follows from the foregoing that there are certain operators—certain additional operators, that is, over and above update operators as already discussed—that apply to variables and not to values. The operators in question are called *referencing* and *dereferencing,* respectively. Here are rough definitions:

Definition: Given a variable *V*, the **referencing** operator applied to *V* returns the value that's the address of *V*.

Definition: Given a value *v* of type address, the **dereferencing** operator applied to *v* returns the variable whose address is *v*.

As you can see, these operators rely (by definition) on support for a type whose values are addresses or pointers. Such types are usually called **REF types**. *Note:* In practice we would probably have not just one REF type but many (one for each individual type), so that pointers themselves would be typed in turn: pointers to variables of type INTEGER, pointers to variables of type CHAR, and so on. In other words, REF here isn't really a type as such at all, but rather a type *generator*. However, I don't want to get into details of *that* topic here (I'll leave it for yet another future paper).

Syntax for referencing and dereferencing typically looks something like the following.

- *Referencing:* The expression REF(*V*), where *V* is a variable, returns a pointer to *V*. For example:

```
VAR VP POINT ;
VAR PADDR REF_POINT ;           /* type REF_POINT = pointers */
                                /* to variables of type POINT */
PADDR := REF ( VP ) ; /* PADDR now contains a pointer to VP */
```

Note: REF is a rather unusual operator, in that it does require its argument *V* to be a variable specifically, even though it's read-only. What's more, that argument must indeed be a variable and not a pseudovariable (probably).

- *Dereferencing:* The expression DEREF(*v*), where *v* is a pointer, returns the variable *v* points to. For example (following on from the REF example above):

```
VAR VQ POINT ;

VQ := DEREF ( PADDR ) ;                 /* assigns VP to VQ */
DEREF ( PADDR ) := VQ ;                 /* assigns VQ to VP */
```

Note: DEREF too is a rather unusual operator, in at least two ways. First, although its argument can in principle be an arbitrary pointer-valued expression, in practice it's almost always a variable specifically, as in both of the DEREF invocations in the example. Second, it returns—or denotes—a *variable*, not a value; this fact allows a DEREF invocation to appear on the left side of an assignment, as in the second assignment in the example.[8] (Of course, such an invocation can also be regarded, harmlessly, as returning the *value* of that variable, if the invocation appears in a position—e.g., on the right side of an assignment, as in the first assignment in the example—where a value is all that's required.)

Before going any further, I'd like to offer a brief comment on terminology here. I've "gone with the flow" and used the kind of terminology that's used in most of the literature on this topic, but I'm bound to say I don't think much of it for at least three reasons:

---

8. More generally, it allows it to appear as an argument to some update operator, where the argument in question is supposed to be a variable specifically. Note, however, that such an appearance does *not* constitute a pseudovariable reference in our sense of that term (even though it looks like one), because the overall assignment isn't shorthand for anything. As a consequence, we need to extend our definition (both syntactic and semantic) of the assignment operator. The details are left as an exercise.

1. The "referencing" terminology is very reminiscent of foreign keys in the relational model, but foreign keys and "references" in the present sense aren't the same thing at all (another logical difference here, in fact).

2. Languages already have a concept (a very different concept!) of *variable reference;* in fact, I've used the term myself several times in this very chapter. To be specific, the use of the variable name *V* to denote either that variable *per se* or its current value—as on the left and right sides of an assignment, respectively, in particular—is a variable reference in the more usual sense.

3. As we've seen, the expression DEREF(*v*) must be understood (at least in certain contexts) as returning a *variable, V* say. As a consequence, that **de**referencing expression might very reasonably be interpreted as a *reference* to the variable *V!* (After all, in the DEREF examples above, the expression DEREF(PADDR) does effectively denote the variable VP both times it appears.)

To return to the main thread of the discussion: We've seen that variables typically imply the existence of at least one REF type, or in other words support for *values of type pointer.* In principle, therefore, we're faced with the possibility that such values—like values of any other kind—might be stored in the database. In practice, however, such a possibility is very strongly contraindicated (in fact, of course, the relational model expressly prohibits it).

Note: Since *relation* variables in particular (see the next section) are indeed variables, they have addresses, at least in principle. However, *the relational model provides no corresponding REF and DEREF operators.* Thus, there's no way in the relational model of obtaining a pointer to a relation variable, and hence *a fortiori* no way in the relational model of storing such a pointer in the database. As far as the relational model is concerned, in fact, relation variables are sufficiently identified by their *name,* and the concept of a relation variable having an address is unnecessary.

Relation Values and Variables

In the relational world, relations themselves provide the obvious example of the importance of the value *vs.* variable distinction. (*Note:* I've included a discussion similar to the one that follows in several other writings. Nonetheless, I believe it bears repeating here. The concepts are important.)

Consider the usual suppliers-and-parts database; to fix our ideas, let's focus on parts specifically (see Figure 6-1). Suppose we execute the following DELETE statement:

```
DELETE P WHERE CITY = 'London' ;
```

The result is shown in Figure 6-2.

P	P#	PNAME	COLOR	WEIGHT	CITY
	P1	Nut	Red	12.0	London
	P2	Bolt	Green	17.0	Paris
	P3	Screw	Blue	17.0	Oslo
	P4	Screw	Red	14.0	London
	P5	Cam	Blue	12.0	Paris
	P6	Cog	Red	19.0	London

Figure 6-1. *Relvar P—initial value*

P	P#	PNAME	COLOR	WEIGHT	CITY
	P2	Bolt	Green	17.0	Paris
	P3	Screw	Blue	17.0	Oslo
	P5	Cam	Blue	12.0	Paris

Figure 6-2. *Relvar P after deleting parts in London*

Now, I hope it's obvious to you that P here is really a variable—a **relation variable,** to be precise, or in other words a variable whose values are **relation values** (different relation values at different times). Conceptually, what the DELETE does in the example is *replace one such relation value by another.* In fact, of course, that DELETE is basically just shorthand for a certain **relational assignment** operation that might look like this:

```
P := P WHERE NOT ( CITY = 'London' ) ;
```

As in all assignments, what's happening here, conceptually, is that (a) the expression on the right side is evaluated, and then (b) the result of that evaluation is assigned to the variable on the left side, with the effect already explained.

In analogous fashion, relational INSERT and UPDATE operations are also basically just shorthand for certain relational assignments. For example, the INSERT statement

```
INSERT P RELATION { TUPLE { P#    P# ('P7'),
                            PNAME  NAME ('Bolt'),
                            COLOR  COLOR ('Red'),
                            WEIGHT WEIGHT ( 15.0 ),
                            CITY   'London' } } ;
```

is shorthand for:[9]

```
P   :=  P UNION RELATION { TUPLE { P#     P# ('P7'),
                                   PNAME  NAME ('Bolt'),
                                   COLOR  COLOR ('Red'),
                                   WEIGHT WEIGHT ( 15.0 ),
                                   CITY   'London' } } ;
```

By the way, note that the expression RELATION {...} appearing in both the original INSERT and the assignment equivalent is an example of a *relation selector invocation* (a relation literal, in fact). Likewise, the expression TUPLE {...} in both cases is an example of a *tuple* selector invocation (a tuple literal, in fact).

In similar fashion, the UPDATE statement

```
UPDATE P WHERE CITY = 'Paris' ( CITY := 'Rome' ) ;
```

is shorthand for:

```
P   :=  WITH ( EXTEND P
                  ADD ( IF CITY = 'Paris' THEN 'Rome' ELSE CITY )
                  AS NEW_CITY ) AS T1,
               T1 { ALL BUT CITY } AS T2 :
        T2 RENAME ( NEW_CITY AS CITY ) ;
```

Now, historically we've tended to use the term *relation* when we really meant *relation variable* (as well as when we meant a relation *per se*—that is, a relation *value*). But the practice is unfortunate, and has certainly led to some confusion (I'll give some examples later in this chapter). In *The Third Manifesto,* therefore, Hugh Darwen and I introduced the term **relvar**— short for relation variable—and we took care to phrase our remarks in terms of relvars, not relations, when it really was relvars that we meant. We also took the unqualified term *relation* to mean a relation value specifically (just as we take, e.g., the unqualified term *integer* to mean an integer value specifically), and we took care to phrase our remarks in terms of relations, not relvars, when it really was relations that we meant.

As an aside, I remark that, given that we now have the term *relvar* to mean a relation variable, it might be useful to go a step further and introduce the term *relcon* ("relation constant") to refer to a relvar whose value, by design, never changes. Indeed, I'll make use of this term occasionally in future writings.

A remark on SQL: SQL, of course, doesn't make the foregoing distinctions at all (not explicitly, at any rate); instead, it uses the single term *table* to refer to both relation values and relation variables.[10] In particular, the keyword TABLE in CREATE TABLE refers to a *variable* specifically (more precisely, it refers to what we might call a *base tablevar*). In **Tutorial D,** by contrast, we

---

9. Note that the "longhand" version (i.e., the explicit assignment) will succeed if the specified tuple for part P7 already exists. In practice, we might want to refine the semantics of INSERT in such a way as to raise an exception in such a situation. For simplicity, however, I'll ignore this possibility here. Analogous remarks apply to DELETE and UPDATE also.

10. Of course, it's a bit of a stretch to say the term *table* in SQL stands for either a relation or a relvar!—we have to overlook all kinds of SQL quirks (the possibility of nulls, the possibility of duplicate rows, the fact of left-to-right column ordering, and so on) if we're even to contemplate the notion that SQL's tables have anything to do with relations as such.

deliberately use the keyword VAR—short for variable—in the definition of variables of all kinds. For example, the **Tutorial D** counterpart to the SQL statement

```
CREATE TABLE P ... ;        /* P is a "base table variable" */
```

is

```
VAR P RELATION ... ;        /* P is a relation variable    */
```

I'd like to elaborate for a moment on the foregoing example. Here again is the **Tutorial D** definition of relvar P, now shown complete:

```
VAR P RELATION { P# P#, PNAME NAME, COLOR COLOR, WEIGHT WEIGHT, CITY CHAR }
    KEY { P# } ;
```

The expression RELATION {...} here denotes a certain *relation type:* namely, the type of the relation variable P, and (of course) the type of all possible relations that might ever be assigned to that variable. The braces enclose a set of attribute-name/type-name pairs; braces are used to emphasize the fact that what they contain is indeed a set, with no ordering to its elements and no duplicate elements.

Another point: Don't make the mistake of thinking a relation variable is a collection of tuple variables! A relation variable is a single variable, just as an array variable is a single variable (see the section "Pseudovariables" earlier in this chapter). A relation variable is a variable whose value is a relation value. A relation value in turn contains a set of tuple values (or just tuples for short; we abbreviate *tuple value* to *tuple,* just as we abbreviate *relation value* to *relation*). What a relation value *doesn't* do, and couldn't possibly do, is contain any tuple variables (or indeed variables of any kind—in fact, the whole notion of a value of any kind containing a variable of any kind is a logical absurdity).

Of course, the foregoing paragraph mustn't be taken to mean there's no such thing as a tuple variable (*tuplevar* for short). A tuplevar is simply a variable whose values are tuples. Here's an example:

```
VAR PTV TUPLE { P# P#, PNAME NAME, COLOR COLOR, WEIGHT WEIGHT, CITY CHAR }
```

Values of the tuplevar PTV are part tuples. So (to repeat) tuplevars are certainly legal. *But such variables aren't allowed in a relational database;* the only kind of variable recognized in the relational model is the relvar, and the only kind of variable allowed in a relational database is the relvar (see the discussion of *The Information Principle* in Chapter 8).

In closing this section, let me point out what I'm sure you've already realized for yourself—namely, that the term *relvar* is not in common usage. But it should be! It really is important to be clear about the distinction between relation values and relation variables in particular, just as it's important to be clear about the distinction between values and variables in general.

Examples of Confusion: Values *vs.* Variables

Confusion over types *vs.* values *vs.* variables is rife in the object world in particular, and so I'll use the object world as the source for most (not all) of the examples I'll be discussing in the rest of this chapter.

First of all, I want to focus on the difference between values and variables specifically. Now, you might find it hard to believe that people could get confused over the difference between notions as fundamental and as straightforward as these two. In fact, however, it seems to be all too easy to fall into traps in this area. Consider, for example, the following somewhat compressed extract from a tutorial on object databases (Stanley B. Zdonik and David Maier, "Fundamentals of Object-Oriented Databases," in Zdonik and Maier (eds.), *Readings in Object-Oriented Database Systems*, Morgan Kaufmann, 1990):

> *We distinguish the declared type of a variable from ... the type of the object that is the current value of the variable ... We distinguish objects from values ... A* mutator *[is an operation such that it's] possible to observe its effect on some object.*

Let's examine this quote in detail.

- First, the phrase "the object that is the current value of the variable" clearly implies that a value is an object. (At least, it implies that some objects are values and that some values are objects.)

- Second, the assertion that "[we] distinguish objects from values" clearly implies that a value isn't an object. (More precisely, it implies that no objects are values and that no values are objects.)

- Third, the existence of mutators—that is, operations that have an "effect on some object," or in other words update some object[11]—clearly implies that the object in question is a variable; so some objects, at least, are variables.

What *are* we supposed to make of such a muddle?

Before going any further, I need to head off another confusion off at the pass. Throughout this chapter so far, I've used the term *variable* in its conventional programming language sense (and of course I'll continue to do so in what follows). Be aware, however, that some object languages and systems use that same term to mean, very specifically, *a variable whose value is an object ID*—that is, a variable whose value is a pointer to some object (*object ID* being the usual object term for what I called a *reference* in the section "Variables Have Addresses, Values Don't" earlier in the chapter). You can get into some very confusing conversations if you're not aware of this fact.

Back to the values *vs.* variables issue. Actually, some object systems and texts draw a distinction between *mutable* and *immutable* objects, and it seems to me that "mutable objects" are exactly variables and "immutable objects" are exactly values. Indeed, in *Database Systems: The Complete Book*, by Hector Garcia-Molina, Jeffrey D. Ullman, and Jennifer Widom (Prentice Hall, 2002), we find a statement to that precise effect:

---

11. The object term *mutator* thus corresponds to our *update operator*. The object term for *read-only operator* is *observer*. I remark in passing that SQL uses the terms mutator and observer too, but SQL's mutators are not really mutators in the usual object sense of the term (i.e., they are not update operators). However, they can be used in such a way as to achieve mutator functionality. For example, the SQL statement SET P.X = Z (which, believe it or not, does not explicitly contain a mutator invocation) is defined to be shorthand for the statement SET P = P.X(Z) (which does).

A class consists of a type and possibly one or more functions or procedures ... that can be executed on objects of that class. The objects of a class are either values of that type (called immutable objects*) or variables whose value is of that type (called* mutable objects*).*

But if they're truly just variables and values as suggested, then why drag in the new terminology? What does it buy us, other than additional complexity and confusion? (In any case, writers on object matters often talk as if objects are always mutable, and forget about the immutable ones.)

Note: I said earlier in this chapter that to say that *V* is a variable is to say that *V* is assignable to, no more and no less. It might therefore be claimed that a mutable object isn't really a variable because the available "methods" typically don't include one for assigning a value (sorry, an immutable object) to it.[12] As we saw in the section "Pseudovariables," however, any method that allows us to "zap" any "component" of an object is really shorthand for one that allows us to assign to the entire object (and if there aren't any such methods, then the object isn't mutable in the first place!). So I stand by my position that mutable and immutable objects are really just variables and values, respectively.

Other object systems use different terminology in an attempt to get at the same value *vs.* variable distinction. ODMG, for example, regards all objects as mutable and uses the term *literal* for an immutable object.[13] But this latter term illustrates a confusion of a different kind; as we saw earlier in this chapter, a literal (at least as that term is conventionally understood) just isn't a value; rather, it's a *symbol* that *denotes* some value.

While I'm on the topic of ODMG, incidentally, I note that ODMG regards objects and literals as being fundamentally different things, in the sense that no object is of the same type as any literal! The (weird) implications of *this* state of affairs are well beyond the scope of the present discussion, however.

Back to objects *per se*. Here's another extract from that same object database tutorial by Zdonik and Maier that manages to confuse values and variables and several other things besides:

A class (sometimes called a type*) is a template for its* instances. *Often the terms* type *and* class *are used interchangeably, but when the two terms are used in the same system,* type *usually refers to specifications, whereas* class *refers to the extension (i.e., all current instances) of the corresponding type. Every object is an instance of some class ...* [Later:] *Some types might also support operations that will alter the state of [their] instances.*

---

12. And why that term *method*, anyway? Considered purely as a regular English word, it doesn't mean what the object advocates seem to want it to mean—not to mention the fact that there are already several perfectly good terms for the concept, including the term *operator* in particular.

13. In this connection, you might care to meditate on the following quotes from the first edition of the ODMG book (R. G. G. Cattell, ed., *The Object Database Standard: ODMG-93*, Morgan Kaufmann, 1994). Page 16: "[The] type *Denotable_Object* [has disjoint subtypes] *Object* and *Literal* [so a denotable object isn't necessarily an object, and no object is a literal, and no literal is an object] ... Objects are mutable; literals are immutable." Page 20: "Literals are objects ..." [*???*].

Points arising:

- First, notice that we now have another term for *object* ("instance"),[14] and another term for *value* ("state"), and a certain amount of confusion over the terms *type* and *class*. I see no need for either *instance* or *state* at all. As for type *vs.* class, let me remind you of the brief discussion of that topic in Chapter 4. Let me also draw your attention to the slightly different (?) meanings those terms seem to have in the extract from Garcia-Molina, Ullman, and Widom quoted earlier.

- Second, the term *extension* is usually understood to refer to a set of values: to be specific, the set of values that satisfy some given **predicate,** often called a *membership* predicate. For example, the extension of the predicate "*i* is an integer such that $0 < i < 6$" is precisely the set of values 1, 2, 3, 4, 5. Thus, the phrase "extension (i.e., all current instances)" strongly suggests that an "instance" is a value. But the final sentence in the extract clearly implies that an "instance" is a variable.

By the way, a type that *didn't* "support operations that will alter the state of [its] instances" would seem not to be very useful, since apparently we wouldn't be able to define variables of that type. (Well, perhaps we could *define* them, but we could never assign anything to them!) This next quote is from the same source once again:

An intensional specification is a template specifying all possible objects with a given structure ... [Objects have] an object identity *... that remains invariant across all possible modifications of the object's value.*

The phrase "all possible objects with a given structure" means an object is a value (for example, think of "all possible integers" or "all possible relations that can be assigned to the relvar P").[15] The phrase "all possible modifications of the object's value" means an object is a variable. *Note:* That same phrase also confuses values and variables (you can't modify values), but perhaps this is nitpicking; perhaps we're to understand the phrase to mean simply "all possible modifications of the object."

The next two quotes are taken from an interview with Mary Loomis in *Data Base Newsletter 22*, No. 6 (November/December 1994):

One of the simplest ways to think about state is as the current values of the properties of an object—much like the values of a record's variables at a particular point in time.

Comment: A "record" must be either a record value or a record variable. If it's the former, it obviously can't contain any variables. If it's the latter it can't either!—a record variable, like an array variable or a tuple variable or a relvar, is *a single variable.* So what does the phrase "a record's variables" mean?

Note: I think I know what's going on here, though. Objects in the object world are supposed to include a set of components, variously known as *properties* or *attributes* or *members* or *instance variables,* and those components are indeed thought of as variables in their own right. (At least, they are if the objects in question are mutable. I don't know what the "instance variables"

---

14. The same tutorial elsewhere uses yet a third term: *object instance* (!).
15. The same phrase also confuses *type* and *representation!*—still another logical difference that I plan to discuss in a future paper.

in an immutable object might be.) It seems to me, therefore, that the concept of a "mutable object" is flawed at the very outset, since we've already seen in this chapter that it's logically wrong to think of any variable as containing others.

By the way: If "one of the simplest ways to think about state" is in terms of values, why not *use* the term "values" (or "value," singular, rather)? And what other ways are there that might be simpler?

An object can be viewed as a dynamic instance that changes over time as it is operated upon.

Comment: So now we have another term for object ("dynamic instance")? Presumably this term means a *mutable* object, however; do we therefore have to refer to immutable objects as "static instances"? (At least I'm pleased to see the use of the phrase "operated upon" instead of some strange circumlocution involving "methods," however.)

Logical Sameness

This subsection is a small digression from my main topic, but I think it's worth including. As you'll surely have realized by now, what we're looking at in this area is a minor epidemic of the "logical sameness" problem. We have:

- Type *vs.* class—not to mention the term *interface*, which, as I mentioned in Chapter 5, is used in ODMG, at least, to mean another kind of type (or class?)

- Value *vs.* immutable object *vs.* state *vs.* static object

- Variable *vs.* mutable object *vs.* dynamic object

- Operator *vs.* method *vs.* function *vs.* procedure[16]

- Read-only operator *vs.* observer

- Update operator *vs.* mutator

- Object *vs.* "instance" *vs.* value and/or variable

Regarding this last one, by the way, you might care to ponder over the following definitions (they're taken from *The Unified Modeling Language User Guide,* by Grady Booch, James Rumbaugh, and Ivar Jacobson, Addison-Wesley, 1999):

Object: A concrete manifestation of an abstraction; an entity with a well-defined boundary that encapsulates state and behavior; an instance of a class.

Instance: A concrete manifestation of an abstraction; an entity to which a set of operations can be applied and that has a state that stores the effects of the operations.

---

16. *Procedures* resemble our update operators in that they have to be explicitly called, but they don't necessarily update anything. *Functions* resemble our read-only operators in that they can be invoked inline, but they aren't necessarily read-only (also, the term "functions" is used even for operators that aren't true functions, in that they return more than one result). We prefer our generic term *operator,* with *read-only* and *update* as qualifiers when appropriate; in other words, we believe the distinction between read-only and update operators is an important logical difference, whereas that between procedures and functions is more just one of syntax.

The same book includes a rather strange definition for *value* and no definition at all for *variable*. (It also has numerous definitions relating, more or less, to the type *vs.* class issue; see Chapter 4 for further discussion.)

By the way, the SQL standard uses the fuzzy term "instance" as well, and "defines" it thus:

Instance: *A physical representation of a value.*

I have no idea what the standard means by "physical representation" here; however, I do know it actually uses the term "instance" to refer to variables as well as values—possibly even to variables exclusively.

A Hypothesis

I have a possible explanation for the widespread failure in the object world to distinguish properly between values and variables. As I've indicated elsewhere (see in particular the paper "Why the Object Model Is Not a Data Model," in my book *Relational Database Writings 1994–1997*, Addison-Wesley, 1998), it seems to me that "the object model" is closer to being a model of *storage* than it is to being a model of *data*. Certainly this conjecture, if true, would explain a lot about the "the object model"!—its provision of so many different ways of structuring data, for example, also its heavy reliance on pointers. In fact, it seems to me undeniable that object advocates try to achieve *good performance*—always one of their key objectives—by "moving users closer to the metal," so to speak (the relational model, by contrast, being "further from the metal" and at a higher level of abstraction).

Now, the distinction between values and variables doesn't make much sense at the storage level—in fact, the concepts don't really even exist, as such, at that level. Instead, what we have is *storage locations*, and those storage locations can be used to hold bit patterns, or in other words encoded representations of values. But there's nothing in general to stop us over-writing any storage location at any time; thus, *all* storage locations effectively correspond to variables in this sense. And I could be wrong, but I strongly suspect that the concept of "objects" grew out of this notion of storage locations. Whence, it seems to me, the lack of emphasis—if not the total lack of appreciation—in the object world regarding the logical difference between values and variables.

Examples of Confusion: Types *vs.* Values and/or Variables

Now I'd like to turn to examples of other confusions: specifically, confusions between types, on the one hand, and values, variables, or both, on the other. My first example is taken from an article by John Taschek entitled "ODBMSs Take On Relational Models" [*sic!*] in *PCWeek*, October 9th, 1995:

The term "classes" describes the behavior of groups of objects ... object classes correspond to relational tables, object attributes map to columns, and instances of objects correspond to rows and columns ... ODBMS vendors ... offer products that bridge object databases and current relational databases. These databases, called hybrids, extend relational databases and add support for objects, which appear as another data type.

Points arising:

- First and foremost, object classes categorically do **not** "correspond to relational tables"! An object class is (as near as I can tell) a *type*. What Taschek calls a "relational table" is either a *value* or—more likely, in this context—a *variable*. A type isn't a value, nor is it a variable. In fact, the idea of equating classes and tables was referred to in early editions of the *Manifesto* book as a **Great Blunder**: the *first* great blunder, to be precise, because there's another one too, which we'll get to in the next section. It's true that some products have embraced that equation, but those products are bound to fail (in fact, some already have). Here's an edited extract from those early editions of the *Manifesto* book: "Obviously, systems can be built that are based on this equation. Equally obviously, those systems (like a car with no oil in its engine, or a house that's built on sand) might even provide useful service, for a while—but they're doomed to eventual failure."

- Next, consider the assertion that "instances of objects [*sic!*] correspond to rows and columns." On the face of it, this claim makes no sense at all. Taken in conjunction with the assertion that "object attributes map to columns," however, I think what the writer meant to say was that "instances of objects" map to *rows*, not "rows and columns." But if that's indeed what he meant to say, then what he meant to say is simply wrong, for many, many reasons. Those reasons are discussed in detail in the *Manifesto* book; here I'll mention just one of them, which is that in the context at hand "instances of objects" are almost certainly variables, but rows are values.

- Given the errors mentioned in the first two comments above, the claim that "object attributes map to columns" has to be wrong too, and it is.

- "These databases ... extend relational databases and add support for objects, which appear as another data type." So now objects are a data type? (Incidentally, by "databases" here, I believe the writer means "DBMSs," but I'll let that one pass for now.)

In sum, this first quote manages to confuse (a) types *vs.* variables (or possibly types *vs.* values), (b) variables *vs.* values, and (c) values and/or variables *vs.* types again (as well as making other logical mistakes that I've chosen not to discuss here).

I turn now to a slide presentation by Jim Melton entitled "ANSI SQL3: New Directions for the SQL Standard." Jim Melton was for many years the editor of the SQL standard, and he gave this presentation, describing what subsequently became SQL:1999, at the second annual Object/Relational Summit conference (Boston, Mass., August 3rd–6th, 1997). The presentation explains among other things SQL's support for abstract data types (ADTs), which were apparently introduced with the intention of making SQL more "object like." Here are two short bullet items from the sides (edited just slightly here):

- ADTs are passed by reference

- But are ADTs objects?

The first of these bullet items is meant to explain the rule by which an argument is passed to an invocation of some operator (or method?) if that argument is of some abstract data type. But it talks about the "ADT" as if it actually were that argument! Two problems: First, arguments must be either values or variables, so there's a confusion here over types *vs.* values and/or variables. Second, "pass by reference" means passing the *address* of the argument, so that argument had better be a variable specifically! (So what happens if it's a value I don't know, but I suspect there's simply a failure here to distinguish between values and variables.)

As for the second bullet item: Well, ADTs are types and objects are values or variables, so once again we have a confusion over types *vs.* values and/or variables. (Of course, I presume what Melton really meant by his rhetorical question was "Does SQL's support for ADTs constitute full object support?" But it's not what he *said.*)

Now, to be fair to Melton here, I need to say that it isn't just him; the literature in general tends to use the terms ADT and UDT (= user-defined type) extremely sloppily, treating both of them as if they meant sometimes a value, sometimes a variable, of the type in question, rather than the type *per se.* The following examples, which are quite typical, are all taken from the same conference as the Melton quotes; they mostly come from presentation slides, a fact that explains the rather choppy style (though I've edited them slightly here). The first two are from "DB2 Extenders and the Universal Database," by Nelson Mattos (note the use of "database" in that title to mean "DBMS," by the way):

- How should we replicate UDTs?

- UDTs are cached close to the application

Both of these use "UDTs" to refer to values and/or variables *of* some user-defined type, rather than to UDTs *per se.*

The next few are from "Object/Relational: Separating the Wheat from the Chaff," by Bruce Lindsay:

- ADTs are mutable

- ADTs/objects live in repository

- Applications manipulate ADTs in queries

- Object/relational databases permit:

  - User-defined types in columns

  - User-defined types in queries

  - User-defined types in applications

The first three of these use "ADTs" to refer to variables (probably) or values (possibly)—though the reference to "manipulating" ADTs in queries is slightly puzzling, since queries are read-only and "manipulating" is usually understood to mean updating. The fourth uses "user-defined types" in the same way; here I'd just like to add that it shouldn't be necessary to say what Lindsay is trying to say, anyway, if UDT support is (as of course it should be) properly orthogonal.

My next exhibit consists of a series of quotes from a paper by Andrew E. Wade entitled "Object Query Standards" (*ACM SIGMOD Record 25*, No. 1, March 1996):

> *A basic difference between an object and traditional data is that the object also includes operations.*

Comment: I don't think so! What operations does the object 3 "include"? Or the object N, where N is a variable? I think all that Wade's trying to say here is that "objects" of type *T* can be operated upon by means of the operators defined for type *T* (where, as earlier in this chapter, by "defined for type *T*" I mean, precisely, that the operator in question has a parameter of type *T*). In other words, I think he's using the term "object" to mean a type instead of a value or a variable. If I'm right, then where's the claimed "basic difference"? Traditional data too can be operated upon by operators defined for the relevant type, no more and no less. It looks like another example of logical sameness to me.

By the way: If Wade's trying to say rather that "objects" actually *include the code* for the operators, then I disagree still further, on at least two counts. First, it's not the "object" *per se* that includes the code, it's the "object" *descriptor* (sometimes called the *class-defining object* or CDO).[17] Second, where the code resides is purely an implementation matter—it has nothing to do with the model, and it shouldn't even be mentioned in the context at hand.

> *Collections can be thought of as multi-valued attributes, [with] individual values, or members, of the collections comprising various, possibly complex, data types, as well as objects.*

Comment: A "collection" is, e.g., an array or a set; in other words, it's a value (unless the term "collection" is meant to stand for a collection *variable,* in which case it's a variable). Attributes, multi-valued or otherwise, are components of a type. Components of a type are neither values nor variables. So it makes no sense to say that collections are—or "can be thought of" as—attributes, multi-valued or otherwise. I suppose I can agree that some attribute *A* of some nonscalar type *T* might be "collection-valued" (much as certain attributes of certain relations are relation-valued), meaning that for all values *v* of type *T*, the *A* component of *v* is some collection *c*. But then I don't understand at all the notion that "members" of that collection *c* might be "data types as well as objects"—especially since (a) *c* is definitely a value here, and in any case (b) Wade himself says those "members" are in fact values! (I think he's using "objects" in this context to mean variables, though it's hard to be sure.)

> *The type of the result of the query may be a scalar (including tuples), an object, or a collection of objects, with ... rules specifying which operations on which types produce which other types.*

Comment: First, the sentence needs to be rephrased in order to avoid "type *vs.* value or variable" errors, perhaps as follows: "The result of the query may be a scalar (including tuples), an object, or a collection of objects, with ... rules specifying which operations on operands of which types produce results of which other types." Second, I thought it was a basic tenet in the object world that "everything's an object"; so what does "a scalar (including tuples), an object, or a collection of objects" mean? Aren't scalars, tuples, and collections objects? Third, what does "a scalar (including tuples)" mean? Scalars aren't tuples and tuples aren't scalars. Fourth, the result of a query is always a value; so "scalar," "tuple," "object," and "collection" here all refer to values—which would be fine, except that such terms are widely used elsewhere in the article to mean variables. (By the way, operations were called methods earlier in the same paragraph as the sentence quoted.)

---

17. More likely, the class-defining object includes a pointer to some library somewhere and the code physically resides in that library. Be that as it may, the claim that "unlike traditional data, objects include code" is frequently heard but seems to me to be simply wrong, on several levels at once.

[I've edited this extract somewhat, but not in such a way as to alter the intended meaning.] *ODMG attempted to make OQL completely compatible with SQL, in the sense that any SQL query would be a legal OQL query, with the same syntax, semantics, and result* [given the same input, presumably!]. *Although this was achieved to a large extent (perhaps 90%, some suggest), full compatibility was not reached ... For example, if X is of type T, then the type of the result of the query SELECT X FROM ... is MULTISET(ROW(T)) in SQL but MULTISET(T) in OQL.*

Comment: If the final sentence is correct here, I would say that the degree of compatibility between SQL and OQL is not 90 percent but 0 percent.[18] All logical differences are big differences.

The addition of object capabilities [to SQL] includes the ability to define and access Abstract Data Types (ADTs), which have much the same functionality as ... objects ... The intent is to add "OO-ness" to rows in tables ... These rows may contain ADTs. A mechanism to reference ADTs in other rows exists ...

Comment: "The ability to access ADTs" suggests confusion over types *vs.* values and/or variables; so does "ADTs have much the same functionality as objects." "These rows may contain ADTs" suggests confusion over types *vs.* values, unless "rows" is being used (confusingly) to mean row *variables*, in which case it suggests confusion over (a) types *vs.* variables, (b) the fact that row variables are *not* collections of component variables, and (c) the fact that there's no such thing as a row variable in the relational model. Analogous remarks apply to the final sentence in the quote (which incidentally does suggest quite strongly that "rows" is being used to mean row variables).

For my final examples in this section, I return to that interview with Mary Loomis in *Data Base Newsletter 22*, No. 6 (November/December 1994):

True object-oriented support means extending the database schema to include specifications of operators that act upon data types defined to the DBMS.

Comment: First, operators "act upon" values and/or variables, not data types. Second (and perhaps more important), I'm not at all sure I agree that "specifications of operators" should appear in "the database schema," because this latter term—at least as usually understood— applies to *one particular database*, and I don't think that either data types or operators should be specific to one particular database, in general. (What database does type INTEGER belong to? What database does the operator "+" belong to?) I think, rather, that definitions of types and associated operators should be completely separate from, and sharable by, definitions of (= schemas for) specific databases.

Question (interviewer): *C. J. Date [has] argued that object type equates to the relational notion of domains—and not to relations or tables. Do you agree?* Answer: *That is absolutely true ...* Question: *What corresponds to a relational table in the object model?* Answer: *A table is an extent, which is the set of instances of a given type.*

---

18. You might have noticed that the extract quoted doesn't illustrate any "type *vs.* value or variable" errors as such and thus doesn't really belong in this section—but I found it so staggering that I couldn't resist including it anyway.

Comment: I agree completely with that first answer! I can *partly* agree with the second answer too, provided that (a) in the question, "a relational table" means a relation variable, not a relation value, and (b) in the answer, "the set of instances of a given type"—*T,* say—means the set of all values of type *T* that are currently represented in the database. But "instances" usually means "objects," and "objects" usually means variables ... So once again there might be some confusion over type *vs.* either value or variable, and I'm not sure I'm right to agree, after all.

Furthermore (and perhaps more important), even if I'm right to agree, I must now qualify that agreement by adding that I certainly reject the subsidiary implication that "rows in relational tables" correspond to objects. And I must qualify it further by pointing out that, in the relational world, we don't usually find the notion of "the set of all values of type *T* that are currently represented in the database" particularly useful! For example, what would be the point of keeping an "extent" or table that contained the set of all integers that are currently represented in the database? Or the set of all money values? Or the set of all names? Etc., etc.

Let me close this section by admitting that I'm well aware that many people will simply dismiss the criticisms I've been articulating here as mere quibbles: "Yes, the phrasing might be a little sloppy, but what does it matter? We all know what the writer really means, don't we?" And so on.

Well, I think it does matter, and I don't think we can just assume we always know what the writer really means. I agree with Bob Boiko when he says (in an article entitled "Understanding XML," `http://metatorial.com/papers/xml.asp`, 2000) that "Even in the smallest organization, most conflicts stem from a lack of clearly defined and shared meaning for the words we use." I also agree with the following remarks by Richard Mitchell (from his book *Less than Words Can Say,* Little, Brown and Company, 1979):

> *It is no coincidence that the Greeks who first devised discursive prose also constructed formal logic ... Thinking is coherent discourse, and the logic and the prose require one another ... [We] have to suspect that coherent, continuous thought is impossible for those who cannot construct coherent, continuous prose ... The logic of writing is simply logic; it is not some system of arbitrary conventions interesting only to those who write a lot. All logical thought goes on in the form of statements and statements about statements ... If we cannot make those statements and statements about statements logically, clearly, and coherently, then we cannot think and make knowledge. People who cannot put strings of sentences together in good order cannot think.*

(I've had occasion to quote these remarks before, in an article entitled "Good Writing Does Matter"—Chapter 3 in the present book.)

Consequences of Such Confusions

What are the consequences of confusing values and variables? Well, here's one. Consider the following quote (it's taken from an article entitled "On Marrying Relations and Objects: Relation-Centric and Object-Centric Perspectives," by Won Kim, in *Data Base Newsletter 22,* No. 6, November/December 1994):

> *[Some] relational database systems ... assign tuple identifiers to tuples in relations ...*

I note in passing that "relational" here should probably be *SQL* and "relations" should certainly be *relvars*, but I don't want to pursue those issues further here. Rather, the point is that the systems in question are clearly thinking of the relvars in question as consisting of collections of tuple variables or "tuplevars"—there wouldn't be any point in "assigning identifiers to" (or, better, associating identifiers with) tuple *values!* So the systems in question are based on a logically flawed concept; as we know, relvars don't contain tuplevars, they contain relation values, which contain tuple values.

Even this flaw might not matter, however (I mean, it might not be a concern at the model level), were it not for the following:

- First, the systems in question typically expose those "tuple IDs" to the user (indeed, if they don't, then from the user's point of view those tuple IDs don't exist—they aren't part of the model, and we don't need to talk about them). Exposing them to the user means the user can access and exploit them in a variety of ways. Unless they're represented to the user as just another relational attribute, however (which they might or might not be), we have a violation of *The Information Principle* on our hands.

- Second, so far as I'm aware, the systems in question universally associate such IDs with tuples in *base* relvars only, not with tuples in other kinds of relvar (e.g., views), and certainly not with tuples in relations produced as the result of evaluating some general relational expression (e.g., the result of some query). Users thus see a logical difference between base relvars and other kinds, and between base relations and other kinds (where by the term *base relation* I mean a relation that happens to be the value of some base relvar). And so we have a violation of *The Principle of Interchangeability* on our hands. *Note: The Principle of Interchangeability* (of base and derived relvars) is discussed in depth in my book *An Introduction to Database Systems*. Basically what it says is simply that the user shouldn't be able to tell the difference between base relvars and other kinds.

Following on from the foregoing discussion, I now claim that it was at least partly a confusion over the value *vs.* variable distinction that led to the introduction of object IDs into the object world. *The Third Manifesto* rejects the concept of object IDs, finding them to be both unnecessary and undesirable. The argument to show they're *unnecessary* goes like this:

- By definition, every value is distinct from every other value (i.e., is in fact self-identifying).

- Values thus have no need to carry around with themselves some hidden, secret identifier that's somehow separate from the value itself, and indeed they don't do so.

- Variables, by contrast, do need some identity that's separate from their current value, and that identification is provided, precisely and sufficiently, by the variable's **name**.

As for the *undesirability* of object IDs, it's sufficient here to say simply that they're logically indistinguishable from pointers, and I've already said we don't want pointers in the database. (I don't think I need to give a detailed justification of this latter position here, though I might do so in some future paper.)

Of course, the relational world too has been guilty in the past of some confusion over values and variables: over *relation* values and variables, to be specific. And that fact has led to some confusion over *normalization* in particular. In the second edition of my book *An Introduction to Database Systems*, for example, I wrote:

Given a relation R, we say that attribute Y of R is functionally dependent on attribute X of R if and only if each X value in R has associated with it precisely one Y value in R (at any one time).

I should have said *relvar*, not *relation!*—then I could (and should, and would) have deleted "(at any one time)." In other words: If we call a relvar a relation, what do we call a relation?

Confusions have also arisen over *update*. In the sixth edition of that same book (though only in the first printing!), I wrote:

Tuple assignments are performed (implicitly) during [relational] UPDATE operations.

No, they're not! As we know, relational UPDATE operations—and INSERT and DELETE operations too, of course—are really shorthands for certain relational assignments, which replace the current value (a relation) of the target relvar by another value (another relation). The target of such assignments is categorically *not* a tuplevar (as it would have to be in a genuine tuple assignment)—not even in the special case where we're trying to DELETE or UPDATE a relvar that currently contains just one tuple.

Further examples of confusion over updating are provided by SQL. Consider first the SQL INSERT statement. In its simplest and probably commonest form, that statement looks like this:

```
INSERT INTO <table name> ( <column name commalist> )
               VALUES ( <expression commalist>  ) ;
```

For example:

```
INSERT INTO EMP ( EMP#,        DEPT#,        SALARY )
        VALUES ( EMP#('E1'), DEPT#('D1'), MONEY(50000) ) ;
```

This example would widely be regarded as "inserting a row" into table EMP, but it really shouldn't be!—see the discussion of INSERT in the section "Relation Values and Variables" earlier in this chapter.

A more serious issue is raised by the "positioned" forms of the DELETE and UPDATE statements (i.e., DELETE and UPDATE via a cursor). For example:

```
UPDATE EMP
SET    SALARY = SALARY * 1.1
WHERE  CURRENT OF EXC ;
```

This statement is *defined* to be a single-row operation—it updates the particular row that cursor EXC happens to be positioned on (I'm assuming that EXC here is a cursor running over the EMP table, of course). But "updating a row" means by definition that the row in question must be a row *variable!*—and there's no such thing, in the relational model. In other words, I'm suggesting that SQL's positioned DELETE and UPDATE statements are and always were a logical mistake. In fact, they would probably never have been included in the language in the first place if the original SQL designers had understood the logical difference between relation (or table) values and variables.

By the way, it's relevant to mention in passing that certain cursor-based updates can never work, anyway. As a trivial example, suppose table EMP is subject to the constraint that employees E1 and E2 must always be in the same department. Then any cursor-based (and hence single-row) update that attempts to change the department number for either E1 or E2 will necessarily fail.

Let me now turn to the issue of confusion over types and either values or variables or both. I've already alluded to the fact that a failure to distinguish between types and variables—in fact, between *scalar* types and *relation* variables, if you think about it!—constitutes **The First Great Blunder**. I don't want to discuss that blunder any further here, except to stress the point that it really is a blunder of huge proportions ... If you want to learn more about it, a detailed discussion can be found in *An Introduction to Database Systems*. But I do want to say something about **The Second Great Blunder,** which can be characterized, informally, as *mixing pointers and relations*—that is, "allowing an attribute in one relation to contain pointers to tuples in another."

Now, I hope you realize immediately that this notion makes no sense, because "pointers to tuples" has to mean pointers to tuple *variables*, and there's no such thing as a tuple variable in a relational database (hence the quotation marks in the previous paragraph). So we really are talking about another huge blunder ... Again, I don't want to discuss the issue in detail here (if you're interested, you can find such a discussion in *An Introduction to Database Systems*). Instead, I just want to make the following points:

- A system that commits the first great blunder is inevitably led into committing the second as well. That is, the second is a logical consequence of the first, and so it's also, logically, a consequence of confusing types and variables.

- However, a system that avoids the first great blunder can still commit the second, anyway. To that extent, therefore, the second is independent of the first. Since we've already seen that the second involves "pointers to tuples," however, we can say that the second is also a consequence of confusing values and variables, as well as a consequence of confusing types and variables.

- Third, as I've written elsewhere, if SQL doesn't quite commit the two great blunders, it certainly sails very close to the wind ... To be specific, SQL does include support for "REF types," it does include support for dereferencing (though, oddly, not for referencing), and it does allow rows in one table to contain "references" to rows in another. Now, advocates of these SQL features claim that they (i.e., the features in question) are all really just shorthand for various combinations of features that already exist in the language. But even if we accept this claim as valid (which it patently isn't, by the way), the fact remains that the new features have the effect of making SQL much more complicated than it was before—as if it wasn't complicated enough already!—and (to say it again) they're all consequences, in the last analysis, of confusing types, values, and variables.

Concluding Remarks

I began this chapter by identifying types, values, variables, and operators as "the four core concepts." They're "core concepts" because they do indeed form the core of the vast majority of traditional programming languages (among other things), and database and programming language professionals really ought to be thoroughly familiar with them—though I believe the body of the chapter has amply demonstrated that there's room for improvement in this regard. Let me therefore say a little more about them here by way of additional justification:

- We must have *variables*, because without them everything would be totally static; in particular, we couldn't update the database to reflect changes in the real world.

- We must have *values*, because values are what we assign to variables. Without them, we couldn't do anything at all.

- We must have *operators*, because, again, without them we couldn't do anything at all. In particular, we must have update operators (at least assignment), because without them we couldn't update the database.

- We must have *types*, because without them we can't catch stupid errors (the SQL example SELECT ... WHERE SHOE_SIZE = AGE is frequently quoted in this connection). *Note:* Types not only allow such errors to be caught—they usually allow them to be caught at compile time.

Once we realize the need for types, we realize further that types are, in a sense, the most fundamental of the four core concepts; to repeat from the section "Types Are Fundamental," values are typed, variables are typed, and operators apply to typed arguments and (if they return a value) are themselves typed as well. In other words, values, variables, and operators all rely on types.

Now, we've seen that there are major logical differences between these concepts. In fact, there are a number of subsidiary, or related, logical differences as well that arise from the ones I've been discussing. Here are a few of them (in alphabetic order):

- Argument *vs.* parameter

- Declared type *vs.* most specific type

- Object *vs.* reference

- Object ID *vs.* tuple ID *vs.* surrogate

- Type *vs.* representation

- Type *vs.* type generator

- Value *vs.* appearance *vs.* encoding

I plan to treat most if not all of these (as well as others) in a series of future writings.

PART 3

■ ■ ■

Relational Database Management

This part of the book consists of nine chapters. Chapters 7 through 10 are essentially detailed tutorials on certain fundamental aspects of the relational model that don't seem to be as generally understood or appreciated as they ought to be (in fact, the SQL standard currently violates all of them). Chapter 11, too, has to do with a fundamental feature of the relational model; in this case, however, the feature in question is one for which the necessity has only recently become apparent. (The feature in question is multiple assignment, and it would be fair to say that, while it's my opinion that the relational model always had an implicit need for such a feature, it was a long time before that fact was realized.) Chapters 12 and 13 address the question of relational database design, focusing on the reduction of data redundancy as the goal of such design. Finally, Chapter 14 discusses the use of the relational model in dealing with tree-structured data, and Chapter 15 discusses the relationship between the relational model and "business rules."

CHAPTER 7

■ ■ ■

Why We Need Type BOOLEAN

This is just a brief technical note, but it does answer a question I get asked very frequently. In our book *Foundation for Future Database Systems: The Third Manifesto*, 2nd edition (Addison-Wesley, 2000), Hugh Darwen and I claimed that support for the data type BOOLEAN was essential in any decent, self-respecting DBMS. To quote:

> *We require that at least one built-in scalar type be supported, namely the—absolutely fundamental!—type **truth value**, [also known as] type BOOLEAN.*

And in our book *Relational Database Writings 1989–1991* (Addison-Wesley, 1992), we said this:

> *[We] find it much easier to imagine a [DBMS] that fails to support numbers, than one that fails to support a truth-valued data type!*

In my seminars and elsewhere, however, I often get asked to justify this strong position. So I thought it was time to set the answer down in writing. Hence this short note.

The basic point is very simple: If the system lets me write an expression X that evaluates to a value v of type T, it should surely also let me declare a variable V or a column C that's of that same type T!—for otherwise the system can hardly be said to be very coherent (it would violate obvious and well-known principles of language design: orthogonality, for example). In other words, it's surely obvious that expressions should always evaluate to values of types that are known within the system.

Now, in the database world, for all kinds of reasons, *we need to be able to perform comparisons.* In other words, we need to be able to write boolean expressions. It follows that BOOLEAN needs to be a type that's known within the system. QED.

Let me immediately add that most SQL implementations fail in this connection. Of course, such systems certainly do let you write boolean expressions (for instance, in a WHERE clause). Here are a couple of more or less self-explanatory examples:

```
1. SELECT S.*              /* get suppliers in Paris          */
   FROM   S
   WHERE  S.CITY = 'Paris' ;

2. SELECT S.*              /* get suppliers who supply part P2 */
   FROM   S
```

```
WHERE  EXISTS ( SELECT SP.*
                FROM    SP
                WHERE   SP.S# = S.S#
                AND     SP.P# = P#('P2') ) ;
```

But those same systems don't let you write those same boolean expressions in a SELECT clause. In other words, the following potentially useful counterparts to Queries 1 and 2—

```
3. SELECT ( S.CITY = 'Paris' ) AS X
   FROM   S
   WHERE  S.S# = S#('S2') ;

4. SELECT EXISTS ( SELECT SP.*
                   FROM    SP
                   WHERE   SP.S# = S.S#
                   AND     SP.P# = P#('P2') ) AS X
   FROM   S
   WHERE  S.S# = S#('S2') ;
```

—are typically not supported. *Note:* Loosely speaking, Query 3 means "Is supplier S2 in Paris?" and Query 4 means "Does supplier S2 supply part P2?" I'm sure you'll agree that both of these queries are useful, and it would be nice to be able to express them; but SQL products prohibit them because (if supported) they would return a result table with a column X of type BOOLEAN, and the products in question don't support that type—which means, among other things, that the following CREATE TABLE is also illegal:

```
CREATE TABLE T ( ... , X BOOLEAN , ... ) ;
```

One last point on SQL: In fact, the SQL standard did introduce a BOOLEAN data type—only 25 years after the language was first defined!—with the 1999 version of the standard (SQL:1999). As far as I know, however, none of the SQL vendors (at least, none of the major ones) support it at the time of writing. Perhaps worse, it suffers from a major logical flaw: namely, it uses NULL to represent "the third truth value." But that's a topic for another day.

CHAPTER 8

■ ■ ■

What First Normal Form Really Means

Normal: see *abnormal.*

—From an early IBM PL/1 reference manual, *circa* 1969

The relational model requires all tables to be in first normal form (abbreviated 1NF). Everybody knows that. Yet few people seem to know what that requirement really means! In fact, there's a great deal of confusion on the issue, as the following "definitions" (taken from various sources on the Web) clearly demonstrate:

- If there are no repeating groups of attributes, then [the table] is in 1NF.

- To achieve first normal form, each field in a table must convey unique information.

- An entity is in *first normal form* if there are no attributes (or groups of attributes) that repeat for a single occurrence of the entity.

- First normal form [requires that you]:

  - Eliminate duplicative columns from the same table.

  - Create separate tables for each group of related data and identify each row with a unique column or set of columns (the primary key).

- First Normal Form ... means the table should have no "repeating groups" of fields ... A repeating group is when you repeat the same basic attribute (field) over and over again. A good example of this is when you wish to store the items you buy at a grocery store ... [*and the writer goes on to give an example—presumably meant to illustrate the concept of a repeating group—of a table called Item Table with columns called Customer, Item #1, Item #2, Item #3, and Item #4*].

To my mind, these "definitions" are, at best, unclear and imprecise and, at worst, just plain wrong (the one thing they're not is atypical). So what then *is* first normal form? In what follows, I'll do my best to provide a clear, precise, and accurate answer to this question. I'll also explore in detail certain implications, both practical and theoretical, of that answer.

Some Preliminaries

If there's a common thread that can be said to run through the foregoing "definitions" (such as they are), it's that 1NF means *no repeating groups*. (If you're too young to be familiar with this concept, then I envy you, and assure you that the meaning will soon become clear enough. Please read on!) And I therefore have to admit that the confusions I'm complaining about are partly my fault, because I'm on record as saying very much the same thing myself ... In the sixth edition of my book *An Introduction to Database Systems* (Addison-Wesley, 1995[1]), I wrote:

> Relations do not contain repeating groups. *A relation satisfying this condition is said to be **normalized,** or equivalently to be in first normal form.*

In other words, for many years I was as confused as anyone else. What's worse, I did my best (worst?) to spread that confusion through my writings, seminars, and other presentations. By the early 1990s, however, I'd seen the light, thanks in large part to the efforts of Hugh Darwen, who wrote an article around that time entitled "Relation-Valued Attributes; *or,* Will the Real First Normal Form Please Stand Up?" (included in my book *Relational Database Writings 1989–1991,* Addison-Wesley, 1992). Since that time, I've done my best to set the record straight, again in both writings and presentations. With regard to the writings in particular, see especially:

- Pages 152–153 and 373–375 of my book *An Introduction to Database Systems,* 8th edition (Addison-Wesley, 2004)

- "Nested Relations" (an article in two parts that originally appeared in *DBP&D 8,* Nos. 3–4, March–April, 1995, republished in my book *Relational Database Writings 1994–1997,* Addison-Wesley, 1998)

However, most of what follows is new and isn't covered in either of those previous publications. A few further preliminary remarks to conclude this section:

- First of all, I want this discussion to reach as wide an audience as possible. For that reason, I've decided to use the comparatively "user-friendly" terminology of *tables, rows,* and *columns* (albeit not exclusively), even though I prefer the more precise terms *relations, tuples,* and *attributes.* I'll have a little more to say on this issue of terminology in Appendix A.

---

1. Publication dates are strange beasts; the copyright date on that book was 1995, but it appeared in 1994, and the text in question was written in 1992.

- Second, good database design discipline generally requires tables to be, not just in 1NF, but also in some higher normal form (usually fifth normal form, 5NF[2]). However, 1NF differs from those higher normal forms in that it is *mandated by the relational model;* that is, relational operators such as join *require* their operands to be normalized, meaning they must be in at least 1NF. And while the database will be generally easier to manage and deal with if the tables are in some higher normal form, the relational model as such doesn't care—it just requires the tables to be in *at least* 1NF, and join and the other operators will then work as expected. For this reason, I'll have little to say in what follows regarding those higher normal forms. For the record, however, let me at least spell the point out explicitly that a table that's in a given normal form (say 5NF) is—necessarily and by definition—in all lower normal forms as well, including 1NF in particular.

- Third, I'd like to stress the point that, technically speaking, the term "normalized" and the term "first normal form" *mean exactly the same thing;* that is, all 1NF tables are normalized, and all normalized tables are in 1NF. Thus, while it's common informally to use the term "normalized" to mean some higher level of normalization (perhaps 5NF), such usage is sloppy and strictly speaking incorrect.

- Fourth, you might be a little surprised at the length of this chapter. After all, isn't 1NF a pretty simple thing? Well, yes, it is; but it turns out that there's rather more to say about it than you might think. Certainly I believe it's important, given the fundamental importance of the subject matter, not to skimp on any of the examples, definitions, or discussions.

"Data Value Atomicity"

Now let's get down to business. Since Codd was the inventor of 1NF in the first place, the obvious place to start is with Codd's own definition of the concept. Oddly enough, however, it's quite difficult to find such a definition in his published writings; after some searching, the only one I could find was tucked away in an appendix to his paper "Further Normalization of the Data Base Relational Model," in Randall J. Rustin (ed.), *Data Base Systems: Courant Computer Science Symposia Series 6* (Prentice-Hall, 1972). (This was the paper in which Codd introduced second and third normal form, 2NF and 3NF. Unfortunately, it—or the book that contains it, rather—seems to be currently out of print.) Anyway, here's the definition I found:

> *A relation is in* first normal form *if ... none of its domains has elements which are themselves sets. An* unnormalized relation *is one which is not in first normal form.*

Note that, according to this definition, a relation—or table, rather, in our "more user-friendly" terminology—fails to be in 1NF only if at least one of its columns contains values that are, quite specifically, *sets.* Thus, a table without any such column but *with* a column that contains, say, bags or arrays is apparently in 1NF! In a later publication, however (namely, his book *The Relational Model for Database Management Version 2*, Addison-Wesley, 1990), Codd says more explicitly:

---

2. You might or might not be interested to know that Hugh Darwen, Nikos Lorentzos, and I have recently come up with a new *sixth* normal form, 6NF (see our book *Temporal Data and the Relational Model,* Morgan Kaufmann, 2003).

The values in the domains on which each relation is defined are required to be atomic with respect to the DBMS.

Although this statement makes no explicit mention of the term "first normal form," I think it's clear that first normal form is the concept Codd's trying to get at here. And the key point is clearly that values in domains, and hence values at row-and-column intersections in a 1NF table, are supposed to be *atomic*[3] (or "atomic with respect to the DBMS," at least). So what exactly does *atomic* mean?

Well, elsewhere on the same page of his book, Codd says:

Atomic data [is data that cannot] be decomposed into smaller pieces by the DBMS (excluding certain special functions).

While I have to admit that I don't know exactly what Codd means by "excluding certain special functions" here, I don't think that exclusion is very important for our purposes. Let's look at some examples. What about character strings? Are character strings atomic? Well, SQL provides several operators on such strings—SUBSTRING, LIKE, "||" (concatenate), and so on— that clearly rely on the fact that character strings in general *are* decomposable by the DBMS (in other words, such strings have an internal structure that's at least potentially of interest to the user). And SQL isn't alone in this regard, of course; every language I know of that supports character strings at all provides analogs of SUBSTRING and the rest. So are character strings atomic? What do you think?

Here are some other examples of values whose atomicity is at least open to question and yet can certainly appear in columns of SQL tables:

- Integers, which might be regarded as being decomposable into their prime factors (yes, I know this isn't the kind of decomposability we usually consider in this context; I'm just trying to show that the notion of decomposability is itself open to a variety of interpretations)

- Fixed-point numbers, which might be regarded as being decomposable into integer and fractional parts

- Dates and times, which might be regarded as being decomposable into year/month/day and hour/minute/second components, respectively

- SQL expressions—think of, e.g., view definitions in the catalog—which certainly are "decomposable by the DBMS" (because otherwise there wouldn't be any point in keeping them in the catalog in the first place)

Now I'd like to examine what some might regard as a more startling example. Consider the table T1 in Figure 8-1, which shows that supplier S2 supplies part P1, supplier S2 supplies part P2, supplier S4 supplies part P2, and so on. *Note:* I'll be referring to table T1 repeatedly in subsequent discussions, and it might be worth your while to make a copy of it now and keep that copy close to hand.

---

3. Codd's famous 1970 paper "A Relational Model of Data for Large Shared Data Banks" (*CACM 13*, No. 6, June 1970) also talks about atomic values, but it never actually comes out and *requires* such atomicity— it merely says that "the possibility of eliminating [values that are not atomic] appears worth investigating."

T1	S#	P#
	S2	P1
	S2	P2
	S4	P2
	S4	P4
	S4	P5

Figure 8-1. *Table T1 (all columns contain "atomic values")*

For the sake of the example (and in fact for the sake of all of the examples to follow), let's agree that supplier numbers and part numbers are indeed atomic values. Table T1 is thus in 1NF according to Codd's definition. Now suppose we replace that table by the table T2 in Figure 8-2; that table shows that supplier S2 supplies parts P1 and P2 and supplier S4 supplies parts P2, P4, and P5. In other words, the values in column P#_SET in table T2 are *sets* of part numbers.

T2	S#	P#_SET
	S2	{P1,P2}
	S4	{P2,P4,P5}

Figure 8-2. *Table T2 (column P#_SET contains sets)*

Now, table T2 is surely not in 1NF by Codd's definition (certainly the domain underlying column P#_SET has "elements [*in other words, values*] which are themselves sets"). In fact, doesn't column P#_SET contain *repeating groups?*—after all, each row of T2 contains a "group" of part numbers, and different rows contain different numbers of part numbers, in general. And didn't we see earlier that repeating groups are the one thing that almost everybody agrees 1NF is supposed to prohibit? In other words, aren't repeating groups the prize example of what the atomicity requirement is supposed to outlaw? I answer these questions as follows:

- Yes, it could be argued that column P#_SET does contain repeating groups.

- Yes, repeating groups are the one thing that almost everybody does agree 1NF is supposed to prohibit.

- Yes, repeating groups are indeed the prize example of what the atomicity requirement is supposed to outlaw.

Nevertheless, I claim that **table T2 is in 1NF!** For consider:

- First, note that—of course deliberately—I've shown the sets of part numbers in column P#_SET in Figure 8-2 enclosed in set braces {}, to emphasize the fact that each such set is indeed *a single value:* a set value, to be sure, but a set is still, at a certain level of abstraction, a single value. (I didn't stress the point earlier, but in fact the notion that a set can legitimately be regarded as a single value underpinned Codd's original definition of 1NF. As you will recall, that definition was expressed in terms of "domains [that have values that] are themselves sets.")

- Second (and regardless of what you might think of the previous point), the fact is that *a set like {P2,P4,P5} is no more and no less decomposable by the DBMS than a character string is.* Like character strings, sets do have some internal structure; as with character strings, however, it's convenient to ignore that internal structure for certain purposes. In other words, if character strings are compatible with the requirements of 1NF—i.e., if character strings are atomic—then sets must be so, too.

The real point I'm getting at here is that the notion of atomicity *has no absolute meaning*[4]—it simply depends on what we want to do with the data. Sometimes we want to deal with an entire set of part numbers as a single thing; at other times, we want to deal with individual part numbers within that set—but then we're descending to a lower level of detail (in other words, a lower level of abstraction). The following analogy might help to clarify this point. In physics—which after all is where the terminology of atomicity comes from—the situation is precisely parallel: Sometimes we want to think about individual physical atoms as indivisible objects; at other times, we want to think about the protons, neutrons, and electrons that go to make up those atoms. *Note:* Those protons and neutrons aren't really indivisible, either—they contain a variety of "subsubatomic" particles called *quarks.* And so on, possibly (?).

It follows that the notion of absolute atomicity has to be rejected. And, since it relies on that rejected notion, it further follows that the notion of 1NF really ought to be rejected as well—at least in a relational context, because (as we'll see later) relations are *always* in 1NF! However, it can still be useful and meaningful to say that some *non*relational data structure isn't in 1NF; see the section "A Definition" later in this chapter for further explanation of this point. Moreover (and despite the foregoing remarks), it can be argued that the notion of 1NF does still have a useful role to play, even in a relational context. I'll come back to this latter possibility in the section "Concluding Remarks," later.

One last point: It might perhaps be claimed that the notion of atomicity does have an absolute meaning after all. To be specific, we might say that a value is *not* atomic if and only if operators exist to "take the value apart," as it were. Thus, a character string is not atomic because it can be taken apart by means of the SUBSTRING operator; a set is not atomic because it can be taken apart by means of operators that extract either elements or subsets from the set; and so on. By contrast, a fixed-point number is atomic if there are no operators to extract its integer

---

4. One reviewer of an earlier draft of this chapter wondered whether the adjective "absolute" here would be understood by all readers. Well, here's a definition (taken from *Chambers Twentieth Century Dictionary*): "**absolute,** *adj. ...* capable of being conceived independently of anything else." That's what I mean.

and fractional parts (say). But even if we were to accept this argument, it seems to me we would then also have to accept the argument that the very same value might be atomic today and nonatomic tomorrow! Such would be the case for a fixed-point number, for example, if there were originally no operators to extract its integer and fractional parts but such operators were subsequently introduced. And it further seems to me that if the notion of atomicity is time-dependent in this way, then (as already claimed) it really doesn't have any absolute meaning.

Relation-Valued Attributes

Let's return for a moment to table T2 in Figure 8-2. In that figure, I showed P#_SET values as general sets. But it's much more useful in practice if they're, more specifically, *relations* (see Figure 8-3, where I've renamed the column as P#_REL and the table accordingly as T3). Why is it more useful? Because relations, not general sets, are what the relational model is all about.[5] As a consequence, the full power of the relational algebra immediately becomes available for the relations in question—they can be restricted, projected, joined, and so on. By contrast, if we use general sets instead of relations, then we need to introduce new operators (set union, set intersection, and so on) for dealing with those sets ... Much better to get as much mileage as we can out of the operators we already have!

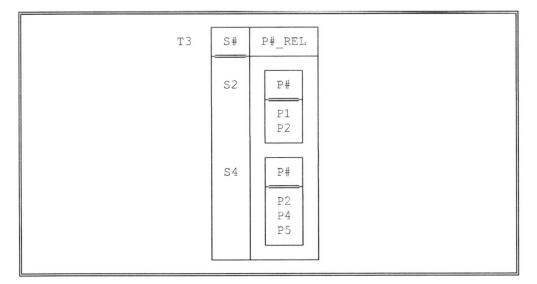

Figure 8-3. *Table T3 (column P#_REL contains relations)*

Column P#_REL in table T3 is an example of a **relation-valued attribute** (abbreviated RVA). Points arising:

---

5. In case you're wondering, the difference is that general sets can contain anything, whereas relations contain tuples specifically. Note, however, that a relation certainly resembles a general set in that it too can be regarded as a single value.

- "RVA" is the usual abbreviation, which is why I'm now talking in terms of relations and attributes instead of tables and columns. For present purposes, you can regard the terms as interchangeable (but see Appendix A).

- If A is an RVA and D is the domain underlying A, then the values in D are relations too, of course.

- In general, the relations that are values of some given RVA can have attributes that are RVAs in turn, and so we can have relations that contain other relations nested inside themselves, and those other relations can contain still further relations nested inside them, and so on, recursively, to any number of levels. All without violating 1NF!

Just as an aside, I remind you that, as noted earlier, the 6th edition of my book *An Introduction to Database Systems* said (paraphrasing) that 1NF meant *no repeating groups*. But it also said that 1NF allowed RVAs—and you might feel these two statements contradict each other somewhat. In fact, however, I was attempting to draw a distinction between repeating groups, which weren't very precisely defined, and RVAs, which were. With hindsight, I think that attempt was probably a mistake on my part. (Though possibly not, if "repeating groups" still aren't precisely defined. See later in this chapter for further discussion of this latter point.)

Of course, we need a way to map between tables without RVAs (like table T1) and tables with them (like table T3), and that's the purpose of the GROUP and UNGROUP operators of the relational algebra. I don't want to go into too much detail on those operators here; let me just say that, given tables T1 and T3 as shown in Figs. 1 and 3, respectively, the expression

```
T1 GROUP ( { P# } AS P#_REL )
```

will produce table T3, and the expression

```
T3 UNGROUP ( P#_REL )
```

will produce table T1. *Note:* All coding examples in this chapter are expressed in a language called **Tutorial D,** which is described in detail in a book by Hugh Darwen and myself, *Databases, Types, and the Relational Model: The Third Manifesto*, 3rd edition (Addison-Wesley, 2006)—referred to hereinafter as just *The Third Manifesto*. In the interests of familiarity I would have preferred to use SQL (though it's not much to my taste); however, SQL doesn't support all of the constructs I need to discuss, so I'm more or less forced into using a language of my own. This state of affairs is a little unfortunate, but I believe the examples are all more or less self-explanatory anyway.

There are a few more points I'd like to make in connection with GROUP and UNGROUP. First of all, Codd himself in fact proposed a grouping operator—he called it *factoring*—in an appendix to his paper "Relational Completeness of Data Base Sublanguages," which appeared in the same book as the further normalization paper mentioned near the beginning of the previous section. I don't think he regarded that operator as part of the relational algebra, however, precisely because it produced a result with an RVA. His actual words were:

> For presentation purposes, it may be desirable to convert a normalized relation to unnormalized form. The operation of factoring accomplishes this.

In other words, Codd saw factoring as converting a relation into something that wasn't a relation but might perhaps be called a *report* (note the words "For presentation purposes").

And, presumably because in his view a report wasn't a relation, I don't think he ever proposed an operator for "going the other way" (i.e., for "unfactoring" an "unnormalized" relation into a normalized one). *Note:* It's certainly true that RVAs can be useful in reports. In my opinion, however, it would be better to bring those reports into the relational fold, as it were, and regard them as relations just like any others—which is what RVAs and the GROUP and UNGROUP operators effectively let us do. (Of course, I don't mean to imply by these remarks that all of the formatting, highlighting, and so forth that reports typically entail should be treated as relational issues. My concern here is only with RVAs as such.)

Second, SQL does have a GROUP operator (actually spelled GROUP BY, as we all know), but it doesn't have any corresponding UNGROUP operator. Of course, the reason it has no UNGROUP operator is that it has no RVAs. But consider the consequences of these omissions: Among other things, they mean that SQL's GROUP BY actually produces a result that (as the SQL standard itself openly admits) *isn't a valid SQL table!* In other words, the all-important *closure* property of the relational algebra is violated, albeit only temporarily (because the GROUP BY result is always converted immediately, through the action of the associated SELECT operator, to something that *is* a valid SQL table). Here's the actual wording from the SQL standard:

> *A grouped table* [which is what GROUP BY yields] *is a set of groups ... A grouped table may be considered as a collection of tables.*

And neither a set of groups nor a collection of tables is logically the same thing as a table in the normal SQL sense. In other words, SQL has to go "outside the relational box," as it were, in order to explain the operation of GROUP BY—and it has to do so precisely because it fails to support RVAs.

Third, suppose that, despite everything I've been saying, we nevertheless try to argue that 1NF does mean "no RVAs" and that a table with RVAs should be regarded as "unnormalized"— or perhaps in "zeroth normal form," 0NF? Now consider the progression from "0NF" to 1NF to 2NF to 3NF ... (and so on). As we all know, the general effect of going from 1NF to 2NF is to decrease redundancy; the general effect of going from 2NF to 3NF is to decrease redundancy further; and so on. But the general effect of going from "0NF" to 1NF is to *increase* redundancy!— for example, the supplier number S4 appears just once in the "0NF" table T3 (see Figure 8-3) but three times in the corresponding 1NF table T1 (see Figure 8-1). This fact thus seems to me to be another good reason, though admittedly only an intuitive one, for not regarding tables with RVAs as unnormalized. *Note:* As a matter of fact, table T3 is not only *not* "unnormalized"— it's actually normalized to the highest possible degree (in fact it's in 6NF); so to say it's only in some hypothetical "0NF" really makes no sense at all.

I'll have a lot more to say on the topic of RVAs in subsequent sections.

Domains Can Contain *Anything!*

Now, I chose the example in the previous section of relations containing relations—tables containing tables, if you prefer—deliberately, for its shock value. After all, we've seen that relations containing relations look rather like relations with repeating groups, and we've always "known" (incorrectly, as it turns out) that repeating groups are supposed to be a no-no in the relational world. But I could have used any number of different examples to make my point; I could have had domains (and therefore attributes, or columns) that contained arrays; or bags;

or lists; or photographs; or audio or video recordings; or X rays; or fingerprints; or XML documents; or any other kind of value, "atomic" or "nonatomic," that you might care to think of. Domains, and therefore attributes or columns, can contain *anything* (any *values*, that is). All of which goes a long way toward explaining why I'm on record as stating, on many different occasions and in many different places (see, e.g., *The Third Manifesto*), that a true "object/relational" system would be nothing more nor less than a true *relational* system—which is to say, a system that supports the relational model, with all that such support entails. After all, the whole point about an "object/relational" system is precisely that we can have columns in tables that contain values of arbitrary complexity. Perhaps a better way to say this is: A proper object/relational system is just a relational system with proper **type** support (see Appendix A)—which simply means it's a proper *relational* system, no more and no less.

But now I'm beginning to stray off topic a little. To return to the main thread of my argument: Having said all of the foregoing—in particular, having said that domains (and therefore attributes, or columns) can contain anything—I'll focus in the remainder of this chapter on domains, and therefore attributes or columns, that contain relations specifically, because:

- First, as I pointed out in the previous section, we already have the operators we need for dealing with relations. By contrast, if we decide to use, e.g., array-valued domains and attributes, then we'll have to introduce an additional set of operators for dealing with arrays; and if we decide to use, e.g., list-valued domains and attributes, then we'll have to introduce an additional set of operators for dealing with lists; and so on. And the effect of all of those additional operators is to introduce a lot of additional complexity[6]—queries become more complex, and so do constraints, and so do updates (and so on). Thus, although such domains and attributes are certainly legal in theory, they might not be a very good idea in practice.

- Second, there are a number of interesting points to be made in connection with RVAs in particular, as we'll see in the next few sections.

Relation-Valued Attributes Make Outer Join Unnecessary

The first of those "interesting points" is that *RVAs make outer join unnecessary.* Consider the tables T4 and T5 shown in Figure 8-4; table T4 shows there are three suppliers at this time, and table T5 is identical to table T1 from Figure 8-1. Note in particular that supplier S5 currently supplies no parts at all.

---

6. Note that what they don't do is introduce any more *power.* To be more specific, there's no data that can be represented with arrays, lists, and so on, that can't be represented without them. Likewise, there's no useful processing that can be done on data represented with arrays, lists, and so on, that can't be done on data represented without them.

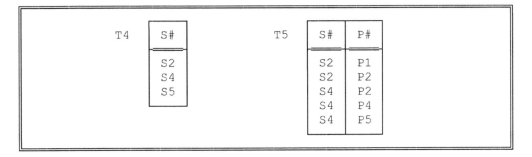

Figure 8-4. *Tables T4 and T5 (supplier S5 supplies no parts)*

Now, if we were to form the *left outer join* of tables T4 and T5 over supplier numbers, we would obtain the result shown in Figure 8-5, in which the fact that supplier S5 currently supplies no parts is represented by a *null* in the P# position (shown in the figure as two dashes, "--"). As an aside, I must point out that the result is thus not a relation, because relations are required to contain a value at every row-and-column intersection, and nulls aren't values. The result also has no key, for essentially the same reason. *Note:* Here and elsewhere in this chapter I use the unqualified term "key" to mean a *candidate* key—possibly but not necessarily a primary key specifically (primary keys are just a special case of candidate keys, of course).

S#	P#
S2	P1
S2	P2
S4	P2
S4	P4
S4	P5
S5	--

Figure 8-5. *Left outer join of tables T4 and T5 over S#*

Now, I've argued on many occasions and in many places that nulls are bad news, and I don't want to repeat all of those arguments here—I just want to say that surely it would *obviously* be better if we could find another way of dealing with the problem that outer join is supposed to solve, one that avoids the apparent need for nulls. And we can. To be specific, we can write an expression that, when evaluated, returns the table T6 shown in Figure 8-6.[7] *Note:* As with table T1, I'll be referring to table T6 repeatedly in what follows, and it might be worth making a copy of it for future reference.

---

7. In case you're interested, the expression in question looks like this: (EXTEND (T4 RENAME (S# AS X)) ADD (T5 WHERE S# = X){P#} AS P#_REL) RENAME (X AS S#). While this expression might seem a little complicated, there are ways in which it can be simplified. For further discussion, see *The Third Manifesto*.

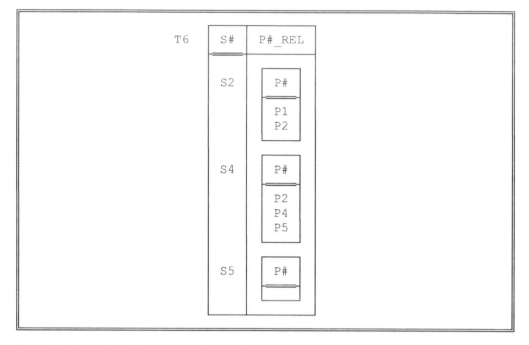

Figure 8-6. *Preserving information for supplier S5 (a better way)*

Observe in particular in Figure 8-6 that the empty set of parts supplied by supplier S5 is represented by an empty set, not (as in Figure 8-5) by some bizarre "null." To represent an empty set by an empty set seems like such an obviously good idea! In fact, *there would be no need for outer join at all* if RVAs were properly supported. Thus, one great advantage of RVAs is that they deal more elegantly with the problem that outer join is intended to solve than outer join does itself—and I'm tempted to say that this fact all by itself, even if there were no other advantages, is a big argument in favor of supporting RVAs.

To pursue the point just a moment longer: How are we supposed to *interpret* the nulls that appear in the result of an outer join, anyway? What do they mean in Figure 8-5, for instance? They certainly don't mean either "value unknown" or "value doesn't apply"; in fact, the only interpretation that does make any logical sense is, precisely, "value is the empty set." (I remark in passing that this fact suggests that we have still another problem on our hands in connection with outer join: Values in column P# in Figure 8-5 are supposed to be part numbers, not sets of part numbers. I regard this issue as yet another nail in the nulls coffin, and I don't propose to discuss it in any more detail here.)

Relation-Valued Attributes in Base Tables?— The Bad News

To summarize so far: We've seen that domains, and therefore columns in tables, can contain values of any kind whatsoever—values of arbitrary complexity, in fact—and we've seen that they can contain relations in particular. One issue I've ducked so far, however, is this: Do we really want relation-valued attributes in *base* tables? In other words, we've seen that RVAs can be useful in *derived* tables (like table T6, for example); but do we really want to design our database in such a way as to include such attributes in "nonderived" or base tables?

As a basis for discussing this issue, suppose table T6 from Figure 8-6 is meant to be a base table instead of, as previously, a derived one. Then it's easy to see that, considered *as* a base table, it suffers from a variety of problems (in other words, it isn't very well designed). In fact, that base table looks very much like a **hierarchy,** with parts subordinate to suppliers, as might be found in (e.g.) an IMS design; as a direct consequence, all of the old arguments against IMS designs in particular or hierarchic designs in general—arguments that were originally raised well over 30 years ago!—thus apply immediately. In the remainder of this section, partly for purposes of future reference, I want to rehearse some of those "old arguments against hierarchies."

Those arguments can be summed up in one word: **asymmetry**. That asymmetry in turn leads to numerous practical and theoretical problems. In the case of table T6, for example, suppliers and parts are treated asymmetrically. As a consequence, the (symmetric) queries—

1. Get S# for suppliers who supply part P2

2. Get P# for parts supplied by supplier S2

—have asymmetric formulations:

1. ((T6 UNGROUP (P#_REL)) WHERE P# = P# ('P2')) { S# }

2. ((T6 WHERE S# = S# ('S2')) UNGROUP (P#_REL)) { P# }

Not only do these two formulations look rather different from each other, they're both more complicated than their (symmetric) counterparts for the symmetric design of Figure 8-1:

1. (T1 WHERE P# = P# ('P2')) { S# }

2. (T1 WHERE S# = S# ('S2')) { P# }

Moreover, it's at least possible—even likely—that the T6 queries will perform worse than their T1 counterparts. *Note:* In fact, of course, performance is an implementation issue, not a model issue, and strictly speaking I shouldn't even be mentioning it in a discussion of this nature. But people are often confused over the difference between implementation and model issues; indeed, performance is often cited as an argument in favor of hierarchic designs! For that reason, I think it's at least legitimate to mention the fact that, contrary to popular opinion, such designs can actually lead to *worse* performance, given the way most systems are actually implemented today.

Like queries, integrity constraints also can be more complex with a hierarchic design. By way of example, suppose, reasonably enough, that table T1 of Figure 8-1 involves a foreign key constraint that looks like this:

```
FOREIGN KEY { P# } REFERENCES P
```

("every shipment refers to an existing part"). The analog of this constraint for table T6 might look something like this:

```
( T6 UNGROUP ( P#_REL ) ) { P# } ⊆ P { P# }
```

Not only is this latter constraint harder to state than its foreign key analog, it's likely to perform worse too (by which I mean that checking it for possible violations is likely to be less efficient).

Matters are even worse for update operations. For example, consider the following two updates:

1. Add the fact that supplier S6 supplies part P5 to the database

2. Add the fact that supplier S2 supplies part P5 to the database

With table T1, there's no qualitative difference between these two—both involve the insertion of a single row into the table:

1. `INSERT T1 RELATION { TUPLE { S# S# ('S6'), P# P# ('P5') } } ;`

2. `INSERT T1 RELATION { TUPLE { S# S# ('S2'), P# P# ('P5') } } ;`

With table T6, by contrast, they differ in kind significantly (not to mention the fact that, again, they're both more complicated than, and might well perform worse than, their T1 counterparts):

1.
```
INSERT T6 RELATION
    { TUPLE { S# S# ('S6'),
                P#_REL RELATION { TUPLE { P# P# ('P5') } } } } ;
```

2.
```
UPDATE T6 WHERE S# = S# ('S2')
    ( INSERT P#_REL RELATION { TUPLE { P# P# ('P5') } } ) ;
```

Note in particular that one of these formulations involves an INSERT operation while the other involves an UPDATE operation instead.

Yet another problem with hierarchic designs is that it's usually unclear as to why any given hierarchy should be chosen over any other. For example, why shouldn't we nest suppliers inside parts instead of the other way around? Note in particular that there isn't any formal design discipline (like the principles of normalization) available to help with such decisions. In fact, of course, hierarchic designs usually arise from a limited perspective on the overall problem— they represent a point of view that happens to be good for some applications but turns out to be bad for others. Nonhierarchic designs, by contrast, are more *application-neutral.* Note too that if we're given some neutral nonhierarchic design, it's easy to *impose* any hierarchic structure we like on the data dynamically, if we want to, using the relational operators (the GROUP operator in particular). The situation is different with systems like IMS that are *inherently* hierarchic, where users are typically locked into whatever particular hierarchies the designer happens to have "hard-wired" into the system at the time he or she defined the database.

Still another point on the question of design: Even when the data has a "natural" hierarchic structure, as—it might be argued—is the case with, say, departments and employees, it doesn't follow that it should be *represented* hierarchically, because the hierarchic representation isn't suitable for all of the kinds of processing that we might need to do on the data. In the case mentioned, for example, if we follow the "natural" hierarchy and nest employees inside departments, then queries like "Get all employees in the sales department" might be quite easy, but queries like "Get all departments that employ clerks" might be quite hard.

Now, one reason I've discussed these "old arguments against hierarchies" at such length is that we're starting to see a variety of newer hierarchic DBMSs emerge in the marketplace, *and all of those old arguments apply directly to those newer systems*. Examples of such systems include XML DBMSs, object-oriented DBMSs, and "multi-value" DBMSs. In all of these cases, the fundamental data object is hierarchic in nature and can be regarded—at least to a first approximation—as a table with RVAs.[8] And I'm well aware that there are those who would use this fact, and the arguments of this chapter, to buttress claims to the effect that relational systems are inadequate, or that hierarchic designs are a good idea, or that "multi-value" systems are really true relational systems (or—worse!—"extended" relational systems), and so on and so forth. So I want to confront such claims head on:

- First, as I've tried to show, hierarchic designs are usually not a good idea anyway.

- Second, even if we do agree to regard those hierarchic data objects as tables (albeit ones that include RVAs), it doesn't follow that the system is relational! The point cannot be emphasized too strongly that **tables alone do not a relational system make**. Rather, we need support for everything else in the relational model as well, including in particular support for all of the operators of the relational algebra. *Note:* In this regard, it's worth pointing out that the ability to form, say, a join of two tables over some RVA requires support for *relational comparisons*—e.g., the ability to test whether two relations are equal or whether one is a subset of the other—and even SQL doesn't provide any such support at the time of writing (though **Tutorial D** does). It's also worth pointing out that there are some things we certainly *don't* want in a relational system: for example, user-visible pointers or "object IDs," which many of those hierarchic systems most definitely do support.

Relation-Valued Attributes in Base Tables?— The Good News

For reasons such as those articulated in the previous section, RVAs in base tables are usually contraindicated. Usually, but not always—there *are* cases, albeit comparatively rare ones perhaps, where a base table with an RVA is exactly the right design. One simple example, table T7, is shown in Figure 8-7. The intended meaning of the table is that the persons identified within any given PERSONS value are all siblings of one another (and have no other siblings). Thus, Amy and Bob are siblings; Cal, Don, and Eve are siblings; and Fay is an only child. Note that the table has just one column (an RVA) and three rows. Note too that the sole key involves an RVA![9]

---

8. Please note that phrase "at least to a first approximation." The truth is, to suggest that the hierarchies in such systems might be regarded as tables with RVAs is *extremely* charitable to the systems concerned! See Appendix D for further discussion.

9. The following remark from Codd's 1970 paper is interesting in the light of this observation: "The writer knows of no application that would require some key to have a relation-valued component." (I've reworded the original just slightly here.)

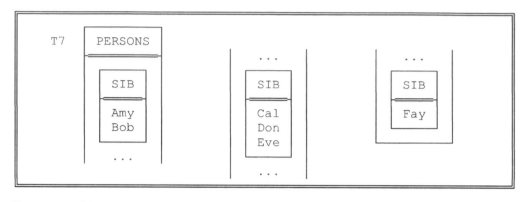

Figure 8-7. *Table T7 (representing persons who are siblings)*

Of course, it would be possible to come up with a different design—specifically, one not involving RVAs—to represent the same information, more or less (see table T8 in Figure 8-8). But please note that "more or less"! The fact is, tables T7 and T8 really represent different things; to be specific, the design of table T8 really means the specified person *belongs to the specified family,* a concept that isn't represented in the design of table T7. The designs thus can't be said to be equivalent in any formal sense. (To be more specific, note that table T7 can be derived from table T8, but the converse isn't true—there's no way table T8 can be derived from table T7.)

	FAMILY	SIB
T8	Mozart	Amy
	Mozart	Bob
	Walton	Cal
	Walton	Don
	Walton	Eve
	Dvorak	Fay

Figure 8-8. *Table T8*

I would argue that table T7 is conceptually easier to deal with than table T8, too. For example, consider the query "Who are Don's siblings?" For simplicity, let's agree to treat Don himself as one of his own siblings. With table T7, this query simply involves finding the unique PERSONS value (a relation) that includes Don, loosely speaking. With table T8, by contrast, it involves finding all of the tuples that contain the same FAMILY name as does the tuple whose SIB value is Don (again loosely speaking). Similar remarks apply to integrity constraints and update operations as well.

Now, you might think the foregoing example is a little contrived. Myself, I rather like it, because it illustrates the point I wanted to make—namely, that RVAs can sometimes be useful, even in base tables—without dragging in any issues that are irrelevant to that main point. Be that as it may, let me now bolster my argument with what some people might feel is a more realistic example. Figure 8-9 shows part of a *catalog* table T9 that documents the tables in the database and their keys (I'm assuming that one of those tables is called MARRIAGE, and it has columns HUSBAND, WIFE, and wedding DATE; I'm also assuming that the MARRIAGE table has three keys, each involving two of those three columns). Attribute KEY of table T9 is relation-valued.

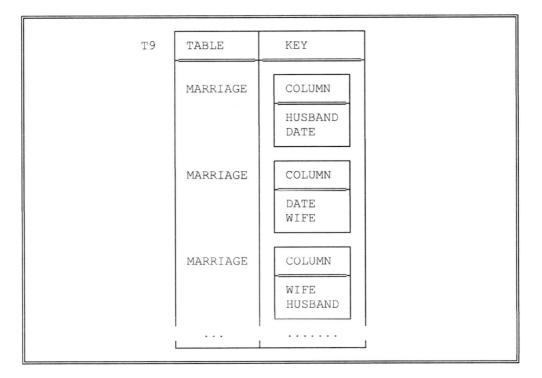

Figure 8-9. *The catalog table T9*

Again, of course, it would be possible to come up with an alternative design that avoids RVAs (see Figure 8-10)—but again the designs won't be formally equivalent. To be specific, we need to introduce *key names* (MK1, MK2, etc.) in the design of Figure 8-10, and there's no counterpart to those key names in the design of Figure 8-9.

T10	TABLE	KEY	COLUMN
	MARRIAGE	MK1	HUSBAND
	MARRIAGE	MK1	DATE
	MARRIAGE	MK2	DATE
	MARRIAGE	MK2	WIFE
	MARRIAGE	MK3	WIFE
	MARRIAGE	MK3	HUSBAND
	. . .	. . .	. . .

Figure 8-10. *Table T10*

I'd like to consider one more example. The requirement this time is to design a table to represent integers and their prime factors. There are two immediate problems:

1. Different integers have different numbers of prime factors. For example, 6 = 2 * 3 (two prime factors), while 30 = 2 * 3 * 5 (three prime factors).

2. A given integer can have the same prime factor repeated any number of times. For example, 45 = 3 * 3 * 5 (two occurrences of prime factor 3).

In general, then, the prime factors of a given integer *i* can be represented by a table in which each row contains (a) some prime factor *p* of *i* and (b) the number of times *p* occurs in the factorization of *i*. An "obvious" overall design thus involves an RVA as illustrated in Figure 8-11.

Once again, of course, it would be possible to come up with a design that doesn't involve any RVAs; in fact, all we have to do in this case is replace table T11 by its ungrouped counterpart T12, as indicated in Figure 8-12. This time, however, *the two designs are formally equivalent.* That is, the following identities hold:

```
T12 ≡ T11 UNGROUP ( FACTORS )
T11 ≡ T12 GROUP ( { P, OCCS } AS FACTORS )
```

In other words, the ungrouping is *reversible* in this example—ungrouping T11 on FACTORS and then (re)grouping the result on P and OCCS takes us back to T11 (so long as we call the RVA produced in that regrouping "FACTORS" again, of course).

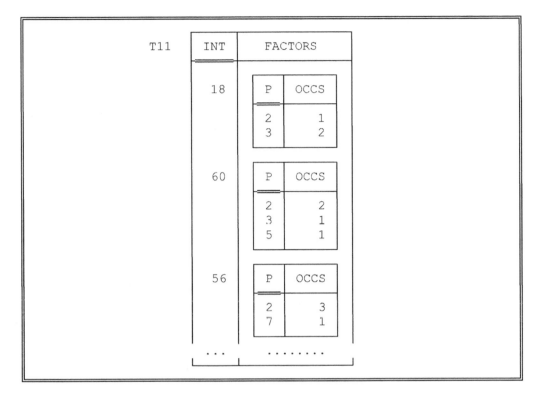

Figure 8-11. *Table T11 (integers and their prime factors)*

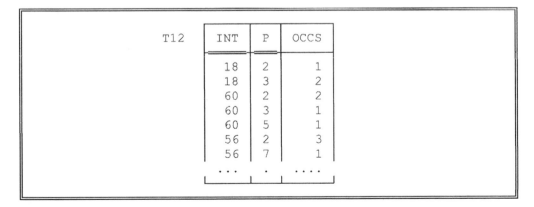

Figure 8-12. *Table T12 (T11 ungrouped on FACTORS)*

The reason why table T11 is "reversibly ungroupable" on FACTORS is that both of the following properties hold in that table:

- There's a functional dependency from INT to FACTORS:

  `{ INT } → { FACTORS }`

  That is, for any given INT value, there's just one corresponding FACTORS value; in fact, this property *obviously* holds, because INT is a key in table T11. (So is FACTORS, as a matter of fact.)

- No FACTORS value is an empty relation.

By contrast, if we return for a moment to the previous two examples, we find that analogous properties do *not* both hold. As a consequence, ungrouping tables T7 and T9 both cause a loss of information, and there's therefore no way to get back to T7 and T9 from the result of those ungroupings. (To be specific, if we ungroup T7, we lose the information as to who is the sibling of whom; if we ungroup T9, we lose the information as to which combinations of columns constitute keys.) That's why we had to introduce *family names* in table T8 and *key names* in table T10. Note that there's nothing analogous to those introduced names in table T12.

Precisely because table T11 is "reversibly ungroupable" in the foregoing sense, there seems little point in choosing the RVA design T11 over its non-RVA counterpart T12. (Observe in particular that queries and so forth against table T11 aren't noticeably easier to formulate and deal with than their counterparts against table T12. By way of example, consider the query "What's the factorization of 60?") Thus, the message of this example is: Just because there's an "obvious" RVA design, it isn't necessarily a good idea to go for it.

A Remark on "NF² Relations"

I include this section mainly for completeness—also, perhaps, to head off a possible misconception at the pass. The fact is, over the years many people have proposed the possibility of supporting, in some shape or form, what in this chapter I've been calling RVAs. Such proposals often go by the name of "NF² relations," where NF² (pronounced "NF squared") is short for NFNF and stands for "non first normal form." But there are at least two major differences between such proposals and what I've been describing:

- First, advocates of the NF² idea assume that RVAs are prohibited in the relational model and therefore advertise their proposals as "extensions" to that model (see, e.g., the paper "Extended Algebra and Calculus for Nested Relational Databases," by Mark A. Roth, Henry F. Korth, and Abraham Silberschatz, *ACM TODS 13*, No. 4, December 1988; note the title in particular). By contrast, what I've been describing involves no extensions to the relational model, as such, at all. (Even the GROUP and UNGROUP operators are just shorthand, in the final analysis, for combinations of other relational operators that don't involve GROUP or UNGROUP *per se*. For further explanation, see *The Third Manifesto*.)

- Second, the NF² advocates are correct—they *are* extending the relational model! For example, they propose an extended form of union that, in our terms, (a) ungroups both operands recursively until they involve no RVAs at all, either directly or indirectly; (b) constructs the regular union of those ungrouped operands; and (c) finally, recursively (re)groups the result again. And it's those two "recursively"s that constitute the extension. That is, while any *specific* extended union is certainly shorthand for some *specific* combination of existing relational operators, it isn't possible to say that extended union *in general* is just shorthand for some combination of existing operators.

  Note: In case the foregoing point isn't very clear, let me elaborate on it a little. Suppose table *T* is nested to two levels, meaning—to speak *extremely* loosely!—that *T* has an RVA whose values are relations with an RVA in turn. Then we can clearly write an expression involving exactly two UNGROUPs that will map *T* into a table with no RVAs at all. But an *arbitrary* table *T* will be nested to *N* levels, where *N* is greater than or equal to zero but is otherwise arbitrary. To map such a table *T* into a table with no RVAs at all will therefore involve *N* UNGROUPs. But *we physically can't write* those *N* UNGROUPs, if we don't know the value of *N;* that is, we physically can't write the set of UNGROUPs that will work for an arbitrary table *T*. That's why it isn't possible to say that extended union *in general* is just shorthand for some combination of existing operators.

It follows from the foregoing that what I've been describing in this chapter is *not* "NF² relations," as that term is usually understood.

A Definition

At last I'm in a position to give my own definition of first normal form. Here it is:

> *A table is normalized—equivalently, it is in first normal form, 1NF—if and only if it is a direct and faithful representation of some relation.*

Explanation: Relations are in 1NF by definition (see Appendix E). Thus, the "tables" in a true relational system might be said to be in 1NF by definition too, since those tables are really just a way of thinking about, or *depicting*, the relations in that system; in fact, we might say that a table is in 1NF if and only if it can be supported in a true relational system, or in other words if and only if it represents some relation. But the trouble with this definition is that, in a sense, *any* data structure can be said to represent some relation!—for any given array there's a corresponding relation, for any given list there's a corresponding relation, and so on. What we really want is for the table in question to be *isomorphic* to some relation, and that's what I mean when I say in my definition that the representation must be "direct and faithful." More specifically, I mean the table in question must satisfy the following five conditions:

1. There's no top-to-bottom ordering to the rows.

2. There's no left-to-right ordering to the columns.

3. There are no duplicate rows.

4. Every row-and-column intersection contains exactly one value from the applicable domain (and nothing else).

5. All columns are regular.

Now, most people's understanding of 1NF is both weaker and stronger than the foregoing definition, so let's take a closer look at it. As I've already indicated, the overriding requirement, to the effect that the table must directly and faithfully represent a relation, follows from the fact that 1NF was originally defined as a property of relations, not tables. The five more specific requirements are all direct consequences of this general one. I'll take them one at a time.

1. *No row ordering:* There shouldn't be any disagreement over this one, even though it isn't usually mentioned in the context of normalization as such. It does mean, however, that the files of a system such as dBase II or the so-called "multi-value" systems (probably!— see Appendix D) aren't relations and so can't possibly be normalized, and hence that such systems aren't relational. It also means that the result produced by SQL's ORDER BY operator isn't normalized either, since that result definitely has a row ordering and thus isn't a relation. It also means (even more so, in a sense) that the result produced by Oracle's CONNECT BY operator isn't normalized, either, since that result has an "essential" row ordering—i.e., a row ordering that (in general) can't be obtained just by applying a simple ORDER BY. *Note:* For a detailed explanation of the important notion of *essentiality,* see my book *The Database Relational Model: A Retrospective Review and Analysis* (Addison-Wesley, 2001).

2. *No column ordering:* Strictly speaking, this requirement means that SQL tables aren't in 1NF!—since such tables always do have such an ordering. (The next chapter in this book, Chapter 9, elaborates on this issue.) Now, if we can guarantee that no attempt, intentional or unintentional, will ever be made to exploit that ordering, then we might agree to overlook the point for the purpose at hand. But it's impossible to provide any such guarantee, of course.

3. *No duplicate rows:* This one also isn't usually mentioned in the present context. But a table with duplicate rows doesn't directly and faithfully represent a relation,[10] and so it can't be in 1NF by definition.

4. *One value per row-and-column intersection:* This is what most people think of as *the* defining feature of 1NF, and so of course it is, so let's analyze it a little more carefully. Here's a more precise statement: Let column *C* of table *T* be defined on domain *D.* Then every row of *T* must contain exactly one value in the column *C* position, and that value must be a value from domain *D.* (The value in question can be arbitrarily complex—in particular, it might be a relation—but, to say it again, there must be exactly one such.)

---

10. Unless redundant duplicate rows can be removed without altering the information content, which is almost never the situation. In any case, I note that there's no way in the relational model to perform such a removal! If rows *r1* and *r2* are duplicates (if such a thing were possible), any relational DELETE operation that removes either of them will necessarily remove the other as well—there's no way to DELETE just one. What's more, even in SQL, where we might try positioning a cursor on *r1* (say) and issuing a DELETE via that cursor, there's no guarantee—at least according to my reading of the standard—that the effect won't be to delete *r2* instead (!).

By way of example, consider Figure 8-13 (a revised version of Figure 8-2 from earlier in this chapter). Assume column P# is defined on domain P# (i.e., the domain whose contained values are part numbers). Then it's clearly not the case that every row-and-column intersection contains exactly one value from the pertinent domain, and we therefore have a violation of first normal form on our hands.

S#	P#
S2	P1,P2
S4	P2,P4,P5

Figure 8-13. *A non-1NF data structure*

By the way, the fact that there must be exactly one value at each row-and-column intersection also rules out nulls (as noted earlier in this chapter, nulls aren't values). Thus, if table *T* is to be in 1NF, then every column *C* of *T* must have "nulls not allowed."

Note further that we now have a basis for a precise definition of the term *repeating group*. To be specific, we might say that column *C* is a "repeating group" column if it is defined on domain *D* and legal values that can appear within *C* are *sets* (or lists or arrays or ...) of values from domain *D*. Repeating groups in this sense are definitely outlawed in the relational model.

5. *No irregular columns:* This is another issue that doesn't usually get mentioned explicitly. The point is, however, that certain systems support certain data structures that clearly don't meet the spirit of 1NF, and yet conditions 1–4 above are insufficient in themselves to rule such structures out. So here goes: No row contains anything extra, over and above the regular column values prescribed under condition 4 above. In particular, there are no "hidden" components (a) that can be accessed only by invocation of some special operator instead of by regular column name references, or (b) that cause invocations of the regular operators on rows or tables to have irregular effects. Thus, for example, rows have no *identifiers* other than regular candidate key values (no hidden "row IDs" or "object IDs"). They also have no hidden *timestamps* as have been proposed for "temporal databases" in much of the research literature.[11]

To sum up: If any of the foregoing conditions 1–5 are violated, then the table does *not* "directly and faithfully" represent a relation, and all bets are off. In particular, join and the other relational operators can no longer be guaranteed to work as expected! As a trivial illustration of this point, note that the SQL expressions A NATURAL JOIN B and B NATURAL JOIN A aren't equivalent—i.e., they don't return the same result—although of course their relational counterparts do.

---

11. In fact, any such separate identifiers or other hidden components would constitute a violation of *The Information Principle*. See Appendix B.

Another point that's worth calling out explicitly is this: *You can't tell whether a given table is in 1NF just by looking at it*[12] (though you might be able to tell that it's not—for example, if it contains any nulls). Rather, you have to know what the table *means*. To be specific, you have to know whether any significance attaches to row or column ordering, you have to know whether duplicate rows or nulls are allowed, and you have to know what the domains are.

Concluding Remarks

There are several things I want to say in conclusion:

- First of all, arguments in favor of supporting RVAs frequently appear in the trade press and elsewhere, but those arguments usually boil down to *physical* or performance arguments in some shape or form. By contrast, the arguments I've presented in this chapter—at least, the vast majority of them—are *logical* arguments. (What's more, even when those physical arguments in the trade press and elsewhere do have some logical component to them, they usually smack of "suboptimization"; that is, they usually involve designs that are optimized for some particular "preferred" application, and they fail to recognize the negative impact of those designs on applications other than that preferred one.)

- Second, we've seen that RVAs can lead to complexity, complexity that's unnecessary more often than not. Codd not unreasonably tried to avoid that complexity by defining it away, via his notion of 1NF—but he didn't get it quite right. To be specific, he defined 1NF in terms of another notion, atomicity, that wasn't well-defined and ultimately (we now realize, with 20:20 hindsight) *can't* be well-defined. And in doing so, he (slightly) threw the baby out with the bathwater: Not only did he apparently outlaw RVAs in particular—which as we've seen can sometimes be useful—but he apparently also threw out array-valued attributes, list-valued attributes, string-valued attributes, and a host of other things that might possibly be useful on occasion.[13]

- Third, as I said earlier in this chapter, I think the term "1NF" does still have a role to play in a relational context, despite the fact that there's actually no such thing as a relation that's not in 1NF. To be specific, I think the term can still be useful, informally, to describe a relation or table that's "only" in 1NF—i.e., one that's not in 2NF, and therefore not in 3NF or any higher normal form either. As we all know, when we describe some table as being in (say) 2NF, we often mean, informally, that the table is in 2NF but not in 3NF (etc.). In the same kind of way, I propose that the term "1NF" can be used, informally, to mean a table that's in 1NF but not 2NF (etc.). However, don't lose sight of the fact that, strictly speaking, *all* tables are in 1NF, just so long as they do directly and faithfully represent relations as explained in the previous section. Formally, in other words, the term "1NF" and the term "normalized" still mean exactly the same thing—just as they always have done, in fact.

---

12. More generally, of course, you can't tell whether a given table is in *any* particular normal form just by looking at it.

13. It's worth mentioning in this connection that the SQL standard does now support array-valued columns, and row-valued columns, and columns of arbitrarily complex user-defined types, and columns whose values are bags of rows—though it does *not* support table-valued columns as such (oddly enough).

- Fourth, it might be argued that if "1NF" and "normalized" mean the same thing, and if all tables are therefore normalized (as indeed they are), then the terms *unnormalized* and *denormalized* aren't very useful. Again, however, I think they do still have a role to play: They can be used with reference to *higher levels* of normalization. For example, we might replace two 3NF tables by a single 2NF table (obtained by joining the two 3NF tables together) and thereby carry out an act of denormalization from 3NF to 2NF.

- Fifth, I've now taken many pages to explain what 1NF *is*, but you might have noticed there's one question I haven't raised at all, let alone answered: namely, **why is 1NF a good idea?** I justify the omission as follows. Given that (as we've seen) all relations are 1NF relations, the question is logically equivalent to this one: Why are *relations* a good idea? Or, more generally, why is the relational model a good idea? And while it might be a useful exercise to write something that answers this latter question at length, such is not the purpose of the present chapter.

- Sixth, the point is worth spelling out explicitly that *all* of the tables shown in this chapter (including the ones with RVAs in particular) aren't just in 1NF—in fact, they're all in the highest possible normal form.[14] RVAs do not in and of themselves constitute a violation of *any* particular level of normalization.

- Seventh, there's a term I've deliberately avoided in this chapter so far: **predicate**. However, I hope you're aware that every table corresponds to some predicate, which is (loosely) what the table *means*. For example, consider tables T1 and T3 from earlier in this chapter. The predicate for T1 is "Supplier S# supplies part P#," while the (more complicated!) predicate for T3 is "Supplier S# supplies exactly that set of parts whose part number is mentioned in relation P#_REL, no more and no less." Observe that the parameters of a given predicate correspond to the columns of the corresponding table. And since—so far as I know—nothing in logic limits the kinds of parameters that can appear in a predicate, so nothing in the relational model limits the kinds of columns that can appear in a table. It follows that RVAs in particular must be legitimate.

- Eighth, my own research recently has concerned *temporal databases,* and it would be very remiss of me not to mention that RVAs are actually required (at least conceptually) as a basis for temporal database support. See the book—mentioned in passing earlier in this chapter—*Temporal Data and the Relational Model,* by Hugh Darwen, Nikos Lorentzos, and myself (Morgan Kaufmann, 2003), for further explanation.

---

14. Except for those in Figures 8-5 and 8-13, neither of which "directly and faithfully" represented a relation at all. In fact, you might have noticed that I deliberately never called those particular examples "tables," since the only tables I'm really interested in are normalized ones.

- My last point is this: Supporting RVAs involves comparatively little in the way of additional learning on the part of the user![15] We need tables anyway "on the outside" (as it were); and if we need them on the outside, we have to understand them anyway, and we have to know how to carry out relational algebra operations, and relational comparisons, and relational assignments (and so on) on them anyway. By contrast, if we were to introduce, say, arrays "on the inside," then users would necessarily have to understand arrays, and a whole set of array operations, *in addition to* the relational ones. Thus, if we need any kind of "collection" data type at all on the inside as well as on the outside, then surely tables are the one requiring the minimum of extra learning; and the minimum amount of extra syntax in the query language; and the minimum number of extra pages in the documentation; and so on.

I'll close with an exercise (due to Hugh Darwen) that might help you appreciate the occasional usefulness of RVAs, even in base tables:

> I decided to throw a party, so I drew up a list of people I wanted to invite and made some preliminary soundings. The response was good, but several people made their acceptance conditional on the acceptance of certain other invitees. For example, Bob and Cal both said they would come if Amy came; Hal said he would come if either Don and Eve both came or Fay came; Guy said he would come anyway; Ian said he would come if Bob and Amy both came; and so on. Design a table to show whose acceptance is based on whose.

Acknowledgments

I'd like to thank Hugh Darwen and Fabian Pascal for helpful comments on earlier drafts of this chapter, and Hugh again for the party invitations exercise. Thanks also to Jonathan Leffler, who discovered a few errors in the first publicly released version.

Appendix A: Terminology

Near the beginning of this chapter, I said that (somewhat against my better judgment) I'd be using the terminology of *tables*, *rows*, and *columns*, even though I preferred the more precise terminology of *relations*, *tuples*, and *attributes*. In this appendix, I'd like to explain these remarks briefly.

First of all, of course, it's undeniable that *table*, *row*, and *column* are more intuitive and informal than *relation*, *tuple*, and *attribute*. The trouble is, though, those "more user-friendly" terms carry a lot of baggage with them. For example, although a relation can obviously be pictured as a table, a relation **isn't** a table (a picture of a thing isn't the same as the thing!). One problem with thinking of a relation as a table is that it suggests that certain properties of tables—for example, the property that the rows are in a certain top-to-bottom order—apply to relations too, when in fact they don't.

In the same kind of way, tuples can be pictured as rows, but tuples aren't rows; and attributes can be pictured as columns, but attributes aren't columns.

---

15. Not to mention comparatively little in the way of additional work on the part of the implementer as well.

Please understand, therefore, that throughout the body of this chapter, when I used the terms *table*, *row*, and *column*, what I meant by those terms were exactly the relational concepts *relation*, *tuple*, and *attribute*, respectively (except that, in the case of *table*, I was a little slippery, using that term sometimes to mean a relation *value* and sometimes a relation *variable*—see the next paragraph). In particular, the tables I was talking about had no top-to-bottom row ordering; they had no left-to-right column ordering; they involved no duplicate rows; and they contained no nulls.

Another important point that tends to get glossed over by the terminology of tables is that we really need to distinguish between relation *values* and relation *variables*. A relation variable is a variable whose permitted values are relation values (just as, for example, an integer variable is a variable whose permitted values are integer values). A relational database contains relation variables,[16] and those variables have different values at different times. When we update the database, what we're really doing is replacing the current values of certain of those relation variables by different values. Likewise, when we specify an integrity constraint (e.g., the constraint that supplier numbers are unique), we're really imposing a limit on the values that can legally be taken by certain relation variables. And (most important!) when we discuss normalization—when we consider 1NF in particular—what we're really talking about is relation variables, not relation values: It's relation variables, not relation values, that the concept of normalization is applicable to (at least primarily).

The net of the previous paragraph is that there's an important **logical difference**—see *The Third Manifesto* for an extensive discussion of this useful and important concept—between relation values and relation variables. In the world of SQL, however, the same term *table* is used to refer to both ... and that fact is, sadly, the source of a very great deal of confusion—not least in connection with the subject of this chapter! In fact, if you've been reading very carefully and attentively, you might have noticed one or two places where that confusion unfortunately reared its head. Precisely because I wanted to use those "user-friendly" terms, however, I was more or less forced into the position (as already noted) of having to use the same term *table* to mean different things at different times. I'm still not sure I made the right decision! I really do prefer the more precise terms.

One last point of terminology: I also very much prefer the term *type* over the term *domain*. I've argued elsewhere—see, e.g., *The Third Manifesto* once again—that what the relational community calls a domain and what the programming language community calls a type are exactly the same thing. Yet, precisely because two distinct terms are used, perhaps, various people (including Codd himself, as a matter of fact) have argued on occasion that the concepts are distinct as well, and this fact too has been the source of a great deal of confusion.

Appendix B: *The Information Principle*

The Information Principle—which I heard Codd refer to more than once as *the* fundamental principle underlying the relational model—is tightly bound up with the subject of this chapter. It can be stated in many different but equivalent forms, of which the following is one of the most succinct:

> *The database contains relations, and nothing but relations.*

---

16. And *no other* kinds of variables (see Appendix B).

In order to explain this principle (as well as its connection to 1NF), I need to digress for a moment. We saw in Appendix A that we really need to distinguish between relation *values* and relation *variables*. Well, a similar remark applies at the database level as well: We really need to distinguish between *database* values and variables, too. A database, as that term is commonly understood, is really a giant variable—a database variable, in fact—and a database value is a value that can be assigned to that variable. Updates have the effect of replacing the current value of that database variable by another database value. And when we look at the database at some particular point in time, what we see is a particular database value. More precisely:

- A database variable is a set of relation variables.

- A database value is a set of relation values, one such relation value for each of those relation variables.

(I'm assuming here that the database in question is a relational database specifically, of course.)

Given the foregoing clarification of the notion of "the database," I can now state *The Information Principle* a little more precisely, thus:

> **At any given time,** the database contains relations, and nothing but relations.

Here are some implications of this restatement:

- The only kinds of variables permitted in a relational database are, very specifically, *relation* variables.

- The total information content of a relational database at any given time is represented in one and only one way: namely, by explicit attribute values within tuples within relations (where by "relations" I mean relation *values* specifically). *Note:* It should now be clear that when I said earlier that tables should "directly and faithfully" represent relations, I was tacitly appealing to *The Information Principle.* In order for a table to represent a relation "directly and faithfully," it mustn't encode any information in row ordering, or column ordering, or row duplication; furthermore, every row-and-column intersection must contain exactly one value, and that value must *be* a value (not a null) and must be of the applicable type; finally, all columns must be "regular" columns.

- Given the foregoing, it has to be said, just as an aside, that *The Information Principle* might better have been called *The Principle of Uniform Representation* (thanks to Hugh Darwen for this observation). But I'll stick to the original name for the remainder of this appendix.

Anyway, I can now explain something that might possibly have been bothering you. If you were already familiar with *The Information Principle,* especially in the form in which I first quoted it above ("the database contains relations only"), you might well have been puzzled about the continual references in the body of this chapter to the effect that we might have array-valued attributes, list-valued attributes, and so on. Don't such possibilities constitute an obvious violation of *The Information Principle?*

Well, no, they don't. What that principle says is that the only kind of *variable* permitted in the database (considered in turn as a *variable*) is the *relation* variable. But a relation variable can have *attributes* of any type whatsoever ... including array types, list types, and so on.

Thus, the database at any given time might include a relation *value* that in turn includes array *values*, list *values*, and so on ... But there are still no array or list *variables* (etc.) anywhere in sight.

Incidentally, here is as good a place as any to remind you that (as stated in a footnote earlier) there is *no* information that can be represented by arrays, or lists, or anything else you might think of, that can't be represented by relations. As explained in *The Third Manifesto*, relations are both **necessary** and **sufficient** to represent absolutely any information you like (at the logical level, of course). In other words, arrays, lists, etc., certainly add *complexity*, but they don't add any *functionality*.

Appendix C: Definitions from the Literature

In this appendix, I simply quote, for interest and without further commentary (I leave that to you), 1NF definitions from some of the better-known database textbooks.

> *Raghu Ramakrishnan and Johannes Gehrke,* Database Management Systems, *3rd edition, McGraw-Hill, 2003: "A relation is in **first normal form** if every field contains only atomic values, that is, no lists or sets."*

> *Hector Garcia-Molina, Jeffrey D. Ullman, and Jennifer Widom,* Database Systems: The Complete Book, *Prentice-Hall, 2002: "First normal form is simply the condition that every component of every tuple is an atomic value."*

> *Ramez Elmasri and Shamkant B. Navathe,* Fundamentals of Database Systems, *3rd edition, Benjamin/Cummings, 2000: "**First normal form (1NF)** ... states that the domain of an attribute must include only atomic (simple, indivisible) values and that the value of any attribute in a tuple must be a single value from the domain of that attribute ... Hence, 1NF disallows having a set of values, a tuple of values, or a combination of both as an attribute value for a single tuple."*

> *Abraham Silberschatz, Henry F. Korth, and S. Sudarshan,* Database System Concepts, *4th edition, McGraw-Hill, 2002: "A domain is **atomic** if elements of the domain are considered to be indivisible units ... We say that a relation schema* R *is in **first normal form** (1NF) if the domains of all attributes of* R *are atomic."*

Finally, here is the definition from the 8th edition of my own book *An Introduction to Database Systems* (Addison-Wesley, 2004):

> *[Every] tuple in every relation contains exactly one value for each of its attributes ... A relation that satisfies this property is in **first normal form,** 1NF ... A [relation variable] is in 1NF so long as all of its possible [relation values] are in 1NF.*

Note that, as this definition indicates, it does make sense (and, the remarks on this point in Appendix A notwithstanding, it can occasionally be useful) to apply the concept of first normal form to both relation *values* and relation *variables*.

Appendix D: So What About "Multi-Value Systems"?

In the body of this chapter, in the section entitled "Relation-Valued Attributes in Base Tables?—The Bad News," I observed that some people might try to claim that *multi-value systems* effectively support relations with RVAs, and hence that such systems are really just relational systems after all (except that those same people would probably also claim that such systems are somehow "better" than relational systems, or at least SQL systems, precisely because of that RVA support). In this appendix, I'd like to respond to such claims. I'd *like* to, I say—but I can't, not really, because my attempts to educate myself regarding multi-value systems from material available on the Web were an utter failure (I had more questions when I'd finished reading than I did when I started). So all I can do here is sketch my limited understanding of what multi-value systems are, and then raise (but not answer) what seem to me to be some pertinent questions. *Note:* For the remainder of this appendix, I'll use *MVS* as an abbreviation for "multi-value system."

First of all, then, an MVS *database* (also called a *file*) consists of a collection of *records* (also called *items*). Each record contains two or more *field* values (also called *attribute* values)—two or more, because the system automatically prefixes every record as presented to it by the user with an *item-ID* (unique at least within the file), which becomes the first field value in the record, and it's my belief that records as presented by the user must already contain at least one field value. The following points arise immediately:

- As the phrase "the first field value" suggests, MVS fields are ordered left to right (and so MVS files are certainly not relations, and the system is certainly not relational).

- Whether item-ID values are visible to the user is unclear (if they're not, then MVS files are certainly not relations—see Appendix B—and the system is certainly not relational).

- Whether item-ID fields can be updated by the user is unclear.

- Two records can be duplicates as far as the user is concerned and yet distinct as far as the system is concerned (because they're given distinct item-ID values). The full implications of this state of affairs are unclear.

- Item-ID values are hashed to determine where records are physically stored (note the mixture of logical and physical considerations here!). Whether records can be accessed sequentially, using either physical or logical sequence, is unclear.

- Does the collection of records in a given file constitute a set? Or a bag? Or an array? Or a sequence? Or what? Note that if it's anything other than a set, then the file is certainly not a relation, and the system is certainly not relational.

- What file-level operators exist? E.g., is there anything analogous to join or union? Note that if there are no such operators, then the system is certainly not relational.

Next, a given MVS field can be "multi-valued"—that is, a given record can contain any number N of values of the same type in a given field position, where N is a positive, or possibly a nonnegative, integer (i.e., whether N can be zero is unclear). In other words, MVS fields can apparently contain "repeating groups." Also, individual values can have "subvalues," which I think just means the values in question don't have to be "atomic" but can be what some languages call *structs* (though the material I read was extremely unclear on this point; in fact, it was almost certainly incorrect). Questions:

- How do you do MVS database design?

- MVS apparently allows one level of nesting. Does it allow two or more? If not, the system is certainly not relational.

- Can a given "multi-valued field value" be operated upon as a single value, or does it always have to be operated on piece by piece, one component value at a time? If the latter, then the system is certainly not relational.

- Is a given "multi-valued field value" a *set* of component values? Or a bag? Or an array? Or a sequence? Or what?

To sum up: The material I read on multi-value systems focused almost exclusively on the structural aspects of such systems and said essentially nothing regarding the manipulative or integrity aspects. And even on the structural aspects, the material was very incomplete, not to say confused. Thus, the only thing I feel comfortable in saying is that, based on what I've seen so far, the chance of multi-value systems being "truly relational," let alone being "more relational than SQL systems," is vanishingly small. In fact, it looks to me as if such systems will almost certainly be more complex—complex for the user, that is, and probably for the DBA as well—than true relational systems (or even SQL systems) should ever be.

Appendix E: Formal Definitions

In this appendix, I give for purposes of reference formal definitions of the terms *tuple* and *relation*. They're taken from the 8th edition of my book *An Introduction to Database Systems* (Addison-Wesley, 2004).

First, given a collection of types Ti ($i = 1, 2, ..., n$), not necessarily all distinct, a **tuple value** (tuple for short) on those types—t, say—is a set of ordered triples of the form $<Ai,Ti,vi>$, where Ai is an **attribute name,** Ti is a **type name,** and vi is a **value** of type Ti, and:

- The value n is the **degree** of t.

- The ordered triple $<Ai,Ti,vi>$ is a **component** of t.

- The ordered pair $<Ai,Ti>$ is an **attribute** of t, and it is uniquely identified by the attribute name Ai (attribute names Ai and Aj are the same only if $i = j$). The value vi is the **attribute value** for attribute Ai of t. The type Ti is the corresponding **attribute type.**

- The complete set of attributes is the **heading** of t.

- The **tuple type** of t is determined by the heading of t, and the heading and that tuple type both have the same attributes (and hence the same attribute names and types) and the same degree as t does. The **tuple type name** is, precisely,

```
TUPLE { A1 T1, A2 T2, ..., An Tn }
```

Second, a **relation value** (relation for short), *r* say, consists of a *heading* and a *body*, where:

- The **heading** of *r* is a tuple heading as defined above. Relation *r* has the same attributes (and hence the same attribute names and types) and the same degree as that heading does.

- The **body** of *r* is a set of tuples, all having that same heading; the cardinality of that set is said to be the **cardinality** of *r*.

- The **relation type** of *r* is determined by the heading of *r*, and it has the same attributes (and hence attribute names and types) and degree as that heading does. The **relation type name** is, precisely,

  RELATION { A1 T1, A2 T2, ..., An Tn }

Note in particular that:

1. Every tuple contains exactly one value for each of its attributes.

2. It follows that every tuple in every relation contains exactly one value for each of its attributes.

3. A relation that satisfies this latter property is said to be **normalized,** or equivalently to be in **first normal form** (1NF).

4. It follows that all relations are in 1NF.

CHAPTER 9

■ ■ ■

A Sweet Disorder

So long as we are in the right column

—T. S. Eliot

John Muir once said "When we try to pick out anything by itself, we find it hitched to everything else in the universe" (often quoted in the form "Everything is connected to everything else"). John Muir was referring to the natural world, of course, but he might just as well have been talking about the relational model. The fact is, the various features of the relational model are highly interconnected—remove just one of them, and the whole edifice crumbles. Translated into concrete terms, this metaphor means that if we build a "relational" DBMS that fails to support some aspect of the model, the resulting system (which really shouldn't be called relational, anyway) will be bound to display behavior on occasion that's certainly undesirable and possibly unforeseeable. I can't stress the point too strongly: Every feature of the model is there *for solid practical reasons;* if we choose to ignore some detail, then we do so at our own peril. In this chapter, I want to illustrate this thesis by considering one particular feature of the model (one that might seem almost trivial, at first sight) and exploring some of the consequences of ignoring it. The feature in question is the rule that says:

> *There's no left-to-right ordering to the columns of a table.*

A note on terminology: In the previous chapter, "What First Normal Form Really Means" (referred to hereinafter as "the first normal form chapter"), I wrote: "I want this discussion to reach as wide an audience as possible. For that reason, I've decided to use the comparatively user-friendly terminology of *tables, rows,* and *columns* (albeit not exclusively), even though I prefer the more precise terms *relations, tuples,* and *attributes.*" The same remarks apply here too. For further elaboration on such terminological issues, see Appendix A in the first normal form chapter.

SQL Tables

Everybody knows that tables in the relational model have no ordering to their rows, top to bottom. However, not everybody seems to know that such tables also have no ordering to their columns, left to right—perhaps because tables in SQL *do* have such an ordering. Note, therefore, that we instantly run into a conflict over terminology; clearly, we need to distinguish between tables in the relational model and tables in SQL. In this chapter, I'll use the unqualified term "table" to mean a table in the relational sense (with no left-to-right column ordering), and I'll use the qualifier "SQL" when I want to talk about an SQL table in particular—except where the context makes it clear that the table in question is indeed an SQL table.

The following points arise immediately:

- First, the relational model is often said to be an *abstraction* (note in particular that it deliberately doesn't prescribe any specific user-level syntax), and SQL is usually regarded as a concrete realization of that abstract model.[1] As we've just seen, however, there's a difference between SQL tables and tables in the relational sense—the former have a left-to-right column ordering and the latter don't (actually there are other differences as well, but this particular one is my primary focus here). The abstraction of which SQL is a concrete realization thus can't be said to be the relational model (at least, not honestly). For want of a better term, therefore, I'll say it's the *SQL* model. This chapter can thus be characterized as dealing with problems that exist in the SQL model but not in the relational model. *Note:* My primary interest, as always, is in matters that directly affect the user, and that means (by definition) matters that affect the model, not matters of implementation.

- Second, the discussions in what follows concentrate on SQL for obvious reasons, but my criticisms don't apply just to SQL *per se*. Rather, they apply to any model in which tables have a left-to-right column ordering, as they do in the SQL model specifically.

- Third, from this point forward I'll abbreviate "left-to-right column ordering" to just "column ordering," for simplicity. Please don't be misled by this abbreviated term into thinking I'm talking about the top-to-bottom ordering of values *within* some column, as might be obtained (e.g.) by carrying out some ORDER BY operation.

The "SELECT *" Problem

One immediate problem that column ordering causes in SQL is what we might call the "SELECT *" problem. Let me say immediately that there are much worse problems than this one!—but this one is easy to understand, and the discussion that follows lays the groundwork for more searching discussions to come.

Consider the following SQL definition for the usual suppliers table (more precisely, the usual suppliers *base* table—note that the keyword TABLE in CREATE TABLE does mean a base table specifically):

```
CREATE TABLE S
     ( S#     CHAR(5),
       SNAME  CHAR(20),
       STATUS INTEGER,
       CITY   CHAR(15),
     PRIMARY KEY ( S# ) ) ;
```

---

1. Despite the fact that the SQL standard never mentions the relational model, nor even the term *relation!*

For simplicity I've given every column a built-in type, though user-defined types might be more appropriate in practice for at least some of the columns.

Now suppose the user defines a cursor CX as follows:

```
DECLARE CX CURSOR FOR
   SELECT * FROM S ;
```

Or equivalently:

```
DECLARE CX CURSOR FOR
   TABLE S ;
```

In case you're unfamiliar with SQL's TABLE *T* construct, I should explain that the expression TABLE *T* is semantically equivalent to the expression SELECT * FROM *T*—where *T* must be a table name specifically, not some more general table expression. *Note:* In practice, cursor definitions and other embedded SQL statements require an EXEC SQL prefix. I've omitted those prefixes in this chapter as irrelevant to my main purpose.

Here now is a corresponding FETCH:

```
FETCH CX INTO :S#, :SNAME, :STATUS, :CITY ;
```

For simplicity I've given each target variable the same name as the corresponding column.

So far, so good. But suppose now that for some reason—the exact reason isn't important here but probably has to do with performance[2]—we change the column ordering in the suppliers table, perhaps as follows:

```
CREATE TABLE S
    ( S#      CHAR(5),
      CITY    CHAR(15),
      SNAME   CHAR(20),
      STATUS INTEGER,
    PRIMARY KEY ( S# ) ) ;
```

What happens? *Answer:* Run-time error on the FETCH!—the DBMS attempts to convert an SNAME value to type INTEGER, and that attempt presumably fails. (Note, by the way, that *not* getting the run-time error would be even worse, in a sense. Suppose the column ordering rearrangement merely involved interchanging the SNAME and CITY columns. Then the FETCH might "succeed," but if it did it would clearly, albeit "silently," have the effect of assigning the wrong values to the SNAME and CITY host variables.)

The problem here, of course, is that the "*" in "SELECT *" stands for "column names for all columns of the relevant table," *in the left-to-right order in which those columns appear in that table.* So, if that left-to-right order changes, the meaning of that "*" changes too.

---

2. To elaborate briefly: As far as I can see, the only "good" reason for including column ordering in the SQL model is to give the person creating the table control over *physical* ordering of columns on the disk. Of course, this isn't really a good reason at all, since it mixes model and implementation issues horribly—not to mention the fact that it presupposes a certain rather unsophisticated style of implementation in the first place. Be that as it may, the specific change in the example will have the effect in certain products of reducing data space requirements from 47 to 44 bytes per row, and might thus be carried out for that very reason.

Analogous problems arise with INSERT. For example, consider the following INSERT statement:

```
INSERT INTO S
VALUES ( 'S6', 'Lopez', 30, 'Madrid' ) ;
```

This INSERT succeeds with the original column ordering but fails (possibly "silently," too) when that column ordering is changed.

Of course, it would be easy enough to fix the foregoing problems by changing the syntax of the FETCH and INSERT statements appropriately. In the case of FETCH, for example, the following syntax would be an improvement:

```
FETCH CX S# INTO :S#, SNAME INTO :SNAME,
        STATUS INTO :STATUS, CITY INTO :CITY ;
```

And for INSERT:

```
INSERT INTO S
VALUES ( S# FROM 'S6', SNAME FROM 'Lopez',
        STATUS FROM 30, CITY FROM 'Madrid' ) ;
```

In fact, revisions along these lines would mean that FETCH and INSERT no longer relied on SQL's column ordering at all.

Now, I began the discussions in this section by referring to what I called the "SELECT *" problem. However, the fact is that column ordering can cause problems even if we don't use "SELECT *" in the cursor definition. For example:

```
DECLARE CX CURSOR FOR
    SELECT S#, SNAME, STATUS, CITY FROM S ;

FETCH CX INTO :STATUS, :CITY, :S#, :SNAME ;
```

As for INSERT, SQL does in fact already provide syntax that lets us avoid the INSERT counterpart to the "SELECT *" problem:

```
INSERT INTO S ( S#, SNAME, STATUS, CITY )
VALUES ( 'S6', 'Lopez', 30, 'Madrid' ) ;
```

Note, however, that the matching up of column names with values (STATUS with 30, for example) in this revised INSERT statement is still being done on the basis of ordinal position. As Hugh Darwen once remarked (in a private communication): "In case it might be observed that dependence on ordinal position in [this example] really is no problem [*because the two ordered lists, of column names and values, are both explicitly specified by the user as part of the same statement*], I would refer to the idea that the syntax of a language should be in all places *in the spirit of* that language. Then it's easier to learn, because people get to know what to expect. A proper relational language attaches no significance to column ordering. Not *anywhere*." I agree!

Duplicate Column Names

Regardless of what you might think of the problems discussed in the previous section, the fact is that (as already mentioned) column ordering gives rise to much worse ones as well. Most of the remainder of this chapter is concerned with illustrating and examining some of those further problems.

First of all, there has to be *some* way to identify individual columns, of course. And, precisely because its tables did have a column ordering, SQL assumed from the outset that the necessary identification could be performed by **ordinal position**. That assumption, though perhaps never spelled out explicitly, led directly to the possibility of *duplicate* column names (duplicate column names within a single table, that is). As a trivial example, consider the following query (which isn't at all unrealistic, by the way): "Get pairs of supplier numbers for suppliers who are located in the same city." Here's a possible SQL formulation:

```
SELECT SX.S#, SY.S#
FROM   S AS SX, S AS SY
WHERE  SX.CITY = SY.CITY ;
```

The result of this query is a table with two columns, both called S#. How then can they be distinguished? *Answer:* By ordinal position, of course—but (once again) ordinal position of columns is a concept deliberately excluded from the relational model. I'll have more to say on the reasons for that exclusion in the section "The Relation Type Issue," later.

Of course, we can avoid the duplicate column names in this example (and I'd say we ought to, too) by introducing new names—e.g., as follows:

```
SELECT SX.S# AS X#, SY.S# AS Y#
FROM   S AS SX, S AS SY
WHERE  SX.CITY = SY.CITY ;
```

Now the result columns do have distinct names, *viz.*, X# and Y#. To repeat, therefore, we can avoid the duplicate names if we want to. The problem is, we don't have to, and so SQL does have to deal with the possibility that a given table might have column names that aren't unique.

As an aside, I should explain that the reason we don't have to use the "AS column name" construct is because it wasn't part of the original standard (it was introduced with SQL:1992), and compatibility therefore dictates that its use has to be optional. (I should also note in passing that—believe it or not—names introduced by AS don't have to be unique! Thus, for example, SELECT SX.S# AS Z#, SY.S# AS Z# is legal.)

By the way, don't make the mistake in the foregoing example—the original version, that is, without the AS clauses—of thinking the result column names are SX.S# and SY.S#, respectively. They aren't. In fact, SX.S# and SY.S# aren't what the standard calls *regular identifiers* at all. Thus, for example, the following isn't a legal CREATE TABLE statement:

```
CREATE TABLE T
     ( SX.S# ..., SY.S# ..., ... ) ;
```

Missing Column Names

The assumption discussed in the previous section—the assumption, I mean, that columns could be identified by ordinal position—also led directly to the possibility of columns that had no name at all. Here's an example:

```
SELECT S#, SUBSTRING ( CITY FROM 1 FOR 1 )
FROM   S ;
```

The result of this query is a table with two columns, one called S# and the other unnamed (this latter contains the first letter of the city name for the supplier identified by the S# value).

In the interests of accuracy (and for the benefit of any barrack-room lawyers who might be reading this chapter), I should now explain that the "unnamed column" in the example isn't *really* unnamed. To quote the SQL standard:[3]

> *Case:*
>
> **a)** *If the ith <derived column> in the <select list> specifies an <as clause> that contains a column name CN, then the <column name> of the ith column of the result is CN.*
>
> **b)** *If the ith <derived column> in the <select list> does not specify an <as clause> and the <value expression> of that <derived column> is a single <column reference>, then the <column name> of the ith column of the result is the <column name> of the column designated by the <column reference>.*
>
> **c)** *Otherwise, the <column name> of the ith column of [the result] is implementation-dependent and different from the <column name> of any column, other than itself, of [any] table referenced by any <table reference> contained in the SQL-statement.*

As an aside, I note that the reference to "the SQL-statement" in the foregoing extract raises several further questions! I don't want to get into those questions here; however, I do need to explain what the term *implementation-dependent* (as in "the <column name> ... is implementation-dependent") means. The standard defines that term as follows:

> *Possibly differing between SQL-implementations, but not specified by this International Standard and not required to be specified ... for any particular SQL-implementation.*

Not required to be specified, in turn, means the implementer doesn't have to document what the implementation does; in fact, the implementation would be within its rights to do different things depending on whether it's a weekday or whether there's an R in the month. Thus, it seems to me that a column that has an "implementation-dependent" name really has, to all intents and purposes, no name at all.

Note: In case you might want to dispute the foregoing conclusion, observe that such "implementation-dependent" names aren't known to the user and can't be used as an explicit reference to the pertinent column elsewhere in the overall SQL expression. Consider again the following example:

```
SELECT S#, SUBSTRING ( CITY FROM 1 FOR 1 )
FROM   S ;
```

If we knew the column corresponding to the SUBSTRING invocation was called X (say), we could at least write a query like this one:

---

3. All quotes from the standard in this chapter are from the 1992 version. The wording might have changed in more recent versions, but not the substance.

```
SELECT S#, X
FROM ( SELECT S#, SUBSTRING ( CITY FROM 1 FOR 1 )
       FROM   S ) AS POINTLESS
WHERE  X BETWEEN 'C' AND 'W'
AND    X <> 'F'
AND    X <> 'K'
AND    X <> 'Q' ;
```

Of course, the name wouldn't be X in practice but something much more complex (e.g., SYS_COL_4A3EC076 or something similarly obscure). As for that "AS *POINTLESS*" specification, please don't even ask about it.

So what's wrong with the idea of a column having no name at all? As we've just seen, the obvious problem is that there's no immediate way for the user to refer to such a column—e.g., as an argument in a function invocation, or in a SELECT clause, or in a WHERE clause. It's odd, really: The standard assumes that columns are identified by ordinal position, but then provides almost no way for users to make use of such ordinal positions to *refer* to those columns. (Just about the only exception in this regard is the construct ORDER BY *n*, and that construct was officially labeled a "deprecated feature" in SQL:1992 and was dropped in SQL:1999.)

To sum up this section and the previous one, then, we can say that:

- Every SQL table has a left-to-right column ordering.

- Every column in every *named* SQL table (i.e., base table or view) has a user-known name, and that name is unique within the table in question. But neither of these properties holds, in general, for *unnamed* tables (i.e., intermediate and final result tables).

Now, you might be thinking the second of these bullet items can't be quite correct—surely a view (as opposed to a base table) *could* have duplicate or missing column names? For example, suppose we try to define a view thus:

```
CREATE VIEW SC              /* warning: invalid! */
    AS SELECT S#, SUBSTRING ( CITY FROM 1 FOR 1 )
       FROM   S ;
```

However, the committee responsible the SQL standard foresaw the problem here (even though it didn't in most other places!). Our putative CREATE VIEW statement fails on a syntax error. To avoid that error, we have to introduce a "view column list" (i.e., we have to introduce names for the columns of the view), as here:

```
CREATE VIEW SC ( S#, CITY_INITIAL )
    AS SELECT S#, SUBSTRING ( CITY FROM 1 FOR 1 )
       FROM   S ;
```

Here's the pertinent quote from the standard:

If any two columns in the table specified by the <query expression> have the same <column name>, or if any column of that table has an implementation-dependent name, then a <view column list> shall be specified ... The same <column name> shall not be specified more than once in the <view column list>.

Of course, I feel bound to point out that, even here, SQL is still relying on ordinal position—the name in the *i*th position in the <view column list> becomes the name of the *i*th column of the view. Let me remind you of that quote from Hugh Darwen: "A proper relational language attaches no significance to column ordering. Not *anywhere.*"

In closing this section, I'd like to point out that duplicate and missing column names both constitute a fairly egregious violation of *The Naming Principle:*

Everything we need to talk about must have a name.

This principle might seem pretty obvious, but it's often violated in practice (not just in SQL, incidentally). See the article "Database Graffiti" in my book *Relational Database Writings 1994–1997* (Addison-Wesley, 1998), for further discussion.

Implications for the UNION Operator

Column ordering has serious implications for the operators UNION, INTERSECT, and MINUS ("EXCEPT" in SQL). For definiteness, let's concentrate on UNION (but everything I'm going to say regarding UNION in particular applies equally well, *mutatis mutandis,* to INTERSECT and EXCEPT as well). In the relational model, we can define UNION quite simply as follows:

Let tables *a* and *b* be of the same type *TT.* Then the union of those two tables, *a* UNION *b*, is a table of the same type *TT*, with body consisting of all rows *r* such that *r* appears in *a* or *b* or both. (Of course, *a* and *b* here aren't necessarily base tables; they might, for example, be the results of previous queries.)

This definition is based on one given in the 8th edition of my book *An Introduction to Database Systems* (Addison-Wesley, 2004). The *body* of a table is the set of rows in that table.

Figure 9-1 shows a trivial example of two tables, T1 and T2, together with their union. I've assumed for simplicity that all columns are of type INTEGER.[4]

---

4. One reviewer wanted me to use a "more realistic" example here. The trouble is, more realistic examples tend to involve a lot of unnecessary baggage that makes it hard to see what's really going on (you can't see the forest for the trees). I'm a great fan of examples that illustrate exactly the point(s) at hand, no more and no less. But if you want a *slightly* more realistic example, take T1 and T2 to be the projection of suppliers over CITY and the projection of parts over CITY, respectively. Of course, T1 and T2 will then have one column each, not two, and that column will be of type CHAR, not INTEGER.

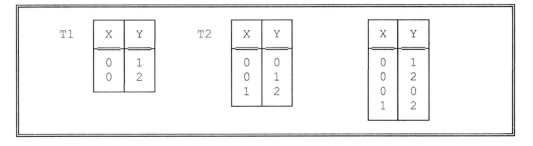

Figure 9-1. *Tables T1 and T2 and their union*

Here now by contrast is the definition of UNION from the SQL standard (though I need to explain immediately that I've shortened, paraphrased, and in fact considerably simplified[5]—not to mention corrected!—that definition here):

Let tables a and b be of the same degree. Let the column descriptor of the ith column of a be the same as the column descriptor of the ith column of b, except possibly for the <column name>s contained in those column descriptors. Then the union of those two tables, a UNION b [not meant to be actual SQL syntax], is a table defined as follows:

- *Let CN be the <column name> of the ith column of a. If the <column name> of the ith column of b is CN, then the <column name> of the ith column of the result is CN. Otherwise, the <column name> of the ith column of the result is implementation-dependent and different from the <column name> of any column, other than itself, of any table referenced by any <table reference> contained in the SQL-statement.*

- *The data type of the ith column of the result is determined by applying [the rules defined in the section on] "set operation result data types" to the data types of the ith column of a and the ith column of b.*

- *The result contains rows as follows (and no other rows):*

  - *Let r be a row that is a duplicate of some row in a or of some row in b or both.*

  - *Then the result contains exactly one duplicate of r.*

(Again the reference to "the SQL-statement" in this extract raises further questions that I don't want to get into here. As for the matter of "set operation result data types" and the issue of "duplicates"—here meaning duplicate rows, of course, not duplicate column names—these are topics I plan to explore in a future paper.)

Obviously the SQL definition is much longer and more complex than the relational definition, but that's not the end of the story. Additional issues are examined in the two subsections immediately following.

---

5. In particular, I've ignored everything to do with "UNION ALL." I'm interested here only in the genuine union operator ("UNION DISTINCT," in SQL terms).

Type *vs.* Degree

The first and overriding point is this:

- The relational definition is expressed in terms of *tables of the same type*—meaning in particular that columns from the two tables are matched up because they have the same name and same type and are in fact (in a certain precise sense, the details of which we don't need to go into here) the same column.

- The SQL definition, by contrast, is expressed in terms of *tables of the same degree*—meaning they have the same number of columns, and more specifically that columns are matched up not because they're "the same column" but, rather, because they have the same ordinal position.

This difference is the root cause of the complexity in the SQL definition, of course.

As a matter of fact, the SQL definition *can't* reasonably be expressed in terms of matching columns with the same name, precisely because (a) either *a* or *b* or both might include two or more columns with the same name, and (b) either *a* or *b* or both might include columns with no name at all (or, at least, with "implementation-dependent" names). As a consequence, the result too might include duplicate or missing column names. All of these facts serve to complicate the definition further.

Which Union?

Take another look at the example in Figure 9-1. Suppose now that column X is the "first" column in table T1 but the "second" in table T2, and column Y is the "second" column in table T1 but the "first" in table T2:

```
CREATE TABLE T1 ( X ..., Y ... ) ;
CREATE TABLE T2 ( Y ..., X ... ) ;
```

Suppose further that we want to form a union of T1 and T2, matching the two X columns with each other and the two Y columns with each other. Note my use of the indefinite article here (**a** union)! The point is, of course, that the expression "*the* union of T1 and T2" isn't well-defined, in SQL; given any two SQL tables, there are typically many distinct tables that can all be regarded as a union of the two given ones. (In my opinion, this fact in itself constitutes a huge defect, but let that pass for now.)

To repeat, then: Suppose we want to form a union of T1 and T2 that matches the X columns with each other and the Y columns with each other. Observe first that the following formulation *doesn't* do what we want:

```
SELECT * FROM T1
UNION
SELECT * FROM T2 ;
```

Or equivalently:

```
TABLE T1 UNION TABLE T2 ;
```

Each of these formulations has the effect of matching X in T1 with Y in T2 and Y in T1 with X in T2, which isn't what we want. (What's more, the columns in the result will have "implementation-dependent" names.) By contrast, the following formulation does do the trick:

```
TABLE T1 UNION SELECT X, Y FROM T2 ;
```

So does the following:

```
SELECT Y, X FROM T1 UNION TABLE T2 :
```

But these two formulations give different results ("different unions") in SQL: The first gives a result with columns X and Y, in that order, while the second gives a result with columns Y and X, in *that* order.

Alternatively, we could use this formulation:

```
TABLE T1 UNION CORRESPONDING TABLE T2 ;
```

The CORRESPONDING option here causes columns to be matched up on the basis of their names; thus, the overall formulation now does more closely approximate what a true relational UNION would do. (Of course, there'd be no need to include such an option in the language at all if SQL tables didn't involve column ordering in the first place.) But suppose we had formulated the query thus:

```
TABLE T2 UNION CORRESPONDING TABLE T1 ;
```

The difference between the two CORRESPONDING formulations is that (again) the first gives a result with columns X and Y, in that order, while the second gives a result with columns Y and X, in *that* order. So now we have the situation that the expressions

```
TABLE T1 UNION CORRESPONDING TABLE T2
```

and

```
TABLE T2 UNION CORRESPONDING TABLE T1
```

aren't equivalent, and the fundamental **commutativity** property of union has been violated. That's like having an arithmetic in which 1+2 isn't the same as 2+1!

As an aside—I'm supposed to be talking about union here, but I can't resist mentioning this point in passing—I note that an analogous remark applies to join also. That is, the SQL expressions

```
T1 NATURAL JOIN T2
```

and

```
T2 NATURAL JOIN T1
```

are also not equivalent, in general, thanks to SQL's insistence on column ordering (this point was also noted in the first normal form chapter).

As a further aside (I know this is an aside within an aside, but I simply can't let the point go by unremarked), I'd like to draw your attention to another syntactic oddity in SQL. Here it is. With UNION, the syntax TABLE T1 UNION TABLE T2 is legal and the syntax T1 UNION T2 isn't; with JOIN, however, it's the other way around—the syntax T1 NATURAL JOIN T2 is legal while the syntax TABLE T1 NATURAL JOIN TABLE T2 isn't. Ho hum.

To return to UNION: Hugh Darwen makes some interesting observations in this connection (again, in a private communication) that I'd like to paraphrase here. He begins by pointing out that UNION CORRESPONDING wasn't part of SQL originally but was added in SQL:1992, some 12 or so years after SQL products first appeared. Presumably the functionality introduced by that new construct was felt to fill some gap (i.e., to meet some need not met by SQL prior to that time). But suppose it had been the other way around; suppose SQL's original UNION had been defined in terms of matching column names (like UNION CORRESPONDING) instead of in terms of column ordering. When—if ever—would the need have emerged to introduce a UNION based on column ordering instead?

Hugh goes on to observe that questions like the foregoing apply to a whole host of constructs that have been added to SQL since it was originally defined:

Would HAVING have been added if "derived tables in the FROM clause" had been there from the outset? Would "unnatural join" (comma in the FROM clause) have been added if SQL's original join—however spelled—had been the natural one? And so on.

Such questions are rhetorical, of course, but no less thought-provoking for that.

Relation Types

What I've said in this chapter so far should be more than enough to convince you that problems certainly do arise from SQL's concept of column ordering. But I haven't really faced up yet to the fundamental issue underlying all of those problems (at least, not explicitly). Now it's time to do so. And to do it properly, I need to switch, at least partly, to my preferred terminology of *relations, tuples,* and *attributes.*

I'll begin with some remarks concerning *operators.* As you know, every operator requires its operand(s) to be of type(s) that are appropriate to the operation in question. Here are a few examples:

- The operator "-" (subtract) requires its operands to be numbers.

- The operator "||" (concatenate) requires its operands to be strings.

- The operator CIRCLE, which returns a circle, requires its operands to be of types POINT and LENGTH, respectively (the POINT operand specifies the center, and the LENGTH operand the radius, for the desired circle).

And so on.

There are a couple more points I need to make regarding operators in general; I'll use the "subtract" example to illustrate them. The first is that some operators (not all) are *polymorphic,* meaning, loosely, that they work for operands of several different types. "Subtract" is polymorphic in this sense—it can take operands that are integers (in which case it returns an integer result); it can take operands that are rational numbers (in which case it returns a rational result); and so on.

The second point is that, in general, expressions are recursively built out of subexpressions. This fact implies that we need to be able to *infer* the type of any expression from the operator(s) involved and the types of their operand(s), because the expression in question might be used as a subexpression within some other (outer) expression. For example, consider this expression:

```
7 - ( 5 - 2 )
```

In this example, we need to know the type of the result of the subexpression "5-2" in order to be sure that the outer expression is legitimate (more specifically, that it's a legitimate invocation of the subtract operator). To spell out the details:

- The subexpression "5-2" is an invocation of "subtract," requesting the subtraction of one number from another.

- That subexpression is thus syntactically legal, and the result it produces is a number.

- The outer expression is thus (again) an invocation of "subtract," requesting the subtraction of one number from another; that outer expression is thus syntactically legal in turn, and the result it produces is again a number.

Thus, the overall expression can be said to be *well-formed*.

Now, everything I've said so far regarding operators and expressions in general applies to relational operators and expressions in particular. For example, UNION is a polymorphic relational operator; it actually works for relations of any type whatsoever (though it does require its operands to be of the *same* type). So what's the type of a relation? Well, this question is easily answered; the type of any given relation is determined by the types of the attributes of that relation. For example, suppose the suppliers relation has attributes as follows:

```
S#     CHAR(5)
STATUS INTEGER
CITY   CHAR(15)
```

(I'm ignoring the supplier name attribute, SNAME, for simplicity.) Then the type of that relation is, precisely,

```
RELATION { S# CHAR(5), STATUS INTEGER, CITY CHAR(15) }
```

The braces enclose a set of attribute-name/type-name pairs; braces are used to emphasize the fact that what they contain is indeed a *set*, with no ordering to its elements and no duplicate elements. The complete expression, including the opening RELATION keyword, is the name of a specific **relation type**.

We also need to be able to infer the type of any relational expression from the operator(s) involved and the types of their operand(s), because—to say it again—the expression in question might be used as a subexpression within some outer expression. Here's a trivial example:

```
( T1 UNION T2 ) { X }
```

("form the union of T1 and T2 and project the result over X"). In other words, we need a set of **relation type inference rules,** such that if we know the type(s) of the input relation(s) for any given relational operation, we can infer the type of the output from that operation. Given such a set of rules, it will follow that an arbitrary relational expression, no matter how complex, will produce a result that also has a well-defined relation type; in particular, it will have a well-defined set of attribute names.

Defining such a set of rules turns out to be straightforward. This isn't the place to go into details; let me just give some examples in order to illustrate the general idea. A complete treatment can be found in the book already mentioned, *An Introduction to Database Systems,* 8th edition.

- If we restrict the suppliers relation to just the suppliers in Paris, the type of the result is the same as the type of the original suppliers relation.

- If we project the suppliers relation over the supplier number and city attributes, the type of the result is, precisely,

  ```
  RELATION { S# CHAR(5), CITY CHAR(15) }
  ```

- In the case of union, intersection, and difference, the input relations must be of the same type; the result is then of that same type too. For example, we might restrict the suppliers relation to just the suppliers in Paris; restrict it again to just the suppliers in London; and then form the union of those two restrictions. Thus, the rule is that the input relations must have exactly the same attributes—i.e., the same attribute-name/type-name pairs— and the result will then have the same attributes too.

  As an aside, I observe that there's an issue that might possibly be bothering you here. Suppose column Y of table T2 in Figure 9-1 were called Z, not Y. Then tables T1 and T2 would be of different types—so how could we form their union? The answer is that the relational model provides a "column rename" operator to help with such matters. In the example, we could obtain the desired union by means of the expression T1 UNION (T2 RENAME (Z AS Y)). The result would have columns called X and Y.

Now, how does SQL measure up to the foregoing requirements? The first point is that SQL never talks in terms of relation (or table) types, as such, at all![6] Indeed, it's a little hard to see how it could, given its reliance on column ordering. For example, consider the following two CREATE TABLE statements:

```
CREATE TABLE SSC              |  CREATE TABLE SCS
    ( S#     CHAR(5),         |      ( S#     CHAR(5),
      STATUS INTEGER,         |        CITY   CHAR(15),
      CITY   CHAR(15) ) ;     |        STATUS INTEGER ) ;
```

SQL would presumably have to say—if it had the concept of "table type" at all—that these two tables are of different types: Table SSC is of type

```
TABLE ( S# CHAR(5), STATUS INTEGER, CITY CHAR(15) )
```

---

6. Actually it talks in terms of *row* types instead.

and table SCS is of type

```
TABLE ( S# CHAR(5), CITY CHAR(15), STATUS INTEGER )
```

Here I'm inventing a kind of SQL counterpart to the relation type notation I used earlier. Note in particular the use of parentheses instead of braces. The parentheses enclose an ordered list, not a set, of column-name/type-name pairs; thus, duplicate column names are allowed, and missing column names presumably have to be allowed as well.

Another way of saying the same thing is this: Consider a relation type with N attributes (i.e., of degree N). Corresponding to that single relation type, then, SQL has factorial N different table types! For example, if $N = 10$, there's just one unique relation type, but well over three million distinct SQL table types.

Now consider the implications of all of the above for union in particular. Tables SSC and SCS are of different types, and yet it does seem reasonable that we should be able to apply UNION to them; therefore, we can't just say, as we do in the relational case, that UNION requires its operands to be of the same type and produces a result of the same type as well. Instead, we have to define a rather complex set of rules to say just when UNION can be applied, and then we have to have a mechanism—a user-visible mechanism, be it noted—for specifying *as part of the specific UNION invocation in question* just how columns of the operands are to be matched up ... And we also have to have another complex set of rules for specifying (in effect) what the type of the result is ... And we also have to accept the possibility that there might be many *different* "unions" that can be defined for a given pair of tables ... And so on. And we've already seen in the previous section some of the complications that such considerations can lead to.

Now consider the fact that complications analogous to those identified above apply to all of the other relational operators, as well. Well ... actually, we're touching on another big issue here. Since SQL tables have a column ordering, they aren't what I called in the first normal form chapter "direct and faithful representations" of relations; in fact, they aren't really relations at all. As a consequence, SQL doesn't really support the relational operators project, join, union, and all the rest; in fact it *can't* do so, because its basic data objects aren't relations. Instead, therefore, it supports what might be called *SQL analogs* of those operators. Thus, SQL's project isn't relational project;[7] SQL's join isn't relational join; SQL's union isn't relational union; and so on.

One consequence of the foregoing is that we can't be sure that properties that apply to relational objects and operators also apply to SQL's analogs of those objects and operators. In fact, as we've already seen, sometimes they don't—recall that certain SQL unions and joins aren't commutative, unlike their relational counterparts. Thus, all of the efforts that have gone into studying the properties of relational objects and operators (in particular, the vast amount of research that's gone into the question of implementing the relational model) **can't be guaranteed to apply to SQL**. In fact, it's clear that, in general, SQL is harder to implement than the relational model, and offers fewer opportunities for optimization than the relational model,

---

7. Hugh Darwen claims (in the same private communication mentioned earlier) that SQL doesn't really have anything we could call project. "I mean, SELECT DISTINCT in which every SELECT item is a simple column reference, none of them repeated, is really too much of a special case to be characterized as *SQL's project*. Rather, if anybody asks what SQL's counterpart of project is, we just have to say that it doesn't have one, but if you really want to do it you can write SELECT DISTINCT followed by a column name list that adheres to certain rules."

precisely because of its departures from the prescriptions of that model. This fact is ironic, given that "relational" systems are often criticized for poor performance! Clearly, part of the blame here needs to be laid at SQL's door.

Note: There are other factors that contribute to the foregoing sorry state of affairs, among them SQL's support for nulls and its support for duplicate rows. Regarding the first of these factors, see the book *An Introduction to Database Systems* once again. Regarding the second, see the article "Double Trouble, Double Trouble" (Chapter 10 in the present book).

Predicates Revisited

As I've explained in the first normal form chapter (and many other places), every relation—every table, if you prefer—corresponds to some **predicate,** which is, loosely, what the relation or table *means.* For example, the suppliers relation, with its attributes S#, SNAME, STATUS, and CITY, corresponds to a predicate that might look like this:

> *The supplier with supplier number S# is under contract, is named SNAME, has status STATUS, and is located in city CITY.*

Note carefully that the parameters to this predicate (i.e., S#, SNAME, STATUS, and CITY, corresponding to the attributes of the relation) are identified by *name,* not by ordinal position. For example, the following predicate is logically equivalent to the one just shown:

> *The supplier with supplier number S# is under contract, is located in city CITY, has status STATUS, and is named SNAME.*

In fact, it's highly desirable, for human factors reasons not least, that parameters be identified by name and not position. To take a simpler example, the (equivalent) predicates "*A* is the father of *B*" and "the father of *B* is *A*" are both preferable to the expression "father_of(*A,B*)"; in this latter case, we need to be told what *roles* the parameters *A* and *B* are playing in order to understand what the expression means. And then, once we've been told what those roles are—perhaps like this:

```
father_of ( A = father, B = child )
```

—we've effectively replaced the "positional predicate" by one that doesn't rely on positional addressing after all!

It follows from all of the above that if we want to be able to say in a similar manner that some SQL table corresponds to some predicate, we have to face up to the question of what the column ordering in that SQL table means (i.e., what the significance of that column ordering is for the predicate). And it seems to me that once we've done that, the need for the column ordering goes away!—just as it did in the "father_of" example. So why was that column ordering there in the first place? What does it buy us? I do think anybody who believes column ordering is a good idea owes us answers to these questions.[8]

---

8. In fact, I think an argument could be made that reliance on positional addressing—either in a predicate like father_of(*A,B*) or in an SQL table with its column ordering—constitutes a violation of *The Information Principle.* See Appendix B of the first normal form chapter for further discussion of this issue.

Where Did Column Ordering Come From?

In my opinion, column ordering as found in SQL is a bigger mistake than is commonly realized. So why was that mistake made? Where did it come from? In this section, I speculate that the source—that is, the cause of the error—might be *an insufficiently careful reading of certain of Codd's early papers*. In his very first paper on the relational model ("Derivability, Redundancy, and Consistency of Relations Stored in Large Data Banks," IBM Research Report RJ599, August 19th, 1969), Codd defined the term *relation* as follows (I've reworded his definition just slightly here):

> *Given sets* S1, S2, ..., Sn *(not necessarily distinct),* R *is a* relation *on those sets if it is a set of tuples, each of which has its first element from* S1, *its second element from* S2, *and so on. We shall refer to* Sj *as the* j*th attribute of* R.

In other words, relations according to this definition do have a left-to-right ordering to their attributes. (For reasons that need not concern us here, relations in mathematics, unlike their counterparts in the relational model, do have such an ordering. A similar remark applies to tuples also.)

Now, in the much more widely distributed and better known 1970 successor to his 1969 paper ("A Relational Model of Data for Large Shared Data Banks," *CACM 13*, No. 6, June 1970), Codd went on to say that users shouldn't have to deal with relations as such (with their left-to-right attribute ordering), but rather with "their [attribute]-unordered counterparts" (which he called *relationships* in that paper, but just *relations* in most subsequent papers). But that refinement seems to have escaped the attention of certain members of the database community, including—as we know, and very unfortunately—the designers of the SQL language in particular.

A couple of years later, Codd wrote another important paper: "Relational Completeness of Data Base Sublanguages," in Randall J. Rustin (ed.), *Data Base Systems, Courant Computer Science Symposia Series 6*, Prentice-Hall, 1972. In that paper, he again assumed, for "notational and expository convenience," that attributes were identified by ordinal position, not by name (though he did also explicitly recognize that names were better in practice). And again it's possible that this assumption on Codd's part in this paper had an unfortunate influence on the designers of SQL.

Please understand that I don't mean to imply, by the remarks in this section, that Codd was the source of the column ordering mistake. Far from it! I only mean, to say it again, that an insufficiently careful reading of what Codd wrote might have been the source of that mistake. Codd always wrote carefully, and his readers owe it to him to exercise the same degree of care in reading what he wrote. Indeed, it's worth mentioning that there was at least one section of the database community that did pay attention to what he said on the topic at hand; I refer to the team who designed and built the early relational prototype IS/1, together with its successor PRTV, at the IBM (U.K.) Scientific Centre in the early 1970s. Their user language ISBL (Information System Base Language)—see P. A. V. Hall, P. Hitchcock, and S. J. P. Todd, "An Algebra of Relations for Machine Computation," Conf. Record of the 2nd ACM Symposium on Principles of Programming Languages, Palo Alto, Calif., January 1975—did indeed avoid all reliance on column ordering.

Concluding Remarks

In closing, I'd like to repeat something I said in the introduction to this chapter:

> *[The] various features of the relational model are highly interconnected—remove just one of them, and the whole edifice crumbles. Translated into concrete terms, this metaphor means that if we build a "relational" DBMS that fails to support some aspect of the model, the resulting system (which really shouldn't be called relational, anyway) will be bound to display behavior on occasion that's certainly undesirable and possibly unforeseeable. I can't stress the point too strongly: Every feature of the model is there for solid practical reasons; if we choose to ignore some detail, then we do so at our own peril.*

Well, we've certainly seen that SQL's failure to support the "no column ordering" rule leads to a lot of complexity. Let me conclude by briefly considering some of the consequences of that complexity.

- First of all, the language, and therefore the specifications, are both much bigger than they need have been.

- That fact increases the likelihood of errors and inconsistencies (and indeed it's undeniable that the SQL standard does include many such errors and inconsistencies; see, e.g., C. J. Date and Hugh Darwen, *A Guide to the SQL Standard*, 4th edition, Addison-Wesley, 1997, Appendix D, for a lengthy discussion of some of them).

- As a consequence of the foregoing, the language becomes harder than it might have been to document, to teach, to learn, to remember, to use—and to standardize! (Although the standard as such includes inconsistencies, real implementations have to resolve those inconsistencies somehow. Do you think they all resolve them the same way? Do you believe every vendor implements exactly the same SQL dialect?)

- The language is also harder to *extend* than it should have been, because every proposed extension has to be assessed in terms of its interactions with everything already included in the language. Thus, if the language includes features it really ought not to have done, such as column ordering, then there's clearly more work involved in adding new features— even when they're good ones.

- Finally, the language is also harder to **implement** (harder to *optimize* in particular) than it might have been—largely for the very same reasons that make it harder to teach, learn, and so on.

Acknowledgments

I'd like to thank Hugh Darwen and Fabian Pascal for helpful comments on earlier drafts of this chapter.

Appendix A: Row Comparisons

Note: This appendix is based on material that first appeared in the book *A Guide to the SQL Standard,* 4th edition, by Hugh Darwen and myself (Addison-Wesley, 1977).

Tuples in the relational model have no left-to-right ordering to their components; as a consequence, the only comparison operators that make sense for tuples are "=" and "≠" (equals and not equals, respectively). By contrast, rows in SQL do have a left-to-right ordering to their components; as a consequence, it becomes possible to attach significance to other comparison operators for rows, and SQL does so.[9] To be specific, SQL supports *row comparisons* of the form

```
<row expression> <comparison operator> <row expression>
```

where the *<comparison operator>* must be "=", "<", "<=", ">", ">=", or "<>" (this last being the SQL syntax for "not equals"). The semantics are as follows:

- Let the two *<row expression>*s evaluate to rows *Left* and *Right,* respectively. *Left* and *Right* must be of the same degree, meaning they must contain the same number, *n* say, of components each.

- Let θ be the specified *<comparison operator>.*

- Let *i* range from 1 to *n,* and let the *i*th components of *Left* and *Right* be *Li* and *Ri,* respectively. The data types of *Li* and *Ri* must be such that the comparison "*Li* θ *Ri*" is valid. (They don't actually have to be of the same *type,* because SQL supports coercion, or implicit type conversion. Coercion implies that a comparison between, e.g., an integer and a floating-point number might be valid.)

- Let *j* also range from 1 to *n.*

- Then the result of the row comparison is defined as follows:

  - "*Left* = *Right*" gives TRUE if and only if for all *i,* "*Li* = *Ri*" gives TRUE

  - "*Left* <> *Right*" gives TRUE if and only if there exists some *j* such that "*Lj* <> *Rj*" gives TRUE

  - "*Left* < *Right*" gives TRUE if and only if there exists some *j* such that "*Lj* < *Rj*" gives TRUE and for all *i* < *j,* "*Li* = *Ri*" gives TRUE

  - "*Left* > *Right*" gives TRUE if and only if there exists some *j* such that "*Lj* > *Rj*" gives TRUE and for all *i* < *j,* "*Li* = *Ri*" gives TRUE

  - "*Left* <= *Right*" gives TRUE if and only if "*Left* < *Right*" gives TRUE or "*Left* = *Right*" gives TRUE

---

9. In other words, we're talking about yet another SQL departure from the prescriptions of the relational model. Incidentally, it's worth mentioning that when this functionality was originally proposed, the SQL standardizers had great difficulty in defining the semantics correctly; in fact, it took them several attempts before they got it right.

- "*Left >= Right*" gives TRUE if and only if "*Left > Right*" gives TRUE or "*Left = Right*" gives TRUE

- "*Left = Right*" gives FALSE if and only if "*Left <> Right*" gives TRUE

- "*Left <> Right*" gives FALSE if and only if "*Left = Right*" gives TRUE

- "*Left < Right*" gives FALSE if and only if "*Left >= Right*" gives TRUE

- "*Left > Right*" gives FALSE if and only if "*Left <= Right*" gives TRUE

- "*Left <= Right*" gives FALSE if and only if "*Left > Right*" gives TRUE

- "*Left >= Right*" gives FALSE if and only if "*Left < Right*" gives TRUE

- "*Left θ Right*" gives UNKNOWN ("the third truth value") if and only if it gives neither TRUE nor FALSE

Exercise: What do the following give?

```
( 1, 2, NULL ) = ( 3, NULL, 4 )
( 1, 2, NULL ) < ( 3, NULL, 4 )
( 1, 2, NULL ) = ( 1, NULL, 4 )
( 1, 2, NULL ) > ( NULL, 2, 4 )
```

CHAPTER 10

■■■

Double Trouble, Double Trouble

As tedious as a twice-told tale

—William Shakespeare

I've stated in many places and on many occasions that duplicate rows (hereafter usually abbreviated to just *duplicates*) are, and always were, a mistake in SQL. In fact, it's my position that (a) duplicate rows should never have been permitted in the first place, but (b) given that they *were* permitted, they ought to be avoided in practice. In what follows, I give some solid reasons for this position. Thus, what follows is far from new; I just feel, sadly, that it needs to be aired still one more time ... The immediate cause for my feeling this way was a letter I received from a colleague in Finland, Lauri Pietarinen, which read in part as follows:

> *I just came back from the [September 2001] VLDB Conference in Rome ... I was talking to <name suppressed to protect the guilty> about why we should stick to "real" relations instead of the current tuple-bag implementations [in other words, why we should outlaw duplicate tuples] ... It was his opinion that from the optimization point of view we have nothing to gain from using relations as compared to the current situation. He referred to the book* Database System Implementation *by Hector Garcia-Molina, Jeffrey D. Ullman, and Jennifer Widom, where he said a tuple-bag algebra had been presented ... Could you please summarize the reasons for using relations ... I know you have addressed this matter in numerous writings, but just to summarize the issue (?) ... The point of view mainly of interest was that of optimization (that is, can we do more optimization with relations?).*

Well, it's certainly true that I've addressed this matter in numerous writings, and I really don't think I can do better to summarize the issue than repeat some material that originally appeared in two of my regular columns for *DBP&D* ("Toil and Trouble," *DBP&D* 7, No. 1, January 1994 and "And Cauldron Bubble," *DBP&D* 8, No. 6, June 1995).[1] What follows, therefore, consists in large part of a lightly edited version of those two earlier columns. However, the chapter does also contain some new material, including in particular an appendix that discusses the

---

1. These two installments were republished—the second under its original title "The Department of Redundancy Department"—by permission of Miller Freeman Inc. in my books *Relational Database Writings 1991–1994* and *Relational Database Writings 1994–1997* (Addison-Wesley, 1995 and 1998, respectively).

tuple-bag algebra of Garcia-Molina *et al.* in some detail; among other things, that appendix does consider the implications of that algebra for optimization, as requested. As we'll see from that appendix, as well as from material in the body of the chapter, the answer to Lauri Pietarinen's question—"Can we do more optimization with relations?"—is very definitely *yes*.

The Cat Food Example

The following extract from an article by David Beech ("New Life for SQL," *Datamation,* February 1st, 1989) is typical of the arguments that are advanced by duplicate row advocates:

> *For example, the row "cat food 0.39" could appear three times [on a supermarket checkout receipt] with a significance that would not escape many shoppers ... At the level of abstraction at which it is useful to record the information, there are no value components that distinguish the objects. What the relational model does is force people to lower the level of abstraction, often inventing meaningless values to be inserted in an extra column whose purpose is to show what we knew already, that the cans of cat food are distinct.*

Apart from the remark regarding "lowering the level of abstraction," which I think is just arm waving,[2] this seems to me to be exactly the straw man argument I gave in my article "Why Duplicate Rows Are Prohibited" (in *Relational Database Writings 1985–1989,* Addison-Wesley, 1990), under the heading "Why Duplicates Are Good (?)"—to wit:

1. Duplicates occur naturally in practice.

2. Given that this is so, it's a burden on the user to have to invent some artificial identifier in order to distinguish between them.

In a subsequent section of that same article, titled "Why Duplicates Are Bad: The Fundamental Issue," I went on to refute this argument as follows:

1. Individual objects *must* be identifiable (that is, distinguishable from all other objects)— for if an object is not identifiable, then it's impossible even to talk about it, let alone perform any kind of operation upon it or use it for any sensible purpose. In other words, objects must have **identity**. *Note:* Here and throughout this chapter, I use the term *object* in its ordinary English sense, not in the special rather loaded sense in which it's used in the OO world.

---

2. If anything, in fact, the relational representation *raises* the level of abstraction, because it eliminates irrelevant details—details, that is, that have to do merely with the way data is presented to the end user. After all, the checkout receipt is really just a *report* (it certainly isn't part of the database!), and there's no particular reason why we should have to represent data in the same way in the database and in a report; in fact, there are good reasons not to. (Thanks to Fabian Pascal for these observations, and more generally for his review of—and helpful comments on—an earlier draft of this chapter.)

2. In a collection of objects in which there are no duplicates (in other words, a mathematical set), objects obviously do have identity, because they are in fact **self-identifying**. For example, in the set of integers {3,6,8,11}, there's no ambiguity as to which element of the set is "6" and which is "8" (etc.). However, in the collection (3,6,6,8,8,8,11), which is certainly not a mathematical set (it is a *multiset* or *bag* instead), we cannot make an analogous statement; both "6" and "8" are now ambiguous.

3. So what *is* the identification mechanism in a collection that permits duplicates (in other words, a bag)? For example, in the bag just shown, how can we distinguish the two "6"s from one another? Note that there must still *be* an identification mechanism; if we cannot distinguish the two "6"s from one another somehow, **we cannot even tell there are two of them** (an illustration of what I believe is known in the world of philosophy as *The Principle of Identity of Indiscernibles*). In other words, we wouldn't even know there *were* any duplicates in the first place!

Now, a common reaction to this argument is "But I really *don't* need to distinguish among the duplicates—all I want to do is be able to count them." The point I'm trying to make is that you do need to distinguish them, even just to count them (for otherwise how do you know which ones you've already counted?). This point is crucial, of course, and I really don't know how to make it any more strongly than I already have.

How then do we distinguish duplicates such as the two "6"s in the bag shown above? The answer, of course, is that we do so *by their relative position;* we say something like "this 6 is **here** and that 6 is **there**," or "this one is the **first** 6 and that one is the **second**."

And so we have now introduced a totally new concept, one that is quite deliberately omitted from the relational model: *positional addressing.* Which means we're now quite beyond the pale!—that is, we've moved quite outside the framework of relational theory. Which means that there's *no guarantee whatsoever* that any results that hold within that framework still apply. For example, does JOIN still work? (As a matter of fact, it doesn't.) What about UNION? EXTEND? SUMMARIZE? Are the theorems of normalization still valid? What about the quantifiers EXISTS and FORALL? What about the rules for functional dependency inference? What about expression transformation and optimization? Etc., etc., etc.

Furthermore, we now definitely need certain additional operators, such as "retrieve the *n*th row" or "insert this new row *here*" or "move this row from *here* to *there*." In my opinion— *pace* Beech—these operators constitute a much greater burden on the user than does the occasional need to invent an artificial identifier.

The relational model, by contrast, adopts the position that, since objects do have to be identifiable *somehow,* then we might as well represent their identity in exactly the same way as everything else: namely, by values in columns. (Especially as there will often be a "natural" identifier that is usable as such a column value anyway, which means that the problem of having to invent an artificial value might not arise all that often in practice.) In this way we can stay securely within the context of relational theory, and all of the desirable properties of that theory will thus still be directly applicable.

To return for a moment to the cat food argument, Beech goes on to say:

We are not being less than respectable mathematically if we consider collections containing duplicates, because mathematicians deal with such collections, called multisets or ... bags.

The point here seems to be that the usual advantage claimed for the relational model, to the effect that the model is at least "mathematically respectable," can be claimed by the duplicate row advocates for their "model" too. But all of the mathematical "bag theory" treatments I've ever seen start off by assuming there's a way to count duplicates! And that assumption, I contend, effectively means that *bags* are defined in terms of *sets*—each bag element really has a hidden identifying tag that distinguishes it somehow, and the bag is really a *set* of tag/element pairs. I see no advantage, and definite disadvantages, in introducing this extra level of complexity.

Expression Transformation

The foregoing argument should be sufficient (I hope) to show why I think it was a mistake—for both theoretical **and practical** reasons—to include duplicate support in SQL in the first place. Now I'd like to go on to argue that, even though duplicates *are* supported, you should take care to avoid them in practice. (The following argument is based on an example originally due to Nat Goodman.)

The fundamental point is that—as I hinted in the previous section—expression transformations, and hence optimizations, that are valid in a relational context are *not* necessarily valid in the presence of duplicates. Here's an example. Consider the database shown in Figure 10-1.

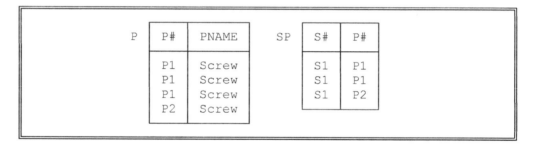

Figure 10-1. *A database with duplicates*

Perhaps I should begin by asking the question: What does it *mean* to have three "(P1,Screw)" rows in table P and not two, or four, or seventeen? It must mean *something,* for if it means nothing, then why are the duplicates there in the first place? To paraphrase a point first nicely made by Codd (in a live presentation): If something is true, saying it twice doesn't make it any *more* true.

So let's assume that there is indeed some meaning attached to the existence of duplicates, even though that meaning, whatever it is, is hardly very explicit. (I note in passing, therefore, that duplicates contravene another of the objectives of the relational model, namely the objective of *explicitness:* that is, the meaning of the data should be as explicit as possible. The presence of duplicates implies that part of the meaning is hidden.) In other words, given that duplicates do have some meaning, there are presumably going to be business decisions made on the basis of the fact that, for example, there are three "(P1,Screw)" rows in table P and not two or four or seventeen. (For if not, then why are the duplicates there in the first place?)

Now consider the query "Get part numbers for parts that either are screws or are supplied by supplier S1, or both." Here are some candidate SQL formulations for this query, together with the output produced in each case.[3]

```
1. SELECT P#
   FROM   P
   WHERE  PNAME = 'Screw'
   OR     P# IN
          ( SELECT P#
            FROM   SP
            WHERE  S# = 'S1') ;
```

Result: P1 * 3, P2 * 1.

```
2. SELECT P#
   FROM   SP
   WHERE  S# = 'S1'
   OR     P# IN
          ( SELECT P#
            FROM   P
            WHERE  PNAME = 'Screw') ;
```

Result: P1 * 2, P2 * 1.

```
3. SELECT P.P#
   FROM   P, SP
   WHERE  ( S# = 'S1' AND
            P.P# = SP.P# )
   OR     PNAME = 'Screw' ;
```

Result: P1 * 9, P2 * 3.

```
4. SELECT SP.P#
   FROM   P, SP
   WHERE  ( S# = 'S1' AND
            P.P# = SP.P# )
   OR     PNAME = 'Screw' ;
```

Result: P1 * 8, P2 * 4.

---

3. Thanks to Jim Panttaja for checking these results for me, using Microsoft SQL Server Release 4.2a running on OS/2. See also Chapter 4, Section 4b, of Fabian Pascal's book *Practical Issues in Database Management: A Reference for the Thinking Practitioner* (Addison-Wesley, 2000), which reports on the results of running a similar experiment. In the interests of accuracy, I should add that a couple of the "candidate formulations" (which ones?) are perhaps not true candidates, inasmuch as they assume that every part that is a screw is supplied by at least one supplier (thanks to Hugh Darwen for this observation). However, this point has no material effect on the argument.

```
5. SELECT  P#
   FROM    P
   WHERE   PNAME = 'Screw'
   UNION   ALL
   SELECT  P#
   FROM    SP
   WHERE   S# = 'S1' ;
```

Result: P1 * 5, P2 * 2.

```
6. SELECT  DISTINCT P#
   FROM    P
   WHERE   PNAME = 'Screw'
   UNION   ALL
   SELECT  P#
   FROM    SP
   WHERE   S# = 'S1' ;
```

Result: P1 * 3, P2 * 2.

```
7. SELECT  P#
   FROM    P
   WHERE   PNAME = 'Screw'
   UNION   ALL
   SELECT  DISTINCT P#
   FROM    SP
   WHERE   S# = 'S1' ;
```

Result: P1 * 4, P2 * 2.

```
8. SELECT  DISTINCT P#
   FROM    P
   WHERE   PNAME = 'Screw'
   OR      P# IN
         ( SELECT P#
           FROM   SP
           WHERE  S# = 'S1') ;
```

Result: P1 * 1, P2 * 1.

```
9. SELECT  DISTINCT P#
   FROM    SP
   WHERE   S# = 'S1'
   OR      P# IN
         ( SELECT P#
           FROM   P
           WHERE  PNAME = 'Screw') ;
```

Result: P1 * 1, P2 * 1.

```
10. SELECT P#
    FROM   P
    GROUP  BY P#, PNAME
    HAVING PNAME = 'Screw'
    OR     P# IN
        ( SELECT P#
          FROM   SP
          WHERE  S# = 'S1') ;
```

Result: P1 * 1, P2 * 1.

```
11. SELECT P.P#
    FROM   P, SP
    GROUP  BY P.P#, PNAME, S#, SP.P#
    HAVING ( S# = 'S1' AND
             P.P# = SP.P# )
    OR     PNAME = 'Screw' ;
```

Result: P1 * 2, P2 * 2.

```
12. SELECT P#
    FROM   P
    WHERE  PNAME = 'Screw'
    UNION
    SELECT P#
    FROM   SP
    WHERE  S# = 'S1' ;
```

Result: P1 * 1, P2 * 1.

The obvious first point to make is that the twelve different formulations produce nine different results!—different, that is, with respect to their *degree of duplication.* (I make no claim, incidentally, that either the twelve different formulations or the nine different results are the only ones possible; indeed, they aren't, in general.) Thus, if the user really cares about duplicates, then he or she needs to be *extremely* careful in formulating the query appropriately in order to obtain exactly the desired result.

Furthermore, of course, analogous remarks apply to the system itself: Because different formulations can produce different results, the system optimizer too has to be *extremely* careful in its task of expression transformation (that is, transforming one formulation into another). In other words, duplicate rows act as a significant **optimization inhibitor** (see Part 2 of my article "Expression Transformation" in *Relational Database Writings 1989–1991,* Addison-Wesley, 1992). Here are some implications of this point:

- First, the optimizer code itself is harder to write, harder to maintain, and probably more buggy—all of which combines to make the product simultaneously more expensive and less reliable, as well as late in delivery in the marketplace.

- Second, system performance is likely to be worse than it might otherwise be.

- Third, the user is going to have to get involved in performance issues; for instance, the user might have to spend time and effort on figuring out *the best way* to express a given query (a state of affairs that the relational model was expressly designed to avoid).

Just as an aside, you might want to try out the twelve formulations—and any others you can think of—on your own DBMS. You might discover some interesting things about your optimizer! For my part, I've certainly encountered products that do not handle the degree of duplication correctly in all cases—presumably because they're making some expression transformations that are technically incorrect. In this connection, let me also draw your attention to another article of mine, "Fifty Ways to Quote Your Query," in *DBP&D 11*, No. 7, July 1998 (reprinted in my self-published book *Relational Database Writings 1997–2001*).

To get back to the main thread of my argument: The foregoing state of affairs (regarding the fact that duplicates serve as an optimization inhibitor) is particularly frustrating in view of the fact that, in most cases, the user probably does *not* really care how many duplicates appear in the result. In other words:

a. Different formulations produce different results, as demonstrated above; however,

b. The differences are probably irrelevant from the user's point of view; *but*

c. The optimizer is not aware of this latter fact and is therefore prevented—unnecessarily— from performing the transformations it would like to perform.

On the basis of examples like the foregoing, I would conclude among other things that users should *always* ensure that query results contain no duplicates—for example, by always specifying DISTINCT at appropriate points in the query—and thus simply forget about the whole problem. (And if this advice is followed, of course, then there can be no good reason for allowing duplicates in the database in the first place.)

Note: The alternative in SQL to SELECT DISTINCT is SELECT ALL (and SELECT ALL is unfortunately the default). The discussion of the foregoing sections suggests that a more apt alternative might have been SELECT *IN*DISTINCT ... On a more serious note: The trouble is, of course, that SELECT DISTINCT often takes longer to execute than SELECT ALL, even if the DISTINCT is effectively a "no op." But this problem arises because SQL systems are typically unable to optimize properly over duplicate elimination, owing to their lack of knowledge of key inheritance (see my article "The Power of the Keys," in *Relational Database Writings 1989–1991*, Addison-Wesley, 1992). And even if duplicate elimination does sometimes give rise to some performance overhead, I would still argue that such overhead is a very minor matter when regarded from the point of view of "the big picture."

A couple of further points to close this section: First, one reviewer of an earlier draft objected that users don't *really* have duplicates in base tables, and the example discussed above thus intuitively fails. Well, OK; but the trouble is, SQL can *generate* duplicates in the results of queries! Indeed, different formulations of "the same" query can produce results with different degrees of duplication, even if the input tables themselves don't have any duplicates. By way of example, consider the following formulations of the query "Get supplier numbers for suppliers who supply at least one part" on the usual suppliers-and-parts database:

```
SELECT  S.S#              |    SELECT  S.S#
FROM    S                 |    FROM    S, SP
WHERE   S.S# IN           |    WHERE   S.S# = SP.S# ;
      ( SELECT SP.S#       |
        FROM   SP ) ;      |
```

So if you don't want to think of the tables in Figure 10-1 as base tables specifically, fine: Just take them to be the output from certain previous queries, and the rest of the analysis goes through unchanged.

The second point is this. Suppose a given table *T* does permit duplicates. Then we can't tell the difference between "genuine" duplicates in *T* and duplicates that arise from errors in data entry operations on *T*! For example, what happens if the person responsible for data entry unintentionally—that is, *by mistake*—enters the very same row into *T* twice? (Thanks to Fabian Pascal again for drawing my attention to this problem.)

Rows Represent Propositions

There's yet another point to be made on this subject. As I've explained in many places and on many occasions, any given relational table denotes a certain **predicate,** and the rows of that table denote certain **true propositions,** obtained from the predicate by substituting certain *arguments*—that is, values of the appropriate type—for the *placeholders* or *parameters* of that predicate ("instantiating the predicate"). For example, consider the relational table EMP {EMP#, ENAME, DEPT#, SALARY}. The predicate here looks something like this:

Employee EMP# is named ENAME, works in department DEPT#, and earns salary SALARY.

(The parameters are EMP#, ENAME, DEPT#, and SALARY, corresponding of course to the four EMP columns.) And the corresponding true propositions might look like this:

Employee E1 is named Lopez, works in department D1, and earns salary 40K.

Employee E2 is named Cheng, works in department D1, and earns salary 42K.

And so on.

Now, the logical operator AND is *idempotent.* Among other things, what this means is that if *p* is a proposition, then *p* AND *p* is equivalent to just *p*. For example, if I say "the sun is shining here today" and "the sun is shining here today," I'm simply telling you the sun is shining here today! And from this perspective, the notion of duplicate rows—as that notion is usually understood—*obviously* makes no sense.

The Conclusion So Far

Duplicate row support should be dropped. A strategy for doing so gracefully was outlined by Codd in his book *The Relational Model for Database Management Version 2* (Addison-Wesley, 1990):

1. Implement an installation-time switch in the DBMS so that the DBA can specify whether duplicates are to be eliminated (a) in all cases—in other words, automatically—or (b) only on user request.

2. Announce that support for Case (b) will be dropped in (say) two or three years' time.

3. Drop that support at the appropriate time, simultaneously upgrading the optimizer to take advantage of the now guaranteed lack of duplicates.

Rats and Ratlets

After the foregoing discussion first appeared in my original *DBP&D* series, I received a letter from Chuck Reinke of Concord, California, who felt that I had not responded satisfactorily to the cat food example. In an attempt to clarify his objections, he suggested the following example:

> *Let's consider* rats *and* ratlets. *Whenever there's a new litter, I want to create an entry for each new ratlet. When just born they are indistinguishable ... Yet, as they grow, I can distinguish certain ones by color or behavior—it's time to assign them a unique key.*

> *As Date would have it, prior to this stage ratlets should be banned from relational representation. Assigning each ratlet an arbitrary unique key implies nonexistent information, that the ratlets are distinguishable ... The inadequacy of SQL is a poor argument for prohibiting duplicates in relational design. I want to keep track of practical real world information, not create mathematical abstractions of Aristotelian purity.*

Space constraints at the time required me to keep my response short, so I refrained from pointing out that (a) the arguments against duplicates have nothing to do with the inadequacies of SQL *per se*, (b) the distinguishability of the ratlets is a fact, not "nonexistent information," and (c) "keeping track of practical real world information" in a database *necessarily* involves creating some kind of "mathematical abstraction"! Instead, I simply replied by observing that the obvious design for the ratlets problem is:

```
LITTERS ( LITTER_ID, #_OF_RATLETS )
        PRIMARY KEY ( LITTER_ID )


RATLETS ( RATLET_ID, LITTER_ID )
        PRIMARY KEY ( RATLET_ID )
        FOREIGN KEY ( LITTER_ID ) REFERENCES LITTERS
```

When there's a new litter, we make the obvious entry in LITTERS. When an individual ratlet becomes "interesting" (unlike Mr. Reinke, I do not say "distinguishable," because distinguishability presupposes identity), we make the obvious entry in RATLETS.

The Pennies Example

Following my original *DBP&D* articles, I also received a long letter from Robert Alps of Evanston, Illinois, which raised further questions about some of the arguments I'd been making. And it seemed to me that it might be worth airing some of the comments from Alps's letter, and my responses to them, before a wider audience; hence the discussion that follows. *Note:* I should make it clear that Alps wasn't saying duplicates were a good thing. To quote his letter:

> *I am not arguing in favor of duplicates, rather against some of your arguments opposing [them]. I only want to be sure the arguments are sound before concluding "Out, damned duplicate."*

Now, I said earlier that individual objects must be identifiable—in other words, distinguishable from all other objects—because if an object isn't identifiable, it's impossible even to talk about it, let alone perform any kind of operation upon it or use it for any sensible purpose. Alps countered with the following example:

> *Imagine a bag of 100 newly minted pennies. You can reach into the bag and pull one out and while it is in your hand it has a special identity (of being the penny in your hand). But as soon as you place that penny back in the bag, it loses that special identity and becomes, once again, indistinguishable from the others. Is there some useful operation we can perform on indistinguishable objects? Certainly. To the extent that we have information regarding their number, we may perform mathematical operations using that information. If we know that one bag contains 100 pennies and another contains 200 pennies then we know that the combination of the two bags holds 300 pennies. This is a useful operation.*

Now, obviously I agree that the individual pennies in a bag of 100 pennies can be regarded as indistinguishable from one another **at a certain level of discourse** (in other words, at a certain level of abstraction). Surely, however, the point is that the entities under discussion here aren't individual pennies; rather, they're the *collective* entities "bags of pennies." Those collective entities in turn have a certain property (namely, cardinality), with values 100, 200, and so on. Furthermore, those collective entities have some **id**entity, because otherwise (as I said before) we can't even refer to them; at the very least, we have to say something like "This is **this** bag of pennies and that is **that** one."

But suppose we ask ourselves the question "How are values of the cardinality property determined?" Then I contend that we have to descend to a lower level of discourse and consider individual pennies as entities. And at this level we **must** be able to distinguish those individual pennies in order to be able to count them! As I put it earlier:

> *[A] common reaction to this argument is "But I really don't need to distinguish among the duplicates—all I want to do is to be able to count them." The point I'm trying to make is that you do need to distinguish them, even just to count them (for otherwise how do you know which ones you've already counted?). This point is crucial, of course, and I really don't know how to make it any more strongly than I already have.*

I further contend that Alps's example of a "useful operation"—namely, the operation of combining the bag of 100 pennies and the bag of 200 pennies to obtain a bag of 300 pennies, which is a union operation, of course[4]—is self-evidently an operation on bags of pennies, not an operation on individual pennies *per se*.

To continue with what I said earlier: I observed that the way we distinguish duplicates in general is *by their relative position;* in a bag (*aka* multiset) containing two 6's, for example, we say something like "This 6 is **here** and that 6 is **there**," or "This is the **first** 6 and that 6 is the **second**." Alps countered by claiming that "the suggestion that we place a positional ordering on duplicates in all situations appears highly artificial and patently false." Well, perhaps I should turn the argument around at this point; specifically, if you're one of those people who think that duplicates "truly exist" in some sense, then please tell me exactly—**exactly, please!**—how you propose to count those 100 "duplicate" pennies. I do think that anyone who advocates

---

4. A *set* union, that is, not a *bag* union (pun intended).

the position that duplicates are a good idea needs to provide a good, convincing answer to this question.[5]

Bag Theory

Recall that, loosely speaking, a *bag* in mathematics is a set that permits duplicates. Duplicate advocates thus sometimes claim that their approach is just as respectable as the relational approach because it too is based on solid theory (bag theory instead of set theory). Earlier in this chapter, however, I claimed that mathematical "bag theory" treatments usually start by assuming there's a way to count duplicates! I further claimed that that assumption effectively means that *bags* are defined in terms of *sets*.

Alps replied by constructing an outline bag theory that—he claimed—didn't start with such an assumption. But I think it does! One of the three primitives of his theory is an expression of the form "count *xA*" which (to quote) "is intended to denote the number of times the [object] *x* occurs in the bag *A*." Now, this quote might have been meant only as an informal, intuitive remark, not as part of the theory as such, but I'm still suspicious.

In any case, the question of whether such an assumption is necessary is perhaps a red herring (and I was perhaps wrong to raise it in the first place). The point rather is that bag theory:

- Is necessarily more complex than set theory

- Includes set theory as a proper subset (perhaps I should say *subbag?*)

- Is reducible to set theory

Occam's Razor would thus clearly suggest that we stay with sets and not get into the unnecessary complexities of bags. (As so often in a database context, Occam's Razor is peculiarly apt here. One simple way of stating it is: "Entities should not be multiplied beyond necessity." A simpler way still is just: "No unnecessary entities.")

The Performance Issue

I also recommended earlier in this chapter that users should always ensure that query results contain no duplicates—for instance, by always specifying DISTINCT at appropriate points in the query—and thus simply forget about the whole problem. However, I also pointed out that SELECT DISTINCT might take longer to execute than SELECT ALL, even if the DISTINCT is effectively a "no op." Alps commented that the performance problem doesn't go away if the system is (re)defined to eliminate duplicates automatically:

> *Imagine an address table containing street, city, state, and zip data. If a query is performed selecting city from the table under a system that [eliminates duplicates automatically], the system is going to have to go through all the same checking for duplicates that would be required if [it didn't eliminate duplicates automatically but] the query asked for DISTINCT cities.*

---

5. It's now been many years since I first issued this challenge, and nobody has yet come up with a cogent response to it. See Appendix B ("More on Counting Pennies"), later.

Here I think Alps missed my point slightly. What I meant was that, because it appears that always eliminating duplicates implies performance problems, there was a strong motivation for the SQL language designers to make *not* eliminating duplicates the default. (In fact, I very specifically pointed out that support for duplicates can actually have a *negative* impact on performance, and my reason for doing so was precisely to provide a counterbalance to this familiar argument.) But the full implications, psychological and otherwise, of this very bad language design decision weren't thought through at the time. It's my belief that the *occasional* overhead that *might* be incurred (in a well-implemented system) in always eliminating duplicates would be vastly outweighed by the benefits—including performance benefits—that such a system would provide.

Of course I understand that checking for duplicates is required regardless of whether (a) the system prohibits them or (b) the system permits them but the user specifies DISTINCT. But note that if the language is *defined* always to eliminate duplicates, at least conceptually, then the system will sometimes be able *not* to eliminate them—for intermediate results, at least, though not of course for final results—as an optimization, where appropriate.

Some More SQL Problems

At this juncture I'd like to digress for a moment and talk about a couple of problems that are caused by duplicates in the SQL standard specifically. The following discussions are based on material from Appendix D ("Some Outstanding Issues") from the book by Hugh Darwen and myself on the SQL:1992 standard (*A Guide to the SQL Standard,* 4th edition, Addison-Wesley, 1997).

The first problem concerns Cartesian product. Part of the standard's explanation of the SQL FROM clause reads as follows:

> *[The] result of the <from clause> is the ... Cartesian product of the tables identified by [the] <table reference>s [in that <from clause>]. The ... Cartesian product, CP, is the multiset of all rows r such that r is the concatenation of a row from each of the identified tables ...*

Note, therefore, that *CP* is not well-defined!—the fact that the standard goes on to say that "The cardinality of *CP* is the product of the cardinalities of the identified tables" notwithstanding. Consider the tables T1 and T2 shown below:

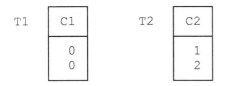

Either of the following fits the above definition for "the" Cartesian product *CP* of T1 and T2 (that is, either one could be "the" multiset referred to):

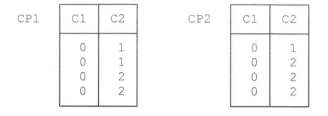

As an exercise, I suggest you try your hand at fixing up the wording of the standard appropriately. If you do try this exercise, I believe you'll find you're inevitably led into using the language of sets, not bags, in order to get around the errors and ambiguities.

Here's the second SQL problem. Consider the following cursor definition, which is intended to apply to the usual suppliers-and-parts database:

```
DECLARE X CURSOR
    FOR SELECT SP.S#, SP.QTY
        FROM    SP
```

Note that:

- Cursor X permits updates.

- The table that is visible through cursor X permits duplicates.

- The underlying table (table SP) does *not* permit duplicates.

Now suppose a "positioned UPDATE or DELETE" operation is executed via cursor X (UPDATE or DELETE ... WHERE CURRENT OF X). Then there's no way, in general, of saying precisely which row of table SP is being updated or deleted by that operation. How would you fix *this* problem?

(After you've given solutions to these two SQL problems, please write out one googol times "There's no such thing as a duplicate.")

Concluding Remarks

The letter from Alps concluded: "Whether or not to allow duplicates in SQL and relational databases seems to me to be more a practical question than a theoretical one." Well, regular readers of my database writings will know that I don't subscribe to the notion that "theoretical" and "practical" issues are at odds with one another. *Au contraire,* it's my strong position that theory—meaning relational theory specifically—is a highly practical matter. Thus, I want the system to be built on a solid, well-established theoretical foundation, for all the obvious good *practical* reasons. I further contend that bag theory, even if it could be made independent and respectable, simply doesn't enjoy the same long pedigree and high level of acceptance that set theory does. Thus, I want to build on set theory, not bag theory—*and I don't want duplicates!*

In this connection, I'd like to draw a possibly enlightening parallel ... The following remarks are due to Lauri Pietarinen (see the introduction to this chapter). In his review of an earlier draft, Lauri wrote:

It came to my mind that one way to look at the issue is to compare it to the GOTOless programming episode that started with Dijkstra's [letter] in 1968 ... Replace "programmer" by "query issuer" and "GOTOs" by "duplicates" in the following discussion:

Programmers used to use GOTOs because that seemed like a natural way to transfer control to another place in the program. Dijkstra declared GOTOs harmful in his landmark [letter], giving ways to eliminate them. Programmers resisted, because they felt they could not do all necessary things without GOTOs. They felt something had been taken away from them. However, programs with GOTOs were much harder to understand, and ... the compilers were bigger, buggier, and had a harder time optimizing the code.

*Little by little, new programming methodologies appeared that did away with GOTOs, and some newer programming languages did not even have GOTOs in the first place ... The old programmers had a hard time **not** using GOTOs, but the new ones were not even told about GOTOs and they managed to make perfectly decent programs without them (to say the least!).*

I'd like to close with the following argument (it's based on some remarks made by Hugh Darwen some years ago in a private letter to myself, and it effectively sums up my position on this whole business of duplicates):

1. We all agree that databases are made up of collections of "records"—or "rows," or "tuples," or whatever—of similar format, where each record has exactly one value for each item in the format (*aka* 1NF).

2. We all agree that different kinds of collections are useful for different purposes. Sometimes lists are wonderful, sometimes arrays, sometimes queues or stacks, sometimes sets, sometimes bags, etc.

3. Of these different kinds of collections, only one is *known* to provide, singlehanded, a basis for a complete model of data. And all of the others can be mapped, if need be, to this one.

4. To insist on supporting bags is equivalent to at least one of the following (probably more than one):

   - To insist on using at least two kinds of collection in one's model of data

   - To fall back on one of those kinds of collection for which no complete model of data has yet been developed, and therefore to have to go to the trouble of developing that theory (if it is available to be developed)

   - To be like SQL and attempt to apply the theory of relations to bags of tuples without fully checking its applicability, consequently making mistakes (like taking relational theorems to hold equally well for such bags, or misdefining UNION), failing to provide interpretations for operations whose relational interpretations don't hold for such bags (for example, Cartesian product is no longer just AND, and projection is no longer existential quantification), and delivering inferior products to the folks who are sensible and knowledgeable enough to stay with relations only

We don't need to argue against the (occasional) utility of bags of tuples, any more than we need to argue against the occasional utility of lists of tuples (why, those are what SQL cursors deliver!), or even stacks of tuples, queues of tuples, and arrays of tuples for that matter. In fact, why do the duplicate advocates specifically single out *bags* of tuples (only) for inclusion in their approach?

Appendix A: A Tuple-Bag Algebra?

In this appendix, I'd like to offer a few comments on the tuple-bag algebra presented in the book by Hector Garcia-Molina, Jeffrey D. Ullman, and Jennifer Widom (*Database System Implementation*, Prentice-Hall, 2000). That algebra, you might recall, was referenced in the letter from Lauri Pietarinen that I quoted in the opening to this chapter. Here first is an extract from page 237 of the book in question:[6]

> *[The relational] algebra involves operations on relations ... However, SQL uses a bag (multiset) model, rather than a set model. Also, there are operations in SQL, such as aggregation, grouping, and ordering (sorting), that are not part of the classical relational algebra. Thus, we need to reconsider this algebra in the light of its role as a representation for SQL queries.*

A few comments right away:

- So SQL uses "a bag (multiset) model," does it? OK: Where's that model defined? *Note:* Perhaps this question is unfair. Probably all that Garcia-Molina *et al.* mean is that the basic SQL construct is a bag, not a set, of rows. Well, OK again; but then I wish they wouldn't use such high-flown language to make such a simple point. As I've written elsewhere— see my article "Models, Models, Everywhere, Nor Any Time to Think" (Chapter 25 in the present book—I think the word "model" is one of the most grotesquely overused in the whole IT field.

- I don't quite know what Garcia-Molina *et al.* mean when they talk about "the classical relational algebra," but aggregation and grouping have been part of the algebra ever since the early 1970s; that seems classical enough to me! (In case you're interested, the reference I have in mind here is the paper by Patrick Hall, Peter Hitchcock, and Stephen Todd titled "An Algebra of Relations for Machine Computation," which appeared in the Conference Record of the 2nd ACM Symposium on Principles of Programming Languages, Palo Alto, Calif., January 1975. See also Stephen Todd's paper "The Peterlee Relational Test Vehicle—A System Overview," *IBM System Journal 15*, No. 4, 1976.)

- Ordering, by contrast, is *not* part of the relational algebra; nor can it be, because its result isn't a relation. This doesn't mean you can't have an ORDER BY operator, of course— it just means that operator isn't part of the algebra as such, and it can't be used in an expression that's nested inside some other (relational) expression, or more generally in any context where the result is indeed required to be a relation. That's why you can't use ORDER BY in a view definition, for example.

---

6. Most if not all of the quotes in this appendix are paraphrased just slightly from the original, mainly for typographical reasons. Of course, I've tried not to change the sense of any of them.

- "Reconsider this algebra"? No, "this algebra" is fine. What the authors need to do instead is define **a whole new algebra** that works on tuple-bags instead of relations.

- In fact, SQL isn't even based on a tuple-bag algebra, because SQL's "tuples" aren't tuples!—they have a left-to-right ordering to their components. As a consequence, for example, *R* JOIN *S* and *S* JOIN *R* give different results, in SQL. (I don't mean to suggest that *R* JOIN *S* is valid SQL syntax, of course—though you might be surprised to learn that *R* NATURAL JOIN *S* is.) Since my primary focus in the present chapter is on duplicates specifically, I won't make a big deal of this left-to-right ordering business here, but it *is* a significant issue in its own right. See Chapter 9 in the present book.

Anyway, a few pages later, in Section 6.1 of their book (the section is titled "An Algebra for Queries"), Garcia-Molina *et al.* proceed to present their tuple-bag algebra. Another quote:

> *[Relational] algebra was originally defined as if relations were sets* [sic!—boldface added]. *Yet relations in SQL are really* bags ... *Thus, we shall introduce relational algebra as an algebra on bags.*

Comment: Well, all right ... I think it was Chesterton who said you can call black white if you want to, and furthermore I would defend your right to do so—but I think I'd have to question your wisdom and your sanity if you actually did. The plain fact is, relations simply *are* sets,[7] not bags, and I don't think you do the cause of communication and understanding much of a service if you insist on pretending otherwise.

Furthermore, I don't think it's a good idea to try to define a theory to fit (force-fit?) established practice, especially if that established practice is bad. Rather, I think we should define a good theory first—the relational model suggests itself as a candidate[8]—and then try to get practice to follow that theory.

Be that as it may, it's an unfortunate fact that, so far as I can tell, the tuple-bag algebra presented by Garcia-Molina *et al.* completely ignores the relational algebra as currently understood in the relational world. Instead, it reinvents—not always terribly well, either—a variety of concepts that have been thoroughly investigated in the relational literature; the "aggregation and grouping" stuff is a case in point. It also bundles together certain constructs that, speaking personally, I would have much preferred to keep apart. Here are some specific quotes, with commentary:

> Projection ... *We shall extend this operator beyond classical relational algebra to allow renaming of attributes and construction of attributes by calculation ... just as the SQL SELECT clause does.*

Comment: I think it would be cleaner to keep "projection" to mean what it always did mean, and to use separate RENAME and EXTEND operators in order to achieve "renaming and construction of attributes" ... just as the relational algebra does. Another example of force-fitting the theory to bad established practice?

---

7. More precisely, the *body* of a relation is a set.
8. A heavy-handed attempt at humor on my part.

Product. *This operator is the set-theoretic Cartesian product ...*

Comment: No, it isn't!—it's the *bag*-theoretic Cartesian product. And as I pointed out earlier, in the section "Some More SQL Problems," it's hard to define, too. Indeed, Garcia-Molina *et al. don't* define it, they simply assume we all know what it is. What's more, they go on to say:

> *If* R *and* S *are relations, the* product R *TIMES* S *is a relation whose schema consists of the attributes of* R *and the attributes of* S. *Should there be an attribute name, say* a, *found in both schemas, then we use* R.a *and* S.a *as the names of the two attributes in the product schema.*

Comment: The proposed naming scheme is seriously flawed (and in any case it's unnecessary). As one example of the kind of problem it leads to, what are the names of the attributes "in the product schema" for the product *R* TIMES *R?* More important, what if the input relations *R* and *S* are derived relations?—in other words, what if they're represented by subexpressions that are more complex than just simple "relation names" and thus have no simple names of their own (implying that names of the form *R.a* are not even possible)? Indeed, the naming mechanism proposed by Garcia-Molina *et al.* here serves as strong evidence to support my earlier claim that the designers of this algebra cannot have paid much attention to the existing literature in this area. To be specific, the naming problem they're wrestling with was solved as far back as 1975—well over a quarter of a century ago!

> Union ... *For* R *UNION* S, *a tuple* t *is in the result as many times as the number of times it is in* R *plus the number of times it is in* S.

Comment: Here I just note that the operator defined isn't the usual bag union; it isn't the regular SQL UNION, either (in fact it's the SQL "UNION ALL" operator). The second of these points is acknowledged by Garcia-Molina *et al.*, but the first—which is more serious, in a way—isn't.

I could say quite a lot more regarding deficiencies in the proposed tuple-bag algebra, but we're supposed to be concentrating here specifically on why duplicates are a bad idea, so let me move on ... Now, I claimed in the body of this chapter that duplicates are an *optimization inhibitor.* And, of course, Garcia-Molina *et al.* do recognize this fact. In Section 7.2 ("Algebraic Laws for Improving Query Plans"), there are several points where they explicitly admit that dealing with bags instead of sets can get in the way of optimization, in one way or another. Some quotes:

> R *JOIN* S = S *JOIN* R ... *We might imagine that the order of [attributes] will be different [for the results of] the left and right [expressions here], but formally, tuples in relational algebra have no ... order of attributes.*

Comment: Actually, the problem here is not that we're dealing with bags instead of sets, but rather that the bags or sets in question don't contain tuples as such (see my earlier remarks in this appendix regarding left-to-right ordering of tuple components). But note the sneaky appeal to *relational* algebra in the middle of what's supposed to be an exposition of *tuple-bag* algebra! The sorry truth is that—as noted earlier—*R* JOIN *S* and *S* JOIN *R* are *not* equivalent, in SQL.

For instance, you may have learned set-theoretic laws such as A *INTERSECT (*B *UNION* C*) = (*A *INTERSECT* B*) UNION (*A *INTERSECT* C*), which is formally the "distributive law of intersection over union." This law holds for sets, but not for bags.*

Comment: Quite right. And this is just a "for instance"! It would be much more interesting— not to say more useful—to give an exhaustive list of such laws that hold for sets but not for bags.

R *WHERE* c1 *OR* c2 = *(*R *WHERE* c1*) UNION (*R *WHERE* c2*) ... [This] law ... works only if the relation* R *is a set* [sic!].

Comment: Yes. See my previous comment.

[Projection] keeps the number of tuples the same and only reduces the length of the tuples. In fact, ... sometimes a projection actually increases the length of tuples.

Comment: True *relational* projection doesn't "keep the number of tuples the same," it *reduces* the number of tuples (in general); thus, "doing projections early" is a good optimization tactic—in the relational world, but not in the tuple-bag world. As for projection "increasing tuple length": Well, no, true *relational* projection never does that, it's EXTEND that does that. As I said earlier, I think it would be better to treat these two as separate operators (and the confusions exhibited in the foregoing claim by Garcia-Molina *et al.* show why, in part).

I don't think I need to comment any further on this particular tuple-bag algebra here; I think I've made my point. That point might be summed up as follows:

- It doesn't matter whether an algebra can be defined for tuple bags.

- It doesn't matter whether expression transformation laws can be defined for such an algebra.

- What does matter is that the range of possible results that can be obtained from any given database is vastly expanded, though not usefully so.

- What matters further is that the range of logically distinct query expressions that can be formulated is vastly expanded, too, though again not usefully so. (Quite apart from anything else, think of the increased costs in terms of user education here!)

- What matters still further is that numerous logically distinct expressions *are* logically distinct only inasmuch as they produce different degrees of duplication in their results; those expressions thus can't be transformed into one another, even when it would be advantageous from a performance point of view to do so, and even when the user doesn't really care about the differences in the degree of duplication in their results. Note that even "law-abiding citizens"—that is, users who make sure always to avoid duplicates entirely—suffer here; that is, they still pay some price, simply because the system *permits* duplicates, even though they themselves never "take advantage" of this particular "feature" of the system.

- What also matters is that the optimizer itself is harder to write and harder to debug. DBMS product releases are thus delayed, and cost more, and are buggier, when they do appear. Again, law-abiding citizens pay a price for this.

- What also matters is that extensions to the language—probably SQL—are harder to define. Indeed, every time the SQL standards bodies consider the addition of some new construct to the SQL language, they have to consider the impact of duplicates on that new construct (view updating provides a good example of this problem). Again, we all pay a price for this ... The standard takes longer to appear, and is buggier when it does appear, than would otherwise have been the case. I say again: We all pay for this. (*Somebody* has to pay the standardizers for the extra time involved, too!)

- Finally, from my own current research interests, I know that all of the foregoing problems are going to be exacerbated yet again when the standard and the products start including support for temporal data.

So I make my plea one final[9] time: **Let's drop duplicates, once and for all!**

Appendix B: More on Counting Pennies

Following the original publication of the article on which this chapter is based, Andrew S. wrote:

> *Date [says]: "Please tell me exactly—**exactly**, please!—how you propose to count those 100 'duplicate' pennies. I do think that anyone who advocates the position that duplicates are a good idea needs to provide a good, convincing answer to this question ..."*
>
> **1.** *Weigh a penny.*
> **2.** *Weigh the bag.*
> **3.** *Weigh the bag of pennies.*
>
> *I haven't seen this challenge as originally issued, but obviously it must have actually referred to "duplicates" of nonphysical things.*

I replied to the foregoing as follows. First, it was good of Andrew to give me an "out" in his final sentence: "[Obviously the challenge as originally issued] must have referred to 'duplicates' of nonphysical things," or in other words to things for which the weighing trick won't work. In fact, however, I don't believe I need to appeal to this particular "out" in order to defend my position. The fact is, I don't find the weighing algorithm convincing at all. Consider the first step ("weigh a penny"). What does Andrew mean by "a penny"? Suppose I give him two pennies but assert that I'm giving him just one. **How does he know I'm wrong?** The answer has to be: **by counting.** *Thus, I submit that he has to be able to count pennies in order to be able to execute the first step of his algorithm.*

To the foregoing response Fabian Pascal, editor of the http://www.dbdebunk.com website, added the following (somewhat reworded here):

> *The following alternative formulation of the penny counting example might throw more light on the problem: "Suppose you have to count a pile of pennies, but suppose you also have to throw each penny back into the pile after you've counted it. How do you know when you're done?"*

---

9. "Final" here is wishful thinking, I expect.

Fabian also quoted the following from his own book *Practical Issues in Database Management: A Reference for the Thinking Practitioner* (Addison-Wesley, 2000):

What is the distinguishing attribute of otherwise identical entities, such as cake-mix boxes? In the real world, we distinguish ... such entities visually by their distinct locations in physical space. The lack of such distinction would mean there was only one entity! Indeed, entities are countable only if they are distinguishable! Since in the real world all entities are so distinguishable, duplicates represent "indistinguishable multiple enti-ties" and are, therefore, an inaccurate representation of reality. In a correct representation, propositions about individual boxes would, therefore, have to include a box identifier, say a box number, the representative in the database of the visual "this" vs. "that" distinction in the real world. Such identifiers are represented in the database by surrogate keys.

And he concluded:

[Note carefully that Andrew S.'s weighing] method implies no interest in the individual pennies, only in their count. And as I argue in the same [book], there should be one database row for the entity type "box in general," with the count made explicit in a column. Thus, whether there is interest in individual entities, or their count, rows must always be unique and there is no justification for duplicates. Note also that [Andrew S.'s] reference to "nonphysical entities"—which cannot be weighed—is particularly pertinent to database rows.

CHAPTER 11

■■■

Multiple Assignment

To targets properly defined
Separate values are assigned;
Disbelief we can suspend—
Constraints are checked at statement end.

—From *Where Bugs Go* (anon.)

We[1] have argued elsewhere—in particular in our book *Databases, Types, and the Relational Model: The Third Manifesto*, 3rd edition (Addison-Wesley, 2006), referred to hereinafter as just *The Third Manifesto* for short—that the only update operator that's logically necessary is **assignment**. All other update operators are just shorthand for certain assignments (and this remark is true of the familiar relational INSERT, DELETE, and UPDATE operators in particular). From the point of view of the underlying model, therefore, assignment is the only update operator we need consider; in the case of the relational model, in fact, this state of affairs is recognized explicitly. But it's the thesis of this chapter that the assignment operator in question needs to be what we call a **multiple** assignment, not the more conventional "single" form we're all familiar with. Loosely speaking, multiple assignment means we can assign to several variables at the same time. Here's a trivial example:

```
X := 1 , Y := 2 ;
```

The comma separator means the constituent assignments (to X and Y, respectively, in the example) are bundled up into a single statement. *Note:* We take it as axiomatic throughout this chapter that "statements are atomic." More precisely, we assume that no statement execution is ever allowed to fail in the middle (barring remarks, either explicit or implicit, to the contrary); statements either execute successfully in their entirety or have no effect at all, except possibly for raising an exception.

Now, the foregoing example is not particularly interesting (certainly it fails to convey any hint of the importance we attach to multiple assignment in general), because it's equivalent, more or less, to the following sequence of two separate single assignments:

```
X := 1 ;   Y := 2 ;
```

---

1. This chapter was written jointly by Hugh Darwen and myself.

As we'll see later, however, that qualifier "more or less" is definitely needed. To be more specific:

- With the two separate assignments, a certain notion of *betweenness* can be defined; that is, we can sensibly talk about the state of affairs that exists in the system after the first assignment has been executed and before the second has. For example, we can sensibly ask what the value of X is between the two assignments.

- With the original multiple assignment, by contrast, there's no such notion; the concept of there being some intermediate state between the two constituent assignments has no meaning, and thus we cannot (for example) sensibly ask what the value of X is "after the first assignment and before the second."

Here's another example, perhaps a little more convincing than the previous one:

```
X := Y , Y := X ;
```

This statement has the effect of interchanging the values of X and Y (regardless of what those values might be). Without multiple assignment, we can achieve this effect only indirectly—namely, by introducing an intermediate variable, as here:

```
Z := X ;  X := Y ;  Y := Z ;
```

What's more, there are some things that can't be done at all without multiple assignment, as we'll see later. In other words, multiple assignment is truly a primitive operator.

A Little History

We begin by briefly reviewing the concept of single assignment (which is just a special case of multiple assignment, of course). What exactly do we mean by the term "single assignment"? Well, we can surely agree that any assignment statement *S* specifies a set of *sources* and a set of *targets*, where the sources are values and the targets are variables[2] (and note that these remarks are valid even if *S* is specified in terms of some INSERT, DELETE, UPDATE, or similar shorthand). Usually, of course, there's just one source and one target, but the whole point of this chapter is to present arguments in favor of dropping this limitation. For the sake of definiteness, then, we define an assignment to be *single* if it specifies precisely one source and one target.

All imperative programming languages include support for single assignment, though the syntax varies considerably from language to language. Here are some examples of the various syntactic styles currently in use:

```
ALGOL:    X := Y
APL:      X <- Y
COBOL:    MOVE Y TO X
FORTRAN:  X = Y
POP-2:    X -> Y
SQL:      SET X = Y
```

---

2. Or *pseudovariables* (see later in this section for an explanation of this term). We'll ignore pseudovariables until further notice.

All of these examples (even the POP-2 one) have the effect of assigning the value of the expression Y to the variable X. *Note:* We've deliberately omitted from those examples all of the various statement terminators (new line, semicolon, period, etc.) that are usually needed in practice. When we need to show an explicit terminator symbol later (especially in SQL contexts), we'll use a semicolon, as we did in our examples in the previous section. Also, we'll use the ALGOL symbol for assignment (":="), except when giving examples in specific languages that use some other syntax. (Just as an aside, we note that the syntax originally proposed for ALGOL was actually the reverse of what we see today; for example, the assignment "X := Y" would originally have been written "Y =: X" instead.)

Turning now to semantics, we define the effect of the single assignment

```
target := source
```

as follows: First, the expression *source* on the right side is evaluated; second, the result of that evaluation—i.e., the value denoted by that expression—is assigned to the variable *target* on the left side. Note further that:

- We assume for simplicity that *target* and *source* are of the same type. In other words, we ignore:

  a. The possibility that the value denoted by *source* might be implicitly converted ("coerced") to the type of *target*

  b. The possibility that the value denoted by *source* might be of some proper subtype of the declared type of *target*

  Neither of these simplifying assumptions has any significant impact on the discussions to follow.

- We also assume that if the variable denoted by *target* is declared to be of type *T*, then the assignment assigns to that variable a value of type *T*. In other words, we do not embrace the semantics, found in some object languages, according to which declaring a variable to be of type *T* really means the variable contains the *address* of some object of type *T*, and "assigning Y to X" really means assigning the *address*, not the *value*, of Y to X.

- We abide by *The Assignment Principle*, which can be stated thus:

  Following assignment of *source* to *target*, the boolean expression *source* = *target* evaluates to TRUE.

  Now, this principle is so obvious, even trivial, that it might seem hardly worth stating, let alone dignifying with such a grand name. But it's violated so ubiquitously!—especially in SQL. For example:

  a. Let X be an SQL variable of type CHAR(3), and let Y be the string 'AB' (of length 2). After the assignment SET X = Y, then, the comparison X = Y does *not* necessarily evaluate to TRUE. (To be precise, it evaluates to TRUE if and only if PAD SPACE applies to the pertinent "collation"; otherwise it evaluates to FALSE. See *A Guide to the SQL Standard*, 4th edition, Addison-Wesley, 2000, by C. J. Date and Hugh Darwen, for further explanation.)

b. Let X be an SQL variable of any type, let Y be an SQL variable of the same type as X, and let Y currently be NULL. After the assignment SET X = Y, then, the comparison X = Y certainly does not evaluate to TRUE (in fact it evaluates to UNKNOWN).

That said, however, we now have to add that *The Assignment Principle* is not particularly relevant to the discussions of this chapter as such. We mention it here mainly for reasons of completeness.

For the remainder of this section, we take the unqualified term "assignment" to mean single assignment specifically, barring explicit statements to the contrary.

Now, assignment as originally defined in most languages was a *scalar* operator specifically, meaning the source was a scalar expression and the target was a scalar variable. Subsequently, however, some languages introduced various kinds of nonscalar assignments. For example, in PL/I (which uses the same syntactic style as FORTRAN for assignment), the following code fragment is valid:

```
DECLARE H (10) INTEGER ;
DECLARE K (10) INTEGER ;

H = K ;
```

Explanation: H and K here are one-dimensional array variables of ten elements each, and the assignment assigns the current value of K to H. But that assignment is really just shorthand—its overall effect is defined to be equivalent to that of the following loop:

```
DO I = 1 TO 10 ;
   H(I) = K(I) ;
END ;
```

The fact that such assignments are just shorthand leads to complications, however. Suppose we revise the example thus:

```
DECLARE H (10) INTEGER ;
DECLARE K (10) INTEGER ;

H = K + H(1) ;
```

The first thing that happens in the expanded form of the assignment here is that a "new" value is assigned to H(1). But what happens next? To be more specific, in the implicit assignments to H(2), H(3), ..., and H(10), which value of H(1) is used—the "old" one or the "new" one? In other words, which of the following code fragments more accurately represents the semantics of the original array assignment?

```
                              |    TEMP = H(1) ;
DO I = 1 TO 10 ;              |    DO I = 1 TO 10 ;
   H(I) = K(I) + H(1) ;       |       H(I) = K(I) + TEMP ;
END ;                         |    END ;
```

Considerations such as the foregoing quickly lead to the conclusion that nonscalar assignment needs to be genuinely defined as such: namely, as a "lock, stock, and barrel" assignment of a certain *single* (albeit nonscalar) value to a certain *single* (albeit nonscalar) variable. In the example, the effect of such a definition would be as follows (conceptually, at any rate): First, the "old" value of the first element, H(1), of the array variable H would be added to each and every element of the array variable K to yield a "new" array value, *v* say; second, that "new" array value *v* would then be assigned to the array variable H. In other words, the overall assignment would really just be a new kind of single assignment.[3]

Another extension to assignment as originally defined involves the use of *pseudovariables* (this term is taken from PL/I; *virtual variables* might be a little more apt). Pseudovariables are discussed at length in Chapter 6 in the present book, so we content ourselves here with a very brief review of a few salient points from that chapter. Essentially, a *pseudovariable reference* consists of an operational expression appearing in the target position of an assignment (i.e., on the left side, in our preferred syntax). Consider the following PL/I code fragment:

```
DECLARE CS CHAR(6) ;

CS = 'Middle' ;
SUBSTR ( CS, 2, 1 ) = 'u' ;
```

Variable CS here is defined to contain character strings of length exactly six characters. After the first assignment, the variable has the value 'Middle'; after the second, it has the value 'Muddle'—the effect of that second assignment is to "zap" the second character position within the variable, replacing the 'i' by a 'u'. The expression on the left side of that second assignment is a pseudovariable reference.

Now, it should be clear that the second assignment in the foregoing example is really shorthand for the following longer one:

```
CS := SUBSTR ( CS, 1, 1 ) || 'u' || SUBSTR ( CS, 3, 4 ) ;
```

Here the left side is a simple variable reference, as is normally required for assignment. As for the right side, the expression on that side denotes the character string obtained by concatenating, in left-to-right order, the first character of the current value of CS, the character 'u', and the last four characters of the current value of CS. It follows that the overall assignment has the effect already explained.

Note: The fact that the original assignment in the foregoing example is really just shorthand for some longer assignment isn't just a fluke; rather, it's *always* the case that an assignment that involves a pseudovariable reference is logically equivalent to some other assignment that does not. Thus, pseudovariables aren't logically required—they act merely as shorthand—but they can be extremely useful in practice.

One form of pseudovariable that we regard as particularly important makes use of what we call *THE_ operators*. Consider the following code fragment, expressed in **Tutorial D** (the language we use for examples in *The Third Manifesto*):

```
TYPE POINT      /* geometric points in two-dimensional space */
     POSSREP { X RATIONAL, Y RATIONAL } ;

VAR P POINT INIT POINT ( 0.0, 0.0 ) ;

THE_Y ( P ) := 5.0 ;
```

---

3. We note in passing that the original (IBM) version of PL/I and the ANSI standard version differ on this issue. In terms of our example, the IBM version would indeed use the "new" value of H(1) in the implicit assignments to H(2), H(3), ..., and H(10), while the standard version would not.

Explanation: Values of type POINT can "possibly be represented" by x and y coordinates, each of which is a rational number (see the POSSREP specification). Variable P is declared to be of type POINT and has initial value the origin—i.e., the point whose x and y coordinates are both zero (see the INIT specification). The assignment statement then sets P's y coordinate to the value five.

As you can see, the assignment statement in this example does involve assignment to a pseudovariable. Overall, that statement is shorthand for the following expanded form:

```
P := POINT ( THE_X ( P ), 5.0 ) ;
```

The expression on the right side here is a *selector invocation,* in *The Third Manifesto* terms. (To be specific, it's an invocation of that unique selector that corresponds to the possible representation we declared for type POINT; by default, that possible representation has the same name as the type—*viz.,* POINT—and the selector in turn has the same name as that possible representation.) Selectors are operators that are used to "select," or specify, values of some specified type; every type has exactly one selector for each possible representation that's declared for the type in question. In the example, the selector invocation selects exactly that point whose x coordinate is that of the point value contained in variable P and whose y coordinate is five. (As a matter of fact, we've already seen another example of a POINT selector invocation: namely, the expression POINT(0.0,0.0), which appears in the INIT specification in the definition of variable P.)

For further explanation of possible representations, selectors, THE_ operators, and related matters, we refer you to either Chapter 6 or *The Third Manifesto.*

Assigning to Several Variables at Once

We turn now to multiple assignment. Earlier, we characterized multiple assignment as an operator that lets us assign to several variables at the same time, loosely speaking. Now, the idea of "assigning to several variables at the same time" is far from new—many languages provide some such facility already. In ALGOL, for example, we can say:

```
A := B := C := D ;
```

The effect of this statement is to assign the value of the source expression D to each of the target variables A, B, and C. More precisely, the statement is defined to be shorthand for a sequence of statements along the following lines:

```
TEMP := D ;
A := TEMP ;
B := TEMP ;
C := TEMP ;
```

In other words, the source expression is evaluated just once, and the result of that evaluation is then assigned to each of the target variables in sequence. *Note:* Actually there's a slight complication here if any of the targets involves a subscript, but we can safely ignore the details of that complication for present purposes.

Analogously, in PL/I we can say:

```
A, B, C = D ;
```

Again the effect is to assign the value of D to each of A, B, and C.[4] *Note:* The same complication regarding subscripts applies here as well. Moreover, there are additional complications in the PL/I case that don't apply to the ALGOL counterpart. For example, what does the following do?

```
SUBSTR ( CS, 1, 2 ), SUBSTR ( CS, 2, 2 ) = 'co' ;
```

But, again, such matters need not concern us here.

Next, some languages also support certain nonscalar assignments, as we already know. If those assignments are regarded as, in effect, assigning to several scalar variables "at the same time," they might be thought of as another kind of multiple assignment. As already explained, however, we believe they should *not* be so regarded but should rather be defined as true nonscalar assignments, in which case they aren't multiple assignments at all but single assignments instead.

Third, in his book *A Discipline of Programming* (Prentice-Hall, 1976), Edsger W. Dijkstra briefly discusses what he calls a *concurrent* form of assignment, according to which, e.g., the statement

```
X, Y := Y, X ;
```

has the effect of interchanging the values of X and Y. (Near the beginning of this chapter, we used a statement of the form

```
X := Y , Y := X ;
```

to achieve the same effect.) In other words, the syntax of Dijkstra's concurrent assignment looks something like this:

```
target-commalist := source-commalist ;
```

The two commalists must contain the same number, n say, of sources and targets.[5] The semantics are as follows: First, all n sources are evaluated; second, the result of evaluating the ith source is assigned to the ith target ($i = 1, 2, ..., n$). Note carefully, however, that the targets must all be distinct. As Dijkstra puts it, "it would be foolish to attach to X, X := 1, 2 any meaning other than *error*" (we've reworded Dijkstra's remarks just slightly here).

Last, consider the following SQL UPDATE statement:

```
UPDATE  EMP
SET     SALARY = 1.1 * SALARY ,
        BONUS = SALARY
WHERE   DEPT = 'Programming' ;
```

The effect of this statement, loosely, is to set the bonus equal to the current salary and to increase the salary by ten percent for every employee in the programming department. It might be claimed, therefore, that we have here yet another example of multiple assignment: The UPDATE assigns to

---

4. PL/I even uses the term *multiple assignment* to refer to this kind of facility. By contrast, Robert W. Sebesta (in his book *Concepts of Programming Languages*, Benjamin/Cummings, 1989) refers to it as *multiple target assignment*, which is actually a better term for this particular construct (because it captures the essence of what's going on a little better).

5. In case you're not familiar with the useful term *commalist*, here's a rough definition: The expression *<xyz commalist>* denotes a sequence of zero or more *<xyz>*s in which each pair of adjacent *<xyz>*s is separated by a comma (as well as, optionally, one or more blanks).

several portions of several rows "at the same time" within table EMP.[6] It resembles Dijkstra's concurrent assignment in that:

a. All of the expressions on the right sides of assignments in the SET clause are evaluated before any of those assignments are performed.

b. No two of those assignments are allowed to specify the same target column. (Actually, we're simplifying matters just slightly here. See Appendix A for further discussion of this point.)

Incidentally, please note that we said "it might be claimed" that the SQL UPDATE statement constitutes an example of multiple assignment. We should make it clear, however, that we wouldn't make any such claim ourselves. In fact, we've argued at length, in *The Third Manifesto* and elsewhere, that UPDATE in SQL—and in a relational language like **Tutorial D,** come to that—is best understood as shorthand for assigning *a single value* (namely, a relation value) to *a single variable* (namely, a relation variable); in other words, it's really another case of nonscalar single assignment. Analogous remarks apply to INSERT and DELETE, of course.

Be that as it may, we can summarize the discussions of this section by observing that there are at least four constructs in the literature already that might lay some claim to being called "multiple assignment":

1. An assignment that assigns the same source value (more precisely, the result of evaluating the same source expression) to several targets

2. Nonscalar assignment

3. Dijkstra's concurrent assignment

4. SQL's UPDATE statement

However, the kind of multiple assignment we believe we need, and the kind we'll be discussing in the rest of this chapter, is different from all of these! Dijkstra's notion of concurrent assignment is, perhaps, closest to what we have in mind. Unlike Dijkstra, however, we do not require that the target variables all be distinct; in some cases, in fact, we explicitly want to be able to specify the same target variable more than once, for reasons that should become clear as we proceed.

---

6. In this chapter we use the terms *table, row,* and *column* in SQL contexts (mainly in Appendix A), the more formal terms *relation, tuple,* and *attribute* elsewhere.

A Multiple Assignment Example

At this point, it would be nice if we could say exactly what our multiple assignment operator is. As you might expect, however, the fact that we want to be able to specify the same target variable more than once causes complications, and we aren't yet in a position to explain just what those complications are. Until further notice, therefore, we focus not so much on what the operator actually is, but rather on why we need it and why systems should support it—and we hope our examples will be sufficient, for now, to give some idea as to how it's supposed to work.

As a basis for our first example, consider the usual suppliers-and-parts database, with definition as follows (**Tutorial D** syntax):

```
VAR S RELATION          /* suppliers */
    { S#     S#,
      SNAME  CHAR,
      STATUS INTEGER,
      CITY   CHAR }
    KEY { S# } ;

VAR P RELATION          /* parts */
    { P#     P#,
      PNAME  CHAR,
      COLOR  COLOR,
      WEIGHT WEIGHT,
      CITY   CHAR }
    KEY { P# } ;

VAR SP RELATION         /* shipments */
    { S#     S#,
      P#     P#,
      QTY    QTY }
    KEY { S#, P# }
    FOREIGN KEY { S# } REFERENCES S
    FOREIGN KEY { P# } REFERENCES P ;
```

S, P, and SP here are *relation variables* or **relvars** (see *The Third Manifesto* for further explanation). Sample values for those relvars are shown in Figure 11-1.

S	S#	SNAME	STATUS	CITY		SP	S#	P#	QTY
	S1	Smith	20	London			S1	P1	300
	S2	Jones	10	Paris			S1	P2	200
	S3	Blake	30	Paris			S1	P3	400
	S4	Clark	20	London			S1	P4	200
	S5	Adams	30	Athens			S1	P5	100
							S1	P6	100
							S2	P1	300
							S2	P2	400

P	P#	PNAME	COLOR	WEIGHT	CITY		S3	P2	200
							S4	P2	200
	P1	Nut	Red	12.0	London		S4	P4	300
	P2	Bolt	Green	17.0	Paris		S4	P5	400
	P3	Screw	Blue	17.0	Oslo				
	P4	Screw	Red	14.0	London				
	P5	Cam	Blue	12.0	Paris				
	P6	Cog	Red	19.0	London				

Figure 11-1. *The suppliers-and-parts database (sample values)*

Suppose now that this database is subject to the constraint "Supplier S1 and part P1 must never be in different cities." Here's a **Tutorial D** formulation of this constraint:

```
CONSTRAINT S1_P1_COLOCATED
    COUNT ( ( S WHERE S# = S# ('S1') ) { CITY }
            UNION
            ( P WHERE P# = P# ('P1') ) { CITY } ) ≤ 1 ;
```

Paraphrasing: If relvars S and P contain tuples for supplier S1 and part P1, respectively, then those tuples must contain the same CITY value (if they didn't, the COUNT invocation would return the value two); however, it's legal for relvar S to contain no tuple for S1, or relvar P to contain no tuple for P1, or both.

Given the sample values shown in Figure 11-1, then, each of the following UPDATEs will fail:

```
UPDATE S WHERE S# = S# ('S1') ( CITY := 'Paris' ) ;
```

```
UPDATE P WHERE P# = P# ('P1') ( CITY := 'Paris' ) ;
```

By contrast, the following UPDATE will succeed (note the comma separator):

```
UPDATE S WHERE S# = S# ('S1') ( CITY := 'Paris' ) ,
UPDATE P WHERE P# = P# ('P1') ( CITY := 'Paris' ) ;
```

Explanation: Of course, UPDATE is really assignment, and the various statements in this example are basically all assignment statements. For example, the statement

```
UPDATE S WHERE S# = S# ('S1') ( CITY := 'Paris' ) ;
```

(the one that attempts to move supplier S1 to Paris) is shorthand for the following:

```
S := WITH ( S WHERE S# = S# ('S1') ) AS T1 ,
          ( EXTEND T1 ADD ( 'Paris' AS NEWCITY ) ) AS T2 ,
          ( T2 { ALL BUT CITY } ) AS T3 ,
          ( T3 RENAME ( NEWCITY AS CITY ) ) AS T4 :
          ( S MINUS T1 ) UNION T4 ;
```

It follows that the successful UPDATE in the example is indeed a multiple assignment; in fact, it involves precisely two target variables, relvar S and relvar P, and it assigns one value to one of these variables and another to the other. By contrast, the UPDATEs that failed were both single assignments. And so we have here our first example of a multiple assignment that can't be simulated by a sequence of single assignments; as we claimed in the introduction, there are some things that can't be done at all without multiple assignment, and multiple assignment thus truly is a new primitive operator.

Aside: In case you're not familiar with the WITH construct (see the expanded version of the first UPDATE in the foregoing discussion), we digress for a moment to explain it. Basically, WITH allows us to introduce names for subexpressions and thereby to break a large, complicated expression into smaller, more digestible pieces. The introduced names can be regarded as denoting compiler-generated temporary variables. In the example, therefore, the overall assignment to relvar S can be thought of as equivalent to the following sequence of assignments—

```
T1 := S WHERE S# = S# ('S1') ;
T2 := EXTEND T1 ADD ( 'Paris' AS NEWCITY ) ;
T3 := T2 { ALL BUT CITY } ;
T4 := T3 RENAME ( NEWCITY AS CITY ) ;
S  := ( S MINUS T1 ) UNION T4 ;
```

—with the important distinction, of course, that the overall assignment is indeed a single statement, not a sequence of five separate statements. Alternatively, and more accurately, we could say that the original assignment to relvar S is equivalent to the following *single* assignment:

```
S := ( S MINUS ( S WHERE S# = S# ('S1') ) ) UNION
     ( ( ( EXTEND ( S WHERE S# = S# ('S1') )
           ADD ( 'Paris' AS NEWCITY ) ) { ALL BUT CITY } )
       RENAME ( NEWCITY AS CITY ) ) ;
```

End of aside.

Let's get back to the example. As that example correctly suggests, it's the fact that certain constraints are in effect that makes it impossible for certain multiple assignments to be replaced by a sequence of single assignments. But you might also have realized that we're making a tacit assumption here: To be specific, we're assuming that **all constraint checking is immediate,** meaning it's done at end-of-statement or, loosely, "at semicolons." You might therefore be thinking that if we had deferred the checking instead (to end-of-transaction), there would have been no need for the multiple assignment. And of course you'd be right in thinking that way. But we have good reasons for insisting that checking never be deferred in this sense—reasons that we'll be discussing in detail in the next section—and thus we believe the multiple assignment was necessary in the example after all.

Incidentally, the foregoing discussion serves to highlight a significant difference in emphasis (not the only one) between our multiple form of assignment and Dijkstra's concurrent form.

Our major reason for wanting to be able to perform several separate—though presumably interrelated—assignments as a single operation is to ensure that no integrity checking is done until all of the assignments in question have been executed. This emphasis on our part on the importance of integrity checking is understandable, given our database background. By contrast, Dijkstra's language presumably didn't support integrity constraints (in the usual database sense) at all; hence, the problems solved by our multiple assignment proposal presumably didn't arise.

To say it again, therefore: Given our assumption regarding immediate checking, there's no way the multiple assignment in the example we've been discussing can be simulated by any sequence of single assignments, and so multiple assignment really is a new primitive operator. *Note:* We first proposed such an operator in *The Third Manifesto,* but we didn't get it quite right—in fact, we got it wrong twice, in two different ways! We'll elaborate on this point in the section on semantics, later.

Why We Need Multiple Assignment

We saw in the previous section that one important reason—in fact, the overriding one—why we need multiple assignment is that we want to be able to perform several individual assignments without checking any constraints until all of the assignments in question have been executed. However, that's not the only reason. In this section, we identify several others.

Convenience: As we've already seen, the multiple assignment

```
X := Y , Y := X ;
```

is more convenient (more user-friendly, possibly less error-prone too) than its single-assignment counterpart

```
Z := X ;  X := Y ;  Y := Z ;
```

Note: This first point is perhaps not very compelling; however, it does become a little more so if the variables X and Y are nonscalar. Consider what happens if they're array variables, for example, when even the matter of having to declare the auxiliary variable Z becomes a little painful.

Assigning to several attributes at once: Suppose supplier S5 acquires a new name (Clark) and a new status (45) and moves to Paris. The statement

```
UPDATE S WHERE S# = S# ('S5')
    ( SNAME := 'Clark' , STATUS := 45 , CITY := 'Paris' ) ;
```

is preferable for several reasons to the following sequence of statements:

```
UPDATE S WHERE S# = S# ('S5') ( SNAME := 'Clark' ) ;
UPDATE S WHERE S# = S# ('S5') ( STATUS := 45 ) ;
UPDATE S WHERE S# = S# ('S5') ( CITY := 'Paris' ) ;
```

Note: Like the previous point, this point also is not very compelling, but for a different reason. It should be clear by now that each of the four UPDATEs just shown—including the first one in particular—is really a *single* assignment; each of them assigns a single relation value to the single relation variable (relvar) S. Thus, to think of the first of those UPDATEs in particular as somehow being a "multiple" assignment to the "variables" SNAME, STATUS, and CITY is strictly incorrect. (On the other hand, UPDATE does share with multiple assignment the property that all of the source expressions are evaluated before any targets are updated, a fact that can become significant if any of the source expressions include a reference to any of the targets.)

Assigning to several relvars at once (I): Suppose we want to enforce a "cascade delete" rule that says that when a supplier is deleted, all shipments for that supplier must be deleted too. For example:

```
DELETE S  WHERE S# = S# ('S1') ,
DELETE SP WHERE S# = S# ('S1') ;
```

Of course, we might expect the system (on request, of course) to perform such compensating actions on our behalf; if so, however, it simply means that multiple assignment is needed by the system as well as by the user—under the covers, in other words, as well as above them.

Assigning to several relvars at once (II): Consider the following database definition:

```
VAR EMP RELATION
  { EMP# EMP#, ENAME CHAR, DEPT# DEPT#, ... }
    KEY { EMP# }
    FOREIGN KEY { DEPT# } REFERENCES DEPT ;

VAR DEPT RELATION
  { DEPT# DEPT#, DNAME CHAR, EMP# EMP#, ... }
    KEY { DEPT# }
    FOREIGN KEY { EMP# } REFERENCES EMP ;
```

The semantics are that every employee works in exactly one department and every department has exactly one manager (and attribute EMP# in relvar DEPT# identifies the manager in question). Observe, therefore, that each of EMP and DEPT includes a foreign key that references the other. As a consequence, the multiple assignment

```
INSERT EMP  RELATION { TUPLE { EMP#  EMP# ('E1') ,
                               DEPT# DEPT# ('D1') } } ,
INSERT DEPT RELATION { TUPLE { EMP#  EMP# ('E1') ,
                               DEPT# DEPT# ('D1') } } ;
```

might well succeed where the following pair of assignments will fail (no matter which is executed first):

```
INSERT EMP  RELATION { TUPLE { EMP#  EMP# ('E1') ,
                               DEPT# DEPT# ('D1') } } ;
INSERT DEPT RELATION { TUPLE { EMP#  EMP# ('E1') ,
                               DEPT# DEPT# ('D1') } } ;
```

Assigning to several relvars at once (III): Consider the suppliers-and-parts database once again. Given the design illustrated in Fig. 1, every part is required to have a color. Suppose, however, that for some parts the color is irrelevant (and so need not be recorded), while for others the color is relevant but unknown. Then the following alternative design might be preferable[7] (for simplicity we ignore part names, weights, and cities):

```
VAR P RELATION          /* master parts list */
    { P# P# }
    KEY { P# } ;

VAR PCOL RELATION       /* parts with known color */
    { P#      P#,
      COLOR COLOR }
    KEY { P# }
    FOREIGN KEY { P# } REFERENCES P ;

VAR PNCOL RELATION      /* parts with no color */
    { P# P# }
    KEY { P# }
    FOREIGN KEY { P# } REFERENCES P ;

VAR PUCOL RELATION      /* parts with unknown color */
    { P# P# }
    KEY { P# }
    FOREIGN KEY { P# } REFERENCES P ;
```

Of course, the foregoing definitions ought also to include an explicit constraint to the effect that every part number appearing in relvar P must also appear in exactly one of the other three relvars. We omit the details of that constraint for simplicity (though we do assume it's being enforced). It should be clear, then, that, e.g., "inserting a new part" will require two updates: one on relvar P, and one on one of the other three relvars. (The situation is similar but not identical to that illustrated by the EMP/DEPT example above—the difference is that there's no foreign key, as such, from relvar P to any other relvar in this design.)

View updating: Consider a view V defined as A UNION B, for some A and B. Without going into details, it should be clear that an update to V will require updates to both A and B, in general, and hence that such an update to V is really shorthand for some multiple assignment (perhaps under the covers again).

Performance: Strictly speaking, we shouldn't even mention this point, since our primary concern is—as always—with getting the model right first before worrying about the implementation. But it does seem reasonable to expect that executing a multiple assignment will often be more efficient than executing an equivalent sequence of single ones (not to mention the fact that such an equivalent sequence might not even exist). In particular, such an expectation seems reasonable if the same target variable is specified more than once. For if the same target

---

7. Such designs are proposed in the presentation "How to Handle Missing Information Without Using Nulls," by Hugh Darwen (slides available at http://www.thethirdmanifesto.com). See also the paper "Nothing from Nothing" (in four parts), by David McGoveran, in the book *Relational Database Writings 1994–1997*, by C. J. Date, Hugh Darwen, and David McGoveran (Addison-Wesley, 1998).

variable, *V* say, is specified *n* times in a given multiple assignment, we can surely expect the implementation to access *V* just once, while *n* separate single assignments will probably involve *n* separate accesses.

Why Integrity Checking Must Be Immediate

Note: The material of this section previously appeared, in somewhat different form, in *An Introduction to Database Systems*, 8th edition, by C. J. Date (Addison-Wesley, 2004).

We now proceed to justify our position that all constraint checking must be done immediately (i.e., at end-of-statement), not deferred to end-of-transaction. The first and biggest point is this: As we've shown elsewhere—see, e.g., Hugh Darwen's paper "What a Database *Really* Is: Predicates and Propositions," in C. J. Date, Hugh Darwen, and David McGoveran, *Relational Database Writings 1994–1997* (Addison-Wesley, 1998)—a database can be regarded as *a collection of propositions* (assumed by convention to be ones that evaluate to TRUE). And if that collection is ever allowed to include any inconsistencies, **then all bets are off**. We can never trust the answers we get from an inconsistent database! While it might be true, thanks to the well-known isolation property of transactions, that no more than one transaction will ever see any particular inconsistency, the fact remains that that particular transaction does see the inconsistency and can therefore produce wrong answers. Indeed, it's precisely because inconsistencies can't be tolerated, not even if they're never visible to more than one transaction at a time, that the constraints need to be enforced in the first place.

Note: In our opinion, the foregoing argument is strong enough to stand on its own. In case you're still not convinced, however, here are some further arguments in support of our position.

- It's well known that transactions are supposed to be isolated from one another. Unfortunately, however, the term *isolation* doesn't mean the same in the world of transactions as it does in ordinary English; to be specific, it doesn't mean that transactions can't communicate with one another. If transaction T1 produces some result that's subsequently read by transaction T2, then T1 and T2 aren't truly isolated from each other (and this remark applies regardless of whether the transactions in question run concurrently or otherwise). In particular, therefore, if (a) T1 is allowed to see an inconsistent state of the database and hence produces an incorrect result, and (b) that result is then seen by T2, then (c) the inconsistency seen by T1 has effectively propagated to T2. In other words, it can't really be guaranteed that a given inconsistency (if such a thing were permitted) *will* be seen by just one transaction, anyway.

- Second, it's often thought that constraints that involve just one relvar ("relvar constraints") should be checked immediately but constraints that span relvars ("database constraints") should be checked at end-of-transaction. But the very same real-world constraint might be a relvar constraint with one design for the database and a database constraint with another. For example, consider two possible designs for the suppliers-and-parts database, one as illustrated in Figure 11-1 and one in which suppliers are represented by four separate relvars, thus:

```
SS { S# }
SN { S#, SNAME }
ST { S#, STATUS }
SC { S#, CITY }
```

This latter design requires (among many other things) a database constraint—actually a foreign key constraint—to say that every supplier number appearing in relvar SS must also appear in relvar ST ("every supplier must have exactly one status"). With the design of Figure 11-1, by contrast, the desired effect is achieved by the primary key constraint on relvar S (a relvar constraint). Thus, if we agree that relvar constraints must be checked immediately, it follows that database constraints must be checked immediately as well.

- Third, the ability to perform "semantic optimization" requires the database to be consistent *at all times* (more precisely, at statement boundaries), not just at transaction boundaries. *Note:* Semantic optimization is a technique for using integrity constraints to simplify queries in order to improve performance. Clearly, if the constraints aren't satisfied, then the simplifications won't be valid. See the book mentioned at the beginning of this section (*An Introduction to Database Systems*) for further discussion.

- Fourth, we don't want every application and the code of every user-defined operator to have to cater for the possibility that the database might be inconsistent. There is a severe loss of orthogonality if a procedure that assumes consistency becomes unsafe to use while constraint checking is deferred.

Having presented all of these arguments, we now have to admit that—of course—the conventional wisdom is that database constraint checks, at least, surely *have* to be deferred. By way of example, consider again the constraint from the section "A Multiple Assignment Example" to the effect that supplier S1 and part P1 must never be in different cities, implying among other things that if supplier S1 moves to Paris, then part P1 must move to Paris as well. The conventional solution to this problem is (a) to define the constraint to be "deferred" (meaning it's checked only at end-of-transaction) and then (b) to wrap the two updates up into a single transaction, like this:

```
BEGIN TRANSACTION ;
    UPDATE S WHERE S# = S# ('S1') ( CITY := 'Paris' ) ;
    UPDATE P WHERE P# = P# ('P1') ( CITY := 'Paris' ) ;
COMMIT ;
```

In this conventional solution, the constraint is checked at COMMIT, and the database is inconsistent between the two UPDATEs.[8] Note in particular that if the transaction were to ask the question "Are supplier S1 and part P1 in different cities?" between the two UPDATEs, it would get the answer *yes*. And this fact is a major reason why we want to support multiple assignment! With multiple assignment, as we know, we can perform both UPDATEs as a single operation, thus:

```
UPDATE S WHERE S# = S# ('S1') ( CITY := 'Paris' ) ,
UPDATE P WHERE P# = P# ('P1') ( CITY := 'Paris' ) ;
```

Now no integrity checking is done until both UPDATEs have been done (i.e., "until we reach the semicolon"), and there's no way for the transaction to see an inconsistent state of the database between the two UPDATEs, because the notion of "between the two UPDATEs" now has no meaning.

---

8. The conventional solution therefore can't be expressed in **Tutorial D**—even though we've pretended for the sake of the example that it can—precisely because **Tutorial D** doesn't support deferred constraints.

Assigning to a Variable More Than Once

Recall that assignment to a THE_ pseudovariable (like assignment to any pseudovariable, in fact) is really shorthand for a longer assignment that doesn't involve pseudovariables at all. For example, the assignment

```
THE_Y ( P ) := 5.0 ;
```

is shorthand for the following expanded form:

```
P := POINT ( THE_X ( P ), 5.0 ) ;
```

Suppose now that the initial value of the variable P is the origin, which we will denote by (0.0,0.0) for brevity, and consider the following multiple assignment:

```
THE_X ( P ) := 7.0 , THE_Y ( P ) := 5.0 ;
```

Expanding the two constituent assignments gives:

```
P := POINT ( 7.0, THE_Y ( P ) ) ,
P := POINT ( THE_X ( P ), 5.0 ) ;
```

What are the semantics of this expanded version? Well, suppose we apply the usual rule—namely, we evaluate all of the right sides first (i.e., before doing any assignments), and then we go on to perform the actual assignments. Then the net result is that P is assigned the point value (0.0,5.0)—*not* the point value (7.0,5.0) as required; in other words, the assignment to THE_X has had no lasting effect. (To be more precise, it does have an effect in the first of the two constituent assignments, but the second of those assignments then causes the result of the first to be overwritten.)

Clearly, what we need to do is collect together the two constituent assignments somehow, such that the result of the first is *combined* with that of the second instead of being overwritten by it. We'll show how this can be done in the next section. First, however, we want to say a little more regarding the foregoing example specifically.

Now, you've probably realized for yourself that the example in question involves, precisely, a multiple assignment in which the same variable, P, appears as a target more than once. What's more, this state of affairs is exactly what we want; we *want* to assign to the same variable more than once—though, admittedly, we want to assign to different *portions* of that variable in different constituent assignments (speaking a trifle loosely). Thus, while we might agree with Dijkstra that a multiple assignment of the form

```
X := 1 , X := 2 ;
```

doesn't make much sense, we don't agree that assigning to the same variable more than once is necessarily an error. In particular, therefore, we don't want to impose a syntax rule to that effect.

Let's look at a couple more examples. First, here's one involving arrays:

```
VAR IA ARRAY INTEGER [5]
      INIT ARRAY INTEGER [ 1, 2, 3, 4, 5 ] ;

IA[4] := 0 , IA[2] := 8 ;
```

Expanded version of this assignment:[9]

```
IA := ARRAY INTEGER [ IA[1], IA[2], IA[3], 0, IA[5] ] ,
IA := ARRAY INTEGER [ IA[1], 8, IA[3], IA[4], IA[5] ] ;
```

The constituent assignments here both involve the same target variable: namely, the array variable IA. Of course, we would like the overall multiple assignment to be equivalent to the following:

```
IA := ARRAY INTEGER [ IA[1], 8, IA[3], 0, IA[5] ] ;
```

Again, we'll explain how this effect can be achieved in the next section.

For a final example, we return to suppliers and parts. Suppose that for some (bizarre!) reason, relvar S is subject to the constraint that suppliers S2 and S3 must have total status 40. Then each of the following single assignments will fail (we use the UPDATE shorthand for convenience):

```
UPDATE S WHERE S# = S# ('S2') ( STATUS := 15 ) ;
UPDATE S WHERE S# = S# ('S3') ( STATUS := 25 ) ;
```

But the following multiple assignment will succeed (again we use the UPDATE shorthand):

```
UPDATE S WHERE S# = S# ('S2') ( STATUS := 15 ) ,
UPDATE S WHERE S# = S# ('S3') ( STATUS := 25 ) ;
```

Again both of the constituent assignments involve the same target variable, here relvar S. (This time we leave the desired single-assignment equivalent as a—somewhat nontrivial—exercise for the reader.)

Semantics

The previous section should be sufficient to hint at some of the complications involved in getting the semantics of multiple assignment right; indeed, in *The Third Manifesto,* we got them wrong twice, as already mentioned. Partly because we believe that examining blind alleys can be instructive (and partly just for the record), we summarize our failed attempts here. Let multiple assignment *MA* consist of single assignments, in sequence, *A1, A2, ..., An.* Then:

- In *The Third Manifesto,* first edition, we simply defined *MA* to be equivalent to executing *A1, A2, ..., An* in sequence (except that no constraint checking was done until the end, of course). This definition didn't work because it meant (for example) that the assignment

  ```
  X := Y , Y := X ;
  ```

  would fail to interchange the values of X and Y (it would set X equal to Y but then leave Y unchanged).

---

9. Note the implication here that an expression such as IA[4] on the left side of an assignment is a pseudovariable reference; logically, it is.

- In the second edition, by contrast, we required all of the right sides to be evaluated first; then we required *A1, A2, ..., An* to be executed in parallel (followed by the constraint checking). This definition didn't work because it meant (for example) that the assignment

```
X := Y , X := Z ;
```

would have an unpredictable effect.

And in the book *Temporal Data and the Relational Model,* by C. J. Date, Hugh Darwen, and Nikos A. Lorentzos (Morgan Kaufmann, 2003), we got the semantics wrong *again* ... To be specific, we required all of the right sides to be evaluated first, and then we required *A1, A2, ..., An* to be executed in sequence instead of in parallel (followed by the constraint checking as usual). This definition didn't work because it meant (for example) that the assignment

```
THE_X ( P ) := 7.0 , THE_Y ( P ) := 5.0 ;
```

would have no effect on THE_X(P), as explained in the previous section.

Here then is our current last word (!) on the subject. Again, let *MA* be the multiple assignment

```
A1 , A2 , ... , An ;
```

Then the semantics of *MA* are defined by the following pseudocode (steps 1-4):

1. For $i := 1$ to n, expand any syntactic shorthands involved in *Ai*. After all such expansions, let *MA* take the form

```
V1 := X1 , V2 := X2 , ... , Vz := Xz ;
```

for some $z \geq n$, where *Vi* is the name of some variable not defined in terms of any others and *Xi* is an expression of declared type the same as that of *Vi*. Here:

   a. *Vi* ($i = 1, 2, ..., z$) is the name of some declared variable (not a pseudovariable) that's not defined in terms of any others. *Note:* We say "not defined in terms of any others" in order to take care of assignment to views. Views are variables that are defined in terms of others; thus, assignments to views are replaced by assignments to the relevant view-defining expressions, and *those* assignments are then replaced by assignments to the relvars in terms of which the views are defined. This process is repeated until all of the assignments have base relvars as their targets.

   b. *Xi* ($i = 1, 2, ..., z$) is an expression whose declared type is the same as that of *Vi. Note:* The declared type of an operational expression is the declared type of the result of the outermost operator involved in that expression.

2. Let p and q ($1 \leq p < q \leq z$) be such that *Vp* and *Vq* are identical and there is no r ($r < p$ or $p < r < q$) such that *Vp* and *Vr* are identical. Replace *Aq* in *MA* by an assignment of the form

```
Vq := WITH Xp AS Vq : Xq
```

   and remove *Ap* from *MA*. Repeat this process until no such pair p and q remains. Let *MA* now consist of the sequence

```
U1 := Y1 , U2 := Y2 , ... , Um := Ym ;
```

   where each *Ui* is some *Vj* ($1 \leq i \leq j \leq m \leq z$).

3. For $i := 1$ to m, evaluate Yi. Let the result be yi.

4. For $i := 1$ to m, assign yi to Ui.

We elaborate briefly on step 2, since the implications of that step might not be immediately apparent. Consider once again the multiple assignment

```
THE_X ( P ) := 7.0 , THE_Y ( P ) := 5.0 ;
```

In accordance with step 1, we first expand the two constituent assignments:

```
P := POINT ( 7.0, THE_Y ( P ) ) ,
P := POINT ( THE_X ( P ), 5.0 ) ;
```

Now we have two assignments with the same target. In accordance with step 2, therefore, we remove the first and replace the second by:

```
P := WITH POINT ( 7.0, THE_Y ( P ) ) AS P :
        POINT ( THE_X ( P ), 5.0 ) ;
```

This latter assignment in turn is equivalent to:

```
P := POINT ( THE_X ( POINT ( 7.0, THE_Y ( P ) ) ), 5.0 ) ;
```

And *this* assignment is equivalent to:

```
P := POINT ( 7.0, 5.0 ) ;
```

The desired result is thereby obtained.

By way of another example, suppose type POINT corresponds to points in *three*-dimensional space and can "possibly be represented" by coordinates x, y, and z, and consider the multiple assignment:

```
THE_X ( P ) := 7.0 , THE_Y ( P ) := 5.0 , THE_Z ( P ) := 6.0 ;
```

(where P is, of course, a variable of type POINT once again). Step 1 yields:

```
P := POINT ( 7.0, THE_Y ( P ), THE_Z ( P ) ) ,
P := POINT ( THE_X ( P ), 5.0, THE_Z ( P ) ) ,
P := POINT ( THE_X ( P ), THE_Y ( P ), 6.0 ) ;
```

Step 2 then yields:

```
P := WITH POINT ( 7.0, THE_Y ( P ), THE_Z ( P ) ) AS P :
      WITH POINT ( THE_X ( P ), 5.0, THE_Z ( P ) ) AS P :
          POINT ( THE_X ( P ), THE_Y ( P ), 6.0 ) ;
```

This assignment in turn is equivalent to:

```
P := POINT (
       THE_X ( POINT ( THE_X ( POINT ( 7.0,
                                       THE_Y ( P ),
                                       THE_Z ( P ) ) ),
                       5.0,
                       THE_Z ( POINT ( 7.0,
                                       THE_Y ( P ),
                                       THE_Z ( P ) ) ) ) ),
       THE_Y ( POINT ( THE_X ( POINT ( 7.0,
                                       THE_Y ( P ),
                                       THE_Z ( P ) ) ),
                       5.0,
                       THE_Z ( POINT ( 7.0,
                                       THE_Y ( P ),
                                       THE_Z ( P ) ) ) ) ),
       6.0 ) ;
```

And *this* assignment—if you analyze it carefully—turns out to be equivalent to:

```
P := POINT ( 7.0, 5.0, 6.0 ) ;
```

Syntax

In this section we summarize the syntax we've been using in our examples thus far. The syntax is based on that of **Tutorial D** but is deliberately simplified somewhat for the purposes of this chapter. In particular, we've tried to choose names for syntactic categories that are suggestive of the intended semantics; we've therefore felt free to omit numerous rules that would need to be stated (perhaps in prose form) in a more complete definition. We've included a few explanatory comments, however.

```
<assignment>
    ::=   <assign> [ , <assign commalist> ] ;
```

Comment: We reject the "obvious" syntax of Dijkstra's concurrent assignment (using a source commalist, a target commalist, and a single assignment symbol between them) because that syntax doesn't work very well when some of the constituent assignments are expressed as INSERTs or DELETEs or UPDATEs.[10]

---

10. In any case, **Tutorial D** generally spurns reliance on ordinal position as a basis for pairwise matching; left-to-right ordering of attributes of relations is expressly prohibited in the relational model, and it seemed a good design principle to apply the same rule to other constructs in the language. (The sole exception is found in invocations of prefix operators, where ordinal position is used, as in many other languages, to match up arguments and parameters.)

```
<assign>
    ::=    <scalar assign> | <nonscalar assign>

<scalar assign>
    ::=    <scalar target> := <scalar exp>

<scalar target>
    ::=    <scalar var ref> | <scalar pseudovar ref>
```

Comment: A *<scalar var ref>* is just a scalar variable name. We omit further details of *<scalar pseudovar ref>*.

```
<nonscalar assign>
    ::=    <relation assign>
```

Comment: The only kind of nonscalar assignment we discuss here is relational assignment, but we could clearly include other kinds if we wanted to (e.g., *<tuple assign>*, *<array assign>*, and so on).

```
<relation assign>
    ::=    <relation target> := <relation exp>
        |  <relation insert>
        |  <relation update>
        |  <relation delete>

<relation target>
    ::=    <relation var ref> | <relation pseudovar ref>
```

Comment: It is not our aim in this chapter to get into details of what *<relation pseudovar ref>*s might look like.

```
<relation insert>
    ::=    INSERT <relation target> <relation exp>

<relation delete>
    ::=    DELETE <relation target> [ WHERE <bool exp> ]
```

Comment: The *<bool exp>* is allowed to include an *<attribute ref>* wherever a literal would be allowed. An analogous remark applies to the production rule immediately following as well.

```
<relation update>
    ::=    UPDATE <relation target> [ WHERE <bool exp> ]
                ( <attribute update>
                  [ , <attribute update commalist> ] )

<attribute update>
    ::=    <attribute ref> := <exp>
```

Comment: The *<exp>* is allowed to include an *<attribute ref>* wherever a literal would be allowed.

Assigning to Several Components at Once

We have a significant piece of unfinished business to attend to. Suppose we're given a type ELLIPSE, defined as follows:

```
TYPE ELLIPSE
    POSSREP { A INTEGER, B INTEGER, CTR POINT
              CONSTRAINT A ≥ B } ;
```

Explanation: Ellipses can "possibly be represented" by their major semiaxis *a*, their minor semiaxis *b*, and their center (where we assume for simplicity that semiaxes are just integers and centers are points in two-dimensional space). For brevity, we will refer to the semiaxes and center of a given ellipse as its components. Please note immediately, however, that this usage is more than a little sloppy; the components in question aren't really components of the ellipse as such, they're components of the specified *possible representation* of that ellipse. But the usage is convenient, and we'll stay with it in this section.

Observe now that ellipses are subject to a **type constraint:** namely, the constraint that *a* must not be less than *b*. (It's the presence of that type constraint that makes this example different in kind from the POINT examples we've been using in earlier sections of the chapter.) Now let E be a variable of declared type ELLIPSE—

```
VAR E ELLIPSE ;
```

—and consider the following multiple assignment:

```
THE_A ( E ) := 7 , THE_B ( E ) := 3 ;
```

The intended effect, presumably, is to make the current value of E an ellipse with *a* = 7, *b* = 3, and center unchanged (i.e., the center should be the same as it was before the assignment). In other words, we want to "zap" the *a* and *b* components of E while leaving the center component alone. But what actually happens?

Well, let's expand the two constituent assignments:

```
E := ELLIPSE ( 7, THE_B ( E ), THE_CTR ( E ) ) ,
E := ELLIPSE ( THE_B ( E ), 3, THE_CTR ( E ) ) ;
```

Now we remove the first assignment and replace the second by:

```
E := WITH ELLIPSE ( 7, THE_B ( E ), THE_CTR ( E ) ) AS E :
          ELLIPSE ( THE_B ( E ), 3, THE_CTR ( E ) ) ;
```

Suppose the previous value of E had *a* = 10 and *b* = 4; then this assignment will work perfectly. But suppose the previous value of E had *a* = 10 and *b* = 8. Then the expression in the WITH clause—

```
ELLIPSE ( 7, THE_B ( E ), THE_CTR ( E ) )
```

—will raise a run-time error! To be specific, it will attempt to produce an ellipse with *a* = 7 and *b* = 8, thereby violating the type constraint on ellipses to the effect that *a* must not be less than *b*. To elaborate: The expression in question is a selector invocation once again. As you'll recall, selectors are operators that are used to "select," or specify, values of some specified type. By definition, such operators *cannot* yield a value that violates any type constraint that applies to the type in question. Type constraints are thus an exception to the general rule that constraint checking is done at end-of-statement ("at semicolons"); we can *never* countenance the existence of a value that is in violation of some pertinent type constraint, because such a value is a contradiction in terms (i.e., it's simply not a value of the pertinent type).

Now, we could avoid the problem in the case at hand by simply replacing the original multiple assignment to THE_A(E) and THE_B(E) by a *single* assignment, thus:[11]

```
E := ELLIPSE ( 7, 3, THE_CTR ( E ) ) ;
```

This solution is unattractive in general, however (imagine a type with a possible representation involving hundreds of components). We therefore propose another shorthand[12] (in syntactic terms, an additional form of *<scalar assign>*):

```
UPDATE <scalar target> ( <assign> [ , <assign commalist> ] )
```

Every *<assign>* target must be a component of the same possible representation for the declared type of the *<scalar target>*. For example:

```
UPDATE E ( A := 7, B := 3 ) ;
```

This example is an assignment statement, or in other words an *<assignment>*. That *<assignment>* in turn contains just one *<assign>*—in fact, a *<scalar assign>*—and that *<scalar assign>* takes the particular form under discussion. The overall statement is shorthand for the single assignment shown earlier:

```
E := ELLIPSE ( 7, 3, THE_CTR ( E ) ) ;
```

More generally, the *<scalar assign>*

```
UPDATE <scalar target> ( <assign> [ , <assign commalist> ] )
```

is defined as follows:

- Let the specified *<scalar target>* be *ST;* let its declared type be *T;* let the pertinent possible representation for *T* be *PR;* and let *PR* have components *C1, C2, ..., Cn* (only). Note that the name *PR* also denotes the selector operator corresponding to the possible representation *PR* (recall that possible representations and corresponding selectors have the same name).

- Syntactically, the commalist of *<assign>*s appearing between the braces is itself a multiple assignment, except that there is no terminating semicolon and hence no constraint checking (except for the special case of type constraints, of course).

- The *<assign>*s are processed in accordance with steps 1 and 2 of the definition given in the section "Semantics," earlier. After that processing is done, the resulting commalist of *<assign>*s must be such that every *<assign>* specifies some component *Ci* as its target. (Note that no two distinct *<assign>*s will specify the same target, thanks to step 2.)

---

11. Of course, we can't avoid the problem with the original multiple assignment by interchanging the two constituent assignments (consider what would happen if the previous value of E had $a = 2$ and $b = 1$, for example).
12. Patterned after a construct, *<tuple update>*, that already exists in **Tutorial D**. Observe, incidentally, that we're overloading the keyword UPDATE here (in fact it was already overloaded, being used for both *<tuple update>*s and *<relation update>*s, but now we're using it for *<scalar assign>*s as well).

- Then the specified *<scalar assign>* is defined to be semantically equivalent to the *<scalar assign>*

```
ST := PR ( X1, X2, ..., Xn )
```

The arguments Xi (i = 1, 2, ..., n) are defined as follows:

    a. If an *<assign>* exists for Ci, then let the source in that *<assign>* be X. For all j (j = 1, 2, ..., n), replace references in X to Cj by (THE_Cj(ST)). The version of X that results is Xi.

    b. Otherwise, Xi is THE_Ci(ST).

We close with a slightly more complicated example. Let variable E be of declared type ELLIPSE; recall that ellipses have a possible representation with components *a, b,* and center, this last being of declared type POINT. Then the statement—

```
UPDATE E ( A := 3, UPDATE CTR ( X := 5.0 ) ) ;
```

—is defined to be shorthand for the following:

```
E := ELLIPSE ( 3, THE_B ( E ),
               POINT ( 5.0, THE_Y ( THE_CTR ( E ) ) ) ;
```

Concluding Remarks

We have defined a new primitive operator that we call *multiple assignment.*[13] The fundamental purpose of that operator is, in effect, to allow the checking of certain constraints to be deferred for a little while, without the possibility that the user will ever see an inconsistent state of the database. However, the operator does have a number of subsidiary uses as well, which the chapter has also briefly examined.

Appendix A: Multiple Assignment in SQL

The SQL standard includes several features that can fairly be regarded as multiple assignment support. Some of those features are new with the most recent version of the standard (SQL:2003); others go all the way back to the very first version (SQL:1986); the rest were introduced at various points along the way. This appendix briefly surveys the features in question.

One point that's worth making right away is this: As just indicated, SQL's multiple assignment features were incorporated into the language piecemeal, and they don't seem to have been perceived as different aspects of the same general problem. As a consequence, they do suffer from a certain lack of orthogonality and parsimony in their design, as will be seen. The reader (or, more to the point, the user) is warned.

---

13. By the way, the word "multiple," which in practice is very often abused, is indeed the *mot juste* here. In general, a good way to tell whether the word is being used appropriately is to see whether it makes sense to replace it by, say, "triple" or "quadruple." This simple test shows immediately that remarks such as "There are multiple reasons to vote for Arnold" are not well expressed ("triple reasons"?). By contrast, "triple assignment" is a perfectly reasonable construction, and so is "multiple assignment."

The appendix is divided into four subsections. In the first, we present an overview of SQL's support for assignment in general, in order to lay some necessary groundwork. In the next two, we discuss the principal SQL assignment statement—i.e., the SET statement—in detail; the first covers single assignment and the second multiple. Finally, the fourth subsection describes certain relevant aspects of the regular SQL UPDATE statement.

Overview

SQL has always supported the well-known INSERT, DELETE, and UPDATE statements, of course (more recently it has added support for a MERGE statement, which is shorthand for a certain combination of INSERT and UPDATE). These statements can all be characterized as table-level assignments, though obviously they don't use conventional assignment syntax. Furthermore, they're all *single* assignments (i.e., they all assign a single source value to a single target variable).[14]

Second, SQL has also always supported the SELECT INTO and FETCH statements, which in fact are *multiple* assignments. For example, the following statement against the suppliers-and-parts database—

```
SELECT S.STATUS, S.CITY
INTO   XST, XSC
FROM   S
WHERE  S# = S#('S1') ;
```

—effectively assigns values to the two variables XST and XSC "at the same time." *Note:* Whether SELECT INTO and FETCH are scalar or nonscalar assignments (or even a mixture) depends on the types of the source expressions and the types of the target variables. The one thing they're not, though, is table-level assignments, because SQL does not permit tables to contain columns that contain further tables in turn.

Third, SQL also supports a variety of miscellaneous statements (e.g., GET DESCRIPTOR, GET DIAGNOSTICS) that can also be regarded as assignments of a kind. For simplicity we ignore such statements for the remainder of this appendix.

Fourth, and most important, SQL now includes an explicit assignment statement called SET (introduced with the Persistent Stored Modules feature, SQL/PSM). SET as originally defined supported single assignment only, but SQL:2003 extends it to support multiple assignment as well. It also supports both scalar and (some) nonscalar assignments, but "nonscalar" here unfortunately does *not* include tables; in fact, it includes arrays, rows, and nothing else.[15] It follows that SET cannot normally be used to update the database.

Fifth and last, SQL's regular UPDATE statement might be regarded as a kind of multiple assignment (see the discussion of this issue near the end of the section "Assigning to Several Variables at Once" in the body of the chapter). It also provides implicit support for multiple *table* assignment through (a) its ability to perform certain "compensating actions" (e.g., cascade delete) and (b) its ability to update certain views (join views in particular). We do not discuss

---

14. How best to characterize the "positioned" or CURRENT forms of DELETE and UPDATE we leave as an exercise for the reader.

15. Some might argue that it also includes "structured types." Certainly SET can be used to assign "structured values" to "structured variables" (as we'll see), but whether such values and variables are scalar or nonscalar is a matter of some debate. The issue is explored in detail in *An Introduction to Database Systems*, 8th edition, by C. J. Date (Addison-Wesley, 2004).

this implicit support any further in this appendix; however, we do have more to say regarding the UPDATE statement in particular (that's the subject of the final subsection).

The SET Statement: Single Assignment

As we saw in the body of the chapter, the single-assignment version of the SQL SET statement takes the form

```
SET target = source ;
```

The target can be a variable or a pseudovariable.[16] We consider the variable case first. Here are some examples. First a self-explanatory scalar example:

```
DECLARE I INTEGER ;

SET I = 0 ;
```

Note: All DECLARE statements shown in this appendix are SQL statements specifically (i.e., they have the effect of defining some SQL variable). Like SET, DECLARE was introduced into the SQL standard as part of the Persistent Stored Modules feature, SQL/PSM.

Next, an array example:

```
DECLARE H INTEGER ARRAY [10] ;
DECLARE K INTEGER ARRAY [10] ;

SET H = K ;
```

Note carefully that the SET statement here is indeed a single assignment (see the discussion of this issue in the section "A Little History" in the body of the chapter). It's also a nonscalar assignment. Incidentally, though it's not relevant to our main purpose in this chapter, we remark that arrays in SQL are "varying-length"; thus, the two "[10]"s in the declarations of H and K each define an *upper bound*, and the variables can each contain any number N of elements ($N \geq 0$), up to but not greater than that upper bound. And if, for example, the variable H currently contains exactly three elements, then those elements are precisely H[1], H[2], and H[3].

Third and last, a row example:

```
DECLARE NAME ROW ( FIRST VARCHAR(25), LAST VARCHAR(25), MI CHAR(1) ) ;

SET NAME = ROW ( 'Truman', 'Harry', 'S' ) ;
```

Again the SET statement here is a single, nonscalar assignment (in fact it's SQL's counterpart to **Tutorial D**'s *<tuple assign>*, which was mentioned in the body of this chapter, though not discussed in detail). The expression on the right side is a *row value constructor*. The keyword ROW is optional in such constructors.

---

16. It can also be a parameter (within the body of some procedure). And in certain kinds of triggered procedures it can be specified as a column reference, in which case SET can be used to achieve a database updating effect after all (albeit only indirectly).

Now we turn to pseudovariables. SQL supports three kinds: elements of arrays, fields within rows, and something analogous (somewhat) to our THE_ pseudovariables.[17] We consider each in turn. Here first is an example involving an array element:

```
DECLARE IA INTEGER ARRAY [5] ;

SET IA    = ARRAY [ 0, 0, 0, 0, 0 ] ;
SET IA[4] = 8 ;
```

The first SET statement here assigns an array of five elements, all of them zero, to the array variable IA (the expression on the right side is an *array value constructor*). The second SET statement then replaces the value of the fourth element of that array variable by the value eight. In fact, that second SET statement is effectively shorthand for this one:

```
SET IA = ARRAY [ IA[1], IA[2], IA[3], 8, IA[5] ] ;
```

Note: We could replace the first SET statement in the example by an appropriate DEFAULT clause on the variable declaration, as here:

```
DECLARE IA INTEGER ARRAY [5] DEFAULT ARRAY [ 0, 0, 0, 0, 0 ] ;
```

The keyword DEFAULT is a little misleading, however, inasmuch as what SQL's DEFAULT clause really does is assign an *initial* value to the variable in question (just as the INIT specification does in **Tutorial D**).

Now we turn to an example involving assignment to a field within a row variable:

```
DECLARE NAME ROW ( FIRST VARCHAR(25), LAST VARCHAR(25), MI CHAR(1) ) ;

SET NAME.LAST = 'Potter' ;
```

Expanded form of the SET statement:

```
SET NAME = ROW ( NAME.FIRST, 'Potter', NAME.MI ) ;
```

A note on terminology: The term *field*—referring to a component of a row type, row value, or row variable—was first introduced into SQL when explicit row type support was added, in SQL:1999. Of course, tables contain rows too, and the components of *those* rows were historically, and rather awkwardly, called *columns*. Now, however, they too are referred to as fields.

Now we consider SQL's analog of our THE_ pseudovariables. Here first is an example:

```
CREATE TYPE POINT AS ( X REAL, Y REAL ) ;

DECLARE P POINT ;

SET P.Y = 5.0 ;
```

This SET statement expands to:

```
SET P = P.Y ( 5.0 ) ;
```

This expansion requires a certain amount of explanation.

---

17. Note, incidentally, that it does *not* support anything analogous to PL/I's SUBSTR pseudovariables.

- First, type POINT is what's called a *structured type;* it has a representation with two components, X and Y, which are called *attributes. Note:* The representation is not a "possible representation" in the **Tutorial D** sense, however (in particular, there's no possibility that a given type can have more than one of them), and the attributes are nothing to do with attributes in the relational sense. Also, SQL requires the definition of a structured type to include a specification of whether the type is FINAL or NOT FINAL; this specification has nothing to do with the topic of this chapter, however, and we therefore omit it from our examples, for brevity.

- Second, the "Y" in the expression on the right side of the expanded form does *not* denote the Y attribute, as such, of type POINT, nor the Y attribute of the variable P, nor the Y attribute of the point contained within that variable P. Rather, it denotes a *method* of the same name as those attributes (where a *method* is really just a special kind of operator). Each attribute definition causes automatic definition of two methods with the same name as the attribute, one *observer* and one *mutator*. We can explain the effect of such methods in terms of our POINT example as follows:

  - The observer invocation P.Y returns the Y coordinate for the point value in the point variable P. *Note:* Possible appearances to the contrary notwithstanding, no such observer invocation appears in either of the SET statements in our example.

  - The mutator invocation P.Y(5.0) returns the point whose X coordinate is that of the point value in the point variable P and whose Y coordinate is five. *Note:* The SQL term *mutator* is thus a misnomer, because an SQL mutator doesn't actually mutate anything—instead, it returns a value. In fact, an SQL mutator is what the object community calls an *observer* (!), or what *The Third Manifesto* calls a *read-only operator*.

The expanded form of the SET assignment in our example—

```
SET P = P.Y ( 5.0 ) ;
```

—thus has the desired effect.

Note: In addition to the observers and mutators, the definition of a structured type also causes automatic definition of a (niladic) *constructor* method, with name the same as that of the type in question. Invoking that method returns that unique value of the type in question whose attributes all have the applicable default value (often null). For example, the expression POINT() returns the point with default X and Y values (both of which are, by default, null, since we didn't specify anything else in the attribute definitions). It follows that, e.g., the following sequence of assignments—

```
SET P = POINT ( ) ;
SET P = P.X ( 7.0 ) ;
SET P = P.Y ( 5.0 ) ;
```

—will have the effect of assigning the point with X coordinate seven and Y coordinate five to the variable P. What's more, we can collapse the entire sequence into a single assignment, thus:

```
SET P = POINT () . X ( 7.0 ) . Y ( 5.0 ) ;
```

To return to our original POINT example: The SQL term for an expression such as P.Y, if it appears on the left side of an assignment, is *mutator reference*—despite the fact that, as we'll see in a few moments, the method involved (Y in the example) doesn't have to be a mutator method as such. Importantly, such references can be *nested*.[18] For example:

```
CREATE TYPE ELLIPSE AS ( A INTEGER, B INTEGER, CTR POINT ) ;

DECLARE E ELLIPSE ;

SET E.CTR.Y = 5.0 ;
```

The SET statement here is shorthand for

```
SET E.CTR = E.CTR.Y ( 5.0 ) ;
```

And this one in turn is shorthand for

```
SET E = E.CTR ( E.CTR.Y ( 5.0 ) ) ;
```

Now, structured types in general can have user-defined methods associated with them in addition to the system-defined ones we've been discussing so far. We deliberately included no user-defined methods in our original POINT example; however, suppose we now do define such a method, *m* say. Then a SET statement of the form

```
SET P.m = exp ;    /* for example */
```

will be legal if and only if all three of the following are true:

1. *m* is not a constructor method.

2. *m* returns a value of type POINT.

3. Exactly one parameter, of the same type as *exp*, is defined for *m* in addition to the distinguished parameter, SELF, that is common to every nonconstructor method. *Note:* The argument corresponding to SELF in an invocation of *m* is specified by the expression immediately preceding the dot preceding the method name. In the invocation P.Y(5.0), for example, the argument corresponding to SELF in the invocation of the mutator method Y is P.

In other words, SQL doesn't just support analogs of our THE_ pseudovariables—it supports what are in effect *user-defined* pseudovariables as well. On the other hand, SQL's analogs of our THE_ pseudovariables are supported only for structured types; they aren't supported for other user-defined types, nor for system-defined types, nor for array or row types. Furthermore, they can't be used with SELECT INTO or FETCH (array elements and fields, by contrast, can).

---

18. The same is true for our own THE_ pseudovariables, though we didn't stress the point in the body of the chapter.

The SET Statement: Multiple Assignment

Now (at last!) to the multiple assignment version of SET. The syntax has the following general form:

```
SET ( target-commalist ) = row-expression ;
```

Note carefully that the right side here consists of a single (row-valued) expression, not a commalist of separate expressions. The ith field value within the row denoted by that expression is assigned to the ith target. More precisely, let the row denoted by the expression on the right side be

```
ROW ( S1, S2, ..., Sn )
```

and let the target commalist on the left side be

```
T1, T2, ..., Tn
```

The overall assignment then reduces to something like Dijkstra's concurrent assignment (see the body of the chapter):

```
SET ( T1, T2, ..., Tn ) = [ ROW ] ( S1, S2, ..., Sn ) ;
```

(However, the SQL operator differs from Dijkstra's in that the targets don't all have to be distinct.) The semantics are as indicated by the following *compound statement* (pseudocode):[19]

```
BEGIN
    DECLARE TEMP ROW ( F1 ..., F2 ..., ..., Fn ... ) ;
    SET TEMP = ROW ( S1, S2, ..., Sn ) ;
    SET T1 = TEMP.F1 ;
    SET T2 = TEMP.F2 ;
        .........
    SET Tn = TEMP.Fn ;
END ;
```

We'll give some examples involving pseudovariables in just a moment (examples not involving pseudovariables are essentially trivial and are left as an exercise for the reader).

Now, the foregoing definition in terms of a single compound statement does ensure that all source expressions are evaluated before any assignment takes place; curiously, however, it fails to ensure that the compound statement in question is atomic—even though all that would be needed to make it so would be to add the keyword ATOMIC immediately following the keyword BEGIN.[20] What makes the situation even odder is that there's a workaround that not only evaluates all source expressions first but guarantees atomicity as well. For example, the statement

```
SET ( U, V ) = ROW ( 1, 2 ) ;
```

is not atomic, but the following one, which has more or less the same effect, is:

---

19. Like SET and DECLARE, compound statements were introduced into SQL with SQL/PSM.
20. We should note that there was an error in SQL:1999 (persisting in SQL:2003), as a result of which ATOMIC actually has no effect. However, a correction for this error has already been agreed upon and is expected to appear in the first Technical Corrigendum for SQL:2003.

```
SELECT 1, 2 INTO U, V FROM ( VALUES 0 ) AS POINTLESS ;
```

Note: The sole purpose of the FROM clause here is to ensure that the SELECT clause operates on a table containing exactly one row. The value of that row is immaterial, because there aren't any column references in the SELECT clause. As for the specification AS *POINTLESS*, it's pointless, but it's required by SQL's syntax rules.

Here now are the promised examples involving pseudovariables. First, one involving array elements:

```
DECLARE IA INTEGER ARRAY [5] DEFAULT ARRAY [ 1, 2, 3, 4, 5 ] ;

SET ( IA[4], IA[2] ) = ROW ( 0, 8 ) ;
```

First we apply the rule for expanding multiple assignment, to obtain:

```
BEGIN
   DECLARE TEMP ROW ( F1 ..., F2 ... ) ;
   SET TEMP = ROW ( 0, 8 ) ;
   SET IA[4] = TEMP.F1 ;
   SET IA[2] = TEMP.F2 ;
END ;
```

Next we apply the rule (twice) for expanding assignment to an array element pseudovariable, to obtain:

```
BEGIN
   DECLARE TEMP ROW ( F1 ..., F2 ... ) ;
   SET TEMP = ROW ( 0, 8 ) ;
   SET IA = ARRAY [ IA[1], IA[2], IA[3], TEMP.F1, IA[5] ] ;
   SET IA = ARRAY [ IA[1], TEMP.F2, IA[3], IA[4], IA[5] ] ;
END ;
```

Thus, the final value of IA is:

```
ARRAY [ 1, 8, 3, 0, 5 ]
```

By way of a second example, let P be a variable of type POINT once again, and consider the assignment

```
SET ( P.X, P.Y ) = ROW ( 7.0, 5.0 ) ;
```

First expansion:

```
BEGIN
   DECLARE TEMP ROW ( F1 ..., F2 ... ) ;
   SET TEMP = ROW ( 7.0, 5.0 ) ;
   SET P.X = TEMP.F1 ;
   SET P.Y = TEMP.F2 ;
END ;
```

Second expansion:

```
BEGIN
   DECLARE TEMP ROW ( F1 ..., F2 ... ) ;
   SET TEMP = ROW ( 7.0, 5.0 ) ;
   SET P = P.X ( TEMP.F1 ) ;
   SET P = P.Y ( TEMP.F2 ) ;
END ;
```

The first assignment to P here sets the X coordinate to seven, leaving the Y coordinate unchanged; the second then sets the Y coordinate to five, leaving the X coordinate unchanged. The final result is thus that P contains the point with coordinates (7.0,5.0), as desired. Note carefully that, in contrast with the analogous example in the body of the chapter, we do *not* have to "collect together" the two constituent assignments in order to achieve the desired result. Why not? Well, in order to answer this question, it helps to examine a more complex example:

```
CREATE TYPE ELLIPSE AS ( A INTEGER, B INTEGER, CTR POINT ) ;

DECLARE E ELLIPSE ;

SET ( E.A, E.B ) = ROW ( 7, 3 ) ;
```

For brevity, let's combine the two expansions this time. The overall result looks like this:

```
BEGIN
   DECLARE TEMP ROW ( F1 ..., F2 ... ) ;
   SET TEMP = ROW ( 7, 3 ) ;
   SET E = E.A ( TEMP.F1 ) ;
   SET E = E.B ( TEMP.F2 ) ;
END ;
```

Now suppose the previous value of E had $a = 10$ and $b = 8$. Then the first assignment to E yields an ellipse with $a = 7$ and $b = 8$—in other words, an ellipse with $a < b$. However, this state of affairs does *not* cause a run-time error (and the second assignment to E thus goes on to yield an ellipse with $a = 7$ and $b = 3$, as required). Why is there no run-time error? Because SQL is unaware of the **type constraint** to the effect that a must be greater than or equal to b (observe that the definition of type ELLIPSE included no such constraint); in fact, SQL doesn't support the concept of type constraints at all (we can't even state them).

In our opinion, this lack of type constraint support on SQL's part constitutes a very serious flaw. While it does make it easier to support multiple assignment, as we've just seen,[21] it also means there are many "real world" types that can't be properly specified in SQL! For example, suppose we want to define a type called LENGTH (with the obvious meaning). Then we might specify, say, integers as the associated representation, and of course that specification does impose an *a priori* constraint on the values that go to make up the type. Considered as type constraints, however, such *a priori* constraints are extremely weak. In the case at hand, for example, there's no

---

21. As we'll see in the next subsection, however, it turns out (in another context) that SQL still has to do the same kind of thing we do anyway—i.e., it still has to collect various constituent assignments together—so it can hardly be argued that the fact that it doesn't have to do so in the case of multiple assignment is a significant advantage.

way to specify that lengths mustn't be negative. As we've shown elsewhere (in *The Third Manifesto* in particular), therefore, SQL necessarily permits negative lengths, noncircular circles, nonsquare squares, and all kinds of similar nonsenses. *Note:* Possible reasons why type constraint support is omitted from SQL are discussed in the book mentioned several times already, *An Introduction to Database Systems*, 8th edition, by C. J. Date (Addison-Wesley, 2004).

We close this subsection by noting that, owing to its lack of proper support for multiple *table* assignment, SQL can't directly handle either (a) the example discussed in the section "A Multiple Assignment Example," or (b) the example discussed at the end of the section "Assigning to a Variable More than Once," in the body of the chapter. Instead, it has to use several separate assignment statements in both cases, and bundle those statements up into a transaction. It also has to make sure the pertinent constraint checking is deferred.[22]

The SQL UPDATE Statement Revisited

As noted in the body of this chapter, we do not regard SQL's UPDATE statement as a true multiple assignment. However, it does have some points in common with multiple assignment, as we'll see in this subsection, and in fact the SET clause in UPDATE is now permitted to include multiple assignments as such. We illustrate these points by means of a slightly abstract example. Let table T have columns C1, C2, C3, C4, and C5 (and possibly others), where C1 is of type INTEGER, C2 is of type POINT, C3 is of type INTEGER ARRAY, and C4 and C5 are of the same type as each other. Now consider the following UPDATE statement (WHERE clause omitted for simplicity):[23]

```
UPDATE T
SET C1 = 2 ,
    C2.X = 7.0 ,
    C2.Y = 5.0 ,
    C3 [ 2 ] = 2 ,
  ( C4, C5 ) = ROW ( C5, C4 ) ; /* true multiple assignment */
```

The SET clause here is applied to each row *r* of T as follows:

1. Syntactic substitutions are applied until the left side of each assignment consists of a simple column reference. With one addition (having to do with the two assignments to C2—see below), these substitutions are essentially as described for the SET statement earlier in this appendix.

2. The right sides of those assignments are evaluated for *r*.

3. A row *r'* is formed by copying *r* and then replacing the values for columns C1-C5 in that copy by the corresponding results of those evaluations.

The value assigned to T is the bag of rows *r'* thus computed.

---

22. Yes, SQL does support "deferred constraints"—but it doesn't allow all constraints to be deferred (some *must* be checked immediately). The apparent arbitrariness of this state of affairs might be seen as yet another argument in favor of our position that all constraint checking should be immediate.

23. We remark in passing that, while as already noted the syntax of the SET *statement* broadly follows the Dijkstra style, the syntax of the SET *clause* in the UPDATE statement is more in the style of **Tutorial D**'s multiple assignment.

Now, under the substitutions described earlier in this appendix, our example expands to the following:

```
UPDATE T
SET C1 = 2 ,
    C2 = C2.X ( 7.0 ) ,
    C2 = C2.Y ( 5.0 ) ,
    C3 = something complicated ,
    C4 = C5 ,
    C5 = C4 ;
```

Note: The last two assignments here really do interchange the values of the columns C4 and C5, because the right sides are evaluated before any assignments are done.

The complications surrounding the assignment to the array column C3 need not concern us here (they have to do with the fact that SQL arrays are varying-length). The two assignments to C2 need further attention, however, because no column is allowed to appear as a target in any given SET clause more than once (precisely because all right sides are evaluated before any assignments are done). A further substitution therefore has to occur, according to which assignments to the same column *that have arisen under the previous substitution process* are collected together. Without going into details—the process is essentially similar to the one described in the section on semantics in the body of this chapter—the net effect in our example is that the two assignments to C2 are replaced by this one:

```
C2 = C2.X ( 7.0 ) . Y ( 5.0 )
```

Thus, if the "old" value of C2 is the point (2.0,3.0), then the invocation X(7.0) on that point yields the point (7.0,3.0), and the invocation Y(5.0) on *that* point then yields the point (7.0,5.0).

Finally, you might be wondering why our example included no column C6 of some row type and an assignment to some field F of that column, as here:

```
C6.F = 3
```

Such columns are indeed permitted. Sadly, however, SQL does not support the updating of fields within such columns in the manner suggested—i.e., it does not permit such an assignment in the SET clause. (These observations were valid for SQL:1999 and are still valid for SQL:2003.)

CHAPTER 12

■■■

Data Redundancy and Database Design

What I tell you three times is true.

—Lewis Carroll

Redundant: *de trop,* diffuse, excessive, extra, inessential, inordinate, padded, periphrastic, pleonastical, prolix, repetitious, supererogatory, superfluous, supernumerary, surplus, tautological, unemployed, unnecessary, unneeded, unwanted, verbose, wordy

I found the foregoing splendid list of synonyms in *Chambers Twentieth Century Thesaurus* (which also gives the following nice list of antonyms: concise, essential, necessary). I quoted it in an earlier two-part paper, "Grievous Bodily Harm" (*DBP&D 11*, Nos. 5 and 6, May/June 1998, reprinted in my self-published book *Relational Database Writings 1997–2001*). In that paper, however, I was concerned with redundancy in the SQL language; here, by contrast, I'm concerned with *data* redundancy, and hence, by extension, with the question of (logical) database design. Throughout this chapter, therefore, I take the term "redundancy" to mean data redundancy specifically, and the term "database design," or just "design" for short, to mean logical database design specifically (barring explicit statements to the contrary in both cases, of course).

Now, I've said many times that database design is not my favorite subject; it's simply too, well, subjective for my taste. Of course, there *is* some solid design theory that can be brought to bear on the problem (and I want to examine that theory in this chapter), but there are many issues the theory just doesn't address at all. In other words, database design in general is still mostly an artistic endeavor, not a scientific one—a state of affairs that, to repeat, I at any rate find less than fully satisfactory.

Be that as it may, design theory in general can be regarded as a set of principles and techniques for **reducing redundancy** (thereby reducing the potential for certain inconsistencies and update anomalies that might otherwise occur). But what exactly *is* redundancy? We don't seem to have a very precise definition of the term; we just have a somewhat vague idea that it can lead to problems, at least if it isn't managed properly.

Note: I remark as an aside that similar remarks could be made in connection with the associated term "update anomaly," which has become sanctified by use but also suffers from the lack of a universally agreed and precise definition. In his paper "A Normal Form for Relational Databases that Is Based on Domains and Keys" (*ACM TODS 6,* No. 3, September 1981),

Ronald Fagin gives precise definitions for the related terms *insertion anomaly* and *deletion anomaly*, and those definitions might be used as a basis for a good definition of the more general term *update anomaly*. However, it's not my aim in this chapter to attempt such a thing.

Back to the main thread of the discussion. In order to get a slightly better handle on what redundancy really means, the first thing we need to do is distinguish clearly between the logical and physical levels of the system. Obviously the design goals are different at the two levels. At the physical level, redundancy will almost certainly exist in some shape or form. Here are a couple of reasons why:

- Indexes and other such "access path" structures necessarily entail some redundancy, because certain data values are stored both in those auxiliary structures and in the structures to which they provide that "fast access."

- Derived relations that are physically stored in some way—what are known variously as *snapshots* or *summary tables* or *materialized queries* or *materialized views*—also obviously involve some redundancy.

The reason for redundancy at the physical level is performance, of course. But such redundancy has (or should have!) no effect on the logical level; it's managed by the DBMS, in the sense that the DBMS assumes responsibility for keeping redundant copies of the same data consistent, and it's never directly seen by the user. In this chapter, however, I'm more interested in the question of redundancy at the logical level; from this point forward, therefore, I'll take the term *database* to refer to the logical level, meaning the database as it's perceived by the user (barring explicit statements to the contrary).

At the logical level, then, it's tempting just to say that *redundancy is always bad*. But of course this statement is much too simplistic, thanks to the availability of the view mechanism if nothing else. Let me digress for a moment to elaborate on this latter point. It's well known, but worth stating explicitly nevertheless, that views serve two rather different purposes:

1. The user who actually defines view *V* is, obviously, aware of the expression *X* in terms of which *V* is defined. That user can use the name *V* wherever the expression *X* is intended, but such uses are basically just shorthand (like the use of macros in a programming language).

2. By contrast, a user who's merely informed that *V* exists and is available for use is supposed[1] *not* to be aware of the expression *X*; to that user, in fact, *V* is supposed to look and feel just like a base relvar. *Note:* I hope you're familiar with the term *relvar* (see the section "Some Prerequisites," later). It's short for *relation variable*. A *base* relvar—also known as a *real* relvar—is the relational model's counterpart to what SQL would call a base table.

As an example of Case 1, suppose the user perceives the database as containing two relvars *A* and *B* and goes on to define their join *A* JOIN *B* as a view *V*; clearly, then, *V* is redundant so far as that user is concerned, and it could be dropped without any loss of information. For definiteness, therefore, I'm going to assume from this point forward (barring explicit statements to the contrary) that no relvar in the database is defined in terms of any others, so that at least this

---

1. Emphasis on *supposed*—I'm describing an ideal situation here; the reality is a little messier. The true state of affairs is analyzed in detail by Hugh Darwen and myself in our book *Databases, Types, and the Relational Model: The Third Manifesto*, 3rd edition (Addison-Wesley, 2006).

particular kind of redundancy isn't present. With this possibility ruled out, then, it's tempting to set a stake in the ground and say again that redundancy at the logical level is always undesirable. In order to adopt such a position, however, we need to be able to say what we mean by redundancy—for otherwise the position can't possibly make sense. And even if we can come up with a good definition of the term, is the position that redundancy at the logical level is always bad really tenable? Is it possible to eliminate all redundancy? Is it even desirable?

These are questions of considerable pragmatic importance, of course. Indeed, I think it's noteworthy that Codd called his very first paper on the relational model "Derivability, *Redundancy*, and Consistency of Relations Stored in Large Data Banks" (IBM Research Report RJ599, August 19th, 1969; emphasis added). And his second paper, "A Relational Model of Data for Large Shared Data Banks" (*CACM 13*, No. 6, June 1970)—this is the one that's usually regarded as the seminal paper in the field, though that characterization is a little unfair to its 1969 predecessor—was in two parts of almost equal length, the second of which was called "Redundancy and Consistency" (the first was "Relational Model and Normal Form"). In both of these papers, in other words, Codd regarded his thoughts on redundancy as a major part of the contribution of his relational work: rightly so, in my opinion, since he did at least provide us with a framework in which we could begin to address the issue precisely and systematically.

Here then are some attempts at pinning down the notion of redundancy a little more precisely:

- The database involves some redundancy if and only if it can be divided into two disjoint partitions such that the very same relation can be derived from both.

- The database involves some redundancy if and only if there exists at least one relation or attribute or tuple that can be removed without having any effect on the set of relations that can be derived from it (the database, that is).

- The database involves some redundancy if and only if it says the same thing twice. (As a matter of fact this attempt isn't too bad, if only we can pin down precisely what it means for the database to "say" something. Part of the purpose of this chapter is to address this very issue.)

Other characterizations are doubtless possible, too. Without further ado, therefore, let's embark on our investigation.[2]

The Running Example

I'll base most of my examples on the usual suppliers-and-parts database. Definitions of the relvars in that database, expressed in **Tutorial D** (see the next section), follow immediately; sample values are shown in Figure 12-1.

---

2. "Investigation" is indeed the *mot juste* here; the chapter is far from definitive. In particular, you shouldn't read it without reading the "further thoughts" in the next chapter as well.

```
VAR S BASE RELATION /* suppliers */
  { S# S#, SNAME NAME, STATUS INTEGER, CITY CHAR }
    KEY { S# } ;

VAR P BASE RELATION /* parts */
  { P# P#, PNAME NAME, COLOR COLOR, WEIGHT WEIGHT, CITY CHAR }
    KEY { P# } ;

VAR SP BASE RELATION /* shipments */
  { S# S#, P# P#, QTY QTY }
    KEY { S#, P# }
    FOREIGN KEY { S# } REFERENCES S
    FOREIGN KEY { P# } REFERENCES P ;
```

S	S#	SNAME	STATUS	CITY
	S1	Smith	20	London
	S2	Jones	10	Paris
	S3	Blake	30	Paris
	S4	Clark	20	London
	S5	Adams	30	Athens

P	P#	PNAME	COLOR	WEIGHT	CITY
	P1	Nut	Red	12.0	London
	P2	Bolt	Green	17.0	Paris
	P3	Screw	Blue	17.0	Oslo
	P4	Screw	Red	14.0	London
	P5	Cam	Blue	12.0	Paris
	P6	Cog	Red	19.0	London

SP	S#	P#	QTY
	S1	P1	300
	S1	P2	200
	S1	P3	400
	S1	P4	200
	S1	P5	100
	S1	P6	100
	S2	P1	300
	S2	P2	400
	S3	P2	200
	S4	P2	200
	S4	P4	300
	S4	P5	400

Figure 12-1. *The suppliers-and-parts database—sample values*

Some Prerequisites

In order to keep this chapter to a comparatively reasonable length, I'm going to have to assume you're familiar with the relational model in general and all of the following in particular:

- The logical difference between relation values (relations for short) and relation variables (relvars for short)

- The logical difference between base and derived relvars, and the fact that views or "virtual relvars" in particular are derived

- The fact that every relation is of a certain *relation type,* represented in **Tutorial D** by syntax of the form

  `RELATION { attribute commalist }`

  (where every *attribute* consists of an *attribute name* and a *type name,* separated by at least one blank—though for brevity I often omit the keyword RELATION and the type names later in this chapter and show just the attribute names)

- The fact that every relvar is likewise of a certain relation type—namely, the type that's common to all possible values of that relvar

- The fact that keys are *sets* of attributes (which is why I always show them enclosed in braces "{" and "}")

- The fact that every relvar, base or derived, has an associated *relvar constraint,* being, loosely, the logical AND of all declared integrity constraints that include any reference to the relvar in question

- The fact that every relvar, base or derived, has an associated *predicate* (the "relvar predicate"), which is the intended interpretation or meaning for the relvar in question

- The fact that every tuple appearing in a given relvar at a given time represents a certain *proposition,* that proposition being an instantiation of the relvar predicate for the relvar in question that (by convention) is understood to be true at the time in question

- *The Closed World Assumption,* which says that if a certain tuple plausibly could appear in relvar *R* at a given time but in fact doesn't, then the corresponding proposition is assumed to be false at the time in question

- The fact that "subtuples are tuples" (loosely, a tuple is a set of attribute:value pairs, and every subset of such a set of pairs is also a tuple)

- *The Principle of Interchangeability* (of base and virtual relvars), which states that there should be no arbitrary and unnecessary distinctions between base relvars and views

- The logical difference between a value and an appearance of that value (for example, the value that's the integer 3 is unique—there's just one such integer "in the universe," as it were—but any number of variables can contain an *appearance,* or *representation,* of that value, at the same time or at different times)

The foregoing points are all explained in numerous places, including in particular my book *Database in Depth: Relational Theory for Practitioners* (O'Reilly Media Inc., 2005). Observe in particular that the system doesn't understand the relvar predicate for relvar *R* but does understand the corresponding relvar constraint; this latter can be regarded as the system's approximation to the relvar predicate. (For precisely this reason, in fact, I've referred elsewhere to the relvar predicate and the relvar constraint as the external predicate and the internal predicate, respectively.) Note, incidentally, that even though the system doesn't understand the relvar predicate, it does at least know exactly which tuples satisfy it at any given time—they're exactly the tuples that appear in the relvar at that time.

In addition to all of the above, I assume you're familiar with:

- The basic ideas of normalization (but I'll review these briefly in the section after next)

- **Tutorial D,** which is the language used by Hugh Darwen and myself as a basis for examples in our book on *The Third Manifesto* (but the language is, I hope, pretty much self-explanatory anyway)

These matters also are discussed in the O'Reilly book mentioned earlier.

Database Design Is Predicate Design

As I've already said, the relvar predicate for relvar *R* is the intended interpretation or meaning for *R*, and the relvar constraint for *R* can be regarded as the system's approximation to that predicate. Given that a database is supposed to be a faithful representation of the semantics of what might be called "the microworld of interest," therefore, it follows that predicates and constraints are highly relevant to the business of database design—predicates are the informal,[3] and constraints the formal, representation of those semantics. Overall, then, the design process goes like this:

1. Pin down the relvar predicates as carefully as possible.

2. Map those predicates into relvars and constraints.

As a consequence of the foregoing, we can see that another way to think about design theory—normalization and so forth—is as follows: *It's a set of principles and techniques for helping with the business of pinning down predicates* (and hence constraints). I'll have occasion to refer to this alternative perspective from time to time in what follows.

Here for reference are the predicates for the relvars in the suppliers-and-parts database:

Suppliers: *Supplier S# is under contract, is named SNAME, has status STATUS, and is located in city CITY.*

Parts: *Part P# is used in the enterprise, is named PNAME, has color COLOR and weight WEIGHT, and is stored in city CITY.*

Shipments: *Supplier S# supplies QTY of part P#.*

A Brief Review of Normalization

The discipline of further normalization involves several well-established principles, which I'll spell out here for purposes of reference even though (as I've said) you're supposed to be familiar with them already:

---

3. They're informal because they're expressed in natural language instead of some formal language like **Tutorial D;** nevertheless, they should still be stated as precisely as possible. Indeed, what I'm here calling "predicates" are what some people like to call *business rules* (see Chapter 15).

1. A relvar that's not in fifth normal form (5NF) should be decomposed into a set of 5NF projections.

2. The original relvar should be reconstructable by joining those projections back together again.

3. The decomposition process should preserve dependencies.

4. Every projection should be needed in the reconstruction process.

A detailed explanation of all of these principles can be found in many places; see, for example, my book *An Introduction to Database Systems,* 8th edition (Addison-Wesley, 2004). However, I'd like to elaborate briefly on certain aspects of them here.

First of all, I need to be clear on my use of the terms "projection" and "join" in this context. Basically, of course, projection and join are operators that apply to relations, not relvars—but of course they certainly apply to the relations that happen to be the current values of relvars in particular. So it obviously makes sense to talk about, for example, "the projection on attributes S# and CITY of relvar S," meaning the relation that results from taking the projection on those attributes of the relation that's the current value of the suppliers relvar S. In some contexts, however (the present context in particular), it's more convenient to use expressions like "the projection on attributes S# and CITY of relvar S" in a slightly different sense. For example, suppose we define a view SC of the suppliers relvar S that consists of just the S# and CITY attributes of that relvar. In **Tutorial D,** that view definition might look like this:

```
VAR SC VIRTUAL ( S { S#, CITY } ) ;
```

Here we might say, loosely but very conveniently, that the view (or virtual relvar) SC is "the projection on attributes S# and CITY of relvar S"—meaning, more precisely, that the value of SC at any given time is the projection on S# and CITY of the value of relvar S at the time in question. In a sense, therefore, we can talk in terms of projections of relvars *per se,* rather than just in terms of projections of current values of relvars—and (following convention in such matters) that's what I'll be doing for the rest of this chapter.

Second, it's usual to use the term *nonloss decomposition* to refer to a decomposition (into projections) that satisfies the second principle. For example, we can clearly nonloss-decompose the suppliers relvar S into projections as follows—

```
SN { S#, SNAME }
   KEY { S# }

ST { S#, STATUS }
   KEY { S# }

SC { S#, CITY }
   KEY { S# }
```

—because S is equal to the join of those projections. Thus, the set of relvars (projections) consisting of SN, ST, and SC is a nonloss decomposition of relvar S.

Suppose, however, we were to decompose relvar S into projections as follows:

```
SN  { S#, SNAME }
    KEY { S# }

SNT { S#, SNAME, STATUS }
    KEY { S# }

SC  { S#, CITY }
    KEY { S# }
```

Again the decomposition is nonloss, because S is certainly equal to the join of the specified projections. However, the decomposition violates the fourth principle (every projection should be needed in the reconstruction process), because projection SN clearly *isn't* needed—S is equal to the join of SNT and SC alone, and SN adds nothing. In fact, of course, SN is redundant; and given that the overall aim of normalization is precisely to reduce redundancy, this particular nonloss decomposition isn't very sensible. **Please note carefully, therefore, that from this point forward in this chapter I'll use the term *nonloss decomposition* to mean, specifically, a decomposition into projections that satisfies the fourth principle as well as the second** (since those that don't aren't very interesting—at least, not as far as we're concerned).

Finally, I'd like to say a word about the third principle, since it often gets overlooked in treatments of normalization. The third principle asks us to *preserve dependencies,* and "dependencies" here basically means *join* dependencies.[4] Now, the general objective of normalization is, as I've already said, to reduce redundancy. The third principle is *not* about reducing redundancy, however; sadly, in fact, it can actually conflict with that objective. The following example is taken from the book mentioned earlier, *An Introduction to Database Systems.* We're given a relvar SJT with attributes S, J, and T and predicate:

Student S is taught subject J by teacher T.

In addition, the following constraints apply:

- For each subject, each student of that subject is taught by only one teacher.

- Each teacher teaches only one subject (but each subject is taught by several teachers).

A sample value is shown in Figure 12-2. Note the redundancy: For example, the fact that Prof. White teaches Math appears twice. (Actually this is the *only* redundancy in the figure, but of course the sample value in that figure is unrealistically simple.)

---

4. I'll have more to say about join dependencies later in this chapter. For now, all you need to know is that *functional* dependencies are a special case. Relvar *R* satisfies the functional dependency $A \to B$ (where *A* and *B* are each sets of attributes of *R*) if and only if, in every relation that's a legal value for *R*, whenever two tuples have the same value for *A*, they also have the same value for *B*.

SJT	S	J	T
	Smith	Math	Prof. White
	Smith	Physics	Prof. Green
	Jones	Math	Prof. White
	Jones	Physics	Prof. Brown

Figure 12-2. *Relvar SJT—sample value*

Observe now that relvar SJT satisfies the following functional dependencies (why?):

```
{ S, J } → { T }
{ T }    → { J }
```

Because of the second of these in particular, the relvar isn't in 5NF (in fact, it isn't even in Boyce/Codd normal form, BCNF, though it is in 3NF); it therefore suffers from redundancy problems, as we already know, and so the first normalization principle would recommend that we decompose it into projections as follows:

```
ST { S, T }
   KEY { S, T }

TJ { T, J }
   KEY { T }
```

But if we do, the functional dependency {S,J} ⟶ {T} disappears! Well, it doesn't disappear exactly, but it does cease to be a functional dependency as such; rather, it becomes *a constraint that spans two relvars*. It might be stated thus in **Tutorial D** (and as you can see, it's not straightforward at all):

```
CONSTRAINT S_AND_J_DETERMINES_T
   COUNT ( ST JOIN TJ ) = COUNT ( ( ST JOIN TJ ) { S, J } ) ;
```

This state of affairs constitutes a violation of the third principle of normalization, precisely because the functional dependency hasn't been preserved: at least, not as a single-relvar constraint—it has become a multi-relvar constraint instead. The tacit and not unreasonable assumption underlying the third principle is that single-relvar constraints are easier to enforce (as well as state) than multi-relvar ones. In the case at hand, for example, suppose we try to insert a tuple for Smith and Prof. Brown into relvar ST. Then that insert must fail, because Prof. Brown teaches physics and Smith is already being taught physics by Prof. Green; but the system cannot detect this fact without examining relvar TJ.

We see, therefore, that the first and third normalization principles can occasionally be in conflict—and I for one am not aware of any good theory that can be used to decide which principle should "win" in such a situation: Is it better to reduce redundancy and lose the dependency, or is it better to preserve the dependency and live with the redundancy? Right here, then, is one place where it would be nice to have a little more science to help in the design process.

Normalization Is Not Enough

The message in the title of this section should already be clear from the SJT example. However, I want to make two further observations as part of the same overall point. The first is this: Contrary to popular misconception, normalization is certainly not enough to eliminate redundancy entirely (even if we ignore the "preserve dependencies" principle)—by definition, the best it can do is eliminate redundancies that can be eliminated by means of nonloss decomposition. Here's a counterexample, again taken from *An Introduction to Database Systems*. We're given a relvar CTXD, with attributes COURSE, TEACHER, TEXT, and DAYS, with predicate:

> *Teacher TEACHER spends DAYS days with text TEXT on course COURSE.*

Figure 12-3 shows a sample value for this relvar.

CTXD	COURSE	TEACHER	TEXT	DAYS
	Physics	Prof. Green	Basic Mechanics	5
	Physics	Prof. Green	Principles of Optics	5
	Physics	Prof. Brown	Basic Mechanics	6
	Physics	Prof. Brown	Principles of Optics	4
	Math	Prof. Green	Basic Mechanics	3
	Math	Prof. Green	Vector Analysis	3
	Math	Prof. Green	Trigonometry	4

Figure 12-3. *Relvar CTXD—sample value*

Observe in Figure 12-3 that (for example) the fact that Prof. Green teaches physics and the fact that the physics course uses the textbook "Basic Mechanics" both appear twice. Observe further that we can't eliminate those redundancies by nonloss decomposition—the relvar satisfies the functional dependency

```
{ COURSE, TEACHER, TEXT } → { DAYS }
```

and attribute DAYS thus can't appear in a relvar with anything less than all three of the other attributes. In fact, relvar CTXD is in 5NF,[5] and it can't be nonloss-decomposed at all.

Note: Actually it's not quite true to say that relvar CTXD can't be nonloss-decomposed at all. *Any* relvar can always be nonloss-decomposed, albeit trivially, into what's called the corresponding *identity* projection. The identity projection of a given relation or relvar is the projection of that relation or relvar on all of its attributes; it's called the identity projection because, obviously enough, it's identically equal to the original relation or relvar. Of course, it's a bit of a stretch to talk about "decomposition" in such a situation, because there really isn't any decomposing, as such, going on at all. Nonetheless, I will occasionally appeal to this notion of identity projection as a possible nonloss decomposition later in this chapter.

---

5. Actually it's in *sixth* normal form (6NF) as well. See Example 11 in the section "Other Kinds of Redundancy," later in this chapter.

Now I turn to my second point. Consider the following decomposition of relvar S:

```
SNT { S#, SNAME, STATUS }
   KEY { S# }

STC { S#, STATUS, CITY }
   KEY { S# }
```

Sample values are shown in Figure 12-4. As the figure shows, this decomposition is hardly very sensible (in particular, the fact that any given supplier has a given status appears twice), and yet it satisfies all of the normalization principles—both projections are in 5NF, the decomposition is nonloss (in the strong sense of satisfying the fourth principle as well as the first), and dependencies are preserved.

SNT	S#	SNAME	STATUS	STC	S#	STATUS	CITY
	S1	Smith	20		S1	20	London
	S2	Jones	10		S2	10	Paris
	S3	Blake	30		S3	30	Paris
	S4	Clark	20		S4	20	London
	S5	Adams	30		S5	30	Athens

Figure 12-4. *Relvars SNT and STC—sample values*

Again, therefore, normalization by itself isn't enough; we need something else to tell us what's wrong with this decomposition (something else *formal*, that is; we all know what's wrong with it informally). The point is, the normalization discipline provides a set of formal principles to guide us in our attempts to reduce redundancy, but that set of principles by itself is inadequate, as the example plainly shows. We need another principle.

Orthogonality (I)

Intuitively, the problem with the design illustrated in Figure 12-4 is clear: It has the property that (to use an obvious shorthand notation for tuples) the tuple *<s#,n,st>* appears in SNT if and only if the tuple *<s#,st,c>* appears in STC; equivalently, the tuple *<s#,st>* appears in the projection of SNT on S# and STATUS if and only if that very same tuple *<s#,st>* appears in the projection of STC on S# and STATUS—meaning the projections in question are equal. In other words, the design implies some redundancy. So the principle we're looking for is obviously going to say something along the lines of: Don't do that! Here's a first attempt:

Let *A* and *B* be distinct projections arising from nonloss decomposition of some relvar *R*. Then there should not exist nonloss decompositions of *A* and *B* into projections *A1, A2, ..., Am* and *B1, B2, ..., Bn*, respectively, such that some *Ai* (*i = 1, 2, ..., m*) is identically equal to some *Bj* (*j = 1, 2, ..., n*).

Or equivalently (my reason for the following restatement should become clear in the section "Orthogonality (II)" later in this chapter):

> Let A and B be distinct projections arising from nonloss decomposition of some relvar R. Then there should not exist nonloss decompositions of A and B into projections $A1$, $A2$, ..., Am and $B1$, $B2$, ..., Bn, respectively, such that a given tuple appears in some Ai ($i = 1, 2, ..., m$) if and only if it appears in some Bj ($j = 1, 2, ..., n$).

Now, we could think of this principle, if we liked, as a "fifth principle of normalization"; in fact, however, it's really just a special case—or a logical consequence, rather—of *The Principle of Orthogonal Design,* which I'll be discussing in detail in the section "Orthogonality (II)." Be that as it may, it should be obvious right away that there's no need to limit our attention to the situation in which A and B are obtained via nonloss decomposition from the same relvar R—it applies to pairs of relvars in general. More generally, therefore, we have:

> Let A and B be distinct relvars. Then there should not exist nonloss decompositions of A and B into projections $A1$, $A2$, ..., Am and $B1$, $B2$, ..., Bn, respectively, such that a given tuple appears in some Ai ($i = 1, 2, ..., m$) if and only if it appears in some Bj ($j = 1, 2, ..., n$).

As an aside, it's interesting to note that Codd himself attempted to deal with the kind of redundancy under discussion here in his very first two papers. In the 1969 paper, he said this:

> *A set of relations is* strongly redundant *if it contains at least one relation [that] is derivable from the rest of the [relations in the set].*

And he tightened up this definition somewhat in the 1970 paper:

> *A set of relations is* strongly redundant *if it contains at least one relation that possesses a projection [that] is derivable from other projections of relations in the set.*

I should explain that when Codd says a relation r is *derivable* from a set S of relations, he means r is equal to the result of applying some sequence of relational operations—join, projection, and so forth—to relations from S. I do have a few comments on his definitions, however:

- First, the term *relation* should be replaced by the term *relvar* throughout (of course, this latter term wasn't introduced until many years later, and Codd never used it at all).

- Second, I think we can ignore the qualifier *strongly;* Codd was distinguishing between "strong redundancy" and something he called *weak* redundancy, but I don't think that distinction is relevant for present purposes (I mean, I don't think we need to consider "weak redundancy" here at all).

- The 1969 definition is subsumed by the 1970 definition, of course, because as we know every relvar R is identically equal to a certain projection of R—namely, the identity projection.

- More to the point, the 1970 definition is still deficient as a definition of redundancy in general for at least the following reasons:

  - It includes certain possibilities that we normally wouldn't regard as redundancies at all. For example, suppose the suppliers-and-parts database is subject to the constraint that every part must be supplied by at least one supplier. Then the projection SP{P#} of relvar SP on P# will be equal to the projection P{P#} of relvar P on P#, and we'll have a "strong redundancy" on our hands. *Note:* Perhaps a more realistic example to illustrate the same point would be a constraint on a personnel database to the effect that every department must have at least one employee.

  - At the same time, it excludes many possibilities that we certainly would regard as redundancies—see several later sections in this chapter for examples.

- Even more to the point, the references to *projections* in the 1970 definition should be replaced by references to *projections obtained via nonloss decomposition.* (The first of the two objections in the previous bullet item would then go away.) If this replacement is made, then my "fifth principle of normalization" becomes very close to saying: There shouldn't be any strong redundancies. However, I haven't yet said all I want to say about that principle, and what I have to add will mean it isn't really as simple as just avoiding strong redundancy.

One last point on Codd's definitions: Codd did at least say (in both papers) that "we shall associate with [the database] a collection of statements [that] define all of the redundancies" in that database. In other words, he certainly wanted the system to be aware of the redundancies, and he wanted those redundancies to be managed. Unfortunately, however, he went on to say:

> *The generation of an inconsistency[6] ... could be logged internally, so that if it were not remedied within some reasonable time ... the system could notify the security officer* [sic]. *Alternatively, the system could [inform the user] that such and such relations now need to be changed to restore consistency ... Ideally, [different remedial actions] should be possible ... for different subcollections of relations.*

I have argued elsewhere, however—see, for example, the book mentioned a couple of times already, *Database in Depth: Relational Theory for Practitioners*—that the database must *never* be allowed to contain any inconsistencies, at least as far as the user is concerned. In other words, "remedying inconsistencies" needs to be done immediately, on an individual statement-by-statement basis (not even on a transaction-by-transaction basis). See the section "Managing Redundancy" later in this chapter.

Another Kind of Decomposition

Informally, normalization has to do with "vertical" decomposition of relvars (that is, decomposition via projection). But "horizontal" decomposition (that is, decomposition via restriction) is clearly possible, too. Consider the example shown in Figure 12-5, in which the parts relvar P

---

6. "Inconsistencies" (or, as I would prefer to call them, integrity violations) can certainly be caused by redundancy, of course—more precisely, by redundancy that's inadequately managed—but of course not all integrity violations are caused by redundancy.

has been split horizontally—in fact, partitioned—into two relvars, one ("light parts," LP) containing parts with weight less than 17 pounds and the other ("heavy parts," HP) containing parts with weight greater than or equal to 17 pounds. The predicates are:

> LP: *Part P# is used in the enterprise, is named PNAME, has color COLOR and weight WEIGHT (which is less than 17 pounds), and is stored in city CITY.*

> HP: *Part P# is used in the enterprise, is named PNAME, has color COLOR and weight WEIGHT (which is greater than or equal to 17 pounds), and is stored in city CITY.*

Note that the original relvar P can be recovered by taking the (disjoint) union of relvars LP and HP.

LP	P#	PNAME	COLOR	WEIGHT	CITY
	P1	Nut	Red	12.0	London
	P4	Screw	Red	14.0	London
	P5	Cam	Blue	12.0	Paris

HP	P#	PNAME	COLOR	WEIGHT	CITY
	P2	Bolt	Green	17.0	Paris
	P3	Screw	Blue	17.0	Oslo
	P6	Cog	Red	19.0	London

Figure 12-5. *Relvars LP and HP—sample values*

Why might we want to perform such a horizontal decomposition? Frankly, I'm not aware of any good *logical* reason for doing so, though of course that's not to say no such reason exists. But there are certainly plenty of *physical* reasons, given today's DBMS implementations; in those systems, the logical and physical levels tend to be in lockstep, pretty much, and there's not nearly as much data independence as relational systems are theoretically capable of. Since there are often pragmatic reasons (having to do with recovery, security, performance, and other such matters) for partitioning data at the physical level, it follows that there are likely to be pragmatic reasons for partitioning the data at the logical level as well, in such systems.

Now, regardless of what you might think of the foregoing argument, at least there's nothing logically wrong with the design of Figure 12-5. But suppose we were to define relvar LP just a little differently; to be specific, suppose we defined it to contain those parts with weight less than *or equal to* 17 pounds (adjusting the predicate accordingly, of course). Figure 12-6 is a revised version of Figure 12-5, showing what happens with this revised design.

LP	P#	PNAME	COLOR	WEIGHT	CITY
	P1	Nut	Red	12.0	London
	P2	Bolt	Green	17.0	Paris
	P3	Screw	Blue	17.0	Oslo
	P4	Screw	Red	14.0	London
	P5	Cam	Blue	12.0	Paris

HP	P#	PNAME	COLOR	WEIGHT	CITY
	P2	Bolt	Green	17.0	Paris
	P3	Screw	Blue	17.0	Oslo
	P6	Cog	Red	19.0	London

Figure 12-6. *Relvars LP (revised) and HP—sample values*

Now there definitely is something wrong with the design. To be specific, observe that the tuples for parts P2 and P3 each appear in both relvars in Figure 12-6 (in other words, there's now some redundancy). Observe further that they *must* appear in both relvars! For suppose, contrariwise, that (say) the tuple for part P2 appeared in HP and not in LP. Then, noting that LP contains no tuple for part P2, we could legitimately conclude from *The Closed World Assumption* that it's not the case that part P2 weighs 17 pounds. But then we see from HP that part P2 in fact does weigh 17 pounds, and the database is thus inconsistent (it contains a contradiction). And as I've shown elsewhere—see, for example, the O'Reilly book once again—we can never trust the answers we get from an inconsistent database! In fact, we can derive *absolutely any result whatsoever* (even nonsensical results like 1 = 0) from such a database.

Fairly obviously, then, we need another design principle to help us avoid situations like that illustrated in Figure 12-6. In order to see what that principle must be, we need to take a closer look at the relationship between tuples and propositions.

Tuples *vs.* Propositions

Let me begin by reminding you that every tuple appearing in relvar *R* at a given time represents a certain proposition, where the proposition in question is an instantiation of the relvar predicate for *R* that (by convention) is understood to be true at the time in question. In the case of relvar HP from Figures 12-5 and 12-6, for example, the relvar predicate is:

> *Part P# is used in the enterprise, is named PNAME, has color COLOR and weight WEIGHT (which is greater than or equal to 17 pounds), and is stored in city CITY.*

And the tuple for part P6 (for example) represents the following instantiation of that predicate:

> *Part P6 is used in the enterprise, is named Cog, has color Red and weight 19.0 (which is greater than or equal to 17 pounds), and is stored in city London.*

I also suggested earlier that the database involves some redundancy if and only if it says the same thing twice. Now I can make this statement a little more precise:

The database involves some redundancy if and only if it contains two representations of the very same proposition.

Now, given that tuples represent propositions, it's tempting to translate this latter statement into the following one: The database involves some redundancy if and only if it contains two appearances of the very same tuple. Unfortunately, this "definition" is, at best, considerably oversimplified. Let's examine it more carefully.

First of all, it's at least true that we don't want the same tuple to appear more than once within the same relation (and here I do mean relation, not relvar), because such a state of affairs would certainly constitute "saying the same thing twice." (As I once heard Codd remark: If something is true, saying it twice doesn't make it any more true.) Of course, the relational model itself takes care of this requirement—by definition, relations never contain duplicate tuples.[7]

As an aside, I observe that we now have a precise characterization of the notion of "duplicate tuples" (people use this phrase all the time, and yet I very much doubt whether many of them would be able to define it precisely if pressed). Strictly speaking, of course, two tuples are duplicates if and only if they're the very same tuple—just as two integers are duplicates if and only if they're the very same integer—and the phrase "duplicate tuples" thus doesn't really make much sense from a logical point of view. What people really mean when they use that phrase is duplicate *appearances* of the *same* tuple—recall from the section "Some Prerequisites" that value *vs.* appearance is one of the great logical differences (tuples are certainly values, of course).

To get back to the main discussion: Second, it's easy to see that the very same tuple can represent any number of distinct propositions. As a trivial example, let SCITY and PCITY be the projections of suppliers on CITY and parts on CITY, respectively. Given the sample data values of Figure 12-1, then, the tuple <London> appears in both SCITY and PCITY, but it represents two different propositions—in SCITY, it represents the proposition *There's at least one supplier in London*, in PCITY it represents the proposition *There's at least one part in London* (simplifying slightly for the sake of the example).

What's more—and here I have to get a little more formal on you for a moment—the same proposition can be represented by any number of distinct tuples, too. That's because, formally, the pertinent *attribute names* are part of the tuple. Thus, for example, we might have our usual relvar SP with its attributes S#, P#, and QTY, and predicate:

Supplier S# supplies QTY of part P#.

We might additionally have a relvar PS with attributes SNO, PNO, and AMT, with predicate:

Supplier SNO supplies AMT of part PNO.

And then (to use **Tutorial D** syntax) the following tuples might appear in these two relvars, respectively:

---

7. In other words, it might be argued that a desire to avoid redundancy is one of the motivations (perhaps a minor one) for choosing sets—which don't contain duplicate elements, by definition—instead of "bags," which do, as the right mathematical abstraction on which to found a solid database theory. SQL apologists please note!

```
TUPLE { S#  S#('S1'), P#  P#('P1'), QTY QTY(300) }
TUPLE { SNO S#('S1'), PNO P#('P1'), AMT QTY(300) }
```

These are clearly different tuples, but they both represent the same proposition:

Supplier S1 supplies 300 of part P1.

In fact, either of the two relvars SP and PS can be defined in terms of the other, as the following constraints both show:[8]

```
CONSTRAINT PS_SAME_AS_SP
   PS = SP RENAME ( S# AS SNO, P# AS PNO, QTY AS AMT ) ;

CONSTRAINT SP_SAME_AS_PS
   SP = PS RENAME ( SNO AS S#, PNO AS P#, AMT AS QTY ) ;
```

A database that contained both relvars would thus clearly involve some redundancy.

Here's a simpler example to illustrate essentially the same point. Suppose we replace attribute CITY in the suppliers relvar S by two distinct attributes CITYA and CITYB, with the constraint that the CITYA and CITYB values are equal in every tuple (both of them representing the city for the applicable supplier). Here's a sample tuple:

```
TUPLE { S# S#('S1'), SNAME NAME('Smith'), STATUS 20,
                     CITYA 'London', CITYB 'London' }
```

Then the following tuples—both of them projections of the tuple just shown[9]—are certainly distinct, but they clearly represent the same proposition:

```
TUPLE { S# S#('S1'), SNAME NAME('Smith'), STATUS 20, CITYA 'London' }

TUPLE { S# S#('S1'), SNAME NAME('Smith'), STATUS 20, CITYB 'London' }
```

Of course, the foregoing design would be extremely unlikely in practice. Note in particular that the principles of normalization militate against it; to be specific, the relvar satisfies the functional dependencies

```
{ CITYA } → { CITYB }
```

and

```
{ CITYB } → { CITYA }
```

and is thus not in 5NF (in fact, it isn't even in 3NF). But normalization *per se* doesn't solve the problem in this example (why not?), nor does it alter the fact that any number of distinct tuples can indeed represent the same proposition.

Now, I said earlier that we can think of design theory as a set of principles and techniques for helping to pin down predicates (and hence constraints), and so it is. If we try to write down the predicate for the revised suppliers relvar (the one with attributes CITYA and CITYB), the fact that the design is bad becomes obvious:

---

8. By the way, note the relational comparisons in these constraints. How would you formulate them in SQL?

9. Here I'm overloading the projection operator by allowing it to apply to tuples as well as to relations (or relvars). I'll assume the availability of this "tuple projection" operator elsewhere in this chapter as well.

Supplier S# is under contract, is named SNAME, has status STATUS, is located in city CITYA, and is located in city CITYB.

Here also, repeated, are the predicates for the two different shipments relvars SP and PS:

Supplier S# supplies QTY of part P#.

Supplier SNO supplies AMT of part PNO.

These two examples suggest an obvious rule of thumb: When carrying out the initial design process—in other words, when writing down the predicates or business rules—*always use the same name for the same property;*[10] don't "play games" by using both S# and SNO to refer to supplier numbers, QTY and AMT to refer to quantities, CITYA and CITYB to refer to cities, and so on. Following this rule will make it less likely that two distinct tuples will represent the same proposition.

Orthogonality (II)

The net of the discussions in the previous section is that, in general, there's nothing like a one-to-one correspondence between tuples and propositions. Thus, we can't say categorically that the database involves some redundancy if and only if it contains two appearances of the same tuple. What we can say, however, is that if the database does contain two appearances of the same tuple, then there's at least a possibility—maybe even a strong possibility, especially if the tuple in question is of degree greater than one[11]—that it involves some redundancy. In support of this claim, I observe that conventional normalization is precisely about eliminating redundant appearances of the same tuple. For example, suppose our usual suppliers relvar S is subject to an additional constraint to the effect that STATUS is functionally dependent on CITY:

$$\{ \text{ CITY } \} \rightarrow \{ \text{ STATUS } \}$$

Figure 12-7 shows a sample value for the relvar that conforms to this additional constraint (I've changed the status of supplier S3 from 10 to 30 to make it do so).

S	S#	SNAME	STATUS	CITY	
	S1	Smith	20	London	
	S2	Jones	*30*	Paris	⟵ note the
	S3	Blake	30	Paris	change
	S4	Clark	20	London	
	S5	Adams	30	Athens	

Figure 12-7. *Revised suppliers relvar—sample value*

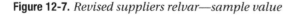

10. I apologize for my use of the term *property* here, which (because it's so vague) is a term I usually prefer to avoid, but I'm only using it in the context of a rule of thumb anyway.

11. The *degree* of a tuple (or relation or relvar) is the cardinality of the set of attributes of that tuple (or relation or relvar).

Note that the relation in Figure 12-7 does include duplicate appearances of the same tuple; to be specific, the tuples <20,London> and <30,Paris> both appear twice (of course, these two tuples are both "subtuples," but I remind you that a subtuple is a tuple, just as a subset is a set). What's more, the two <20,London> appearances do represent the same proposition,[12] as do the two <30,Paris> appearances, and so we do have some redundancy on our hands.

Now, conventional normalization would get rid of the redundancies in this example by decomposing the relvar into projections as illustrated in Figure 12-8. As you can see, therefore, normalization is indeed, as claimed, a process of eliminating redundant (sub)tuples and thus reducing *data* redundancy.

SNC	S#	SNAME	CITY		CT	CITY	STATUS
	S1	Smith	London			Athens	30
	S2	Jones	Paris			London	20
	S3	Blake	Paris			Paris	30
	S4	Clark	London				
	S5	Adams	Athens				

Figure 12-8. *Decomposing the relvar of Figure 12-7—sample values*

Several earlier examples in this chapter also illustrate redundancies that arise from the fact that some (sub)tuple appears more than once. To be specific:

- The database of Figure 12-4—the one involving relvars SNT and STC—contains two appearances of each of five subtuples (one for each of the five suppliers), where the subtuples in question are the projections of the corresponding tuples of the suppliers relvar S on S# and STATUS. Again the database involves some redundancy, and again normalization comes to our rescue (so long as we pay attention to "the fifth normalization principle," that is—but as we'll soon see, it's really orthogonality, not normalization as such, that we're talking about here).

- The database of Figure 12-3—the one involving relvar CTXD—also contains several appearances of each of several subtuples (for example, the subtuple <Math,Prof.Green>) and also involves some redundancy. Unfortunately, we already know that normalization as such is of no help with this example.

- The database of Figure 12-6—the one involving relvar HP and a revised version of relvar LP—contains two appearances of the tuple for part P2 and two appearances of the tuple for part P3 and therefore also involves some redundancy. Normalization as conventionally understood is of no help with this example, either. But in this case the problem is easy to see, and the solution looks as if it should be reasonably straightforward, too. Let's think about it.

---

12. To spell it out, the proposition in question is essentially this: *There exists a supplier S# and a name SNAME such that supplier S# is under contract, is named SNAME, is located in city London, and— precisely because the city is London—has status 20.*

The problem with the database of Figure 12-6 is that the predicates for relvars LP and HP "overlap," in the sense that what is effectively the very same proposition can be a valid instantiation of both of them. Clearly, we would like to prevent such a state of affairs if we could. Unfortunately we can't (at least, not exactly)—as I've already said, the system doesn't understand relvar predicates. But it does understand relvar constraints, which (to say it one more time) are the system's approximation to the corresponding predicate. In particular, if tuple *t* satisfies the relvar predicate for relvar *R*, we can safely say it satisfies the relvar *constraint* for *R* as well; thus, if the relvar constraints for relvars *A* and *B* are such that the very same tuple *t* can satisfy both of them, there's at least a possibility that the corresponding predicates overlap and redundancy can thereby occur. Thus, we might reasonably consider adopting the following rule:

The Principle of Orthogonal Design (first version): No two distinct relvars should be such that their relvar constraints permit the same tuple to appear in both.

Adherence to this rule in the case at hand (Figure 12-6) would certainly avoid the redundancies involved in that database. (As it is, the relvar constraints for the relvars in that database are identical, except that one includes the condition "weight ≥ 17 pounds" and the other the condition "weight ≤ 17 pounds"; they can thus indeed be satisfied by the very same tuple.)

As a matter of fact we can extend the rule to take care of "the fifth normalization principle" as well:

The Principle of Orthogonal Design (second version): Let *A* and *B* be distinct relvars. Then there should not exist nonloss decompositions of *A* and *B* into projections *A1, A2, ..., Am* and *B1, B2, ..., Bn*, respectively, such that the relvar constraints for some *Ai* (*i* = *1, 2, ..., m*) and some *Bj* (*j* = *1, 2, ..., n*) are such as to permit the same tuple to appear in both.

This second version of the rule subsumes "the fifth normalization principle" because, if the database satisfies it, it certainly satisfies that "fifth principle" as well. What's more, this second version subsumes the first version of the rule, too, because one nonloss decomposition that always exists for any given relvar *R* is that into the corresponding identity projection.

I'll close this section with a few miscellaneous remarks. First, I should explain why the principle has the name it does: *The Principle of Orthogonal Design*. Basically, the term *orthogonal* derives from the fact that what the principle says is that relvars should all be independent of one another—which they won't be, if their constraints "overlap," as it were. *Note:* I remind you that what we would really like to do is prohibit overlapping *predicates*—but we can't, not properly, because the system doesn't understand predicates. Prohibiting overlapping *constraints* is the best approximation we can get to what we would really like to do.

Second, orthogonality complements normalization, in a sense: Normalization is about reducing redundancy within a given relvar; orthogonality is about reducing redundancy across distinct relvars. We might therefore consider trying to unify them into some kind of grand *redundancy reduction principle*—but I won't attempt any such unification in the present chapter (at least, not formally).

Next, orthogonality implies that if we want to decompose some relvar via restriction instead of projection, we should take care to ensure that the restrictions in question are pairwise disjoint (as well as ensuring that their union gets us back to the original relvar, of course). *Note:* In *An Introduction to Database Systems,* I referred to a decomposition that satisfies this requirement as an *orthogonal decomposition*—but I now think it would be better to generalize this term and use it to mean any decomposition that satisfies *The Principle of Orthogonal Design*. This revised definition includes the earlier one as a special case.

Finally, I remind you that there don't seem to be any strong *logical* reasons for decomposing some relvar "horizontally," via restriction (though that's not to say that no such reasons exist). Orthogonality differs from normalization in this regard; normalization does offer strong reasons for decomposing "vertically," but (to repeat) orthogonality doesn't seem to offer any comparably strong reasons for decomposing "horizontally." What's more, decomposing horizontally leads to the need for additional integrity constraints to be declared and enforced, precisely in order to enforce the required disjointness. For example, if we replace our usual suppliers relvar by a separate restriction for each supplier city, then we'll need a constraint to the effect that no supplier number appears in more than one of those restrictions. (Of course, decomposing vertically leads to the need for additional constraints, too—typically foreign key constraints.)

What About Views?

According to *The Principle of Interchangeability* (of base and virtual relvars), there should be no arbitrary and unnecessary distinctions between base relvars and views; in other words, views are supposed to look and feel just like base relvars. (In accordance with the assumptions spelled out earlier in this connection, by "views" here I don't mean views defined as mere shorthands, I mean views that are meant to insulate the user from the "real" database in some way.) In general, in fact, any given user interacts not with a database that contains base relvars only (the "real" database), but rather with what might be called a *user database* that contains some mixture of base relvars and views. By definition, however, that user database is supposed to look and feel like the real database to that user, and so it follows that **all of the design principles discussed in this chapter—including the principles of normalization and orthogonality in particular— apply equally well to such user databases,** not just to the real database.

Second, *The Principle of Interchangeability* also implies that views must be updatable. Now, it's well known that view updatability is a contentious issue, and I certainly don't want to get into that issue here, at least not in detail. All I want to do here is make the following points:

- An appendix to the *Third Manifesto* book includes my own proposals for a set of view updating rules. (Those rules are based on, but are not identical to, an earlier set described in a pair of papers by David McGoveran and myself—"Updating Union, Intersection, and Difference Views" and "Updating Joins and Other Views," both of which can be found in my book *Relational Database Writings 1991–1994*, Addison-Wesley, 1995.)

- The rules in question satisfy certain desirable properties.

- The properties in question include the following among several others:

  - *All* views are potentially updatable (barring integrity constraint violations); there's no such thing as a view that's inherently nonupdatable.

  - The result of applying a given update to a given view is always predictable.

  - The result of performing a given update on a given view is usually (though possibly not always) just what one would intuitively expect.

And (most important for the purposes of the present chapter):

- If the database abides by *The Principle of Orthogonal Design*, then the number of cases—it is tempting to call them pathological—in which results are *not* as one would intuitively expect is significantly reduced.

Note carefully that the view updating rules I'm referring to don't *require* the database to abide by *The Principle of Orthogonal Design*—they just work a little better, as it were, if it does.[13] What's more, if the database violates that principle (see the section immediately following), it's still unlikely in practice that view updating will produce unexpected results, precisely because it's unlikely that views that might give such results will actually be updated (or even defined, possibly).

Violating Orthogonality

Everybody knows there can sometimes be good reasons for violating the principles of normalization—good *logical* reasons, I mean; I'm not a fan of "denormalizing for performance," which should never be necessary anyway, in a properly architected DBMS (but that's another topic I don't want to get into in detail on here). I described one such reason earlier in this chapter, in the section "A Brief Review of Normalization," where I showed there can be a conflict between the objective of full normalization and the objective of dependency preservation; in other words, we might decide it's worth living with some redundancy in order to make certain update procedures simpler,[14] and certain constraints easier to state and maintain, than they would otherwise be. There might be other good reasons, too.

In the same kind of way, sometimes there'll be good reasons for violating *The Principle of Orthogonal Design*. In particular, recall from the section "Tuples *vs.* Propositions" earlier in this chapter that the very same tuple can represent any number of distinct propositions. One consequence of this fact is that a design that violates orthogonality might sometimes be acceptable. The following simple example is due to Hugh Darwen. Consider the predicates *Employee E# is on vacation* and *Employee E# is awaiting phone number allocation.* The obvious design for this situation involves two unary relvars—that is, relvars of degree one—that look like this (in outline):

```
ON_VACATION { E# }
          KEY { E# }

NEEDS_PHONE { E# }
          KEY { E# }
```

---

13. I mention this point because the principle has been criticized as having been defined purely to bolster up the view updating mechanism. I reject this criticism. As I've tried to show, orthogonality would still be a good idea even if view updating weren't an issue at all.

14. I remark in passing that this observation suggests another possible characterization of redundancy (or at least another way to think about it, if only informally): *Reducing* redundancy makes more single-tuple updates logically acceptable than would otherwise be the case—because the presence of redundancy implies that sometimes we have to update several tuples "at the same time," as it were, meaning that what would otherwise be single-tuple updates have to become multi-tuple updates instead.

Clearly, the very same employee can be represented in both of these relvars at the same time, and the design thus violates orthogonality. But even if the very same tuple *t* appears in both relvars, those two appearances represent two different propositions, and there's no redundancy involved. Violating orthogonality doesn't *necessarily* imply redundancy—as indeed we already know.

(On the other hand, it would be remiss of me not to point out that there is at least a difference in kind between the example just discussed and the examples of light *vs.* heavy parts—LP *vs.* HP—discussed, and illustrated in Figures 12-5 and 12-6, earlier in this chapter. In the LP *vs.* HP examples, we can write a formal constraint, to the effect that the WEIGHT value has to lie in a certain range, that a given part tuple has to satisfy in order for it to be accepted into LP or HP or both. However, there's no formal constraint we can write that a given "E# tuple" has to satisfy in order for it to be accepted into ON_VACATION or NEEDS_PHONE or both. If the user asserts that a certain "E# tuple" is to be inserted into, say, ON_VACATION, then the system simply has to trust the user; there's no check it can perform to ascertain that the tuple does indeed belong in ON_VACATION instead of or as well as NEEDS_PHONE.)

Here's another example, also due to Hugh Darwen, that might mistakenly be thought to violate orthogonality[15] but in fact doesn't. It's based on an example from his presentation "How to Handle Missing Information Without Using Nulls" (slides available at http://www.thethirdmanifesto.com, May 9th, 2003). We're given three relvars that look like this (in outline):

```
EARNS      { E#, SALARY }
           KEY { E# }

SALARY_UNK { E# }
           KEY { E# }

UNSALARIED { E# }
           KEY { E# }
```

Sample values are shown in Figure 12-9.

EARNS		SALARY_UNK	UNSALARIED
E#	**SALARY**	**E#**	**E#**
E1	85,000	E2	E4
E3	70,000		

Figure 12-9. *Relvars EARNS, SALARY_UNK, and UNSALARIED—sample values*

---

15. Indeed, I thought as much myself at one time, which is why I include the example here.

The predicates for these three relvars are as follows:

- EARNS: *Employee E# has salary SALARY.*

- SALARY_UNK: *Employee E# has a salary, but we don't know what it is.*

- UNSALARIED: *Employee E# doesn't have a salary.*

Now, even if the same employee could be simultaneously represented in both SALARY_UNK and UNSALARIED, there would be no redundancy, because the tuples in question would represent two different propositions. In fact, however, the semantics of the situation are such that no employee *can* be simultaneously represented in both relvars. We therefore need an integrity constraint—part of the relvar constraint for both relvars—to express this fact:

```
CONSTRAINT SALARY_UNK_AND_UNSALARIED_DISJOINT
    IS_EMPTY ( SALARY_UNK JOIN UNSALARIED ) ;
```

In a nutshell, then: Let *t* be a tuple and let *t1* and *t2* be extensions of *t* (tuple *b* is an extension of tuple *a* if and only if tuple *a* is a projection of tuple *b*). Let *t1* and *t2* appear in relvars *R1* and *R2*, respectively (*R1* and *R2* distinct), and let those appearances denote propositions *p1* and *p2*, respectively. Let *q1* be that portion of *p1* that mentions attributes of *t* only, and let *q2* be that portion of *p2* that mentions attributes of *t* only. Then, if propositions *q1* and *q2* are distinct, it's all right to have *t1* appear in *R1* and *t2* appear in *R2* at the same time, even if such a state of affairs violates orthogonality. In other words, *The Principle of Orthogonal Design* is sometimes stronger than it needs to be; adherence to it is likely to reduce redundancy, but it can be violated with impunity—logical impunity, at least—if such violation doesn't *increase* redundancy.

But Isn't It All Just Common Sense?

Perhaps I should have addressed this issue earlier. The fact is, database design theory in general, and normalization and orthogonality in particular, have often been criticized on the grounds that they're all basically just common sense. By way of example, consider Figure 12-4 again, which shows a design for suppliers in which the suppliers relvar has been split into two projections, SNT (on S#, SNAME, and STATUS) and STC (on S#, STATUS, and CITY). Now, that design is obviously bad; the redundancies are obvious, the consequences are obvious too, and any competent human designer would "naturally" avoid such a design. But what does "naturally" mean here? What principles is the designer applying in opting for the more "natural" design (the one illustrated in Figure 12-1)? The answer is: They're exactly the principles of normalization and orthogonality. That is, competent designers already have those principles in their brain, as it were, even if they've never studied them formally and can't put a name to them. So yes, the principles are common sense—but they're *formalized* common sense. (Common sense might be common, but it's not so easy to say exactly what it is!) What design theory does is *state in a precise way what certain aspects of common sense consist of.* In my opinion, that's the real achievement of the theory: It formalizes certain commonsense principles, thereby opening the door to the possibility of mechanizing those principles (that is, incorporating them into mechanical design tools). Critics of design theory usually miss this point; they claim, quite rightly, that the ideas are really just common sense, but they typically don't realize that it's a significant achievement to state what common sense means in a precise and formal way.

That said, I'd like to add that common sense might not be all that common, anyway. The following is a quote from a very early—1970s?—paper on database design by Robert R. Brown of Hughes Aircraft[16] (he's claiming that redundancy is a real life problem):

[The following design represents] a simplified real example ...

```
EMP  { E#, ENAME, PHONE#, D#, MGRNAME }
     KEY { E# }

DEPT { D#, DNAME, MGRNAME, MGRPHONE# }
     KEY { D# }
```

The actual database on which this example is based had many more files and fields and much more redundancy. When [the designer] was asked his reasons for such a design, he cited ... performance and the difficulty of doing joins ... Even though the redundancy should be clear to you in my example, it was not that evident in either the program or [the] schema documentation. In large databases with many more files and fields, it is impossible to find the duplications without doing extensive information analysis ... and without having extended discussions with the ... experts in the user organizations.

Other Kinds of Redundancy

This brings me to the end of my discussion of normalization and orthogonality as such. In order to illustrate my claim that design theory as a field of investigation in general is still wide open, however, in this section I want to give a few examples of designs that are fully normalized and fully orthogonal and yet still suffer from various kinds of redundancy.

Example 1: Consider the following self-explanatory name-and-address relvar:

```
NADDR { NAME, ADDR }
      KEY { NAME }
```

Suppose attribute ADDR in this relvar is *tuple-valued,* where the tuples in question have attributes STREET, CITY, STATE, and ZIP. A sample value is shown in Figure 12-10. If we assume (as is conventional in such examples) that whenever two ADDR values have the same ZIP component, they also have the same CITY and STATE components, then this design clearly involves some redundancy—yet there's no violation of normalization here. In particular, the functional dependency

$$\{ \text{ZIP} \} \rightarrow \{ \text{CITY, STATE} \}$$

does not hold, since functional dependencies are defined to hold among attributes, not among components of attributes.

---

16. Unfortunately I lost my original copy of this paper in the Loma Prieta earthquake and can no longer cite the original source.

Figure 12-10. *Relvar NADDR (ADDR is tuple-valued)—sample value*

Example 2: Now, Codd would probably have prohibited the design of Example 1 on the grounds that values of attribute ADDR aren't "atomic." I don't fully agree with this position myself, for reasons explained in detail in Chapter 8 in the present book—but maybe my disagreement isn't important, because we can obviously replace that tuple-valued attribute by a simple text-valued attribute as shown in Figure 12-11. Codd presumably would have allowed that revised design, and yet it suffers from redundancies precisely analogous to those in Example 1.

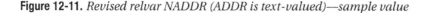

Figure 12-11. *Revised relvar NADDR (ADDR is text-valued)—sample value*

Example 3: Redundancies similar to those in Example 2 can arise in connection with attributes of type DATE, if those attributes include the day of the week as well as a calendar date (as in, for example, "Wednesday, February 22nd, 2006").

Example 4: This next example is an extremely simple version of the familiar employees-and-programmers example, in which all programmers are employees but some employees aren't programmers.[17] Here's the conventional design:

---

17. Some would say that employees and programmers in this example correspond to an *entity supertype* and an *entity subtype,* respectively. Like the term *property,* however (see earlier in this chapter), I regard the term *entity* as unpleasantly vague and choose not to use it, for the most part.

```
EMP  { E# }
     KEY { E# }

PGMR { E#, LANG }
     KEY { E# }
```

I'm assuming for simplicity that nonprogrammers have no attributes of interest apart from E# (if they do, it makes no significant difference to the example), and programmers have just one additional attribute, LANG (programming language skill). Now we have a choice: Record all employees in EMP, or record just the nonprogrammers in EMP. Which is better?

- If we record just the nonprogrammers in EMP, the processing involved when an employee becomes or ceases to be a programmer is slightly nontrivial—in both cases we have to delete a tuple from one relvar and insert a tuple into the other. (Also, note the implications if we want some other relvar to include a reference to employees. Normally that reference would be a simple foreign key; but if employees are split across two relvars, EMP and PGMR, it can't be.)

- On the other hand, if we record all employees in EMP, we have some redundancy in our design (if *e* is a programmer, *e* is certainly an employee, so why say so explicitly?).

Note, incidentally, that there's no violation of orthogonality in this example, even if we do record all employees in EMP. Suppose we do; then it's clearly the case that PGMR has a projection, on E#, with the property that the very same tuple can (and in fact must) appear both in that projection and in EMP—but that projection isn't derivable from PGMR *via nonloss decomposition*, which it would have to be in order to violate orthogonality. Thus, a database can satisfy *The Principle of Orthogonal Design* and yet still exhibit some redundancy.

Now, it's pertinent to remind you at this point that I'm using the term *nonloss decomposition* to mean, specifically, a decomposition that additionally satisfies the requirement that every projection is needed in the reconstruction process. If we were to use a weaker definition of the term, one that didn't impose that additional requirement, then the foregoing paragraph would be incorrect. To be specific:

- Clearly, PGMR is equal to the join of its projections on (a) E# and (b) E# and LANG.

- PGMR could thus be nonloss-decomposed into those two projections; in particular, therefore, the projection of PGMR on E# *could* be obtained from PGMR via nonloss decomposition.

- The second design (the one involving some redundancy) would thus violate orthogonality after all.

But of course this decomposition of PGMR does fail to satisfy the requirement that every projection is needed in the reconstruction process (to be specific, the projection on just E# is obviously unnecessary). On balance, my strong preference is to stick with nonloss decomposition, and hence orthogonality, as previously defined. In fact, if we didn't, then **every foreign key** would constitute a violation of orthogonality!—as the foregoing example suggests (note that {E#} is a foreign key in PGMR, referencing the sole key {E#} in EMP, in the design in which EMP does represent all employees).

Example 5: Now I'd like to extend Example 4 slightly in order to make an additional point. Suppose relvar EMP does include at least one additional attribute after all, JOB, such that a given employee is a programmer, and is represented in relvar PGMR, if and only if the JOB value in that employee's tuple in EMP has the value 'Pgmr' (maybe other values of JOB—'Janitor', for example—correspond to other relvars). This kind of situation is not at all uncommon in practice, by the way. Once again, then, the design exhibits some redundancy, because it satisfies the following constraint (as well as many similar ones):

```
CONSTRAINT PGMR_CONSTRAINT
   ( EMP WHERE JOB = 'Pgmr' ) { E# } = PGMR { E# } ;
```

Example 6: In his RM/T paper ("Extending the Database Relational Model to Capture More Meaning," *ACM TODS 4*, No. 4, December 1979), Codd proposed a certain design discipline, a simplified form of which can be described thus:[18]

- Let *E* be an entity type, and let *ID* be a data type such that every entity of type *E* has exactly one *primary identifier* (my term, not Codd's), of type *ID*. For example, *E* and *ID* might be the entity type "suppliers" and the data type "supplier numbers," respectively.

- Let *P1*, *P2*, ..., *Pn* be a set of property types such that every entity of type *E* has at most one property of each of the types *P1*, *P2*, ..., *Pn*. In the case of suppliers, for example, *P1*, *P2*, ..., *Pn* might be the types "name," "status," and "city" (so *n* = 3 in this example). *Note:* I'm assuming here that a given supplier can have any subset of the three properties, including the empty set in particular (of course!).

- Then the database should include:

  - Exactly one **E-relvar,** containing *ID* values for those entities of type *E* extant at any given time

  - Exactly one **P-relvar** for each *Pi* (*i* = 1, 2, ..., n), containing *ID*-value:*Pi*-value pairs for each entity of type *E* that is extant at any given time and has a property of type *Pi* at that time

Applying this "RM/T discipline" (as I'll call it) to the case of suppliers specifically, we obtain a design that looks like this:

```
VAR S  BASE RELATION { S# S# }
       KEY { S# } ;

VAR SN BASE RELATION { S# S#, SNAME NAME }
       KEY { S# }
       FOREIGN KEY { S# } REFERENCES S ;

VAR ST BASE RELATION { S# S#, STATUS INTEGER }
       KEY { S# }
       FOREIGN KEY { S# } REFERENCES S ;
```

---

18. Details of the simplifications aren't important for present purposes. Once again, however, I feel obliged to apologize, slightly, for my use of the vague terms *entity* and *property*—but here I'm simply following the usage in Codd's paper.

```
VAR SC BASE RELATION { S# S#, CITY CHAR }
       KEY { S# }
       FOREIGN KEY { S# } REFERENCES S ;
```

Each of these relvars is *irreducible,* or equivalently in *sixth normal form,* 6NF (see Example 11 later in this section for further discussion of this concept). Figure 12-12 shows a set of sample values. *Note:* Those values aren't meant to be the same as our usual sample values, though they're close. Observe in particular that (a) supplier S3 has no status, (b) supplier S4 has no status and no city, and (c) supplier S5 has no name, no status, and no city.

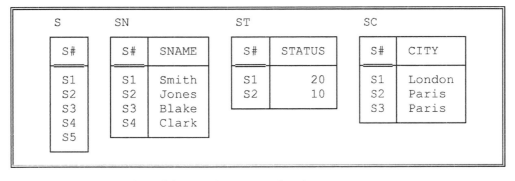

Figure 12-12. *An "RM/T design" for suppliers—sample values*

Now, this kind of design actually has a lot to recommend it (at least, it would in a well-architected system). For present purposes, however, all I want to do is call your attention to the following: So long as every entity of type *E* has at least one of the *n* properties, then the design certainly involves some redundancy—arguably, in fact, *strong* redundancy as defined by Codd himself in his 1970 paper—because, at any given time, the value of the E-relvar will be equal to the union of the projections of the P-relvars over the identifier attribute. This kind of redundancy would apply to Figure 12-12, for example, if we deleted supplier S5 (that is, if every supplier had at least one of the three properties name, status, and city). *Exercise for the reader:* How does the redundancy here differ from that discussed under Example 4? *Does* it differ? Would it make any difference if the employees of Example 4 had additional properties (for example, names)?

Observe further that the design becomes "even more redundant," as it were, in the (common?) special case in which every entity of type *E* in fact has all of the *n* properties. Figure 12-13 is a revised version of Figure 12-12 that illustrates this situation. Note in that figure that—speaking a trifle loosely—{S#} is now a foreign key in each of the relvars that references the sole key {S#} in each of the others; equivalently, the projection on S# of any of the relvars is equal to the projection on S# of any of the others. Note carefully, however, that even in this extreme case, the design doesn't violate orthogonality. What's more, I say again that this kind of design would in fact have a lot to recommend it in a well-architected system.[19] In particular, the redundancies would be properly managed in such a system (see the section "Managing Redundancy," later).

---

19. I have in mind here, primarily, a system implemented using the facilities of *The TransRelational*[TM] *Model.* You can find a preliminary description of this model in Appendix A of my book *An Introduction to Database Systems,* 8th edition (Addison-Wesley, 2004).

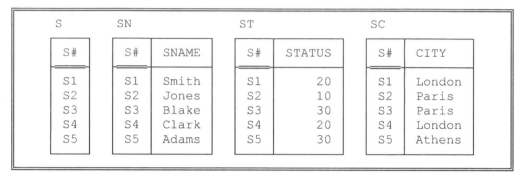

Figure 12-13. *A revised version of Figure 12-12*

Example 7: Consider a company in which every employee is required to be in exactly one department and every department is required to have at least one employee. Figure 12-14 shows sample values (in outline) for an RM/T design for this situation.[20]

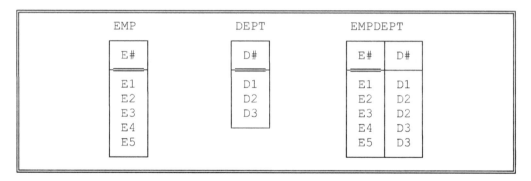

Figure 12-14. *Employees and departments*

With reference to those sample values, however, note that:

- The DEPT relvar shows there are exactly three departments (D1, D2, and D3).

- We're told there's a rule to the effect that every employee must be in exactly one department.

- So why not define one of those departments—D3, say—to be the "default" one, and adopt a rule that says that any employee mentioned in relvar EMP and not in relvar EMPDEPT is in that default department? In terms of Figure 12-14, this rule would allow us to omit employees E4 and E5 from relvar EMPDEPT.

---

20. *Exercise for the reader:* Is EMPDEPT in that figure a P-relvar for employees, departments, or both? Justify your answer!

Indeed, if we don't adopt such a rule, then the design clearly involves some redundancy once again—to be specific, it satisfies the following constraints:

```
CONSTRAINT EVERY_EMP_HAS_A_DEPT
   EMP { E# } = EMPDEPT { E# } ;

CONSTRAINT EVERY_DEPT_HAS_AN_EMP
   DEPT { D# } = EMPDEPT { D# } ;
```

There seem to me to be at least two factors that militate against adopting such a "default department" rule, however. The first is that the choice of which department to make the default is likely to be arbitrary. The second is that now we need to be extremely careful over the meaning of relvar EMPDEPT! The obvious predicate *Employee E# is in department D#* doesn't work. Why not? Because, under that predicate (and assuming department D3 is the default), omitting the tuple, say, <E5,D3> would mean—thanks to *The Closed World Assumption*—that employee E5 *isn't* in department D3! So the predicate has to be something along the following lines:

> *Employee E# is in department* D#, *and there exists exactly one department* d *that appears in relvar DEPT and not in relvar EMPDEPT, and for all employees* e *that appear in relvar EMP and not in relvar EMPDEPT, employee* e *is in department* d.

I doubt very much whether users would want to have to deal with unwieldy predicates like this one.

Example 8: Consider the design illustrated in Figure 12-15 (a revised, somewhat "RM/T-like" version of Figure 12-9). In that design, either relvar SALARY_UNK or relvar UNSALARIED is redundant—any employee represented in relvar EMP and not in relvar EARNS must be represented in precisely one of the other two; thus, we could eliminate, say, relvar SALARY_UNK without any loss of information. Yet there doesn't seem to be any good reason for choosing either of SALARY_UNK and UNSALARIED over the other as the one to be eliminated, and considerations of symmetry would argue in favor of retaining both.[21]

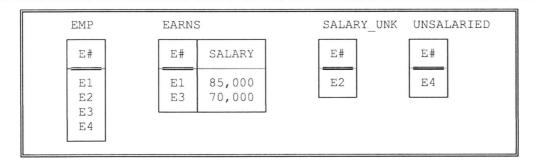

Figure 12-15. *A revised version of Figure 12-9*

---

21. Symmetry is usually a good design principle. To quote Polya (G. Polya: *How To Solve It*, 2nd edition, Princeton University Press, 1971): "Try to treat symmetrically what is symmetrical, and do not destroy wantonly any natural symmetry." But Example 8 and others like it suggest that symmetry and nonredundancy might sometimes be conflicting objectives.

Example 9: This example is also due originally to Hugh Darwen; it's a greatly simplified version of a real life situation that arises in connection with the Open University in the U.K. We're given a relvar that looks like this:

```
VAR SCT BASE RELATION { S# S#, C# C#, T# T# }
    KEY { S#, C#, T# } ;
```

The predicate is: *Student S# is enrolled in course C# and is tutored on that course by tutor T#.* Figure 12-16 shows a sample value for this relvar. The redundancies are obvious: For example, the fact that student S1 is enrolled in course C1, the fact that course C1 is tutored by tutor T1, and the fact that tutor T1 tutors student S1 are all represented more than once in the sample value of Figure 12-16.

SCT

S#	C#	T#
S1	C1	T1
S1	C1	T2
S2	C1	T1
S2	C1	T2
S1	C2	T1
S2	C2	T1

Figure 12-16. *Relvar SCT—sample value*

One way to reduce redundancy in examples like that of Figure 12-16 is by introducing *surrogate keys* (surrogates for short).[22] For example, we might introduce a surrogate SC#, say, to represent the combination of a particular student and a particular course, as illustrated in Figure 12-17.

SCSC

SC#	S#	C#
abc	S1	C1
def	S2	C1
ghi	S1	C2
jkl	S2	C2

SCT

SC#	T#
abc	T1
abc	T2
def	T1
def	T2
ghi	T1
jkl	T1

Figure 12-17. *Using surrogates for S#-C# combinations*

22. As a matter of fact, Codd advocated the use of surrogates in his RM/T discipline (in connection with *all* entity types, that is, not just those with composite keys). In this recommendation he was following the pioneering work of Hall, Owlett, and Todd in their paper "Relations and Entities," in G. M. Nijssen (ed.), *Modelling in Data Base Management Systems* (North-Holland/Elsevier Science, 1975).

One problem with the idea of introducing surrogates in this example is: On what basis do we decide to use surrogates for S#-C# combinations and not for C#-T# combinations or T#-S# combinations? Whichever choice we make is asymmetric. Moreover, surrogates are not without problems of their own, as I've explained elsewhere (see the paper "Composite Keys" in my book *Relational Database Writings 1989–1991*, Addison-Wesley, 1992).

Example 10: Another way to reduce redundancy in examples like that of Figure 12-16 is by means of *relation-valued attributes* (RVAs). Figure 12-18 gives an example. The problem with this approach—quite apart from all of the usual problems that always attend the use of RVAs— is again asymmetry: How do we choose whether to use an RVA for tutors rather than students or courses?

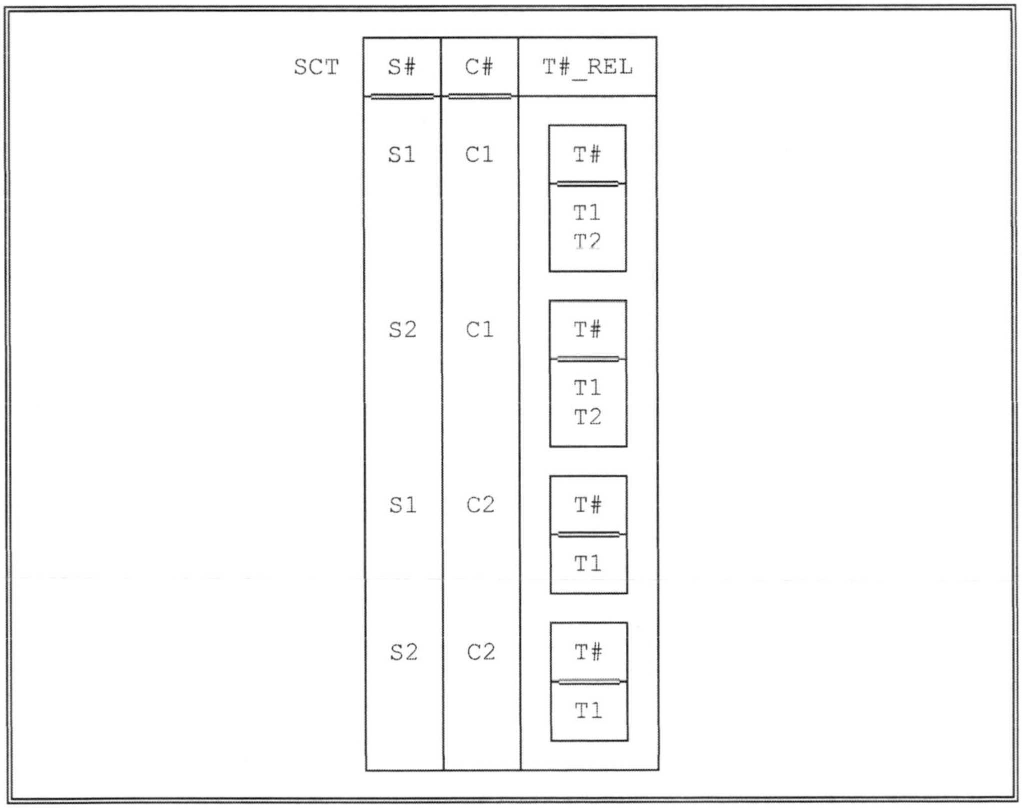

Figure 12-18. *Using an RVA for tutors*

Example 11: This one is essentially just a placemarker. In our book *Temporal Data and the Relational Model* (Morgan Kaufmann, 2003), Hugh Darwen, Nikos Lorentzos, and I show that several further kinds of redundancy can arise in connection with temporal data, and we propose a number of design principles and techniques—including a new normal form, 6NF—for dealing with them. Space prohibits detailed discussion of such matters here; all I want to do here is explain what 6NF means for "regular" (that is, nontemporal) data. Here's the definition:

Relvar *R* is in 6NF if and only if it satisfies no nontrivial join dependencies at all.

Just to remind you, here's the definition of *join dependency:* Let A, B, ..., Z be subsets of the heading of R.[23] Then R satisfies the *join dependency* (JD) ✩$\{A,B,...,Z\}$ if and only if every relation that's a legal value for R is equal to the join of its projections on A, B, ..., Z. Moreover, that JD is *trivial* if and only if at least one of A, B, ..., Z is equal to the entire heading of R (implying that the corresponding projection is in fact the identity projection).

It's immediate from the definition that a nontemporal relvar R that consists of a key (a *single* key, that is) plus at most one additional attribute is in 6NF. A 6NF relvar is also said to be *irreducible*, because it can't be nonloss-decomposed via projection at all, other than trivially. Points arising:

- Any 6NF relvar is necessarily also in 5NF.

- In the RM/T discipline as I described it under Example 6, the E- and P-relvars are in fact in 6NF. (In the interests of historical accuracy, I note that P-relvars as described by Codd in his RM/T paper weren't necessarily in 6NF, however, because he didn't insist that each P-relvar involve just a single "property.")

- I remind you once again that design theory can be seen as a set of principles and techniques for helping to pin down predicates. 6NF in particular can be seen as assisting in the process of identifying what might be called *atomic* predicates: that is, predicates that (a) serve as building blocks from which larger ones can be constructed and (b) cannot themselves be broken down into smaller ones. I would like to say too that, for my own part, I find the discipline of insisting that all relvars be in 6NF an increasingly attractive one.

Example 12 (for there must always be twelve): My final example is typical of a common practical situation. It's loosely based on an example in Fabian Pascal's book *Practical Issues in Database Management: A Reference for the Thinking Practitioner* (Addison-Wesley, 2000). We're given two relvars that look like this:

```
VAR PAYMENTS BASE RELATION
   { CUST# CUST#, DATE DATE, AMT MONEY }
     KEY { CUST#, DATE } ;

VAR TOTALS BASE RELATION
   { CUST# CUST#, TOTAL MONEY }
     KEY { CUST# }
     FOREIGN KEY { CUST# } REFERENCES PAYMENTS ;
```

Attribute TOTAL in relvar TOTALS is an example of what's often called *derived data*, since its value for any given customer is derived by summing all of the payments for the customer in question. Derived data is clearly redundant—though note once again that there are no violations of either normalization or orthogonality here (in particular, both relvars are in 6NF). I'll analyze this example in more detail in the section immediately following.

---

23. The *heading* of a relation or relvar is the set of attributes of that relation or relvar. Observe that every subset of a heading is itself a valid heading also.

Managing Redundancy

The fact that the design of Example 12 from the previous section is redundant is clearly shown by the fact that it satisfies the following constraint (C12):

```
CONSTRAINT C12
   TOTALS = SUMMARIZE PAYMENTS BY { CUST# } ADD ( SUM ( AMT ) AS TOTAL ) ;
```

There are four basic approaches to dealing with the kind of redundancy illustrated by this example:

1. Raw design only

2. Declare the constraint

3. Use a view

4. Use a snapshot

Let's take a closer look.

1. Raw Design Only

This is the approach most likely to be encountered in practice, given the limited functionality provided by most of today's DBMS implementations. The idea is simply that:

a. Relvars PAYMENTS and TOTALS are defined exactly as shown in the previous section.

b. Constraint C12 is *not* declared to the DBMS.

c. Maintaining the derived data is the user's responsibility one hundred percent. (Or some user's responsibility, at any rate; the maintenance might be done by means of a triggered procedure, but some user still has to write that procedure.)

In effect, this approach trades off (a) the extra work involved on the part of the user in executing certain updates (as well as the associated performance hit) against (b) the improved performance obtained when executing certain queries. But there are no guarantees—if the user makes a mistake during some update that (in effect) causes Constraint C12 to be violated, well, tough.

2. Declare the Constraint

In this approach Constraint C12 is explicitly declared to the DBMS and the DBMS takes the responsibility for enforcing it. Maintaining the derived data is still the user's responsibility, though. What's more, if the user carries out this task reliably and correctly, the constraint checking will never fail, and it will thus, in effect, constitute pure overhead on the user's updates. But we can't dispense with the constraint, of course, precisely because we need the system to check that the user *is* carrying out the maintenance task reliably and correctly.

By the way, proper support for this approach will require the system to support, and the user to use, multiple assignment in the maintenance task (see Chapter 11).

3. Use a View

Clearly it would be better if, instead of simply declaring the constraint, we could actually inform the system of the rule by which the derived data is defined and have the system perform the derivation process automatically. And we can; that's exactly what the view mechanism does. To be specific, we can replace the base relvar TOTALS by a view of the same name, thus:

```
VAR TOTALS VIRTUAL
  ( SUMMARIZE PAYMENTS BY { CUST# } ADD ( SUM ( AMT ) AS TOTAL ) ) ;
```

Now the user no longer has to worry about maintaining the derived data; moreover, there's now no way that Constraint C12 can possibly be violated, and there's no need even to state it any more, except perhaps informally (as a means of telling the user the semantics of the view, perhaps). Note, however, that the user does have to be explicitly told not to try to maintain the totals! This fact doesn't mean the user has to be told that relvar TOTALS is a view, though; it just means the user has to be told that the maintenance task will effectively be performed by the system.

4. Use a Snapshot

The drawback to the view solution, however, is that the derivation process is performed every time the view is referenced. Thus, if the object of the exercise is (in effect) to do that work at update time in order to improve subsequent query performance, the view solution is clearly inadequate. In that case, we should use a *snapshot* instead of a view:

```
VAR TOTALS SNAPSHOT
  ( SUMMARIZE PAYMENTS BY { CUST# } ADD ( SUM ( AMT ) AS TOTAL ) )
    REFRESH ON EVERY UPDATE ;
```

The snapshot concept has its origins in a paper by Michel Adiba ("Derived Relations: A Unified Mechanism for Views, Snapshots, and Distributed Data," Proc. 1981 Int. Conf. on Very Large Data Bases, Cannes, France, September 1981; see also the earlier version "Database Snapshots," by Michel E. Adiba and Bruce G. Lindsay, IBM Research Report RJ2772, March 7th, 1980). Basically, snapshots, like views, are derived relvars; unlike views, however, they're real, not virtual—that is, they're represented not just by their definition in terms of other relvars, but also (at least conceptually) by their own separately materialized copy of the data.[24] In other words, defining a snapshot is much like executing a query, except that:

a. The result of the query is kept in the database under the specified name (TOTALS in the example) as a *read-only relvar* (read-only, that is, apart from the periodic refresh—see point b. immediately following).

b. Periodically (ON EVERY UPDATE in the example) the snapshot is *refreshed*—that is, its current value is discarded, the query is executed again, and the result of that new execution becomes the new snapshot value.

---

24. As I mentioned earlier in this chapter, snapshots are also referred to (at least in some circles) as *materialized views*. In my opinion, this terminology should be firmly resisted. A large part of the point about views, at least as far as the relational model is concerned, is precisely that they aren't materialized—in other words, they're virtual—and "materialized view" is simply a contradiction in terms.

The general form of the REFRESH clause is

`REFRESH EVERY <now and then>`

where <*now and then*> might be, for example, MONTH or WEEK or DAY or HOUR or *n* MINUTES or MONDAY or WEEKDAY (and so on). In particular, the specification REFRESH [ON] EVERY UPDATE means the snapshot is kept permanently in synch with the relvar(s) from which it is derived—which is presumably just what we want, in the case of Example 12.

Now, in this section so far I've concentrated on Example 12 and "derived data." However, the fact is that *all* forms of redundancy can be thought of as derived data: If *x* is redundant, then by definition *x* can be derived from something else in the database. (Limiting use of the term *derived data* to the kind of situation illustrated by Example 12 is thus misleading and not recommended.) It follows that the foregoing analysis—in particular, the four different approaches to dealing with derived data—can be generalized to apply to all kinds of redundancy, at least in principle. Note in particular that the third and fourth of those approaches, using views and snapshots respectively, both constitute examples of what's sometimes called *controlled* redundancy. Redundancy is said to be controlled if it does exist (and the user is aware of it), but the task of "propagating updates" to ensure that it never leads to any inconsistencies is managed by the system, not the user. Uncontrolled redundancy can be a problem, but controlled redundancy shouldn't be. In fact, I want to go further—I want to say that while it's probably impossible, and possibly not even desirable, to eliminate redundancy one hundred percent, any redundancy that isn't eliminated ought at least to be controlled. We need support for snapshots!

Concluding Remarks

Near the beginning of this chapter, I mentioned some attempts at characterizing the notion of redundancy. I'm still not sure we have a good operational definition of the term—in principle, it's surely the case that something involves redundancy if and only if it can be "made smaller" in some way—but this statement isn't much use as any kind of guidance on how to deal with the problem. On balance, I think the most useful statement is:[25]

> The database involves some redundancy if and only if the same proposition can be derived from it in two different ways.

In particular, we don't want the same tuple *t* to appear in two different places if those two appearances denote the same proposition. (Obviously we'd like to prohibit duplicate propositions as such; unfortunately, however, the DBMS doesn't understand propositions.) But it's all right for the same tuple to appear twice if those two appearances *don't* denote the same proposition; and in any case we can have redundancy without any tuple appearing twice at all, as we've seen.

Normalization and orthogonality seem to be all we have by way of a scientific attack on the issue at the present time. Unfortunately, we've seen that normalization and orthogonality don't solve the whole problem—they can be used to reduce redundancy, but they can't eliminate it entirely, in general. (In the section "Other Kinds of Redundancy," we saw several examples of designs that fully conformed to the principles of normalization and orthogonality and yet involved redundancy, and that section was certainly far from exhaustive.) We need more science!

---

25. But see Chapter 13.

Given the foregoing state of affairs, it seems that redundancy will definitely exist in most databases. If it does:

- It should at least be controlled, in the sense that the DBMS should take responsibility for guaranteeing that it will never lead to inconsistency.

- If it can't be controlled, then appropriate constraints should at least be declared and enforced to ensure (again) that it never leads to inconsistency.

- If it can't be controlled and constraints can't be declared and enforced, then you're on your own—and woe betide you if you make any mistakes.

Sadly, this last scenario is the one most likely to apply in practice, given the state of today's commercial implementations.

I'll close with a couple of acknowledgments. First, I'd like to thank Hugh Darwen for continually prodding me to tighten up my thinking on this topic. His criticisms of, and objections to, orthogonality in particular were what spurred me to get my thoughts on the subject into some kind of order and to write the present chapter (which he also reviewed, and I thank him for that review, too). Second, I want to acknowledge the contributions of David McGoveran in this area. It was David who originally came up with *The Principle of Orthogonal Design*, which he and I first described in a joint paper, "A New Database Design Principle," in my book *Relational Database Writings 1991–1994* (Addison-Wesley, 1995). I need to warn you, however, that the definition of orthogonality has changed over the years, and I have reason to believe that David's definition and mine now differ somewhat. Please note too that all remarks in the present chapter regarding my own definition are subject to refinement as explained in the next! *Caveat lector.*

CHAPTER 13

■ ■ ■

Data Redundancy and Database Design: Further Thoughts Number One

Second thoughts are best.

—Sixteenth century English proverb

This chapter is a sequel to the previous one. One reviewer of the previous chapter—referred to in what follows as ADR—produced a series of comments and criticisms that were so carefully thought out, for the most part, that I was more or less forced to make a few minor revisions and corrections right away. However, the majority of ADR's comments were along the lines of "Amplify this discussion ... Elaborate on this point ... There's more to be said here ..." (and so on). Now, I wasn't trying to be either exhaustive or definitive in Chapter 12; all I was trying to do was start an enquiry into the general nature of data redundancy, with special reference to its significance for logical database design. For that reason, I didn't want to incorporate all of ADR's suggested elaborations into that chapter as such (for one thing, it was already longer than I'd hoped it would be when I first set out to write it). On the other hand, I did think ADR was raising several interesting and important points. I also felt that similar points might have occurred to other readers, also that still others might be interested in them. I therefore decided to treat them in this separate sequel to the original (which is, of course, still a long way from being the last word on the subject—hence the title).

A couple more preliminary points:

- You won't understand very much of what follows if you haven't read Chapter 12. Prerequisites, terminology, definitions, ground rules, and so forth are all as they were in that chapter, barring explicit statements to the contrary.

- I've quoted at length here and there from ADR's comments on Chapter 12; however, I've taken the liberty of editing those comments when necessary—sometimes lightly, sometimes not so lightly—in order to make them fit the flow of the present chapter better (though naturally I've tried never to change the original sense).

More on Predicates

I used the following example in Chapter 12 to illustrate the concept of nonloss decomposition. Given our usual suppliers relvar S, with definition as follows (in outline)—

```
S  { S#, SNAME, STATUS, CITY }
   KEY { S# }
```

—we can clearly nonloss-decompose that relvar into projections as follows:

```
SN { S#, SNAME }
   KEY { S# }

ST { S#, STATUS }
   KEY { S# }

SC { S#, CITY }
   KEY { S# }
```

The decomposition is valid (i.e., nonloss) because S is clearly equal to the join of the three projections SN, ST, and SC.

ADR commented on this example as follows:

> *Personally, with such examples, I always like to mention the precise business rule[1] that makes the decomposition nonloss. In this case, it is that every supplier who is under contract has exactly one name, exactly one status, and exactly one city, and every supplier who has a name is under contract (and so has a status and a city too), and every supplier who has a status is under contract (and so has a name and a city too), and every supplier who has a city is under contract (and so has a name and a status too).*

I agree. Here's my attempt:

> *Every supplier S# under contract has exactly one name SNAME and exactly one status STATUS and exactly one city CITY; further, no supplier S# has a name SNAME or a status STATUS or a city CITY without being under contract.*

ADR also observed that it's precisely because this rule is in effect that we don't actually *need* to decompose relvar S into its projections SN, ST, and SC; the single relvar S can effectively serve as shorthand for the combination of the three relvars SN, ST, and SC. Note carefully, therefore, that I did not mean to suggest that relvar S *should* be replaced by those three projections; I meant only to illustrate the concept of nonloss decomposition as such—though elsewhere in the chapter I did say I found the discipline of insisting that all relvars be in sixth normal form, or *irreducible,* an increasingly attractive one. In particular, such a discipline (in the case at hand) would allow us to deal adequately with the following weaker version of the rule:

> *Every supplier S# under contract has at most one name SNAME and at most one status STATUS and at most one city CITY; further, no supplier S# has a name SNAME or a status STATUS or a city CITY without being under contract.*

---

1. See Chapter 15 for more on business rules.

(The difference is that each "exactly" in the previous version has been replaced by "at most." See Chapter 12, Example 6.)

Identity Decompositions

While I'm on the subject of nonloss decomposition, let me recall something else I said in the previous chapter (in the section "Normalization Is Not Enough"):

> *Any relvar can always be nonloss-decomposed, albeit trivially, into what's called the corresponding* identity *projection. The identity projection of a given relation or relvar is the projection of that relation or relvar on all of its attributes; it's called the identity projection because (obviously enough) it's identically equal to the original relation or relvar.*

And I added:

> *Of course, it's a bit of a stretch to talk about "decomposition" in such a situation, because there really isn't any decomposing, as such, going on at all.*

ADR commented:

> *Your degenerate decomposition, yielding only one projection, fails to merit the appellation "decomposition." Even if you feel more sanguine about this state of affairs than I do, the remedy is simple and straightforward—the other projection is a variable of type RELATION{}.*

Well, it seems I do "feel more sanguine about this state of affairs" than ADR does; I see it as no different in kind from the familiar convention according to which (for example) the SUM, AVG, MAX, and MIN of a single number N are all just N, or the union, join, intersection, and product of a single relvar R are all just R. But it's certainly true that any given relvar R is identically equal to the join of $R1$ and $R2$, where:

1. $R1$ is the projection of R on all of its attributes (i.e., the applicable identity projection).

2. $R2$ is the projection of R on *none* of its attributes.

$R2$ here is, as ADR says, of type RELATION{}; it has no attributes at all, and its value is either TABLE_DUM, if R is empty, or TABLE_DEE otherwise.[2] I observe, however, that the combination of $R1$ and $R2$ isn't a valid nonloss decomposition of R, because it fails to satisfy the requirement that both projections are needed in the reconstruction process.

While I'm on the subject of identity decompositions, let me remark that any relvar can always be decomposed—again trivially, but this time horizontally instead of vertically—into the corresponding identity *restriction*. The identity restriction of a given relation or relvar R is the restriction of R to just those tuples that satisfy the simple boolean expression TRUE, thus:

---

2. TABLE_DUM and TABLE_DEE are pet names for, respectively, the unique relation with no attributes and no tuples and the unique relation with no attributes and one tuple. For further discussion, see, e.g., my book *Database in Depth: Relational Theory for Practitioners* (O'Reilly Media Inc., 2005).

```
R WHERE TRUE
```

It's called the identity restriction because (obviously enough) it's identically equal to the original relation or relvar.

I note in passing that a given relation or relvar also always has an *empty* restriction, which we can denote thus:

```
R WHERE FALSE
```

The (necessarily disjoint!) union of the identity restriction and the empty restriction of a given relation or relvar *R* is of course identically equal to *R*.

More on Propositions

Another example I discussed in the previous chapter is repeated in Figure 13-1. Here the parts relvar P has been replaced by two relvars, one ("light parts," LP) containing parts with weight less than or equal to 17 pounds and the other ("heavy parts," HP) containing parts with weight greater than or equal to 17 pounds. The predicates are:

LP: *Part P# is used in the enterprise, is named PNAME, has color COLOR and weight WEIGHT (which is less than or equal to 17 pounds), and is stored in city CITY.*

HP: *Part P# is used in the enterprise, is named PNAME, has color COLOR and weight WEIGHT (which is greater than or equal to 17 pounds), and is stored in city CITY.*

LP

P#	PNAME	COLOR	WEIGHT	CITY
P1	Nut	Red	12.0	London
P2	Bolt	Green	17.0	Paris
P3	Screw	Blue	17.0	Oslo
P4	Screw	Red	14.0	London
P5	Cam	Blue	12.0	Paris

HP

P#	PNAME	COLOR	WEIGHT	CITY
P2	Bolt	Green	17.0	Paris
P3	Screw	Blue	17.0	Oslo
P6	Cog	Red	19.0	London

Figure 13-1. *Relvars LP and HP—sample values*

As I pointed out in the previous chapter, the database as shown in Figure 13-1 contains two appearances of the tuple for part P2 and two appearances of the tuple for part P3 and thereby involves some redundancy. And I went on to say that the problem with the design was obvious: The predicates for relvars LP and HP "overlap," in the sense that the very same proposition can be a valid instantiation of both of them. But ADR commented:

"The very same proposition"? Not quite! For example, in the case of part P2 the two propositions are as follows:

Part P2 is used in the enterprise, is named Bolt, has color Green and weight 17.0 (which is less than or equal to 17 pounds), and is stored in city Paris.

Part P2 is used in the enterprise, is named Bolt, has color Green and weight 17.0 (which is greater than or equal to 17 pounds), and is stored in city Paris.

We need to know that 17 is neither less than nor greater than 17, and then apply some logic, in order to conclude that these two propositions are indeed saying the same thing.

Of course I agree with these observations; I was merely abbreviating my example in what I thought was an acceptable manner, given my goals in writing Chapter 12 in the first place. But as ADR went on to remark, what's obvious to humans isn't necessarily obvious to a machine, and I should really have spelled out the missing steps in my argument.

Somewhat analogous remarks apply to another of the examples in Chapter 12: Suppose we replace attribute CITY in the suppliers relvar S by two distinct attributes CITYA and CITYB, with the constraint that the CITYA and CITYB values are equal in every tuple (both of them representing the city for the applicable supplier). I gave the following as the corresponding predicate:

Supplier S# is under contract, is named SNAME, has status STATUS, is located in city CITYA, and is located in city CITYB

I also observed that it was obvious from this predicate that the design was bad. To belabor the point, I gave the following as a sample tuple:

```
TUPLE { S# S#('S1'), SNAME NAME('Smith'), STATUS 20,
                     CITYA 'London', CITYB 'London' }
```

Then I went on to give the following as two projections of this tuple[3] that were certainly distinct and yet clearly represented the same proposition:

```
TUPLE { S# S#('S1'), SNAME NAME('Smith'), STATUS 20, CITYA 'London' }
```

```
TUPLE { S# S#('S1'), SNAME NAME('Smith'), STATUS 20, CITYB 'London' }
```

Here ADR commented:

---

3. As in the previous chapter, I'm overloading the projection operator here by allowing it to apply to tuples as well as to relations (and/or relvars).

I strongly recommend spelling out how you arrive at the conclusion that the two tuples represent exactly the same proposition. The predicate to be instantiated by the tuple with both CITYA and CITYB components includes something like this: "... and is located in CITYA, which is the same city as CITYB." The propositions which the two projected tuples are supposed to represent are:

Supplier S1 is under contract and has exactly one name (Smith) and exactly one status (20) and exactly one city (London), and there exists exactly one city CITYB such that London is the same city as CITYB ...

Supplier S1 is under contract and has exactly one name (Smith) and exactly one status (20) and exactly one city (London), and there exists exactly one city CITYA such that CITYA is the same city as London ...

It might not be clear to a machine that these two propositions are effectively identical.

Again I agree; again, however, I was merely abbreviating my example in what I thought was an acceptable manner, given my goals in writing Chapter 12 in the first place (I wasn't really concerned at that point in the chapter with what might or might not be automatable). But ADR's point is well taken.

More on Normalization

Yet another example I discussed in the previous chapter is repeated in Figure 13-2, which shows sample values for the following decomposition of the suppliers relvar S:

```
SNT { S#, SNAME, STATUS }
   KEY { S# }

STC { S#, STATUS, CITY }
   KEY { S# }
```

SNT	S#	SNAME	STATUS	STC	S#	STATUS	CITY
	S1	Smith	20		S1	20	London
	S2	Jones	10		S2	10	Paris
	S3	Blake	30		S3	30	Paris
	S4	Clark	20		S4	20	London
	S5	Adams	30		S5	30	Athens

Figure 13-2. *Relvars SNT and STC—sample values*

As I said in the previous chapter, this decomposition is hardly very sensible (in particular, the fact that any given supplier has a given status appears twice), and yet it satisfies all of the classical normalization principles. *Note:* Just to remind you, let me summarize those principles here:

1. A relvar that's not in fifth normal form (5NF) should be decomposed into a set of 5NF projections.

2. The original relvar should be reconstructable by joining those projections back together again.

3. The decomposition process should preserve dependencies.

4. Every projection should be needed in the reconstruction process.

On the basis of this example, I claimed that normalization by itself wasn't enough; we needed something else to tell us what's wrong—what's *formally* wrong, I mean—with this decomposition. In fact, I claimed that what we needed was another principle (and later in the chapter, I claimed that the principle in question was essentially *The Principle of Orthogonal Design*). ADR commented:

> *How about a principle stating that no attribute of the relvar being decomposed is to appear as a nonkey attribute in more than one projection? But I would not elevate such a simple and obvious rule to the status of a* principle; *I would just add it to the definition of the decomposition procedure. (That said, I admit that at the moment I'm still wondering if there are pathological cases that my suggested wording doesn't cater for.)*

There are several things I want to say in response to this particular suggestion:

- First, a small point: It seems to me that the proposed rule, if we accept it, would be just as much of a principle as the four existing ones (even ADR says it should be "added to the definition of the decomposition procedure"). In other words, I don't agree with ADR's apparent objection that it's too "simple and obvious" to merit such an extravagant epithet.

- In any case, even if the rule is "simple and obvious," certainly I've never seen it previously articulated. The field of computing is littered with examples of unwarranted and undocumented assumptions being made because some "simple and obvious" principle wasn't spelled out. Examples that come to mind include (a) the normalization requirement that all projections should be needed in the reconstruction process; (b) *The Assignment Principle*, which states that after assignment of the value v to the variable V the comparison $V = v$ should give TRUE; (c) the claim (which Codd makes in at least one of his early papers) that there exist relations that aren't the join of any relations at all. (In case you're wondering, the fact that any relation r is identically equal to r JOIN r is sufficient to show that this last claim is false as stated.)

- If ADR's proposed rule is equivalent to the one I later propose myself, then we aren't talking about a logical difference (see Part 2 of this book), we're just talking about alternative formulations for something. While I'm always on the lookout for formulations that are intuitively easy to understand, finding the ergonomically best formulation wasn't and isn't my primary concern in this context at this time. And if the proposed rule *isn't* equivalent to the one I later propose myself, then I think we're barking up the wrong tree anyway.

But my major concern is that I think the proposed rule is too strong (and it's not equivalent to the rule I later propose myself). By way of example, suppose suppliers are partitioned into classes (C1, C2, etc.), so that the suppliers relvar has an additional attribute CLASS. Suppose also that (a) each class has just one associated status, and (b) each city has just one associated status as well, but (c) classes and cities are otherwise quite independent of each other. Then the relvar satisfies these two functional dependencies (FDs):

```
{ CLASS } → { STATUS }
{ CITY }  → { STATUS }
```

(Perhaps this is an example of one of the "pathological cases" that ADR refers to in his comment.) Anyway, I'll leave the details as an exercise, but it should be apparent that the following is a valid nonloss decomposition for this revised suppliers relvar (I ignore attribute SNAME for simplicity):

```
SCC { S#, CLASS, CITY }
    KEY { S# }

CLS { CLASS, STATUS }
    KEY { CLASS }

CTS { CITY, STATUS }
    KEY { CITY }
```

Observe in particular that attribute STATUS appears here as a nonkey attribute in more than one projection, and the decomposition thus violates ADR's proposed rule. Yet, to repeat, the decomposition is surely valid, and the proposed rule is thus not quite right. What's more, it seems to me that the more difficult it is to get it right, the more reasonable it is to regard the correct version, if and when we find it, as indeed another principle.

More on Dependencies

I made the claim in Chapter 12 that functional dependencies were a special case of join dependencies.[4] But ADR wrote:

> *I find this claim very misleading ... I believe such claims ... make 4NF and 5NF more difficult to understand than they should be ... You only have to look at a functional dependency (FD) and a join dependency (JD) to see that an FD isn't a JD. However, we can indeed derive from an FD the projections of a binary JD. (I tried to write down the derivation rule but realised that it's not that trivial and I would be likely to make a mistake.)*

These comments gave me furiously to think! I was very surprised at the suggestion that an FD might not be a JD, and had to go back and revisit some very basic concepts in order to convince myself that my claim that every FD *is* a JD was indeed correct. Let me elaborate. Of course, it's true that we typically use different formalisms—different syntax, in other words— to express FDs and JDs. For example, let's go back to the original suppliers relvar S:

---

4. I assume you're familiar with these concepts. Definitions are given in the previous chapter; more detailed explanations can be found in many places—see, e.g., the O'Reilly book mentioned earlier (*Database in Depth: Relational Theory for Practitioners*).

```
S { S#, SNAME, STATUS, CITY }
   KEY { S# }
```

As we know, this relvar can be nonloss-decomposed into projections as follows:

```
SN { S#, SNAME }
   KEY { S# }

ST { S#, STATUS }
   KEY { S# }

SC { S#, CITY }
   KEY { S# }
```

Thus, we can say that relvar S satisfies the following FDs:

```
{ S# } → { SNAME }
{ S# } → { STATUS }
{ S# } → { CITY }
```

We can also say it satisfies the following JD:

```
✪ { { S#, SNAME }, { S#, STATUS }, { S#, CITY } }
```

And these two assertions are clearly different in form—but they *are* logically equivalent. In fact, there's a theorem (Heath's theorem) that effectively says as much:

> Let A, B, and C be subsets of the heading of relvar R such that the (set-theoretic) union of A, B, and C is equal to that heading. Let AB denote the (set-theoretic) union of A and B, and similarly for AC. If R satisfies the FD $A \rightarrow B$, then R is equal to the join of its projections on AB and AC.

Observe that the third (final) sentence here can equivalently be written:

> If R satisfies the FD $A \rightarrow B$, then R satisfies the JD ✪$\{AB,AC\}$.

Observe too that this same sentence addresses the last part of ADR's comment (regarding the rule by which we can derive the projections of a binary JD from a given FD).

Incidentally—the following point is a little tangential to the main topic under discussion, but I think it's interesting—there's a very pleasing parallelism (first noted by Ron Fagin) among the definitions of:

- *Boyce/Codd normal form,* BCNF, which is "the" normal form so long as we limit our attention to functional dependencies only

- *Fourth* normal form, 4NF, which is "the" normal form when we take multi-valued dependencies, MVDs, into account as well

- *Fifth* normal form, 5NF, which is "the" normal form when we take general join dependencies into account as well

It goes like this:

- Relvar *R* is in BCNF if and only if every nontrivial FD satisfied by *R* is implied by the keys of *R*.

- Relvar *R* is in 4NF if and only if every nontrivial MVD satisfied by *R* is implied by the keys of *R*.

- Relvar *R* is in 5NF if and only if every nontrivial JD satisfied by *R* is implied by the keys of *R*.

For an explanation of exactly what it means for an FD or MVD or JD to be nontrivial or to be implied by keys, see the O'Reilly book mentioned a couple of times already (*Database in Depth: Relational Theory for Practitioners*).

More on Dependency Preservation

As already mentioned, the third normalization principle is: *The decomposition process should preserve dependencies.* Here's a simple example to illustrate the point. Consider the original suppliers relvar S once again; for simplicity, let's ignore attribute SNAME, but let's also assume that suppliers satisfy the following additional FD:

```
{ CITY } → { STATUS }
```

The obvious decomposition here is as follows:

```
SC { S#, CITY }
   KEY { S# }

CS { CITY, STATUS }
   KEY { CITY }
```

Now consider by contrast the following alternative decomposition:

```
SC { S#, CITY }
   KEY { S# }

ST { S#, STATUS }
   KEY { S# }
```

(Projection SC is the same in both decompositions; the difference is in the other projection.)

Now, the second decomposition here is certainly nonloss (S is certainly equal to the join of SC and ST); what's more, projections SC and ST are both in 5NF. However, the FD from CITY to STATUS has been "lost" in this decomposition. What do I mean by "lost" here? I mean the pertinent constraint—to the effect that CITY determines STATUS—*is no longer an FD as such;* rather, it has become a constraint that spans two distinct relvars. Here's a precise formulation of that constraint in terms of the SC/ST decomposition:

```
CONSTRAINT CITY_DETERMINES_STATUS
   COUNT ( ( SC JOIN ST ) { CITY } ) =
   COUNT ( ( SC JOIN ST ) { CITY, STATUS } ) ;
```

(Awful, isn't it?) In other words, the original FD, which was a constraint on a single relvar, has become a multi-relvar constraint instead. What's more, not only is the constraint now harder to state, it's probably harder for the system to enforce as well—by which I mean there's likely to be a performance penalty to pay in enforcing it, compared with what's involved in enforcing the original FD.

Now, I didn't discuss the foregoing example in detail in Chapter 12, because I assumed that readers were probably familiar with the general idea of dependency preservation already. (It might be a little late to be saying this!) What I did do, however, was show that the objective of preserving dependencies could actually be in conflict with the objective of reducing redundancy. I used the following example. We're given a relvar SJT with attributes S, J, and T and (simplified) predicate: *Student S is taught subject J by teacher T.* In addition, the following constraints apply:

- For each subject, each student of that subject is taught by just one teacher (so the FD $\{S,J\} \to \{T\}$ holds).

- Each teacher teaches just one subject (so the FD $\{T\} \to \{J\}$ holds).

And I showed that if we decompose the relvar (in order to reduce redundancy) into 5NF projections as follows—

```
ST { S, T }
   KEY { S, T }

TJ { T, J }
   KEY { T }
```

—then the FD $\{S,J\} \to \{T\}$ is lost, in the sense that it's replaced by the following multi-relvar constraint:

```
CONSTRAINT S_AND_J_DETERMINES_T
   COUNT ( ST JOIN TJ ) = COUNT ( ( ST JOIN TJ ) { S, J } ) ;
```

ADR commented on this example:

But after the decomposition into ST and TJ we have the opportunity to represent teachers (in relvar TJ) who teach a subject that nobody studies. What's more, that opportunity is one of the justifications given for doing such decompositions. If we grasp that opportunity, then how can we say that the FD is "preserved"? (In any case, I find it difficult to think of preserving the FD when we are discarding the very relvar in which that FD holds!) I suppose we have preservation in the sense that the FD in question does hold in ST JOIN TJ, but (ST JOIN TJ){T,J} is no longer equal to TJ if TJ represents teachers who teach subjects that nobody studies. I think this point needs to be added.

Several responses once again:

- It's true that the decomposition gives us the opportunity to represent teachers who teach a subject that nobody studies. It's also true that just such an opportunity is one of the justifications given for doing such decompositions in the first place[5] (however, this observation applies to further normalization in general—it has nothing directly to do with the topic of dependency preservation as such). But even if relvar TJ does include tuples for teachers who teach a subject that nobody studies, it's still the case that SJT is equal to the join of its projections ST and TJ (equivalently, the FD $\{T\} \to \{J\}$ still holds in that join). So the opportunity to represent teachers who teach a subject that nobody studies doesn't in and of itself constitute any dependency loss; *pace* ADR's (rhetorical?) question, the dependency is indeed preserved even if we do "grasp the opportunity."

- "In any case, I find it difficult to think of preserving the FD when we are discarding the very relvar in which that FD holds!" But I didn't say the FD was preserved—in fact, it was precisely my complaint that discarding the relvar SJT meant we were *not* preserving the FD $\{S,J\} \to \{T\}$. That was precisely the problem.

- "I suppose we have preservation in the sense that the FD in question does hold in ST JOIN TJ, but (ST JOIN TJ)$\{T,J\}$ is no longer equal to TJ if TJ represents teachers who teach subjects that nobody studies. I think this point needs to be added." Well, the FD in question is $\{S,J\} \to \{T\}$, and this FD does indeed hold in ST JOIN TJ, as ADR says. It's also true that (ST JOIN TJ)$\{T,J\}$ isn't equal to TJ if TJ represents teachers who teach subjects that nobody studies; and I thus consider the point made as requested.

Following on from all of the above, I gave another example (Example 1) in Chapter 12 that might also be regarded, loosely, as having something to do with the concept of dependency loss. We're given a relvar looking like this:

```
NADDR { NAME, ADDR }
     KEY { NAME }
```

Attribute ADDR here is *tuple-valued,* where the tuples in question have attributes STREET, CITY, STATE, and ZIP. Further, I assume for the sake of the example that whenever two ADDR values have the same ZIP component, they also have the same CITY and STATE components. Then the design clearly involves some redundancy, and yet there's no violation of normalization involved. In particular, the FD

```
{ ZIP } → { CITY, STATE }
```

does *not* hold, since FDs are defined to hold among attributes, not among components of attributes. However, ADR pointed out that the FD does hold in R = NADDR UNWRAP (ADDR). *Note:* UNWRAP is an operator prescribed by *The Third Manifesto*. Its semantics are supposed to be more or less self-explanatory (in the case at hand, it returns a relation with attributes NAME, STREET, CITY, STATE, and ZIP).

---

5. Indeed, Codd himself made this same point in his very first paper on this subject, "Further Normalization of the Data Base Relational Model," in Randall J. Rustin (ed.), *Data Base Systems, Courant Computer Science Symposia Series 6* (Prentice Hall, 1972).

Generalizing Key Constraints

Key constraints as conventionally understood (and as currently supported in **Tutorial D**) are, specifically, constraints on relvars; that is, the syntax

```
KEY { <attribute ref commalist> }
```

is specifically limited to appearing only within some relvar definition. (Note, however, that there's no requirement that the relvar in question be a base relvar in particular; it might, for example, be a virtual relvar or view.)

Now consider again the following constraint from the section "More on Dependency Preservation":

```
CONSTRAINT S_AND_J_DETERMINES_T
   COUNT ( ST JOIN TJ ) = COUNT ( ( ST JOIN TJ ) { S, J } ) ;
```

ADR commented on this constraint:

I would much prefer to say more clearly that {S,J} is a key for ST JOIN TJ. Giving the longhand (or rather, a possible longhand) for what KEY is short for is a little obscure, especially in the present context ... It is a bit annoying that we can use the KEY shorthand only as part of a relvar definition, where the syntax obviously doesn't require a specification of the relvar to which the constraint applies. Really it should be possible to use the KEY shorthand in a named constraint defined outside of any relvar definition. And then we would be able support keys for arbitrary expressions and not just relvars.

I agree completely. Indeed, I'm on record as saying something very similar myself (see my paper "A Normalization Problem," in my book *Relational Database Writings 1991–1994*, Addison-Wesley, 1995). Here then is a syntax proposal for **Tutorial D** ... Currently, a constraint is defined in **Tutorial D** by means of syntax of the form:

```
CONSTRAINT <constraint name> <bool exp> ;
```

Now I suggest the following as an additional alternative form:

```
CONSTRAINT <constraint name> <relation exp>
           KEY { <attribute ref commalist> } ;
```

Of course, this format is subject to certain syntax rules, of which the most important is as follows: Suppose the *<relation exp>* were used to define a view *V;* then every *<attribute ref>* in the KEY specification must refer to an attribute of that view *V*.

Given support for this format, constraint S_AND_J_DETERMINES_T could be expressed as follows:

```
CONSTRAINT S_AND_J_DETERMINES_T ( ST JOIN TJ ) KEY { S, J } ;
```

Likewise, constraint CITY_DETERMINES_STATUS from the same section ("More on Dependency Preservation") could be expressed as follows:

```
CONSTRAINT CITY_DETERMINES_STATUS
   ( ( SC JOIN ST ) { CITY, STATUS } ) KEY { CITY } ;
```

With regard to this latter example, I'm assuming relvar S has been decomposed into its projections SC and ST on {S#,CITY} and {S#,STATUS}, respectively. If this decomposition isn't done, the constraint is just a simple FD:

```
CONSTRAINT CITY_DETERMINES_STATUS ( S { CITY, STATUS } ) KEY { CITY } ;
```

As this example suggests, the proposed KEY syntax provides a simple way of stating FDs. Of course, the usual $A \to B$ syntax is simpler still; it might thus profitably be considered as a basis for extending the syntax of **Tutorial D** constraint definitions still further.

If the proposed KEY syntax is accepted, then (as ADR goes on to point out in his comments) "dependency loss" doesn't mean the dependency in question is actually lost—it just means it applies to some different relvar (possibly a virtual relvar or view, more generally what *The Third Manifesto* calls a *pseudovariable*).

Orthogonality Revisited

I've left the biggest issue till last. ADR took exception to *The Principle of Orthogonal Design*, or at least to my formulation thereof; to be specific, he found it too strong, in the sense that it regarded certain situations as violating orthogonality that he didn't. His comments read in part:

> *One of your definitions appears to single out precisely those cases of the same tuple appearing in more than one place that do indeed represent redundancy, thus addressing my complaints ... But later in the chapter you appear to return to [a] version I object to ... If you revised the principle in line with [the definition referenced in the first sentence of this extract], then my complaints would disappear; effectively, the principle would advise against duplicate appearances of a tuple representing the same proposition rather than mere repetition of tuples.*

Clearly, then, ADR and I agree on wanting to prevent the existence of any constraint that requires a tuple representing some given proposition to appear in more than one place. Here then is my attempt to state this requirement more precisely:

> *The Principle of Orthogonal Design:* Let A and B be distinct relvars. Replace A and B by nonloss decompositions into projections $A1, A2, ..., Am$ and $B1, B2, ..., Bn$, respectively, such that every Ai ($i = 1, 2, ..., m$) and every Bj ($j = 1, 2, ..., n$) is in 6NF. Let some i and j be such that there exists a sequence of zero or more attribute renamings with the property that (a) when applied to Ai, it produces Ak, and (b) Ak and Bj are of the same type.[6] Then there must not exist a constraint to the effect that, at all times, $Ak' = Bj'$ (where Ak' and Bj' are specified nonempty restrictions of Ak and Bj, respectively).

In other words, if there's a constraint to the effect that some such Ak' and Bj' do exist, then that fact constitutes a violation of the principle. *Note:* Perhaps I should say explicitly that the projections and restrictions referred to in the definition might very well be identity projections and restrictions, respectively.

---

6. *R1* and *R2* are of the same type if and only if they have the same headings (i.e., if and only if they have the same attribute names, and attributes of the same name are defined over the same type in turn).

What's the difference between the principle as just defined and the version I gave in the previous chapter? Well, here's the definition from that chapter:

The Principle of Orthogonal Design (previous version): Let *A* and *B* be distinct relvars. Then there should not exist nonloss decompositions of *A* and *B* into projections *A1, A2, ..., Am* and *B1, B2, ..., Bn,* respectively, such that the relvar constraints for some *Ai* (*i* = *1, 2, ..., m*) and some *Bj* (*j* = *1, 2, ..., n*) are such as to permit the same tuple to appear in both.

Observe that any database that satisfies the new version of the principle certainly satisfies the old version, but the converse is not true; a database could satisfy the old version and not the new one. In other words, the old version was strictly stronger than the new one—and that was the problem; as I observed earlier, the old version was too strong, and regarded as violations certain designs that were in fact perfectly reasonable. Note in particular that simply having the same tuple *t* appear in two distinct relvars could constitute a violation of the old version; in the new version, by contrast, having tuple *t* appear in two distinct relvars is a violation only if that tuple is *not allowed* to appear in one and not the other (in other words, only if there's a constraint to the effect that a certain degree of redundancy must exist).

By way of example, consider relvars LP and HP once again, with predicates (to repeat) as follows:

LP: *Part P# is used in the enterprise, is named PNAME, has color COLOR and weight WEIGHT (which is less than or equal to 17 pounds), and is stored in city CITY.*

HP: *Part P# is used in the enterprise, is named PNAME, has color COLOR and weight WEIGHT (which is greater than or equal to 17 pounds), and is stored in city CITY.*

This database violates the new version of the principle because the following constraint clearly applies to it:

```
CONSTRAINT LP_AND_HP_OVERLAP
   ( LP WHERE WEIGHT = WEIGHT ( 17.0 ) ) =
   ( HP WHERE WEIGHT = WEIGHT ( 17.0 ) ) ;
```

By way of another example (also repeated from the previous chapter), consider the predicates *Employee E# is on vacation* and *Employee E# is awaiting phone number allocation.* The obvious design for this situation involves two relvars:

```
ON_VACATION { E# }
          KEY { E# }

NEEDS_PHONE { E# }
          KEY { E# }
```

Clearly, the very same employee can be represented in both of these relvars at the same time—and in the previous chapter I claimed that this state of affairs constituted a violation of *The Principle of Orthogonal Design* (and so it did, given the definition I was appealing to in that chapter). But I also pointed out that even if the very same tuple appeared in both relvars, those two appearances represented two different propositions, and there wasn't any redundancy involved. And I tried to finesse the situation by claiming that there were occasions on which it was acceptable to violate the principle. Note clearly, however, that the example under discussion *doesn't* violate the new version of the principle! That's because *there's no formal constraint we can write* that a given "E# tuple" has to satisfy in order for it to be accepted into ON_VACATION or NEEDS_PHONE or both. (And I did point this fact out explicitly in the previous chapter, without realizing it was precisely this fact that was the key to revising the principle appropriately.)

What impact do the discussions of the present section have on the discussions of the previous chapter? The answer is: Very little, apart from revisions already explicitly considered. In other words, most of the material in that chapter—in the section titled "Violating Orthogonality" in particular—is still applicable, even given the new definition of the orthogonality principle.

Concluding Remarks

I have one small piece of unfinished business to attend to. In the section "Concluding Remarks" in the previous chapter, I said I thought the most useful statement we could make regarding redundancy was as follows:

> The database involves some redundancy if and only if the same proposition can be derived from it in two different ways.

With hindsight, I realize this sentence wasn't very well put! It's not only possible, but probable, that a given proposition can be derived from a given database (if it can be derived at all) in many different ways, at least in the sense that there are usually many different but equivalent ways of formulating a given query. That wasn't what I meant. I used the word *derived* because I had in mind the fact that the proposition in question might be represented, not directly by some tuple in some base relation, but rather by some tuple in some relation that could be derived from the base relations. So perhaps a better way to say it is:

> The database involves some redundancy if and only if it includes two distinct representations (either direct or indirect) of the same proposition.

Tree-Structured Data

The insane root that takes the reason prisoner

—William Shakespeare

One child makes you a parent.

—Sir David Frost

An often-heard question in the relational world is this: How can tree-structured data be dealt with in a relational context? In fact, can relational systems deal with such data at all? Such data occurs very commonly in practical applications: Organization charts (showing who reports to whom), bill-of-materials structures (showing which parts are contained in which other parts), and family trees are all familiar examples. So do we have to give up on such applications if we're using a relational system? It's my position that the answer to this question is *no*, and the purpose of this chapter is to present arguments in support of that position.

Note: What follows is far from being an exhaustive treatment; essentially it's just a series of examples. However, those examples should be sufficient to help you visualize relational approaches to a variety of tree-related applications.

The structure of the chapter is as follows. After definitions of terms in the section immediately following, the next two sections discuss certain common and generic tree-processing algorithms: one involving the use of trees for sorting, and several involving different tree-traversal sequences. The next section discusses the bill-of-materials problem specifically. Finally, the last two sections, immediately prior to the concluding remarks, discuss the rather different kinds of trees found in hierarchic databases (IMS and XML databases in particular).

Definitions

I'm sure you know what we mean by the term *tree* in computing contexts, but let me give a precise definition here for purposes of reference:

A **tree** *T* consists of a finite set *N* of **nodes** and a finite set *E* of **edges** (also known as *arcs*). *T* is **empty** if *N* is empty (in which case *E* is necessarily empty too), otherwise it is **nonempty**. Each edge in *E* connects exactly two distinct nodes in *N* and represents a directed path from one of those two nodes to the other; the "from" node is a **parent** node and the "to" node is a **child** node. Each parent node is connected by edges to one or more child nodes. Each child node is connected by an edge to exactly one parent node. A node connected to no child nodes is a **leaf** node. A node connected to no parent node is a **root** node. If *T* is nonempty, it has exactly one root node, otherwise it has no root node at all.

For example, in the nonempty tree shown in Figure 14-1, we have:

- Nine nodes and eight edges (a nonempty tree always has one more node than it has edges)

- Four parent nodes—*A, B, D,* and *G*

- Eight child nodes—every node except *A* (a nonempty tree always has exactly one node, the root, that isn't a child)

- One root node—*A*

- Five leaf nodes—*C, F, E, H, I*

The nodes themselves can be anything at all: integers, character strings, records, etc. (even trees!).

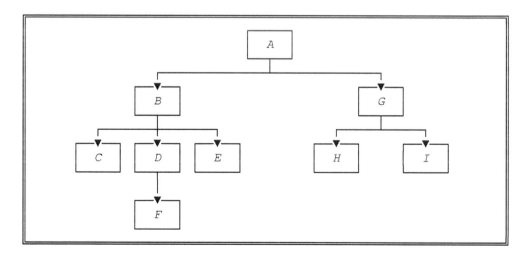

Figure 14-1. *A typical tree*

Incidentally, note that we do usually draw trees as shown in Figure 14-1, with the root at the top, despite the fact that nature would dictate otherwise. The point isn't completely trivial, either, because we often use terms like *up* and *down* and *top* and *bottom* in connection with trees, and we obviously need to be clear as to what we mean by such terms.

Now, it's well known that trees have a recursive structure (just as trees in nature have a fractal structure, in fact). As a consequence, it's possible to give an alternative definition—a recursive, and in some ways preferable, definition—of the term. (It's preferable because, as we'll see, many algorithms exploit the recursive nature of trees and are thus recursive in turn.) Here it is:

A **tree** *T* consists of a finite set *N* of **nodes**. *T* is **empty** if *N* is empty, otherwise it is **nonempty**. If *T* is nonempty, then *N* is partitioned into:

- A distinguished node called the **root** node

- Disjoint sets of nodes *S1, S2, ..., Sm* ($m \geq 0$), each of which is a nonempty tree in turn (a **subtree** of the root)

Assuming *T* is nonempty, then (a) if $m > 0$, the root node is a **parent** node, and the root nodes of its subtrees are **child** nodes; (b) if $m = 0$, the root node is a **leaf** node.

For example, referring to Figure 14-1 again, we have a root node *A* with two subtrees. Those subtrees are themselves trees, of course, and their roots are *B* and *G*, respectively. Next, the tree rooted at *B* has three subtrees, with roots *C, D,* and *E*, respectively ... and so on. *Exercise:* As you might have noticed, the recursive definition mentions the nodes but not the edges. So where did the edges go?

A few final points to close this section:

- Observe that the term *child* refers to what might be called an "immediate" child specifically. In terms of Figure 14-1, for example, it would *not* be usual to refer to *F* as a child of either *B* or *A;* rather, *F* is a grandchild of *B* and a great-grandchild of *A*.

- Trees as I've defined them have the property that the children (and therefore the subtrees) of any given parent are *unordered*. Sometimes, however, we do want them to be ordered, so that we can refer unambiguously to the first, second, ..., *M*th child (or *M*th subtree) of any given parent. A tree for which the children of each parent are ordered in this way is called an **ordered tree**. The trees that are the subject of the two sections immediately following are ordered in this sense.

- The definitions I've given are in accordance with those found in any good book on computer science. But the terminology of trees is also used in connection with certain other data structures—including in particular IMS databases, XML documents, and "containment hierarchies" in the object world—that don't exactly conform to those definitions. I'll discuss these other kinds of trees later in the chapter.

A Tree-Based Sort Technique

The first application of trees I want to discuss is a sorting technique called **treesort**. First I'll show in outline how the technique works; then I'll show a relational representation for the data involved (input and output lists and the associated tree structure); then I'll propose some appropriate relational operators; finally, I'll show how those operators might be implemented. *Note:* Different writers use the name *treesort* to refer to a variety of different algorithms. I use it here in the sense in which, e.g., David Harel uses it in his book *Algorithmics: The Spirit of Computing* (Addison-Wesley, 1987).

How Treesort Works

The basic idea behind treesort is very simple: Given a list of values to be sorted, we arrange those values, in a manner to be explained, into a tree that represents the desired sort order. The tree in question is both:

- *Binary*, which means no parent has more than two children

- *Ordered*, which, because the tree is binary, means we can refer unambiguously to the children of a given parent as the left and right child, respectively (assuming both exist, of course)

The tree in question is constructed in such a way as to satisfy what I'll call **the ordering property,** by which I mean that the value at any given node is both:

- Greater than or equal to every value in the left subtree of that node

- Less than every value in the right subtree of that node

By way of example, suppose the given list of values—let's assume for simplicity that they're positive integers—is:

5, 17, 12, 42, 44, 2, 17, 1, 6, 12, 17, 4

Then the tree we want to build might look as shown in Figure 14-2. *Exercise:* Verify that the tree in Figure 14-2 does indeed satisfy the ordering property. (Doing this exercise is recommended because it will give you some insight as to what's involved in building the tree in the first place.)

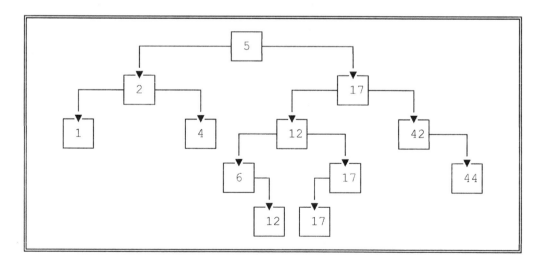

Figure 14-2. *Treesort example*

The process of building the tree can be regarded as the sort process *per se*. Once the tree is built, we can produce the desired output—i.e., a list of the input values in order—by means of the following simple recursive procedure (pseudocode):

```
operator inorder ( root ) ;
   emit inorder ( left child ( root ) ) ;
   emit root ;
   emit inorder ( right child ( root ) ) ;
end inorder ;
```

Note: I'll explain the reason for the name *inorder* in the next section.

So how do we build the tree?—in other words, how do we do the actual sort? Well, that's a recursive process too. Pseudocode:

```
tree := empty ;
i := 0 ;
do i := i + 1 until no more input values ;
   if i = 1 then insert ith value into tree ; /* root */
            else call add_to_tree ( root ) ;
   end if ;
end do ;


operator add_to_tree ( root ) ;
   if ith value ≤ root value
      then if root has no left child
            then insert ith value as left child ( root ) ;
            else call add_to_tree ( left child ( root ) ) ;
            end if ;
      else if root has no right child
            then insert ith value as right child ( root ) ;
            else call add_to_tree ( right child ( root ) ) ;
            end if ;
   end if ;
end add_to_tree ;
```

Data Structures

Treesort clearly involves three data structures: the input list, the output list, and the tree. How can we represent these structures relationally? Well, the input and output lists are easy:

```
INLIST  { P INTEGER, V INTEGER }
        KEY { P }

OUTLIST { P INTEGER, V INTEGER }
        KEY { P }
```

Explanation: If there are n values (integers, by our earlier assumption) to be sorted, INLIST and OUTLIST each contain or will contain n tuples, and attribute P ("position") takes or will take exactly the values 1, 2, ..., n. For INLIST, P = i corresponds to the value appearing in the ith position in the input. For OUTLIST, P = i corresponds to the value appearing in the ith position in the sorted result.

What about the tree? One simple design is:

```
TREE { ID INTEGER, V INTEGER, LEFT INTEGER, RIGHT INTEGER }
    KEY { ID }
```

Explanation: After it's built, the tree will contain n nodes—i.e., there will be n tuples in TREE—and attribute ID ("node identifier") will take exactly the values 1, 2, ..., n. For a given node, LEFT and RIGHT refer to the left and right child, respectively; I adopt the convention that a LEFT or RIGHT value of zero means no corresponding child exists.

Note: As I've explained elsewhere (see, e.g., my book *An Introduction to Database Systems*, 8th edition, Addison-Wesley, 2004), INLIST, OUTLIST, and TREE are strictly speaking not relations as such but, rather, relation *variables* (*relvars* for short). From this point forward I'll be careful always to use the term *relvar* when it really is a relvar I'm talking about, and reserve the term *relation* to mean a relation *value* (in particular, the value of some relvar).

Relational Operators

Essentially I want to propose just one new relational operator here, which I'll call (unsurprisingly) TREESORT. TREESORT takes a single relation as input and produces another as output. The input relation has two attributes, which I'll assume for the moment are called ID and V and have semantics as explained in the previous subsection, and the output relation has the same heading as the input one. Thus, if INLIST is as in the previous subsection, the expression

```
TREESORT ( INLIST )
```

yields a relation looking like, and having the same semantics as, OUTLIST in the previous subsection. Points arising:

- In practice we would need a way to specify "which attribute is which," as it were, in the input relation, so that TREESORT knows which is the "identifier" attribute and which the "value" one. I omit such details here for simplicity.

- In practice we wouldn't want TREESORT to be limited to sorting lists of integers but to work for values of any ordinal type (where an ordinal type is simply a type for which the operator "<" is defined). I limit my attention to integers here for simplicity.

It should be clear that the user of TREESORT needs to know the structure of the input and output relations but not the structure of the tree relation, which is purely internal to the TREESORT implementation. Of course, we could make the structure of that tree relation externally visible (and provide user-visible BUILD and INORDER operators as well) if we had some good reason to do so.

One final point: Remarks similar to those of the present subsection apply to the discussions of the next section ("Traversing the Nodes of a Tree") also, *mutatis mutandis*, and I won't bother to spell the details out again in that section.

Implementing TREESORT

I now show how TREESORT might be implemented.[1] The intention is, of course, that this implementation code should be provided as part of the DBMS—but if it isn't, then it could be provided by some application programmer and then invoked as if it *were* part of the DBMS after all. *Note:* I make no claim that the following code is particularly efficient; my primary concern is just to show that TREESORT is indeed implementable. There are some fairly obvious improvements that could be made if desired (as doubtless they would be in practice).

Essentially what we have to do is (a) build the tree from the input list and then (b) build the output list from the tree. Here then is the code to build the tree (which I'll assume is initially empty):

```
VAR I INTEGER ;                 /* node number within TREE   */
VAR N INTEGER ;                 /* total number of nodes     */
VAR X INTEGER ;                 /* current value from INLIST */

IF NOT ( IS_EMPTY ( INLIST ) )
   THEN
      BEGIN ;
         N := COUNT ( INLIST ) ;
         DO I := 1 TO N ;
            BEGIN ;
               X := V FROM
                     ( TUPLE FROM ( INLIST WHERE P = I ) ) ;
               INSERT TREE RELATION
                     { TUPLE { ID I, V X, LEFT 0, RIGHT 0 } } ;
               IF I > 1
                  THEN CALL ADD_TO_TREE ( 1 ) ;
               END IF ;
            END ;
         END DO ;
      END ;
END IF ;

OPERATOR ADD_TO_TREE ( M INTEGER ) ;
   BEGIN ;
      VAR T TUPLE { ID INTEGER, V INTEGER,
                    LEFT INTEGER, RIGHT INTEGER } ;
      T := TUPLE FROM ( TREE WHERE P = M ) ;
      IF X ≤ ( V FROM T )
         THEN
            IF ( LEFT FROM T ) = 0
               THEN UPDATE TREE WHERE P = M ( LEFT := I ) ;
               ELSE CALL ADD_TO_TREE ( LEFT FROM T ) ;
            END IF ;
```

---

1. Barring explicit statements to the contrary, all coding examples in the body of this chapter are expressed in a self-explanatory language called **Tutorial D**. As you might know, **Tutorial D** is the language used for examples by Hugh Darwen and myself in our book *Databases, Types, and the Relational Model: The Third Manifesto*, 3rd edition (Addison-Wesley, 2006).

```
            ELSE
               IF ( RIGHT FROM T ) = 0
                  THEN UPDATE TREE WHERE P = M ( RIGHT := I ) ;
                  ELSE CALL ADD_TO_TREE ( RIGHT FROM T ) ;
               END IF ;
         END IF ;
      END ;
END OPERATOR ;
```

And here's the code to build the output list, which, like the tree, I'll assume is initially empty:

```
IF N > 0
   THEN
      BEGIN ;
         I := 0 ;
         CALL INORDER ( 1 ) ;
      END ;
END IF ;


OPERATOR INORDER ( M INTEGER ) ;
   BEGIN ;
      VAR T TUPLE { ID INTEGER, V INTEGER,
                    LEFT INTEGER, RIGHT INTEGER } ;
      I := I + 1 ;
      T := TUPLE FROM ( TREE WHERE P = M ) ;
      IF ( LEFT FROM T ) ≠ 0
         THEN
            CALL INORDER ( LEFT FROM T ) ;
      END IF ;
      INSERT OUTLIST
            RELATION { TUPLE { P I, V ( V FROM T ) } } ;
      IF ( RIGHT FROM T ) ≠ 0
         THEN
            CALL INORDER ( RIGHT FROM T ) ;
      END IF ;
   END ;
END OPERATOR ;
```

Integrity Constraints

Note: This subsection can be skipped on a first reading.

It's a little bit of a digression from the main thrust of this chapter, but I think I should say something about the integrity constraints that apply to relvar TREE. Please note, however, that I'm not saying the constraints I'm going to show would need to be stated explicitly in practice;[2]

---

2. A good thing, you might think, since (as we'll soon see) some of them are a little complex. But this observation raises another point: The complexities in question are *not* due to the fact that we've chosen to represent the tree relationally—they're inherent (for the most part) in the very nature of trees, and they need to be enforced somehow, regardless of whether the system is relational or otherwise.

they might not be, if the only code that ever updates TREE is the ADD_TO_TREE code we've been discussing (and if we're sure that code is correct!). But it's still interesting to examine the constraints in question, if only to get some sense of what integrity constraints for trees in general might look like.

Here to remind you is the structure of relvar TREE:

```
TREE { ID INTEGER, V INTEGER, LEFT INTEGER, RIGHT INTEGER }
    KEY { ID }
```

One constraint that obviously applies is that if TREE contains exactly n tuples, then ID must take exactly the values 1, 2, ..., n. I won't bother any further with this one, since it isn't particularly tree-specific. Rather, I want to focus on attributes LEFT and RIGHT; until further notice, in fact, I'll concentrate on LEFT only, since the constraints that apply to RIGHT will obviously be very similar. For any given node *GN* of the tree, then, either LEFT must be zero (meaning node *GN* has no left child) or there must exist another node that *is* the left child of node *GN* whose ID is equal to LEFT in node *GN*:

```
CONSTRAINT LEFT_CHILD_IN_TREE
    ( ( TREE WHERE LEFT ≠ 0 ) { LEFT } RENAME ( LEFT AS ID ) ) ⊆ TREE { ID } ;
```

Explanation: The relational comparison here requires one specified relation (*a*, say) to be a subset of another (*b*, say).[3] Relation *a* is computed by eliminating tuples from TREE where LEFT = 0, projecting the result over LEFT, and renaming the sole attribute of that projection as ID; relation *b* is just the projection of TREE over ID. Overall, therefore, the constraint simply says that every nonzero LEFT value in TREE must also appear as an ID value in TREE.

Next, given the way the tree is constructed—IDs are assigned in a numerically increasing manner as nodes are inserted, and no child can be inserted before its parent—every child must have an ID greater than that of its parent:

```
CONSTRAINT LEFT_CHILD_ID_GT_PARENT_ID
    IS_EMPTY ( TREE WHERE LEFT ≠ 0 AND LEFT ≤ ID ) ;
```

This constraint additionally ensures that:

- If a given node *GN* does have a left child *LC*, then nodes *GN* and *LC* are distinct.

- There are no cycles in the structure—no node *GN* has *GN* itself as a child or grandchild or great-grandchild (etc.)

Next, no two distinct nodes have the same left child:

```
CONSTRAINT LEFT_CHILD_HAS_ONE_PARENT
    COUNT   ( TREE WHERE LEFT ≠ 0 ) =
    COUNT ( ( TREE WHERE LEFT ≠ 0 ) { LEFT } ) ;
```

This constraint ensures that if the total number of nodes with a nonzero LEFT value is *a* and the total number of distinct nonzero LEFT values is *b*, then *a* = *b*; in other words, no two distinct nodes have the same nonzero LEFT value. (Informally, we might characterize this constraint

---

3. In fact it will be a *proper* subset unless TREE is empty, and we could refine the constraint to say as much if we wanted.

by saying that if we delete those TREE tuples for which LEFT = 0, then what remains has LEFT for a key.)

Finally, no node is both a left and a right child:

```
CONSTRAINT LEFT_AND_RIGHT_CHILDREN_DISTINCT
   WITH ( TREE WHERE LEFT  ≠ 0 ) { LEFT  } AS T1 ,
         ( TREE WHERE RIGHT ≠ 0 ) { RIGHT } AS T2 ,
         ( T1 RENAME ( LEFT  AS CHILD ) ) AS T3 ,
         ( T2 RENAME ( RIGHT AS CHILD ) ) AS T4 :
      IS_EMPTY ( T3 INTERSECT T4 ) ;
```

As an aside, I remark that we could even write a constraint—I mean a nonrecursive constraint—to ensure that TREE satisfies the ordering property. The details are left as an exercise.

Traversing the Nodes of a Tree

There are several distinct ways of traversing, or sequencing, the nodes of an ordered tree. Three important ones are described in the literature: **preorder, postorder,** and **inorder**. They can be explained by means of the following recursive procedures (pseudocode again):

```
operator preorder ( root ) ;
   emit root ;
   do for each child ( root ) left to right ;
      emit preorder ( child ( root ) ) ;
   end do ;
end preorder ;

operator postorder ( root ) ;
   do for each child ( root ) left to right ;
      emit postorder ( child ( root ) ) ;
   end do ;
   emit root ;
end postorder ;

operator inorder ( root ) ;
   emit inorder ( first child ( root ) ) ;
   emit root ;
   do for each child ( root ) left to right after the first ;
      emit inorder ( child ( root ) ) ;
   end do ;
end inorder ;
```

For example, consider the tree shown in Figure 14-1 once again. Assume it's ordered as that figure suggests. Then:

- *Preorder* yields: *A, B, C, D, F, E, G, H, I*

- *Postorder* yields: *C, F, D, E, B, H, I, G, A*

- *Inorder* yields: *C, B, F, D, E, A, H, G, I*

Actually, any ordered tree is equivalent in a specific sense to a certain ordered *binary* tree (see, e.g., Donald E. Knuth's book *The Art of Computer Programming Volume I: Fundamental Algorithms,* 3rd edition, Addison-Wesley, 1997, pages 334–335). We could make life a little simpler, therefore, by defining the foregoing operators in terms of ordered binary trees only:

```
operator preorder ( root ) ;
   emit root ;
   emit preorder ( left child ( root ) ) ;
   emit preorder ( right child ( root ) ) ;
end preorder ;

operator postorder ( root ) ;
   emit postorder ( left child ( root ) ) ;
   emit postorder ( right child ( root ) ) ;
   emit root ;
end postorder ;

operator inorder ( root ) ;
   emit inorder ( left child ( root ) ) ;
   emit root ;
   emit inorder ( right child ( root ) ) ;
end inorder ;
```

As you can see, the simplified version of *inorder* in particular here is identical to the pseudocode procedure of the same name in the previous section, which explains why I used that name in that section.

I'll now show how to do the generalized—i.e., nonbinary—version of *preorder* relationally. (I'll leave *postorder* and *inorder* as exercises. They're very similar, of course.) First, here in outline is an appropriate database design. I've assumed for simplicity that the values in the nodes are integers.

```
NODE { ID INTEGER, V INTEGER }
    KEY { ID }

PC { PARENT INTEGER, FIRST_CHILD INTEGER }
   KEY { PARENT }
   KEY { FIRST_CHILD }

LR { LEFT INTEGER, RIGHT INTEGER }
   KEY { LEFT }
   KEY { RIGHT }

NODE { ID, V, FIRST_CHILD, NEXT_SIB }
    KEY { ID }
```

Explanation: NODE contains a tuple for each node in the tree. PC contains a node for each parent in the tree; PARENT gives the ID of that parent and FIRST_CHILD gives the ID of that parent's first child. LR contains a tuple for each child except the last for each parent in the tree; LEFT gives the ID of such a child and RIGHT gives the ID of the next child to the right. Node IDs are positive integers 1, 2, ... (as in the previous section). Observe that PARENT, FIRST_CHILD, LEFT, and RIGHT are never zero (there's no need with this design to use zero to mean some node doesn't exist).

Note: For completeness, I ought really to state the integrity constraints that apply to relvars NODE, PC, and LR. I've omitted those constraints here for space reasons, but you might like to try formulating them yourself before reading any further. By the same token, I've also omitted the code for populating those relvars.

Here now is the **Tutorial D** *preorder* code (it might look a little complicated, but it can easily be improved in a variety of ways). Assuming relvar NODE is nonempty (implying that the tree is nonempty), the **Tutorial D** expression PREORDER(1) will return the desired result as a relation with attributes P and V (where, as in the previous section, P = *i* corresponds to the value appearing in the *i*th position in the sequenced result).

```
OPERATOR PREORDER ( M INTEGER )
        RETURNS RELATION { P INTEGER, V INTEGER } ;
    BEGIN ;
      VAR OUTLIST RELATION
                { P INTEGER, V INTEGER } KEY { P } ;
      VAR TN  TUPLE { ID INTEGER, V INTEGER } ;
      VAR TPC TUPLE { PARENT INTEGER, FIRST_CHILD INTEGER } ;
      VAR TLR TUPLE { LEFT INTEGER, RIGHT INTEGER } ;
      VAR X INTEGER ; /* OUTLIST tuple number */
      X := ( IF M = 1
                THEN 1
                ELSE MAX ( OUTLIST, P ) + 1
             END IF ) ;
      TN := TUPLE FROM ( NODE WHERE ID = M ) ; /* root */
      INSERT OUTLIST
             RELATION { TUPLE { P X, V ( V FROM TN ) ) } } ;
      IF NOT ( IS_EMPTY ( PC WHERE PARENT = M ) )
         THEN
            BEGIN ;
               TPC := TUPLE FROM ( PC WHERE PARENT = M ) ;
               INSERT OUTLIST
                     PREORDER ( FIRST_CHILD FROM TPC ) ;
               IF NOT ( IS_EMPTY
                 ( LR WHERE LEFT = ( FIRST_CHILD FROM TPC ) ) )
                  THEN
                     BEGIN ;
                        TLR := TUPLE FROM ( LR WHERE LEFT =
                                ( FIRST_CHILD FROM TPC ) ) ) ;
```

```
              LOOP : WHILE TRUE
                      BEGIN ;
                          INSERT OUTLIST
                             PREORDER ( RIGHT FROM TLR ) ;
                          IF NOT ( IS_EMPTY
                            ( LR WHERE LEFT =
                               ( RIGHT FROM TLR ) )
                             THEN
                                 TLR := TUPLE FROM
                                       ( LR WHERE LEFT =
                                           ( RIGHT FROM
                                                   TLR ) ) ;
                             ELSE
                                 LEAVE LOOP :
                          END IF ;
                      END ;
                  END WHILE ;
              END ;
          END IF ;
        END ;
     END IF ;
     RETURN OUTLIST ;
  END ;
END OPERATOR ;
```

Note: Even if you agree with me that this code looks a bit complicated, that's not really the point. Rather, the point is that (as already mentioned) the simple expression PREORDER(1) can now be used to produce the preorder, and of course that expression can be freely incorporated into other expressions—in particular, into *ad hoc* queries—as desired. Also, it's not impossible that the code that implements PREORDER might be provided by the system instead of by some application programmer (meaning PREORDER could become a built-in operator, just like, e.g., JOIN).

Bill-of-Materials Processing

Consider Figure 14-3, which shows in tree form how a certain part—namely, part P1—is constructed from certain other parts. To be specific, it shows that part P1 contains parts P2, P3, and P4 as immediate components; part P2 contains parts P5 and P6 as immediate components; and so on. *Note:* If you'd prefer a more concrete example, take part P1 to be a bicycle wheel; then parts P2, P3, and P4 might be a hub, a spoke, and a rim, respectively (and so on).[4] Incidentally, note that the tree of Figure 14-3, unlike those we were considering in the previous two sections, is *unordered;* for example, interchanging the two subtrees rooted at the node for part P2 has no effect (no effect on the interpretation of the tree, that is).

---

4. In practice, of course, we'd also want to know *how many* of each immediate component we need for a given part; for example, a bicycle wheel has one hub but many spokes. I omit such considerations here for space reasons.

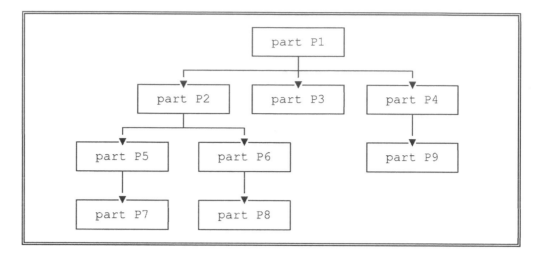

Figure 14-3. *Structure of part P1 represented as a tree*

Now, we can see from Figure 14-3 not only that part P1 contains parts P2, P3, and P4 as immediate components (i.e., components at the first level), but also that it contains parts P5, P6, and P9 as components at the second level, and parts P7 and P8 as components at the third level. Also, of course, it shows that part P2 contains parts P5 and P6 as immediate components, and so on.

An important application of trees such as that shown in Figure 14-3 arises in connection with the so-called **bill-of-materials** problem (also known as the *part explosion* problem). This problem—in its simplest form, at any rate, which is all I have room to discuss here—is the task of determining, for any given part, what the components are of that part, regardless of level. So what's involved in producing a relational solution to this problem?

Well, observe first of all that it's very easy to represent the tree of Figure 14-3 in relational form. All we need is a relation—I'll call it MM—with two attributes, MAJOR_P# and MINOR_P#, with a tuple for each edge in the tree, showing which parts are immediate components of which parts. Refer to Figure 14-4.

MM	MAJOR_P#	MINOR_P#
	P1	P2
	P1	P3
	P1	P4
	P2	P5
	P2	P6
	P4	P9
	P5	P7
	P6	P8

Figure 14-4. *Relational analog of Figure 14-3*

Now I need to confess that I've been practicing a slight deception on you ... The fact is, part-structure "trees" like the one we've been talking about are not, in general, trees at all! That's because the same part might appear at more than one point in the overall structure. Figure 14-5 is a revised version of Figure 14-3 in which part P6 has been replaced by part P4 (and part P8 has therefore been replaced by part P9 as well). While it's true that the revised structure still looks like a tree, *it does so only because I've drawn it with repeated nodes.* The fact is, the node for part P4 is now a child with two distinct parents—the nodes for part P2 and part P1— and the structure thus violates the definitions I gave for a tree structure earlier in this chapter. Thus, a more accurate rendition of the structure in question is the **graph** shown in Figure 14-6. A relational analog of that graph is shown in Figure 14-7. *Note:* The relation in that figure is an example of what's sometimes called a *digraph relation*, because it can be represented as a graph of nodes and directed edges (as Figure 14-6 indicates).

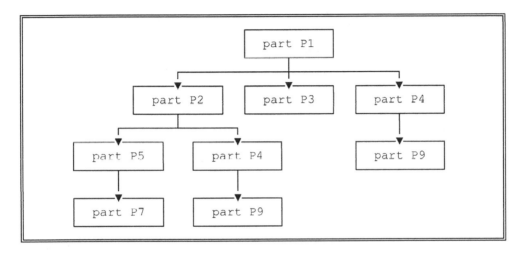

Figure 14-5. *A revised version of Figure 14-3*

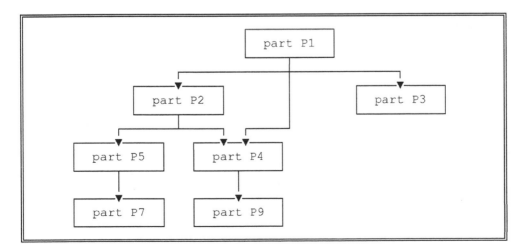

Figure 14-6. *A revised (graph) version of Figure 14-5*

MM	MAJOR_P#	MINOR_P#
	P1	P2
	P1	P3
	P1	P4
	P2	P5
	P2	P4
	P5	P7
	P4	P9

Figure 14-7. *Relational analog of Figure 14-6*

Now let's think about the bill-of-materials problem as it applies to part P1. From either Figure 14-5 or Figure 14-6, we can easily see that part P1 contains parts P2, P3, P4, P5, P7, and P9 as components (at some level or other); in fact, a given part *p* contains another part *q* as a component if and only if there's a path of one or more edges connecting the node for part *p* to the node for part *q*. Figure 14-8 is an extended version of Figure 14-7, showing a tuple for every such path (instead of just for every edge, as Figure 14-7 does; of course, an edge is just a special case of a path).

TC	MAJOR_P#	MINOR_P#
	P1	P2
	P1	P3
	P1	P4
	P2	P5
	P2	P4
	P5	P7
	P4	P9
	P1	P5
	P1	P7
	P1	P9
	P2	P7
	P2	P9

Figure 14-8. *Transitive closure of relation MM from Figure 14-7*

The relation in Figure 14-8, relation TC, is said to be the *transitive closure* of the relation MM in Figure 14-7. Note that (as I've more or less said already) it's a superset of relation MM. Here's the definition:

Let *r* be a binary relation with attributes *X* and *Y*, both of the same type *T*. Then the **transitive closure** of *r* is a relation r^+ defined as follows: The tuple *<x,y>* appears in r^+ if and only if (a) it appears in *r* or (b) there exists a value *z* of type *T* such that the tuple *<x,z>* appears in *r* and the tuple *<z,y>* appears in r^+.

In other words, the tuple *<x,y>* appears in r^+ if and only if there's a path in the graph from node *x* to node *y*, loosely speaking.

Transitive closure is important for the obvious reason that it enables us to obtain a solution to the bill-of-materials problem very directly. Thus, what we need is a way of computing the transitive closure of a relation like MM. The following not very sophisticated **Tutorial D** code will suffice:

```
OPERATOR TRANCLO ( XY RELATION { X P#, Y P# } )
             RETURNS RELATION { X P#, Y P# } ;
   RETURN
    ( WITH
      ( XY UNION
        ( ( XY JOIN
          ( XY RENAME ( Y AS Z, X AS Y ) ) ) ) { X, Z }
               RENAME ( Z AS Y ) ) ) AS TC :
      IF TC = XY
        THEN TC
        ELSE TRANCLO ( TC )
      END IF ) ;
END OPERATOR ;
```

If relation MM is as shown in Figure 14-7, the expression

```
TRANCLO ( MM RENAME ( MAJOR_P# AS X , MINOR_P# AS Y ) )
              RENAME ( X AS MAJOR_P# , Y AS MINOR_P# )
```

will now return the result shown in Figure 14-8. *Explanation:* The following nonrecursive pseudocode might help you understand how TRANCLO works:

```
TC := XY ;
do until TC reaches a "fixpoint" ;
   TC := TC UNION ( XY <*> TC ) ;
end ;
```

Loosely speaking, this procedure works by repeatedly forming an intermediate result consisting of the union of (a) the previous intermediate result and (b) the join of XY and that previous intermediate result, until that intermediate result reaches a *fixpoint*—i.e., a point at which it ceases to grow. The expression "XY <*> TC" is shorthand for "join XY and TC over XY.Y and TC.X and project the result over XY.X and TC.Y"; for brevity, I'm ignoring here the attribute renaming operations that **Tutorial D** would require in order to make this operation work. *Exercise:* Try working through this algorithm (both nonrecursive pseudocode and recursive **Tutorial D** versions) using the sample data of Figure 14-7. Compare your results with Figure 14-8. Can you see any coding improvements that could be made in the interests of efficiency?

I must now quickly add that **Tutorial D** includes *built-in* support for the transitive closure operator, in accordance with which we could obtain the transitive closure of relation MM by means of the simpler expression

```
TCLOSE ( MM )
```

The query "Get components at all levels for part P1" (for example) can thus be formulated as follows:

```
( TCLOSE ( MM ) ) WHERE MAJOR_P# = P#('P1')
```

Loosely speaking, the TRANCLO code shown earlier might be regarded as possible *implementation code* for the TCLOSE operator.

At this point I'd like to mention a couple of asides (which you might want to skip on a first reading). First, I remark that—although it's certainly not relational, and it doesn't support transitive closure as such—the SQL standard does allow us to write recursive expressions. (This feature was introduced with SQL:1999.) Thus, for example, the query "Get components at all levels for part P1" might be formulated in SQL as follows:

```
WITH RECURSIVE TC ( MAJOR_P#, MINOR_P# ) AS
  ( ( SELECT MM.MAJOR_P#, MM.MINOR_P#
      FROM   MM )
    UNION
    ( SELECT TC.MAJOR_P#, MM.MINOR_P#
      FROM   TC, MM
      WHERE  TC.MINOR_P# = MM.MAJOR_P# ) )
SELECT DISTINCT MINOR_P#
FROM   TC
WHERE  TC.MAJOR_P# = P#('P1') ;
```

Lines 2–3 and lines 5–7 of this expression constitute *the initial subquery* and *the recursive subquery*, respectively; between them, they construct the transitive closure. Lines 8–10 constitute *the final subquery*. Please don't ask me to explain the example further.

Second, I remark that the commercial Oracle product has had proprietary support for recursive queries for many years. For example:

```
SELECT  LEVEL, MINOR_P#
FROM    MM
CONNECT BY MAJOR_P# = PRIOR MINOR_P#
START   WITH MAJOR_P# = P#('P1') ;
```

Given the sample data of Figures 14-5 through 14-7, this expression yields the result shown in Figure 14-9 (LEVEL in that result shows the level below part P1 at which the component MINOR_P# appears in the tree—see Figure 14-5). Note very carefully, however, that the result in question suffers from the serious defect that *it's not a relation* (which is why there's no primary key marked by double underlining in the figure). To be specific:

LEVEL	MINOR_P#
1	P2
2	P5
3	P7
2	P4
3	P9
1	P3
1	P4
2	P9

Figure 14-9. *Recursive Oracle query result*

- It's not a relation because the result involves what's called *essential ordering*. For example, suppose we were to interchange the rows <2,P5> and <2,P4>; then P7 would apparently be a component of P4 instead of P5. See my book *The Database Relational Model: A Retrospective Review and Analysis* (Addison-Wesley, 2001), if you need an explanation of the important concept of *essentiality*.

- It's also not a relation because it might contain what look like duplicate rows, and yet the rows in question don't have the same meaning. Consider what would happen, for example, if P3 were to contain P4 as a component; the result would have two <2,P4> rows, one showing that P4 was a component of P2 and the other showing that it was a component of P3.

In a nutshell, the result isn't a relation because it violates *The Information Principle*, and the crucial relational **closure** property—not the same thing as transitive closure, by the way!—is thereby violated too. The implications of this state of affairs are beyond the scope of the present chapter; see, e.g., my book *An Introduction to Database Systems*, 8th edition (Addison-Wesley, 2004), pages 61–62, for further discussion.

A point that's often forgotten in discussions of bill-of-materials and related matters is that the bill-of-materials problem *per se* is only one side of the coin; the other side is the **where-used** problem, also known as the *part implosion* problem, which is the task of determining, for any given part, what parts that part is a component of (again, regardless of level). The interesting point about the where-used problem is that trees or graphs like those of Figures 14-3, 14-5, and 14-6 are of no help with it! Why? Because they're "the wrong way up," as it were; equivalently, the edges "go the wrong way." Clearly, what we need is the appropriate *inverse* structure (after all, the where-used problem is the inverse of the bill-of-materials problem, in a sense). By way of example, Figure 14-10 shows the inverse of the graph in Figure 14-6.[5] Note that, since Figure 14-6 had three leaf nodes, Figure 14-10 has three root nodes; in other words, Figure 14-10

---

5. Of course, we could obtain an inverse picture by simply repeating Figure 14-6 but reversing all of the arrows, but the result would violate our convention for drawing trees with the root at the top.

shows a *set* of trees, or what's sometimes called a **forest** (a forest of three trees, in this particular case—if we agree for the moment to overlook the fact that they're not really trees at all, that is).

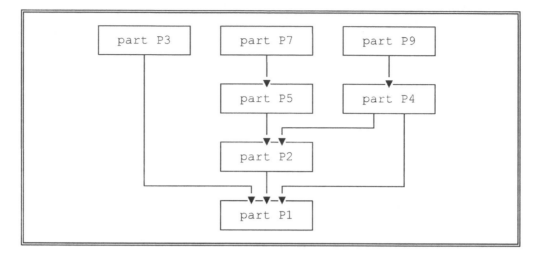

Figure 14-10. *Inverse of Figure 14-6*

We see, therefore, that the trees or graphs we've been discussing have a *direction* to them, so to speak. But relations don't! The very same transitive closure relation TC from Figure 14-8 can be used for where-used queries just as well as it can for bill-of-materials queries. For example:

```
( TCLOSE ( MM ) ) WHERE MINOR_P# = P#('P2')
```

("get parts that contain part P2 at some level"). I would argue, therefore, that not only can relations handle bill-of-materials and related processing just as well as trees can, they actually do it better than trees do. I might add that the relational solutions are easier to understand as well. For evidence in support of this claim, see the book mentioned earlier, *An Introduction to Database Systems*, 8th edition (Addison-Wesley, 2004), pages 887–888; see also the 3rd edition of that same book (Addison-Wesley, 1981), pages 356–360.

An obvious constraint on a part-structure tree is that no part can contain itself as a component at any level (in other words, there mustn't be any cycles in the graph). We can state this constraint formally as follows:

```
CONSTRAINT NO_CYCLES
    IS_EMPTY ( ( TCLOSE ( MM ) ) WHERE MAJOR_P# = MINOR_P# ) ;
```

Of course, this formulation does assume that TCLOSE is defined (and implemented) in such a way that it still works if the graph includes cycles. If you can't be sure of this assumption, use TRANCLO instead, which certainly does work in the presence of cycles. *Exercise:* Check this latter claim.

Don't assume, however, that cycles in such graphs are always invalid. A simple counterexample is provided by the case of a transportation network, where, if there's a path from *A* to *B*, there's certainly a path from *B* to *A* as well. Of course, suitable care must be taken over the design of algorithms that process such graphs; otherwise you might find that, for example, the system suggests one possible airline route from SFO (San Francisco) to JFK (New York) is SFO - SJC (San Jose) - SFO - JFK.

Another Kind of Tree

There's another kind of tree in common use (especially in database contexts) that's logically different in several ways from the ones we've been discussing so far: namely, the kind of tree found in, e.g., IMS databases. I'll use IMS as the basis for my discussions until further notice. *Note:* IMS uses the term *hierarchy* instead of *tree*, but the terms are more or less interchangeable (at least their meanings overlap considerably); I'll stay with *tree* in what follows. In fact, from this point forward I'll simply ignore all IMS-specific details, terminological or otherwise, if they're irrelevant to my main purpose.

The first thing I have to say is that the picture gets muddied instantly, because IMS actually involves two different kinds of trees, which I'll refer to as *type* trees and *occurrence* trees, respectively.[6] An IMS database contains a set of occurrence trees, each of which is basically a tree—in fact, an *ordered* tree —in the sense of that term as used in this chapter thus far. (More or less, anyway; actually there are a few differences, which I'll get to in a moment.) By way of example, consider Figure 14-11, which shows an occurrence tree from a certain IMS education database (which is based on a real application, incidentally). That figure is meant to be interpreted as follows:

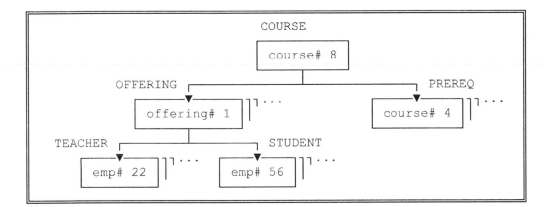

Figure 14-11. *Sample occurrence tree from an IMS database*

---

6. Don't confuse the term *type tree* as used here and the term *type hierarchy* as used in connection with type inheritance matters. *Type hierarchies* are used to represent the fact that certain types are subtypes of certain other types; they have nothing to do with the subject of the present chapter.

- A certain education course (course number 8) has a set of offerings and a set of immediate prerequisite courses. One such offering (offering number 1) and one such prerequisite
(course number 4) are represented in the figure. *Note:* The figure deliberately shows
explicit edges only where it also shows the corresponding child nodes explicitly.

- Offering 1 of course 8 has a set of teachers and a set of students. One such teacher
(employee number 22) and one such student (employee number 56) are represented in
the figure. *Note:* The education system represented by this database is purely internal to
the company in question; thus, all teachers and all students are indeed employees of the
company.

To repeat, an occurrence tree like the one shown in Figure 14-11 is just a tree in the sense
in which I defined that term near the beginning of this chapter (to a first approximation, anyway).
But there's another kind of tree involved here, too. To be specific, every occurrence tree in a
given IMS database is supposed to conform to the corresponding *type* tree. Figure 14-12 shows
the type tree corresponding to Figure 14-11. To elaborate:

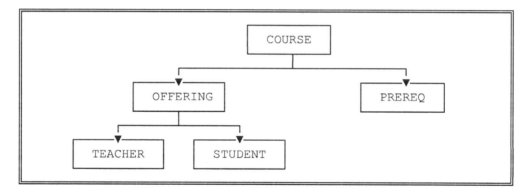

Figure 14-12. *Type tree corresponding to Figure 14-11*

- COURSE, OFFERING, TEACHER, STUDENT, and PREREQ are *record types* (and their
counterparts in an occurrence tree are *record occurrences,* or just *records* for short). In
other words, the nodes in a type tree represent record types, and their counterparts in
an occurrence tree represent record occurrences. Note too that both the type tree and
all of its corresponding occurrence trees differ in kind from the ones discussed earlier
in this chapter, inasmuch as different nodes in those type and occurrence trees are of
different types. The trees in question are thus *heterogeneous.* (Precisely for this reason,
the nodes need to be *named;* observe by contrast that nodes in our earlier discussions
were never named.)

- COURSE is the root record type; COURSE and OFFERING are parent record types;
OFFERING, TEACHER, STUDENT, and PREREQ are child record types; and all of these
latter except OFFERING are also leaf record types.

- Every course has a set of offerings and a set of immediate prerequisite courses, and every
offering has a set of teachers and a set of students. Of course, any of these sets might be
empty, in general; thus, it follows that an occurrence (in an occurrence tree) of a parent

record type might not be a parent as I defined that term near the beginning of this chapter, because it might not actually have any children. For example, a given offering might have no students enrolled in it at this time.

- Just as a given node in the type tree corresponds to many nodes in each of many occurrence trees (in general), so a given edge in the type tree corresponds to many edges in each of many occurrence trees (again in general). In fact, an edge in the type tree can be thought of as representing a one-to-many relationship (where "many" includes the zero case).

- Another difference between these IMS-style heterogeneous trees and the homogeneous trees discussed in earlier sections is that those homogeneous trees were of potentially unlimited depth. For example, a given part might "explode" to any number of levels. By contrast, the depth of an IMS-style type tree is fixed (it's three in the education example), and the depth of any corresponding occurrence tree is equal to or less than that of the type tree.

- Although IMS-style trees can still be regarded as having an element of recursion in their make-up, that fact is much less important than it was for homogeneous trees, precisely because (a) different nodes are of different types, and (b) there's a limit on the depth, in the case of heterogeneous trees.

As an aside, it's ironic to note, given the state of affairs just explained, that IMS—or what subsequently became IMS, at any rate—was originally intended *precisely* to address the bill-of-materials problem! Only later was it extended to become the general-purpose system that it was marketed as by IBM. As should be clear from the discussions in this chapter, IMS-style trees are not well suited to bill-of-materials—not least because, in general, part-structure "trees" aren't true trees anyway—and the machinations one has to go through in order to use IMS-style trees for the purpose are, to my mind, baroque in the extreme. See the paper "A Hierarchic System: IMS" in my book *Relational Database Writings 1991–1994* (Addison-Wesley, 1995), for further discussion of this topic.

One final remark: I haven't bothered to show the internal structure of the various record types and occurrences in Figures 14-11 and 14-12. For the sake of subsequent discussion, however, I'll assume that:

- Courses have a course number and title.

- Offerings have an offering number, a date, and a location.

- Teachers have just an employee number.

- Students have an employee number and a grade.

I've concentrated on IMS in this section so far for definiteness. For the record, however, let me now observe that (a) *containment hierarchies* as found in the world of object orientation and (b) *XML documents* (in which there is so much current interest) are both essentially "occurrence trees" in the sense discussed above. It follows that:

- Everything I've said or will say in this chapter regarding IMS-style trees applies equally well, *mutatis mutandis*, to containment hierarchies and XML documents as well.

- Relational systems can provide XML-like functionality if desired (because they can certainly provide IMS-like functionality, as I'll show in a moment).

- With respect to both object and XML databases, we're—sad to say—revisiting a lot of ancient territory (though I have to say too that most of the current literature doesn't seem to recognize this fact).

- The "semistructured data model," on which XML is supposed to be based, is essentially just the old IMS data model in a different guise.

But now I'm beginning to stray from the principal topic of the present chapter; let me leave these issues for some future publication (which I do plan to produce as soon as I can).

The usual technique for representing IMS-style trees relationally is well known, of course; indeed, it was discussed by Codd himself in his famous 1970 paper "A Relational Model of Data for Large Shared Data Banks" (*CACM 13*, No. 6, June 1970). The technique isn't worth discussing in detail here; in essence, all it involves is simply (a) extending each record type (i.e., each node) in the type tree with the key of its parent, if any, and then (b) mapping each resulting record type to a separate relvar. In the case of the type tree of Figure 14-12, this process yields the following relvars (in outline):

```
COURSE { COURSE#, TITLE }
      KEY { COURSE# }

OFFERING { COURSE#, OFF#, DATE, LOCATION }
        KEY { COURSE#, OFF# }
        FOREIGN KEY { COURSE# } REFERENCES COURSE

TEACHER { COURSE#, OFF#, EMP# }
       KEY { COURSE#, OFF#, EMP# }
       FOREIGN KEY { COURSE#, OFF# } REFERENCES OFFERING

STUDENT { COURSE#, OFF#, EMP#, GRADE }
       KEY { COURSE#, OFF#, EMP# }
       FOREIGN KEY { COURSE#, OFF# } REFERENCES OFFERING

PREREQ { MAJOR_COURSE#, MINOR_COURSE# }
       KEY { MAJOR_COURSE#, MINOR_COURSE# }
```

The usual techniques for mapping IMS-style operations on IMS-style trees into relational analogs are equally straightforward, and I omit further discussion here.

What About Relation-Valued Attributes?

Following on from the previous section, I'd now like to remind you that there is in fact another way—arguably a more direct way—to represent IMS-style trees relationally: namely, by using

relation-valued attributes (here abbreviated RVAs). Here, for example, is the outline of a definition for a relvar directly corresponding to the type tree of Figure 14-12:

```
COURSE { COURSE#,
         TITLE,
         OFFERING { OFF#,
                    DATE,
                    LOCATION,
                    TEACHER { EMP# },
                    STUDENT { EMP#,
                              GRADE } },
         PREREQ { COURSE# } }
       KEY { COURSE# }
```

OFFERING and PREREQ here are RVAs, and the relations that are values of OFFERING involve TEACHER and STUDENT as RVAs in turn.

Now, the foregoing design *is* a valid relational design for the education database; however, it's of a form that's usually contraindicated. Why? Because it's essentially isomorphic to the original tree, and it suffers from essentially the same problems as the original tree does. I discussed such problems in detail in my paper "What First Normal Form Really Means" (Chapter 8 in the present book), and I don't want to repeat all of those arguments here. Suffice it to say that trees, and isomorphic relvars with RVAs, are both asymmetric structures; thus, while they might make some problems "easy," they make others much more difficult. For example, given either the COURSE relvar just shown or the tree of Figure 14-11, the query "Get all students on course number 8" is comparatively straightforward, but the query "Get all courses attended by employee number 56" isn't. As I put the matter earlier (in a different context), "the tree is often the wrong way up." *Note:* It's relevant to mention that IMS in particular goes to extraordinary lengths, via what it calls *logical databases* (as opposed to physical ones, of course) and *secondary data structures,* in its attempts to overcome this inherent problem with trees. Again, see the paper "A Hierarchic System: IMS" in my book *Relational Database Writings 1991–1994* (Addison-Wesley, 1995), for examples and further explanation.

Let me add that RVAs could be used in connection with homogeneous trees as well as IMS-style ones. For example, Figure 14-13 shows two relations, BM and WU, both representing the same information as relation MM from Figure 14-7 and both involving an RVA; relation BM ("bill-of-materials") shows, for each part, which parts that part contains as immediate components, and relation WU ("where-used") shows, for each part, which parts contain that part as immediate components. Note, however, that:

- Both of these relations suffer from the problems of asymmetry referred to above.

- Both of these relations represent just *a single level of nesting*. Clearly, we can use RVAs to represent any depth of nesting, just so long as that depth is known ahead of time (as it is in the case of the education database); however, we can't use them to represent an *arbitrary* depth, as is typically the case in homogeneous trees.

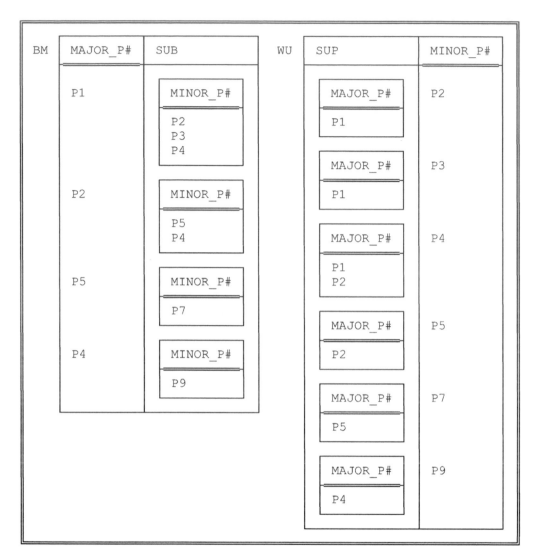

Figure 14-13. *Relations BM and WU*

On the other hand, it's worth pointing out that relations BM and WU are each easily obtained from relation MM by means of simple **Tutorial D** expressions:

```
BM ≡ MM GROUP ( { MINOR_P# } AS SUB )
WU ≡ MM GROUP ( { MAJOR_P# } AS SUP )
```

And the converse is true too:

```
MM ≡ BM UNGROUP ( { SUB } )
   ≡ WU UNGROUP ( { SUP } )
```

The consequences of choosing a relational design that involves RVAs are thus not as severe as the consequences of having to use IMS-style trees. In IMS and similar systems, we're stuck with whatever trees the designer has decided to give us (operators for transforming such trees into one another or into relations without RVAs are usually not supported in such systems). In a relational system, by contrast, we can transform the structures we're given into whatever other structures we like, and we can perform such transformations whenever we like, too (in other words, at run time).

Concluding Remarks

I hope I've covered enough ground to give you reason to believe as I do that trees and tree processing can be handled perfectly well in a relational system. First, of course, it's clearly possible to write procedural code for such tasks. Second, and more important, it's also possible to define high-level relational operators (e.g., the proposed TREESORT operator) that can raise the level of abstraction to a level comparable to that supported by more familiar relational operators such as join. Of course, it won't have escaped your notice that recursion is important in this connection—but recursion is a time-tested and well-respected technique in other areas of computer science, and there's no reason why relational systems shouldn't provide good support for recursion too.

Acknowledgments

I'd like to thank Hugh Darwen and Fabian Pascal for their comments on earlier drafts of this chapter.

■■■

Twelve Rules
for Business Rules

No rules, however wise, are a substitute for affection and tact.

—Bertrand Russell

This chapter has to do with what are commonly called *business rules*. Its aim is to propose a set of rules about such rules—rules that, it is suggested, a "good rule engine" really ought to abide by. Such rules about rules might well be called *metarules;* they might equally well be described as *objectives;* however, the chapter refers to them as **prescriptions**.[1]

Disclaimer: The original version of this chapter was prepared under a contract with Versata Inc., a company that has a business rule product to sell. However, it was categorically *not* written in such a way as to "make Versata look good"; the various prescriptions it describes were designed without any special reference to the current commercial scene in general or Versata's product in particular. In other words, the chapter serves to document my own opinion merely—my opinion, that is, as to what business rule products ought to strive for in the future.

Assumptions

It is convenient to begin by stating some underlying assumptions and introducing some terminology:

- The purpose of any given piece of application software—an **application** for short—is to implement some **enterprise work item** (i.e., some piece of functionality that is relevant to the enterprise in question).

---

1. I decided to include this chapter in this part of the book because rule engines—i.e., software systems that support the development of applications by means of "business rules"—can be regarded as implementing a large piece of the relational model that ought by rights to have been implemented many years ago by the "relational" DBMS vendors, but in fact never was. Part II ("A Relational Perspective") of my book *WHAT Not HOW: The Business Rules Approach to Application Development* (Addison-Wesley, 2000) elaborates on this claim and explains it in depth.

Note: The term *application* is used here and in what follows in a very loose kind of way; thus, a given application might be a simple subroutine (e.g., a function to calculate withholding), or a large collection of mutually interacting programs (e.g., a fully integrated corporate accounting system), or anything in between.

- The enterprise work item in question is specified as a set of **definitions** (data definitions, access definitions, form definitions, and so forth).

- To the maximum extent logically possible, those definitions are **declarative**—i.e., nonprocedural—in nature. They are also **formal** (necessarily so, of course). In what follows, they are referred to as **business rules,** or just **rules** for short.

  Note: The reason for the slight degree of hesitancy in the foregoing paragraph ("To the maximum extent logically possible") is that the rules in question might include certain *stimulus/response* rules, which do include an element of procedurality (see Prescription 3, later).

- Business rules are **compilable**—i.e., mechanically convertible into executable code— and hence, loosely, **executable**. In other words, the set of rules constituting the declarative specification for a given application **is** the source code for that application, by definition (pun intended). Thus, the activities of (a) *specifying* or *defining* the application, and (b) *developing* or *building* it, are in fact one and the same.

  Note: It follows from the foregoing that, so far as this chapter is concerned, the terms *rules* and *business rules* are reserved to mean **rules that can be automated.** Other writers use the term more generally. For example, the final report of the GUIDE Business Rules Project [3] defines a business rule to be "a statement that defines or constrains some aspect of the business." By this definition, a statement to the effect that the last person to leave the premises must turn off the lights might qualify as a business rule—but not one that is very interesting from the point of view of business automation. To put the matter another way, not all business policies and protocols are capable of being automated, and this chapter is concerned only with ones that are.

- Finally, the software system that is responsible for compiling and overseeing the execution of such declaratively specified applications is called the **rule engine.**

A Note on Terminology

It is, unfortunately, undeniable that the term *rules* is not a very good one (certainly it is not very specific, nor very descriptive). And the term *business rules* is not much better; in particular, not all enterprises are businesses. As already indicated, this chapter does make use of these terms; however, it does so primarily because other publications in the field do so too! Be that as it may, the really important point is that the technology under discussion is a **declarative** one. To be more specific, rules, whatever they might be called, are *declarative,* not *procedural,* in nature: Application software—possibly some system software too—is specified declaratively, and the resulting declarative specifications are directly compilable and executable.

Further Preliminary Remarks

It might be felt that prescriptions such as the ones to be discussed in this chapter ought all to be independent of one another. After all, such independence is surely desirable for the same kinds of reasons that the prescriptions themselves demand certain kinds of independence in business rule systems. However, it turns out to be more convenient to state the prescriptions in a kind of layered fashion, with later ones building on earlier ones; thus, the various prescriptions are not, nor are they claimed to be, fully independent of one another, despite any possible advantage that might follow from trying to make them so. What is more, some of the prescriptions overlap others (that is, some requirements are stated in more than one place, in more than one way).

Now, many readers will be aware that there are precedents for a proposal of this nature. What is more, some of those precedents have become a little discredited over time, and the writer is therefore sensitive to the possibility of criticism (especially criticism along the lines of "oh no, not again"[2]). But business rule systems are becoming increasingly important, and it does therefore seem worthwhile—the foregoing comments notwithstanding—to attempt to provide some structure for the debates that will inevitably arise in the marketplace. Thus, what follows is offered as a kind of yardstick, or framework, that might conveniently be used to orient such debates; equally, it is proposed as a basis against which business rule systems might be "carefully analyzed, criticized, evaluated, and perhaps judged" (wording cribbed from reference [2]).

That said, however, there are a couple of important caveats that need to be spelled out immediately:

- The prescriptions that follow are emphatically **not** intended as a basis for any kind of "checklist" evaluation. To say it again, they are offered as a framework for structuring discussion and debate; they are definitely not meant as a basis for any kind of scoring scheme. (Statements to the effect that "Product P is x percent of a good business rule system" are not only absurd but positively harmful, in this writer's very firm opinion.)

- There is no claim that the prescriptions that follow are complete or exhaustive in any absolute sense. Indeed, they are meant to be open-ended, in general. That is to say, anything not explicitly prescribed is permitted, unless it clashes with something explicitly prohibited; likewise, anything not explicitly prohibited is permitted too, unless it clashes with something explicitly prescribed.

The list of prescriptions follows immediately. *Note:* Some of those prescriptions (the first two in particular) just repeat certain assumptions already spelled out above; however, the assumptions in question are sufficiently important as to deserve elevation to the status of prescriptions *per se*. The final section of the chapter (before the acknowledgments and list of references) presents a summary of the entire set of prescriptions.

---

2. Especially since, as it happens, the number of prescriptions is exactly *twelve*.

Prescription 1: Executable Rules

Rules shall be **compilable**—see Prescription 10—and **executable** (even when the rule in question is basically just a data definition rule, as in the case of, e.g., CREATE TABLE in SQL).

Prescription 2: Declarative Rules

Rules shall be stated **declaratively**. The *rule language*—i.e., the language or interface that supports such declarative specifications—shall be **expressively complete;** that is, it shall be at least as powerful as a sorted, two-valued, first-order predicate logic. To elaborate:

- "Sorted" here might better be *typed* (but *sorted* is the term logicians use for the concept). It refers to the fact that any given placeholder in any given predicate must be of some specific "sort" or type; i.e., its permitted values must be exactly the values that make up some specific data type (or domain—the terms *type* and *domain* mean exactly the same thing [1,2], and they are used interchangeably herein).

- "Two-valued" refers to the two truth values TRUE and FALSE.

- "First-order" refers to the fact that (as already stated under the first bullet above) any given placeholder in any given predicate must take its values from, specifically, the set of values that make up some data type, not, e.g., the set of values—i.e., the set of *relation* values—that is the set of relations currently appearing in the database.

In addition, the rule language shall be constructed according to well-established principles of **good language design,** as documented in, e.g., reference [2]. In particular, it shall exhibit both (a) **syntactic** and **semantic consistency** and (b) **conceptual integrity** (again, see reference [2] for elaboration of these desirable properties).

Prescription 3: Kinds of Rules

Rules shall be loosely divisible into three kinds, as follows:

- **Presentation rules:** Presentation rules have to do with interactions with the application user (they include rules for displaying interactive forms to the user, rules for accepting filled-out forms from the user, rules for controlling form transitions, rules for displaying error messages to the user, and so forth).

- **Database rules:** Database rules have to do with defining database data, retrieving and updating database data in response to user requests and user entries on interactive forms, specifying legal values for such database data, and so forth.

- **Application rules:** Application rules have to do with the processing the application needs to carry out in order to implement the enterprise work item. (Application rules are sometimes referred to as *business*—or *application*—*logic,* but these terms are deprecated and are not used further in this chapter.)

Note: It is not always easy to say whether a given rule is a database rule or an application rule, which is why the foregoing categorization is proposed as a loose one only.

Database and application rules shall include **computations, constraints,** and **inference rules:**

- A **computation** is an expression to be evaluated. The result can be named or can be assigned to one or more variables.

- A **constraint**—frequently referred to more specifically as an **integrity** constraint—is a truth-valued expression (also known as a *conditional, logical,* or *boolean* expression) that, given values for any variables mentioned in the expression, is required to evaluate to TRUE.

- An **inference rule** is a statement of the form $p \vdash q$ (where p and q are truth-valued expressions and "$\vdash$"—sometimes pronounced "turnstile"—is a metalinguistic or metalogical operator) that, given the truth of p, allows the truth of q to be inferred. *Note:* If q is regarded, as it clearly can be, as a truth-valued *function,* then the inference rule can be regarded as a (not necessarily complete) *definition* of that function.

By the way, inference rules as just defined should not be confused with truth-valued expressions of the form $p \Rightarrow q$ (where p and q are truth-valued expressions and "$\Rightarrow$"—sometimes pronounced "implies"—is the *material implication* operator of predicate logic). The expression $p \Rightarrow q$ is defined to evaluate to TRUE if and only if p is FALSE or q is TRUE (equivalently, it evaluates to FALSE if and only if p is TRUE and q is FALSE). Such an expression might constitute an integrity constraint (e.g., "*e* is an accountant $\Rightarrow$ *e* earns more than \$45,000 a year"). By contrast, the inference rule $p \vdash q$ actually *defines q* in terms of p (e.g., "*e* is an accountant $\vdash$ *e* is a white-collar worker").

Note: The following (lightly edited) extract from reference [4] might help to clarify the foregoing distinction:

> Do not confuse $\vdash$ with $\Rightarrow$. The sign $\vdash$ is a symbol of the metalanguage, the language in which we talk about the language that the formation rules have to do with. It makes sense to speak of the formula $p \Rightarrow q$ as being TRUE in some state of affairs or FALSE in some other state of affairs. However, it makes no sense to speak of $p \vdash q$ as being TRUE in such-and-such state of affairs; the truth of $p \vdash q$ has nothing to with states of affairs but with whether the system of logic in which we are operating allows us to infer q from p.[3]

(A *state of affairs* can be thought of, loosely, as an assignment of truth values to available atomic formulas.)

The foregoing discussion notwithstanding, it might be desirable in practice (for reasons of user-friendliness, perhaps) for inference rules and material implication expressions both to use the same syntax, *viz.,* IF p THEN q. Thus, "IF *e* is an accountant THEN *e* is a white-collar worker" could be an inference rule, asserting that the fact that *e* is a white-collar worker can validly be inferred from the fact that *e* is an accountant. By contrast, "IF *e* is an accountant THEN *e* earns more than \$45,000 a year" could be an integrity constraint, asserting that the database must show *e*'s salary as being more than \$45,000 a year if *e* is an accountant (and any update operation that would cause this constraint to be violated must be rejected). Of course, if inference and material implication do both use the same syntax, then context will have to provide a means of distinguishing between the two.

---

3.   Yet another way of thinking about the statement "$p \vdash q$" is as a *proof:* "q is *provable* from p."

Database and application rules might possibly also include **stimulus/response rules**—i.e., rules of the form IF *p* THEN DO *q*, where *p* is a truth-valued expression and *q* is an action (of arbitrary complexity, in general; e.g., "send an email message to the customer" might be a valid action, in suitable circumstances). However, such rules at least partially violate Prescription 2, inasmuch as they are at least partially procedural, and they should be used sparingly and with caution. *Note:* Stimulus/response rules correspond to what are more frequently referred to as *triggers*. The idea is that the *triggered action q* is to be carried out whenever the *triggering event p* (meaning "*p* is TRUE") occurs. The keyword IF might more appropriately be spelled WHEN or ON in some situations.

By the way, it is not necessary that rules be "atomic" in any sense, at least from the user's point of view. That is, if *p* and *q* are business rules, then (e.g.) *p* AND *q* is a business rule too. (Rule atomicity might be important from the point of view of the underlying theory or from the point of view of some implementation or both, but it should not be of much concern to the user.)

Rules shall impose **no artificial boundary** between the database and main memory (i.e., the user shall not be required to be aware that the database and main memory constitute different levels of the storage hierarchy under the covers).

Prescription 4: Declaration Sequence *vs.* Execution Sequence

Business rules will depend on one another, in general, in a variety of different ways; for example, rule *A* might refer to a data item that is defined via rule *B*. This fact notwithstanding, it shall be possible to declare the rules in **any physical sequence**. (Equivalently, it shall be possible to change the sequence in which the rules are physically declared without affecting the meaning.) Determining the sequence in which the rules are to be executed ("fired") shall be the responsibility of the rule engine solely.

Observe that this prescription implies that inserting a new rule or updating or deleting an existing rule will require the rule engine to recompute the rule execution sequence, in general.

Prescription 5: The Rule Engine Is a DBMS

Database and application rules, at least (and to some extent presentation rules as well), are all expressed in terms of constructs in **the database schema**. Logically speaking, in fact, they are an integral part of that schema; indeed, it could be argued that the schema *is* the rules, nothing more and nothing less. It follows that the rule engine is just a special kind of database management system (DBMS), and rules *per se* are just a special kind of data (or metadata, rather). By virtue of Prescription 10, however, that DBMS can be thought of as operating at some kind of "middleware" level within the overall system; in other words, it is a DBMS that is at least capable of using other DBMSs and/or file systems to hold its stored data (thereby effectively running "on top of" those other DBMSs and/or file systems—possibly several such at the same time). *Note:* As noted previously, this last point is further elaborated under Prescription 10.

As just stated, "rules are data" (*database* data, to be precise). It follows that the well-known external *vs.* conceptual *vs.* internal distinctions apply (thanks to Ron Ross for drawing my attention to this point). To be more specific:

- The external form of a given rule is the source form of that rule (i.e., the form in which it is originally stated to the rule engine by the rule definer).

- The conceptual form is a canonical representation of the rule, perhaps as one or more statements of pure predicate logic (a formalism that might not be suitable at the external level for ergonomic reasons).

- And the internal form is whatever form—or forms, plural—the rule engine finds it convenient to keep the rule in for storage and execution purposes.

These three levels shall be rigidly distinguished and not confused with one another.

The external and conceptual versions of any given rule shall include absolutely nothing that relates to, or is logically affected by, the internal (or *physical* or *storage*) level of the system. In particular, those versions shall include nothing that has to do with **performance**.

Since (to say it again) "rules are data," all of the services that are provided for database data in general—including, e.g., conceptually centralized management, access optimization, physical and logical data independence, and recovery and concurrency controls—shall be provided for rules in particular. In other words, **standard DBMS benefits** shall apply. Here are some specific implications of this point:

- Any given user shall need to be aware only of those rules that are **pertinent to that user** (just as any given user needs to be aware only of that portion of the data in a given database that is pertinent to that user).

- Rules shall be **queryable** and **updatable** (see Prescription 7).

- Rule **consistency** shall be maintained (again, see Prescription 7).

- Rules shall be **sharable** and **reusable** across applications (and *vice versa*—see Prescription 9).

Prescription 6: The Rule Engine Is a *Relational* DBMS

It is well known—see, e.g., reference [2]—that domains (or types) and relations are together both *necessary* and *sufficient* to represent absolutely any data whatsoever, at least at the conceptual level. It is also well known that the relational operators (join, etc.) are closely related to, and have their foundation in, the discipline of first-order predicate logic; they therefore provide an appropriate formalism for the declarative statement of rules, at least at the conceptual level. It follows that it is necessary and sufficient that the rule engine shall be, specifically, a **relational** DBMS,[4] at least at the conceptual level.

---

4. Not necessarily, and ultimately not even desirably, an SQL DBMS specifically. (Considered as an attempt at a concrete realization of the constructs of the abstract relational model, SQL is very seriously flawed. Again, see, e.g., reference [2].)

Here are some specific consequences of the foregoing:

- *The Information Principle:* The totality of data in the database shall be represented at the conceptual level by means of relations (and their underlying domains) *only*. To say the same thing in another way, the database at any given time shall consist of a collection of **tuples;** each such tuple shall represent a **proposition** that (a) is an instantiation of the **predicate** corresponding to the relation in which it appears and (b) is understood by convention to be TRUE.

- *The Principle of Interchangeability of Views and Base Relations:* The system shall support relational **views,** which, as far as the user is concerned, "look and feel" exactly like base relations; that is, as far as the user is concerned, views shall have *all* and *only* the properties that base relations have (e.g., the property of having at least one candidate key). In particular, views, like base relations, shall be **updatable** [1,2].

- *Database* **is a purely logical concept:** The term *database* throughout this chapter refers to the database as perceived by the user, not to any kind of physical construct at the physical storage level. In the extreme, one logical database, as the term is used herein, might map to any number of physically stored databases, managed by any number of different DBMSs, running on any number of different machines, supported by any number of different operating systems, and connected together by any number of different communication networks.

- Overall, the rule engine shall function from the user's point of view as **an abstract machine.** It shall not be necessary to go to a lower level of detail in order to explain any part of the functioning of that abstract machine (i.e., the definition of that abstract machine shall be logically self-contained).

Prescription 7: Rule Management

Since rules are not just data but, more specifically, *metadata,* the portion of the database in which they are held shall conceptually be some kind of *catalog*. It is convenient to refer to that portion of the database as **the rule catalog** specifically. By definition, the rule catalog shall be relational. Suitably authorized users shall be able to access that catalog (for both retrieval and update purposes) by means of their regular data access interface. *Note:* This prescription does not prohibit the provision of additional, specialized interfaces for rule catalog access.

To the maximum extent logically possible, the rule engine shall:

- Detect and reject **cycles** and **conflicts** in the rule catalog

- Optimize away **redundancies** in the rule catalog

- Permit rule catalog updates to be performed **without disruption** to other system activities, concurrent or otherwise

See also the discussion of "standard DBMS benefits" under Prescription 5.

Prescription 8: Kinds of Constraints

Integrity constraints shall be divisible into four kinds, as follows [1,2]:

- A **type constraint** is, logically speaking, nothing more nor less than a definition of the set of values that constitute the type (domain) in question. Such a constraint shall not mention any variables.

  Note: The constraint that one type is a subtype of another (which provides the basis for supporting *inheritance* of certain properties from one type to another, of course) is a special kind of type constraint [2]. That is, type constraints shall include what are sometimes called "IS A" constraints (not to be confused with "HAS A" constraints!—again, see reference [2]) as a special case.

- An **attribute constraint** is a constraint on the values a given attribute is permitted to assume. More precisely, an attribute constraint shall specify that the attribute in question is of a given type (domain).

- A **relation constraint**[5] is a constraint on the values a given relation is permitted to assume. Such a constraint shall be of arbitrary complexity, except that it shall mention exactly one variable (*viz.*, the relation in question).

- A **database constraint** is a constraint on the values a given database is permitted to assume. Such a constraint shall be of arbitrary complexity, except that it shall mention at least two variables, and all variables mentioned shall be relations in the database. *Note:* The distinction between relation constraints and database constraints is primarily a matter of pragma—it can be helpful in practice, but it is not all that important from a theoretical standpoint.

In the case of database and relation constraints (only), the constraint shall also be allowed to constrain **transitions** from one value to another. A constraint that is not a transition constraint is a **state** constraint. In no case shall a constraint explicitly mention the update events that need to be monitored in order to enforce the constraint; rather, determining those events shall be the responsibility of the rule engine.

All constraints shall be satisfied **at statement boundaries**. That is, no statement shall leave the database in such a state as to violate any state or transition constraint, loosely speaking. *Note:* See reference [2] for a more precise formulation of this requirement—in particular, for a precise explanation of exactly what it is that constitutes a "statement" here.

As well as enforcing constraints, the rule engine shall make its best attempt to use them for purposes of **semantic optimization** [1].

---

5. More correctly referred to as a *relation variable,* or *relvar,* constraint (see references [1] and [2]). The term *relation* is unfortunately used in common database parlance to mean sometimes a relation *value,* sometimes a relation *variable* (i.e., a relvar). While this practice can lead to confusion, it is followed in the present chapter—somewhat against my better judgment!—for reasons of familiarity.

Prescription 9: Extensibility

Within any given rule, it shall be possible to invoke existing applications[6] as if they were built-in operators. In other words, the system shall be **extensible,** and applications, like rules, shall be **sharable** and **reusable.**

Prescription 10: Platform Independence

The rule language, and rules expressed in that language, shall be **independent** of specific software or hardware platforms (other than the rule engine itself, possibly).[7] The rule engine shall be responsible (a) for converting—i.e., compiling—rules into executable code that is appropriate to whatever hardware and software environment happens to pertain and (b) for assigning individual portions of that executable code to processors within that environment appropriately. The concept of platform independence thus embraces at least all of the following (see reference [1]):

- Independence of the overall implementation environment ("system architecture independence")

- Hardware independence

- Operating system independence

- Transaction monitor independence

- Network independence

- Location, fragmentation, and replication independence

- DBMS independence

Regarding the last of these in particular, note that it shall be possible for an application to **span** several distinct backend subsystems, running several distinct DBMSs and/or file systems. It shall also be possible for an application (declaratively built, of course) to access **preexisting** databases and/or files. In all cases, the necessary **mappings** between backend database schemas and the rule engine's own database schema (and/or the rule catalog) shall themselves be specified by means of appropriate business rules.

Prescription 11: No Subversion

If an interface is supported that provides access to the database at a level below the conceptual level (in effect, below the level of the abstract machine that is the rule engine), then it shall be possible to **prevent use of that interface** for purposes of subverting the system. In particular, it shall be possible to prevent the bypassing of any integrity constraint.

---

6. Refer back to the "Assumptions" section for an explanation of the term *application* as used in this chapter.

7. It could be argued that this prescription is a straightforward logical consequence of the requirement, already articulated under Prescription 6, that the rule engine shall function as an abstract machine.

Prescription 12: Full Automation

Applications developed using business rules shall be **complete** (loosely, "everything automatable shall be automated"). That is, the total set of rules for all of the applications that are pertinent to the enterprise in question shall constitute a **complete model of the business,** or in other words an abstract definition of the entire enterprise and its workings. In fact, because rules are shared across applications and *vice versa*—see Prescriptions 5 and 9—the activity of defining rules in general can be seen not so much as a process of developing individual applications, but rather as one of developing **entire integrated application systems.**

Summary

By way of conclusion, here is a brief (and somewhat simplified) summary of the twelve prescriptions.

1. **Executable Rules:** Rules are compilable and executable.

2. **Declarative Rules:** Rules are stated declaratively. The rule language is well designed and expressively complete.

3. **Kinds of Rules:** Rules are divided into presentation, database, and application rules. They include computations, constraints, inference rules, and stimulus/response rules (possibly).

4. **Declaration Sequence *vs.* Execution Sequence:** Rules can be declared in any sequence. The rule engine determines the corresponding execution sequence.

5. **The Rule Engine Is a DBMS:** Rules are expressed in terms of constructs in the database schema. The rule engine is a special kind of DBMS; it can act as middleware, using other DBMSs and/or file systems to hold its stored data (possibly several such subsystems at the same time). Rules exist in external, conceptual, and internal forms; the first two of these, at least, include nothing to do with performance. Rules are shared and reused across applications.

6. **The Rule Engine Is a *Relational* DBMS:** At the conceptual level, at least, the rule engine is relational. It acts from the user's point of view as an abstract machine.

7. **Rule Management:** Rules can be queried and updated. Insofar as is logically possible, the rule engine detects and rejects cycles and conflicts (and optimizes away redundancies) among the rules, and permits rule updates to be done without disrupting other system activities.

8. **Kinds of Constraints:** Constraints are divided into type, attribute, relation, and database constraints. Transition constraints are supported. Constraints are satisfied at statement boundaries.

9. **Extensibility:** Rules can invoke existing applications.

10. **Platform Independence:** The rule engine provides independence of hardware and software platforms. It also provides independence of the overall system architecture, by assigning compiled code to available processors appropriately. Applications can span backend subsystems (possibly preexisting ones).

11. **No Subversion:** The database cannot be accessed below the conceptual level in such a way as to subvert the system.

12. **Full Automation:** The rule engine supports the development of entire integrated application systems.

Acknowledgments

Thanks to Manish Chandra, Hugh Darwen, Mike DeVries, Val Huber, Gary Morgenthaler, Ron Ross, and Gene Wong for helpful comments on earlier drafts of this chapter and other technical assistance.

References

1. C. J. Date: *An Introduction to Database Systems* (8th edition). Reading, Mass.: Addison-Wesley (2004).

2. C. J. Date and Hugh Darwen: *Databases, Types, and the Relational Model: The Third Manifesto* (3rd edition). Boston, Mass.: Addison-Wesley (2006).

3. GUIDE Business Rules Project: *Final Report*, revision 1.2 (October 1997).

4. James D. McCawley: *Everything that Linguists Have Always Wanted to Know about Logic (but were ashamed to ask).* Chicago, Ill.: University of Chicago Press (1981).

PART 4

SQL Database Management

This part of the book consists of three chapters. Chapter 16 highlights some of the complexities surrounding the SQL UNION operator. Chapter 17 has to do with a question of SQL subquery optimization; In particular, it shows how that question illustrates the logical difference between model and implementation. Finally, Chapter 18 discusses, and criticizes, three- and four-valued logic (the discussions of that chapter thus do apply to SQL to some extent, but are in fact more general).

CHAPTER 16

■ ■ ■

Two Remarks on SQL's UNION

A little while back I published a paper on left-to-right column ordering ("A Sweet Disorder"—Chapter 9 in the present book). The basic message of that paper was that

> **a.** SQL includes such a notion but the relational model doesn't,

and therefore

> **b.** SQL runs into a lot of complications that the relational model doesn't.

Part of my argument had to do with the UNION operator, which is *much* more complicated in SQL than it ought to be, in part because of that business of column ordering (see Chapter 9 for the specifics). In the course of examining the SQL UNION operator, however, I realized there were some additional complications involved, ones that didn't arise from column ordering as such and so didn't belong in the earlier paper, but ones I felt were still worth documenting somewhere. Hence this short chapter.

The complications in question arise from two sources: the fact that SQL permits implicit data type conversions (also known as *coercions*), and the fact that SQL permits duplicate rows. I'll discuss each in turn. *Note:* I focus here on UNION for definiteness. As I'm sure you would expect, however, similar complications arise with the operators INTERSECT and MINUS— "EXCEPT" in SQL—as well.

Union in the Relational Model

For purposes of reference, I give first a definition of the *relational* UNION operator:

> Let tables *a* and *b* be of the same type *TT*. Then the union of those two tables, *a* UNION *b*, is a table of the same type *TT*, with body consisting of all rows *r* such that *r* appears in *a* or *b* or both.

(Of course, *a* and *b* here aren't necessarily base tables; they might, for example, be the results of previous queries.) This definition is based on one given in the 8th edition of my book *An Introduction to Database Systems* (Addison-Wesley, 2004). The *body* of a table is the set of rows in that table.

Figure 16-1 shows a trivial example of two tables, T1 and T2, together with their union. I've assumed for simplicity that all columns are of type INTEGER. Observe in particular that the union in this example has four rows, not five (because "duplicates are eliminated").

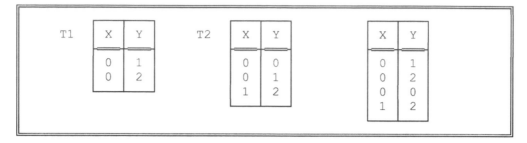

Figure 16-1. *Tables T1 and T2 and their union*

Data Type Conversion

UNION as defined in the SQL standard relies on something called Subclause 9.3, "Set operation result data types." I certainly don't want, nor do I need, to explain that subclause in detail here; however, I'd like to give a simple example. Consider the tables T3 and T4 shown in Figure 16-2.

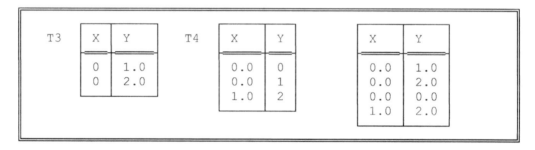

Figure 16-2. *A very strange "union"*

Now, I need to pin down the example in Figure 16-2 a little more precisely before I can make my point. So:

- Let column X be of type INTEGER in table T3 but type NUMERIC(p,1) in table T4, and let column Y be of type NUMERIC(p,1) in table T4 but type INTEGER in table T3. (The symbol p here denotes the maximum possible NUMERIC precision, whatever that might be in the implementation at hand.)

- Also, let columns X and Y be the "first" and "second" column, respectively, in both tables. (We can refer unambiguously to "the first column," "the second column," and so forth in SQL precisely because SQL tables do have a left-to-right ordering to their columns.)

- Finally, let's agree to limit our attention to the "original" version of the SQL UNION operator, which matches up columns based on their ordinal position. (Various extended versions of the operator were added in later iterations of the standard—see Chapter 9—but they're irrelevant for present purposes.)

Now consider the SQL query:

```
SELECT * FROM T3
UNION
SELECT * FROM T4 ;
```

Or the semantically equivalent query:

```
TABLE T3 UNION TABLE T4 ;
```

In accordance with Subclause 9.3 of the standard, then:

- Columns X and Y in the result of this query are both of type NUMERIC(p,1).

- All values in those columns are obtained by first implicitly converting ("coercing") some INTEGER value from either T3 or T4 to type NUMERIC(p,1).

- **The overall result thus consists exclusively of rows that appear in neither T3 nor T4!**

A very strange kind of union, you might be forgiven for thinking.

Note: In order to head off a possible objection here, let me address the question "So what would the relational model do in this example?" In fact, there are two possibilities:

- Suppose INTEGER and NUMERIC(p,1) have a common supertype; without any serious loss of generality, let that common supertype be NUMERIC(p,1). Then columns X and Y in the result will indeed be of type NUMERIC(p,1), as in SQL, *but every row in that result will be a row from T3 or T4 or both.* (See the book *Databases, Types, and the Relational Model: The Third Manifesto*, 3rd edition, Addison-Wesley, 2006, by Hugh Darwen and myself, for further explanation.)

- Alternatively, suppose INTEGER and NUMERIC(p,1) have no common supertype. Then the union won't be permitted in the first place. It can still effectively be performed by carrying out some *explicit* data type conversions first, of course.

Duplicate Rows

The SQL definition of UNION also relies on the concept of *duplicate rows*. (Actually the relational definition does too, in a sense, but the concept of "duplicate rows" doesn't have the same bizarre meaning in the relational world that it does in SQL.) Here's the pertinent part of the SQL definition (*a* and *b* here denote the tables to be "unioned"):

- Let *r* be a row that is a duplicate of some row in *a* or some row in *b* or both.

- Then the result contains exactly one duplicate of *r*.

Before I go any further, let me make it crystal clear that I'm not interested here in "UNION ALL"; that is, I'm not interested in the case where we want to preserve duplicate rows, somehow, in the result of the union. I'm also not interested in the case where the input tables already include duplicate rows, though whether they do or not doesn't really affect the present discussion. Rather, the point is that even "UNION DISTINCT" does necessarily rely on SQL's concept of duplicate rows. *Note:* In case you weren't aware of the fact, the SQL standard does allow DISTINCT to be specified in UNION as an explicit alternative to ALL. Also, DISTINCT is the default for UNION, although ALL is the default for SELECT.

So what exactly is it about SQL's concept of duplicate rows that warrants the characterization "bizarre"? Well, the basic point is that two rows *r1* and *r2* can be distinct—meaning, to spell the point out explicitly, that they're not the same row—and yet be regarded as "duplicates" of one another! Several factors contribute to this strange state of affairs:

- One has to do with nulls (as you might expect), but I certainly don't want to get into *that* can of worms here.

- Another has to do with the notion, already touched on in the discussion of Subclause 9.3 earlier, that two *scalar* values—for example, the integer 2 and the rational number 2.0— can be regarded as equal even though they're of different data types.

- A third has to do with yet another SQL weirdness: namely, the fact that two scalar values of the *same* type can be distinct and yet be regarded as "equal."

And this third phenomenon has at least three manifestations in turn:

- Suppose X and Y are of types CHAR(2) and CHAR(3), respectively, and suppose their current values are 'PQ' and 'PQ ', respectively (note the trailing blank in the latter case). Then those values are certainly distinct, but the comparison X = Y gives TRUE if PAD SPACE applies to the pertinent "collation." See the book *A Guide to the SQL Standard*, 4th edition, Addison-Wesley, 2000, by Hugh Darwen and myself, for further explanation.

- Suppose X and Y are both of type CHAR(3), and suppose their current values are 'PQR' and 'pqr', respectively. Then those values are certainly distinct, but the comparison X = Y gives TRUE if the pertinent "collation" is case-insensitive. Again, see the book *A Guide to the SQL Standard*, 4th edition, Addison-Wesley, 2000, by Hugh Darwen and myself, for further explanation.

- In the case of certain user-defined types (the so-called *structured* types, to be specific), the corresponding "=" operator is user-defined as well, and there's no requirement that it have the semantics that two values are equal if and only if they're the very same value. (Actually, there's no requirement that an "=" operator even be defined! Discussion of the implications of *that* point would take us way beyond the scope of this chapter, however.)

As a result of such considerations, again it's possible for the result of a union to include rows that don't appear in either of the operands! (In fact, I might say, perfectly accurately but possibly confusingly, that the result includes rows that don't appear in the *union* of those operands.) Figure 16-3 gives an example.

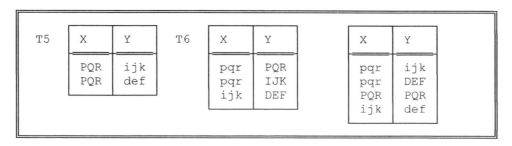

Figure 16-3. *An even stranger "union"*

Actually, the example shown in Figure 16-3 is even weirder than you might have realized. Since I'm assuming for the sake of that example that we're operating under a case-insensitive collation (so that, e.g., the strings 'PQR' and 'pqr' are regarded as equal), *the result of the union isn't even well-defined!* For example, we could replace every appearance of the string 'PQR' in the result shown in Figure 16-3 by the string 'pqr'—or 'PQr', or 'PqR', or any of four other possibilities—and the result would still be valid according to the standard. In the example, in fact, there are a total of 8 to the power 8 = 16,777,216 equally valid results (!).

Concluding Remarks

SQL is a case study in how not to design a language. The weirdnesses highlighted in this short chapter serve as just one tiny illustration of this general point; in fact, they serve as a textbook example of what happens when the principle of *conceptual integrity* is violated (see the book *The Mythical Man-Month*, 20th anniversary edition, Addison-Wesley, 1995, by Frederick P. Brooks, Jr., for an explanation of this term).

CHAPTER 17

■ ■ ■

A Cure for Madness

Though this be madness, yet there is method in't.

—William Shakespeare

Ⅰ originally wrote this short piece in response to a paper titled "Subquery Madness,"[1] in which the author, Jonathan Gennick, raises a question about subqueries in SQL and their implementation in Oracle. The following is an edited version of his question. We're given a table called SUBTEST with two columns, FLAG and NUM, both containing character data, with the constraint that if FLAG = 'N' then NUM represents a numeric value. Figure 17-1 shows some sample values.

```
                    SUBTEST

            ┌───────┬───────┐
            │ FLAG  │  NUM  │
            ├───────┼───────┤
            │   N   │  123  │
            │   X   │  123  │
            │   Y   │  pqr  │
            │   N   │  456  │
            │   Z   │  ijk  │
            └───────┴───────┘
```

Figure 17-1. *Table SUBTEST*

Now consider this SQL query:

```
SELECT FLAG, TO_NUMBER ( NUM ) AS NUM
FROM    SUBTEST
WHERE   FLAG = 'N' ;
```

Given the sample data of Figure 17-1, this query returns the result table (let's call it R1) shown in Figure 17-2.

---

1. See http://gennick.com/madness.

```
                                  R1

                          FLAG    NUM

                           N      123
                           N      456
```

Figure 17-2. *Table R1*

Now suppose we use the original query as a subquery within the FROM clause of another query:

```
SELECT *
FROM ( SELECT FLAG, TO_NUMBER ( NUM ) AS NUM
       FROM    SUBTEST
       WHERE   FLAG = 'N' )
WHERE   NUM > 0 ;
```

According to Gennick, this query fails in Oracle with the following error message:

```
ERROR:
ORA-01722: invalid number
```

Gennick suggests in his paper that the failure occurs because the outer query attempts to evaluate the condition NUM > 0 on one of the nonnumeric values in column NUM. To quote: "[The] optimizer is free to test ... rows against [the] NUM > 0 predicate first, if that's deemed more efficient."

As Gennick subsequently points out, however, the foregoing explanation cannot be correct, because the condition NUM > 0 involves a type error (one that should be caught at compile time, moreover)—NUM is of type character string and 0 is of type numeric. What has really happened is that the optimizer has rewritten the original query as follows:

```
SELECT FLAG, TO_NUMBER ( NUM ) AS NUM
FROM    SUBTEST
WHERE   TO_NUMBER ( NUM ) > 0
AND     FLAG = 'N' ;
```

Now it's clear that the failure occurs as soon as the system tries (in the WHERE clause) to convert some nonnumeric NUM value—say 'pqr'—to a number. The question is, then: Is this rewriting on the part of the optimizer valid? The short answer is *no*. But the question does merit a lengthier response and discussion, and such is the intent of the rest of this chapter.

The Syntax and Semantics of
SELECT - FROM - WHERE

First I want to make an obvious point about SELECT - FROM - WHERE expressions in SQL. To do so, I don't need to consider such expressions in all of their full generality and complexity—the following simple form will suffice:

```
SELECT expression, expression, ..., expression
FROM   table
WHERE  condition
```

Note in particular that I've mentioned just one table, *T* say, in the FROM clause. I also want to impose the limitation that there are no subqueries in either the SELECT clause or the WHERE clause (this query is *really* simple). Note carefully, then, that **every column mentioned in the SELECT clause or the WHERE clause must be a column of table *T* specifically**.

Observe now that I deliberately didn't rule out the possibility of subqueries in the FROM clause. The fact is, the foregoing syntax rule regarding columns in the SELECT and WHERE clauses applies no matter how table *T* is specified. Here again is Gennick's original query:

```
SELECT *
FROM ( SELECT FLAG, TO_NUMBER ( NUM ) AS NUM
       FROM    SUBTEST
       WHERE   FLAG = 'N' )
WHERE  NUM > 0 ;
```

This query is logically equivalent to:

```
SELECT *
FROM   R1
WHERE  NUM > 0 ;
```

(you will recall that R1 is the result of the subquery in the FROM clause). It should be clear, then, that the reference to column NUM in the WHERE clause is a reference to a column of table R1, *not* a reference to the column of the same name in table SUBTEST. (In fact, the two NUMs even have different data types—SUBTEST.NUM is of type character string, while R1.NUM is numeric.)

Note: The foregoing point might be easier to understand if we had introduced a different name, XYZ say, in the original query, thus:

```
SELECT *
FROM ( SELECT FLAG, TO_NUMBER ( NUM ) AS XYZ
       FROM    SUBTEST
       WHERE   FLAG = 'N' )
WHERE  XYZ > 0 ;
```

(boldface for emphasis). Using XYZ instead of NUM makes no logical difference to the query, but I think it does make a psychological difference—it's obvious, now, that XYZ is a column of R1, and SUBTEST has no such column at all.

Now, the SQL standard makes it perfectly clear that the result of the query

```
SELECT *
FROM   R1
WHERE  NUM > 0 ;
```

is defined as follows:

1. Evaluate R1.

2. Restrict the result of the previous step to just those rows satisfying NUM > 0.

3. Project the result of the previous step over all of its columns (which is effectively a no op, of course).

In other words, the inner subquery must be evaluated *before* the outer WHERE and SELECT clauses are executed (hence my unequivocal *no* to the question "Is this rewriting on the part of the optimizer valid?"). But there's still a little more to be said.

Model *vs.* Implementation

Part of the reason I wanted to discuss Gennick's question is that it illustrates very well my thesis that model *vs.* implementation is one of the great **logical differences**. I have argued this point in many places and on many occasions; in fact, I recently published a paper with the title "On the Logical Difference Between Model and Implementation" (Chapter 5 in the present book). In most of my discussions of this topic, however, I have concentrated on the relational model specifically (contrasting it with implementations—perhaps I should say would-be implementations—of that model). In the case of Gennick's question, however, the relational model is involved only somewhat incidentally; rather, the model we're dealing with is *a formal language definition* (of the language SQL, to be precise), and the implementation is what Gennick refers to in his paper as *the database engine* (also known as the optimizer). In other words, Gennick's question is a language question, not a relational one.[2]

Any formal language definition, if it's worth its salt, will specify the precise syntax and semantics of the language in question. The pertinent portion of the SQL language definition reads as follows (I'm quoting here from the SQL:1992 version of that standard):

```
<table expression> ::=
      <from clause>
      [ <where clause> ]
      [ <group by clause> ]
      [ <having clause> ]
```

The result of a <table expression> is a derived table in which the descriptor of the i-th column is the same as the descriptor of the i-th column of the table specified by the <from clause> ... If all optional clauses are omitted, then the result of the <table expression> is the same as the result of the <from clause>. Otherwise, each specified clause is applied to the result of the previously specified clause and the result of the <table expression> is the result of the application of the last specified clause.

---

2. But see the section "Further Thoughts," later.

In the case at hand, therefore (in which there is a WHERE clause but no GROUP BY or HAVING clause), we see that (a) we have the syntax correct[3] and (b) the semantics are as previously stated: First execute the FROM clause, then execute the WHERE clause. That's the formal model. That's what the query *means*.

Now, the algorithm given in the formal definition—first execute the FROM clause, then execute the WHERE clause, in the case at hand—is purely conceptual in nature. In effect, the standard is just saying "*If* you execute this algorithm, *then* you'll get the right answer." But that *if* is a pretty big *if!* There's no implication that the implementation (the "database engine") has to do exactly what the formal definition says. In fact, the implementation is free to use any algorithm it chooses, just so long as whatever algorithm it does use is guaranteed to give the same answer as the specified conceptual algorithm. And, of course, there are often very good reasons—usually performance reasons—for using a different algorithm, thereby (for example) executing clauses in a different order or otherwise rewriting the original query. But the implementation is free to do such things **only if it can be proved that the algorithm used is logically equivalent to the conceptual one specified in the formal definition**. In Gennick's example, however, the optimizer has clearly used an algorithm that is *not* logically equivalent to the conceptual algorithm specified in the SQL standard, and the implementation is incorrect.

Nested Functions

There's another way to articulate the foregoing argument, and some readers might like this alternative formulation better. In general, we can regard an SQL SELECT - FROM - WHERE expression as a *nested expression*, or *nested set of function invocations*, of the form

    s (w (f (x)))

Explanation:

- The expression $f(x)$—f for FROM—is a function invocation that returns a table (x here stands for anything that's legal in a FROM clause).

- w (WHERE) is a function that operates on a table and returns a table.

- s (SELECT) is a function that operates on a table and returns a table.

This hypothetical notation of nested function invocations makes it very clear that, at least conceptually, s can't be invoked before w (because s's input is w's output), and w can't be invoked before f (because w's input is f's output). Thus, if the implementation does want to invoke the functions in some different sequence (perhaps in some kind of coroutine fashion), then it must guarantee that the semantics are preserved; in other words, it must guarantee that it produces the result that would have been produced if the original nested sequence had been adhered to. And again we see, in the example at hand, that this requirement is not met and the implementation is in error.

---

3. Actually, another portion of the SQL standard, not quoted here, would require the explicit introduction of a name to refer to the result of the subquery in the FROM clause, like this: SELECT * FROM (...) *AS R1* WHERE ... (italics for emphasis)—even though that name *R1* isn't referenced anywhere else in the query! Oracle, not unreasonably, appears not to enforce this requirement.

Further Thoughts

Further reflection on Gennick's problem made me realize there was more that could usefully be said on this matter; hence the present section.

Let's agree to ignore SQL as such until further notice and switch to relational algebra (and relational terminology) instead. In relational algebra, if r and p are a relational expression and a truth-valued expression, respectively, then the expression

    r WHERE p

evaluates to a relation with the same heading—i.e., the same attributes—as r and with a body containing just those tuples of r for which p evaluates to TRUE.[4] That result relation is said to be a restriction of r, and the operation that computes it is called a restriction operation. Loosely, what the restriction operation does is *filter out certain tuples from its operand relation*.

Now suppose the expression r itself denotes another restriction operation, so that the overall expression takes the form, say,

    (s WHERE q) WHERE p

for some relational expression s and some truth-valued expression q. Then it's well known that this overall expression can be legitimately transformed into

    s WHERE (q) AND (p)

And this transformation is useful for optimization purposes, because the original expression implies that the implementation must perform two passes over the s-relation while the transformed version shows that one pass suffices. Moreover, the original expression suggests that the implementation must check q first when filtering out tuples, but the transformed version shows it can check p first if it likes, because AND is commutative. (And it presumably would like to check p first if, for example, p is easier to evaluate than q, or if it's likely that most tuples satisfy q but very few satisfy p.)

Suppose now, however, that we have a situation in which the q-filtering *must* be done before the p-filtering (as it were). Then the relational expression that represents this state of affairs is **not**

    (s WHERE q) WHERE p

—because this expression does not capture the requirement that q must be applied first, as we have just seen. So what is to be done?

Well, in fact a situation of this same general nature occurs in connection with the issue of *type inheritance*. Let's look at an example. *Note:* The discussion that follows is based on one given in the book *Databases, Types, and the Relational Model: The Third Manifesto*, 3rd edition, by Hugh Darwen and myself (Addison-Wesley 2006), where further details can be found.

By way of example, then, let CIRCLE be a subtype of type ELLIPSE, and let relation s have an attribute E that's declared to be of type ELLIPSE. In general, then, some tuples of s will have a value for attribute E that is in fact a circle instead of just a (noncircular) ellipse. Now consider the following query:

---

4. Strictly speaking, p must be quantifier-free and its parameters must be some subset of the attributes of r, but there's no need to get into the fine detail of such matters here.

Get tuples of *s* where the E value is in fact a circle and the radius of that circle is greater than two.

Observe immediately that the following "obvious" formulation of the query doesn't work:

```
( s WHERE IS_CIRCLE ( E ) ) WHERE THE_R ( E ) > LENGTH ( 2.0 )
```

(I'm assuming here that (a) for a given tuple *t* of *s*, IS_CIRCLE(E) returns TRUE if the value of E in *t* is a circle and FALSE otherwise, and (b) THE_R is an operator that takes a circle as its operand and returns the corresponding radius, a value of type LENGTH.) The reason the formulation shown above doesn't work is because it's logically equivalent to the following one:

```
s WHERE THE_R ( E ) > LENGTH ( 2.0 ) AND IS_CIRCLE ( E )
```

And this expression will fail as soon as it tries to invoke the operator THE_R on a value of E (in some tuple *t* of *s*) that's just an ellipse and not a circle, because THE_R isn't defined for ellipses that aren't circles; in other words, there's no guarantee that the system will apply the IS_CIRCLE filtering before attempting to check the radius. *Note:* In fact, if static type checking is performed, then the expression will fail at *compile* time, because the compiler will know that the argument E to THE_R is of type ELLIPSE but the corresponding parameter is of type CIRCLE.

Clearly, then, what we need to do, for any given tuple *t* of *s*, is make sure the E value is a circle *before* we check to see whether the radius of that circle is greater than two (indeed, we mustn't even perform this latter check if the E value *isn't* a circle). To that end, Hugh Darwen and I (in the book mentioned previously) invented some new syntax, such that the query under discussion can be correctly formulated as:

```
( s : IS_CIRCLE ( E ) ) WHERE THE_R ( E ) > LENGTH ( 2.0 )
```

The expression *s*:IS_CIRCLE(E) is defined to return a relation *r* that's identical to *s* except that:

- The body of *r* contains just those tuples of *s* for which the E value is a circle.

- Attribute E in the heading of *r* is of type CIRCLE, not type ELLIPSE (so the compile-time type checking on THE_R(E) will now succeed).

Moreover, the operator precedence rules are defined in such a way that—even if we don't enclose it in parentheses as above—the expression *s*: IS_CIRCLE(E) is guaranteed to be evaluated *before* the restriction specified in the WHERE clause is performed. The overall effect is thus as desired.

Abstracting somewhat from the foregoing example, then, we can say that the relational expression

```
( s : q ) WHERE p
```

is such that the *q*-filtering will definitely be done before the *p*-filtering (even if the parentheses are omitted); that is, the expression *cannot* legally be transformed into

```
( s WHERE p ) : q
```

or

```
s WHERE ( p ) AND ( q )
```

(and not into (*s*:*p*):*q* either, come to that).

The relevance of the foregoing discussion to Gennick's example should be obvious, but let me spell the details out. (So now I'm switching back to SQL—but I want to simplify the original example and abstract from it, somewhat.) Consider the following SQL expression:

```
SELECT * FROM ( SELECT * FROM s WHERE q ) WHERE p
```

Rather counterintuitively (at least, so it seems to me), then, this expression is **not** just SQL syntax for

```
( s WHERE q ) WHERE p
```

(!)—precisely because, as we saw in the body of this chapter, it can't always be legally transformed into the SQL expression

```
SELECT * FROM s WHERE q AND p
```

In fact, the SQL standard makes it clear (albeit not in these terms, of course) that the expression under discussion—

```
SELECT * FROM ( SELECT * FROM s WHERE q ) WHERE p
```

—is really SQL syntax for

```
( s : q ) : p
```

So the problem with SQL (and I regard this state of affairs as yet another SQL deficiency) is that it provides syntax for $(s{:}q){:}p$ but not for (s WHERE q) WHERE p. Thus, users are effectively forced to write $(s{:}q){:}p$ even when what they really mean is (s WHERE q) WHERE p. And in Oracle, at least, the optimizer apparently assumes that users *always* mean the latter and therefore performs the logically incorrect transformation—which happens to work, most of the time, because most of the time users really do mean (s WHERE q) WHERE p! A somewhat topsy-turvy situation, you might be forgiven for thinking.

A Final Observation

It's worth noting that SQL does in fact support something along the lines of the $s{:}IS\_T(A)$ operator described briefly in the previous section (where s is a relation, A is an attribute of s, and T is some subtype of the type of A). Here's the query from that section expressed in SQL ("Get s rows where the E value is in fact a circle and the radius of that circle is greater than two"):

```
SELECT *
FROM ( SELECT A, ..., TREAT E AS CIRCLE AS E, ..., Z
       FROM   s
       WHERE  TYPE ( E ) IS OF ( CIRCLE ) )
WHERE  THE_R ( E ) > LENGTH ( 2.0 )
```

Note: I'm assuming here that s has attributes A, ..., Z in addition to the specific attribute E that's of interest to this particular query.

Do note, however, how clumsy the SQL support is! In particular, the operations of (a) picking out just the tuples of s in which the E value is a circle and (b) changing the type of attribute E in the result from ELLIPSE to CIRCLE—I'm speaking pretty loosely here—are expressed separately (in the WHERE clause and the SELECT clause, respectively). By contrast, these two operations are bundled together in our syntax *s*:IS_CIRCLE(E) and *cannot* be separated. As a consequence, there's scope for additional errors in SQL ... For example, the expression

```
SELECT *
FROM ( SELECT *
       FROM   s
       WHERE  TYPE ( E ) IS OF ( CIRCLE ) )
WHERE  THE_R ( E ) > LENGTH ( 2.0 )
```

fails on a type error (how, exactly?).

■ ■ ■

Why Three- and Four-Valued Logic Don't Work

Nothin' ain't worth nothin'.

—Kris Kristofferson

I've written many times and in many places—to excess, some might say—on problems inherent in the use of three- and four-valued logic (3VL and 4VL) in connection with "missing information" (a term I'll elaborate on later). This chapter presents a brief description of some of those problems. The material it contains is thus not new, but the issues it raises aren't widely discussed in the database literature, so far as I know. The issues in question are inherent, for the most part; I mean, they have to do with 3VL and 4VL as such, not merely with the use of those logics in connection with "missing information" specifically.

I'll begin by laying a little groundwork: first of all, by discussing the notion of logical connectives.

Some Basic Concepts

Connectives is the term logicians use for logical operators such as NOT, OR, and AND. As is well known, such connectives can be defined by means of *truth tables*. For example, here are the truth tables for NOT, OR, and AND in conventional two-valued logic (2VL):

p	NOT p
t	f
f	t

p	q	p OR q
t	t	t
t	f	t
f	t	t
f	f	f

p	q	p AND q
t	t	t
t	f	f
f	t	f
f	f	f

(t = true, f = false).

Now, truth tables are indeed usually shown in the form just illustrated. For the purposes of this chapter, however, it turns out to be more convenient to show them in a slightly different form, as suggested by the following revised tables for NOT, OR, and AND in 2VL:

NOT	
t	f
f	t

OR	t	f
t	t	t
f	t	f

AND	t	f
t	t	f
f	f	f

NOT, OR, and AND aren't the only possible connectives, of course. For obvious reasons, in fact, there are exactly as many distinct connectives as there are distinct truth tables. It follows that, in 2VL, there are exactly four *monadic* connectives (i.e., connectives that take one operand), as defined by the following truth tables:

t	t
f	t

t	t
f	f

t	f
f	t

t	f
f	f

I haven't shown names for these four connectives because most of them don't have names in common use; however, the third truth table corresponds to the NOT connective, and the second (where, for all inputs, the output is the same as the input) corresponds to what might be called the *identity* connective.

In the same kind of way, there are exactly 16 *dyadic* connectives in 2VL (i.e., connectives that take two operands); OR and AND are two such. Two particularly important dyadic connectives are *logical equivalence* and *logical implication*, which I'll denote by IF AND ONLY IF (or just IFF) and IF ... THEN (or just IF), respectively. Here are the 2VL truth tables for these connectives:

IFF	t	f
t	t	f
f	f	t

IF	t	f
t	t	f
f	t	t

As you can see, IFF is essentially just *equality*, as that operator applies to truth values—it returns true if its operands are equal and false if they aren't. As for IF, in this case the truth table needs some explanation, since (unlike all of the other dyadic ones we've seen so far) it isn't symmetric. It's meant to be read as follows. Let operands p and q have truth values as indicated down the left side and across the top of the table, respectively; then the expression IF p THEN q has truth value as indicated in the body of the table. More specifically, IF p THEN q is false if and only if p is true and q is false; more specifically still, IF p THEN q is logically equivalent to (NOT p) OR q—which illustrates the point that the connectives aren't all primitive; in fact, as you probably know, all 20 connectives in 2VL can be expressed in terms of suitable combinations of NOT and either AND or OR.

I remark in passing—the point isn't directly germane to the main argument of this chapter, but it's interesting—that the 20 2VL connectives can actually all be expressed in terms of just one primitive: *viz.*, either NOR or NAND. NOR (also known as the *Peirce arrow* and usually written as a down arrow, "↓") is a dyadic connective that evaluates to true if and only if both of its operands are false; that is, the expression $p{\downarrow}q$ is equivalent to NOT (p OR q). NAND (also known as the *Sheffer stroke* and usually written as a vertical bar, "|") is a dyadic connective that evaluates to false if and only if both of its operands are true; that is, the expression $p|q$ is equivalent to NOT (p AND q).[1] It's an interesting exercise, here left to the reader, to show that either of these connectives can serve as a "generating" connective for the whole of 2VL.

Tautologies, Identities, and Contradictions

Let me now point out explicitly what you probably know already: *viz.*, that p and q are equivalent if and only if each implies the other. In symbols:

(p IFF q) IFF ((IF p THEN q) AND (IF q THEN p))

This overall expression is an example of a *tautology*, or in other words an expression that's guaranteed to evaluate to true, regardless of the truth values of any operands involved (here p and q). What's more, it's a tautology of the following special form:

x IFF y

Tautologies of this form can be taken as *identities*, in the sense that the expressions x and y are clearly logically identical—they're guaranteed to have the same truth value, regardless of the truth values of any operands they might involve. And, very importantly, such identities can be used in *transforming expressions:* Any expression involving x can be transformed into a logically equivalent expression by replacing all appearances of x by y. Again as you probably know, such transformations (among others) lie at the heart of the *query rewrite* process that's performed by relational DBMS optimizers.

Now, we can, of course, write down on paper any logical expression we like. Here are a few examples (I've numbered them for purposes of subsequent reference):

1. IF p THEN q

2. IF (p AND q) THEN p

3. IF p THEN (p OR q)

4. p OR NOT p

5. p IFF (NOT (NOT p))

6. (p IFF q) IFF ((IF p THEN q) AND (IF q THEN p))

7. p AND NOT p

---

1. Elsewhere (e.g., in my book *An Introduction to Database Systems*, 8th edition, Addison-Wesley, 2004), I've said the Sheffer stroke corresponds to NOR, not NAND. I don't accept full responsibility for this mistake, however!—the logic text I was using at the time got it wrong, too.

Clearly, just writing a given expression down on paper isn't the same as saying the expression in question is a tautology. In order to say a given expression *is* a tautology, we need another symbol, "⊨" ("it is the case that"). To express the fact that Example 2 above is a tautology, for example (which it clearly is—check the truth tables if you're not sure), we would write:

⊨ IF (*p* AND *q*) THEN *p*

As you can easily verify, Examples 2–6 are all tautologies; of these, however, only Examples 5 and 6 are identities (tautologies of the form *x* IFF *y*). Example 7 is an example of a *contradiction*, or in other words an expression that's guaranteed to evaluate to false, regardless of the truth values of any operands involved.

A note on terminology: The operator "⊨" ("it is the case that") is an example of a *metalogical* operator, because it enables us to make logical observations about logic itself. Other metalogical operators exist, but they're beyond the scope of this discussion.

De Morgan's Laws

Two useful and familiar identities are *De Morgan's Laws*. These laws can be stated in various equivalent ways, of which the following are most convenient for present purposes:

⊨ (NOT (*p* AND *q*)) IFF ((NOT *p*) OR (NOT *q*))
⊨ (NOT (*p* OR *q*)) IFF ((NOT *p*) AND (NOT *q*))

These two laws can easily be verified by appealing to the truth tables for NOT, OR, and AND.

Note: In the interests of accuracy, I should explain that De Morgan's Laws were originally formulated in the context of set theory, not logic. To be specific, if *a* and *b* are sets, then De Morgan's Laws state that (a) the complement of the union of *a* and *b* is equal to the intersection of the complements of *a* and *b*, and (b) the complement of the intersection of *a* and *b* is equal to the union of the complements of *a* and *b*. However, to quote *The Facts on File Dictionary of Mathematics* (Market House Books Ltd., 1999): "Parallel laws exist in other areas; e.g., [the identities shown above] are also known as De Morgan's Laws."

Codd's Three-Valued Logic

In his paper "Extending the Database Relational Model to Capture More Meaning" (*ACM TODS 4*, No. 4, December 1979)[2]—hereinafter referred to as "the RM/T paper"—Codd proposed the use of a three-valued logic as a basis for dealing with missing information in databases. In that paper, he gave the following as the 3VL truth tables for NOT, OR, and AND (or, to be absolutely precise, he gave definitions for those connectives that are equivalent to the truth tables I show here):

---

2. Note the title of this paper, which refers explicitly to "extending" the relational model. Codd first defined the relational model in 1969 and didn't add the requirement that it support 3VL until he wrote this paper; thus, the model managed perfectly well—in my opinion, better—for some ten years without any notion of 3VL at all (and early implementations managed perfectly well without it, too). Partly for reasons documented in the present chapter, my own very strong opinion continues to be that 3VL has no place in a clean formal system such as the relational model is meant to be.

NOT	
t	f
a	a
f	t

OR	t a f
t	t t t
a	t a a
f	t a f

AND	t a f
t	t a f
a	a a f
f	f f f

Here a is "the third truth value"; to quote from page 236 of Codd's book *The Relational Model for Database Management Version 2* (Addison-Wesley, 1990)—hereinafter referred to as "the RM/V2 book"—it stands for "missing and applicable," or (as I would frankly prefer to call it) just "unknown." It corresponds to what the SQL standard calls the UNKNOWN truth value; in particular, it's the truth value returned in SQL from (among many other things) a comparison of the form $u = v$ if u is null or v is null or u and v are both null.

Now, what happens to the IF ... THEN ... and IF AND ONLY IF connectives, given the foregoing definitions? Both the RM/V2 book and the SQL standard are silent on this question; in fact, neither of them gives a definition of, nor even mentions, these important connectives. From numerous private discussions over the years, however, I can safely say that, in both Codd's 3VL and SQL, IF p THEN q is meant to be equivalent to (NOT p) OR q, and p IF AND ONLY IF q is meant to be equivalent to (IF p THEN q) AND (IF q THEN p)—just as in conventional 2VL in both cases. Given these identities, then, here are the corresponding truth tables:

IF	t a f
t	t a f
a	t a a
f	t t t

IFF	t a f
t	t a f
a	a a a
f	f a t

Two serious problems arise immediately.

- In ordinary discourse, and in 2VL, the expression IF p THEN p ("p implies p") is clearly true for all p; in fact, it's a tautology. For example, "if it's raining, then it's raining" is clearly a true statement. But with IF as just defined, IF p THEN p is unknown ("the third truth value") if p in turn has truth value unknown. *Note:* Since we've effectively just defined IF p THEN p to be equivalent to (NOT p) OR p, therefore, we have the situation that this latter expression, which is a simple and well-known tautology in 2VL, isn't a tautology in 3VL. It follows that not all tautologies in 2VL are tautologies in 3VL. Likewise, not all contradictions in 2VL are contradictions in 3VL (consider p AND NOT p, for example). It seems to me that these are facts that ought to give us some pause.

- In ordinary discourse, and in 2VL, the expression p IF AND ONLY IF p ("p is equivalent to p") is clearly true for all p (indeed, it's another tautology). For example, "it's raining if and only if it's raining" is clearly a true statement. But with IFF as just defined, p IF AND ONLY IF p is unknown ("the third truth value") if p in turn has truth value unknown, and remarks similar to those of the previous bulleted paragraph apply again here.

In connection with the second of these points, incidentally, I note that according to page 138 of Nicholas Rescher's book *Many-Valued Logic* (McGraw-Hill, 1969)—the standard text on the subject, hereinafter referred to as "the Rescher book"—equivalence is required to be *reflexive,* meaning that *p* IF AND ONLY IF *p* is indeed required to be true for all *p*; but this requirement is violated by 3VL as here described, if *p* has truth value unknown (i.e., *a*).

Now, one way to address the foregoing difficulties might be to define implication and equivalence differently, in order to guarantee that IF *p* THEN *p* and *p* IF AND ONLY IF *p* do indeed evaluate to true for all *p*:

IF	*t*	*a*	*f*
t	*t*	*a*	*f*
a	*t*	*t*	*a*
f	*t*	*t*	*t*

IFF	*t*	*a*	*f*
t	*t*	*a*	*f*
a	*a*	*t*	*a*
f	*f*	*a*	*t*

With these definitions, the expressions IF *p* THEN *p*, *p* IF AND ONLY IF *p*, and

(*p* IFF *q*) IFF ((IF *p* THEN *q*) AND (IF *q* THEN *p*))

are indeed all tautologies, as required. Sadly, however, this one isn't:

(IF *p* THEN *q*) IFF ((NOT *p*) OR *q*)

What are the consequences of this state of affairs? One is that users are likely to make mistakes in formulating queries (because they probably think that this last expression *is* a tautology, or in other words that the identity does hold). Another is that the optimizer is likely to make incorrect expression transformations, for essentially the same reason. Either way, the system is likely to deliver *wrong answers*.

Note: As you might be aware, I've made the foregoing point in different ways in many other writings. I could sum it up by saying that the *pragmatic* problem with three-valued logics in general is not that they can't be defined and implemented in a consistent way, but rather that the answers they say are correct are not always correct in the real world. A couple of simple examples are discussed in my book *Database in Depth: Relational Theory for Practitioners* (O'Reilly Media Inc., 2005), pages 54–56. What's more, a literally infinite number of analogous examples can be constructed to illustrate the same overall point. The nub of the matter is this: All bets are off! You can never trust a system that's based—even if, unlike today's SQL systems, it's *correctly* based—on some 3VL, because you never know whether what the system is telling you is true. In my view, this state of affairs is a complete showstopper.

The Unknown Truth Value and A-marks

There's one point that might be bothering you in connection with the foregoing discussion. To be specific, you might be thinking that the fact that *p* IFF *p* gives unknown, not true, if *p* is unknown is no big deal; after all, isn't it rather like the situation we already have in SQL according to which the comparison *v* = *v* gives unknown, not true, if *v* is null?

Well—not to mention the fact that I have major problems with the fact that "null = null" gives unknown anyway—the two situations aren't the same at all. In the RM/V2 book, Codd talks about what he calls *A-marks,* which are essentially the same as SQL-style nulls, and he makes it very clear that *A-marks aren't values.* At the same time, he makes it very clear that "the third truth value" definitely is a value; as the RM/V2 book puts it, "*t, f,* ... and *a* are actual values, and should not be regarded as marked values." Now, by "marked values" here, Codd means, among other things, A-marks, which he had previously stated explicitly aren't values at all; thus, "marked values" is actually a contradiction in terms. I don't really want to pursue that point here, though I do think that careful analysis of the term "marked value" leads inexorably to the position that many-valued logics don't solve the problem of missing information at all. But never mind that; the point is, as Codd does make clear, "the third truth value" and A-marks are logically different things. It follows that to confuse them is a logical mistake. The following is an edited version of a discussion of this point from my book *An Introduction to Database Systems*, 8th edition (Addison-Wesley, 2004):[3]

> *It's important to understand that an A-mark (an SQL null, if you prefer) and* a *(the unknown truth value) aren't the same thing. Indeed, this state of affairs is an immediate consequence of the fact that* a *is a value, while an A-mark isn't a value at all. But let's be a little more specific. Suppose X is a variable of type truth value. Then X must have one of the values* t, a, *or* f. *Thus, the statement "X has the value* a*" means the value of X is known to be "the unknown truth value,"* a. *By contrast, the statement "X is A-marked" means X has no value at all (because we don't know what value to assign to X, and therefore we don't assign a value to it but "mark" it instead).*

To repeat, to confuse A-marks and *a* (or nulls and UNKNOWN, in SQL terms) is a logical mistake. Indeed, using an A-mark instead of *a* to represent "the third truth value" is exactly as serious an error as using an A-mark instead of 0 to represent zero! As Hugh Darwen and I have argued in many places (see, e.g., my paper "On the Notion of Logical Difference," Chapter 4 in the present book), logical mistakes are *big* mistakes—and, sadly, this particular big mistake has been committed both by the SQL standard and by Codd himself, in the RM/T paper.

How Many 3VLs Are There?

You might have been a little surprised by my earlier use of the phrase "three-valued logics in general." How many 3VLs are there? Isn't there just one?

Well, in a sense there is just one. Let's think about the connectives again. As I said earlier, there are exactly as many distinct connectives as there are distinct truth tables, and of course this remark is just as true of 3VL as it is of 2VL. Since 3VL has three truth values, there are $3 * 3 * 3 = 27$ monadic 3VL connectives, because each of the three possible inputs *t*, *a*, and *f* can map to each of the three possible outputs *t*, *a*, and *f*. And there are $3^9 = 19,683$ possible dyadic 3VL operators, as the following table suggests:

---

3. Honesty compels me to point out that the text quoted, if carefully analyzed, fails the coherency test. To say that a variable has no value is to say, by definition, that the variable is not a variable after all—as can easily be seen by checking the definition of the term *variable*. The truth is, the very act of trying to state precisely what nulls and 3VL are all about is (or should be) sufficient to show why the idea is not exactly coherent. As a consequence, it's hard to explain it coherently, too. In fact, the entire topic illustrates perfectly something I've elsewhere called *The Principle of Incoherence* (sometimes referred to, unkindly, as *The Incoherent Principle*)—*viz.*, it's hard to criticize something coherently if what you're trying to criticize is itself not very coherent in the first place.

	t	a	f
t	$t/a/f$	$t/a/f$	$t/a/f$
a	$t/a/f$	$t/a/f$	$t/a/f$
f	$t/a/f$	$t/a/f$	$t/a/f$

So each and every 3VL has exactly these 19,710 connectives in total and in common. But the question is: Which of those connectives do we call NOT, and which OR, and which AND, ... and, very importantly, which do we call implication and which equivalence? Different choices will give rise to "different 3VLs"—different in the sense that (e.g.) in some 3VLs IF p THEN q will be equivalent to (NOT p) OR q but IF p THEN p won't be a tautology, while in others IF p THEN p will be a tautology but IF p THEN q won't be equivalent to (NOT p) OR q. Furthermore, there's no 3VL that's universally accepted as "the" 3VL, partly because, as David McGoveran shows in his paper "Nothing from Nothing" (in four parts, in C. J. Date, Hugh Darwen, and David McGoveran, *Relational Database Writings 1994–1997*, Addison-Wesley, 1998), there's *no* 3VL that preserves all of the desirable properties of conventional 2VL. That's precisely the problem!—or one of the problems, at any rate.

Codd's Four-Valued Logics

I turn now to 4VL. Just as there are many 3VLs (in a sense), there are, of course, many 4VLs: vastly more of them, in fact. Again let's start with the connectives. It should be clear that, in general, n-valued logic for any $n > 1$ involves n to the power n monadic connectives and n to the power n^2 dyadic connectives, as the following table indicates:

	monadic connectives	dyadic connectives
2VL	4	16
3VL	27	19,683
4VL	256	4,294,967,296
...	....	....
nVL	$(n)**(n)$	$(n)**(n^2)$

By the way, the foregoing table raises certain questions that I think it incumbent on any supporter of nVL for some $n > 2$ to have a good answer for:

- What's a suitable set of *primitive* connectives? That is, what connectives must the system support, at a minimum, in order to guarantee that every connective can at least be expressed?

- What's a suitable set of *useful* connectives? (This is an issue of ergonomics, not a logical issue.) For example, in 2VL, either of the sets {NOT,OR} or {NOT,AND} is a suitable primitive set,[4] but the set {NOT,OR,AND} is more user-friendly; it would be very undesirable always to have to express, say, OR in terms of NOT and AND. I remark in passing that such a criticism applies to SQL—not because it supports, e.g., OR and not AND, but because it supports EXISTS and not FORALL (in a finite universe, of course, EXISTS is basically iterated OR and FORALL is basically iterated AND).

These are questions that I've never seen advocates of *n*VL for some *n* > 2 even ask, let alone answer.

Anyway, let's get back to 4VL specifically. As I've said, there are many 4VLs. In particular, there are at least three that can lay some claim to being "Codd's 4VL" (a fact in itself that raises questions about the legitimacy of the whole endeavor, it might be thought, but let that pass). I'll consider each in turn.

4VL Number 1

Codd first spelled out proposals for supporting 4VL in detail in the RM/V2 book. (He had previously talked about the idea of using 4VL in his paper "Missing Information (Applicable and Inapplicable) in Relational Databases" (*ACM SIGMOD Record 15*, No. 4, December 1986), but that paper gave few details; in particular, it gave no 4VL truth tables.) His justification for wanting to use not just three- but four-valued logic was the need, as he saw it, to deal with the fact that information might be missing for two distinct reasons:[5]

- Some "property" is applicable but the value is unknown (as in the example of an employee whose salary is unknown; the employee does have a salary, but we don't know what it is). A-marks (nulls in SQL) are used to deal with this case, and *a* ("missing and applicable") is the corresponding ("third") truth value.

- Some property is inapplicable (as in the example of an employee who has no spouse; the property of having a spouse simply doesn't apply to that employee). *I-marks*—another kind of "marked value"—are introduced to deal with this case, and another ("fourth") truth value, *i* ("missing and inapplicable"), is defined accordingly.

Before going any further, I remark that to refer to the latter situation as an example of "missing information" is rather curious, in a way. If employee Joe has no spouse, it doesn't really make sense to say Joe's spouse information is "missing"; there simply *is* no spouse information in this case. In fact, I think the phrase "missing information" is a contradiction in terms in such a situation. But it isn't my purpose here to try to fix such terminological infelicities, so I'll say no more about them here.

Here then are the 4VL truth tables for NOT, OR, and AND as given in the RM/V2 book:

---

4. In fact either of the sets {NOR} and {NAND} would suffice.
5. Of course there are many other reasons also, in addition to the two articulated here—another point that I think should raise a few warning flags about the desirability or otherwise of the many-valued logic approach.

NOT			OR	t	a	i	f		AND	t	a	i	f
t	f		t	t	t	t	t		t	t	a	i	f
a	a		a	t	a	a	a		a	a	a	i	f
i	i		i	t	a	i	f		i	i	i	i	f
f	t		f	t	a	f	f		f	f	f	f	f

Given these truth tables, here's the truth table for (NOT p) OR q (not explicitly given in the RM/V2 book):

	t	a	i	f
t	t	a	f	f
a	t	a	a	a
i	t	a	i	f
f	t	t	t	t

Does this truth table define logical implication? Well, we clearly don't have t's all down the diagonal from top left to bottom right, which we would have to have if "p implies p" is to be a tautology; so I would say it doesn't (and the Rescher book, page 134, agrees with me).

Following on from the foregoing, here's the truth table for ((NOT p) OR q) AND ((NOT q) OR p):

	t	a	i	f
t	t	a	f	f
a	a	a	a	a
i	f	a	i	f
f	f	a	f	t

Does this truth table define logical equivalence? Clearly not; again we don't have t's all down the diagonal from top left to bottom right, which we would have to have if "p is equivalent to p" is to be a tautology; so I would say it doesn't (and again the Rescher book, page 139, agrees with me).

Another problem with this first 4VL of Codd's is that De Morgan's Laws don't hold. Consider the two expressions

    NOT (p AND q)

and

    (NOT p) OR (NOT q)

These two expressions represent, respectively, the left and right sides, as it were, of the first of De Morgan's Laws as stated earlier in this chapter. Let p and q have truth values i and a, respectively. Then the first expression evaluates to i but the second to a. Note, incidentally, that the truth tables for implication and equivalence play no part here; that is, De Morgan's Laws break down in Codd's first 4VL regardless of how we choose to define these latter operators.

Incidentally, one consequence of the foregoing fact is that the following important identity breaks down also (that is, the expression isn't in fact an identity after all, in Codd's first 4VL):

```
( FORALL x ( p ) ) IFF ( NOT EXISTS x ( NOT p ) )
```

This failure is particularly distressing, given that (as I've already indicated in passing) queries that are most "naturally," or anyway most readily, expressed in terms of FORALL have to be expressed in terms of NOT EXISTS instead, in SQL. *Note:* I don't want to give the impression that the foregoing is the only problem with SQL's support for the quantifiers. As I've written elsewhere—see, e.g., the O'Reilly book mentioned earlier—SQL is supposed to support three-valued logic, but SQL's EXISTS is not a faithful representation of the existential quantifier of that logic. To be specific, SQL's EXISTS never returns UNKNOWN (the third truth value in SQL), even when UNKNOWN is the logically correct answer.

4VL Number 2

Codd subsequently revised his 4VL truth tables, first in a July 1991 reprinting of the RM/V2 book, and later in a 1994 book—really a collection of papers—with the overall title *1994: The 25th Anniversary of the Creation of the Relational Model for Database Management* (published through the auspices of the consulting company Codd & Date Inc.). In the latter, he refers to "the four-valued logic defined by the following truth tables":[6]

NOT	
t	f
a	a
i	i
f	t

OR	t	a	i	f
t	t	t	t	t
a	t	a	a	a
i	t	a	i	i
f	t	a	i	f

AND	t	a	i	f
t	t	a	i	f
a	a	a	i	f
i	i	i	i	f
f	f	f	f	f

As you can see, here Codd has changed the truth table for OR, such that *f* OR *i* and *i* OR *f* are now both defined to return *i* instead of (as formerly) *f*. What effect does this change have? Well, it's easy to see that (NOT *p*) OR *q* still fails to give the definition we'd like for implication; likewise, ((NOT *p*) OR *q*) AND ((NOT *q*) OR *p*) still fails to give the definition we'd like for equivalence. De Morgan's Laws still fail, too. Frankly, in fact, it isn't at all clear why Codd made the changes he did, from his first 4VL to his second—unless it was simply to bring the truth tables for OR and AND a little more into line with each other, as it were.

---

6. This phrasing is rather curious. A logic can't be "defined" by simply specifying a few truth tables. Codd appears to be assuming that all of the operators in the 4VL he's talking about can be derived from the three operators he does define, but he doesn't spell out explicitly what the rules are by which such derivations can be performed. In particular, he doesn't say how the equivalence and implication operators are derived.

4VL Number 3

Although I'm not aware of any generally available publication in which he documented the fact, I have it on good authority that Codd subsequently revised his 4VL tables again, thus:

NOT						OR	t	a	i	f			AND	t	a	i	f
t	f					t	t	t	t	t			t	t	a	i	f
a	i					a	t	a	a	a			a	a	a	i	f
i	a					i	t	a	i	i			i	i	i	i	f
f	t					f	t	a	i	f			f	f	f	f	f

Here the change is in the table for NOT—NOT a and NOT i are now defined to return i and a, respectively, instead of (as formerly) a and i. What effect does this change have? Well, again it's easy to see that (NOT p) OR q still fails to give the definition we'd like for implication, and ((NOT p) OR q) AND ((NOT q) OR p) still fails to give the definition we'd like for equivalence. However, De Morgan's Laws do now work, and I think it not unlikely that this fact was Codd's justification for defining his third 4VL the way he did. But De Morgan's Laws aren't everything, of course.

I have a more formal criticism of Codd's third 4VL. Returning for a moment to *three*-valued logic, it's easy to see that Codd's 3VL truth tables for NOT, OR, and AND reduce to those for *two*-valued logic if we simply delete the rows and columns corresponding to "the third truth value" *a. However, no analogous property holds for Codd's third 4VL.* To be specific, if we delete the rows and columns for "the fourth truth value" *i* from the 4VL truth tables for NOT, OR, and AND, we do *not* obtain the corresponding 3VL tables; to be more specific still, we're left with the fact that NOT *a* is defined to return "the fourth truth value" *i*, a truth value that doesn't exist at all in Codd's 3VL.

Some Questions of Intuition

Most of this chapter has been concerned with various *formal* properties of the logics under discussion. In this final section, however, I want to raise some questions of a more intuitive nature.

Recall that the A-mark is supposed to denote a value that's missing because it's unknown, while the I-mark is supposed to denote a value that's missing because it doesn't apply, and the two truth values a and i are introduced as corresponding truth values. Now, I deliberately didn't try to explain previously what it might mean for a and i to "correspond to" A-marks and I-marks, respectively. That's because I'm not sure I can! It's quite difficult to find a clear statement on the matter in the RM/V2 book. However, let me give it a shot. Let X, A, and I be variables (of the same type, so they can be tested for equality), and let X have some genuine (i.e., "unmarked") value while A is "A-marked" and I is "I-marked." Then I think the following, at least, are true statements (though, frankly, it's hard to be sure):

- The following expressions all evaluate to *i:*

  ```
  X = I
  A = I
  I = I
  ```

- The following expressions both evaluate to *a:*

  ```
  X = A
  A = A
  ```

So *a* ("missing and applicable") is what we get if we ask if an A-mark is equal to anything other than an I-mark, and *i* ("missing and inapplicable") is what we get if we ask if an I-mark is equal to anything at all. Observe in particular, therefore, that (like null in SQL) nothing, not even the A-mark itself, is equal to the A-mark, and likewise for the I-mark.

Given the foregoing state of affairs, I now come to my questions:

- First, what *intuitive*—as opposed to, possibly, formal—justification is there for defining "NOT (missing and applicable)" to be equivalent to "missing and inapplicable"? Certainly the equivalence doesn't seem to make much sense in ordinary colloquial English.

- Likewise, what intuitive justification is there for defining "NOT (missing and inapplicable)" to be "missing and applicable"?

- In a similar vein, what intuitive justification is there for defining *a* OR *i* to be *a* and *a* AND *i* to be *i?*

I don't think formal justifications, even if there are any, will be sufficient to persuade the punters that these rules make sense (remember that all of these matters eventually have to be explained to "the naïve end user").

I have a related question, too. Let *X* and *Y* be variables of type truth value. In Codd's 4VL, the legal values of *X* and *Y* are precisely *t, a, i, f.* But, of course, each of *X* and *Y* might be either A-marked or I-marked. Suppose *X* has the value *t* but *Y* is A- or I-marked. Then what's the value of *X* OR *Y?* It *must* be *t*—*t* OR *anything* is always *t*—but I strongly suspect that Codd would say it has to be *a* or *i* (though again I can't find a clear statement on the matter in the RM/V2 book).

PART 5

■ ■ ■

Further Relational Misconceptions

Over the years I've published quite a few papers on the general subject of relational misconceptions (hence the qualifier "further" in the foregoing title):

- "Some Relational Myths Exploded: An Examination of Some Popular Misconceptions Concerning Relational Database Management Systems" (1984)

- "Relational Database: Further Misconceptions Number One" (1986) and "Relational Database: Further Misconceptions Number Two" (1986), combined into "Further Relational Myths" (1990)

- "Relational Database: Further Misconceptions Number Three" (1992)

The generic abstract for these papers—all of which appeared in one or other of this book's predecessors—looks like this:

> *Relational database management is one of the key technologies for the 1980s (and beyond!), yet the field of relational technology still suffers from a great deal of misunderstanding and misrepresentation. Misconceptions abound. The purpose of [these articles] is to identify some of those misconceptions.*

And the chapters that follow (Chapters 19–22) continue in this tradition. *Note:* Those chapters all originally appeared on the website http://www.dbdebunk.com. Here is what Fabian Pascal, the editor of that website, has to say about it:

> *A lot of what is being said, written, or done in the database management field ... by vendors, the trade press, and "experts" is irrelevant, misleading, or outright wrong ... [This] website ... sets matters straight by telling the truth about database management!*

The chapters in question can indeed be seen as attempts on my part to "set matters straight" with respect to various aspects of (relational) database management.

CHAPTER 19

■■■

There's Only One Relational Model

The misconception that there's no such thing as *the* relational model is, unfortunately, quite widespread (indeed, the term *relational model* often appears in the literature with the indefinite article *a* instead of the definite article *the*). What follows is an attempt to debunk this myth. I wrote it originally as a response to something I read in a book titled—rather curiously, I thought—*Joe Celko's Data and Databases: Concepts in Practice* (Morgan Kaufmann, 1999), by Joe Celko. Chapter 18 of that book is called "Different Relational Models," and the first sentence of that chapter reads as follows:

> *There is no such thing as* the *relational model for databases anymore* [sic] *than there is just one geometry.*

Now, Celko does have a point here, in a way. Here's an extract from a recent book of my own (*The Database Relational Model: A Retrospective Review and Analysis*, Addison-Wesley, 2001):

> *What then exactly* is *the relational model? If you've been following the discussions [in previous chapters] carefully, you'll have noticed that Codd's own definitions evolved somewhat [over the years] ... One consequence of this fact is that critics have been able to accuse Codd in particular, and relational advocates in general, of "moving the goalposts" far too much. For example, Mike Stonebraker has written that "one can think of four different versions" of [the relational model]:*
>
> - *Version 1: Defined by the 1970 CACM paper*
>
> - *Version 2: Defined by the 1981 Turing Award paper*
>
> - *Version 3: Defined by Codd's 12 rules and scoring system*
>
> - *Version 4: Defined by Codd's book*

Let me interrupt myself briefly to explain the references here. First of all, of course, E. F. Codd is the first and onlie begetter of the original model, and all four references are to writings by him. The 1970 CACM paper is "A Relational Model of Data for Large Shared Data Banks," *CACM 13*, No. 6 (June 1970). The 1981 Turing Award paper is "Relational Database: A Practical Foundation for Productivity," *CACM 25*, No. 2 (February 1982). The 12 rules and the accompanying scoring system are described in Codd's *Computerworld* articles "Is Your DBMS Really Relational?" and "Does Your DBMS Run By The Rules?" (October 14th and October 21st, 1985). Finally, Codd's book is *The Relational Model For Database Management Version 2* (Addison-Wesley, 1990). Now back to the quote from my book:

> *Perhaps because we're a trifle sensitive to such criticisms, Hugh Darwen and I have tried to provide [in our book* Databases, Types, and the Relational Model: The Third Manifesto, *3rd edition, Addison-Wesley, 2006] our own careful statement of what we believe the relational model is (or ought to be!). Indeed, we'd like [that]* Manifesto *to be seen in part as a definitive statement in this regard. I refer you to [that book] itself for the details; here just let me say that we see our contribution in this area as primarily one of dotting a few* i*'s and crossing a few* t*'s that Codd himself left undotted or uncrossed in his own original work. We most certainly do not want to be thought of as departing in any major respect from Codd's original vision; indeed, the whole of the* Manifesto *is very much in the spirit of Codd's ideas and continues along the path that he originally laid down.*

To say it again, therefore, Celko does have a point, and a sensible discussion of how—and, more importantly, why—the relational model has evolved over the years could be a useful contribution. His Chapter 18 offers no such discussion, however. On the contrary, it gives the impression that the writer is more interested in scoring a few debating points than he is in conveying truly useful information. What's more, the chapter in question doesn't really define *any* of the alleged "different relational models" at all!—and no such definition can be found anywhere else in the book, either (not even in Chapter 16, which is titled "The Basic Relational Model"). To criticize something without explaining just what it is you're criticizing might be an effective technique, but (in my not unbiased opinion) it's hardly a fair one.

Given the foregoing assessment of Celko's chapter overall, the idea of trying to analyze it at a detailed level might be thought a little pointless. The fact is, however, the chapter contains so many assertions that are misleading, inaccurate, or just plain wrong that—it seems to me— *somebody* ought to try to set the record straight. And since Celko's chapter also takes my name in vain (several times, in fact), it seemed appropriate that that somebody should be me ... Hence the present rebuttal.

All otherwise unattributed quotes in what follows are taken from Celko's Chapter 18. The chapter in question consists of a short untitled preamble and six numbered sections with the following somewhat strange titles:

1. Chris Date = No Duplicates, No NULLs

2. E. F. Codd, RM Version I

3. E. F. Codd, RM Version II

4. SQL-92 = Duplicates, One NULL

5. Duplicates, One NULL, Non-1NF Tables

6. Rick Snodgrass = Temporal SQL

Celko's Preamble

Let me begin my detailed analysis by repeating Celko's opening sentence (which appears in his preamble, of course):

> *There is no such thing as* the *relational model for databases anymore* [sic] *than there is just one geometry.*

Now, it is of course true that there are several different geometries (euclidean, elliptic, hyperbolic, etc.). But is the analogy that Celko is trying to draw here a valid one? That is, do Celko's "different relational models" differ in the same way that those different geometries differ? It seems to me that the answer to this question is *no*. Elliptic and hyperbolic geometries are often referred to quite specifically as *noneuclidean* geometries; for the analogy to be valid, therefore, it would seem that at least five of Celko's six "different relational models" would have to be *nonrelational* models, and hence (by definition) not "relational models" at all.

Note: Actually, I would agree (and will argue in more detail later) that several of Celko's "different relational models" are indeed nonrelational. But then he can hardly go on to claim—at least, he can't claim consistently—that they are then "different *relational* models." So I have a serious problem right away with Celko's overall thesis ... However, let's continue. Here's the next quote:

> *For example, if I draw a triangle on a plane, it always has 180 degrees; if I draw it on the surface of a sphere, it always has more than 180 degrees; and if I draw it on the surface of a trumpet, it always has less than 180 degrees ... Which geometry is true? Well, it depends where I am. My backyard is roughly a plane, the surface of the earth is roughly a sphere, and the gravity well of a star is roughly a trumpet.*

Celko seems to be suggesting here, by analogy, that which of his "different relational models" is "true" depends on where he is: a rather curious argument, I would have thought, and one that betrays a strange interpretation of the nature of truth. In any case, I don't think we can reasonably say that a geometry—or a model—is "true"; at best, we might say it's *consistent*. But we aren't arguing about whether Celko's "different relational models" are consistent; we're arguing about whether they're really "different relational models" in the first place.

"Chris Date = No Duplicates, No NULLs"

On to Celko's Section 18.1:

> *Chris [Date's] version [of the relational model] is the simplest and closest to the "usual file model" of data ... Date's relational model allows no duplicate rows in tables and has no NULL* [uppercase NULL in the original].

Well, it's true that "my" relational model—or, better, **the** relational model!—doesn't permit relations to contain duplicate tuples or nulls. That's because a "relation" that contains duplicate tuples or nulls **is not a relation,** by definition.[1] It follows that a model that permits such "relations"

---

1. Just as an aside, let me say too that a "domain" that contains a null is not a domain and a "tuple" that contains a null is not a tuple. See my book *An Introduction to Database Systems*, 8th edition (Addison-Wesley, 2004), for further explanation.

is not and cannot be relational (again by definition), and hence that the concept of a "relational" model that does permit duplicate tuples or nulls is a contradiction in terms. *Note:* This state of affairs is one of the justifications—not the only one—for my position that most of Celko's "different relational models" aren't in fact relational at all.

Also, I object strongly to Celko's characterization of "my" relational model as being close to "the usual file model." First of all, I'm not even sure what the term "the usual file model" might mean (though I can guess). Second, and more important, I've stated as clearly as I can, on many occasions, that we should *not* think of relations as being somehow "like" files, but rather as being *sets of true propositions.* (See, e.g., my book *WHAT Not HOW: The Business Rules Approach to Application Development,* Addison-Wesley, 2000, for an elaboration of this position.) Indeed, it's precisely because some people do tend to think of relations as being like files that we got into messes like "duplicate rows" in the first place. To be specific, the idea of a file containing duplicate records seems both familiar and innocuous, whereas (as I've already indicated) the idea of a "relation" containing "duplicate tuples" makes no sense at all.

> *Date is also a vocal opponent of the ANSI/ISO SQL standard efforts, although he has never attended a committee meeting or submitted a paper for consideration.*

This quote looks dangerously close to being an *ad hominem* attack, but perhaps I'm being oversensitive. Anyway, I'll admit to being a vocal *critic* (not an "opponent") of the SQL *standard* (not the SQL standard "efforts"). However, I will *not* admit to using the term "the ANSI/ISO SQL standard" (I don't think it's appropriate in this context to give one individual national standards body, ANSI, out of many such, a level of billing that is the same as—or arguably higher than—that of the umbrella organization, which is the international standards body, ISO). As for my participation in the standard "efforts," I'll agree that I haven't participated very much, at least not directly (though it's not quite true to say that I've "never attended a committee meeting or submitted a paper for consideration"[2]). But I do have my reasons for not participating very much. This is not the place to go into those reasons in detail; suffice it to say that they include, but are not limited to, the fact that I couldn't possibly afford the investment required, in terms of either time and money. (I might come back and revisit this particular issue at some future time.)

> *Date has also added other operators and proposed special notation for extensions to an unimplemented language based on the relational algebra. These proposals include the MAYBE postfixed unary logical operator that returns TRUE when its operand is TRUE or UNKNOWN. His SUMMARIZE operator is a generalized columnar function constructor.*

Well, it's true that, along with my colleague Hugh Darwen,[3] I've proposed a number of extensions—I believe useful ones—to Codd's original relational algebra. However:

---

2. In any case, surely the whole point of a standard is that it is *totally defined* by the publicly available standard documentation. It is not necessary to attend committee meetings, nor should it be, in order to know what the standard is, or to comment on it, or to criticize it in an informed manner.

3. In passing, let me acknowledge Hugh Darwen's helpful review of an earlier draft of this chapter.

a. Celko's choice of MAYBE as an example of such an extension is bizarre in the extreme! First of all, MAYBE isn't an extension to the algebra, as such, at all; as Celko himself says, it's a *logical* operator, not a relational one. Second, his definition is wrong (MAYBE returns TRUE when its operand is UNKNOWN, not TRUE or FALSE). Third, MAYBE is a prefix operator, not a "postfixed" one. (Just how carefully did Celko read what I had to say on this particular topic, I wonder?) Fourth—and much the most important point—I **didn't** "propose" the MAYBE operator at all! Rather, I simply pointed out that if you want to support nulls (which I categorically don't want to do), then you have to support the MAYBE operator (and then I went on to explore some of the implications of that state of affairs). That's all.

b. I don't know what a "generalized columnar function constructor" might be, but I'm pretty sure SUMMARIZE isn't one. *Au contraire*, it's a clean, orthogonal, non-*ad-hoc* analog of SQL's grouping-with-aggregation operation. In any case, SUMMARIZE was originally due, not to me, but—as far as I know—to the people who developed the PRTV prototype at IBM U.K. in the early 1970s. See Stephen Todd's paper "The Peterlee Relational Test Vehicle—A System Overview," *IBM System Journal 15*, No. 4 (1976); see also the paper by Patrick Hall, Peter Hitchcock, and Stephen Todd "An Algebra of Relations for Machine Computation," which appeared in the Conference Record of the 2nd ACM Symposium on Principles of Programming Languages, Palo Alto, Calif. (January 1975).

c. "Proposed special notation for extensions to an unimplemented language," eh? What exactly is the reader supposed to make of this wording? I think it would be fairer (not to mention being more accurate and less of an apparent putdown) to say rather that Hugh Darwen and I have defined *additional relational operators*—and then, in order to explain those operators, we have invented some syntax to use as the basis for examples to illustrate their use. After all, when Codd defined his original relational algebra, he too "proposed special notation" for "an unimplemented language." (I might add that Codd's algebra remains essentially unimplemented to this day, at least in commercial form. I might add further that this state of affairs is a major reason why today's commercial products are so plainly unsatisfactory.)

d. Just to add insult to injury, Celko then goes on to give a reference that he says explains MAYBE and SUMMARIZE—and the reference is incorrect! Just for the record, you can find such explanations in my book *An Introduction to Database Systems*, 8th edition (Addison-Wesley, 2004). That book in turn includes references to the original source documents.

"E. F. Codd, RM Version I"

Dr. Codd's original model of the relational database has been given the name "RM Version I" ... This classic model allowed no duplicate rows and [had] one NULL ...

Actually it was Codd himself who gave his original model the name "RM Version 1" (that's supposed to be an Arabic "1", by the way, not a Roman "I"). The expression "model of the relational database" is a curious one—what can it mean but the somewhat circular "model for databases that are constructed according to the relational model"? The expression "classic model" is odd too; indeed, I don't really know what it means.

Anyway, Codd's RM/V1 did indeed allow no duplicate rows. It also had no nulls! In his book *The Relational Model for Database Management: Version 2* (Addison-Wesley, 1990), Codd says: "I refer to the total content of [my] pre-1979 papers as Version 1 of the relational model (RM/V1 for brevity)." The extensions to RM/V1 to support nulls weren't defined until the 1979 paper "Extending the Database Relational Model to Capture More Meaning," *ACM TODS 4*, No. 4 (December 1979). Note, therefore, that the relational model managed perfectly well without nulls for over ten years (Codd's very first paper on the relational model, "Derivability, Redundancy, and Consistency of Relations Stored in Large Data Banks," IBM Research Report RJ599, was dated August 19th, 1969).

"E. F. Codd, RM Version II"

In 1990, Dr. Codd released a second version of his relational model ... He still [did] not allow duplicate rows in a table, but he added two [sic] types of NULL markers.

In fact Codd added the first "type of null marker" in 1979, as explained in the previous section, and the second in 1986—see his paper "Missing Information (Applicable and Inapplicable) in Relational Databases," *ACM SIGMOD Record 15*, No. 4, December 1986. But it is at least true that he included both "types of null markers" in "RM Version 2" (RM/V2), and his book on RM/V2 was indeed published in 1990. However, as I've written elsewhere (see, e.g., my book *The Database Relational Model: A Retrospective Review and Analysis* mentioned earlier in this chapter), I regard nulls and everything to do with them as a mistake—Codd's one big error of judgment in this whole business, in my opinion. Codd and I debated this issue in print (see E. F. Codd and C. J. Date, "Much Ado About Nothing," in C. J. Date, *Relational Database Writings 1991–1994*, Addison-Wesley, 1995).

"SQL-92 = Duplicates, One NULL"

The SQL language was developed by IBM's Santa Teresa labs ... The big debate during development was not over the relational model, but over how NULLs should be handled ... The result was System R and Sequel (Structured English-like Query Language) as their first product ... The language was later extended a bit and became the first version of SQL.

SQL was indeed originally called SEQUEL; the name was an acronym for Structured English (not "English-like") Query Language. The name was subsequently changed for legal reasons. However, the language was originally developed in the research division of IBM (initially at Yorktown Heights, New York, and later at San Jose, California), not "by IBM's Santa Teresa labs." There were many "big debates" during the development of the language; frankly, I very much doubt whether how to handle nulls was "the" big debate, but perhaps it was.[4] System R wasn't a product but a prototype (and it was built in IBM's research laboratory in San Jose, not

---

4. I was never one of the SQL developers myself, but I was in close touch with the people who were—so though I can't be absolutely certain as to what "the" big debate was (if there ever was such a thing), I'm pretty sure I'm right here.

in "IBM's Santa Teresa labs"). For a more accurate account of the historical development of SQL, I suggest you take a look at any of the following:

- Donald D. Chamberlin, Arthur M. Gilbert, and Robert A. Yost: "A History of System R and SQL / Data System," Proc. 7th Int. Conf. on Very Large Data Bases, Cannes, France (September 1981)

- Donald D. Chamberlin *et al.*: "A History and Evaluation of System R," *CACM 24*, No. 10 (October 1981)

- Chapter 1 of Don Chamberlin: *Using the New DB2* (Morgan Kaufmann, 1996)

- Chapter 1 of C. J. Date and Hugh Darwen: *A Guide to the SQL Standard*, 4th edition (Addison-Wesley, 1997)

Note: Along with Raymond Boyce, Don Chamberlin was the original designer of SEQUEL (later SQL), so his accounts can be taken as authoritative.

> *Removing redundant duplicates was considered too expensive and too strange for programmers, so SQL uses a multiset model instead of a pure set model.*

It would be more helpful if Celko could explain why duplicates (or *redundant* duplicates, as he correctly calls them) are a bad idea and really *should* be removed. Too expensive to remove them? I would say it's too expensive not to! It's only too expensive if you take a very narrow view of the world and consider just the performance of certain tiny subexpressions, instead of looking at the overall big picture.

As for SQL using "a multiset model rather than a pure set model": It's true that, in general, SQL tables contain multisets (also known as *bags*) of rows, not sets of rows; however, SQL doesn't provide all of the usual bag operators (for example, "bag union" isn't directly supported, and it's hard to simulate, too). So it's a bit of a stretch to claim that SQL "uses a multiset model"— not to mention the fact that, so far as I'm aware, no such thing has ever been formally defined.

"Duplicates, One NULL, Non-1NF Tables"

> *In a first normal form (1NF) database, all the columns in the rows of a table contain only scalar values ... Roth and Korth (1998) developed a model that extends the SQL model by allowing a table to contain another table within a column ... They added operators for nesting and unnesting these tables and extended some of the existing operators.*

Several points here:

a. Celko's definition of a "1NF database"—meaning, presumably, a database that contains only 1NF relations[5]—is incorrect (attribute values within relations are *not* limited to scalar values only). But he can certainly be forgiven for the error; indeed, I'm on record as saying much the same thing myself in various writings prior to about 1992. However, my own understanding of the true nature of 1NF has improved since then, and I now know that domains (and therefore attributes in relations) can contain *any values whatsoever*, including in particular relation values (and "nested relations" are thus

---

5. Strictly speaking, it's relations (or relation variables, rather), not databases, that can be said to be or not to be in some particular normal form.

legal). The book mentioned a couple of times already, *An Introduction to Database Systems*, 8th edition (Addison-Wesley, 2004), explains the true state of affairs in detail. It also offers a historical perspective on why we originally got the definition wrong. See also Chapter 8 in the present book.

b. Roth and Korth's paper was published in 1988, not 1998, in *ACM TODS 13*, No. 4 (December 1988). Moreover:

- It certainly wasn't the first paper on the subject (others dated back to the mid 1970s and early 1980s), and so Roth and Korth can hardly be said to be the "developers" of the model in question.

- The authors were in fact Roth, Korth, and Silberschatz, not just Roth and Korth alone.

- The paper did indeed extend the relational model (certainly not "the SQL model"!)— its title was "Extended Relational Algebra and Calculus for Nested Relational Databases," by Mark A. Roth, Henry F. Korth, and Abraham Silberschatz—but the extensions were (in my opinion) unnecessary. The pure relational model, *without* any of the extensions in question, in fact provides all of the (useful) functionality that the so-called "non-first-normal-form" model provides.

"Rick Snodgrass = Temporal SQL"

My final quote from Celko's Chapter 18 consists of Section 18.6 in its entirety:

> *Rick Snodgrass (1995) at the University of Arizona has a series of papers that add temporal operations to standard SQL. He is not the only researcher in this area, but his work is the only project that has been brought to the attention of the NCITS H2 Committee for SQL3.*
>
> *The set models used in all of the data models discussed so far are state oriented and lack a temporal dimension. That is, when a fact is entered or changed in the database, the database engine makes no note of when this event occurred. Instead, the database is a model of the current state of the real world as of a moment in time. The real worry is that the model be consistent with logical constraints on the data.*
>
> *Temporal SQL adds extra clauses to the usual SELECT statement that match rows based on when they occurred relative to each other.*

My first reaction to this section is that it's right out of left field! If you're going to consider "the addition of temporal operations to SQL" as somehow defining "a different relational model," then why stop there? Why not examine the addition of pointers, something that several commercial products (and the standard) have already done?[6] Or the addition of OLAP operators? Or the addition of user-defined types and type inheritance support? Or the addition of "subtables and supertables"? Or the numerous additional *departures* (not just the "duplicates and nulls" departures) from the relational model that are already found in SQL? Etc., etc., etc.

---

6. Thereby destroying any claims those products might previously have had to being relational, of course.

Second, Snodgrass's work might indeed be the only temporal database project to have "been brought to the attention of the [ANSI] NCITS H2 Committee," but it's certainly not the only such project to have been brought to the attention of the *international* SQL standards committee. Another such (and one that looks much more promising to me) is reported in—among other publications—Nikos A. Lorentzos and R. G. Johnson, "An Extension of the Relational Model to Support Generic Intervals," in Joachim W. Schmidt, Stefano Ceri, and Michel Missikoff (eds.), *Extending Database Technology* (Springer Verlag, 1988). *Note:* Celko's reference to Snodgrass's work is to the book *The TSQL2 Temporal Query Language,* Richard T. Snodgrass, ed. (Kluwer Academic Publishers, 1995). Lorentzos's work is described in C. J. Date, Hugh Darwen, and Nikos A. Lorentzos: *Temporal Data and the Relational Model* (Morgan Kaufmann, 2003).

Third, Snodgrass's proposals in fact violate "the fundamental principle of the relational model"—*viz., The Information Principle*—and cannot therefore be regarded as being truly relational at all, let alone constituting "a different relational model." *Note:* In case you're unfamiliar with this crucial principle, it runs as follows: *All information in the database must be cast explicitly in terms of values in relations and in no other way.* Snodgrass's proposals violate this principle because they involve a variety of hidden timestamps on rows in tables.[7]

Fourth, I'd like to comment on the remark that "the set models used in all of the data models discussed so far are state oriented and lack a temporal dimension." I don't know what the expression "the set models" means, nor do I know what it could *possibly* mean for such models to be "used in data models," but I do know that temporal data support has nothing to do with whether the underlying data model is set- or record-level, and I also know that the relational model in particular is perfectly capable of dealing adequately with temporal data (and it doesn't need huge extensions to do it, either).

Fifth, "the database engine" certainly does "make a note" of when update events occur (admittedly it does so in the log, not in the database, but at least it does do so). But the point is, when update events occur is—for the most part—not in itself very interesting. What's much more interesting (and much more important) is when certain states of affairs *obtain in the real world. That's* what we want to record in a temporal database.

Sixth, Celko says: "The real worry is that the model be consistent with logical constraints on the data." By *the model* here, I believe he really means *the database,* not one of his "different relational models." And yes, it's vitally important—always!—that the database be consistent, regardless whether we're dealing with temporal data or any other kind. The significance of his remark in this context escapes me, I'm afraid.

Seventh: "Temporal SQL adds extra clauses to the usual SELECT statement that match rows based on when they occurred relative to each other." What on earth does this sentence mean? If Celko really wants to talk about temporal databases, then I think he should make a start by explaining some basic temporal concepts. Then (and only then) he might try to claim that he needs a "different relational model." But then, of course, I would dispute that claim (see above).

How Many Relational Models?

Near the beginning of this chapter, I said the idea of trying to analyze Celko's Chapter 18 at a detailed level might be thought a little pointless. But the relational model is so important!—and I believe it's important also to try to spread the truth regarding that model as far and wide as

---

7. This argument is elaborated in Chapter 28 of the present book.

possible, and I regard such an endeavor as part of my own personal mission. In fact, Celko's book actually includes excerpts from an interview I gave to *DBMS Magazine* back in 1989, and the introduction to those excerpts (included in Celko's book) has this to say: "C. J. Date has made a career of explaining, teaching, and clearing up misunderstandings about the relational model." True enough!—or, at least, the "made a career of" bit is; whether I've been successful in that regard is for others to judge, of course. So let me conclude with my own take on this business of "different relational models." Here goes.

First of all, it's undeniably true that the relational model has changed over the years. But the changes—at least, the ones I believe will stand the test of time—have all been evolutionary, not revolutionary, in nature. It's like mathematics: Mathematics too changes over time, it's not a static thing. Indeed, I think the relational model can be seen as a small branch of mathematics; as such, it grows over time as new theorems are proved and new results discovered. (Moreover, those new contributions can be made by anyone who is competent to do so. Like mathematics again, the relational model, though originally invented by one person, is now a community effort and belongs to the world.) In other words, I do claim there's really only one relational model, even though that model has evolved over time and will continue to do so. And I fully expect database systems still to be based on that model a hundred years from now, because it really is rock solid, thanks to its foundation in mathematics and predicate logic.

So what are those evolutionary changes? Here are some of them:

- A better understanding of the relationship between the model and predicate logic

- A better understanding of the true nature of first normal form

- A better understanding of the fundamental significance of integrity constraints in general (and many good theoretical results regarding certain important special cases)

- Certain important database design principles

- A clear theory of updating, including view updating in particular

- A better understanding of the interactions between the relational model and type theory

For more details on these and other developments, see the *Third Manifesto* book mentioned earlier in this chapter.

Concluding Remarks

I'd like to close with a lightly edited excerpt from my book *The Database Relational Model: A Retrospective Review and Analysis*. Appendix A of that book gives my own definition of the relational model (not "the" definition of "my own" relational model, please note!). The definition is both terse and fairly abstract, but it is at least accurate, so far as I know. Here it is.

[The] relational model consists of the following five components:

1. An open-ended collection of **scalar types** (including in particular the type *boolean* or *truth value*)

2. A **relation type generator** and an intended interpretation for relations of types generated thereby

3. Facilities for defining **relation variables** of such generated relation types

4. A **relational assignment** operator for assigning relation values to such relation variables

5. An open-ended collection of generic **relational operators** for deriving relation values from other relation values

A few additional comments on these five components:

1. The scalar types can be system- or user-defined, in general; thus, a means must be available for users to define their own types (this requirement is implied, partly, by the fact that the set of types is "open-ended"). A means must therefore also be available for users to define their own operators, since types without operators are useless. The only *required* system-defined type is the scalar type BOOLEAN (the most fundamental type of all), but a real system will surely support other built-in scalar types (e.g., type INTEGER) as well.

2. The relation type generator allows users to specify their own individual relation types. The "intended interpretation" for a given relation (of a given relation type) is the corresponding *predicate.*

3. Facilities for defining relation variables *must* be available (of course). Relation variables are the *only* variables allowed inside a relational database. *Note:* This latter requirement is implied by the *Information Principle* (see a couple of sections back).

4. Variables are updatable by definition; hence, every kind of variable is subject to *assignment*, and relation variables are no exception. INSERT, DELETE, and UPDATE shorthands are legal and indeed useful, but strictly speaking they *are* only shorthands.

5. The "generic operators" are the operators that make up the relational algebra, and they are therefore built in (though there is no inherent reason why users should not be able to define additional ones). They are "generic" because they apply to all possible relations, loosely speaking.

The foregoing definition is explained in depth in the book mentioned several times in this chapter already, *An Introduction to Database Systems,* 8th edition (Addison-Wesley, 2004).

Technical Correspondence

Relational misconceptions don't just abound, they *proliferate.* They don't seem to die, either. Here are some more examples, taken from letters written after the foregoing article first appeared on the Database Debunkings website. First, some quotes from a message from SW,[8] with commentary:

A tuple is an ordered list of values, or alternatively an unordered list of key-value pairs.

---

8. I'll use this initials-only style to refer to correspondents in "Technical Correspondence" sections throughout this book.

No, it's not. A tuple is a set of <*A,T,v*> triples, where *A* is an attribute name (and no two triples in the set have the same *A* component), *T* is a type name, and *v* is a value of type *T*. **Immediate consequences:** (a) No left-to-right ordering of tuple components. (b) No left-to-right ordering of attributes in a relation. (c) **No nulls!**—because nulls aren't values. (d) All relations are in first normal form—even if *T* is (for example) a relation type and *v* is therefore a relation value.

> *A relation cannot contain duplicates. In practice, I cannot see how this can be the case ... it is impractical to scan every record* [sic!—a tuple is not a record] *whenever a field* [sic!—an attribute is not a field] *changes.*

Not true. Even today's SQL systems can deal with this requirement (via hashes or indexes), even with very large tables. (This is not to say there aren't better ways to do it.) And even if there is a performance hit in enforcing uniqueness, not enforcing it is worse; it's a suboptimization—it makes overall system performance much worse (I'm including people performance here, though I don't think it's necessary to do so in order for the argument to be valid).

> *[The] relational model ... does not contain any underlying [?] representation of relationships ... Alternate approaches ... allow knowledge to be expressed directly ... [and represent] the relationships within the database schema itself.*

I don't know what SW's background is, but this quote reminds me strongly of Santayana's observation to the effect that those who don't know history are doomed to repeat it. We've *tried* DBMSs in the past that "represent relationships directly." It was a terrible idea! In fact, I thought it had been completely debunked. But it looks as if all of the old arguments need to be dragged out and dusted off again. Perhaps I'll do that, one of these days.

By the way, I hope it's obvious that a relational database does represent relationships; furthermore, it represents them all in the same uniform way. Other databases don't.

> *[An] SQL query is an **assertion** about a relationship between tables ... It does not seem appropriate for application developers ... to be asserting the semantics of the data model.*

No, an SQL query is a set definition. The DBMS effectively returns all of the tuples from the database that satisfy the definition. That's all.

By the way, SQL is not unique in this regard! Even in IMS, for example, you could ask for (e.g.) the set of employees in a given department. The difference was that you had to do it one "tuple" at a time, in a loop. Even SQL does it better.

> *[Can] someone provide some pointers* [sic!] *to any clear comparisons of the pros and cons of the relational model versus the object/relationship* [sic] *model?*

In *Databases, Types, and the Relational Model: The Third Manifesto*, 3rd edition (Addison-Wesley, 2006), Hugh Darwen and I claim—and I think we demonstrate, too—that a true "object/relational" DBMS is *nothing more* and *nothing less* than a true **relational** DBMS. That is, the only sensible interpretation we can give to the term "object/relational model" is to say that it's just another term for "relational model." The trouble is, the term "relational" has been usurped (destroyed?) by SQL, so the industry needed a new marketing term for systems that implemented a little bit more of the relational model—hence the term "object/relational" DBMS. It's hype, really.

By the way, in case it's not obvious, I should add that today's O/R DBMSs are *not* "true O/R DBMSs," because they're not true relational DBMSs. In other words, they're not built on what I claim is the only sensible "O/R model."

Another reader wrote to Fabian Pascal, editor of the website http://www.dbdebunk.com, to ask:

> *How does [the fact that the storage level in a relational system is not itself relational square] with the fundamental principle of the relational model "All information in the database must be cast explicitly in terms of values in relations and in no other way"?*

In his reply, Fabian said in part: "[You are confusing] the logical and physical levels ... The relational model is purely *logical* and has absolutely nothing to do with storage!" This response is 100 percent correct, of course. Unfortunately, Fabian went on to say this:

> *What Date means* [here Fabian is referring to some writings of my own on the same subject] *is that* any *atomic values can be represented by a relational DBMS, no matter how complex the* representation *(e.g., domains can be relation-based).*

Gentle reader, please delete the word *atomic* here! It has no precise definition. What I do claim (and have claimed ever since about 1992, when I first realized that to talk in terms of this fuzzy "atomicity" concept was misleading and counterproductive) is that if *A* is some attribute of some relation, then *A* can be defined in terms of **absolutely any type** (or domain, if you prefer) whatsoever. So you can have attributes whose values are integers, attributes whose values are strings, attributes whose values are polygons, attributes whose values are arrays, attributes whose values are relations, ... and on and on. Of course, it's crucial (as Fabian suggests) that we make a distinction between values of any given type, on the one hand, and the representation of those values under the covers, on the other—but the idea that these two concepts should be kept rigidly apart isn't one that's peculiar to the relational world.

The last letter I want to discuss didn't include any relational misconceptions as such; however, it still makes sense to deal with it here. I'll refer to the writer as CC. CC asks some questions regarding the terminology of "relations" and "relationships" and related matters. To be specific, he or she asks whether "relations" in relational database theory are "equivalent" to "relations" in set theory (quotation marks as in the original letter). I replied as follows.

> *This question requires a rather lengthy answer! I think the overriding point is that **the relation construct as understood in relational database theory is based on, but is not identical to, its mathematical counterpart**. Here are some of the principal points of difference between the two:*
>
> - *RDB relations are typed—they emphasize, much more than mathematical relations do, the significance of the relation heading. Note: Here and throughout the remainder of these remarks I use RDB as a convenient abbreviation for "relational database." An explanation of the term "relation heading" can be found in many places (see, e.g., An Introduction to Database Systems).*

- *The heading of an RDB relation has no left-to-right ordering to its attributes; the heading of a mathematical relation does have such an ordering. (In fact, of course, the term* attribute *is never used in the RDB sense at all in a mathematical context.) In particular, RDB relations have* named *attributes, while mathematical relations don't. Those names in turn play a crucial role in the relational algebra, especially with respect to* relation type inference. *And to spell the point out, those attribute names are conceptually distinct from the underlying domain or type names.*

- *The primary emphasis in mathematics is on binary relations specifically. RDB relations, by contrast, are* n*-ary, where* n *can be 0, 1, 2, 3, ... Note the cases* n = 0 *and* n = 1 *in particular! The case* n = 0 *turns out to be crucially important for all kinds of fundamental reasons.*

- Relational algebra: *Very little work seems to have been done in mathematics or logic on general* n*-ary relational operators, presumably because of the emphasis already noted on binary relations specifically. For example, Patrick Suppes's book* Introduction to Logic *(Van Nostrand, 1957) defines an operator called* relative product: *If* r(A,B) *and* s(B,C) *are two binary relations, then their relative product* t(A,C) *is the binary relation consisting of all pairs* (a,c) *such that, for some* b, *the pair* (a,b) *appears in* r *and the pair* (b,c) *appears in* s. *In RDB terms, this is the projection over* (A,C) *of the join of* r *and* s *over* B.[9] *But notice how the operation is specifically defined to produce a binary relation as its result; the ternary relation that is the intermediate result—the join—is never explicitly mentioned.*

  Thus, although operators such as join (and all of the other operators of the relational algebra) are clearly applicable *to mathematical relations, it's fair to say that they were* first defined *(for the most part) in the context of relations in the RDB sense. Indeed, the theory of such operators (including the laws of expression transformation, the associated principles of optimization, etc.) can reasonably be regarded as a new branch of mathematics, and the theory in question is one that arose specifically as part of the development of the relational approach to the problem of database management.*

- Dependency theory: *To say it again, the emphasis in mathematics tends to be on binary relations specifically, whereas the emphasis in the relational model is on* n*-ary relations instead.* The entire field of what is now usually called dependency theory—*the large body of theorems and techniques concerning such matters as functional dependence, multivalued dependence, join dependence, higher normal forms, candidate keys, etc.*—is crucially dependent on this difference in emphasis. *For example, the concept of Boyce/Codd normal form (BCNF) is relevant only to relations of degree three or more, because all (well, almost all) relations of degree less than three are necessarily in BCNF. In fact, the entire field of dependency theory—like the theory of* n*-ary relational operators already mentioned above—can be regarded as a new branch of mathematics, one that was brought into being by the special requirements of a theory of data and a theory of* n*-ary relations (as opposed to a theory of binary relations merely).*

---

9. In fact, it's the relational *compose* operator (see, e.g., the *Third Manifesto* book).

- Relation values vs. relation variables: *Mathematics has no notion (so far as I know) of a relation variable—it deals with relation values only. RDB theory, by contrast, is crucially dependent on relation variables, at least if we ever want to update the database (that's meant to be a joke). In fact, the dependency theory mentioned under the previous bullet item only really makes sense if we are dealing with relation* variables *specifically—it would be pretty pointless if we had relation values only.*

- Integrity: *To generalize from the previous point, everything having to do with data integrity in general also makes sense only if we are dealing with relation variables specifically.*

- Views *and* view updating theory *are further aspects of "RDB relations" that depend on integrity theory and have no counterpart (so far as I know) in traditional mathematics.*

Back to CC's letter. The writer continues: "And then there comes the 'relationship' thing. Why do we need that?" Well, of course I don't think we do (I was never much of a fan of "entity/relationship modeling"). The term "relationship" was introduced, it seems to me, primarily by people without a mathematical background, or at least by people who prefer fuzzy concepts to precise ones. Though in fairness perhaps I should add that in Codd's original paper on the relational model, we do find the following:

> *[We] propose that users deal, not with relations which are domain-ordered, but with relationships which are their domain-unordered counterparts ... [Users] should interact with a relational model of the data consisting of a collection of time-varying relationships (rather than relations).*

In other words, the domains (and hence attributes) of a relation *were* originally considered to have a left-to-right ordering, but the relational model was concerned with "relationships" instead of relations. In almost all subsequent work, however, Codd used the term "relation" to mean what he originally called a relationship. Thus, I suppose it's at least possible (though I think it's a bit of a stretch) to lay the blame for "relationships" at Codd's door.

The Relational Model Is
Very Much Alive!

Though you wouldn't know it from today's SQL products

I recently had the (dis)pleasure of reading one of the most confused articles I've ever read on the subject of database technology—and I've read quite a few over the years, I can assure you. The article in question was titled "Great News, The Relational Model Is Dead!" No author's name is given, but the article does bear the notice *Copyright 1998, Whitemarsh Information Systems Corporation.*[1] The article's thesis is twofold (I'm quoting here):

- *The relational data model, as we all know it through its linguistic expression, the SQL language, has been "dramatically extended" by the ANSI H2 Technical Committee.*

- *The extensions in question have "taken the SQL data model clearly into the past, and then beyond."*

By the way, I like that "and then beyond." It reminds me of the possibly apocryphal story of the telescope manual that claimed that "The range of focus of your telescope is from fifteen feet to infinity *and beyond*" (quoted in Eli Maor, *To Infinity and Beyond*, Birkhäuser, 1987; my italics).

Some Specific Issues

When I first read the subject article—which, at the risk of being severely misunderstood, I will refer to hereinafter as "The Great News Article"—my initial reaction was to try to produce a blow-by-blow response to it. However, I quickly realized that such an endeavor would take far more time than I had available and would yield a result many times longer than The Great News Article itself. I therefore decided to limit myself to commenting (and commenting only *briefly*, in most cases) on a few specific points. Rest assured, though, that the points in question are quite typical—they haven't been unfairly singled out—and they represent only a fraction of the total number of incorrect assertions in the original article.

A record structure (in [SQL] terms, a table) ...

---

1. I was subsequently told the author was Michael M. Gorman.

Note the type *vs.* value *vs.* variable confusion here! A record structure is a type. An SQL table is (depending on context) either a value or a variable. There are huge logical differences among these concepts (see Chapter 6 in the present book). Confusion over such basic matters does not bode well for what's to come.

> *Relationships are explicit linguistic expressions that defines* [sic] *the basis for interrelating records from different types of record structures.*

To the extent I can construe this quote at all (which is, frankly, not very far), it's simply wrong, on several levels at once. Note in particular that the writer doesn't make it clear whether we're talking about relationship *types* or relationship *instances*. A relationship *type* corresponds **exactly** to a relation heading, in the conventional relational model sense. A relationship *instance* corresponds **exactly** to a tuple—i.e., a row—within such a relation, again in the conventional relational model sense. *Note:* Of course, the relation in question might be a derived one, i.e., one that is derived in some way from the base relations.

As I've remarked on many occasions and in many places, one of the virtues of the relational model is exactly that it allows us to make precise statements and give precise definitions, instead of relying on vague arm-waving statements like the one quoted above. As I've also remarked elsewhere, if we can't be precise in the computing field above all, we're surely lost.

> *Most of the DBMSs that support pointer-based relationships permit any reasonable quantity of different relationships between a given owner and sets of members.*

If this quote is meant to suggest that relational DBMSs *don't* support "any reasonable quantity of relationships" between things, well, that suggestion is flat wrong, of course. More to the point, compare what's involved in adding a *new* relationship to a pointer-based DBMS *vs.* a relational one: major upheaval (if it's even possible) in the pointer-based case, trivial in the relational case. Why? Because pointer-based systems mix logical and physical levels, while relational ones don't.[2]

> *If multiple relationships are needed between an owner record and a set of members [in a relational system] then there must be a different field within the member data record to represent each relationship. For example, there would have to be different fields for current, full-time, hi-achievers, part time, and retired employees. Such a technique generally makes for bad database design, however.*

Baloney. The EMP table contains a row for every employee, with EMP# as primary key. The CURRENT table contains a row for every current employee, with EMP# serving as both primary key and foreign key (the foreign key references the EMP table, of course). The FULL_TIME table contains a row for every full-time employee, with (again) EMP# as both primary key and foreign key ... And so on.

> *DBMSs that employ DBMS defined and controlled relationship mechanisms* [i.e., pointers] *... usually retrieve and traverse data much faster than ... DBMSs ... that are based on primary and foreign keys.*

---

2. At least in principle. Today's SQL systems do sometimes fail to distinguish these levels properly. Even so, they don't fail in this regard as much as pointer-based systems do.

You know, it's truly amazing (or depressing, depending on your point of view, or perhaps your psychological make-up) ... Codd stressed the distinction between logical *vs.* physical issues—or model *vs.* implementation issues, to be more precise—when he first introduced the relational model over 35 years ago, in 1969. Yet we *still* find remarks like this one in the literature! So let me spell out the true situation one more time. Let's agree for the sake of the discussion that pointers are a good—i.e., efficient—implementation mechanism for retrieving and traversing data.[3] *However, there's absolutely no reason why foreign-to-primary-key references shouldn't be implemented by pointers on the disk.* (I know they typically aren't implemented that way in today's SQL products, but that's a defect of those particular products, not a defect of relational systems in general. At least one system, the IBM Starburst prototype, does provide such a pointer-based implementation.)

To say it a different way: (1) *Implementing* references by pointers is very different from (2) *exposing* such pointers in the model. The fact that (1) might be a good idea doesn't imply that (2) is a good idea, and of course it categorically isn't. We *must* keep logical and physical concepts distinct, and not get confused over the two levels in our debates; we've learned the hard way (or some of us have, at least) what happens when this principle is violated.

> *Relationship operations [in pointer-based DBMSs] ... depend directly on whether ... member pointer arrays ... or next, prior, and owner pointers [are] stored in the member data records ...*

Quite right. Whatever happened to data independence?

> *While relational purists may assert that there is some great theoretic need for all this extra work and overhead, there are certainly no database or application compelling reasons to completely separate naturally existing data hierarchies into distinct relational tables.*

The author of The Great News Article would probably regard me as a "relational purist." But I think we need to be *pure*, not *purist!* Be that as it may, at least I do understand relational theory ... and therefore I know that (a) you don't *have* to separate "naturally existing data hierarchies into distinct relational tables," but also that (b) if you don't, you'll probably run into major problems further down the road. But it's your choice.

Also, I categorically reject disparaging remarks like the one at hand regarding theory. The cry that "if something is theoretical, it can't be practical" is heard all too often, usually from people who really ought to know better. Relational theory, to be specific, is not just "theory for its own sake"; rather, every detail of that theory has very solid practical applications. (Referring back to "your choice" in the previous paragraph: What is it that helps you make the *right* choice? Why, a good knowledge of relational theory, of course.)

By the way, exactly what it is that constitutes "all this extra work and overhead" in the relational case is far from clearly identified in The Great News Article.

---

3. Please don't infer that I think pointers are the *best* way of "retrieving and traversing data." They might not even be a *good* way. It all depends! But the whole point is that relational technology doesn't lock you in—you can use different implementation techniques in different contexts, as applicable and as appropriate.

> *The greatest change in the [SQL:1999] standard is that it no longer adheres to the ... relational data model.*

Actually this claim is correct as stated, but not for the reasons cited in The Great News Article. *Au contraire*, it's correct precisely because SQL:1999 has introduced pointers!—pointers, that is, that are visible to the user, and hence part of the model, not just part of the implementation. Oddly enough, however, The Great News Article has virtually nil to say on this—in my opinion, disastrous—extension.[4] Instead, it focuses on a series of SQL:1999 extensions that in fact aren't extensions to the relational model (as such) *at all:* array and row types, abstract data types, user-defined functions, computational completeness, and many others. It seems to me that if you're going to claim that something is an "extension" to the relational model, you really ought to know what the relational model *is* in the first place. But then, almost nobody does.

> *To say that these SQL:1999 extensions are mere "extended interpretations" of the relational data model is like saying that an intercontinental ballistic missile is merely an "extended interpretation" of a spear.*

See my previous comment. Also, I'd like to go on record as saying how much I deplore analogies like the one at hand; surely the author could make his or her point just as well—probably better—with some metaphor of a less military nature.

> *For the past 20 years, database designers and implementers have struggled with highly normalized databases that perform poorly. The only solution is to denormalize ...*

Well, *one* solution—not the only one—is to denormalize. But such denormalization, if it should prove necessary, should be done at the physical level, not at the logical level! Once again we see the writer's total confusion over these two levels.[5]

> *In short, we are returning to the past ... we will see the return of significant designer and analyst time for database design and redesigns.*

Now this quote I agree with!—though probably not for the reasons the writer has in mind (the problem, to say it again, is those user-visible pointers). *Why* on earth did the SQL committee—or anybody—think that such a "return to the past" might be a good idea?

---

4. For a discussion of just why it's so disastrous, see, e.g., my papers "Don't Mix Pointers and Relations!" and "Don't Mix Pointers and Relations—*Please!*", both in C. J. Date, *Relational Database Writings 1994–1997* (Addison-Wesley, 1998).

5. Actually we see some confusion on my part, too. By definition, normalization and denormalization are techniques that apply to design at the relational (i.e., logical) level, not the physical level. However, the reason for wanting to denormalize at the relational level is that the relational level maps so directly to the physical level in most of today's systems, implying that such denormalization has very direct effects on the performance of those systems. Strictly speaking, however, we shouldn't speak of denormalizing, as such, at the physical level at all, but rather of some analogous technique that applies to the design of stored files instead of relations.

Concluding Remarks

So much for a few specific comments on The Great News Article. If you'd like to understand those comments in more depth and/or gain a more extensive understanding of the true state of affairs regarding relational technology in general, I'd like to suggest you take a look at some of my own books on this subject. (I apologize for the inevitable "advertisements for myself" flavor in what follows, but it can't be helped.)

The obvious one to mention first is *An Introduction to Database Systems*, 8th edition (Addison-Wesley, 2004). This book is rather long (sorry about that), but it does include a very careful tutorial—as complete as I could make it—on the relational model specifically, as well as on numerous related topics such as optimization, SQL, transaction management, temporal data, inheritance, and so on.

For a gentler—i.e., less formal, albeit less exhaustive (or exhausting?)—treatment of the same kind of material, I suggest either Fabian Pascal's recent book *Practical Issues in Database Management: A Reference for the Thinking Practitioner* (Addison-Wesley, 2000) or my own more recent book *Database in Depth: Relational Theory for Practitioners* (O'Reilly Media Inc., 2005). And for a brief historical survey of the subject, I'd like to suggest my book *The Database Relational Model: A Retrospective Review and Analysis* (Addison-Wesley, 2001).

I'd like to conclude this short polemic by stating categorically my very strong opinion that—despite the several failures of the major vendors in their attempts to implement the relational model to date, despite the dreadful mess that is the SQL language, and despite numerous ill-informed attacks like those in The Great News Article—**the relational model is alive and well**. It's rock solid, and it isn't going to go away. One hundred years from now, when all the hype regarding pointers, and XML, and "objects," and "hypercubes" (and on and on) has long been forgotten, I expect DBMSs *still* to be based on Codd's relational model.

Technical Correspondence

Shortly after the original publication of the foregoing, I received the following letter (I'll refer to the writer as RS):

> I'm confused, both by the following assertion quoted in your article and the response. A little more background to the original assertion would have been helpful.

> > If multiple relationships are needed between an owner record and a set of members [in a relational system] then there must be a different field within the member data record to represent each relationship. For example, there would have to be different fields for current, full-time, hi-achievers, part time, and retired employees. Such a technique generally makes for bad database design, however.

You replied to this assertion as follows:

> Baloney. The EMP table contains a row for every employee, with EMP# as primary key. The CURRENT table contains a row for every current employee, with EMP# serving as both primary key and foreign key (the foreign key references the EMP table, of course). The FULL_TIME table contains a row for every full-time employee, with (again) EMP# as both primary key and foreign key ... And so on.

> [But] a full-time employee cannot also be part-time—and presumably both are current, not retired. And what has hi-achievement to do with either? Given the current information I would see these as two status fields. I can (vaguely) justify creating temp tables to assist queries at run time.

> On a more general point, I've felt for some time that the problem with relational databases is the language used. Both SQL and any GUI programming tool I've used has demanded explicit column joins on tables. Given that the data dictionary is exposed, we should be able to navigate the foreign key relationships from one table to another, in the same way we navigate hierarchical relationships in (UNIX or DOS) directory structures.

I responded to this letter as follows.

> RS raises two points. First, he or she wants "more background" in connection with a particular quote from the article "Great News, The Relational Model is Dead!" (and in connection with my response to that quote). Here's the original quote:

[Original quote and my response omitted]

> Frankly, I don't know that "more background" is all that helpful here. The assumption in the original quote seems to be that one would bundle all the properties of "current, full-time, hi-achievers, part time, and retired employees" into a single table. My response was simply that no database designer in his or her right mind would do anything of the kind. Instead, you would put common information in the EMP table, information specific to current employees in the CURRENT table, information specific to full-time employees in the FULL_TIME table, and so on, and then you would use the standard relational primary-key/foreign-key mechanism to interrelate those tables appropriately.

> RS's second point is that "The problem with relational databases is the language used ... SQL, [for example,] ... demands explicit column joins ... Given that the data dictionary is exposed, we should be able to navigate the foreign key relationships"—by which I assume from the context that the writer means we should be able to get the system to do the joins implicitly in our behalf.

Now, I have no problem with the idea of such implicit joins as such. However:

- *The issue is, of course, a psychological one merely, not a logical one. Also, it should be a trivial matter to build a front end component on top of SQL that provides the functionality that RS is suggesting.*

- *Any such front end must certainly permit the user to do explicit joins as well, because not all joins are based on "foreign key relationships." And even when they are, there is still the potential for ambiguity (think of bill-of-materials structures, which typically involve two distinct foreign keys involving the same referencing and referenced tables).*

- *I certainly wouldn't agree that lack of support for implicit joins is the problem with relational databases! The problem with relational databases is that nobody has ever seen one (in the commercial world, at any rate). We've all seen SQL databases, but SQL databases aren't relational databases. SQL itself suffers from all kinds of problems (of which nulls and duplicates are two of the worst), but the single biggest—indeed, the overriding—problem with SQL is that it doesn't support the relational model.*

■ ■ ■

What Do You Mean, "Post-Relational"?

[This product] is a relational database management system that literally redefines the meaning of relational.

—Advertisement for a commercial DBMS product

The December 1999 issue of *Database Trends* (Vol. 13, No. 12) included an article titled "The Changing Database Landscape," by Joe DeSantis. The author was identified as Director of Software Development at InterSystems Corporation, and that company in turn was described as "the leading provider of post-relational [*sic*] database technology for high performance transaction processing applications." In his article (hereinafter referred to as *the subject article*), the author claimed that "we are entering a new era of network-centric computing [that requires] a new kind of database technology: the so-called post-relational database."

I have two immediate knee-jerk reactions to this claim, one perhaps minor, the other much less so. The minor one has to do with one of my pet linguistic peeves!—the semantic overloading of the term *database*, which is apparently used here as a synonym for *database technology*. Elsewhere in the subject article, however (fairly ubiquitously, in fact), it's used to mean *DBMS* ... and on at least one occasion (possibly more than one) it's actually used to mean *database. Why* is the IT field so cavalier in its use of terminology? The problem, of course, is this: If we call (say) the DBMS a database, then what do we call the database?

Anyway—regardless of what you might think of the foregoing possibly rather trivial complaint—the second and more important issue is: What on earth does *post-relational* mean anyway? Is the concept defined anywhere? Is it "post"-relational in any sense other than the trivial and overblown one of marketing hype? Please understand that these are not idle questions; it's well known that *domains* and *relations*—the principal kinds of "data objects" provided by the relational model—are between them **necessary** and **sufficient** to represent absolutely any kind of data whatsoever at the logical level (i.e., we must have domains and relations, and we don't need anything else). So anybody proposing something that *isn't* relational—and I have to assume that whatever else it might be, "post-relational" certainly isn't relational—better have an extremely strong argument to buttress his or her rather radical position.

In fact, it appears from remarks elsewhere in the subject article that a "post-relational" DBMS might just be one that supports both a multi-dimensional view and a relational view of the same underlying database. If this hypothesis on my part is correct, then I have no problem with the concept, even if I don't much care for the name; we all know that multi-dimensional views can be useful for certain kinds of processing. However, the subject article seems to be confused over the all-important distinction between the logical and physical levels of the system. In particular, it seems to suggest that the data should be represented multi-dimensionally at both levels (since it doesn't properly distinguish between them), and how a relational view of that same data is supposed to be supported on top of that multi-dimensional representation is nowhere explained.

What About Object Technology?

To get back to the subject article's overall thesis: The author claims that "post-relational" technology, whatever that technology might consist of, is required because "relational ... technology is failing to scale up to today's business needs" (a point I want to come back to later). The author further claims that, by contrast, object technology:

- Is excellent at modeling complex data

- Can be extremely scalable

- Can simplify the development process and decrease time to market

and

- Is [able] to plug into the Internet (a fact that is "probably the most compelling reason for switching to object technology")

Despite these claimed advantages, the subject article nevertheless says that object technology is not "the answer to every enterprise computing need." Why not? Because (to quote further):

- Certain business functions ... may benefit from a centralized data repository. (*The relevance or otherwise of objects—or relations, come to that—to this particular point is unclear, at least to me.*)

- Even more important is the huge investment that most companies have already made in their relational systems ... Objects require a new and different approach to data modeling, and most businesses quail at the thought of retraining their technical staff.

I find it interesting, and telling, that the author doesn't seem to find or mention any *technical* problems with object technology! While objects might have their uses, serving as a basis on which to build databases in the classical sense of that term—i.e., databases that are intended for shared, general-purpose use—is certainly not one of them. See, e.g., my book *An Introduction to Database Systems*, 8th edition (Addison-Wesley, 2004), for arguments in support of this position.

Further Points Arising

Now, at this point you might be saying "Well, clearly, what we really need is *object/relational* technology." And the subject article does discuss this possibility, but only rather superficially (and indeed dismissively). I'll come back to this point a little later. First, however, I'd like to call out some other specific quotes from the subject article and comment on them briefly. So here goes:

[We] are entering an era of network-centric computing typified by web-enabled, distributed computing architectures. As with periods in the past, this new era requires a new kind of database technology: the so-called "post-relational" database [sic]. Such a database [sic] must be inherently scalable, support the use of object technology, and provide a migration path for legacy relational applications.

I agree that "such a database"—the writer means "such a DBMS," of course—must be scalable and must provide a migration path for "legacy" SQL applications (not at all the same thing as "legacy" *relational* applications, please observe!). "Support the use of object technology" is more problematic. In our book *Databases, Types, and the Relational Model: The Third Manifesto*, 3rd edition (Addison-Wesley, 2006), Hugh Darwen and I show that the only good idea of object technology is support for a proper type system. And the relational model doesn't need any extension in order to provide that support!—it's already there, in the form of *domains*. By contrast, object technology includes numerous bad ideas (object IDs being one of the worst), and we certainly don't want those in our future database systems.

The increasing sophistication of applications is creating a demand for complex data types.

I agree. Relational *domain* support does the necessary.

The processing overhead required by the two-dimensional [relational] data model ... makes relational technology unbearably slow for large scale applications.

First of all, I am *so tired* of hearing claims to the effect that "the relational model is two-dimensional," or that relations are "flat" (and so on and so forth), while real data is "multi-dimensional." Anyone who thinks such claims constitute a valid criticism of the relational model clearly doesn't understand that model, and in fact is seriously confused. Of course it's true that a relation looks flat when pictured in tabular form on paper. But a picture of a thing isn't the thing! If a relation has *n* columns, then *each row in that relation represents a point in* n-*dimensional space*—and the relation as a whole represents a set of such points. In other words, a relation of *n* columns is *n*-dimensional, not two-dimensional! **Let's all vow never to say "flat relations" ever again.**

Second, regarding the argument that "relational technology [is] ... slow": Well, I might agree for the sake of the argument that it's true that some, or even all, existing SQL products are slow. But it does *not* follow that relational products *must* be slow! There are *no* intrinsic reasons why such needs to be the case; to argue otherwise is to confuse logical and physical once again. In fact, there are good arguments to say that relational products could actually be faster than nonrelational products, if well designed. (A study of the history of the computing field is illuminating in this regard. Do you remember when people said Fortran was too slow?)

Note: In connection with both of the foregoing paragraphs, I'd like to draw your attention to a forthcoming book of mine titled *Go Faster!—The TransRelational™ Approach to DBMS Implementation* (to appear). This book describes an implementation technology for (among other things) the relational model that (a) is directly *n*-dimensional and (b) is capable of producing truly relational systems that are "blindingly fast."

Object databases avoid two of the big problems that plague their relational counterparts. First, object technology is excellent at modeling complex data. Second, object technology can be extremely scalable ... .

I think *database* means DBMS here. I also think *modeling* simply means *representing* ... "Modeling" is one of the most overworked words in the whole IT industry, so much so that it's almost lost what meaning it ever had (see Chapter 25 in the present book). More to the point: Object technology is no more "excellent" at representing complex data than the relational model is; in fact, it's worse, owing to its reliance on pointers (object IDs), which are both unnatural for most users and technically contraindicated for a variety of reasons. As for scalability, I'll discuss that issue later.

> *[Because] objects bundle and store related data together, an object database can be partitioned across multiple machines without separating information that is closely connected. Contrast this with the relational model, in which related pieces of data are scattered among many tables.*

Here *database* means *database* ... ! Much more to the point, this extract demonstrates a clear lack of understanding of the relational model and relational technology. First, "related pieces of data" might or might not be "scattered among many tables." Second, even if they are, it doesn't follow that "information that is closely connected" needs to be "separated" at the physical level. Logical *vs.* physical again.

> *Objects also shine when it comes to modeling complex data realistically. Natural data relationships are maintained as part of the data itself. Data behavior is also considered part of the data itself. Transactional performance is improved because an object-based application does not have to perform cumbersome and time-consuming joins of data residing in multiple disparate tables.*

Several comments on this extract:

- Objects categorically do not "shine" here (as already mentioned, pointers are the fly in the ointment, or at least the main one).

- "Natural data relationships are maintained as part of the data itself" in the relational case, too (of course!).

- "Data behavior is also considered part of the data itself"—the same is certainly true in the relational case for domains (the relational analog of object classes), and can be true for relations as well if desired.

- The suggestion that relational joins are "cumbersome," even if we accept it as valid for the sake of the argument, overlooks the possibility of using the relational view mechanism or a higher-level interface to hide such joins.

- The suggestion that joins are "time-consuming" betrays a lack of understanding of the relational model and relational technology. (To say that joins are "time-consuming" is a solecism. Joins are part of the model, and the model *per se* can't be said to be either fast or slow; only implementations can be said to possess any such quality. So we might reasonably say that Product X has a faster or slower implementation of a certain specific join than Product Y does, but that's about all.)

> *[The] richness of data types allowed by the object model can simplify the development process and decrease time to market.*

What "object model"? Where is such a thing defined? More to the point, the relational model certainly doesn't preclude "rich data type" support if that's what you want. Domains do the necessary.

The biggest obstacle to adopting object technology [meaning object *database* technology, presumably, from the context] *is the lack of an easy and non-disruptive path from relational to object systems.*

Nonsense. The biggest obstacle is that object technology suffers from major technical problems. For example, did you know that objects and a good model of type inheritance are fundamentally incompatible? See the book mentioned earlier, *Databases, Types, and the Relational Model: The Third Manifesto*, 3rd edition (Addison-Wesley, 2006), for detailed arguments in support of this position.

The object/relational databases [sic] *that are currently available miss out on many of the advantages of object technology, because they do not support features like inheritance and polymorphism.*

I'm not at all convinced that the "advantages" claimed for object technology in this quote do truly constitute strongpoints of today's object products. Certainly I can identify problems in connection with the topics mentioned, at least as implemented in certain of today's object products. Indeed, I would argue that it can't reasonably be claimed that "features like inheritance and polymorphism" confer any positive advantages at all until we know exactly what those features *are*—and, to date, a good (i.e., an abstract, formal, robust, rigorous, implementation-independent) *model* of those features, which would indeed explain exactly what they are, has been conspicuous primarily by its absence. Speaking from a purely personal point of view, I certainly wouldn't want to incorporate any such features into a product before I understood them! In fact, however, the same *Third Manifesto* book referred to a couple of times already does include a carefully designed proposal for such a model; if we can convince the IT world at large that the proposed model is indeed a good one, then—but only then—it might be desirable to implement it in commercial products, thereby achieving certain *well-understood* advantages, for certain *well-understood* costs.

As already mentioned, I'll come back later to the question of object/relational systems in general.

The database [sic] *that can meet the needs of enterprise-wide information processing in the new network-centric era must include a host of advanced features ... [Here are some of them]:*

- *A multidimensional data model, so that data is not constrained to rows and columns, joins are eliminated, and performance enhanced*

Comment: I categorically reject these claims! The data model *must* be relational, for reasons already discussed above. It's not a *constraint* if data is represented in terms of rows and columns! "Joins are eliminated": Confuses logical and physical again.[1] "Performance

---

1. Hugh Darwen has pointed out (in a private communication) that the claim that joins are eliminated, if taken literally, means no query ever contains an "and"!

enhanced": Confuses logical and physical *again* (performance is determined by the implementation, *not* by the model).

- *A complete spectrum of object capabilities, including inheritance, polymorphism, and relationships*

Comment: See my earlier comments regarding the good and bad features of object technology and the lack of a model to explain features like inheritance. "Relationships"? If the suggestion is that relational systems can't handle "relationships," well, that suggestion is clearly absurd. If the suggestion is that "relationships" and "entities" should be treated differently, well, that suggestion was thoroughly discredited over 30 years ago.

- *Support ... to ease the migration ... from a relational to an object model*

Comment: "A" relational model? No, there's only one, and it's *the* relational model.[2] "An" object model? Yes, here the indefinite article is correct; there's no such thing as an object model that's universally agreed on (in fact, if there are *n* systems supporting object technology, then there are probably at least *n* different "object models").

What About Object/Relational Technology?

By way of conclusion, let me come back as promised to the question of whether object/relational technology can serve as the desired "new kind of database technology." What of this possibility? The subject article has the following to say:

> *The traditional relational database vendors are trying to hang onto their customers by adding object-like capabilities to their products ... [The resulting so-called "object/relational" products all provide] a relational database engine, covered by a computational layer that assembles "objects" for presentation to the outside world ... [Just] as mapping objects into tables for SQL access adds processing overhead, so too does assembling objects from relational data.*

The better object/relational products *don't* just "cover" a relational engine with a computational layer in the manner suggested; instead, they've been redesigned and reimplemented from the ground up. As a consequence, they *don't* "add processing overhead" in the manner alleged.

> *[The] object/relational model does not address one of the major drawbacks of relational technology—that of scalability. Regardless of how it is packaged for the outside world, the data contained in an object/relational database is still ultimately stored as a set of two-dimensional tables.*

Regarding "two-dimensional tables," see earlier. Regarding the "lack of scalability" argument, we see here the same old logical *vs.* physical confusion yet again. "The data contained in an object/relational database" is certainly kept in tables from a *logical* point of view—as it must be, for reasons explained in detail in the book already mentioned several times above, *Databases, Types, and the Relational Model: The Third Manifesto*—but it isn't *physically stored*

---

2. See Chapter 19 in the present book.

in tables. Relational (or object/relational) systems can and should be at least as scalable as nonrelational systems. In fact, it's my belief that the largest databases in the world at the time of writing are all SQL databases specifically. (And I do mean databases here, of course, not DBMSs!)

> *There is a crying need for some sort of "unified data architecture" that simultaneously defines data as both objects and tables without adding computational layers.*

I agree, there *is* a "crying need" for unification—the right kind of unification, that is—and it's exactly one of the big objectives of *The Third Manifesto* to delineate just what such unification ought to look like. I strongly suspect, however, that what the subject article is calling for is *not* "the right kind of unification," but rather—not to put too fine a point on it—some kind of kludge.

Technical Correspondence

When the foregoing first appeared, I received a letter from UW, agreeing with the technical points I made, but taking me to task for wasting my time on one specific example of a much more general problem. Here are some edited extracts from UW's letter:

> *What I find unfortunate ... is that you have avoided the fundamental objection to [the original] article—which, as you surely recognize, is [the writer's] intent to deceive his audience in furtherance of his own pecuniary interests.*

> *I'm sure you also realize that [this] is but one isolated example, and that this problem is absolutely pervasive in the computer field ... Given this situation, responding to Mr. DeSantis is not enough ... I'd hope you further agree that your response in this case is not workable as a general approach to combat the problem. You have constructed a conscientious rebuttal of Mr. DeSantis's claims, as if the technical issues were actually the point. One might compare this to a situation where a malfunctioning database application is serving up the wrong phone numbers when names are looked up. Do you turn to alternative sources to find out the right number each time an error arises? Or do you fix the system?*

> *How [can we] fix our "system," in which the profit incentive leads most players to engage in deception—generally with impunity?*

> *As with all problems, the first step is to acknowledge it. Then what's needed is a wake-up call to confront it head-on. Specifically, I'd propose something like the following:*

> *"The pitiful state of today's most popular DBMS products—some 30 years after the foundations of relational database theory were laid out—is a situation that should be impossible in a world where business enterprises are serious about pursuing profit. That it is nevertheless our reality is largely explained by the fact that one of the software industry's most important products is not software at all, but illusion—illusion generated by the army of professional flatterers, seducers, entertainers, and deceivers whom software producers depend upon to sell their products.*

"Why is this army indispensable? In a word, because of the terrible credulousness of corporate America—or more specifically, the IT managers who uncritically swallow the sales pitches of the industry and spend their employers' money on shoddy products, with phony features, backed by misleading claims.

"Let us take a look at a typical example of the type of deceit that has propelled this terribly 'fast-paced' industry—whose glacial progress year after to year continues to cripple the productivity of DBMS users the world over with buggy and ill-designed products. [Now give a brief, nontechnical *description of the 'post-relational' article.]"*

I responded to this letter as follows.

I was delighted to see the letter from UW ... As that letter suggests, the problem is systemic, and it can't be fixed simply by attacking one particular manifestation of the problem (which is all I did in my original article, of course). However, perhaps I might be permitted a few words of additional explanation here.

First of all, I hope it's clear that my target was Mr. DeSantis's opinions *as stated in print, not Mr. DeSantis himself. [My] article was certainly not meant as any kind of* ad hominem *attack. I don't like* ad hominem *attacks, and I tried to stay within appropriate technical bounds.*

Second, UW goes on to say that "the fundamental objection to [the original] article ... is [the writer's] intent to deceive his audience in furtherance of his own pecuniary interests." Well, maybe so. However, I'm a charitable soul, and I wouldn't accuse Mr. DeSantis, or anybody else, of acting in bad faith unless and until the evidence of deliberate deceit was overwhelming. In other words, I would prefer to assume that Mr. DeSantis actually believed what he was saying in his original article. To me, therefore, the "fundamental objection" to that article was not deliberate deceit on the part of the author, but rather the vast lack of understanding it displayed of the very technology it was pontificating about, and the further implications of that lack of understanding (see below).

Anyway: Regardless of whether the problem is one of deliberate intent to deceive or merely one of ignorance, I agree with UW that it can't be solved on an instance-by-instance basis. In other words, I agree that attacking individual writings "is not workable as a general approach to combat the problem." However, I do think people learn from examples. In part, therefore, what I was trying to do in my critique of Mr. DeSantis's article was the following:

- *To suggest that many if not most articles in the trade press on this subject can be similarly deconstructed*

- *To demonstrate the huge confusion, lack of clear thinking, and lack of intellectual rigor to be found in such articles*

- *More generally, to encourage critical thinking on the part of readers*

- *Last but not least, to highlight a number of important technical facts from the field of database technology that don't seem to be nearly as widely understood and appreciated as they need to be*

For purposes of future reference, I'd like to repeat some of those "important technical facts" here:

- *The logical and physical levels of the system must be kept clearly apart (though they often aren't).*

- *Relations are* n-*dimensional, not two-dimensional.*

- *Domains and relations are together both necessary and sufficient to represent absolutely any kind of data whatsoever.*

- *The one good idea of object technology is support for a proper type system, and the relational model already includes such support.*

- *Object technology includes several* bad *ideas (object IDs are one of the worst). Objects and a good model of type inheritance are incompatible.*

- *Object technology is not a good basis on which to build databases in the classical sense of that term.*

And I'd like to add one more, one that I didn't call out explicitly in my original attack:

- *A true "object/relational" DBMS would be nothing more nor less than a true* relational *DBMS.*

Back to UW's letter. In that letter, UW asserts that the real problem is that "the profit incentive leads most players to engage in deception—generally with impunity." Clearly, UW might be right in this claim (my remarks in the foregoing notwithstanding). He or she therefore proposes a specific approach (a "wake-up call") for confronting the problem "head-on," involving the production of what might not unreasonably be called a polemical essay ... Myself, I don't really feel capable of writing an essay of the kind suggested, but I'd very much like to see such a thing, and I'd like to encourage UW (strongly!) to write one. Soon.

Some little time later, I received a letter from the author of the original "post-relational" article, Joe DeSantis himself. The bulk of that letter read as follows:

I have just seen your article responding to my article on "Post-relational" databases. I have only had a chance for a cursory glance but I wanted to let you know that I am flattered to be mentioned!

I have read the "Third Manifesto" and agree with many of the points it raises. I suspect that if I translated my article from "marketingese" to a more technical format we might find that we are closer in agreement on many points than you may currently suspect.

I became involved in the development of a "post-relational" database about four years ago because of my personal frustrations as an application developer: The then-current generation of "object databases" did not deliver any kind of real-world transaction semantics or performance, while the so-called relational databases have nothing to offer for people trying to develop object-oriented applications (as well as terrible performance).

Over the last four years we have built an "object/relational" system with the following characteristics:

- *All data can be viewed (and defined) "relationally": That is, all data in the system can be accessed/modified using standard SQL-92 syntax, which is as close to a "relational" system as exists within the commercial world.*

- *All data can be accessed (and modeled) through objects: That is, entities can be "instantiated" (brought into memory with appropriate locks and concurrency control), operated upon (including "methods" associated with such objects), and saved back into the database following transaction semantics that are useful for object-based applications (e.g., modify a set of objects programmatically and post them back into the database within a transaction). At the same time, operations (and queries) on sets of data can be performed via SQL statements in a natural and efficient way.*

  Object access to data opens the database up directly to application use by a variety of technologies—such as Java, XML, Web, Active-X—without the complexity of "middleware," object-relational wrappers, and transaction monitors that developers typically resort to.

  "Object modeling" simply means that we have defined a "mapping" from object concepts to relational concepts and vice versa. This is a fairly common practice among "object/relational" systems. Ours differs in that it is native and fairly complete. We also wiggle around the "Object ID" debate by allowing both Object IDs and traditional Foreign Key relations.

- *The "type" of data can be determined by the database developer by defining a "datatype" class. Strictly speaking, such a "class" is simply a "type-generator"—it provides a common place to define a set of constraints for a specific data type (and, in some cases, conversion information for external usage).*

- *Physical and Logical structures are completely divorced. One of the most interesting parts of our product is that the physical structure used for data can be defined independently of the logical structure. This means that the physical structure can be changed without application change—including storage within a third party RDBMS.*

I am quite happy with our results to date on this project, though, as always, there is a lot more to do. I am sure our product contains some number of theoretical inconsistencies as well, but this, unfortunately, is a necessary evil in the world of commercial software development.

I responded to this letter as follows.

I'm glad Mr. DeSantis thinks we might be in close agreement on many points. I'm sorry to have to say, however, that I don't think we're "in close agreement" on that point! Not only does his letter fail to respond to most of the issues I mentioned in my original article, it also raises some more questions ... For example, "allowing both object IDs and foreign keys" might indeed "wiggle around the object ID debate," but it doesn't solve the real problem!—unless, I suppose, you regard the real problem just as "how to wiggle around the debate." Note: For the record, the real problem (as I claimed in my original article) is that object IDs are both unnatural for most users and technically contraindicated for a variety of reasons. In particular, object IDs—and therefore objects per se—and a good model of type inheritance are fundamentally incompatible.

I don't want to get into a lot more detail here. Let me just observe that:

- *Mr. DeSantis doesn't really respond to the question that formed the title of my original article. However, he does strongly suggest that "post-relational" means the same as "object/relational"—and yet, in his original article, he was claiming that "post-relational" had to include* multidimensional *data support (not mentioned in his letter), and indeed was rather dismissive of "object/relational" support as such.*

- *InterSystems Corporation's own current ads (see, e.g., page 5 of* Intelligent Enterprise 3, No. 15, September 29th, 2000)—*which, by the way, describe the product in question as neither post-relational nor object/relational but as an "e-DBMS"!—claim "automatic generation of both object classes and relational tables from a single data definition." If this claim is meant to imply that some kind of equivalence exists between object classes and relational tables, then I would like to draw your attention to Chapter 9 of the book* Databases, Types, and the Relational Model: The Third Manifesto, *3rd edition, Addison-Wesley, 2006, by Hugh Darwen and myself. It is a large part of the technical argument of that chapter that such an equivalence does not exist (nor should one be forced).*

I'd like to mention another message I received on this same general subject of proposed "replacements" for relational technology. This one had to do primarily with XML, but it also raised some more general points. I'll refer to the author as MC; here is the reply I gave at the time (slightly edited here).

MC's message has to do with XML and databases. I don't have time to produce a detailed analysis or blow-by-blow response to all of the points MC raises, but I'd like to comment on a few items. Quotes are from MC's original.

> *Free market theory suggests that someone implementing the relational model properly would find some niche ... IF the relational model is all [you say] it is ... and there ARE enough serious players in the database marketplace to allow this to happen. What's wrong with this reasoning?*

*One of the greatest lies ever told is "Build a better mousetrap and the world will beat a path to your door" (Emerson?). It's not sufficient to have a better mousetrap. You have to have a good product version, and you have to package it appropriately, and you have to have good marketing, and you have to have good distribution ... **and you have to face up to the problem of vested interests**. Did you ever see the Alec Guinness movie* The Man in the White Suit? *It's all about vested interests suppressing a better mousetrap (i.e., a technically superior invention).*

In addition to all of the above, you need a target audience that is properly educated and properly informed and thus can properly appreciate what it is that you have to offer. Given the state of the IT world today, that target audience is close to nonexistent.

> *[The] relational model gives ONE scientific foundation ... but is that the last word on the subject?*

I'd never claim anything is "the last word." You never know what's round the next corner. But the scientific foundation the relational model provides is essentially logic, *which has served us supremely well in scientific endeavors for a very long time. (Parts of that foundation go back nearly 2500 years, to Aristotle.) Indeed, much of mathematics is founded on logic—so if there's something wrong with logic, well, I think we have much bigger problems than just database management ... But of course I don't think there is anything wrong with it. More to the point, I don't see any of the current fads (objects, OLAP, XML, etc.) offering anything by way of a foundation that's in the same league—I'm tempted to say the same universe—as that provided by the relational model.*

In other words: Anyone proposing a replacement for the relational model needs to demonstrate that what they're proposing does everything the relational model does (and perhaps more), and does it better. Not only is that a pretty tall order, but it also means that the person concerned needs to understand *the relational model, too, and such people are (sadly) few and far between.*

Net of all this: *We should stay with the relational model until such time as somebody does come along with that better replacement! And I certainly don't expect that to happen any time soon.*

Are you suggesting that [the people trying to build a formal foundation for XML] are wasting their time?

Probably. (Though I suppose it depends on what you mean by wasting time. If it gets them an income, I suppose they could claim they're not wasting their time. But if you mean "Will their efforts have a lasting and positive effect on human society?", I'm pretty sure the answer is no.)

[Why] not exploit a DBMS that understands XML's hierarchical format?

Many points could be made here. Here are some of them.

- *"Understand" is a very loaded word in this context. A proper relational system can certainly* deal *with hierarchic relationships. Moreover, it can deal with hierarchic relationships that are imposed dynamically on the data, not just ones that are hard-coded, as they are with XML.*

- *IBM's IMS product "understood" hierarchic relationships; indeed, in some respects, it did so better than XML does (at least there were some semantics and constraints attached to IMS's analog of XML's tags). And look what happened to IMS.*

- *The most general kind of relationship is many-to-many. Dealing with such relationships is trivial in a relational system but a nightmare in a hierarchic system.*

- *There is some theory available on which hierarchic systems might be constructed, but XML has demonstrably not been constructed on the basis of any such thing. Indeed, the (rhetorical?) question above regarding waste of time shows that the XML people are retroactively trying to impose such a theory on their efforts! I think it's better to have the theory first. Don't you think we should know what we're trying to do before doing it?*

- *If your job is to build a front end or DBMS extension that implements natural language support, or data mining, or OLAP, or temporal data, or a bunch of other things, what kind of system would you prefer to target?—one that's based on a clean, theoretically sound, robust, tried and true, rigorous, well-understood, formally defined logical foundation— or one that's based on something else?*

CHAPTER 22

■ ■ ■

A Database Disconnect

O what a tangled web we weave ...

—Sir Walter Scott

A recent issue of *DB2 Magazine* (Vol. 7, No. 4, 4th quarter 2002) included articles with titles as follows:

- "A SMARTer DB2" (by Sam S. Lightstone, Guy M. Lohman, Bryan F. Smith, Randy Horman, and Jim Teng)

- "Database Technology Leaps Ahead" (by Philip Gunning)

The first, which I'll call the SMART paper, was concerned with a project at IBM to make DB2 more self-managing; the second, which I'll call the Version 8 paper, was concerned with features added to IBM's DB2 Universal Database product in Version 8.1. Both were interesting and informative. However, I couldn't help noticing what might be called a slight *disconnect* between them. *Now read on ...*

The SMART Paper

Here's the opening paragraph from this paper:

> *Wouldn't it be nice if your database were as easy to manage as your refrigerator, automatically regulating its operation based on the settings of a couple of knobs and initiating maintenance operations that would periodically "defrost" your data without your intervention? That's the goal of the Self-Managing And Resource Tuning (SMART) project at IBM: to reduce the cost of tuning and managing DB2 Universal Database (UDB).*

Let me say immediately that I'm in complete agreement with the stated objective here. Today's DBMS products have become *much* too difficult to configure, tune, and maintain (DB2 isn't the only culprit in this regard), and the DBA's job has become virtually impossible. It's sad, really. Codd himself is on record (in his paper "Recent Investigations into Relational Data Base Systems," Proc. IFIP Congress, Stockholm, Sweden, 1974) as stating that one of his objectives in introducing the relational model was "to simplify the potentially formidable job of the database administrator." What would he have made of the present situation? (I used to

joke in seminars that before they were done, the folks at IBM would make DB2 just as complicated as IMS ever was. Well, I think they succeeded. Though, to say it again, it isn't just DB2;
SQL products in general are much too hard to administer.)

The paper goes on to describe a long list of aspects of the SMART project that should eventually help to make DB2 easier to administer. And it concludes as follows:

> *The many self-managing features you enjoy in DB2—and many more you may not even*
> *be aware of—are just the tip of the iceberg. In upcoming releases, look for many more*
> *SMART features in DB2 and increasingly autonomic behavior from many other IBM*
> *hardware and software products. Of course, the ultimate goal is to reduce what you see*
> *and take care of everything behind the scenes—just as your refrigerator does.*

I can only applaud.

The Version 8 Paper

Hats off, then, to the SMART project (*obviously* a good idea). But what's the reality? What
follows is a series of quotes from the Version 8 paper—many of them, though not all, taken
from a section entitled "Manageability" (!). I leave it to you to decide for yourself how many of
the features mentioned require human decisions and thus don't exactly conform to the SMART
objectives. Note the repeated use of words such as *option, select, can*, etc.

- *If you specify the COPY NO option [on online load]* ...

- *With the READ ACCESS option of the load command* ...

- *The new option LOCK WITH FORCE [on the load command]* ...

- *The ... load utility no longer requires the SET INTEGRITY statement* ...

- *The LOAD QUERY command now returns* ...

- *LOAD QUERY can [now] also query table states* ...

- *You can select a Load Wizard* ...

- *You can choose from a list of instances, databases, and tables* ...

- *Make your ... selection and the wizard presents you with an option dialog* ...

- *Select the options you want* ...

- *You can launch* almost *all the new wizards in this way* ... [my emphasis]

- *A new FLUSH PACKAGE CACHE SQL statement* ...

- *This capability will be useful in conjunction with the new online update of database*
  manager (DBM CFG) and database configuration (DB CFG) parameters ...

- *[You] can now specify the logpath through the MIRRORLOGPATH DB CFG parameter* ...
  This new parameter replaces the previous registry variable DB2NEWLOGPATH2 ...

- *The BLK_ON_LOG_DISK_FUL registry variable has been replaced with the new data-*
  base configuration parameter BLK_LOG_DSK_FUL [note the different spellings!] ...

- *Instead, DB2 will retry the write to log every five minutes, giving you time to resolve the disk full condition ...*

- *You no longer have to specify Coordinated Universal Time ... [Instead,] you can now specify local time ...*

- *The level of information is controlled by the new NOTIFYLEVEL database configuration parameter ...*

- *You can use the ... QUIESCE command [to specify a new database maintenance mode] ...*

- *The UNQUIESCE command takes the database out of [this new mode] ...*

- *REORGCHK now includes an ON SCHEMA option ...*

- *RUNSTATS can now collect [new statistics] ...*

- *RUNSTATS can now also accept [further new parameters] ...*

- *The new Health Monitor ... can raise alerts when predefined thresholds are exceeded ...*

- *Simply click on the Launch button to ... analyze [output from the new Health Monitor] ...*

- *You can create event monitors ...*

- *You can write customized queries containing event monitor data and produce reports ...*

- *[You] can now take snapshots through SQL table functions ...*

- *The new INSTEAD OF trigger extends the ability to update views ...*

- *New Informational Constraints [can be specified] ...*

- *New options on the ALTER TABLE statement (ENABLE QUERY OPTIMIZATION or DISABLE QUERY OPTIMIZATION) ...*

- *[Materialized Query Tables] are managed by the user ... and are distinguished by the MAINTAINED BY USER option of the CREATE SUMMARY TABLE statement ...*

- *You can now use block-based buffer pools ... [by specifying the] BLOCKSIZE parameter of the CREATE or ALTER BUFFERPOOL statement ...*

- *You can enable [the new feature for compression of nulls and defaults] ... by using the VALUE COMPRESSION and COMPRESS SYSTEM DEFAULT clause [sic] of the CREATE TABLE statement ...*

- *[Asynchronous I/O] must be enabled before ... installation ... Two ... parameters that you can tune are MINSERVERS and MAXSERVERS ...*

- *You can enable this new feature by setting MAX_CONNECTIONS greater than the value of MAX_COORDAGENTS ...*

- *The NOT LOGGED clause ... is now optional ...*

- *You can now create an index on a temporary table and run RUNSTATS ...*

- *[The new] type-2 indexes are required for online load, online reorganization, and MDC ...*

- *A table can't have a mix of type-1 and type-2 indexes ...*

- *Tables can be migrated to type-2 indexes via index reorganization ...*

- *New commands give you the capability to monitor ...*

- *Reorganization ... can [now] be paused and resumed ...*

- *Note that online table reorganization is only allowed on tables with type-2 indexes ...*

- *A new REORG INDEXES command ...*

- *You can set more than 50 configuration parameters online ...*

- *The GET DB CFG and GET DBM CFG commands now feature a SHOW DETAIL option ...*

- *A few of these parameters* can *be set to automatic ...* [my emphasis]

- *[You can] use the new BEGIN NEW STRIPE SET option of the ALTER TABLESPACE command ...*

- *These operations can be performed online ...*

- *A new INSPECT command ...*

- *A new command ... DB2SUPPORT ...*

- *The Database Analysis and Reporting Tool ... is now supported ... Use [it] to diagnose ... and repair ...*

And finally:

- *Through autonomic computing and the SMART initiative, IBM has made DB2 ... easier to operate and manage ...*

What do you think?

Conclusion

Further comment seems superfluous.

PART 6

■ ■ ■

Subtyping and Inheritance

This part of the book contains just two chapters. Chapter 23 considers the surprisingly controversial question of whether a circle is an ellipse. Chapter 24 reports on an investigation into the *Liskov Substitution Principle*.

Is a Circle an Ellipse?

Yes, of course it is (?)

Common sense and mathematics, which certainly don't always agree with each other, do at least agree in regarding a circle as a special case of an ellipse—a state of affairs that leaves the object community out in the cold, somewhat, since that community seems to think for the most part that a circle is not an ellipse at all. In what follows, I argue that any approach that adopts this latter position is at least *prima facie* less than satisfactory; I also sketch the details of a type inheritance model in which circles certainly are ellipses, and I further suggest that the IT community at large might do well to consider that model as a serious candidate for a "good" model of inheritance.

Preamble

I propose to examine the surprisingly controversial topic of type inheritance. Now, the basic idea of type inheritance does seem pretty straightforward, at least at first sight; after all, we frequently encounter situations in which all values in some given set of values have certain properties in common, while some but not all of those values additionally have special properties of their own. For example, all ellipses have an area, while some ellipses—specifically, those that happen to be circles—have a radius as well. On the face of it, therefore, it does seem reasonable to say that we have two **types,** ELLIPSE and CIRCLE, such that all properties of the former are properties of the latter, but the latter has properties of its own that don't apply to the former. To use the jargon, we say that ELLIPSE and CIRCLE are **supertype** and **subtype,** respectively, and we say that the subtype **inherits** properties from the supertype.

Before I go any further, let me be a little more precise regarding this example, since I intend to appeal to it repeatedly in what follows. In the real world, every ellipse has a "major semiaxis" of length a and a "minor semiaxis" of length b (and we can assume without loss of generality that $a \geq b$). A circle, then, is precisely an ellipse for which $a = b$ (for a circle, in fact, the two semi-axes coincide in the radius). In the real world, therefore, there can surely be no argument that a circle categorically *is* an ellipse—or, more precisely, a circle is a *special case* of an ellipse.

Not everyone agrees with the foregoing, however. In fact, arguments have raged for years in the literature (especially the object literature) over exactly the ellipses-and-circles example just quoted. For example, in Section 23.4.3.1 of his book *The C++ Programming Language,* 3rd edition (Addison-Wesley, 1997), page 703, Bjarne Stroustrup has this to say:

For example, in mathematics a circle is a kind of an ellipse, but in most programs a circle should not be derived from an ellipse or an ellipse derived from a circle. The often-heard arguments "because that's the way it is in mathematics" and "because the representation of a circle is a subset of that of an ellipse" are not conclusive and most often wrong. This is because for most programs, the key property of a circle is that it has a center and a fixed distance to its perimeter. All behavior of a circle (all operations) must maintain this property (invariant; [here Stroustrup gives a reference to Section 24.3.7.1 of his book, which explains the concept of invariants]*). On the other hand, an ellipse is characterized by two focal points that in many programs can be changed independently of each other. If those focal points coincide, the ellipse looks like a circle, but it is not a circle because its operations do not preserve the circle invariant. In most systems, this difference will be reflected by having a circle and an ellipse provide sets of operations that are not subsets of each other.*

The foregoing is the whole of one paragraph from Stroustrup's book, quoted more or less *verbatim,* except that I've deliberately omitted the opening sentence. I want to come back and consider that opening sentence later.

Now, I must immediately make it clear that Stroustrup is not alone in holding such opinions. For example, in an article by James Rumbaugh titled "A Matter of Intent: How to Define Subclasses" (*Journal of Object-Oriented Programming,* September 1996), we find the following:

Is SQUARE a subclass of RECTANGLE? ... Stretching the x-dimension of a rectangle is a perfectly reasonable thing to do. But if you do it to a square, then the object is no longer a square. This is not necessarily a bad thing conceptually. When you stretch a square you do *get a rectangle ... But ... most object-oriented languages do not want objects to change class ... [This] suggests [a] design principle for classification systems:* A subclass should not be defined by constraining a superclass.

Of course, Rumbaugh is talking here about squares and rectangles instead of circles and ellipses, but the general point is the same. Perhaps more to the point, he's also talking about *classes* rather than *types.* For the purposes of this discussion, I take these terms to be synonymous—though not everybody agrees with this position, either.[1] Be that as it may, I therefore take a subclass to be the same thing as a subtype and a superclass to be the same thing as a supertype.

Here are some further publications that seem to agree with the position articulated in the Stroustrup and Rumbaugh quotes:

---

1. In this connection, you might like to meditate on the following remarks (they're taken from Elisa Bertino and Lorenzo Martino, *Object-Oriented Database Systems: Concepts and Architectures,* Addison-Wesley, 1993): "Object-oriented systems can be classified into two main categories—systems supporting the notion of *class* and those supporting the notion of *type* ... [Although] there are no clear lines of demarcation between them, the two concepts are fundamentally different" (!). *Note:* These remarks are considered further in Chapter 4 of the present book.

- A "technical correspondence" item by Kenneth Baclawski and Bipin Indurkhya titled "The Notion of Inheritance in Object-Oriented Programming" (*CACM 37*, No. 9, September 1994). Here's a quote: "[In other approaches,] it is taken for granted that CIRCLE is a subtype of ELLIPSE. A hierarchy in which ELLIPSE is a subtype of CIRCLE is, therefore, considered an aberration ('nonstandard') ... [But we] would like to affirm a stronger point of view in which there are no 'standard' conceptual hierarchies." According to Baclawski and Indurkhya, therefore, we can't simply claim as I did earlier that CIRCLE just *is* a subtype of ELLIPSE. *Note:* I've set the type names CIRCLE and ELLIPSE in the quote in uppercase for clarity (they're in lowercase in the original).

- A paper by Nelson Mattos and Linda G. DeMichiel titled "Recent Design Trade-Offs in SQL3" (*ACM SIGMOD Record 23*, No. 4, December 1994; as you probably know, "SQL3" was the working title for what subsequently became SQL:1999, the version of the SQL standard that was current when this chapter was first written). Again, here's a quote: "[The] most appropriate [approach] is to not permit specialization via constraints" (see the next bullet item below). In essence, what this quote means is that we shouldn't—and indeed in SQL we *can't*—define type CIRCLE to be a "specialization" of type ELLIPSE such that an ellipse is in fact a circle if and only if it satisfies the constraint $a = b$.

- A tutorial by Stanley B. Zdonik and David Maier titled "Fundamentals of Object-Oriented Databases" (in Zdonik and Maier, eds., *Readings in Object-Oriented Database Systems*, Morgan Kaufmann, 1990). Actually, this tutorial isn't 100 percent clear on the matter at hand, but if it doesn't actually adopt the "circles aren't ellipses" position, it certainly comes very close to doing so. To be specific, it first defines something it calls *specialization via constraints*, thus: "*Specialization via constraints* happens whenever the following is permitted:

```
B subtype_of A and T subtype_of S and
f(...b:T,...) returns r:R in Ops(B) and
f(...b:S,...) returns r:R in Ops(A)
```

That is, specialization via constraints occurs whenever the operation redefinition on a subtype constrains one of the arguments to be from a smaller value set than the corresponding operation on the supertype."

Now, the implications of this definition of "specialization via constraints" for the circles and ellipses controversy in particular might not be very clear to you (they certainly aren't to me), but perhaps it doesn't matter, because it's also not clear as to whether Zdonik and Maier want to adopt the concept or not. They do, however, suggest that the concept implies that if we assign a circle value to an ellipse variable, we can't subsequently assign a value to that variable that's "just an ellipse" and not a circle (?)—and this state of affairs certainly has *something* to do with the question of whether a circle is an ellipse.

To repeat, therefore, Stroustrup is not alone in arguing in favor of the position that circles aren't ellipses. For definiteness, however, I want to focus in the rest of this chapter on Stroustrup's argument specifically. Stroustrup is well known and widely respected as the inventor of the C++ language, and his views thus deserve the courtesy of careful attention. But I want to make it as clear as I possibly can that what follows is not meant as any kind of *ad hominem* attack. Nor is it meant as an attack on the C++ language specifically. Rather, I just want to use C++—or the quote from Stroustrup's book on C++, rather—as a convenient hook off which to hang my argument. That argument, of course, is that any approach to inheritance in which "a circle is not an ellipse" is *fundamentally flawed*. This criticism apparently does apply to the C++ approach in particular, but it's very far from being limited to C++ alone.

A Little Background

Let me interrupt myself at this point to say something about the history of this chapter. First of all, I sent a copy of the first draft to Dr. Stroustrup himself, asking if he would like to exercise any "right to reply." I was hoping for either (a) a response that agreed with my position or (b) more likely, one that showed me the error of my ways by providing me with—or providing me with a reference to—a cogent defense of the position that a circle *isn't* an ellipse. Unfortunately, however, I got neither. Instead, Dr. Stroustrup took the draft as an attack on the C++ language specifically, and responded on that basis.[2]

Well, he was right, in a way: Although I never intended to attack C++ specifically—I was merely using C++ as an important example of what I wanted to criticize—it's true that all of my individual comments were based on the quote from his own C++ book. It's also true, with hindsight, that some of those comments might have been seen as being gratuitously offensive. So the chapter you're reading now has been revised somewhat since that earlier draft: I've added some quotes from other (non-C++) sources, I've toned down some of my criticisms, I've added some new points, I've changed the emphasis here and there, and I've made certain other cosmetic changes.

That said, however, I must also make it clear that the general thrust of the chapter remains as it was in the original draft. I still believe the overall message is valid—in fact, I feel this more strongly than I did before, since I never saw a convincing counterargument—and I think that message is worth parading before a wider audience. What's more, the chapter still consists in large part of a detailed examination of the quote from Stroustrup's book, because I believe that's a valid and effective way of bringing the issues to the fore and exploring them. But, to say it again, the chapter is not meant to be *ad hominem*, nor is it meant as an attack on C++ specifically.

The Main Argument

Back to the main argument. As already indicated, it's my position that a circle categorically is an ellipse in the real world—to be specific, it's an ellipse in which the two semiaxes coincide in the radius (i.e., it's an ellipse for which $a = b$). In my opinion, therefore, any "model" of inheritance in which type CIRCLE is not considered to be a subtype of type ELLIPSE can hardly be said to be a good model of reality.

---

2. I replied to that response too, and we wound up exchanging several letters on the subject.

Note: I put "model" in quotation marks in the foregoing paragraph precisely because the "model" in question fails to model reality accurately. And I think it's clear that any system that's based on such a "model" is likely to exhibit very strange behavior—meaning in particular that it's likely to produce *wrong answers*. And this criticism is demonstrably valid; in fact, it applies to SQL! The type inheritance portions of SQL certainly can, and certainly do, produce wrong answers; for example, they can and do produce "circles" with $a \neq b$. For further discussion and analysis of this bizarre "feature" of the SQL standard, see Appendix H of the book *Databases, Types, and the Relational Model: The Third Manifesto*, 3rd edition, by C. J. Date and Hugh Darwen (Addison-Wesley, 2006).

Now, in the book just mentioned, Darwen and I have proposed and defined in detail—and sketched some implementation approaches for—a model of inheritance to which the foregoing criticism doesn't apply; in our model, in other words, a circle most definitely is an ellipse. However, I don't want to describe that model in detail here (though I'll give a brief sketch of it later); rather, what I do want to do is examine the Stroustrup quote piece by piece to see if we can pin down just where our ideas differ, and also why they differ, where possible.

Without further ado, therefore, let me begin that piece-by-piece examination. I've numbered the sentences for purposes of subsequent reference.

> **1.** *For example, in mathematics a circle is a kind of an ellipse, but in most programs a circle should not be derived from an ellipse or an ellipse derived from a circle.*

Sentence Number 1 is, of course, essentially just a summary statement of an overall position. The wording is not very precise, however. To start with, I would delete the phrase "a kind of," or at least replace the word "kind" by the phrase "special case." More important, it's not at all clear—at least, not to me—what it might mean to "derive" a circle from an ellipse.[3] Circles and ellipses are just **values;** like all values, they simply *exist*, they're not "derived" from *anything*. Of course, it's true that a value that happens to be an ellipse (value) might happen to be a circle (value) as well, but I don't think it makes any sense in such a case to say that the circle in question is somehow "derived" from the ellipse in question. In other words, it's my position that if *E* is the set of all ellipses (= all ellipse *values*) and *C* is the set of all circles (= all circle *values*), then *C* is a proper subset of *E* (equivalently, every circle is an ellipse, but some ellipses aren't circles). To say it again, no value in *C* is "derived" from any value in *E* (though in some cases the very same value does exist in both *C* and *E*).

Aside: Perhaps I should say a little more on this business of "deriving values." It's true that we do sometimes talk, loosely, of values being "derived" according to some formula, meaning they're produced as the result of evaluating some expression. For example, we might say that an employee's pay *p* is "derived" by multiplying that employee's hourly wage *w* by the number of hours worked *n*. Clearly, if *w* is 20 and *n* is 40, then *p* is 800 (meaning 800 US dollars, say). But that value 800 already *exists*—it isn't *created* by the "derivation" process. Rather, what that "derivation" process does is (in effect) *pin down* or *select* the particular pay value, out of the set

---

3. In the course of my correspondence with Dr. Stroustrup, I learned that, in C++, "deriving a circle from an ellipse" means "defining type CIRCLE in terms of type ELLIPSE," and most of my comments on Sentence Number 1 are thus based on a misunderstanding on my part. I've left those comments essentially unchanged, however, because I think the points I'm trying to make are still valid and still important (especially since they have to do, in part, with the differences between a type *per se*, on the one hand, and values and variables of the type in question, on the other).

of all possible pay values, that happens to represent the pay for that particular employee. *End of aside.*

Now, some clue as to what Sentence Number 1 might mean when it talks of a circle being "derived" from an ellipse might perhaps be gleaned from its reference to the opposite possibility ("an ellipse [being] derived from a circle"). By definition, no circle—no circle *value,* that is—is "just an ellipse" (where by the term "just an ellipse" I mean an ellipse that's not a circle). On the face of it, therefore, to think of an ellipse as being somehow "derived" from a circle doesn't seem to make any sense at all. **Unless**—and could this be the nub of the matter?—we allow a circle (which has $a = b$, remember) to be somehow **updated** to produce a result with $a > b$ ... *Then* we might perhaps talk, albeit very loosely, of the ellipse that's the output from that update being "derived" from the circle that's the input to that update.

But when we update something, the thing we update is, by definition, a **variable**. (To be updatable is to be a variable and *vice versa.* Certainly we can't update a *value!* The one thing we can't do to *any* value is change it—because if we could, then after the change it wouldn't be that value any more.) In other words, we might have a *variable* that currently contains a circle value (with $a = b$), and we might then update that variable—that is, we might replace the current value by another value. And if the value of the variable after the update has $a > b$, then we might say that the type of the variable was CIRCLE before the update but ELLIPSE after it. And then, as I indicated previously, we might talk, *very* loosely, of the ellipse value that's the output from the update being "derived" from the circle value that's the input to the update.

Now, I don't know if the foregoing text captures the essence of what Sentence Number 1 is getting at,[4] but it does seem plausible, as a hypothesis, to think it does. But observe how much clearer it makes things if we talk explicitly in terms of values and variables! I find it very telling indeed that Sentence Number 1 doesn't mention values or variables at all. And yet the distinction between values and variables is one of the great **logical differences!** (See Part II of the present book—in particular, see Chapter 6—for further elaboration of this useful and important concept.) Sadly, it's also one that's very much overlooked—I'm tempted to say totally ignored—in the object world, a point I'll come back to later.

    2. The often-heard arguments "because that's the way it is in mathematics" and "because the representation of a circle is a subset of that of an ellipse" are not conclusive and most often wrong.

The two "often-heard arguments" quoted here are very different in kind. The first ("because that's the way it is in mathematics") I would have rephrased as *because that's the way it is in the real world.* If someone wants to propose a world in which circles aren't ellipses, then all I can say is that the person in question must be using the terms *circle* and *ellipse* in ways that fly in the face of their conventionally accepted meanings. In other words, I find this first argument, far from being inconclusive and wrong, both conclusive and right.

The second argument ("because the representation of a circle is a subset of that of an ellipse") is rather different, however. In fact, it demonstrates a confusion—again one that seems to be all too common in the object world—between *type* and *representation.* Type *vs.* representation is another of the great logical differences! In database contexts, at least (and, I would argue, in other contexts too, desirably), we try to distinguish carefully between a **type,** on the one hand, and the **representation** of values of that type inside the system, on the other.

---

4. It doesn't. See the previous footnote.

(Incidentally, it's precisely that distinction that makes *data independence* possible in database systems.) *Type* is a model issue; *representation* is an implementation issue (and model *vs.* implementation is yet another of the great logical differences). The second "often-heard argument" thus invokes an *implementation* issue to bolster a *model* conclusion, and I therefore agree that it's wrong (and *a fortiori* inconclusive)—though I suspect that Stroustrup and I have very different reasons for our common position on this point.[5]

3. *This is because for most programs, the key property of a circle is that it has a center and a fixed distance to its perimeter.*

Two comments:

a. The sentence claims that a certain property of circles is relevant "for most programs" (and hence, presumably, irrelevant for certain other programs). But the property in question is *the defining property* for a circle!—it's *intrinsic* to all circles. It thus seems a little strange to suggest that it might be irrelevant for some programs. I mean, the suggestion seems to be that some programs that deal with circles are not interested in circles as circles (?).

b. "[The] key property of a circle is that it has a center and a fixed distance to its perimeter." I would have said, rather, that every point on the perimeter is at the *same* fixed distance from the point that's the center; by definition, a circle is the set of all points in the plane that are at a fixed distance (the radius) from a fixed point (the center). Anyway, regardless of whether you prefer my definition of a circle as just given or Sentence Number 3's definition of a circle's "key property," note carefully that the construct thereby defined is a circle *value* specifically and not a circle *variable* (observe the phrase "fixed distance" in both definitions).

4. *All behavior of a circle (all operations) must maintain this property (invariant; [here Stroustrup gives a reference to Section 24.3.7.1 of his book, which explains the concept of invariants]).*

And here "circle" clearly means a circle *variable*, and we run smack into the values *vs.* variables confusion. Let me explain.

---

5. In fact, the analysis in this paragraph could be claimed to be a trifle charitable to Stroustrup's argument. He suggests that "the representation of a circle is a subset of that of an ellipse." But he doesn't say what those representations are!—and so we can hardly conclude that either "is a subset of" the other. However, we can probably guess from remarks elsewhere in the extract quoted that "the representation of a circle" involves the circle's center, while "that of an ellipse" involves the ellipse's focal points. But the former is *not* "a subset of" the latter!—the former involves one concept (the center), while the latter involves a quite different concept (the focal points). Just because the focal points for a circle happen to coincide in the center doesn't mean the center *is* a focal point (if it were, which one would it be?). The fact is that the circle representation involves a component—the center—that the ellipse representation doesn't involve at all.

a. Yet another of the great logical differences is that between *read-only* and *update operations*. A read-only operation is one that merely "reads" the values of its operands and never tries to update any of those operands; an update operation is one that does update at least one of its operands. It follows that read-only operations apply to values (in particular, they apply, harmlessly, to the values that happen to be the current values of variables); update operations, by contrast, apply very specifically to *variables* (since variables are—to say it again—the only things that can be updated, by definition).[6]

b. "All operations on circles must maintain the property that all points on the perimeter are at the same distance from the center" (paraphrasing the original Sentence Number 4 considerably). Well, read-only operations maintain this property trivially, since they never change anything. So we must be talking about update operations, and therefore we must be talking about variables (circle variables, that is). What the sentence is saying, in other words, is that it's OK to have an update operation that changes the radius of a circle variable (thereby implicitly changing the location of every point on the perimeter of that circle variable), but it's *not* OK to have one that updates some but not all of the points on the perimeter of that circle variable. Note again how much clearer it is to talk explicitly in terms of circle values and circle variables, instead of in terms of just plain old unqualified circles, which might be either.

5. *On the other hand, an ellipse is characterized by two focal points that in many programs can be changed independently of each other.*

Again two comments:

a. "An ellipse is characterized by two focal points": I would have said rather that an ellipse can be *defined* as the set of all points in the plane that are such that the sum of their distances from two fixed points (the focal points or *foci*) is fixed in turn. Hence, every ellipse has two focal points. (For a circle, of course, the two focal points coincide in the center, as we already know.)

b. "[In] many programs, [the focal points] can be changed independently": OK, so here, clearly, we're talking about ellipse *variables*. "Changing one of the focal points of an ellipse" is shorthand for "updating an ellipse variable such that (a) the ellipse value in that variable before the update, and (b) the ellipse value in that variable after the update, differ in one of their focal points."

6. *If those focal points coincide, the ellipse looks like a circle, but it is not a circle because its operations do not preserve the circle invariant.*

Allow me to expand, rephrase, and—with all due respect—*correct* this sentence. If the focal points of an ellipse value coincide, then that ellipse value is a circle value. If an ellipse variable contains such an ellipse value, then in fact it contains a circle value. However, that variable can of course be updated. If, after such an update, the focal points of the ellipse value that is now the current value in that ellipse variable *don't* coincide, then the ellipse variable

---

6. Of course, if some given operand to an update operation is never updated, the operation in question can be regarded as a read-only operation so far as that particular operand is concerned.

now contains an ellipse value that *isn't* a circle value. On the other hand, if, after such an update, the focal points of the value that is now the current value in that ellipse variable *do* coincide, then the ellipse variable now contains an ellipse value that *is* a circle value.

In other words: Some ellipse values are circle values. Every circle value is an ellipse value. Any ellipse variable can contain a circle value (it can also contain "just an ellipse value"). However, a circle variable must contain a circle value specifically (it can't possibly contain "just an ellipse value," because such an ellipse value is *not* a circle value).

Now, I'd be the first to agree that the wording in the previous two paragraphs is intolerably clumsy. It is, however, accurate (and in computing contexts above all others, surely, accuracy is paramount). And distinguishing properly between values and variables is what lets us achieve that accuracy. In the object world, by contrast, people talk in terms, not of values and variables, but of *objects* ... and (it seems to me) therein lies the problem. What *is* an object? Is it a value? Is it a variable? Is it both? Is it something else entirely?[7]

> **7.** *In most systems, this difference will be reflected by having a circle and an ellipse provide sets of operations that are not subsets of each other.*

To begin with, I can't resist pointing out that if "a circle and an ellipse" were to provide "sets of operations" that *were* "subsets of each other," then they'd both be providing exactly the same set of operations! In other words, at least one of those sets must *not* be a subset of the other. But presumably what Sentence Number 7 means is that, in particular, type CIRCLE is not a subtype of type ELLIPSE—at least "in most systems" (?)—and so type ELLIPSE does have some associated operations that type CIRCLE doesn't (as well as type CIRCLE having some associated operations that type ELLIPSE doesn't).

Notice, by the way, that the phrase "a circle and an ellipse" in Sentence Number 7 really means "*type* CIRCLE and *type* ELLIPSE" (operations are associated with types, not with individual values or individual variables). So we see that *within a single paragraph*, the very same word *circle* is used to mean (a) sometimes a circle *value*, (b) sometimes a circle *variable*, and (c) sometimes a circle *type* (and analogously for the word *ellipse*, of course). In fact, type *vs.* "object" (meaning a value? or a variable?) is *another* of the great logical differences, and again it's one that's very often muddled in the literature. No wonder this subject is so confusing, when the literature itself is not only confusing but (apparently) confused as well.

Finally, note the failure in Sentence Number 7 (and throughout the paragraph, in fact) to distinguish between read-only and update operations: another source of confusion, and another reason why (in my opinion) the "model" of inheritance that's being advocated is inadequate as a model of reality.

Software Engineering *vs.* Conceptual Modeling?

Let me now say in fairness that it probably wasn't Stroustrup's goal to advocate an inheritance model that could serve as "a good model of reality." The paragraph I've been examining is taken from Chapter 23 of his book. The title of that chapter is "Development and Design," and it's concerned primarily with the software production process "at a relatively high level" (slightly

---

7. These questions are, of course, rhetorical (somewhat). In any given system, it must presumably be possible to answer them. But the problem is, they have *different* answers in different systems! Certainly there's no consensus. And that's why there's confusion (or, at least, that's one reason why there's confusion).

paraphrased from the original text). Section 23.4.3.1, from which the paragraph I've been examining is taken, is titled "Step 1: Find Classes," and the opening sentence to that paragraph, which I deliberately omitted earlier, runs as follows:

> *Note that the classification should be of aspects of the concepts that we model in our system, rather than aspects that may be valid in other areas.*

The term *classification* here refers to the matter of choosing supertypes and subtypes; thus, what the sentence is saying is that the way we choose supertypes and subtypes depends on what "our system" is meant to do, not on "aspects that may be valid in other areas." In other words, just because circles are ellipses "in other areas," it doesn't necessarily follow that we have to treat them that way in "our system."

The point is perhaps a valid one, in some ways. However, the fact remains that circles *are* ellipses in reality; if we choose not to regard them in that way in "our system," then certainly the things that "our system" calls circles and ellipses differ in some rather important ways from circles and ellipses in the real world. Indeed, they simply *aren't* circles and ellipses (by definition), at least as those constructs are conventionally defined and understood. Of course, you can call an ellipse with $a > b$ a "circle" if you want to—I might even be persuaded to defend your right to do so, though I'd have to question your wisdom if you actually did—but calling such a thing a circle certainly doesn't *make* it a circle (and I'm greatly tempted to say there's an end on't).

Note too that if "our system" includes "ellipses" that aren't ellipses or "circles" that aren't circles, then "our system" is likely to be seriously misunderstood, and possibly misapplied, both by our intended users and by people who might subsequently have to perform maintenance on the system. So if you *really* want to have a system that supports ellipse-like things that aren't ellipses or circle-like things that aren't circles, then I would suggest very strongly that—at the very least—you call those things something other than ellipses and circles.

What About "Colored Circles"?

At this point, I'd like to address another issue that Dr. Stroustrup raised in the course of our correspondence. Here's a quote from one of his letters:

> *[Entities] called "circle" and "ellipse" are quite common in drawing programs and in interactive systems dealing with on-screen representations of a wide variety of entities. These entities can reasonably be called "circle" and "ellipse" because their shapes follow the standard mathematical definitions. However, they typically have additional properties (such as color and associated text) and operations (such as move and stretch). You don't consider anything like that [in your draft].*

I'd like to thank Dr. Stroustrup for reminding me of this issue—which I ought to have addressed in my original draft but didn't—because it gives me the opportunity to address it now. The fact is, I strongly disagree with the suggestion that, for example, the combination of a circle and a color is a circle. By definition, the former (the combination of a circle and a color) is an ordered pair of values of the form *<circle,color>*, while the latter (a circle) is a singleton value of the form *circle*. And there's a huge logical difference between these two concepts!—in fact, the two values are quite clearly of two different types, *neither of which is a subtype of the* *other*. (That's right—a *<circle,color>* value obviously isn't a *circle* value, and a *circle* value isn't a *<circle,color>* value, either.)

Also, with respect to the suggestion that circles might have "operations (such as move and stretch)," I'd like to point out that if you stretch a circle, you get—in general—an ellipse that isn't a circle. And in some cases, if you stretch an ellipse, you get an ellipse that *is* a circle. We believe our model deals correctly with such operations (see the outline description of that model in the section immediately following). We also believe it deals correctly with "colored circles" and similar constructs—but certainly not by pretending they're circles.

A Type Inheritance Proposal

By way of conclusion, let me summarize those features of our own inheritance model[8] that are pertinent to the ellipses-and-circles controversy. Of course, what follows is only a brief sketch, and many features of the model aren't mentioned at all.

- First of all, our model is based on the four classical (and, we hope, widely understood) concepts **type, value, variable,** and **operator.** We find no need to drag in any kind of "object" concept at all, nor do we do so.

- We distinguish these four concepts very carefully; in particular, we draw a very sharp distinction between values and variables.

- Every value has a type—sometimes called the *most specific* type (of the value in question)— that never changes. For example, if *e* is an ellipse value that's "just an ellipse" and not a circle, its most specific type is ELLIPSE. And if *c* is an ellipse value that *is* a circle, its most specific type is CIRCLE. *Note:* It's also of type ELLIPSE, since it *is* an ellipse, but, to repeat, its most specific type is CIRCLE. (In general, in fact, every value has *several* types that never change: the most specific type, as well as all defined supertypes of that most specific type. For simplicity, I'll assume throughout most of what follows that the system includes just the two types ELLIPSE and CIRCLE.)

- Every variable has a type—sometimes called the *declared* type (of the variable in question)— that never changes. For example, if E is a variable of declared type ELLIPSE, then the values that are permitted to be values of E are, precisely, ellipse values (= values of type ELLIPSE). Of course, some of those ellipse values are in fact circles (= values of most specific type CIRCLE), and so we have the notion that a variable of declared type ELLIPSE might in fact have as its current value a value of most specific type CIRCLE.

- Observe, therefore, that we now have another logical difference on our hands: namely, that between the declared type of a given variable, on the one hand, and the most specific type of the current value of that variable, on the other. The former never changes, but the latter *does* change, in general. (The object world seems not to distinguish between these two types but regards a given "object" as having just one type, which is never allowed to change—another reason why object "models" of inheritance are unsatisfactory, in our opinion.)

---

8. "Our own inheritance model" = the model defined by Hugh Darwen and myself in *Databases, Types, and the Relational Model: The Third Manifesto,* 3rd edition (Addison-Wesley, 2006). In passing, let me acknowledge Hugh Darwen's helpful review of earlier drafts of this chapter.

- All read-only operations that apply to ellipse values—"get the area," for example—apply to circle values too (because circle values *are* ellipse values); that is, read-only operations associated with type ELLIPSE are inherited unconditionally by type CIRCLE. However, there are some read-only operations associated with type CIRCLE—"get the radius," for example—that don't apply to type ELLIPSE. In other words, the set of read-only operations that apply to circle values is *a proper superset* of the set of read-only operations that apply to ellipse values.

- Some update operations that apply to ellipse variables—"change the center," for example—apply to circle variables too. Other such operations—"change the *a* semiaxis," for example—*don't* apply to circle variables too (because circle variables *aren't* ellipse variables; that is, a variable of declared type CIRCLE *can't* hold a value that's "just an ellipse," and changing the *a* semiaxis of a circle yields a result that's "just an ellipse," in general). In other words, update operations associated with type ELLIPSE are *not* inherited unconditionally by type CIRCLE. Moreover, there are some update operations associated with type CIRCLE—"change the radius," for example—that don't apply to type ELLIPSE. Thus, the set of update operations that apply to circle variables is neither a subset nor a superset of the set of such operations that apply to ellipse variables.

- Let E be a variable of declared type ELLIPSE. Then updating E in such a way that $a = b$ after the update means the most specific type of the current value of E is now CIRCLE. Likewise, updating E in such a way that $a > b$ after the update means the most specific type of the current value of E is now "just ELLIPSE."

In sum, we believe our model includes many desirable features that seem to be missing from other proposals. We also have reason to believe it's efficiently implementable. We would therefore like the IT community to consider it as a serious contender—a contender, that is, for the role of an inheritance model that's both (a) formally and rigorously defined and (b) robust in its application. I note in closing that such a model seems to be conspicuous by its absence in the industry at large, at least at the time of writing.

Technical Correspondence

The arguments of this chapter, when it first appeared, really seemed to get people going ... I received an unusually large number of responses, responses that were almost universally unclear, badly expressed, and confused (though it was at least clear that they were mostly quite critical of my position and arguments). I've quoted several passages from those letters and messages at length in what follows (*verbatim*—I haven't attempted to correct the originals in any way), and I think the passages in question will give you some idea of what I mean.

The first response, by LH, was forwarded to me by JM, who described LH's message as a "cogent" response to my "complaints" that the object world mostly seems to think a circle isn't an ellipse. Well, my dictionary defines "cogent" as "powerful, convincing," and I don't think LH's argument is even close to being either. And I think a large part of the problem is precisely that LH is talking "object talk"; he or she never addresses my complaint that the object concept is both redundant and unnecessarily confusing, not least when we're trying to resolve the particular issue at hand. In fact, LH never really addresses *any* of the arguments I was making in my original article. He or she does seem to say it's "unwise" to treat a circle as an ellipse in

C++ specifically (actually LH talks in terms of squares and rectangles, not circles and ellipses, but the examples are isomorphic, of course). Well, maybe it is unwise; but if so, then that's a problem with C++ specifically, it's not an argument for saying that circles should never (or "almost" never?) be treated as ellipses.

"That a square is a rectangle is true enough in carefully written code": I don't think code, carefully written or otherwise, has anything to do with the matter. In fact, the argument that code should dictate whether or not a circle is an ellipse seems to me to be 100 percent backward. A circle *is* an ellipse, and if your code doesn't support that fact, then there's something wrong with your code.

By the way, treating circles as ellipses is not only logically correct, it's positively desirable in the context of (at least) spatial or temporal data. Furthermore (as noted in the body of the chapter), Hugh Darwen and I not only think we know how to do it, we think we know how to do it efficiently.

Here are some quotes from a series of responses, all from the same person:

> *I'm not surprised that Dr. S had problems with [the circles and ellipses article] ... Chris Date ... makes two fundamental errors with this article, these stopped me reading less than half the way through.*

I'll reserve judgment on this extract until we find out what the alleged errors are (see later).

> *As a quick point a class is a programming level realization of a type. If in ooa you specify the classification type and some of its properties this could be modelled in any number of ways in any number of languages (of course also non oop's). A class in most oop's refers to the code itself that is a template for instantiation of behaviour ... (As a follow on an object is most often an instantiation of a class, oop language terms vary of course.)*

As I pointed out in my original article—as clearly as I could!—there's no consensus on what a class is and what a type is. For the purposes of that article, I said I was going to take the terms as synonymous. I don't want to quibble over terminology; the *concepts* are what I'm interested in, and playing games with the terms doesn't invalidate any of the points I tried to make.

> [The first error:] *In basing your criticism on the C++ paragraph you miss the context. This is talking about implementation issues NOT about pure theory. Yes people recognise that circles are special kinds of ellipses, the point is within a programming context HOW do you model this, NOT wether outside of this context it is correct.*

I couldn't disagree more. The context was a chapter called "Development and Design," and the section I was quoting was headed "Step 1: Find Classes." We're trying to find classes (= types!) that are useful for the database and/or application at hand. And I would *strongly* suggest that if we think we want some "classes" called ELLIPSE and CIRCLE, then those "classes" had jolly well better correspond pretty closely to ellipses and circles, not to something that just happens to be "a little bit like" ellipses and circles. Frankly, it doesn't seem to me that my position here should even need defending; I find it amazing that some people would want to attack it.

By the way, I can't resist pointing out that the passage quoted includes a use of the verb "to model" that is clearly intended to be understood as "to implement." See my paper "Models, Models, Everywhere, Nor Any Time to Think" (Chapter 25 in the present book).

The issue with invariants is the major problem with such generalisations. The comments on the main key aspects of circles for most programs were ridiculous and appeared nothing more than "I'm bored who can I troll today" ... The point is that if a program is relying on these invariants with a circle but uses the ellipse class' interface its behaviour may vary. As such it would end up checking for the type of the object before expecting behaviour, which is against the point of polymorphism in the first place (look up LSP) ... So you may use inheritance just to provide implementation inheritance. Depending on your applications needs, however, the invariants for a circle may be violated if you operate through an ellipse.

"LSP," or substitutability, is *precisely* what concerns me in this debate.[9] A circle is a special kind of ellipse; therefore, a program that works for ellipses in general ought to work for circles in particular. The inheritance model defined in *The Third Manifesto* satisfies this objective. The "model" I was criticizing in my original article doesn't.

Incidentally, this particular quote illustrates my complaints about the quality of my opponents' criticisms in general. What on earth can it mean to "operate [on a circle] through an ellipse"?

Also, I've never previously encountered the word *troll* used in the sense apparently intended here. My loss, perhaps—but does it mean anything different from *attack*?

Finally, note the suggestion that "you may use inheritance just to provide implementation inheritance." To me, this looks like more evidence in support of my strong suspicion that the object world fails to make a proper distinction between model and implementation.

[The second error:] This notion of variable's and values is outside of oop concerns. Bare in mind that if your oop uses class semantics it is the class itself that governs behaviour not the "data" that may or may not be underneath it (i.e., it may be in other classes and this class assembles behavioural abstractions against them).

I love that "bare in mind" (a Freudian slip, I presume, and a rather telling one). More to the point: It is my claim (and I make this claim *very strongly*) that you must have values and—at least if you're using an imperative language, not a functional one—you must have variables too. **This claim is valid even in the OO world**. So to say that "the notion of variables and values is outside of" OO concerns is—I'm sorry to have to say—to betray a deep lack of understanding of what's really going on (in other words, a deep lack of understanding of fundamentals).

Incidentally, I have to say too that if there's any logical connection at all between the two sentences quoted in the foregoing extract, then it certainly escapes me. So also, even more so, does the *meaning* of the second sentence.

My point is that after taking things out of context the paragraph is then twisted beyond what really means. An example (excuse bad copy and pasteing): [The writer goes on to quote Stroustrup's Sentence Number 6 and my proposed "expanded, rephrased, and corrected" version of that sentence, and then continues:] *Aside from obviously taking liberties (a with respect doesn't really cut it) this is not "correcting" the statement. It was fine to begin with ... If you take it out of an implementation context then yes, this may be true. Further the main point of this, again, is that the paragraph is concerned with LSP and invariants ... I can't believe that Chris Date doesn't know what an invariant is nor a class invariant. This again only leaves the article as a trolling.*

---

9. See the next chapter.

The statement was categorically *not* "fine to begin with." And there was no attempt on my part to "twist the paragraph beyond what [it] really means." I was merely indulging in the fine art of deconstruction—which basically operates on the premise that you can judge a writer's intent only by what he or she has actually said, not by what you might possibly think he or she might possibly have wanted to have possibly said, but didn't.

Here are some quotes from another message:

> *Circles and ellipses are not real world objects, they are mathematical objects.*

Oh dear. I think I can guess what the writer is getting at here, but if my guess is correct then I have to say I don't agree with it at all. Even if you think—as I do not!—that mathematics is not part of "the real world," you must surely agree that much of mathematics is *directly relevant to* "the real world." "Mathematical objects" are precisely what enable us to construct the appropriate theories that in turn let us construct "real world" applications of those theories (computer systems are surely one of the prize examples here, but there are literally thousands of others). Those theories rely hugely on abstractions of various kinds, and that's precisely what "mathematical objects" are (i.e., abstractions). It seems to me, therefore, that any decent, self-respecting theory of type inheritance ought to be able to deal with "mathematical objects" as well as with "real world" ones (though, to repeat, I don't draw that distinction anyway). What's more, "mathematical objects" provide a rich source of good examples, examples that can be used to test the theory without getting sidetracked into distracting irrelevancies (as tends to happen if you use "real world" objects instead, such as employees and managers). In a nutshell, then, I think this criticism is completely off base.

> *Thus, objects are not values ... Date is right that OO people ignore the difference between values and variables; that is because they do everything with variables and do not have real values.*

Yes, but you can't have the concept of *variable* without simultaneously having the concept of *value* (see my comments on the previous set of criticisms above). If OO people truly "do not have real values," it just means they have a concept they don't properly recognize, or name. And they can't truly "ignore" the difference between values and variables; again, it just means there's a concept (in this case, a *logical difference*) that they fail to recognize and name properly.

> *Objects are better models of real world objects than is a value. I can let out some string as I swing an object around my head, and its orbit (a circle) has just changed its radius.*

Yes, the concept of a variable is useful (see above).

> *[My] summary of the paper ... is "I don't like objects. I like relations better." To each his own. They are both Turing complete. But the disagreement is much more profound than ... Date seems to realize.*

I never said "I don't like objects," and I never said "I like relations better"; in fact, the word *relation* didn't appear in my original article at all. Objects and relations aren't directly comparable concepts. I do know that *inside a database* I need relations ("need," not just "like," please note). I also know that relations need to be defined over types (*aka* domains). Since the object *class* concept seems to be vaguely related to the all-important *type* concept, it seems worthwhile to explore a possible marriage between the object and relational worlds, based on this putative connection (that's one of the things Darwen and I did, in depth and detail, in *The Third Manifesto*). **But the crucial point is that we must have a very clear notion of just what types are**—including a very clear notion of what it means for one type to be a subtype of another. In *The Third Manifesto*, we do pin down these notions, very precisely. In the object world, by contrast, we find a great lack of precision and clear thinking in these very areas. My article on circles and ellipses was intended to draw people's attention to such issues.

Some quotes from a message from CC:

> *Perhaps the basic premise is flawed, and a circle is a subset of an ellipse (or in other words an ellipse a super type of a circle)? Yes I know this is contrary, but it too can be argued ... Justifying this in an application-sense would provide examples of both type and object definition representations. What the condition of these two entities are in a mathematical realm is ambiguous if you are dealing with a system which does not obey those same syntactical scriptures.*

I suspect the first sentence in this quote is topsy-turvy; I think CC is trying to suggest that type ELLIPSE might be a subtype of type CIRCLE (but see my earlier remarks on *deconstruction!*). If so, then the suggestion is not new, of course; the idea is that (for example) circles and ellipses might both have a major semiaxis, but ellipses that aren't circles have a minor semiaxis as well. But this suggestion either violates substitutability or (perhaps more likely) violates the type graph as a good model of reality—e.g., it might mean that we have to pretend that ellipses in general have a radius. I don't understand the last two sentences in this quote at all.

> *An example of an ellipse as a type / subset of a circle is as follows*

```
Type Shape
        area
        position
End of Type

Type Circle
        Shape
        dimension1
End of Type

Type Ellipse
        Circle
        dimension2
End of Type
```

Note the phrasing "... an ellipse as a type / subset of a circle." One thing that makes this whole subject so difficult to get your head around, at least in spoken and written debate, is that people *will* insist on using, for example, the term *circle* to mean sometimes a type, sometimes a value, and sometimes a variable (not to mention sometimes an object, and possibly other things besides, and not to mention the use of the term *type* when *subtype*—and *proper* subtype at that—is surely what is intended). This is a plea for precision. Please.

By the way, the term *dimension* is also very definitely not the right term for the concept the writer has in mind.

> *The circle object / type has no second dimension so why force one on it by reversing the definition, it is a waste of space to enforce redundant fields and violates the first (1st) normal form of a database definition (not that this is an inviolate rule but it does help to keep the house work down).*

Note the tacit assumption here that "redundant" "dimensions" imply additional storage space! I never said as much in my article, and I don't believe it, either. There's a confusion here between type and representation (see *The Third Manifesto* once again for further clarification). To spell the point out: The physical representation for a circle could involve just a radius "field," while the physical representation for an ellipse that's not a circle could involve a major semiaxis "field" and a minor semiaxis "field." The operators that return the major semiaxis and the minor semiaxis for type ELLIPSE will then have to be (trivially, and possibly automatically) reimplemented for type CIRCLE to return the radius—that's all.

The remark about first normal form is a red herring. First normal form applies to the design of relations (actually relation *variables*). Types are not relation variables.

> *I don't mean to seem too afronting, but it would appear the Circle as an Ellipse arguement as applied to a database paradigm means to leave us missing the forest for the trees ... Am I wrong?*

Well, yes, I think the writer *is* wrong—at least overall, though frankly I don't know what he or she is getting at by that talk of missing the forest for the trees. Sorry about that.

Another commentator, KU, wrote to say that the article on circles and ellipses, and the ensuing debate, were "at turns enlightening, provocative, and challenging." Well, many thanks! But KU then went on "to propose a second representation [*sic*—*I don't really think representation, as such, is relevant to the matter at hand, but let that pass*] of CIRCLE and ELLIPSE," as follows:

> *In the real plane, take a line D and a point F not on D. Determine the locus of points P such that for every point in P, the distance [P,F] divided by the (tangential) distance [P,D] is a constant E. If E = 0, the locus of points P is a CIRCLE; if 0 < E < 1, then the locus of points is an ELLIPSE.*

Of course, I recognize what's going on here—D is the directrix, F is the focus, and E is the eccentricity. Though I feel bound to add that:

a. I think that parenthetical qualifier "(tangential)" is incorrect—the distance in question is surely just the conventional straight-line distance between two points (?).

b. I also think it's slightly naughty of KU not to state explicitly that in the case of a circle the directrix is supposed to be at infinity.

Be that as it may, the key observation is that all we're really doing here is playing games with *terminology*. The assertion that "0 < E < 1 defines an ellipse" must be understood to mean, precisely, that "0 < E < 1 defines *an ellipse that isn't a circle*"! So what KU is calling an ellipse *tout court* is exactly what I would call, more specifically, a noncircular ellipse.

As an aside, I remark that I could (of course) have done the equivalent thing in terms of semiaxes *a* and *b*. I mean, there's no need to drag in this stuff about eccentricity and the rest in order to make the point that KU is apparently trying to make. To be specific, I could have defined type ELLIPSE to have $a > b$ and type CIRCLE to have $a = b$. And then of course, I would have to agree that CIRCLE isn't a subtype of (this redefined version of) type ELLIPSE.

The question then becomes: Is the foregoing revision to the definition of type ELLIPSE useful? Well, KU doesn't mention any types apart from CIRCLE and that redefined version of ELLIPSE; so if these are the only types we have, we clearly lose value substitutability—I mean, we wouldn't be able to substitute a value of type CIRCLE wherever the system expected a value of type ELLIPSE. Thus, for example, we couldn't have a single AREA operator that computes the area of a general ellipse and can thus be applied, thanks to subtyping and inheritance, to a circle in particular. (And so we would lose some code reuse, too.)

(Still assuming the revised definition of type ELLIPSE:) Of course, we could go on to define a type hierarchy in which ELLIPSE and CIRCLE are distinct immediate subtypes of the same supertype (which might perhaps be called ELLIPSE_OR_CIRCLE). At least such a type hierarchy would mean that we regain some kind of value substitutability, because we would now be able to substitute a value of type CIRCLE (or a value of type ELLIPSE, come to that) for a value of type ELLIPSE_OR_CIRCLE. But then again, type ELLIPSE_OR_CIRCLE wouldn't *have* any values whose most specific type was ELLIPSE_OR_CIRCLE—by definition, every such value would simply be either a value of type ELLIPSE or a value of type CIRCLE (and type ELLIPSE_OR_CIRCLE would be what Hugh Darwen and I call a *union type*). Thus, it might be argued that this revised type hierarchy gives us back at least some of the advantages that our original design (in which CIRCLE *was* a subtype of ELLIPSE) gave us—but it does so at the cost of having an extra type and a more complicated type hierarchy. There might be other costs, too.

KU then goes on to assert that "Every other aspect of the model—whether concerning variables or values, operations or properties—is perfectly preserved." I don't know, here, whether KU is talking about the ellipses-and-circles example in particular or our model of type inheritance in general. If it's the former, well, I think I've discussed the issue sufficiently. If it's the latter, well, I certainly don't think KU's alternative design in any way invalidates our original design. Furthermore, KU doesn't address a crucial aspect of our approach, an aspect in which we clearly differentiate ourselves from just about every other approach I've ever seen described in the literature. I'm referring to the aspect we call **specialization by constraint** (S by C) and **generalization by constraint** (G by C), according to which—to talk *extremely* loosely!— (a) "squeezing" an ellipse to make *a* equal to *b* converts that ellipse into a circle and (b) "stretching" a circle to make *a* greater than *b* converts that circle into a (noncircular) ellipse. I find it extremely interesting that nobody has refuted, or even disputed, our claims that (a) S by C and G by C correspond to what actually happens in the real world and (b) we believe we know how to implement them (efficiently, too).

The last message I want to discuss here came from DN, who wrote a pleasant (and unusually coherent!) commentary on the overall debate; indeed, I found myself in considerable sympathy with much of DN's main argument. To paraphrase somewhat, that argument was that C++ and other OO languages aren't really *trying* to deal with subtyping in their approach to inheritance;

that's not what they want to do. In other words, they're more interested in software engineering matters (in particular, with such issues as code reuse) and not so interested in "models of reality" as such—this latter, perhaps, being a matter of more interest to the database community.

However, DN then went on to say that "A model of inheritance whose purpose was to model subtyping ... would be relatively useless in an OOPL ... There may, of course, be cases where [such a facility] is useful, but in all my C++ programming years I have never come across this." There are a couple of (major) points I want to make in response to these remarks:

a. First, Hugh Darwen and I have never claimed that our brand of type inheritance would be useful "in an OOPL." *Au contraire*, in fact: We recognize that our brand of inheritance doesn't work with objects (at least inasmuch as we can agree on what "objects" are). To be specific, if using "an OOPL" means using objects that have object IDs, then we recognize that *specialization by constraint* (S by C) and *generalization by constraint* (G by C)— see my response to KU, earlier—**can't be made to work**. Since we regard S by C and G by C as essential components of a good model of subtyping and inheritance, we conclude that "OOPLs" (or objects) and a good model of subtyping and inheritance are incompatible concepts. This is one of several reasons why we reject objects, as such, *entirely* in *The Third Manifesto*. (See Appendix F of the book *Databases, Types, and the Relational Model: The Third Manifesto*, 3rd edition, Addison-Wesley, 2006, for arguments and examples in support of the foregoing position.)

b. Second, there's an implicit wider suggestion in DN's letter (possibly unintended) to the effect that a model of inheritance whose purpose was to model subtyping would be relatively useless *in general* (i.e., not just "in an OOPL"). Well, here I'd like to observe that, in sharp contrast with this position, Hugh Darwen and I have discovered the following:

- Our brand of inheritance provides an elegant solution to a certain problem that arises in connection with something we're currently very interested in: namely, the proper handling of *temporal data*. What's more, we haven't seen any other "good" solution to the problem in question in the literature.

- Our brand of inheritance also deals elegantly with a somewhat vexing problem that arises in connection with questions such as this one: Are NUMERIC(3) and NUMERIC(2) different types or not?

- Preliminary investigations seem to show that our brand of inheritance also provides an elegant approach to certain important problems that arise in the world of geospatial applications.

  (We plan to publish our thoughts on these matters as soon as we can, but don't hold your breath.)

Finally, let me add that we *can* do "C++-style inheritance" in our model; we just don't call it inheritance (or subtyping). In fact we don't explicitly call it anything at all, but what I have in mind is akin to what I believe some people call *delegation*. Appendix G of the book already mentioned—*Databases, Types, and the Relational Model: The Third Manifesto*, 3rd edition (Addison-Wesley, 2006)—discusses this issue in some detail.

CHAPTER 24

■ ■ ■

What Does Substitutability Really Mean?

I first published my paper on circles and ellipses (Chapter 23 in the present book) in July 2001. Then I ducked ... Perhaps it's an exaggeration to say that people threw things at me from all directions, but (as noted in that previous chapter) I certainly received an unusually large amount of correspondence, most of it unfavorable. It isn't my intention to give a blow-by-blow response here to all of the criticisms I received, but I do want to respond to one particular claim that ran like a common thread through many of them: namely, that I seemed not to be aware of the *Liskov Substitution Principle*—or (worse!) if I was aware of it, then I didn't understand it.

Well, I freely admit that I wasn't familiar with the *term* "Liskov Substitution Principle" (hereinafter abbreviated to LSP) when I wrote my original paper. However, I was certainly familiar—I venture to say, extremely familiar—with the *concept*, which I had been taught to call **substitutability**.[1] Here's a loose definition (I'll refine this definition at the very end of this chapter):

> *If S is a subtype of T, then wherever the system expects a value of type T, a value of type S can be substituted.*

For example, if AREA is an operator that can be invoked on an ellipse *e*, then we can always substitute a circle *c* for *e* in such an invocation, because circles *are* ellipses (at least, such is my claim).

As I recall, it was Nelson Mattos of IBM who introduced me to the idea of substitutability, way back in 1993; certainly I was already writing about it no later than May of that year, when I was working on the 6th edition of my book *An Introduction to Database Systems* (published by Addison-Wesley in 1994, though with a copyright date of 1995). And I have subsequently studied it in considerable depth in connection with my work with Hugh Darwen on the inheritance model we describe in our book on *The Third Manifesto*. In view of the criticisms I received, however, it clearly seemed to be incumbent on me to take a closer look at LSP *per se*. So I did ... What follows is the result. *Note:* I wrote to Dr. Liskov (twice, in fact) offering to let her see and comment on this material before it was published, but received no reply.

---

1. So perhaps I owe Barbara Liskov an apology, if the concept truly is due to her and I haven't acknowledged that fact in previous writings.

What Is LSP?

My major concern was naturally to discover whether there were any significant differences between substitutability as I understood it and LSP. I began my attempt to answer this question by taking a look at a short article by Stephen R. Tockey titled "What is LSP?" (http://www. otug@rational.com, January 14th, 1998). That article starts by asserting that LSP is described in detail in a paper titled "A Behavioral Notion of Subtyping," by Barbara Liskov and Jeannette Wing (*ACM Transactions on Programming Languages and Systems 16*, No. 6, November 1994), and it goes on to quote from the abstract to that paper as follows. (In fact, the extract quoted consists of the first half of the abstract in its entirety.)

> *The use of hierarchy is an important component of object-oriented design. Hierarchy allows the use of type families, in which higher level supertypes capture the behavior that all of their subtypes have in common. For this methodology to be effective, it is necessary to have a clear understanding of how subtypes and supertypes are related. This paper takes the position that the relationship should ensure that any property proved about supertype objects also holds for subtype objects.*

The wording of this extract put me on my guard right away. I believe strongly—and I've said as much, in many places and on many occasions—that if you want to make precise and formal statements about data and data management in general, then it's a bad idea to try and do so in terms of "objects." Object terminology almost always seems to be fuzzy. There are several reasons for this state of affairs, but one of the biggest is that it (object terminology, I mean) seems never to make the absolutely crucial distinction between *values* and *variables*. (In fact, in our own work on type inheritance, Hugh Darwen and I found it necessary to distinguish two kinds of substitutability, one based on values and the other based on variables; what's more, we showed that if you fail to make that distinction, then at least one, and arguably as many as four, extremely undesirable consequences follow. I'll elaborate on this point later.)

Anyway (I said to myself as I was reading), perhaps the Liskov/Wing paper does deal with the substitutability issue properly and does avoid the many "value *vs.* variable" traps and confusions. We'll see. Meanwhile, I was still studying the Tockey article. The very next thing it said was this:

> *Very simply put, the LSP states that "objects of the subtype ought to behave the same as those of the supertype as far as anyone or any program using supertype objects can tell." In other words, I ought to be able to substitute any subtype of class X in a program that expects a member of class X and the program should still behave reasonably.*

As I expected: *Fuzziness!* Let's examine the two sentences in this quote one at a time. The first one is not *too* bad[2]—I mean, you can make a pretty good guess at what the author is trying to say, even if, like me, you feel the phrase "ought to behave" would be better shortened to just "behave"—but surely it could be better expressed? For example:

> If S is a subtype of T, then wherever the system expects an object of type T, an object of type S can be substituted.

---

2. I subsequently discovered that it was a direct quote from the Liskov/Wing paper.

Much more precise, and—at least to me—much easier to understand, too. (Mind you, I don't necessarily agree with the sentiment this revised version expresses!—it depends, of course, on what the term *object* means. But let that pass for now.)

Now let's look at the second sentence: "In other words, I ought to be able to substitute any subtype of class X in a program that expects a member of class X and the program should still behave reasonably." I have many reactions to this sentence:

- First of all, where did that stuff about classes come from? It wasn't mentioned in the first sentence, and it wasn't mentioned in the Liskov/Wing abstract either. Am I to understand that *class* is just another word for *type*? If so, why introduce the term? If not, how do the concepts differ? And if they do differ, what are we supposed to make of the phrase "any subtype of class X"?

By the way, in "Is a Circle an Ellipse?" I did say that class and type were synonyms—and I got a lot of flak on that one, too. The truth is, however, that there's an amazing amount of confusion over this particular issue. In support of this claim, let me quote some material from Appendix J of *The Third Manifesto*. Appendix J is the "References and Bibliography" appendix, and it includes a reference to a book by Elisa Bertino and Lorenzo Martino titled *Object-Oriented Database Systems: Concepts and Architectures* (Addison-Wesley, 1993). Here's the annotation to that reference from Appendix J (edited just slightly here):[3]

> *Many publications from the object world try to draw a distinction (as we do not) between* type *and* class, *and Bertino and Martino's book is one such: "Object-oriented systems can be classified into two main categories—systems supporting the notion of* class *and those supporting the notion of* type ... *[Although] there are no clear lines of demarcation between them, the two concepts are fundamentally different* [sic!] ... *Often the concepts* type *and* class *are used interchangeably. However, when both are present in the same language, the* type *is used to indicate the specification of the interface of a set of objects, while class is an implementation notion* [so why is it "present in the language" at all?]. *Therefore ... a type is a set of objects which share the same behavior ... [and] a class is a set of objects which have exactly the same internal structure and therefore the same attributes and the same methods.* [But if all objects in a class have the same attributes and the same methods,[4] is not that class a type, by the authors' own definition?] *The class defines the implementation of a set of objects, while a type describes how such objects can be used." (Contrast the ODMG specification, incidentally—see R. G. G. Cattell and Douglas K. Barry (eds.),* The Object Data Standard: ODMG 3.0, *Morgan Kaufmann, 2000—which uses the terms* type *and* class *in almost exactly the opposite way.)*

> *The authors* [i.e., Bertino and Martino] *then go on to say: "With inheritance, a class called a* subclass *can be defined on the basis of the definition of another class called a* superclass." *Surely—in accordance with their own earlier definitions—they should be talking in terms of types here, not classes? And then they add: "The specification hierarchy (often called* subtype hierarchy) *expresses ... subtyping relationships which mean that an instance of the subtype can be used in every context in which an instance of the supertype can correctly appear (substitutability)." Observe that they do now speak of types, not classes ... [Also,] observe the failure to distinguish properly between values and variables (note the fuzzy talk of "instances"), and the consequent failure to distinguish between value substitutability and variable substitutability.*

---

3. I quoted from this annotation in my original paper, too.
4. I prefer the term *operator*, but *method* is much more common in the object world, and so I'll use it here.

> *Of course, it is precisely because of confusions, terminological and otherwise, such as those just illustrated that we felt free—or compelled, rather—to introduce our own terms in* The Third Manifesto *and to define them as carefully as we could.*

- Back to the sentence from the Tockey article. My next complaint is *sloppiness,* as evidenced by the phrasing "substitute any subtype of class [= *type?*] X." To be specific, the author is talking about substituting *a subtype as such,* when presumably what he should be talking about is substituting an *object of* the subtype in question. This is not just a quibble! As I wrote in my original article, our own model of types and inheritance is based on the four classical—and, we hope, widely understood—concepts **type, value, variable,** and **operator.**[5] There are huge logical differences between any two of these concepts, and any article or other writing that confuses them is likely to manifest other confusions as well.

By now you've probably forgotten what the sentence was from Tockey's article that I'm complaining about (I nearly have myself), so let me repeat it again, but with a different emphasis this time:

> *In other words, I ought to be able to substitute* [an object of?] *any subtype of class* [= type?] *X in a program that expects a* **member** *of class* [= type?] *X and the program should still behave reasonably.*

Am I to understand that *member* is just another word for *object?* If so, why introduce the term? If not, how do the concepts differ?

I could say quite a bit more about this sentence of Tockey's—in particular, I'd love to see a definition of what it means for a program to "behave reasonably"—but let's move on. A couple of paragraphs further on, I found this:

> *In order for class X' to be a subtype* [sic!] *of class X, the pre-conditions of the methods of the supertype* [presumably "the supertype" is class X?] *must be at least as restrictive (but possibly more) than the pre-conditions of the corresponding methods of the subtype(s) AND/OR the post-conditions of the methods of the subtype must be at least as restrictive (but possibly more) than the post-conditions of the corresponding methods on the supertype.*

Well, the syntax here is pretty wobbly, but let's focus on the two central claims the author appears to be making. I'll take them one at a time. The first is as follows:

> Let M be a method that applies to objects of type X and therefore—let's assume—to objects of type X' as well.[6] Then the preconditions that apply to M when it's invoked on an object of type X must be "at least as restrictive" as those that apply to M when it's invoked on an object of type X'.

To me, this claim seems to be nonsense. For consider:

---

5. I also said we found no need to drag in any kind of "object" concept at all, and I stand by this claim.
6. Actually this assumption needs to be carefully examined too, but this isn't the place for that examination. Suffice it to say that the distinction between values and variables rears its (very nonugly) head here once again.

- First of all, by definition, there are more values of type X than there are of type X'. After all, to say that X' is a subtype of X is to say that every value of type X' is a value of type X, so there can't be *more* values of type X' than there are of type X; and if the two types have the same number of values, then they're the same type. *Note:* I'm aware that not everyone agrees with the points I'm making here. I'll revisit them later in this chapter.

- The precondition that applies to M when it's invoked on an object O of type X is basically that O must have a value that's a value of type X. The precondition that applies to M when it's invoked on an object O' of type X' is basically that O' must have a value that's a value of type X'. This latter precondition is *obviously* more restrictive than the former, thereby directly contradicting the claim that the former is supposed to be more restrictive than the latter. *Note:* Of course, I'm aware that preconditions might be more complicated in practice than the simple ones I'm describing here, but it's sufficient to consider just the simple case in order to make the point I want to make.[7]

Now here's the second claim:

Again, let M be a method that applies to objects of type X and therefore to objects of type X' as well. Then the postconditions that apply to M when it's invoked on an object of type X' must be "at least as restrictive" as those that apply to M when it's invoked on an object of type X.

This claim, by contrast, does seem reasonable. Assume first that M produces a result R when it's invoked. Then—given the preconditions stated earlier—it's *obvious* that every possible result that can be produced when invoking M on some object O' of type X' can also be produced when invoking M on some object O of type X (because O' is an object of type X, by definition). Thus, the postcondition that applies to M when it's invoked on an object of type X' is *obviously* "at least as restrictive" as the one that applies to M when it's invoked on an object of type X.

Onward. Tockey subsequently gives an example of two methods both called Draw, one of which applies to objects of type GeometricShape and the other to objects of type WildWest-Gunfighter, and observes, correctly, that there's no subtyping, and therefore no substitutability, in that example. (His actual words are as follows: "[According] to LSP, WildWestGunfighter is not a subtype of GeometricShape and I should not expect a program to be well behaved if I substitute a member of WildWestGunfighter in a place where the program expected a GeometricShape.") Well, I agree, but I think the point would have been much clearer if the writer had explicitly introduced the terms *inclusion polymorphism* and *overloading polymorphism* (and explained the difference between them, of course). Let me elaborate.

First of all, an operator (or "method") is said to be **polymorphic** if it's defined in terms of some parameter *P* and the arguments corresponding to *P* can be of different types on different invocations. The equality operator "=" is an obvious example: We can test *any* two values for equality (just so long as the two values are of the same type), and so "=" is polymorphic—it applies to integers, and to character strings, and to ellipses, and to polygons, and in fact to values of

---

7. As an aside, I feel bound to say that I'm not very happy with the terminology of "preconditions," anyway. Given a method M, the preconditions, as such, for M are surely always the same, no matter what types the arguments might happen to have. Thus, the real question is, rather, "Do the arguments satisfy the preconditions?" (Perhaps the reason I'm having difficulties here is that Tockey and I are basing our statements on different unspoken assumptions. Be that as it may, I'll revisit the whole business of preconditions—and postconditions—later in this chapter.)

every type. Analogous remarks apply to the assignment operator ":=" also. Further examples include the well-known aggregate operators of SQL (MAX, COUNT, etc.), the operators of the relational algebra (UNION, JOIN, etc.), and many others.

Next, polymorphism comes in (at least) two distinct flavors, known as *inclusion* polymorphism and *overloading* polymorphism, respectively.[8] To paraphrase some remarks from *The Third Manifesto*, a helpful way of characterizing the difference between these two concepts is as follows:

- **Inclusion** polymorphism means we have one operator with several distinct implementation versions under the covers (but the user does not need to know that the versions in question are in fact distinct—to the user, there is just the one operator). Inclusion polymorphism is what we get with subtyping, and it implies substitutability. For example, the fact that the operator AREA applies to values of type POLYGON implies that the same operator AREA can be invoked on a value of type RECTANGLE (i.e., rectangles can be substituted for polygons), even if there are indeed—as there probably will be, for efficiency reasons—two distinct implementation versions of AREA under the covers. *Note:* The term "inclusion polymorphism" derives from the fact that, e.g., the set of all rectangles is *included* in the set of all polygons (just as the set of all circles is included in the set of all ellipses).

- **Overloading** polymorphism means we have several distinct operators with the same name (and the user does need to know that the operators in question are in fact distinct, with distinct—though preferably similar—semantics). Overloading polymorphism has nothing to do with subtyping, and it doesn't imply substitutability. It shouldn't really even be mentioned in connection with subtyping, except to make it clear (as I'm trying to do here) that it has nothing to do with the subject under discussion. Tockey's "Draw" example is an example of overloading.[9]

Note: The foregoing definitions notwithstanding, I should now warn you that some writers—very unfortunately, in my opinion—use the term *overloading* to mean inclusion polymorphism. *Caveat lector!*

The Liskov Substitution Principle

Tockey's article concludes with a reference to another article, "The Liskov Substitution Principle," by Robert C. Martin (described by Martin himself as "the second of my *Engineering Notebook* columns for *The C++ Report*")—so the next thing I did was take a look at that article, too. Almost the first thing I found was the following "paraphrase of the Liskov Substitution Principle" (uppercase and boldface as in the original):

---

8. The kind of polymorphism displayed by the operators of the relational algebra is called *generic* polymorphism, on the grounds that—loosely speaking—those operators apply to all possible relations, generically.

9. What's more, that example violates the suggested principle that the "several distinct operators" in question should have similar semantics. Indeed, the kind of polymorphism displayed in that example might better be called *punning* polymorphism.

FUNCTIONS THAT USE POINTERS OR REFERENCES TO BASE CLASSES MUST BE ABLE TO USE OBJECTS OF DERIVED CLASSES WITHOUT KNOWING IT.

Numerous objections spring to mind immediately![10] First: "Functions?" Am I to understand that *function* is another word for *method?* If so, why introduce the term? If not, how do the concepts differ? (Actually, it's quite clear that if we're to take the term *function* in its mathematical sense, then not all methods *are* functions, because mutators, at least, do not fit the mathematical definition. See *The Third Manifesto* for further discussion.)

Second, why "pointers or references"? Am I to understand that *reference* is just another word for *pointer?* If so, why are there two terms? If not, how do the concepts differ?

Third, does Martin *really* mean, as he states, "pointers or references to base classes"? Shouldn't it really be "pointers or references to *objects in* base classes"?[11] (See my earlier complaint regarding Tockey's talk of "substituting a subtype" when what he really meant was substituting an *object of* the subtype in question. As I said previously, I don't think this complaint is just a quibble.)

Fourth, shouldn't "use objects of derived classes" really be "use *pointers or references to* objects of derived classes"? Or is there no difference between (a) an object, on the one hand, and (b) a pointer or a reference to an object, on the other? If so, why even mention "pointers or references"?

Fifth, all this talk of "pointers or references" makes me nervous, anyway. In fact, it takes me straight back to the original debate over whether a circle is an ellipse. In *The Third Manifesto*, Hugh Darwen and I demonstrate clearly—and I think conclusively—that if your inheritance model involves "pointers or references," then it's *logically impossible* to deal properly with the idea that a circle is an ellipse! In fact, we strongly suspect that it's this fact (the fact, that is, that pointers and a good model of inheritance are fundamentally incompatible) that's the root of the problem. Given that

a. Most work on inheritance has been done in an object context, and

b. Most if not all "object models" take pointers (in the shape of "object IDs") as a *sine qua non,*

it follows that

c. Most workers in this field are forced into the position that a circle isn't an ellipse (or, at least, isn't *necessarily* an ellipse).

---

10. I'm informed by one reviewer (Dan Muller) that the things I'm objecting to in this paragraph and the next three are all features of C++ that "will be immediately understood by any C+ practitioner"; in fact, they all "have very precise meanings in the context of C++," and "the terms used in [Martin's sentence] are precisely the terms used in the standard that defines the language ... Martin is using them quite correctly." Very well; it follows that my criticisms should be taken, not as criticisms of Martin's article as such, but rather of the C++ language itself. If you happen to be a C++ aficionado and find such criticisms offensive, then I apologize, and suggest you skip to the paragraph beginning "Fifth."

11. I have another problem here, too. As Hugh Darwen and I explain in *The Third Manifesto*, pointers must be pointers to *variables*, not *values*, and so the "objects" in question here must be variables, not values. But then I don't understand what it could possibly mean for a *variable* to be "in" a *class.*

But they don't seem to recognize that it's the pointers (i.e., the object IDs) that are the source of the difficulty.[12] Instead, they give "justifications" for their apparently illogical position that typically look something like the following:

- "Most object-oriented languages do not want objects to change class." In other words, if we update an ellipse such that its semiaxes become equal, "most object-oriented languages" simply "don't want" the ellipse now to be regarded as a circle (I'm speaking pretty loosely here, as you'll probably realize, but you get the idea).

- "It would be computationally infeasible to support a rule-based, intensional definition of class membership, because you would have to check the rules after each operation that affects an object." In other words, if we update an ellipse such that its semiaxes become equal, "it would be computationally infeasible" to do the work needed for the ellipse now to be regarded as a circle (again speaking pretty loosely).

Note: The quotes in the foregoing bullet items are taken from "A Matter of Intent: How to Define Subclasses," by James Rumbaugh (*Journal of Object-Oriented Programming,* September 1996). I quoted from this source in my original ellipses-and-circles article, too, where I also explained why we reject such "justifications."

Anyway, back to the Martin article. A little further on, Martin discusses, not the ellipses-and-circles example as such, but a rectangles-and-squares example (which is isomorphic to the ellipses-and-circles example in all essential respects, of course):

> *It is often said that, in C++, inheritance is the ISA relationship. In other words, if a new kind of object can be said to fulfill the ISA relationship with an old kind of object, then the class of the new object shoud be derived from the class of the old object.*
>
> *Clearly, a square is a rectangle for all normal intents and purposes* [boldface added!]. *Since the ISA relationship holds, it is logical to model the Square class as being derived from the Rectangle class ... However this kind of thinking can lead to some subtle, yet significant, problems ... Our first clue might be the fact that a Square does not need both itsHeight and itsWidth member variables. Yet it will inherit them anyway. Clearly this is wasteful ... Are there other problems? Indeed! Square will inherit the SetWidth and SetHeight functions. These functions are utterly inappropriate for a Square, since the width and height of a square are identical.*

I agree with the overall sense of this quote, up to but not including what comes after "However." But that business of inheriting "member variables" just points up the fact that a *good* "object model" shouldn't involve "member variables," anyway! Objects—"encapsulated" objects, at any rate—should have *behavior* but not *structure.* Then "methods" (behavior) would be inherited but "member variables" (structure) wouldn't, because there wouldn't be any "member variables" (structure) to inherit. After all, it's obvious that squares can be represented more economically in storage than rectangles can, and this fact in itself is, precisely, a good argument for not exposing the "structure" of squares and rectangles in the first place. As it is, Martin is using a bad feature of a particular object model as the basis for arguing that we

---

12. In fact, I might observe, with a touch of malice, that since object IDs seem to be a necessary feature of objects, it's objects *per se* that are the source of the difficulty. In other words, it's my opinion that *objects per se* and a good model of inheritance are logically incompatible.

shouldn't do what is clearly the logically correct thing to do. Myself, I think this argument is completely backward; as I say, it's at least in part because (e.g.) squares are rectangles that we shouldn't expose member variables.

As for the question of Square inheriting the SetWidth and SetHeight functions, here we run smack into the confusion over values and variables yet again. I don't want to get into a lot of detail on this point here, but will just observe once more that the whole picture becomes so much clearer if we frame our arguments and discussions in terms of values and variables instead of objects. And I think our own inheritance model deals with this particular issue—the issue, that is, of "inheriting the SetWidth and SetHeight functions"—in a logically defensible and correct manner, too.

Well, I don't think I want to beat this particular dead horse very much longer. Suffice it to say that Martin perseveres with the rectangles-and-squares example, building epicycles on epicycles, and getting deeper and deeper into confusion, without ever seeming to recognize what the real problem is. In fact, he says the following (in a section titled "What Went Wrong?"):

> So what happened? Why did the apparently reasonable model of the Square and Rectangle go bad? After all, isn't a Square a Rectangle? Doesn't the ISA relationship hold?
>
> No! A square might be [sic!] a rectangle, but a Square object is definitely not a Rectangle object. Why? Because the behavior of a Square object is not consistent with the behavior of a Rectangle object. Behaviorally, a Square is not a Rectangle! And it is behavior that software is really all about ... The LSP makes clear that in [object design] the ISA relationship pertains to behavior.

Well, it seems to me that "what went wrong" was that we got mired in the world of objects. To say it one more time: The inheritance model that Hugh Darwen and I propose (a) does not involve objects and (b) does understand that a square is a rectangle (and a circle is an ellipse). And we would really like to suggest, with all due respect, that the industry leaders in this field, instead of spending so much time and effort in trying to persuade the rest of us that squares aren't rectangles and circles aren't ellipses, would take a look at our model and see how we do it.

Anyway, I more or less stopped reading Martin's paper at this point—except for the following small point, which I noticed on the next page:

> [When] redefining a routine [in a derivative], you may only replace its precondition by a weaker one, and its postcondition by a stronger one.

Actually, Martin says this is a quote from Bertrand Meyer's book *Object Oriented Software Construction* (Prentice Hall, 1988); the text in brackets is thus Tockey's editing of Meyer's original, not editing by me. Anyway, the overall quote looks like something Tockey said in his article too (perhaps Tockey got it from here); in effect, therefore, I've already dealt with it, at least to some extent, but as I promised earlier I'll come back and take a closer look at it later in this chapter.

A Behavioral Notion of Subtyping

It was with a certain sense of relief and anticipation that I turned to the original Liskov/Wing paper, "A Behavioral Notion of Subtyping." Surely here, I thought, I would find much greater precision and clarity of thinking and expression. Nor was I disappointed. Indeed, the paper was so clear that its errors were clear, too! Indeed, I found there were so many comments I wanted to make on that paper that I decided to devote the entire remainder of this chapter (except for the final section, "Substitutability Defined") to the Liskov/Wing paper specifically.

The Liskov/Wing Paper: Assumptions

The Liskov/Wing paper includes a section titled "Model of Computation," in which the authors spell out some—but unfortunately not all—of their background assumptions. The present section represents my own attempt to distill out the essence of those assumptions. To be more specific, the work reported in the Liskov/Wing paper is explicitly cast in an object framework, and I believe the salient features of that framework are as indicated below.

- Objects have values—different values at different times, in general, unless the object in question is "immutable" (see later).

- Objects are accessed via program variables containing pointers (i.e., object IDs). Program variables are subject to assignment, but objects *per se* apparently aren't (?).

- Objects are generally "encapsulated," meaning they have behavior but no user-visible structure—unless such structure is an intrinsic feature of the object type in question, as would be the case if, e.g., the object type in question were some array type. *Note:* The paper doesn't actually say objects are encapsulated—indeed, encapsulation as such isn't mentioned at all—but I think it's at least implied.

- Every object is of some type. In fact, a given object is of *exactly one* type, except in the case where the object in question is of type S and type S is a proper subtype of type T, in which case the object is additionally of type T. *Note:* I believe the second sentence here is true, although the point is nowhere spelled out explicitly in the paper. Also, the term "proper subtype" doesn't appear, so I'd better define it: Type S is a proper subtype of type T if (a) it is a subtype of T and (b) S and T are distinct. (Note, therefore, that any given type T is a subtype of itself but not a *proper* one.)

- Objects cannot change their type. *Note:* Again, this is my assumption—the paper doesn't say as much explicitly, but it does include numerous remarks that make sense only if what I've just said is correct.

- Objects are never destroyed. *Note:* I think this assumption—which *is* stated explicitly— is made purely to simplify other portions of the paper, but I can't be sure.

- Methods are bundled with types. As a consequence, every method has a distinguished parameter, called in the paper (rather loosely, I feel) "the method's object." Mutators are methods that update "the method's object," while observers are methods that don't (instead they return results—i.e., values, not objects, I presume—"of other types" (?)). However, the paper explicitly states that "an observer can also be a mutator," which I take to mean that a mutator can also return a result; also, I find it hard to imagine a mutator that doesn't "observe" as well. So the distinction between observers and mutators isn't very clear to me. However, the distinction, perhaps fortunately, isn't very important for present purposes.

- Following on from the previous point, the paper explicitly defines any given type to consist, in part, of some specific set of methods. Note the (presumably intended) implication: *Adding a new method to a given type changes the type!* This fact would seem to have some rather important consequences, some of which I'll discuss later.

- An object is "immutable" if its value can never change (presumably such an object, unlike other objects, *must* be initialized when it first comes into existence). An object is "mutable" if it isn't immutable.

- A type is immutable "if its objects are" (i.e., if and only if *all* of its objects are, presumably). A type is mutable if it isn't immutable. *Note:* This notion of types *per se*, as opposed to objects, being mutable or immutable seems rather strange to me. At the very least, there seems to be something wrong with the terminology; types *per se* are, among other things, sets of values, and such sets don't change (in fact, sets of values are themselves values, and values *cannot* change, by definition). Also, quite apart from this issue of terminology, I don't really understand what an "immutable type" would be.[13] However, the rest of the paper has little to say regarding "mutable *vs.* immutable types," so perhaps the point isn't very important.

The Liskov/Wing Paper: Objectives

As I see it, the primary aim of the Liskov/Wing paper is not to propose an abstract model, as such, of subtyping and inheritance. Rather, it is to provide certain definitional constructs that allow assertions of the form "S is a subtype of T" to be *formally verified*, in the sense that:

a. Methods associated with type S can be shown to "behave the same as" the corresponding methods associated with type T.

b. "Constraints" associated with type S can be shown to imply those associated with type T.

Note: The paper makes these two statements much more precise. I can't do the same here, because I haven't explained enough of the background—and I don't *want* to explain more of the background just yet, because there are significant parts of it I don't agree with, as I'll make clear soon.

The paper's main contribution is thus that it provides a way of checking whether an assertion on the part of the type definer to the effect that S is a subtype of T is valid, or at least plausible. By way of motivation for their work, the authors offer the following remarks among others:

> *"[Objects] of the subtype ought to behave the same as those of the supertype as far as anyone or any program using supertype objects can tell."* Interestingly, this sentence (which as we saw earlier was repeated in the Tockey article) seems to be as close as the paper comes to actually providing a statement of the Liskov Substitution Principle. Certainly there is no formal statement of LSP, as such, anywhere in the paper.

---

13. Unless it's one you can't add methods to?

"Subtype Requirement: *Let ø(x) be a property provable about objects* x *of type T. Then ø(y) should be true for objects* y *of type S where S is a subtype of T.*" This statement is highlighted in the paper (in the introduction, in fact), and it constitutes clear evidence in support of what I said at the beginning of this section: namely, that the aim of the paper is to provide a mechanism that supports formal verification of claims to the effect that some given type S is a subtype of some other type T.[14] Note: I think the word "true" in the second sentence would better be replaced by the word "provable," but perhaps it's not important.

"[We] were motivated primarily by pragmatics. Our intention [was] to capture the intuition programmers apply when designing type hierarchies in object-oriented languages. However, intuition in the absence of precision can often go astray or lead to confusion. This is why [in the past] it has been unclear how to organize certain type hierarchies such as integers." [Sic! Presumably the authors mean "type hierarchies such as ones involving different kinds of integers."]

I find these remarks regarding pragmatics and intuition very revealing. I could be quite wrong, but it seems to me that what Liskov and Wing are trying to do in their paper is *retroactively* to formalize, and impose some discipline on, a bunch of disparate preexisting notions that are all somehow related to some vague notions of "subtyping" and "type inheritance." The trouble is, there has never been—there still isn't!—any consensus as to what what these latter terms mean. Instead, what there definitely has been is much *confusion* ... To paraphrase some remarks from *The Third Manifesto* once again:

- In "The Object-Oriented Database System Manifesto" (Proc. 1st International Conference on Deductive and Object-Oriented Databases, Elsevier Science, 1990), Malcolm Atkinson *et al.* say: "[There] are at least four types of inheritance: *substitution* inheritance, *inclusion* inheritance, *constraint* inheritance, and *specialization* inheritance ... Various degrees of these four types of inheritance are provided by existing systems and prototypes, and we do not prescribe a specific style of inheritance."

- In his book *An Introduction to Data Types* (Addison-Wesley, 1986), J. Craig Cleaveland says: "[Inheritance can be] based on [a variety of] different criteria and there is no commonly accepted standard definition"—and proceeds to give *eight* (!) possible interpretations. (Bertrand Meyer, in his article "The Many Faces of Inheritance: A Taxonomy of Taxonomy," *IEEE Computer 29*, No. 5, May 1996, gives *twelve*.)

- In a "Technical Correspondence" item in *Communications of the ACM 37*, No. 9 (September 1994), Kenneth Baclawski and Bipin Indurkhya say: "[A] programming language [merely] provides a set of [inheritance] mechanisms. While these mechanisms certainly restrict what one can do in that language and what views of inheritance can be implemented [in that language], they do not by themselves validate some view of inheritance or other. [Types,] specializations, generalizations, and inheritance are only concepts, and ... they do not have a universal objective meaning ... This [fact] implies that how inheritance is to be incorporated into a specific system is up to the designers of [that] system, and it constitutes a policy decision that must be implemented with the available mechanisms." In other words, there simply is no model.

---

14. In case it's not obvious, I should stress the fact that I think this aim is a perfectly valid and interesting one. However, it's rather different from the one Hugh Darwen and I had in mind when we developed our own inheritance model, as I'll explain later.

Thus, it seems to me that most if not all of those earlier notions of subtyping and inheritance were confused and muddled at best. And it also seems to me that at least some of that muddle has, regrettably, carried over to the Liskov/Wing paper. I'll get more specific on this point below, as well as later in this chapter.

Anyway, regardless of whether I'm right about that business of "formalizing and imposing discipline on a bunch of preexisting notions," I would like to emphasize how different our own objectives were when we (i.e., Hugh Darwen and I) developed our own inheritance model. Basically, we worked from first principles; we very deliberately paid very little attention to existing work in the field.[15] We certainly didn't feel constrained by "existing programmer intuition," and very definitely not by "object-oriented languages." Rather, we were concerned with getting the concepts of the model right *first*—i.e., finding a good answer to the question "What does it *mean* to assert that S is a subtype of T?"—before possibly turning our attention to the question of making such assertions formally verifiable in some way. Thus, we started by developing a formal theory of types as such (and considering the impact of such a theory on the relational model of data in particular). Then we extended that theory to incorporate what seemed to us to be logically sound and useful concepts of subtyping and inheritance. In particular— since we were familiar with at least the general idea and aims of LSP, even if not by that name—we took pains to ensure that our theory did indeed support that notion in what seemed to us to be a logically sound, correct, and useful fashion.

In this connection, the Liskov/Wing paper contains another interesting remark: "Our work is most similar to that of America (P. America: "Designing an Object-Oriented Programming Language with Behavioural Subtyping," in J. W. de Bakker, W. P. de Roever, and G. Rozenberg, eds., *Foundations of Object-Oriented Languages,* Springer-Verlag, 1991) ... who has proposed rules for determining based on type specifications whether one type is a subtype of another." In other words, the idea seems to be: Given two type specifications, what conditions must those specifications satisfy for one of the two types to be regarded as a subtype of the other? In our own work, by contrast, we took the diametrically opposite approach: We *assumed* that type S was a subtype of type T, then we spelled out in detail what the properties of type S must logically be, and went on to explore the logical implications of those properties (especially the substitutability implications). *Note:* I'll come back to this difference in approach later, when I discuss the "bags and stacks" example.

The Liskov/Wing Inheritance Model

In this section, I want to sketch and comment on certain features of the inheritance model that the Liskov/Wing paper appears to espouse. Throughout what follows, I'll assume that type S is supposed to be a subtype of type T. I'll also appeal from time to time to a trivial running example in which T is INT (integers) and S is EVEN (even integers)—though I'm not at all sure that Liskov and Wing would agree with this example (that is, I'm not sure they would allow the type "even integers" to be regarded as a subtype of the type "integers in general"!). This is clearly another point I'm going to have to elaborate on later, and I will.

---

15. After a period of initial study, that is. Of course, we did recognize that our decision to work from first principles meant we might be duplicating work already done by somebody else, but there seemed to be so much confusion in the field—not least the confusion over whether a circle was an ellipse!— that we decided we would be better off going it alone, as it were. And so we did, and I think we were.

First of all, then, S and T are allowed to have different "value spaces"; for example, values of type INT might be decimal, while values of type EVEN might be hexadecimal. In such a case, however, an *abstraction function* must be provided to "relate" *[sic]* values of type S to values of type T.

Comment: This first point looks like a model *vs.* implementation confusion to me. I would have said, rather, that (for example) every even integer simply *is* an integer; if for some reason we want to represent "even integers in particular" differently from "integers in general," well, that's an implementation matter, and it has nothing to do with the model. But object systems usually seem not to distinguish model and implementation properly. This first point is thus, perhaps, a consequence of (as I put it earlier) trying to formalize preexisting notions, instead of attempting to define a brand new model.

Next, S is allowed to have more values than T does! Here's a quote (slightly simplified): "Consider pairs and triples. Pairs have methods that fetch the first and second elements; triples have these methods plus an additional one to fetch the third element. *Triple is a subtype of pair*" [my italics].

Comment: **What?** Is this another consequence of trying to "formalize preexisting notions"? Surely, to say that S is a subtype of T is to say that every value of type S is a value of type T (i.e., the set of S values is a subset of the set of T values).[16] Thus, to say that "triple is a subtype of pair" is to say that every triple is a pair, or equivalently that triples are a special case of pairs!

Now, in our own inheritance model, we do take it as axiomatic that there can't be more values of type S than there are of type T (and we find this apparently trivial observation a great aid to clear thinking in this potentially confusing area). Furthermore, it seems to me that Liskov and Wing's rejection of this axiom constitutes in itself a violation of their own "Subtype Requirement"! For example, consider a method that, given an arbitrary object of some specific type T, returns the cardinality—i.e., the number of distinct values—of that type T. That method will clearly give different answers depending on whether it's invoked on a pair or a triple. (Equally clearly, such a method could be defined; I mean, I think the example is legitimate.)

Next (to quote again): "The subtype must provide all methods of its supertype;[17] we refer to these as the *inherited* methods."

Comment: Another model *vs.* implementation confusion! (and another consequence of trying to formalize preexisting notions?). I mean, the statement doesn't seem to need saying, unless there might otherwise have been some possibility that it wasn't true. Let me elaborate:

---

16. In other words, I agree with Robert Martin's remark—or, at least, the general sense of his remark—to the effect that "inheritance is the ISA relationship" (see earlier). Of course, Martin himself made that remark only in order to go on to refute it, but I reject his refutation!

17. Note the tacit assumption that a given subtype has just one supertype (more precisely, just one *immediate* supertype—see *The Third Manifesto*). Liskov and Wing do say they allow multiple supertypes, but there's no serious discussion of the possibility of multiple inheritance in their paper. In *The Third Manifesto*, by contrast, we show that multiple inheritance is not only desirable, it's logically *required* (i.e., single inheritance by itself makes little sense)—and we go on to examine the implications of this fact in considerable detail.

- If S is a subtype of T, then any method that applies to values of type T *must* apply to values of type S, because S values *are* T values. For example, if DOUBLE is a method that applies to integers in general, then certainly DOUBLE is a method that applies to even integers in particular. If it doesn't, then even integers aren't integers!

- Of course, it's true that a method M that applies to values of type T might be—might even *need* to be—*reimplemented* for type S; earlier in this chapter, I gave the example of a "method" called AREA that applies to values of type POLYGON and therefore to values of type RECTANGLE as well, but I also said that the method would probably be reimplemented for type RECTANGLE under the covers for performance reasons. But the fact that there are several implementation versions of an operator is indeed an implementation issue, not a model issue; to the user, there's just one method. (If AREA applies to polygons, it applies to rectangles by definition—because if it doesn't, then rectangles aren't polygons.)

By contrast, to reiterate, Liskov and Wing say "The subtype must provide all methods of its supertype." This remark can only mean that subtype and supertype *versions* of those methods are "provided" *and are user-visible*—and indeed, that's exactly what happens in the bags and stacks example (which I've already promised I'm going to discuss in more detail later). What's more, since those different implementation versions are exposed in the model, it follows *a fortiori* that different implementation version *names* are exposed, too. In the bags and stacks example, for instance, there's a method for adding a new element to the bag or stack, but it's called PUT for bags and PUSH for stacks.

Next, values aren't required to be values of leaf types specifically. In the case of integers and even integers, for example, a value can indeed be just an integer. In other words, there's no requirement that another type ODD be defined, such that ODD and EVEN are both proper subtypes of INT and every INT value is either an ODD value or an EVEN value. I agree with Liskov and Wing on this point. (By the way, if type ODD *were* defined, type INT would become a "virtual" type, or what *The Third Manifesto* calls a union type. Such types are important, but the Liskov/Wing paper has little to say about them—despite the fact that they do raise some rather interesting questions in connection with substitutability.)

Next: "[We allow] subtypes to have more methods than their supertypes." But if S doesn't have more methods than T, then what was the point of defining it as a subtype in the first place? In other words, I want to say that S must have at least one method that isn't defined for T, because otherwise it wouldn't be a proper subtype.

Another quote: "32-bit integers are not a subtype of 64-bit integers ... because a user of 64-bit integers would expect certain method calls to succeed that will fail when applied to 32-bit integers."

Comment: First, I'd really prefer to ignore the stuff about 32 *vs.* 64 bits (it looks like yet another model *vs.* implementation confusion); however, I suppose I can't. Anyway: Presumably what the authors mean by their use of such terms is that if type S consists of integers that *can be represented* using 32 bits and if type T consists of integers that *can be represented* using 64 bits, then S isn't a subtype of T. But I disagree with this claim, strongly! Certainly every integer that can be represented using 32 bits can also be represented using 64 bits, so every value of type S is also a value of type T.[18]

---

18. To say that "32-bit integers aren't a subset of 64-bit integers" is very like saying that the type "sets of cardinality less than or equal to 50" isn't a subtype of the type "sets of cardinality less than or equal to 100." Personally, I find this latter example even weirder than the one involving 32- and 64-bit integers.

So what about that business of "certain method calls succeeding on 64-bit integers but failing on 32-bit ones?" Presumably what the authors have in mind here is methods such as DOUBLE, where the result of doubling a 32-bit integer might be too large to represent using only 32 bits. All right then: Obviously, the result is of type "64-bit integer," not "32-bit integer." What's the problem?[19]

Well ... Actually I need to pursue this example a little further. In the previous paragraph, I was tacitly assuming that DOUBLE was an "observer," not a "mutator." In terms of **Tutorial D**—the language we use to illustrate the ideas of *The Third Manifesto*—DOUBLE might look like this:

```
OPERATOR DOUBLE ( I INT64 ) RETURNS INT64 ;
   RETURN ( I + I ) ;
END OPERATOR ;
```

When invoked, this operator—sorry, method—has no effect on the argument corresponding to its sole parameter I. And note too that, thanks to LSP, that argument can be of type INT32 as well as INT64. (Of course, I'm assuming here that INT32 and INT64 have the obvious semantics and that, *pace* Liskov and Wing, INT32 is indeed a subtype of INT64.)

However, suppose we were to make DOUBLE a *mutator* instead, thus:

```
OPERATOR DOUBLE ( I INT64 ) UPDATES { I } ;
   I := I + I ;
END OPERATOR ;
```

When this revised DOUBLE operator is invoked, it definitely does have an effect on the argument corresponding to its sole parameter I. And if that argument is of type INT32, not INT64, then the invocation might fail on an overflow error.[20] *Note:* I really need to be a bit more precise here. In our model, the problem under discussion can occur only if the argument is of *declared* type INT32. If its current *most specific* type is INT32 but its declared type is INT64, then the problem under discussion doesn't arise. See the subsequent discussion of *generalization by constraint.*

Anyway, it's presumably because of such possibilities (e.g., the possibility that the DOUBLE mutator might give an overflow if invoked on an INT32 "object" when it doesn't do so on a corresponding INT64 "object") that Liskov and Wing claim that INT32 isn't a subtype of INT64. Instead, they say, in effect, that we need to define a type INT consisting of all possible integers and having two distinct proper subtypes INT32 and INT64, neither of which is a subtype of the other. Then different versions of DOUBLE—DOUBLE32 and DOUBLE64, say—can be defined, with different preconditions (see later for a discussion of preconditions and postconditions), and the problem goes away.

But do you see what's happened? We've been forced into defining what's surely a rather strange and counterintuitive type hierarchy,[21] basically because *the model doesn't allow objects to change their type*—as I'll now try to explain.

---

19. In our model, the result will actually be of type "64-bit integer" only if it is indeed too large to represent using 32 bits; otherwise it'll be of type "32-bit integer." See the subsequent discussion of *specialization by constraint.*

20. Just as an aside, therefore, I'd like to point out that examples like this one can be seen as an argument—no pun intended—against the idea of mutators in the first place.

21. I don't even want to get into all of the complexities caused by the fact that the two subtypes INT32 and INT64—neither one of which is a subtype of the other, remember—*overlap*, in the sense that many integers (2^{32} of them, to be precise) are values of both types. Let me just observe that "overlapping types" is yet another topic that our own model does address, gracefully, that isn't even discussed in the Liskov/Wing paper.

Let me switch to the simpler (?) example of types INT and EVEN, and let's consider the DOUBLE method again. In our model, applying DOUBLE to a value of type INT—regardless of whether that value is also a value of type EVEN—will always give a result of type EVEN, automatically. In other words, our model supports what we call **specialization by constraint**, which means, in the case at hand, that any INT value will *automatically* be understood to be an EVEN value if it is in fact even. By contrast, I strongly suspect that Liskov and Wing would say that the result is merely of type INT—or, perhaps more accurately, they would say that EVEN isn't a subtype of INT, precisely because they don't support specialization by constraint and they don't want to deal with the real world fact that doubling any integer always returns an even result. *Note:* I must make it clear that their paper never spells these points out explicitly; so far as I know, however, our own inheritance model is the only one that does support specialization by constraint.

Following on from the previous point: Suppose now that we have an "object" O of type INT whose current value happens to be even (so in our model "the current most specific type"—as opposed to "the declared type" INT—of the object O is EVEN). And suppose we now increase the current value of O by one. In our model, then, the current most specific type of O is now just INT, not EVEN. In other words, our model also supports what we call **generalization by constraint**, which means, in the case at hand, that if the previous value of O was even but the current value is not, then O is *automatically* understood now to contain just an INT value, not an EVEN value. (Specialization by constraint and generalization by constraint—hereinafter abbreviated to S by C and G by C, respectively—go hand in hand. So far as I know, our own inheritance model is the only one that supports either of these concepts.)

Onward. My next point is this: Liskov and Wing tacitly seem to support unconditional inheritance of *mutators,* but they never discuss—in fact, they don't even mention—the logical absurdities that are necessary consequences of such unconditional inheritance. Here are some of those consequences (for further discussion, see *The Third Manifesto*):

- What seem to be "pure retrieval" operations can have the side-effect of updating the database.

- Values of (e.g.) type SQUARE can have sides of different lengths, thereby violating their own "squareness," undermining the database "as a model of reality," and causing programs to produce nonsensical results such as "nonsquare squares."

- S by C and G by C aren't supported.

- Type constraints aren't supported. (This one is fundamental! Type constraints are the mechanism by which legal values of the type in question are specified. Without type constraints, *there can be no check at all on the correctness of values in the database*. See *The Third Manifesto* once again.)

As *The Third Manifesto* makes clear, the common thread running through all of these problems is *a failure to make a clear distinction between values and variables.*

The last criticism I want to make concerning the Liskov and Wing model—not the last one I have, but the last one I want to articulate here—is that it fails to prescribe the semantics of equality! Rather, those semantics appear to be user-defined. In fact, it's not even clear that every type has to have an equality method, though the idea of not being able to tell whether two values of the same type are the same seems bizarre, to say the least.[22] Here's a quote:

---

22. By the way, equality methods illustrate very well the point that the idea of a distinguished parameter ("the method's object") sometimes seems artificial in the extreme.

If objects of the subtype have additional state, x *and* y *may differ when considered as subtype objects but ought to be considered equal when considered as supertype objects.*

And the authors give an example of two triples <0,0,0> and <0,0,1> that are clearly unequal "but are equal if they're considered just as pairs" (paraphrasing the original considerably).

Well, we've been here before. The idea that *equal* might be interpreted to mean *equal ignoring certain differences* is espoused in SQL today—for example, in the rule that says that the two character strings

'AB' (length two characters)

and

'AB ' (length three characters)

can be considered equal. And this rule has led to endless complications—for example, over the semantics of DISTINCT, and GROUP BY, and UNION, and many other operators (not to mention additional rules regarding, e.g., what's legal in integrity constraints and the like). Can't we learn from past mistakes? If not, why not?

Now, Liskov and Wing do go on to say (in the pairs and triples example) that two different methods are needed, "pair_equal" and "triple_equal," and of course that solves the problem in that particular case. But the fact remains that their model has no prescribed semantics for equality—not to mention the fact that it was the idea that the subtype could have more values than the supertype that caused the pair/triple problem in the first place.

Here's another quote that relates to the same point: "The need for several equality methods seems natural for realistic examples. For example, asking whether *e1* and *e2* are the same person is different from asking if they are the same employee. In the case of a person holding two jobs, the answer might be true for the question about person but false for the question about employee." Well, I suppose they're thinking of employees as <person,job> pairs; then two "employees" can be different and yet involve the same person. Nothing wrong with that. But what *is* wrong is to think of two such "employees" that involve the same person but different jobs as *equal!* Rather, the question to which the answer is *yes* is not "Are these two employees (i.e., <person,job> pairs) equal?" but "Do these two employees (i.e., <person,job> pairs) involve the same person?"

We're supposed to be talking about substitutability. Now, there's an extremely important and fundamental principle in logic that says that if *a* and *b* are equal, then *a* can be substituted for *b*—or the other way around—**in absolutely any logical statement whatsoever** (see, e.g., James D. McCawley, *Everything that Linguists Have Always Wanted to Know about Logic (but were ashamed to ask),* University of Chicago Press, 1981). Clearly, the same is not true for two "employees" that involve the same person but different jobs. Thus, the model that Liskov and Wing describe appears to be violating an absolutely crucial *logical* principle of substitutability.

As an aside, perhaps I should make it clear that Hugh Darwen and I do know how to handle examples like "pairs and triples" or "persons and jobs" in our own model; in particular, we know how to get some code reuse in such cases—code reuse, after all, being one of the benefits usually claimed for subtyping and inheritance. But we can achieve that reuse without having to pretend that every triple is a pair!

The Running Example

The Liskov/Wing paper makes extensive use of a running example involving *bags and stacks.* Here's the paper's own introduction to the example:

> *Consider a bounded bag type that provides a* put *method that inserts elements into a bag and a* get *method that removes an arbitrary element from a bag.* Put *has a precondition that checks to see that adding an element will not grow the bag beyond its bound;* get *has a precondition that checks to see that the bag is nonempty.*

> *Consider also a bounded stack type that has, in addition to* push *and* pop *methods, a* swap_top *method that takes an integer, i, and modifies the stack by replacing its top with i. Stack's* push *and* pop *methods have preconditions similar to bag's* put *and* get, *and* swap_top *has a precondition requirng that the stack is nonempty.*

Note: For clarity, from this point forward I'll set the type names and method names in uppercase, even when I'm giving what are otherwise *verbatim* quotes from the Liskov/Wing paper.

Observe, by the way, that the running example involves bags and stacks containing integers specifically; the much more interesting question of *generic* bag and stack types isn't discussed. Anyway, to continue with that example:

> *Suppose we want to show STACK is a subtype of BAG. We need to relate the values of stacks to those of bags. This can be done by means of an* abstraction function ... *A given STACK value maps to a BAG value where we abstract from* [= ignore?] *the insertion order on the elements.*

> *We also need to relate STACK's methods to BAG's. Clearly there is a correspondence between STACK's PUSH method and BAG's PUT and similarly for the POP and GET methods (even though the names of the corresponding methods do not match).*

At this point I'd like to make a few observations about the example. First of all, note the assumption that the two types already exist, and now we're trying to show that one is a subtype of the other. In other words, to paraphrase something I said previously, the emphasis is on *verifying the hypothesis* that STACK is a subtype of BAG. It's not a matter of taking the statement "STACK is a subtype of BAG" as a given and exploring the logical consequences of that fact; rather, it's the exact opposite.[23] (And so I've been quite unfair to the Liskov/Wing paper in this chapter so far, because I've almost totally ignored what the authors regard as its main contribution! But my purpose isn't so much to examine that contribution as such, but rather—to say it one more time—to figure out what the Liskov Substitution Principle is.)

Second, it's presumably because the two types already exist that we get into that business of their having "different value spaces" (see earlier). After all, it's almost certainly the case that bags and stacks will have different storage representations (note the remark about "relating the values of stacks to those of bags"). But I stand by my claim that such questions are an implementation matter merely and shouldn't show through to the model level. We shouldn't even be

---

23. In other words, Liskov and Wing are effectively suggesting that if we have substitutability, then we have subtyping. Our own approach, by contrast, is to say that if we have subtyping, then we have substitutability.

talking about them at the model level, even if we're discussing the two types independently and not considering the possibility that one might be a subtype of the other.

Third, it's also because the two types already exist that "corresponding methods have different names"—i.e., the fact that there are different *versions* of "the same" method is exposed at the model level (note the remark about "relating STACK's methods to BAG's"). Again, however, I stand by my claim that such issues are an implementation matter merely and shouldn't show through to the model level; again, we shouldn't even be *talking* about them at the model level.

The foregoing conjectures on my part are reinforced by the following facts:

- The paper explicitly states that "subtypes must provide [the] expected methods with compatible signatures." This remark too suggests an emphasis on preexisting types, because if we were explicitly *defining* a new type S to be a subtype of an existing type T, there's no way S *couldn't* have "[the] expected methods with compatible signatures." (In our approach, in fact, the question of whether the signatures are "compatible" doesn't even make sense.)

- The paper also states that "a common case [is] that the subtype adds some extra methods [like SWAP_TOP in the example] *but does not change any existing ones*" (italics added). "Changing existing methods" here refers, I'm pretty sure, to the idea that the *implementations* might be different at the supertype and subtype levels—suggesting, again, that we're really talking about distinct *implementation versions* of "the same" method, and thus talking about an implementation concern rather than a model one.

Preconditions and Postconditions

Back to the running example. I assume it's clear, at least in principle, how the necessary mappings of stack values and methods to bag values and methods might be done. Thus, we're close to being able to say that STACK is a subtype of BAG. However, we aren't quite all the way there ... According to Liskov and Wing, we also need to show that:

- The *preconditions* for PUT and GET imply those for PUSH and POP, respectively.

- The *postconditions* for PUSH and POP imply those for PUT and GET, respectively.

For brevity, let's consider just PUT and PUSH and ignore the other two. Informally, the precondition for PUT is simply that the target bag isn't full, or in other words that its current size is less than the maximum size (recall that the bags we're talking about are bounded ones specifically). Analogously, the precondition for PUSH is that the target stack isn't full.[24] So it's easy to see that the precondition for PUT implies that for PUSH.

Likewise, the postcondition for PUSH is that the stack now additionally contains the specified integer in its topmost position, while the postcondition for PUT is that the bag now additionally contains the specified integer (we can't say where, because the concept of position within a bag has no meaning). Thus, it's easy to see that the postcondition for PUSH implies that for PUT.

---

24. Of course, there are other aspects to the preconditions (and postconditions); for example, the operands for PUT must be of type BAG and INT, respectively. I'm ignoring such issues here for simplicity.

Of course, it goes without saying that in order for the foregoing logical implications to be checked, the preconditions and postconditions in question must be explicitly stated somewhere. Liskov and Wing propose a **requires** clause for stating preconditions and an **ensures** clause for stating postconditions; these clauses appear as part of the specification of the method in question. (At run time, then, it should be possible—at least in principle—for the system to check that any given method invocation does indeed satisfy the stated conditions, but such run-time checking isn't the principal point of the clauses.)

Our own type model—our *type* model, please note, not our inheritance model—currently includes nothing corresponding to the **requires** and **ensures** clauses, though there's no reason why we couldn't extend it to do so if we wanted to. What we definitely wouldn't do, however, is have two distinct versions of the same method, a subtype version and a supertype version, both explicitly user-visible, with two distinct sets of preconditions and postconditions. In our view, the need to check the various precondition and postcondition implications arises from a defect in the Liskov/Wing model: more precisely, from the fact that the model exposes certain features (i.e., distinct versions of the same method) that ought really to be hidden.

Covariance and Contravariance

Liskov and Wing also espouse two notions called "covariance" and "contravariance." Our own inheritance model supports covariance, too; in fact, you can't *not* support it if you support substitutability (which is to say, if you support subtyping and inheritance at all, since in our view subtyping and inheritance logically imply substitutability). Covariance—more precisely referred to as *result* covariance—says that if a method M is defined to return a result of type T, then an invocation of M is allowed to return a result of any subtype of T. For example, if "add one" is defined to return a result of type INT, sometimes it will return a result of type EVEN instead. (Here once again INT is integers, EVEN is even integers, and EVEN is a subtype of INT.)

Contravariance is another matter, however. I don't really want to get into a lot of detail here, because the topic is a little complicated; suffice it to say that I strongly suspect Liskov and Wing are forced into considering it because (as noted earlier) they're trying to define subtyping in terms of substitutability, and their model thus necessarily seems to include some features that I believe should be kept firmly under the covers. In our own model, by contrast, where we define substitutability in terms of subtyping, we find no good reason for embracing the concept of contravariance at all, and indeed we explicitly reject it. (In fact, we claim in *The Third Manifesto* that contravariance seems to be a case of *the implementation tail wagging the model dog*.)

Extending the Example

Suppose it's been established that STACK is indeed a subtype of BAG in accordance with all of the requirements of the Liskov/Wing proposal. Now suppose we want to define a new method—more precisely, a new "observer"—called UNION that takes two bags and returns the bag union of those two bags.[25] What happens?

---

25. The bag union of two bags A and B is a bag in which the value v appears exactly n times if and only if it appears exactly a times in A and exactly b times in B and $n = MAX(a,b)$. In fact, the Liskov/Wing paper mentions a union operator for bags in passing, but doesn't give a precise definition for it and doesn't attempt to show it as a method.

Clearly, if the supertype/subtype relationships are to be maintained, UNION has to work when the operands are two stacks, or one stack and one bag, as well as when they're both just bags. (For simplicity, let's agree until further notice to use the term *bag* to mean, specifically, a bag that isn't a stack.) Well, we can obviously write some procedural code—I mean, we can implement versions of the UNION method—that will work for these two cases. However, the result is surely just a bag in both cases; certainly I don't see a sensible way of defining a "union" of two stacks that produces another stack as a result.

The foregoing paragraph notwithstanding, I still don't think there's a problem—not yet, at any rate. But suppose now that the UNION method is defined to be a *mutator*, not an observer (i.e., it actually modifies one of its arguments). According to everything I've understood about the Liskov/Wing model so far, then, UNION will fail if the argument to be modified happens to be a stack, not just a bag! (As I understand it, objects can't change type, and generalization by constraint isn't supported, in that model.) In other words, the Liskov/Wing "Subtype Require-ment" is violated—there's at least one context in which I simply can't substitute stacks for bags. Am I forced to conclude, therefore, that *it's no longer the case that STACK is a subtype of BAG?*

Now, I pointed out earlier that the Liskov/Wing paper explicitly defines a type to consist, in part, of some specific set of methods, and hence that adding a new method to a given type changes the type. Thus, it could logically be argued that adding the UNION mutator method to type BAG yields a brand new type, BAG+ say, and "all bets are off"—meaning that all supertype/subtype relationships now need to be reexamined and reestablished, where appropriate. (In this connection, let me draw your attention to the title of the paper: "A *Behavioral* Notion of Subtyping"—emphasis added. That title does tend to suggest that if the behavior changes, the supertype/subtype relationships change too.)

Such reexamining and reestablishing of existing relationships seems to be a necessary consequence of defining subtyping in terms of substitutability instead of the other way around. So (to say it again) the position might be logically defensible. But is it desirable? Myself, I wouldn't have thought so—though it is admittedly still the case that a program that previously worked for bags, and therefore could previously be invoked on stacks instead of bags, can still be invoked on stacks instead of bags, because (by definition) such a program won't be using the new UNION method anyway.[26]

Extension and Constraint Subtypes

Toward the end of their paper, Liskov and Wing have this to say:

> The requirement we impose on subtypes is very strong and raises a concern that it might rule out many useful subtype relations. To address this concern we looked at a number of examples ... The examples led us to classify subtype relationships into two broad cate-gories. In the first category, the subtype extends the supertype by providing additional methods and possibly additional "state." In the second, the subtype is more constrained than the supertype.

---

26. Except that there aren't any bags now, there are what we might call "bag+"s instead. Or do we have to keep type BAG as it was before, and define BAG+ as a proper subtype of BAG? But then every BAG value would be a BAG+ value too; thus, to say that BAG+ is a "subtype" of BAG looks to me suspiciously like a hack. (In fact, in our own inheritance model, we require that if S is a proper subtype of T, then there must exist at least one value of T that *isn't* a value of S.)

Actually, the requirement that Liskov and Wing impose on subtypes isn't as strong as ours! We require every value of the subtype to be a value of the supertype (in other words, we require proper subtypes to be proper subsets), as explained earlier and as just mentioned in a footnote. Nevertheless, we believe we can handle, cleanly, all of the various problems that—it has been claimed, at one time or another, by one writer or another—a general model of "subtyping and inheritance" ought to be able to handle (though it's true that we don't always handle the problem in question by means of subtyping and inheritance as such).

Be that as it may, let's take a look at the two categories of subtype relationships. The first is called "extension subtypes." This is what Liskov and Wing have to say on this topic:

> *A subtype extends its supertype if its objects have extra methods in addition to those of the supertype. [They] might also have more "state" ... One common example concerns persons, employees, and students ... A person object has methods that report its properties such as its name, age, [etc.]. Student and employee are subtypes of person; in each case they have additional properties, e.g., a student id number, an employee number and salary ... In this example, the subtype objects have more state than those of the supertype as well as more methods.*

As you know by now, in our own model, by contrast, (a) we require subtypes to have extra methods, but (b) we reject the notion of "state" entirely, so subtypes cannot possibly have more of it. So what about the example of, e.g., persons and employees? (Let's ignore students, for simplicity.) Well, one way to approach the problem is to define an EMPLOYEE as a *tuple* of two components, one of which is of type PERSON and the other is of type OTHER_STUFF (employee number, for example). Then EMPLOYEE *isn't* a subtype of PERSON, but any program that operates on PERSONs will work for the PERSON component of an EMPLOYEE, and any program that operates on EMPLOYEEs can reuse the programs that work for PERSONs. In this way, code reuse can still be obtained, without any need to muddy a clear, clean, and logically sensible model of subtyping and inheritance.

I turn now to the second category of subtypes, "constrained subtypes." To quote Liskov and Wing again:

> *The second type of subtype relation occurs when the subtype is more constrained than the supertype. In this case, the supertype specification is written in a way that allows variation in behavior among its subtypes. Subtypes constrain the supertype by reducing the variability ... The subtype may extend those supertype objects that it simulates by providing additional methods and/or state.*

The last sentence here is unfortunate, it seems to me. Again, we would require extra methods and prohibit "state" entirely—but if (for the sake of this discussion only) we accept the possibility of additional "state," it would appear that the two subtype categories are thus not independent of one another. Wouldn't such independence be desirable?[27] Also, I find the use of the term "simulates" a little puzzling; are the authors suggesting that if a certain stack "simulates" a certain bag, *both the stack and the bag are physically materialized in storage?*

---

27. In any case, it seems to me that if "the subtype is more constrained than the supertype," it can't possibly have "additional state." By way of illustration, see Robert Martin's discussion of the rectangles-and-squares example, quoted earlier in this chapter.

Anyway, so far as our own model is concerned, the two subtype categories collapse into one. Indeed, we think subtypes should always be "more constrained" than their supertypes. In fact, we argue in *The Third Manifesto* that logically constraining supertypes is the only logically correct way to define subtypes! And Liskov and Wing seem to like the approach too:

> *[We] prefer the constraint approach ... The constraint approach is appealing because it is simple and direct ... [Including] constraints in specifications makes for a more robust methodology ... Being able to state everything declaratively seems like a particularly important advantage of the constraint aproach.*

Note: Actually, the foregoing remarks apply, not to constrained subtypes as such, but rather to what Liskov and Wing call *the constraint approach to defining subtypes*. However, the two concepts are very much interrelated, and I don't think I'm misrepresenting—at least, I *hope* I'm not misrepresenting—the authors' position here. If I'm wrong, I hope they'll accept my apologies.

Given the foregoing, it's interesting to note that James Rumbaugh, in his article "A Matter of Intent: How to Define Subclasses" (*Journal of Object-Oriented Programming*, September 1996)— which I quoted earlier, as you might recall—says almost exactly the opposite:

> *[Most] object-oriented languages do not want objects to change class ... [This] suggests [a] design principle for classification systems:* A subclass should not be defined by constraining a superclass.

Hmmm ...

Substitutability Defined

I'd like to end this chapter with a precise definition of the concept of substitutability—actually two such definitions, because (as noted earlier) we find it necessary to distinguish between *value* substitutability and *variable* substitutability. That distinction in turn rests on the distinction between read-only operators and update operators—or observers and mutators, to use the object terms, but now I definitely do want to talk in terms of operators, not methods. Also, I'll use the term *polymorphism* to mean *inclusion* polymorphism specifically (as explained earlier, inclusion polymorphism is the kind of polymorphism we get with subtyping and inheritance).

Value Substitutability: Basically, if S is a subtype of T, then every read-only operator that applies to values of type T also applies to values of type S. More precisely:

> Let *Op* be a read-only operator, let *P* be a parameter to *Op*, and let *T* be the declared type for *P*. Then the declared type of the argument expression (and hence *a fortiori* the most specific type of the argument value) corresponding to parameter *P* in an invocation of *Op* can be **any subtype** S of *T*. In other words, the read-only operator *Op* applies to values of type *T* and therefore, necessarily, to values of type S—*The Principle of (Read-only) Operator Inheritance*. It follows that such operators are *polymorphic*, since they apply to values of several different types—*The Principle of (Read-only) Operator Polymorphism*. And it further follows that wherever a value of type *T* is permitted, a value of type S is also permitted—*The Principle of (Value) Substitutability*.

Variable Substitutability: Basically, if S is a subtype of T, then an update operator that applies to variables of declared type T applies to variables of declared type S only in those cases where such application makes sense. More precisely:

Let *Op* be an update operator, let *P* be a parameter to *Op* that is subject to update, and let *T* be the declared type for *P*. Then it might or might not be the case that the declared type (and hence *a fortiori* the current most specific type) of the argument variable corresponding to parameter *P* in some invocation of *Op* can be a proper subtype of type *T*. It follows that for each such update operator *Op* and for each parameter *P* to *Op* that is subject to update, it is necessary to state explicitly for which subtypes of the declared type *T* of parameter *P* operator *Op* shall be inherited—*The Principle of (**Update**) Operator Inheritance*. (And if update operator *Op* is not inherited in this way by type *S*, it is not inherited by any subtype of type *S* either.) Update operators are thus only conditionally polymorphic—*The Principle of (**Update**) Operator Polymorphism*. If *Op* is an update operator and *P* is a parameter to *Op* that is subject to update and *S* is a subtype of the declared type *T* of *P* for which *Op* is inherited, then by definition it is possible to invoke *Op* with an argument variable corresponding to parameter *P* that is of declared type *S*—*The Principle of (**Variable**) Substitutability*.

I'll illustrate these ideas by repeating some remarks I made in "Is a Circle an Ellipse?" (Chapter 23 in the present book). Let types T and S be ELLIPSE and CIRCLE, respectively (of course, I do assume here that CIRCLE is a proper subtype of ELLIPSE). Then:

- All read-only operations that apply to ellipse values—"get the area," for example—apply to circle values too (because circle values *are* ellipse values); that is, read-only operations associated with type ELLIPSE are inherited unconditionally by type CIRCLE. However, there are some read-only operations associated with type CIRCLE—"get the radius," for example—that don't apply to type ELLIPSE. In other words, the set of read-only operations that apply to circle values is *a proper superset* of the set of read-only operations that apply to ellipse values.

- Some update operations that apply to ellipse variables—"change the center," for example—apply to circle variables too.[28] Other such operations—"change the *a* semiaxis," for example—*don't* apply to circle variables too (because circle variables *aren't* ellipse variables; that is, a variable of declared type CIRCLE can't hold a value that's "just an ellipse," and changing the *a* semiaxis of a circle yields a result that's "just an ellipse," in general). In other words, update operations associated with type ELLIPSE are *not* inherited unconditionally by type CIRCLE. Moreover, there are some update operations associated with type CIRCLE—"change the radius," for example—that don't apply to type ELLIPSE. Thus, the set of update operations that apply to circle variables is neither a subset nor a superset of the set of such operations that apply to ellipse variables.

- Let E be a variable of declared type ELLIPSE. Then updating E in such a way that $a = b$ after the update means the most specific type of the current value of E is now CIRCLE. Likewise, updating E in such a way that $a > b$ after the update means the most specific type of the current value of E is now "just ELLIPSE."

For further explanation and discussion of such matters, with many worked examples, please refer to *The Third Manifesto*.

---

28. By the terms "ellipse variable" and "circle variable," I mean a variable of declared type ELLIPSE and one of declared type CIRCLE, respectively. Note too that, in our model, a variable of (for example) declared type ELLIPSE contains ELLIPSE *values*, not "object IDs" that somehow point to ellipses. Our model has no notion of object IDs, nor indeed of objects *per se*.

PART 7

∎ ∎ ∎

Relational *vs.* Nonrelational Systems

This final part of the book consists of four chapters. Chapter 25 addresses the question of what the verb "to model" (much used in nonrelational database writings) means. Chapter 26 is an investigation into the Unified Modeling Language (UML) and the associated Object Constraint Language (OCL). Chapter 27 is a tutorial and critical analysis of the proposals of the Object Data Management Group (ODMG). Finally, Chapter 28 is an investigation into proposals for dealing with temporal data that are based on TSQL2 or variants thereof.

■ ■ ■

Models, Models, Everywhere, Nor Any Time to Think

I wondered in a bewildered manner whether it was my friends or I that were mad.

—Bertrand Russell

model, mod'l, n. *plan, design* (obs.): *a preliminary solid representation, generally small, or in plastic material, to be followed in construction: something to be copied: a pattern: an imitation of something on a smaller scale: a person or thing closely resembling another: one who poses for an artist: one who exhibits clothes for a shop by wearing them: a pattern of excellence: an article of standard design or a copy of one: structural type: a medal* (obs.): *a close covering or mould* (Shak.).—adj. *of the nature of a model: set up for imitation: completely suitable for imitation, exemplary.*—v.t. *to form after a model: to shape: to make a model or copy of: to form in some plastic material: of a mannequin, to display (a garment) by wearing it.*—v.i. *to practice modeling ...* [O.Fr. modelle—It. modello, dim. of modo—L. modus, a measure.]

—*Chambers Twentieth Century Dictionary*

Is it only me that has difficulty in understanding exactly what IT people mean when they use the term *model?* (That's *model,* not muddle.) My own opinion is that the term is grotesquely overused—not to say misused, or abused—in the IT world, especially in the database portions of that world. A while back, I had occasion to read an article titled "Persistence Modeling in the UML," by Scott W. Ambler (it was an installment of his regular column "Thinking Objectively" in the August 1999 issue of the magazine *Software Development*). While that article was neither the first nor the only one to make me wonder over the meaning of the term, it did act as a catalyst to get me to put some thoughts down on paper on the subject. What follows, then, can be seen as an attempt—almost certainly doomed to failure—to alert people to some of the worst excesses in this regard and to try to persuade them to think twice (at least!) before they use the term in future.

Note: All otherwise unattributed quotes in this chapter are taken from Ambler's article (hereinafter referred to as *the subject article*).

"Modeling in the UML"

To repeat, the subject article was titled "Persistence Modeling in the UML." As you probably know, "UML" stands for "Unified Modeling Language." To quote the book *The Unified Modeling Language User Guide* (Addison-Wesley, 1999), by Grady Booch, James Rumbaugh, and Ivar Jacobson (the inventors of UML), UML is "a graphical language"—*methodology* might be a better term—"for visualizing, specifying, constructing, and documenting the artifacts of a software-intensive system." In other words, UML is meant as a tool to help with the task of application design, database design, and so on. And it certainly is, as advertised, *graphical:* It consists in large part of an extensive set of rules, conventions, and techniques for drawing different kinds of diagrams (class diagrams, object diagrams, interaction diagrams, activity diagrams, and many others). It might be characterized, loosely, as "E/R modeling, only more so."

So the term *modeling* in the UML context basically seems to mean "drawing a picture of [*something*]."[1] But then "Persistence Modeling"—the other part of the subject article's title—would seem to mean drawing a picture of *persistence*, a possibility I can't get my head around at all. Perhaps the term is intended to mean, rather, "drawing a picture of *persistent data*." But then, surely, "drawing a picture of persistent data" is nothing more nor less than the process of *designing a database* (at least, that's what many people do when they're designing a database—namely, draw pictures of persistent data). So perhaps the subject article should have been called just "Database Design with UML."

The subject article then goes on to say: "In reality, your persistence strategy can be so complex that you inevitably need to model it." Here "persistence strategy" can only mean database design (at the logical level, presumably), and the phrase *model it* therefore just seems to mean "design—or plan, or specify, or define, or *something*—your database" (again, at the logical level).

"The UML does not explicitly include a data model—more appropriately named a persistence model—in the object world." Hmmm. In my book *An Introduction to Database Systems*, 8th edition (Addison-Wesley, 2004), I wrote:[2]

> *[The] term* data model *is used in the literature with two quite different meanings ... The difference between the two ... can be characterized thus:*
>
> *A data model in the first sense is like a* programming language—*albeit one that is somewhat abstract—whose constructs can be used to solve a wide variety of specific problems, but in and of themselves have no direct connection with any such specific problem. The relational model is a data model in this sense.*

---

1. I feel bound to say immediately that I was never much of a fan of such pictures. E/R diagrams in particular, while they can be useful for explicating the structure of the database at a high intuitive level, are virtually incapable of representing *integrity constraints* (except for a few special cases—including foreign key constraints in particular—that are admittedly important in practice). So far as I'm concerned, by contrast, database design is really all about specifying integrity constraints!—that is, database design *is* constraint definition. I've elaborated on this argument in a recent book (*WHAT Not HOW: The Business Rules Approach to Application Development*, Addison-Wesley, 2000) and elsewhere.
2. As the following extract shows, I do believe the term model can be given a sensible meaning in appropriate contexts (see the next section for further discussion). The trouble is, it's often used in contexts that are utterly inappropriate, with meanings—or intended meanings—that can only be guessed at.

A data model in the second sense is like a specific program *written in the language referred to in the previous paragraph. In other words, a data model in the second sense takes the facilities provided by some model in the first sense and applies them to some specific problem; it is a model of the persistent data of* some particular enterprise. *It can be regarded as a* specific application *of some model in the first sense.*

The subject article's use of the term *data model* in the sentence quoted above ("The UML does not explicitly include a data model ... in the object world") refers, I think, to the first of these two senses. But then it says that it—i.e., the data model—would better be called a *persistence* model! A *data* model is a model of data ... A *persistence* model is a model of persistence (whatever that means). Data ≠ persistence. (Especially "in the object world," where it's generally believed that persistence and data types are, or should be, orthogonal to one another. I don't subscribe to that belief myself—at least, not fully—but that's not the point at issue here.)

"[You] can use class models to model an objectbase's schema ...": I'm not exactly sure what a class model is (it's not mentioned in the index to the UML book I referred to earlier), but I suspect it's something like what's more usually called a *type constructor* or *type generator* (I could be wrong). Anyway, what it might mean to use *anything* "to model an objectbase's schema" I have no idea. Surely a schema *is* a (data) model, in the second of the two senses explained above?

"[Class models] are not immediately appropriate for modeling schema [*sic*] of relational databases": I include this quote merely because I think it supports the suggestion in the previous paragraph to the effect that class models are basically type generators. If UML includes, e.g., SET and BAG and ARRAY and LIST "class models" but no RELATION "class model,"[3] it would indeed not be "immediately appropriate for modeling schema[s] of relational databases."

"[The] only thing that logical persistence models show that standard class models don't is candidate keys, and frankly, modeling candidate keys is a bad idea": I infer from this quote that a "logical persistence model" is something like a RELATION type generator, since it does apparently "show candidate keys" (though persistence has nothing to do with the matter!—relations might or might not be "persistent"). As for "modeling candidate keys" being "a bad idea": Quite apart from the breathtaking implications of this remark—candidate keys are categorically *essential* and *must* be specified!—I don't really know what it means to "model" a key. Does the term "model" really mean anything more in this context than just *specify?*

"Keys form the greatest single source of coupling in relational databases ... It is good practice to reduce coupling within your design [= *your model?*]; therefore, you want to avoid using keys with business meaning. The implication is that you really don't want to model candidate keys." The suggestion to "reduce coupling" here is fatuous, of course. As for the admonition not "to model candidate keys," that piece of advice seems to mean rather that you *should* "model" them, but the keys in question should be surrogate keys, not "natural" ones (see later). And "modeling" such keys just seems to mean *specifying* them.

"Figure 2 shows an example of a physical persistence model, which describes [*models?*] a relational database's schema": **Physical?!?** The whole point about a relational schema is that it's *not* "physical"! Does the writer perhaps mean a *logical* "persistence model"? If so, what's the precise difference between a logical and a physical "persistence model"? And in any case: Is "describes" here, as suggested, really just a synonym for *models?*

---

3. I've no idea whether such is the case, but it does seem likely, given the track record of object methodologies in general. (Note that I do think UML can fairly be regarded as such a methodology. As the subject article itself says, "the Unified Modeling Language [is] the industry standard notation ... for modeling *object-oriented software*" [my italics].)

"Figure 3 shows how to model views, alternative access paths to one or more tables, modeled as class symbols [*classes?*] with the stereotype <<*view*>>": Oh *dear* ... I'm supposed to be concentrating on the subject article's use of the term *model*, but other considerations keep pushing themselves to the fore. Views are just *not* "alternative access paths to one or more tables." It would take me much too far away from what I'm trying to do here to deal with this quote adequately; let me just say that *a view is a table*—not an "access path," alternative or otherwise—and any suggestion that views are somehow different from "tables" betrays a deep lack of understanding of the relational model. Unfortunately, that lack of understanding is all too widespread (it pervades the SQL standard, for example), so the author can perhaps be forgiven. Certainly he isn't alone.

Anyway: What does it mean to "model" a view? And does "modeled" in this extract mean anything other than just "represented"?

"Indices ... are modeled as class symbols [*classes?*] with a <<*primary index*>> or <<*secondary index*>> stereotype. You use indices to implement the primary and secondary [*sic*] keys, if any, in a relational database. A primary key is the preferred access method [*sic!*] for a table, whereas secondary keys provide quick access via alternative paths. Indices are interesting because their attributes, which all have implementation visibility, imply [*sic!*] the attributes that form the primary and secondary keys ... of a given table." Well, I hardly know where to start ... Indices (personally I prefer the variant *indexes,* but it's not a big deal) are, of course, an imple-mentation concept—they have no place at all in a relational schema, which deliberately, and by definition, has absolutely zero to say about implementation matters. So there are many, many things wrong with this quote from a relational perspective. Again, however, I'm supposed to be concentrating on the subject article's usage of the term *model.* So what on earth does it mean to say that indexes are "modeled" (whether by means of "class symbols," with some kind of "stereotype," or by any other means)? I strongly suspect that it simply means that the fact that there's an index on a certain combination of columns is *documented*—nothing more and nothing less.

"Foreign keys are ... clunky because they are effectively [*sic*] columns that depend on columns in another table (either the primary key columns or one [*sic*] of the secondary key columns). [*How does this fact make them "clunky"?*]. To model this properly [*what? the clunkiness?*], you should have a dependency relationship between the two [*sic*] columns, although this [*what does "this" refer to?*] quickly clutters up your diagrams. You could potentially indicate this type of dependency with a constraint, but I suspect this [*what does "this" refer to?*] would unneces-sarily complicate your models." Here *models* apparently means *pictures*—and the gist of the quote reinforces my contention that such pictures are not a good way to "model" the database in the first place. (As indicated earlier, database design is, first and foremost, a matter of capturing integrity constraints, and integrity constraints in general are just not susceptible to representa-tion as simple pictures. But there again, the subject article has very little to say on the subject of integrity constraints at all, in general.)

What *Does* "Model" Mean?

Let's get away from the subject article for a little while ... I should probably explain what *I* think the term "model" means. The following remarks are extracted from a paper of my own, "Why 'The Object Model' Is Not a Data Model" (published in *Relational Database Writings 1994–1997,* Addison-Wesley, 1998):

[A] model (of anything) is basically a construction, as concrete or as abstract as we please, that captures certain aspects of the thing being modeled—where by "capturing certain aspects" I mean that features or properties of the model mimic, in certain specific ways, features or properties of the thing being modeled. Study of the model can thereby lead to improved understanding of the thing being modeled.

In particular, therefore, a model of data *is a construction—necessarily somewhat abstract, since data itself is already a fairly abstract concept—that captures certain aspects of data. What aspects? Well, the aspects we're interested in are clearly those that are intrinsic, as opposed to those that are mere artifacts of some particular representation or implementation. We want to study data in its pure form and not be distracted by irrelevancies. To use the usual jargon, we're interested in the logical aspects of data, not the physical aspects.*

It follows that a good *model of data will be one that (like the relational model) is "logical, not physical"—i.e., one that captures only logical aspects, not physical aspects. (Ideally it would capture* all *of those logical aspects, of course, but this goal I take to be unachievable.) Moreover, it shouldn't include anything else!—i.e., there should be no properties or features that don't correspond to anything intrinsic. In IMS, for example, the very same data item can be interpreted either as a character string or as a packed decimal number; but this oddity is merely an artifact of "the IMS model" (if I might be permitted to use such a term)—it certainly isn't something that's intrinsic to data per se.[4]*

To be more specific, a good data model will include a set of objects *(using the word here in its generic sense, not its object-oriented sense), together with a set of* operators *for operating on those objects. The objects allow us to model the* structure *of data. The operators allow us to model its* behavior. *Taken together, therefore, the objects and operators effectively constitute an* abstract machine—*and we can thus usefully distinguish the model from its* implementation, *which is the physical realization of that abstract machine on some underlying real machine. In a nutshell: The model is what users have to know about; the implementation is what users don't have to know about.*

Next, the objects and operators of the model serve as a basis for further investigations into the nature of data. For example, what does it mean for data to be secure? consistent? redundant? (and so on). And those investigations in turn can lead to (compatible!) extensions to the original model; that is, the model can grow over time to become an ever more faithful abstraction of data "as it really is." In other words, a model of data is really a theory *of data (or at least the beginnings of one), and it's not a static thing.*

Note: With reference to the earlier remarks in this chapter concerning the two meanings of the term *data model,* I hope it's clear that the foregoing extract applies primarily to the term in its first sense.

---

4. In fact, of course, it's a consequence of a failure to distinguish adequately between type and representation.

Miscellaneous Observations

Now let's get back to the subject article. The fact is, that article includes a number of other remarks that, while they mostly don't make use of the term *model* as such, I simply can't let go by without comment.

> *The object paradigm ... is based on the concept of object networks that have both data and behavior, networks that you traverse.*

I couldn't agree more!—the "object paradigm" categorically does involve "networks that you traverse." And that's what's wrong with it (or one of the things that's wrong with it, anyway). Traversing networks was *exactly* what we had to do before relational databases came along. Object databases are a throwback to the prerelational era.

> *Object technology employs concepts that are well supported by the UML such as classes, inheritance, polymorphism, and encapsulation.*

This quote would be funny if it weren't so sad. First of all, there's no universally agreed definition of the term *class*. Second, *inheritance* is generally not well understood (certainly there's no good, formal, robust, rigorous, and universally agreed inheritance *model*[5]). Third, there are many distinct kinds of *polymorphism*, and there's much confusion in the literature over which kind is which and which kind applies when. Fourth and last, *encapsulation* is widely misunderstood, and indeed something of a red herring (as I've claimed elsewhere, in fact; see my article "Encapsulation Is a Red Herring," *DBP&D 12*, No. 9, September 1998, reprinted in my self-published book *Relational Database Writings 1997–2001*). What's more, encapsulation is (by definition) about hiding information; and if the information is hidden, then it can't be "modeled" (at least, not at the user or logical level). So there does seem to be some confusion here.

> *The relational paradigm ... is based on collections of entities that only have data and rows of data that you combine, which you then process as you see fit. Relational technology employs concepts such as tables, columns, keys, relationships between tables, indices on tables, stored procedures, and data access maps.*

The subject article was written (or at least published) in 1999. The relational model was first described in *1969*. How is it possible that there can be such a huge lack of understanding of it—on the part of IT professionals, I mean—over 30 years later? By the way: I would certainly claim to know something about relational technology, and I've never heard of "data access maps."

> *[Subtyping] relationships are indicated* [modeled?] *using inheritance.*

This remark bothers me because it's clear from the context that what the author has in mind is what's usually referred to as "subtables and supertables." In our book on *The Third Manifesto*, Hugh Darwen and I have conclusively demonstrated—in our own not unbiased

---

5. And here I really do mean *model!* A good inheritance model would be a (good) model of inheritance in the same sense that the relational model is a good model of data. Hugh Darwen and I have proposed what we believe to be such an inheritance model in our book *Databases, Types, and the Relational Model: The Third Manifesto*, 3rd edition (Addison-Wesley, 2006).

opinion, of course—that "subtables and supertables," whatever else they might be, are categorically *not* subtyping and inheritance. (What's more, we don't even think they're useful. The problem that they're supposed to solve can much more readily, and much more elegantly, be solved by the conventional relational view mechanism.)

> *[A] row ... is the relational equivalent of an object's data aspects ... [The potential stereotype] <<oid>> [is applied] to a column in a table* [I think the writer means it's applied to a *model* of a column in a *model* of a table!] *to indicate that it is a persistent object identifier, an artificial/surrogate key that has no business meaning.*

A row is categorically *not* "the relational equivalent of an object's data aspects." A relational key, surrogate or otherwise, is categorically *not* "a persistent object identifier." This is not the place to get into a detailed explanation of these matters; they're covered in depth in the same book I've mentioned a couple of times already, on *The Third Manifesto* (and elsewhere). As for surrogate keys, see my comments on the quote immediately following.

> *Experience has shown that natural keys are one of the greatest mistakes of relational theory ... because they have business meaning.*

"Natural keys" here means keys that aren't *surrogate* keys. Now, I might be charitable and agree that surrogate keys are often a good idea (not the same thing as saying natural keys are always a bad idea!); however, I must also point out that (a) natural keys are what we use in the real world,[6] and in any case (b) "relational theory" *per se* has absolutely nothing to say as to whether keys should be "natural" or not.

By the way, surrogate keys aren't *always* a good idea, as I've explained elsewhere (see my paper "Composite Keys," in *Relational Database Writings 1989–1991*, Addison-Wesley, 1992).

> *[The stereotype] <<primary key>> ... is redundant if the primary index is modeled.*

There seems to be some confusion here over logical *vs.* physical considerations (more precisely, over model *vs.* implementation considerations—where by the term *model* I mean the relational model specifically).

> *[The stereotype] <<table>> [is applied] to a class* [model? diagram?] *to indicate that it represents* [models?] *a physical database table.*

If the term means anything at all, a "physical database table" has to be something that's physically stored. Yet it's clear from the context that the author is talking about tables as perceived by the user (i.e., tables—almost certainly *base* tables, in fact—that are part of the database as seen by the user). As I've explained elsewhere, in numerous books and papers and articles, a base table is *not* necessarily something that's physically stored. See, e.g., the book *An Introduction to Database Systems* mentioned earlier.

---

6. Even if we invent surrogates! Such invented surrogates simply *become* "natural" keys. Consider, e.g., license plate numbers, musical opus numbers, social security numbers, etc., etc.

Concluding Remarks

Let's get back to the term *model* as such. As I've indicated, the term can certainly be *given* a respectable interpretation; it's the cavalier way people throw the term around, without any apparent common agreement on its meaning, that bothers me. In the subject article in particular, the term, if it means any one specific thing at all in that context, basically seems to mean a *picture*. "A picture is worth a thousand words"—right? But if that's true, then why do we say it in words?

> *Models, models, everywhere*
> *My mind is on the blink;*
> *Models, models, everywhere*
> *Nor any time to think.*

> *The database is rot: O Christ!*
> *That ever this should be!*
> *Yea, slimy models E'd and R'd*
> *All through the poor DB.*
>
> —With apologies to Samuel Taylor Coleridge and John Lennon

Postscript

As indicated in the introduction, the subject article appeared in the August 1999 issue of *Software Development*. A letter to the editor on the subject appeared in the next issue of the magazine (September 1999). The following is the gist of that letter:

> *Scott Ambler's "Persistence Modeling in the UML" (August 1999) was excellent. I haven't been able to find much information about living with relational databases in an object-oriented world. His article proposed a very elegant and useful solution. Can Ambler recommend further reading on persistence modeling?*

Your comments here.

Basic Concepts in UML:
A Request for Clarification

Rose is a rose is a rose is a rose, is a rose.

—Gertrude Stein

Everybody gets so much information all day long that they lose their common sense.

—Gertrude Stein

This is a report on an investigation I conducted recently into **UML** ("Unified Modeling Language"). According to its inventors, UML has "been accepted throughout the software industry as the standard graphical language for specifying, constructing, visualizing, and documenting software-intensive systems" (I'm quoting from Grady Booch, James Rumbaugh, and Ivar Jacobson, *The Unified Modeling Language User Guide,* Addison-Wesley, 1999). **OCL** ("Object Constraint Language") is a component of UML that can be used to specify constraints. Since my own work recently has been very much tied up with this matter of constraints—see, for example, my book *WHAT Not HOW: The Business Rules Approach to Application Development* (Addison-Wesley, 2000)—I thought it might be useful to investigate the question of how such things are handled in UML and OCL. So I did ... As already stated, this chapter reports on what I found in the course of that investigation, and presents some of my initial reactions to the UML in general and OCL in particular.

Some Immediate Discoveries

Here are a few things I discovered immediately:

1. From a UML point of view, the use of OCL is strictly optional. "Constraints may be written as free-form text. If you want to specify your semantics more precisely [*sic!*], you can use the UML's Object Constraint Language ..." (to quote the book by Booch, Rumbaugh, and Jacobson again). In other words, the UML community doesn't seem to regard constraints— or semantics in general, apparently—as being all that important. My own position, by contrast, is that constraints and semantics are absolutely fundamental! See the book *WHAT Not HOW* already mentioned in the introduction for an elaboration of this position.

2. Although UML in general is, as noted in the previous quote, a graphical language, OCL in particular is not graphical but text-based—not unreasonably, since attempts to represent all but the simplest of constraints in graphical form tend to be spectacularly unsuccessful.

3. Page xix of the introduction to "the OCL book"—I'll explain this terminology in the next section—defines OCL as "an expression language that enables one to describe constraints on object-oriented models and other object modeling artifacts."[1] Note in particular, therefore, that a basic assumption underlying OCL is that (as of course the name suggests) we are indeed operating in an object world. While I'm prepared to accept this fact as a given in the case of OCL *per se,* the idea of constraints in general is, obviously enough, not limited to the object world alone. Moreover, I feel bound to say that some of the complaints I'm going to be making in what follows arise precisely because of that basic assumption (i.e., the assumption that we *are* "operating in an object world"). To be more specific, it seems to me that the object world manages to introduce far too many distracting confusions and irrelevancies into a subject that (some might argue) is complicated enough already. Surely it would be better to avoid those confusions and irrelevancies and deal with a methodology in which the only complications are ones that are *intrinsic* to the topic under investigation?

4. On page 20, the OCL book has this to say: "Constraints specified in OCL are used during modeling or specification and are not an implementation description." Actually I'm not 100 percent sure what this remark means, but I *think* it means we're not talking about constraint specifications that are intended to be compilable and executable—not yet, at any rate, and certainly not primarily.[2] Rather, OCL seems to be intended mainly as a documentation tool. (Of course, the language still needs to be formal and precise despite this fact, as well as being easy to use, easy to understand, and so forth.)

   Note: The foregoing interpretation of OCL as just a documentation tool is supported by a recent article titled "Object-Oriented Business Rules," by Scott W. Ambler (an installment of his regular column "Thinking Objectively" in the June 2000 issue of the magazine *Software Development*). To quote: "An important aspect of OCL is that it is not a programming language—it is a modeling language. You use it to *document* your object design and a language such as Java or C++ to *implement* it" (my italics).

---

1. As I've explained elsewhere—see, e.g., "Models, Models, Everywhere, Nor Any Time to Think" (Chapter 25 in the present book)—I don't much care for the term *modeling* in contexts such as the one under discussion. For present purposes, however, I'll let it go without further comment.
2. Contrast the situation in the relational world, where such specifications most certainly are meant to be compiled and executed (in other words, they're meant to be *enforced by the system*). Constraints in this sense have always been a crucial feature of the relational model—though it's unfortunately true that, until recently at any rate, they haven't been very well supported in commercial SQL products.

The OCL Book

I began my detailed investigations into OCL by studying a book titled *The Object Constraint Language: Precise Modeling with UML* (Addison-Wesley, 1999), by Jos Warmer and Anneke Kleppe (referred to throughout this chapter as "the OCL book"). Here's another quote from the introduction to that book (page xix):

> *[This] book is meant to be a textbook and reference manual for practitioners of object technology who find a need for more precise modeling.*

More precise than *what*, I'm tempted to ask. More precise than UML without OCL, I suppose—which doesn't say much for UML without OCL, I fear. Anyway, since it's meant, at least in part, as a reference manual, the book is presumably also meant to be both *accurate* and *complete*—and since one of the authors, Warmer, is described on the back cover as the primary author of the OCL standard [*sic*], it's presumably meant to be authoritative as well. Unfortunately, however, I very quickly ran into difficulties in trying to understand it; I found myself going round in circles, stumbling up against what seemed to be contradictions, and generally finding a lack of clarity and precision in what is, after all, a field in which such qualities should surely be prized above all others.

While I had numerous problems at the detail level with the OCL book, my biggest difficulties all had to do with the question of *types*, which are, of course, fundamental. I mean, it seemed to me that I didn't have a hope of understanding OCL constraints as such until I understood the types of things that could thereby be constrained ... Here are a few quotes, with commentary, that illustrate some of the difficulties I encountered:[3]

> Page 4: *Invariants are always coupled to classes, types, or interfaces ... An* invariant *is a constraint that states a condition that must always be met by all instances of the class, type, or interface [with which it is coupled].*

This first quote clearly suggests that *class, type,* and *interface* are three different kinds of things (though I should say immediately that I'm not sure that the idea of "interfaces" in particular having "instances" makes much sense, but let that pass for the moment).

> Page 23: *The context of an invariant is always a class, an interface, or a type. In this book, the convention is to show the type of the model element underlined on the line above the [invariant].*

The first sentence here lends further support to the idea that *class, interface,* and *type* are different kinds of things. But then shouldn't "type" in the second sentence really be "class, interface, or type"? After considerable thought, however, I realized that the phrase "the type of the model element" in that sentence should be abbreviated to just "the model element"; the term "type" is being used formally in the first sentence but only very informally—in the vague sense of "kind"—in the second.

---

3. I apologize ahead of time if some of the criticisms that follow seem excessively convoluted or are otherwise hard to understand. In my defense, I appeal to *Chris Date's Principle of Incoherence* (sometimes referred to, unkindly, as *The Incoherent Principle*): *It's hard to criticize something coherently if what you're trying to criticize is itself not very coherent in the first place.*

Note: A "model element" is just a component of the applicable UML diagram (e.g., "Customer"). Accordingly, I think the foregoing interpretation of the second sentence is charitable at best! In fact, I see no *good* reason to include the phrase "the type of" in that sentence at all.

Anyway, the book goes on to give the following example of an invariant, together with its "context":

```
Customer
--------
Name = 'Edward'
```

Meaning: "All customers must be named Edward"—hardly a very realistic example, I would have thought, but never mind that. The context here is the "model element" (not the *type* of the model element!) called Customer.

So far, so good (?). But then I encountered the following:

> Page 29: *The classes, types, interfaces, and datatypes defined in the UML model are, within OCL, considered to be classes of which instances can be made. In other words, all these UML model elements define types within OCL.*

First of all, we now apparently have a fourth category, "datatypes." Second, classes, types, and interfaces (and "datatypes") are now apparently all just classes anyway!—so why all the different terms? (Note in particular that *types* are classes, a point I want to come back to in a few moments.) Third, classes are types! (The first sentence says "types ... are ... classes." The second sentence says "all these UML model elements [*classes in particular*] define types.") So all types are classes and all classes are types. Hence, *type* and *class* mean exactly the same thing, and the terms are interchangeable (?).

In addition to the foregoing, I have to say that I have a severe problem with the idea that "*value* types" in particular—see below—can be regarded as "classes of which instances can be made." I'll come back to this point in my final comment on the quote immediately following.

Now I need to back up a little way ... Elsewhere in the OCL book, we find the following:

> Page 22: *OCL has value types and object types. Both are types (that is, both specify instances), but there is an important difference.* Value types *define instances that never change their value ...* Object types *or classes represent types that define instances that can change their value(s) ... Martin Fowler ... calls object types* reference objects *and* value types value objects.

It seems to me that here the authors of the OCL book are trying to get at the fundamental distinction between values and variables, but, frankly, they aren't making a very good job of it. *Note:* That distinction—which truly is fundamental—is discussed at length in a book by Hugh Darwen and myself titled *Databases, Types, and the Relational Model: The Third Manifesto,* 3rd edition, Addison-Wesley, 2006. As I say, that distinction truly is fundamental; indeed, it underpins all of our thinking in this field, both in *The Third Manifesto* itself and elsewhere.

Let me elaborate. It seems to me that it would be possible to interpret the passage just quoted from page 22, somewhat charitably, as meaning that (a) any given *value* is an "instance" of some given "value type," and (b) any given *variable* is an "instance" of some given "object type." But then, if 'Edward' is a character string *value* and Name is a character string *variable,* they're apparently of different types!—and so we need some rules to say whether they can be compared with each other (and if so, how), and whether the value can be assigned to the variable (and if so, how). Yet the OCL book appears not to include any such rules at all.[4]

To get back to the main issue: Of course, the real point is that the difference between values and variables shouldn't be seen as a difference of *type* at all (at least, certainly not in the usual programming language sense of the term *type*). A type, as the term is usually understood, is a set of values, from which variables of the type in question draw their actual (permitted) values. Values never change (i.e., they can't be updated); variables, by contrast, *can* be changed (i.e., they can be updated), and updating a given variable means, precisely, replacing the current value of the variable by another value, probably a different one. And the rules regarding comparison and assignment are straightforward; basically, they just require the types of the operands to be the same, regardless of whether those operands happen to be values or variables.

In addition to the foregoing serious criticisms, I have a few more detailed comments to make on the page 22 quote:

- First of all, I think the fuzzy talk of "instances" and "objects" is the source of much of the confusion. The terms *value* and *variable* are so much better!—they're well-defined, they're widely understood, and they have a much longer and much more respectable pedigree than the terms *instance* and *object* do.

- Second, I don't think types "specify" or "define" anything (neither "instances," nor anything else); rather, types simply *are* sets of values.

- Third, the phrase "object types or classes" suggests that a type that happens to be an "object type" is a class but a type that happens to be a "value type" isn't. Is it only me that's confused? What *is* the true state of affairs regarding this business of types *vs.* classes? Stay tuned ...

- Fourth, I don't think classes "represent" types; rather, I think, the previous point notwithstanding, that classes *are* types (but see the subsequent quotes from pages 14 and 21 of the OCL book).

- Fifth, I also don't think, *pace* Martin Fowler, that types (of any kind) are "objects" (of any kind). To say it one more time, types are sets of values, and "objects" are, apparently, either values or variables, depending on context and (it sometimes seems) on who's speaking and whether there's an R in the month.[5] Values and types are different things. Variables and types are different things. And values and variables are different things.

---

4. Page 54 does define a set of "Type Conformance Rules," but those rules really amount to nothing more than a definition of *The Principle of Value Substitutability*. A detailed explanation of that principle is beyond the scope of this chapter (such an explanation can be found in the *Third Manifesto* book already mentioned); suffice it to say that it has little to do with the matter at hand. See also Chapter 24 in the present book.

5. Fowler's talk of "reference objects" and "value objects" appears to have something to do with the distinction that's sometimes drawn in the object world between "mutable" and "immutable" objects (a mutable object is basically a variable and an immutable one is basically a value). The idea is that (a) mutable objects are identified by means of *object identifiers* (OIDs), which are separate and distinct from the object *per se*, and those OIDs can be used elsewhere as references to the (mutable) objects in question, while (b) immutable objects don't have such OIDs but are instead self-identifying. Thus, Fowler's "reference objects" sound like they might be mutable ones, while his "value objects" sound like they might be immutable ones. Observe, however, that this manner of speaking does regard values as objects—immutable ones, to be specific—whereas OCL apparently doesn't.

Finally, the excerpts already quoted from pages 22 and 29, taken together, seem to imply that "instances" of "value types" can be "made." But I don't think it makes any sense to think of, say, the "instance" of the "value type" *Integer* that happens to be the integer value 3 as somehow being "made" **at all**. I think, rather, that *values* (as opposed to variables) simply **exist;** nobody "makes" them, they're simply available for use by anyone who wants to use them, whenever and wherever (and for whatever purpose) the person in question needs them.

So what have we learned so far? Well, one thing is that, apparently, all types are classes (page 29). But elsewhere we find:

Page 14: *When the attribute is not of a standard type, such as* Boolean *or* Integer, *but its type is a class itself,* ...

So some types apparently *aren't* classes after all! To be specific, this quote seems to be saying that "standard" (= system-defined?) types aren't classes; rather, classes are types that are *user-defined.* But if this distinction is truly what's intended, then I venture to suggest that the terms *system-defined type* and *user-defined type* capture the distinction better—the point being, of course, that system- and user-defined types are indeed both types (or should be). I see no need for the term *class* at all.

But then what are we to make of the next quote?

Page 21: *Types in OCL are divided into the following groups.*

- *Predefined types, including*

  - *basic types*

  - *collection types*

- *User-defined model types*

The term *user-defined model type* appears to be synonymous with "user-defined type." (I don't think there are any "model types" that *aren't* user-defined, though I could be wrong.) In other words, a model type is a *class* (see the quote from page 14). And so a class is a type after all!—as indeed the second bullet in this quote affirms. Since we saw earlier (page 29) that types are classes, and now we know that classes are types, we apparently have two distinct terms with the same meaning. **Why?**

Page 21: *The predefined basic types are* Integer, Real, String, *and* Boolean ... *The predefined collection types are* Collection, Set, Bag, *and* Sequence ... *Model types ... are defined by the UML models. Each class, interface, or type in a UML model is automatically a type in OCL, including enumeration types that can be used as attribute types.*

Well ...

- First, the "collection types" referred to here aren't really types at all in the usual sense; rather, they're *type generators,* also known as *type constructors* (the OCL book in fact supports this interpretation, referring to such "collection types" on page 94 as *type templates*).

- Second, "enumeration types" seem to be thrown in as an afterthought, and how they fit into the OCL type scheme sketched earlier doesn't seem to be explained at all.

- *Boolean* and *Integer* were previously said to be "standard types"; now they're "predefined basic types." Do these terms mean the same thing? If they do, why do we have both terms? If they don't, what's the difference between them?

Page 22: *Both the predefined basic types and the predefined collection types of OCL are value types. The user-defined model types can be either value types or object types.*

If this quote truly means what it seems to mean, then I don't understand how the user can define "objects"—that is, *variables*—of type (say) *Integer,* or any other "predefined basic type, **at all**. I mean, objects are supposed to be "instances" of "*object* types," but *Integer* is a "*value* type"—?

Page 40: *[A] collection never contains collections but contains only simple objects.*

But I thought collection types—at least, "predefined" ones—were "value types" (implying that collections *per se* are values)? How then can a collection—at least, one of a "predefined" type—contain "objects"? The concept of a *value* containing an *object* makes no sense at all. *Note:* I also have grave misgivings regarding the violation of orthogonality that seems to be implied by the idea of collections not being allowed to contain other collections, but that's a topic for another day.

My final quote from the OCL book is this:

Page 29: *Valid model types are the types, classes, interfaces, association classes, actors, use cases, and datatypes defined in the UML model.*

Your comments here.

The UML Book

After struggling for a long time with the OCL book, it occurred to me that perhaps I wasn't being quite fair in criticizing that book *per se;* perhaps I lacked some necessary prerequisites. So I went back to the book mentioned at the beginning of the chapter (Grady Booch, James Rumbaugh, and Ivar Jacobson, *The Unified Modeling Language User Guide,* Addison-Wesley, 1999, hereinafter referred to as "the UML book") for definitions of some basic concepts. I started out by looking up the term *class:*

Page 459: Class: *A description of a set of objects that share the same attributes, operations, relationships, and semantics.*

OK: If "description" here means—as it appears to do—what logicians refer to as an *intensional definition*, then I can accept this quote as at least confirming that a class, like a type, is indeed a *set*. However, it's apparently a set of "objects," not values. So next I looked up *object:*

> Page 464: Object: *A concrete manifestation of an abstraction; an entity with a well-defined boundary that encapsulates state and behavior; an instance of a class.*

So an object is—among other things[6]—"an instance of a class." But what's an instance?

> Page 463: Instance: *A concrete manifestation of an abstraction; an entity to which a set of operations can be applied and that has a state that stores the effects of the operations.*

We seem to be going round in circles! That is, as far as I can tell, "instances" and "objects" seem to be more or less the same thing (in effect, an object is defined as an instance and an instance is defined as an object)—though I do note in passing that the OCL book, page 29, seems to use the term "instances" to refer to values as well as objects (see Chapter 16).

Types, Classes, and Domains

At this point, I decided to try a different tack: Can we try and pin down whether *type* and *class* are really the same thing or not?

> Page 468: Type: *A stereotype of class used to specify a domain of objects, together with the operations (but not methods) applicable to the objects.*

So a type is *not* a class but, rather, a "stereotype" of "class," and it specifies a "domain" of "objects." (I note in passing that "class" here has neither the definite nor an indefinite article to qualify it, but am uncertain as to the implications of this fact.) Regarding the use of the terms *stereotype* and *domain,* see later. Regarding the phrase "operations (but not methods)," I would accept, and indeed welcome, the idea of maintaining a clear and systematic distinction between the external specification and internal implementation of some piece of functionality. Is that what's going on here? Let's see ...

> Page 463: Method: *The* [sic] *implementation of an operation.*

So an operation (or operator) is apparently permitted to have just one implementation? Well, never mind that unnecessary and undesirable limitation—at least the term "method" does seem to refer to matters of *internal implementation.* So, presumably, the term "operation" refers to matters of *external specification* ... Does it? Well, on the next page we find:

> Page 464: Operation: *The implementation* [sic!] *of a service that can be requested from any object of the class in order to affect* [do the writers perhaps mean "effect"?] *behavior.*

So I'm confused again.

---

6. As an aside, let me reiterate that one of the other things an object is said to be is "a concrete manifestation of an abstraction." Strange!—I would have thought it was exactly the other way around. That is, I would have thought an object, whatever else it might be, was surely an *abstraction* of something *concrete* (or something *more* concrete, at any rate). For example, the customer named Edward is surely something fairly concrete, while the object that corresponds to that customer in some information system is an abstraction of that concrete thing. Oh well, perhaps it's all in the mind.

Let's get back to *type,* which was defined as a "stereotype" of "class." Here's the UML book's definition of *stereotype:*

> Page 466: Stereotype: *An extension of the vocabulary of the UML, which allows you to create new kinds of building blocks that are derived from existing ones but that are specific to your problem.*

So a type, which is a "stereotype" of "class," is apparently ... er, what, exactly?

Well, let's try *domains.* Now, in the database world, a domain and a type are exactly the same thing—they're both sets of values. (So yes, the database world too, like the object world, sometimes has two different terms for the same thing. Guilty as charged! The reason in this particular case is basically a historical one, not too important for present purposes.) But the definition of *type* already quoted from page 468 refers to a domain of *objects,* and it seems to me that objects, whatever else they might be, are much closer to variables than they are to values. So the term "domain" isn't being used in the conventional database sense, nor indeed in the sense of conventional logic (a sense that's very close to the database sense, of course).[7] So what sense is it being used in? Well:

> Page 461: Domain: *An area of knowledge or activity characterized by a set of concepts and terminology understood by practitioners in that area.*

All right, I can accept this very informal definition (for *something*—though I wish the UML community had used some different term for the concept, since the term *domain* already has a very precise meaning in the database world). But then I don't understand what it means to say that a type is used "to specify a domain of objects" (see the definition of *type* quoted earlier); I can't reconcile that statement with the foregoing definition of *domain* at all. Nor can I make any sense of the following definition of *value:*

> Page 468: Value: *An element of a type domain.*

Note in particular that this definition completely fails to capture (or even mention) the defining characteristic—the quintessential feature, the *sine qua non,* the *raison d'être*—of values, which is that they can't be changed! (I.e., they're "immutable," to use the jargon.)

Further Puzzles

Referring back for a moment to the OCL book, you might recall from earlier discussions that there were a couple of other terms that caused me trouble. The first was *interface.* Well, in the UML book we find:

> Page 463: Interface: *A collection of operations that are used to specify a service of a class or a component.*

---

7. The term "type" is likewise not being used in the conventional database or logic sense, nor indeed in the conventional programming language sense either.

I strongly suspect that this definition should refer to a "collection"—by the way, what's wrong with the simple term *set* here? especially since "collection" is somewhat of a loaded term in UML?—of operation *signatures* rather than operations *per se*. More to the point, however, I can't reconcile this definition with the notion, alluded to in my earlier discussion of the OCL book, that an interface can have *instances*. And note too that we now have yet another possible synonym for the term *class!*—*viz.*, "component." Here's the UML book's definition:

> Page 459: Component: *A physical and replaceable part of a system that conforms to and provides the realization of a set of interfaces.*

Given this definition, what's the difference between a component and a class? Are there any classes that aren't "components"? Or any "components" that aren't classes?

Oh well, what about that business of *datatypes?*

> Page 460: Datatype: *A type whose values have no identity* [sic!]. *Datatypes include primitive built-in types (such as numbers and strings), as well as enumeration types (such as Boolean).*

This one demands several responses! First of all, to speak of values as having no identity is *prima facie* absurd. If, e.g., the integer 3 literally had no identity, then we couldn't even talk about it; in fact, **it wouldn't exist**. It's axiomatic that *everything* has an identity of some kind (not necessarily distinct from the thing itself, however). Presumably what the writers mean is that a value like the integer 3 has no identity *apart from the value itself*—in other words, it's *self-identifying* (a position I would strongly agree with, by the way)—but it's not what they say.

Next, the term *type* was previously defined as "specifying a domain of objects." I don't understand at all how to reconcile that definition with the idea that a "datatype" is a type—especially one that apparently contains values, not objects (note the phrase "whose values" in the definition of "datatype" as quoted).

Third, if a datatype is indeed a type (as of course I do believe it should be), what kind of type isn't a datatype? What's the justification for (apparently) distinguishing between types in general and "datatypes" in particular? As a general comment, it seems to me that that there are far too many nonorthogonal concepts floating around in the UML soup—not to mention the fact there seem to be even more *terms* than there are *concepts*.

Fourth, datatypes are said to "include primitive built-in types (such as numbers and strings) as well as enumeration types (such as Boolean)." Some obvious questions arise. For example:

- Are there any other "datatypes," or is the foregoing meant to be an exhaustive list?

- What does "primitive built-in" mean? Are there any primitive types that aren't built-in, or built-in types that aren't primitive?

- What does "primitive" mean anyway?

- Why was Boolean referred to in the OCL book as a "standard" type (also as a "predefined basic" type), but in the UML book as an "enumeration" type?

- In fact, isn't "enumeration" better thought of as a type *generator* rather than a type *per se?*

- What does "standard" mean in this context?

- What about "basic"?

- And "predefined" isn't really the right term either. (*Predefined* just means "defined previously." I suspect that what the authors really mean is not *pre*defined but, rather, *system*-defined.)

And so on (this isn't an exhaustive list).

Concluding Remarks

It seems to me undeniable that the material I've been quoting, both from the UML book and the OCL book, displays, at the very least, an extreme lack of clarity and precision. Now, I suppose it's possible that the underlying *concepts* might be clear—to somebody, at least, though certainly not to me—but if so, then they ought to be capable of clear, precise *definition*. Why, we even use the expression "well-defined" to characterize concepts that are clear and precise. (To quote Wittgenstein: "What can be said at all can be said clearly.") It seems more likely, however, that the lack of clarity and precision is indicative of a much deeper *malaise*. To be specific, it seems to me that the concepts in question are simply *not* well defined; what's more, they don't seem to be properly orthogonal, and they're certainly not agreeably few in number. In other words, the system overall lacks *conceptual integrity*. (See *The Mythical Man-Month*, 20th anniversary edition, by Frederick P. Brooks, Jr., Addison-Wesley, 1995, for an explanation and detailed discussion of this beautiful and important design principle.)

    Note: After this chapter was first written, I came across the abstract to a paper titled *UML: A Modern Dinosaur?—A Critical Analysis of the Unified Modelling Language*, by Klaus-Dieter Schewe. Here's an excerpt from that abstract:

> *UML is far from being new. With respect to syntax it just reinvents many ... concepts and introduces new names for them. With respect to semantics it does not present precise semantic definitions. If these were added, the limitations of the expressiveness of the UML [would] become apparent.*

I'm glad to see, therefore, that it isn't just me that has problems with UML.

    I feel bound to add too that, in my opinion, the real culprit in all of the foregoing is—as strongly suggested earlier—the excessive reliance in UML and OCL on notions and terminology from the object world. The object world is quite notorious for the kinds of shortcomings I've been complaining about in this chapter. *Note:* In this connection, it's relevant to mention, with respects to constraints in particular, that constraints can be defined in an object context only by *breaking encapsulation!* Indeed, UML in general and OCL in particular both openly assume that objects have "public" instance variables (the UML term is *attributes*); in other words, objects can be used as a basis for defining constraints only if we discard what's usually regarded as a *sine qua non* of the object paradigm (*viz.*, encapsulation)—a fact that would be a good argument, one might have thought, in favor of not basing the methodology on objects and object notions.

In conclusion, therefore, it seems to me that if the software industry feels it needs a standard for "specifying, constructing, and documenting software-intensive systems,"[8] then it's a great pity it doesn't see fit to choose one that's based on an agreeably small, carefully chosen, well-defined, orthogonal set of concepts. In this regard, I would have volunteered the work by Hugh Darwen and myself on *The Third Manifesto* as a candidate for consideration, but I suppose it's too late now (is it?).

---

8. Note that I omit "visualizing" here (see the original quote, which appeared near the beginning of the chapter). I have nothing against the idea of using pictures to explicate some design at a high intuitive level, but I don't regard the drawing of such pictures as a substitute for the formal design process *per se*.

■ ■ ■

A Comparison Between ODMG and *The Third Manifesto*

What follows is a lightly edited version of an appendix from *Foundation for Future Database Systems: The Third Manifesto*, 2nd edition (Addison-Wesley, 2000), by C. J. Date and Hugh Darwen. The third edition of that book was published in 2006 (under the revised title *Databases, Types, and the Relational Model: The Third Manifesto*), and the appendix was dropped from that edition (largely for space reasons). However, we did not want to lose it entirely, and we therefore decided to include it in the present book.[1] Readers are assumed to be broadly familiar with *The Third Manifesto*.

Preamble

The term *ODMG* is used, loosely, to refer to the proposals of the Object Data Management Group, a consortium of representatives from "member companies [spanning] almost the entire object DBMS industry."[2] At the time of writing (early 2000), those proposals consist of an *Object Model*, an *Object Definition Language* (ODL), an *Object Interchange Format* (OIF), an *Object Query Language* (OQL), and *bindings* of these facilities to the programming languages C++, Smalltalk, and Java. *Note:* The first two of these components are based, respectively, on the Object Model and Interface Definition Language of the Object Management Group, OMG [6]. Observe that there is no "Object Manipulation Language" component; instead, object manipulation capabilities are provided by whatever language ODMG happens to be bound to (C++, Smalltalk, Java, possibly others as well). The following quote is worthy of note:

---

1. This chapter was written jointly by Hugh Darwen and myself.
2. All otherwise unattributed quotes in this chapter are taken from R. G. G. Cattell and Douglas K. Barry (eds.), *The Object Database Standard: ODMG 2.0* (Morgan Kaufmann, 1997), hereinafter referred to as "the ODMG book" [2]. They are reprinted here by permission of Morgan Kaufmann. We should make it clear that reference [2] is the third edition of the book and thus represents the third version of the ODMG proposals (the previous two were Releases 1.0 and 1.2, respectively). A fourth edition, *The Object Data Standard: ODMG 3.0*—note the slight change of title—was published in 2000. Some of the comments in what follows might not apply to this fourth version.

> *[We] define an* object DBMS *to be a DBMS that integrates database capabilities with object-oriented programming language capabilities. An object DBMS makes database objects appear as programming language objects ... [It] extends the language with transparently persistent data, concurrency control, data recovery, associative queries, and other database capabilities.*

We—i.e., the authors of *The Third Manifesto*—agree with the implication here that "one language, not two" is a desirable goal. However, we do not agree with the further implication that "persistence orthogonal to type" is another, for reasons explained in reference [4] and sketched in the annotation to that reference at the end of this chapter.

Incidentally, reference [2] refers repeatedly, both in its title and throughout the text, to "the ODMG standard." While it is certainly possible that ODMG will someday become a *de facto* standard ("the ODMG ... member companies are committed to support this standard ... by the end of 1998" [*sic*]), it is not a *de jure* one, since the ODMG committee has no official standardization authority; the bodies that do have such authority are the International Organization for Standardization, ISO (for worldwide standards), and national bodies such as the American National Standards Institute, ANSI (for standards in the USA). On the other hand, it is at least true that the ODMG committee has been working with the ANSI SQL committee to try to achieve some degree of convergence between its proposals and the SQL standard as such.

The following quote give some idea of the ODMG committee's *modus operandi* and its own assessment of the significance of its work:

> *We have worked outside of traditional standards bodies for our efforts in order to make quick progress ... The intense ODMG effort has given the object database industry a "jump start" toward standards that would otherwise have taken many years ... It is to the personal credit of all participants that the ODMG standard has been produced and revised [so] expeditiously. All of the contributors put substantial time and personal investment into the meetings and this document. They showed remarkable dedication to our goals.*

And elsewhere: "[Object DBMSs] are *a revolutionary rather than an evolutionary development*" (our italics). Observe the contrast here with *The Third Manifesto*, which is intended very specifically to be evolutionary, not revolutionary, in nature.

It must be said too that the ODMG book includes many remarks that seem either to display a poor understanding of the relational model or to mix matters that are of concern to the model with ones that are more properly of concern to the implementation. Here are some examples (some of which we choose to comment on, though not all):

> *Analogous to the ODMG Object Model for object databases is the relational model for relational databases, as embodied in SQL.*

SQL and the relational model are *not* the same thing. SQL is merely a flawed attempt to realize in concrete syntactic form some (not all) of the components of the abstract relational model.

> *The [ODMG] query language [OQL] is more powerful [than a relational query language].*

OQL is more *complicated*, certainly, but it is not more *powerful*. The added complication derives from the fact that ODMG in general, and OQL in particular, both expose many different data structures to the user—a consequence, in our opinion, of a failure to appreciate the advantages of keeping model and implementation rigidly apart. Analogous remarks apply to most of the next few quotes also:

> *The scope of object DBMSs is more far-reaching than that of relational DBMSs.*

> *We have used the relational standard SQL as the basis for OQL, where possible, though OQL supports more powerful capabilities.*

> *We go further than relational systems, as we support a unified object model for sharing data across programming languages.*

Surely it might reasonably be argued that the *relational* model is precisely a unified model for sharing data across different programming languages?

> *The ODMG Object Model ... includes significantly richer semantics than does the relational model, by declaring relationships and operations explicitly ... Relationships in the Object Model are similar to relationships in entity-relationship data modeling.*

Now this one does demand a response. The point is, the relational model *deliberately* does not "declare relationships explicitly"—instead, it represents both "entities" and "relationships" in the same uniform way.[3] (Incidentally, it is not really true that ODMG relationships are "similar to relationships in entity-relationship data modeling," because (a) they are binary only, and (b) they cannot have properties. See later in this chapter for further discussion.) As for "declaring *operations* explicitly," *The Third Manifesto* makes it clear that, while it is true that the relational model has nothing explicit to say regarding such a capability, it certainly implies it as a requirement as part of its support for *domains* (types).

> *The ODMG data model encompasses the relational data model by defining a TABLE type to express SQL tables. The ODMG TABLE type is semantically equivalent to a collection of structs.[4]*

One major problem with this particular claim is that it totally ignores the relational operators! For example, it is hard to see how we could use the ODMG Object Model to implement a generic join operation—i.e., one that would work on arbitrary "SQL tables." It is worth pointing out too that even if we could implement such an operation, we would then have succeeded only in writing a lot of code that in a relational DBMS would have been provided by the system itself. *Note:* OQL does provide such an operation, but the Object Model *per se* does not.

---

3. Some might feel that relational foreign key definitions constitute explicit relationship declarations. We would argue rather that foreign keys are really just shorthand for certain pragmatically important integrity constraints.
4. See the next section for an explanation of "structs." We remark that, at the very least, the term *collection* here should be replaced by *set* if we are truly talking about the relational model, or *bag* if we are talking about SQL. We note too that those "structs" have object IDs, whereas relational tuples do not.

Overview

It is probably fair to say that few readers will have much familiarity with ODMG. In this section, therefore, we present a general overview of the most important features of the ODMG proposals. For obvious reasons, we concentrate on the Object Model component specifically (for the most part). *Caveat:* The descriptions that follow are, of course, based on our own reading and interpretation of the ODMG book. Naturally we believe those descriptions to be accurate, but it is only fair to warn you that we might have misunderstood, and hence misrepresented, some points of detail; thus, what follows should thus *not* be taken as a definitive statement of the ODMG proposals *per se* (that definitive statement is reference [2] itself, of course).

Objects

ODMG supports *atomic, structured,* and *collection* objects. It is possible to draw some loose—*very* loose!—analogies between these various kinds of objects and certain constructs in *The Third Manifesto*, as follows:

- An ODMG *atomic* object corresponds roughly to a scalar variable, in *Manifesto* terms. (We note that the ODMG book also occasionally talks about variables as such, but an ODMG variable and an ODMG object seem to be different things. It also talks—fairly ubiquitously, in fact—about *instances,* which it seems to use as a synonym for *objects.* For consistency with the ODMG book, therefore, we will do the same ourselves in what follows.)

- An ODMG *structured* object corresponds roughly to a tuple variable, in *Manifesto* terms. (Tuples are called "structs" in ODMG; STRUCT is the ODMG counterpart to the *Manifesto's* TUPLE type generator—see later.)

- An ODMG *collection* object is a set, bag, list, or array of other objects, all of which must be of the same type.[5] Collections have no precise *Manifesto* counterpart. (It is true that relation variables—i.e., relvars—might be thought of as "collections" of a kind, but they are one the Object Model does not directly support.) *Note:* ODMG also supports another kind of collection called a dictionary (defined in the ODMG book as "an unordered sequence [*sic!*] of key-value pairs with no duplicate keys." We ignore dictionaries for simplicity.

  Every object has a unique object ID.

Atomic Objects

The analogies in the previous subsection notwithstanding, there is at least one major difference between ODMG's atomic objects and the *Manifesto's* scalar variables, and that is that, to use object terminology, the former have structure (the ODMG term is *properties*) as well as behavior, while the latter have behavior only. Just why "atomic" objects should have any structure at all—any user-visible structure, that is—is never explained; it seems clear, however, that such a state of affairs violates encapsulation and undermines data independence.

---

5. More accurately, the *value* of such a collection object at any given time is a set, bag, list, or array. ODMG is sometimes a little cavalier regarding value *vs.* variable distinctions (and value *vs.* variable *vs.* type distinctions, come to that).

Note: ODMG does not draw the clear distinction the *Manifesto* does between physical and possible representations. To quote: "[Each] property [maps to] an *instance variable* [in the representation]" (and the context makes it clear that *representation* here means the physical representation specifically). At the same time, the book also states that "separation between [object definition and object implementation] is the way that the Object Model reflects encapsulation." (These two quotes—taken from the same page, though slightly paraphrased here—seem to contradict each other.) And then on a later page we find: "While it is common for [properties] to be implemented as data structures, it is sometimes appropriate for an attribute to be implemented as a method." This quote seems to contradict the first of the previous two. Overall, the true situation is not clear.

Be that as it may, ODMG properties fall into two categories, *relationships* and *attributes*. A relationship is an association between two objects (and is in fact represented by a *pair* of properties, one for each of the objects involved); an attribute is a property that is not part of any such pair. More precisely:

- A *relationship* is, very specifically, a *binary* association (involving, therefore, exactly two objects); it is realized in the Object Model by two properties (one for each of the objects involved), each of which names the other as its *inverse.* The two properties are said to define *traversal paths* between the two objects. For example, a given employee object might have a traversal path to a certain department object, and that department object might have a traversal path to a certain set of employee objects—a set that includes the original employee object, of course. (Note the redundancy here; to be specific, the fact that a given employee is in a given department is represented twice, at least from the user's point of view.) Operators are provided to create, destroy, and traverse relationships (more precisely, relationship "members"). Moreover, those operators "vary according to the traversal path's cardinality"; to be specific, different operators are used depending on whether the relationship is one-to-one or otherwise.

  It has to be said that ODMG's relationships look a lot like a throwback to the days of prerelational systems (and in any case, why the binary limitation?). The only justification for the idea to be found in reference [2]—and it is a fairly weak one, in our opinion—seems to be this: "The object DBMS is responsible for maintaining the referential integrity of relationships. This means that if an object that participates in a relationship is deleted, then any traversal path to that object must also be deleted." (Some might feel there is more to referential integrity than this brief characterization suggests.)

  Relationships are not objects and have no properties (in particular, no user-defined "behavior") of their own, a fact that in itself constitutes a major argument against the idea, one might have thought. (Note that while it is true that *entities* and *relationships* have been useful concepts for many years in database design, the relational model—as pointed out earlier in this chapter—deliberately does not make a formal distinction between the two, because the very same object can quite legitimately be regarded as an entity by one person and as a relationship by another.)

- An *attribute* is any property that is not part of a pair that defines a relationship in the foregoing sense. There are two kinds of attributes: those whose values are *object IDs*, and those whose values are *"literals."*

  - An attribute whose values are object IDs "enables one object to reference another, without expectation of an inverse traversal path or referential integrity." *Note:* Attributes whose values are object IDs are often described—somewhat confusingly, in our opinion—as if their values were in fact those objects *per se*, instead of pointers to those objects.

  - An attribute whose values are "literals" is simply an attribute that contains values that are not pointers but are of some "literal" type (e.g., character strings). See later in this section for a discussion of "literals"—in particular, for an explanation of why we often place the term in quotation marks in an ODMG context.

Structured Objects

A structured object is basically just a tuple variable (it is not encapsulated). The components of such an object—the ODMG term is *elements* or *members*—can be objects (of any kind), "literals" (of any kind), or a mixture. Operators are provided for accessing such components (typically using dot qualification syntax). ODMG does not, however, seem to provide analogs of all of the tuple operators required by *The Third Manifesto*. On the other hand, it does prescribe support for certain *built-in* structured object types—*viz.*, DATE, TIME, TIMESTAMP, and INTERVAL, with semantics "as in the ANSI SQL specification." (This latter claim is unfortunate if true, because the relevant features of "the ANSI SQL specification" are both incomplete and self-contradictory [3].)

Collection Objects

The ODMG terminology in this area is not used consistently.[6] We therefore choose not to use it here, although we recognize that our attempt to explain the concepts might therefore be a little suspect. Anyway, it seems to us that ODMG supports certain *collection type generators*—SET, BAG, LIST, and so on—which can be used (of course) to define certain *generated collection types*. Let *T* be such a generated type; to fix our ideas, assume until further notice that *T* is defined using the type generator LIST. Then objects of type *T* are variables, the value of which

---

6. For example, the ODMG book says: "In the ODMG Object Model, instances of *collection objects* are composed of distinct elements, each of which can be an instance of an atomic type, another collection, or a literal type ... An important distinguishing characteristic of a collection is that *all* the elements of the collection must be of the *same* type. They are either all the same atomic type, or all the same type of collection, or all the same type of literal." The word *collection* occurs five times in this extract. The first occurrence is in the phrase "instances of collection objects," which seems to mean *all objects of any given generated collection type*. The second is in the phrase "another collection," which seems to mean *an object of some distinct generated collection type*. The third occurrence seems to mean *any given generated collection type*. The fourth seems to mean *any object of the given generated collection type*. The fifth occurrence is in the phrase "the same type of collection," which might mean *of a generated collection type defined by means of the same collection type generator*, or it might mean *of the same generated collection type*. (And by the way: What exactly does it mean for two elements of a "collection"—no matter how that term is interpreted—to be "distinct" or not? Especially when the elements in question are objects, not literals, and hence are represented in the collection by their object IDs?)

at any given time is some specific list: either a list of object IDs or a list of "literals," depending on how *T* is defined (that is, either it is true for all time that every object of type *T* has a value that is a list of object IDs, or it is true for all time that every object of type *T* has a value that is a list of "literals").

- In the former case, every object whose object ID can appear in any such list must be of the same type (a type specified in the definition of *T*); in the latter case, every "literal" that can appear in any such list must be of the same type (again, a type specified in the definition of *T*).

- In the former case, the objects whose object IDs appear in a given list are regarded as the elements of that list; in the latter case, the "literals" that appear in a given list are regarded as the elements of that list.

As noted earlier, there is no ODMG "Object Manipulation Language" component as such. However, the Object Model does prescribe support for the following built-in operators (most of which should be fairly self-explanatory) for operating on objects—i.e., lists, under our simplifying assumption—of type *T*:

```
IS_EMPTY
IS_ORDERED
ALLOWS_DUPLICATES
CONTAINS_ELEMENT
INSERT_ELEMENT
REMOVE_ELEMENT
CREATE_ITERATOR
CREATE_BIDIRECTIONAL_ITERATOR
REMOVE_ELEMENT_AT
RETRIEVE_ELEMENT_AT
REPLACE_ELEMENT_AT
INSERT_ELEMENT_AFTER
INSERT_ELEMENT_BEFORE
INSERT_ELEMENT_FIRST
INSERT_ELEMENT_LAST
REMOVE_FIRST_ELEMENT
REMOVE_LAST_ELEMENT
RETRIEVE_FIRST_ELEMENT
RETRIEVE_LAST_ELEMENT
CONCAT   /* concatenate two lists without changing either */
APPEND   /* append list L2 to list L1 (changing list L1)  */
```

Remarks analogous to the foregoing apply to all of the other ODMG collection type generators (SET, BAG, and so on). *Note:* We remark that the built-in operators defined for sets in the Object Model are strictly weaker—*much* weaker—than those defined for relations in the relational model. This fact gives the lie to claims to the effect that the Object Model "is more powerful than" or "encompasses" the relational model. Also, serious questions arise regarding the type of the object that results from (e.g.) set operators such as CREATE_UNION. We remark too that ODMG's collection type generators are really examples of what the *Manifesto* book calls *union types*. As a consequence, if we define (say) two distinct specific list types, one in which the list elements are integers and one in which they are rectangles, we might have to construct two distinct implementations of every single one of the operators prescribed for lists.

Literals

ODMG uses the term "literal" in what seems to the present writers to be a rather unconventional way. In most conventional languages, if *T* is a type, then *variables* can be defined that are of that type *T*, and *values* of those variables are values of that type *T*; further, every such value can be denoted by some *literal* of that type *T*. Note in particular, therefore, that it is normal to distinguish between:

- *Literals*, which are symbols that denote values (usually in some kind of self-explanatory way), on the one hand, and

- The *values* denoted by those symbols, on the other.

For example, the symbol 3.5 might be a literal denoting the value "three and a half." Note in particular that different literals can denote the same value (a fact that points up the distinction we are emphasizing here); for example, the literals TIME ('10:00 am PST') and TIME ('6:00 pm GMT') might very well both represent the same value of some TIME type.

The foregoing distinction, which we might as well call the symbol *vs.* denotation distinction (or, more simply, just the literal *vs.* value distinction) is certainly made in *The Third Manifesto*. ODMG, however, does not seem to make the same distinction, but instead uses the term "literal" to include both senses (which is why we often place the term in quotation marks). And yet we note that ODMG also frequently talks about values *per se*; thus, it is not really clear whether an ODMG value and an ODMG "literal" are the same thing or not.

Be that as it may, ODMG does then go on to distinguish between *literal types* and *object types* (implying among other things that a literal and an object can never be of the same type?). Apparently, instances of a literal type are literals (values?), while instances of an object type are objects (variables?). In fact, LITERAL_TYPE and OBJECT_TYPE are defined as two distinct roots, in two distinct built-in type hierarchies; thus, for example, there is a built-in LONG (i.e., long integer) literal type, but no built-in LONG object type. However, the user could define an "atomic" object type with just one attribute, X say, of literal type LONG; it might then be possible to perform, e.g., comparisons between values of that attribute X and LONG literals.[7] We note in passing that ODMG does agree with the *Manifesto* insofar as it does not support implicit conversions between types (i.e., coercions).

ODMG supports three kinds of literals—*atomic, structured,* and *collection* literals—which we now proceed to describe. First, *atomic* literals. Atomic literals seem to be the ODMG analog of the *scalar value* concept; the ODMG book says they "are not explicitly created by applications, but rather implicitly exist." ODMG prescribes support for certain built-in atomic literal types. Without going into details, we note merely that in addition to the types that one might expect (BOOLEAN, FLOAT, CHAR, etc.), the list includes ENUM ("enumeration"), which is surely better regarded as a *type generator. Note:* Specific enumerated types that are generated by means of that type generator, by contrast, might perhaps be said to be "atomic"—although presumably they will have some user-visible structure (?).

---

7. Reference [2] actually states that "literals ... are embedded in objects and cannot be individually referenced," thereby implying that, e.g., even a simple comparison such as "X = 3" is invalid (though the OQL chapter later in the ODMG book includes plenty of examples of such comparisons).

Next, *structured* literals. As noted earlier, ODMG supports a STRUCT type generator, analogous (somewhat) to the TUPLE type generator of *The Third Manifesto;* hence, "struct" or tuple types can be generated, and instances of such types then seem to be called "structured literals," regardless of whether (in *Manifesto* terms) they are values or variables. "A structured literal ... has a fixed number of elements, each of which has a ... name and can contain either a literal value [*sic!*] or an object [i.e., an object ID]." The idea of a *literal* including a component that is an *object* (i.e., variable) seems to muddle some very basic notions that would surely be better kept separate. *Note:* ODMG requires support for certain built-in structured literal types, namely DATE, TIME, TIMESTAMP, and INTERVAL (not to be confused with the structured *object* types of the same names).

Finally, *collection* literals. Here again the situation seems unnecessarily confusing. Collection literals are really *collection type generators.* "The ODMG Object Model supports collection literals of the following types [*sic!*]: SET, BAG, ... (etc.). These type generators [*sic!*] are analogous to those of collection objects ... Their elements ... can be of literal types or object types." Apparently, therefore, we can have, e.g., a list *object* whose elements are *literals,* and a list *literal* whose elements are *objects* (?). *Note:* The ODMG book also mentions a user-defined UNION literal type, the semantics of which it does not explain (we suspect it refers to heterogeneous collections, although collections are elsewhere stated to be homogeneous). It does not say whether there is an analogous UNION object type.

In sum, we agree wholeheartedly that there is a vast and important logical difference between *values* and *variables,* but that particular difference does not seem to be the one that ODMG draws between *literals* and *objects*—nor does the precise nature of the difference that ODMG does draw in this connection seem very clear, at least to us. At the same time, ODMG also makes use of the value *vs.* variable terminology, but it does not give definitions of these latter concepts.

We conclude this subsection by noting that:

- An ODMG literal (of any kind) is not an object and does not have an object ID.

- Although as noted earlier the Object Model prescribes certain operators for certain *objects* (especially collection objects), it does not appear to prescribe any such operators for *literals.*

- Indeed, if it is really true that object types and literal types are different kinds of things, it would seem that (e.g.) if operator *Op* is defined to work on, say, integer *objects,* it cannot be invoked on integer *literals* (?).

- ODMG also supports a special *null literal.* "For every literal type ... there exists another literal type supporting a null value [*sic*] ... This nullable type is the same as the literal type augmented by the ... value *nil.* The semantics of null are the same as those defined by [the SQL standard]." (This last claim is contradicted later, in the chapter on OQL.)

Types, Classes, and Interfaces

On the face of it, it might have seemed more logical to explain these concepts prior to this point. We deliberately did not do so, however, because (a) the concepts are not as clear as they might be, and (b) it therefore seems necessary to have some appreciation of the material discussed in the foregoing subsections in order to understand them. Consider the following series of quotes:

> *A type has an external* specification *and one or more* implementations. *The specification defines the external characteristics of the type. These are the aspects that are visible to users of the type: the* operations *that can be invoked on its instances [and] the* properties ... *whose values can be accessed ... By contrast, a type's implementation defines the internal aspects of the objects of the type* [or of literals of the type, presumably, if the type in question is a literal type instead of an object type]: *the implementation of the type's operations and other internal details.*

> *An external specification of a type consists of an abstract, implementation-independent description of the operations ... and properties that are visible to users of the type. An* interface *definition is a specification that defines only the abstract behavior of an object type. A* class *definition is a specification that defines the abstract behavior and abstract state of an object type. A* literal *definition defines only the abstract state of a literal type.*

Observe, therefore, that the terms *type* and *class* are being used here in a somewhat unusual way: *Class* is being used to refer to what in the *Manifesto* book, following more orthodox usage, we call a *type,* and *type* is being used to refer to the combination of *class* in this unorthodox sense together with the *implementation* of the class in question.[8] *Note:* We will come back to "literal definitions" in a few moments, and to "interface definitions" in the next subsection.

But then what are we to make of the following, which appears a couple of pages later?

> *Classes are types ... Interfaces are types ...*

Most of the rest of the ODMG book either ignores the distinction between types and classes or observes it in inconsistent ways. In what follows, we will stay with the term "type" (mostly).

As for the assertion that "a literal definition defines only the abstract state of a literal type": This statement seems to suggest that no operations can be performed on literals, which cannot be correct. We suspect that what the ODMG book really means here is that a "literal definition" that is actually *an application of some type generator* (see the previous subsection) defines the unencapsulated logical structure of some generated type but does not define any operators that apply to instances of that generated type (the only operators that do apply being inherited built-in ones).

Inheritance

ODMG includes support for both multiple and (*a fortiori*) single inheritance, though the semantics are not very clear. In fact, it supports both behavioral inheritance (which it calls *subtyping*) and structural inheritance (which it calls *extension* or "the EXTENDS relationship"). We will return to these two kinds of inheritance in a moment. First, however, it is necessary to say something about the difference between interfaces and classes.

---

8. The ODMG terminology derives from that of OMG [6]. Other object texts and systems use the terms the other way around—i.e., they use *type* in our sense and *class* to mean the implementation of a type. See, e.g., references [1] and [5].

ODMG's "interfaces" correspond to the *Manifesto* book's *union types*. In other words, an ODMG interface is a type that is not—in fact, is not allowed to be—the most specific type of any value at all. Such a type *must* have proper subtypes, and every value of the type *must* be a value of one of those subtypes. For example, consider the types ELLIPSE, CIRCLE, and NONCIRCLE, where type CIRCLE and type NONCIRCLE are both proper subtypes of type ELLIPSE (and the obvious semantics apply). Clearly, every instance of type ELLIPSE is also an instance of one of the other two types, and so ELLIPSE is not the most specific type of anything at all.

In ODMG, then, a type like ELLIPSE in this example can be defined by means of an *interface* definition instead of a *class* definition; an interface definition defines behavior (or at least what in the *Manifesto* book we call *specification signatures*) but no structure.[9] The general intent seems to be that, as we travel down any given path in the type graph, operations *must* be explicitly specialized at the point where we first encounter a class instead of an interface. Observe in passing, therefore, that ODMG assigns a very special meaning to what is more usually a very general term (*viz.,* interface).

Reference [2] then goes on to say: "Subtyping pertains to the inheritance of behavior only; thus interfaces may inherit [behavior] from other interfaces and classes may inherit [behavior] from interfaces ... [but] interfaces may not inherit [behavior] from classes, nor may classes inherit [behavior] from other classes ... The EXTENDS relationship is a single inheritance relationship between two classes[10] whereby the subordinate class inherits all of the properties [i.e., structure] and all of the behavior of the class that it extends." In other words, if *T* is a root type and *T'* is a leaf type (to use the terminology of the *Manifesto* book), then the path from *T* to *T'* consists of zero or more *interfaces* followed by one or more *classes* (i.e., once we meet the first class, the rest are all classes). Note too that if every such path contains just one class (i.e., all inheritance is via subtyping, not extension), then all instances are instances of leaf types. *Speculation:* It seems possible that what ODMG calls subtyping refers to "is a" relationships and so does correspond, more or less, to type inheritance in the sense of the *Manifesto* book, while what it calls "the EXTENDS relationship" refers to "has a" relationships instead. More investigation is required to determine whether this speculation is anywhere close to being accurate—but if it is, then some of our **"conforms"** assessments later in this chapter might need to be changed to **"conforms** (partly)" or even to **"fails."**

As already noted, ODMG does support multiple inheritance, but only for interfaces, not for classes (speaking a little loosely). More precisely, a type can have any number of proper supertypes, but at most one of them can be a class, not an interface. Also, note the following: "The ODMG Object Model supports multiple inheritance of object behavior [only]. Therefore it is possible that a type could inherit operations that have the same name, but different parameters, from two different interfaces. The model precludes this possibility [*so in fact the "possibility" is not really a possibility after all*] by disallowing name overloading during inheritance."

---

9. And yet later in the ODMG book we find an extensive example of an interface definition specifically that includes several attribute and relationship—i.e., "structure"—definitions as well as operator definitions as such (?).
10. It could hardly be a *multiple* "inheritance relationship," since it is "between two classes." More to the point, the two sentences quoted here contradict each other—the first says classes cannot inherit behavior from other classes, the second says they can.

While we are on the subject of inheritance, incidentally, the ODMG book includes a nice example of how difficult it can be to get the type hierarchy right: "For example, ASSOCIATE_ PROFESSOR is a subtype of PROFESSOR ... Where an object of type PROFESSOR can be used, an object of type ASSOCIATE_PROFESSOR can be used instead, because ASSOCIATE_ PROFESSOR inherits from PROFESSOR." But surely professors have properties—perhaps *tenure*— that associate professors do not? In other words, is not the hierarchy (at best) upside down?

ODMG does not appear to distinguish between value and variable substitutability.

Object Definition Language

The foregoing subsections summarize the major aspects of the Object Model (though we have skipped over features that we regard as secondary, such as details of the catalog or "metadata" and details of recovery and concurrency control). Now we turn to the Object Definition Language, ODL. ODL is basically a language that provides a concrete syntax for "the specification of object types that conform to the ODMG Object Model." *Note:* ODL supports the definition of operator "specification signatures" (*Manifesto* book terminology)—including the names of any *exceptions* that might be raised by the operation in question—but does not provide a means of writing the code to implement such operations. Presumably that code must be written in a language such as C++ or Java.

The chapter of the ODMG book that discusses ODL gives a number of examples, together with a complete definition of ODL syntax (a BNF grammar), but says almost nothing about semantics. Possibly the reader is supposed to have read the *OMG* specifications (on which ODL is based) first. In any case, we omit the details of ODL here since (as we say in the *Manifesto* book) we do not regard matters of mere syntax as being very important.

Object Interchange Format

To quote the ODMG book, the Object Interchange Format (OIF) is "a specification language used to dump and load the current state of an object database to or from a file or set of files." As such, it is not very germane to the present discussion, and we therefore skip the details.

Object Query Language

The Object Query Language OQL might be characterized as a large superset of a small subset of SQL, with incompatibilities. It is not the ODMG "Object Manipulation Language" (as noted in the introduction to this chapter, no such language exists); rather, it is, specifically, a *query* language that supports nonprocedural retrieval (only)[11] of data stored in an ODMG database. As such, it supports a variety of operators that are not part of the Object Model *per se*. It is not computationally complete.

We choose not to provide anything close to a complete description of OQL here. Suffice it to say that it supports:

- SQL-style SELECT-FROM-WHERE queries against sets, bags, lists, and arrays

- Analogs of the SQL GROUP BY, HAVING, and ORDER BY constructs

---

11. What happens if an OQL query invokes an *update* operator does not seem to be defined.

- Union, intersections, and differences, and special operations for lists and arrays (e.g., "get the first element")

- "Path expressions" for traversing relationships

There appear to be quite a few detail-level incompatibilities, of both style and substance, between OQL and the Object Model. For example, "[certain] expressions yield objects without identity" (but surely objects *always* have identity in the Object Model?); "OQL allows us to call a method" (but methods are defined earlier in the book to be part of the implementation, not part of the model); "[we can retrieve] the *i*th element of an indexed collection" (the term *indexed* here does not mean what it means earlier in the book); and so on. It should be noted too that the semantics of nulls and certain query constructs are—presumably unintentionally— different from those of their SQL counterparts.

Summary

The basic idea behind ODMG, in a nutshell, is (of course) to allow many different data structures—sets, bags, lists, arrays, and so on—to be used for data in the database *and to expose them all to the user* ("persistence orthogonal to type"). We reject this idea for reasons explained in detail in reference [4] and sketched in the annotation to that reference in the final section of this chapter.

We now proceed to consider the question of how ODMG measures up to the various prescriptions, proscriptions, and suggestions defined formally and explained in (the third edition of) the *Manifesto* book. What follows thus consists essentially of a series of point-by-point comparisons of pertinent ODMG features with those prescriptions, proscriptions, and suggestions. The comparisons are presented mostly as bald statements of fact; we (mostly) do not restate opinions, give value judgments, or comment on the relative severity of various points. Also, we use the terms **conforms** and **fails,** in **boldface,** to indicate our general finding in connection with each point. Very often these terms have to be qualified, and sometimes both are used in connection with the same point. For example, ODMG sometimes conforms to (say) a certain prescription in some respects but fails in others; sometimes it conforms as far as it goes but does not go far enough; sometimes it fails not because of specifics of the feature at hand, but rather because that feature depends on some other feature on which it fails in turn. Such dependencies are appropriately indicated.

RM Prescriptions

1. Scalar types

ODMG **conforms,** partly. However, (a) the distinction between literal and object "atomic" types seems unnecessary and confusing;[12] (b) there does not appear to be a way of destroying user-defined scalar types; (c) ODMG's objects have object IDs; (d) ODMG objects have structure as

---

12. In fact, it looks like a serious violation of orthogonality. At best, it requires many specifications— regarding valid operations, for example—to be duplicated; at worst, it introduces undesirable rules and distinctions. (In fact, it seems to us that the ODMG distinction between literals and objects has something to do with another ODMG distinction that we also find unnecessary and confusing: namely, that between structure and behavior.)

well as behavior; (e) instead of supporting *Manifesto*-style selectors, ODMG requires "new object instances" (apparently uninitialized) to be "created" by means of a prescribed NEW operator. *Note:* OQL (as opposed to the ODMG Object Model as such) does include something it calls a "type name constructor" that seems to be more akin to our selector, however.

2. Scalar values are typed

ODMG **conforms,** subject to the reservations indicated under RM Prescription 1.

3. Read-only *vs.* update operators

ODMG **conforms,** partly. However, (a) there does not appear to be a way of destroying user-defined operators; (b) it is not clear whether ODMG conforms to the *Manifesto's* many prescriptions regarding the distinction between read-only and update operators.

4. Physical *vs.* possible representations

ODMG **fails** (it does not clearly distinguish between physical and possible representations).

5. Expose possible representations

ODMG **fails** *a fortiori.* However, it does expose *physical* representations. It is not clear whether it supports anything analogous to the *Manifesto's* nestable THE_ pseudovariables.

6. Type generator TUPLE

ODMG **conforms,** partly. However, (a) the distinction between literal and object tuple types seems unnecessary and confusing; (b) there does not appear to be a way of destroying user-defined tuple types; (c) ODMG's "tuple objects" have object IDs; (d) instead of supporting tuple selectors, ODMG requires "new object instances" (apparently uninitialized) to be "created" by means of a prescribed NEW operator; (e) ODMG does not support tuple-valued possible representation components (because it does not support the concept of possible representations at all); (f) ODMG tuple types have explicit names; (g) it is not clear when two ODMG tuple types are regarded as equal; (h) ODMG's tuple types appear to have a left-to-right ordering to their components; (i) most of the *Manifesto's* required tuple operators are not supported in the Object Model (though it might be possible to simulate them in OQL). *Note:* OQL (as opposed to the ODMG Object Model as such) does include a construct that seems to be somewhat more akin to our tuple selector.

7. Type generator RELATION

ODMG **fails.** The comments under RM Prescription 6 apply here also, *mutatis mutandis.* Note in particular that most of the operators of the relational algebra are not supported in the ODMG Object Model (though they can probably be simulated in OQL).

8. Equality

ODMG **fails** (probably). First, it distinguishes between *identity* and *equivalence* (sometimes called deep equality *vs.* shallow equality, though authorities disagree as to which is which);

second, it distinguishes between literals and objects. Both of these facts muddy the picture considerably. In addition, there does not appear to be any way to prevent users from defining an "=" operator with any semantics they please (note that no "=" operator, as such, is actually prescribed). However, it is least true that support for a SAME_AS operator, with prescribed semantics, is required for objects (though apparently not for literals); SAME_AS tests to see whether two objects are "identical" (i.e., have the same object ID).

9. Tuples

See RM Prescription 6.

10. Relations

See RM Prescription 7.

11. Scalar variables

ODMG **conforms,** partly. At least, it supports *objects* of (user-defined) "atomic" type *T*, and ODMG objects seem to be something like variables and ODMG "atomic" types seem to be something like scalar types. But the values of those "scalar variables" are not exactly values of type *T*, owing to the distinction ODMG draws between literal and object types (in fact, it is quite difficult to say *what* they are). Also, "defining"—i.e., creating, via NEW—a scalar variable (atomic object) does not appear to initialize that variable (atomic object).

12. Tuple variables

The comments under RM Prescription 11 apply here also, *mutatis mutandis.*

13. Relation variables (relvars)

ODMG **fails** in all respects.

14. Kinds of relvars

ODMG **fails** in all respects.

15. Candidate keys

ODMG **fails** *a fortiori,* because it does not support relation values or variables (in the full sense of the relational model) at all. However, it does support something it *calls* keys: "The *extent* of a type is the set of all instances of the type within a particular database ... [The] object database designer can decide whether the object DBMS should automatically maintain the extent of [any given] type. Extent maintenance includes inserting newly created instances in the set ... In some cases the individual instances of a type can be uniquely identified by the values [*sic!*] they carry for some property or set of properties ... A *simple key* consists of a single property. A *compound key* consists of a set of properties. The scope of uniqueness is the extent of the type; thus a type must have an extent to have a key." Points arising:

- Nothing analogous to the extent notion as just described exists in the relational model at all. The closest we might come to it would be something like the following: Let *T* be a type and let *R* be a relvar with an attribute *A* defined on *T*. Then the extent of *T* would be the union of all projections of all such relvars *R* over all such attributes *A*. Note that (a) that extent is itself a relvar (a virtual relvar, in fact), and (b) in general, it does not seem to be particularly useful.

- "Automatic maintenance" of such an extent implies that "creating a new object" of the type in question via NEW has the side effect of updating the database (for indeed the extent is a variable in the database). It also implies that support for a "constructor" operator (like NEW) is required, a notion that the *Manifesto* rejects.

- It is not "instances of a type" that are identified by keys, it is "instances within an extent." The ODMG book does say that "a type must have an extent [*meaning, presumably, an extent that is explicitly defined and automatically maintained—after all,* all *types have an extent, by definition*] to have a key," but the ODL syntax does not enforce this rule.

- We would not draw the distinction ODMG does between simple and compound keys (at least, not in the same way). Keys *always* consist of sets of "properties," by definition. If the set has cardinality one (or zero?), then we might say the key is "simple."

16. Databases

ODMG **conforms,** partly. However, ODMG databases are not "named containers for relvars," they are named containers for *objects* (of any type); also, ODMG database definition and destruction are not done "outside the ODMG environment."

17. Transactions

ODMG **conforms,** more or less.

18. Relational algebra

The Object Model **fails** in almost all respects. However, OQL does support analogs of most of the usual operators of the relational algebra. Unfortunately, it supports many other things as well.

19. Relvar names, relation selectors, and recursion

The comments under RM Prescription 18 apply here also, *mutatis mutandis.* Also, OQL apparently does not support recursion.

20. User-defined tuple and relational operators

ODMG apparently **fails**.

21. Assignments

ODMG **fails**. It does require support for a large number of operators of an updating nature—for example, NEW, DELETE, INSERT_ELEMENT, REMOVE_ELEMENT, REMOVE_ELEMENT_AT, REPLACE_ELEMENT_AT, INSERT_ELEMENT_AFTER, INSERT_ELEMENT_BEFORE, INSERT_ELEMENT_FIRST, INSERT_ELEMENT_LAST, REMOVE_FIRST_ELEMENT, REMOVE_LAST_ELEMENT, and APPEND in the case of lists, and analogous operations in the case of sets, bags, arrays, relationships, and so on—but it does not seem to support assignment *per se* (presumably, assignment support is to be provided by whatever language ODMG is bound to). It also does not support multiple assignment, *a fortiori*.

22. Comparisons

ODMG mostly requires type definers to provide comparison operators. Almost no such operators (not even "=") are built in, with prescribed semantics.

23. Integrity constraints

ODMG **fails** in all respects.

24. Total database constraints

ODMG **fails** in all respects.

25. Catalog

ODMG **conforms,** partly (it does define a catalog, but of course that catalog contains objects, not relvars).

26. Language design

Not directly applicable. The ODMG analog of **D** is a combination of ODL and whatever language ODMG is bound to, plus OQL (which is really rather separate). OQL in particular is hamstrung by its goal of being "SQL-like"; hence, it cannot possibly "be constructed according to well-established principles of good language design," by definition. (To be fair, we should add that OQL nevertheless does seem to be better designed than SQL in certain respects!)

RM Proscriptions

1. No attribute ordering

The Object Model probably **fails**. OQL definitely **fails**.

2. No tuple ordering

ODMG **conforms** for sets and bags (of tuples).

3. No duplicate tuples

ODMG **conforms** for sets (of tuples).

4. No nulls

ODMG **fails**. What is more, ODMG nulls and SQL nulls are different.

5. No nullological mistakes

The Object Model probably **fails** (it is hard to tell). OQL definitely **fails**.

6. No internal-level constructs

ODMG **fails**.

7. No tuple-level operations

ODMG **fails** (it expressly prescribes "iterators" over collections).

8. No composite attributes

ODMG **conforms**.

9. No domain check override

ODMG **conforms**.

10. Not SQL

The Object Model **conforms**. OQL **conforms** (just).

OO Prescriptions

1. Compile-time type checking

ODMG allows, e.g., a parameter type to be specified as ANY, a fact that might possibly undermine the system's ability to perform compile-time type checking. Otherwise, it probably **conforms**.

2. Type inheritance (conditional)

ODMG **fails** by definition here, because it does not abide by the inheritance model described in the *Manifesto* book (in fact, ODMG's "inheritance model" is scarcely defined at all, in the opinion of the present writers). We can be more specific than this, however, and we will be under the various IM Prescriptions (see later in this chapter).

3. Computational completeness

OQL **fails**. Not applicable to the Object Model *per se;* however, we remark that ODMG does share our distaste for the "embedded data sublanguage" approach adopted in SQL: "Note that unlike SQL in relational systems, object DBMS data manipulation languages are tailored to specific application programming languages, in order to provide a single, integrated environment for programming and data manipulation." And: "It is possible to read and write the same database from C++, Smalltalk, and Java, *as long as the programmer stays within the common subset of supported data types*" (italics added). *Note:* The reference here to "the programmer" seems to suggest that ODMG is aimed specifically at application programmers. What about end-user access via OQL?

4. Explicit transaction boundaries

ODMG **conforms**.

5. Nested transactions

ODMG **fails**.

6. Aggregate operators and empty sets

Not applicable to the Object Model. OQL **fails**.

OO Proscriptions

1. Relvars are not domains

ODMG **conforms,** inasmuch as it does at least distinguish between types and collections (where we take "collections" to mean both collection values and collection variables, in *Manifesto* terms).

2. No object IDs

ODMG **fails** (of course).

RM Very Strong Suggestions

1. System keys

ODMG **fails** on both parts of this suggestion. *Note:* An argument might be made that object IDs make system keys unnecessary. Even if this argument is accepted, however, object IDs are still not keys in the relational sense, because:

    a. Unlike keys, object IDs are represented differently (at the *logical* level) from other data; as a consequence,

    b. Unlike access via keys, access to data via object ID is different from access via other properties.

2. Foreign keys

ODMG **fails.**

3. Candidate key inference

ODMG **fails.**

4. Transition constraints

ODMG **fails.**

5. Quota queries

ODMG **fails.**

6. Generalized transitive closure

ODMG **fails.**

7. User-defined generic operators

Not clear.

8. SQL migration

ODMG **conforms,** partly (at least for query operations, via OQL).

OO Very Strong Suggestions

1. Type inheritance

ODMG **fails** *a fortiori,* because it fails on OO Prescription 2.

2. Types and operators unbundled

ODMG **fails.** "An operation is defined on [i.e., bundled with] only a single type ... [We] had several reasons for choosing to adopt this single-dispatch model rather than a multiple-dispatch model. The major reason was for consistency with the C++ and Smalltalk programming languages ... Another reason to adopt the classical object model was to avoid incompatibilities with the OMG ... object model, which is classical rather than general [*sic*]."

3. Single-level store

ODMG **conforms**.

IM Prescriptions

1. Types are sets

ODMG presumably **conforms**—though *object* types seem to be sets of variables, not sets of values (?).

2. Subtypes are subsets

ODMG **conforms,** subject to the reservations indicated under IM Prescription 1. But whether *proper* subtypes are required to be *proper* subsets is not clear (we suspect they are not).

3. "Subtype of" is reflexive

Not clear. Certainly the ODMG book never explicitly mentions the fact that every type is both a supertype and a subtype of itself.

4. Proper subtypes

Not clear. Certainly the ODMG book never explicitly mentions the concept.

5. "Subtype of" is transitive

ODMG **conforms**—but note the class *vs.* interface distinction, not part of our inheritance model (it is *not* identical to our regular type *vs.* union type distinction).

6. Immediate subtypes

Not clear. Certainly the ODMG book never explicitly mentions the concept.

7. Root types disjoint

Not clear. Certainly the ODMG book never explicitly discusses the issue.

8. Scalar values with inheritance

ODMG **conforms**.

9. Scalar variables with inheritance

Not clear. Certainly the ODMG book never discusses the issue of an abstract *model* of a scalar variable, with its *DT, MST,* and *v* components, nor does there seem to be an ODMG term corresponding to our "declared type."

10. Specialization by constraint

ODMG **fails** completely; in fact, as implied by our remarks under RM Prescription 23, it does not support type constraints at all.

11. Assignment with inheritance

Not clear. First of all, the reservations under IM Prescription 9 apply here *a fortiori*. Second, the Object Model does not support assignment as such, anyway. However, the book does say (in connection with the example mentioned earlier involving types PROFESSOR and ASSOCIATE_PROFESSOR) that "where an object of [most specific] type PROFESSOR can be used, an object of [most specific] type ASSOCIATE_PROFESSOR can be used instead," but the semantic implications—for assignment in particular—are left seriously underspecified.

12. Equality etc. with inheritance

Not clear. The comments under IM Prescription 11 apply here also, *mutatis mutandis*. In addition, OQL provides some rules regarding comparisons, but they seem to be (a) incomplete and (b) both less and more than what is required by IM Prescription 12.

13. Join etc. with inheritance

Not clear. Again, the comments under IM Prescription 11 apply here also, *mutatis mutandis*. However, OQL provides some rules regarding joins and similar operations that do seem to **conform** to IM Prescription 13.

14. TREAT

The Object Model **fails** (it never mentions the concept at all). OQL probably **fails** too; it does seem to have something analogous to TREAT, but it is not fully specified, and it cannot be used as a pseudovariable (since OQL is a retrieval-only language).

15. Type testing

ODMG **fails**.

16. Read-only operator inheritance and value substitutability

ODMG **conforms**.

17. Operator signatures

ODMG probably **fails** (in several ways).

18. Read-only parameters to update operators

ODMG **conforms**.

19. Update operator inheritance and variable substitutability

ODMG probably **fails**. Although reference [2] never discusses the issue, it can safely be assumed that unconditional inheritance of update operators is required; moreover, ODMG does not seem to distinguish between value substitutability and variable substitutability.

20. Union, dummy, and maximal and minimal types

ODMG **fails,** except inasmuch as its "interfaces" are counterparts to our union types.

21. Tuple/relation subtypes and supertypes

ODMG **fails**.

22. Tuple/relation values with inheritance

ODMG **fails**.

23. Maximal and minimal tuple/relation types

ODMG **fails**.

24. Tuple/relation most specific types

ODMG **fails**.

25. Tuple/relation variables with inheritance

ODMG **fails**.

References

1. Michael Blaha and William Premerlani: *Object-Oriented Modeling and Design for Database Applications.* Upper Saddle River, N.J.: Prentice-Hall (1998).

2. R. G. G. Cattell and Douglas K. Barry (eds.): *The Object Database Standard: ODMG 2.0.* San Francisco, Calif.: Morgan Kaufmann (1997).

3. C. J. Date (with Hugh Darwen): *A Guide to the SQL Standard* (4th edition). Reading, Mass.: Addison-Wesley (1997).

4. C. J. Date: "Why 'The Object Model' Is Not a Data Model," in C. J. Date, *Relational Database Writings 1994–1997.* Reading, Mass.: Addison-Wesley (1998).

5. Ivar Jacobson (with Magnus Christerson, Patrik Jonsson, and Gunnar Övergaard): *Object-Oriented Software Engineering* (revised printing). Reading, Mass.: Addison-Wesley (1994).

6. Richard Mark Soley and William Kent: "The OMG Object Model," in Won Kim (ed.): *Modern Database Systems: The Object Model, Interoperability, and Beyond.* New York, N.Y.: ACM Press / Reading, Mass.: Addison-Wesley (1995).

■ ■ ■

An Overview and Analysis of Proposals Based on the TSQL2 Approach

It's about time.

—Anon.

In reference [6], the present writers,[1] along with Nikos Lorentzos, describe an approach to the temporal database problem that is firmly rooted in the relational model of data (and we assume here and there in the present chapter that you do have some familiarity with the ideas described in that reference). However, many other approaches have been proposed and described in the literature. In this chapter, we take a brief look at the "temporal query language" **TSQL2,** which is probably the best known and most influential of those alternative approaches—indeed, a version of it was even proposed at one time for inclusion in the SQL standard (see the section immediately following this introduction).[2] The next five sections provide an overview of the major features of TSQL2; the next four then describe what we regard as a series of major flaws in the TSQL2 approach; and the final section offers a few concluding remarks.

With regard to those "major flaws," incidentally, we should say there is one that seems to us so significant—indeed, it underlies all the rest—that it needs to be mentioned right away, and that is that **TSQL2 involves "hidden attributes."**[3] As a direct consequence of this fact, the basic data object in TSQL2 is not a relation, and the approach thus clearly violates *The Information Principle.* In other words, TSQL2, whatever else it might be, is certainly not relational. We should immediately add that TSQL2 is not alone in this regard—most of the other temporal proposals described in the literature do the same thing, in one way or another. What is more, the picture is muddied by the fact that most if not all of the researchers involved refer to their proposals, quite explicitly, as *relational* approaches to the problem, even though they are clearly not (relational, that is).

---

1. This chapter was written jointly by Hugh Darwen and myself.
2. Reference [1] describes a temporal query language very similar to TSQL2 called ATSQL. In this chapter, we use the name *TSQL2* as a convenient generic label to refer to the approach espoused in all or any of references [1] and [11-14].
3. The TSQL2 term is *implicit columns.* Regular attributes are called *explicit* columns.

We will elaborate on this matter of hidden attributes later. And although those later remarks are framed in terms of TSQL2 specifically, it should be clear that they apply with equal force, *mutatis mutandis*, to any approach that attempts to "hide attributes" in the same kind of way that TSQL2 does.

One final preliminary remark: Our discussions of TSQL2—which are not meant to be exhaustive, please note—are based primarily on our own understanding of references [13–15]. Naturally we have tried to make those discussions as accurate as we can, but it is of course possible that we have misinterpreted those references on occasion. If so, we apologize; in our defense, however, we need to say that those references [13–15] do contradict one another on occasion.

TSQL2 and the SQL Standard

First of all, a little background. The body that publishes the international SQL standard is the International Organization for Standardization ("ISO"). That body produced versions of the standard in 1992 (*SQL:1992*, known informally as SQL2) and 1999 (*SQL:1999*, known informally as SQL3). SQL:1999 [8] is the version of the standard that is current at the time of writing; a thorough tutorial description of the previous version, SQL:1992, with an appendix giving an overview of SQL3 as it was around 1996 or so, can be found in reference [5]. The next version is likely to be ratified later this year (2003). *Note added later:* In fact this latter did happen, and SQL:2003 is now the current standard.

The ISO committee with direct responsibility for the SQL standard has delegates representing a variety of national standards bodies. During the 1990s, the United States national body received a proposal for a set of temporal extensions to SQL based on TSQL2. (The name "TSQL2" presumably reflects the fact that the language was designed as an extension to SQL2 specifically [11], which—in the form of SQL:1992—was the official standard at the time.) The U.S. national body in turn submitted that proposal as an "individual expert's contribution" (i.e., not as a formal position paper) for consideration by the ISO SQL committee [13].

The ISO SQL committee proceeded to examine the proposal carefully. As part of that examination, members of the United Kingdom national body in particular came to the conclusion that, while the proposal might look attractive at first glance, that attractiveness did not stand up to close scrutiny. To be specific, they found that TSQL2 departed significantly from both established language design principles in general [2] and relational database theory in particular. What is more, they found that the departures in question were significantly different in kind from SQL's other well-documented departures from those principles and that theory. As a consequence of those findings, the U.K. body prepared a paper [4] and submitted it for consideration at the ISO committee meeting in January 1997.

The U.K. paper demonstrated conclusively that the specific proposals of reference [13] were unacceptable for the working draft of SQL3 at that time. Indeed, it went further: It showed why the U.K. body was unlikely ever to support any proposal that was based on TSQL2. Actually, the U.K. opposition to such an approach had become clear to other participants at previous ISO committee meetings in 1995 and 1996. However, those previous meetings had at least achieved the following positive results among others:

- Agreement had been reached that temporal extensions of some kind were desirable.

- A working draft for a possible Part 7 of the international standard, known informally as "SQL/Temporal," had been established as the base document for such extensions.

- Finally, discussion papers suggesting various ways forward had been considered and debated.

Moreover, despite the arguments of reference [4], several members of the ISO committee remained enthusiastic about the possibility of a TSQL2-based approach—perhaps because of the apparent reluctance on the part of the TSQL2 proponents themselves to acknowledge that the arguments of reference [4] held water. Be that as it may, it was at least agreed that the specific proposals of reference [13] needed a significant amount of revision and left several important questions unanswered, and the U.S. delegates therefore agreed to withdraw the submission.[4] It was further agreed that nobody would submit any more temporal proposals to the ISO committee until SQL3 was formally published. That publication took place at the end of 1999, when the informal name SQL3 was replaced by the official one, SQL:1999.

Following all of the activity described above, ISO interest in temporal extensions waned somewhat; in fact, nobody was prepared to spend any more time on the matter unless and until some positive move was made by the leading SQL vendors. And time ran out toward the end of 2001, when—since no vendor had made any such move, and the committee had therefore done no further work on the project to develop Part 7 of the standard—ISO's own bylaws led to that project being canceled altogether. At the time of writing, therefore, the working draft document mentioned above ("Part 7: SQL/Temporal") is in limbo.

TSQL2 Tables

We begin our description of TSQL2 by describing the basic data objects—to be more specific, the various kinds of "tables"—that TSQL2 supports ("tables" in quotes because those "tables" are certainly not relational tables, as we will quickly see). Then, in subsequent sections, we can go on to explain various detailed aspects of TSQL2 in terms of those different kinds of tables.

Before we can even start to describe those tables, however, we need to say a word about terminology. As previously stated, TSQL2 is designed as an extension to SQL specifically. As a result, we will frequently be forced to use SQL terminology instead of our own preferred terms, as documented in reference [6], in our explanations. However, we will do our best to stay with our preferred terms as much as possible—certainly when we are talking about general concepts rather than TSQL2 specifics.

Here then is a list of our preferred terms and their SQL or TSQL2 counterparts. Note that we do not say "equivalents," because the SQL (or TSQL2) terms are mostly not exactly equivalent to their relational counterparts. For example, a tuple and a row are not the same thing, nor are an attribute and a column.

---

4. In spite of that withdrawal (and in support of our claim above that the TSQL2 proponents themselves seem reluctant to accept the arguments of reference [4]), we observe that (a) Chapter 12 of reference [15], published some three years later, continues to describe the TSQL2-based proposals as if they were part of SQL3, and (b) reference [1], published later still, continues to pursue the idea of *statement modifiers*, even though statement modifiers were one of the TSQL2 ideas that reference [4] showed to be fundamentally flawed (see later).

Our Term	SQL or TSQL2 Term
relvar	table
relation	table
tuple	row
attribute	column
interval	period
stated time	valid time
logged time	transaction time
operator	operator, function

Now to the question of the kinds of tables that TSQL2 supports. Consider Figure 28-1, which shows a sample value for a relvar called S_DURING_LOG, with attributes S# (supplier number), DURING (stated or "valid" time), and X_DURING (logged or "transaction" time). Note our use of symbols of the form *d01, d02*, etc., in that figure; the "*d*" in those symbols can conveniently be pronounced "day," a convention to which we will adhere throughout this chapter. We assume that day 1 immediately precedes day 2, day 2 immediately precedes day 3, and so on; also, we drop insignificant leading zeros from expressions such as "day 1" (as you can see). *Note:* Details of how relvar S_DURING_LOG is meant to be interpreted can be found in reference [6]; here we just note that, for the sake of the example, we have assumed that day 99 is "the end of time." We have also assumed that today is day 10 (and we will stay with that assumption throughout the rest of this chapter).

```
S_DURING_LOG     S#  |  DURING   |  X_DURING
                 ────┼───────────┼───────────
                 S1  | [d01:d01] | [d01:d03]
                 S1  | [d05:d06] | [d04:d10]
                 S2  | [d02:d04] | [d02:d06]
                 S2  | [d02:d04] | [d08:d08]
                 S2  | [d02:d99] | [d09:d10]
                 S3  | [d05:d99] | [d05:d10]
                 S4  | [d03:d99] | [d02:d10]
                 S6  | [d02:d05] | [d01:d02]
                 S6  | [d03:d05] | [d03:d10]
```

Figure 28-1. *Relvar S_DURING_LOG—sample values*

Figure 28-2 shows a table that might be regarded as a TSQL2 counterpart to the relvar shown in Figure 28-1. Note the following points right away:

- The table is named S, not S_DURING_LOG.

- The table has no double underlining to indicate a primary key.

- The "timestamp" columns—i.e., the columns corresponding to attributes DURING and X_DURING—are unnamed.

- Those timestamp columns are separated from the rest of the table by a double vertical line.

S	S#		
	S1	[d01:d01]	[d01:d03]
	S1	[d05:d06]	[d04:d10]
	S2	[d02:d04]	[d02:d06]
	S2	[d02:d04]	[d08:d08]
	S2	[d02:d99]	[d09:d10]
	S3	[d05:d99]	[d05:d10]
	S4	[d03:d99]	[d02:d10]
	S6	[d02:d05]	[d01:d02]
	S6	[d03:d05]	[d03:d10]

Figure 28-2. *A TSQL2 bitemporal table*

The object depicted in Figure 28-2 is an example of what TSQL2 calls a *bitemporal table*. Let us examine it more carefully. First of all, the unnamed timestamp columns are *hidden from the user*, which is why we show them separated from the rest of the table by that double vertical line. (To the user, in other words, the table contains just one column, named S#.) Of course, there has to be a way to access those hidden columns, and so there is, as we will see later; however, that access cannot be done in regular relational fashion—i.e., by simply referring to the columns by name—because, to repeat, they have no names. Indeed, those hidden columns are not relational attributes, and the overall table is not a relation (more precisely, it is not a relvar).

Next, the table is named S, not S_DURING_LOG, because TSQL2 wants to pretend as far as possible that the table is indeed just the usual suppliers table;[5] to say it again, the timestamp columns are hidden. In particular, TSQL2 wants regular SQL statements to operate on the table, so far as the user is concerned, just as if those hidden columns were not there. (Indeed, it wants much more than that, as we will see.)

Next, we have omitted the double underlining we normally use to indicate a primary key, because we clearly cannot pretend to the user that the combination of all three columns is the primary key (as it really is, in effect), while at the same time pretending to that same user that the hidden columns are not there. (In fact, TSQL2 also wants to pretend, in effect, that certain rows are not there either, as we will also see later; as a consequence of this latter pretense, it is able to pretend as well that {S#} alone is the primary key. But this notion is hard to illustrate in a figure like Figure 28-2, and we have not attempted to do so.)

Now we need to explain that both of the hidden columns are in fact optional, in general. As a result, TSQL2 supports at least four kinds of tables:

---

5. We are assuming here a version of "the usual suppliers table" that has just one column, called S# ("supplier number").

- A **bitemporal table** is one that includes exactly two hidden columns, one containing "valid-time" timestamps and the other "transaction-time" timestamps.

- A **valid-time state table**[6] (or just *valid-time table* for short) is one that includes exactly one hidden column, which contains "valid-time" timestamps.

- A **transaction-time state table** (or just *transaction-time table* for short) is one that includes exactly one hidden column, which contains "transaction-time" timestamps.

- A **regular table** (note that we cannot say "just *table* for short," because *table* is a generic term that now has to encompass all of the new kinds of tables introduced by TSQL2 as well as regular tables *per se*) is a table that includes no hidden columns at all.

More terminology: A table with a valid-time hidden column is said to be *a table with valid-time support.* A table with a transaction-time hidden column is said to be *a table with transaction-time support.* A table with either valid-time support or transaction-time support is said to be *a table with temporal support.*

Finally—this is important!—note that in TSQL2 valid- and transaction-time columns are always **hidden by definition**. A user-visible column that happens to contain valid or transaction times is not regarded by TSQL2 as a valid- or transaction-time column as such, but rather as a column that contains what it calls *user-defined times.* From this point forward, therefore, we will assume that all valid-time columns and all transaction-time columns are hidden, barring explicit statements to the contrary (though we will often refer to such columns explicitly as "hidden columns," for clarity). See the annotation to reference [10] for further discussion.

The Central Idea

We now proceed to describe what we perceive to be the central idea of TSQL2. Now, as every student of temporal databases quickly becomes aware, queries involving intervals (temporal or otherwise) can be surprisingly tedious or difficult or both to express. And while it is true that the various operators discussed in reference [6]—Allen's operators, PACK and UNPACK, and (especially) the so-called "U_ operators"—can help in this regard, some degree of both tedium and difficulty still remains, even when those shorthands are used. Accordingly, it is a goal of TSQL2 to simplify matters still further. And it appears that such further simplification might be possible in a certain very special case; to be specific, it might be possible if and only if the query under consideration satisfies all four of the following conditions (labeled *C1-C4* for purposes of subsequent reference).

- **C1:** The output table—i.e., the final result—has at most one (hidden) valid-time column and at most one (hidden) transaction-time column.

- **C2:** The output table has at least one additional (regular) column, over and above any hidden valid- or transaction-time column.

---

6. The term *state* here corresponds to reference [6]'s use of the term **during**—i.e., it refers to the idea that something is true, or believed to be true, throughout some period (interval). It is contrasted with the term *event*, which corresponds to reference [6]'s use of the term **at**—i.e., it refers to the idea that something is true (or believed to be true) at a certain point in time.

C3: Every input or intermediate-result table satisfies these same properties—at most one hidden valid-time column, at most one hidden transaction-time column, and at least one additional regular column.

C4: Every hidden valid-time column in every input, output, or intermediate-result table involved at any point in the query is of exactly the same data type.[7]

Let us examine these conditions a little more carefully. Here again is the first one (now stated a little more simply):

C1: The result has at most one valid-time column and at most one transaction-time column.

This condition clearly derives from the fact that TSQL2 tables have at most one valid-time column and at most one transaction-time column (both hidden, of course). Here by way of example is a **Tutorial D** query that satisfies the condition (though of course the "valid- and transaction-time columns"—i.e., the stated- and logged-time attributes, in the terminology of reference [6]—are not hidden in **Tutorial D**):

```
WITH ( SP_DURING RENAME ( P# AS XP# ) ) AS T1 ,
     ( SP_DURING RENAME ( P# AS YP# ) ) AS T2 :
USING DURING ◄ T1 JOIN T2 ►
```

Note: Relvar SP_DURING represents the predicate "Supplier S# was able to supply part P# throughout interval DURING." Thus, the query returns a result with predicate "Supplier S# was able to supply both part XP# and part YP# throughout interval DURING." That result thus certainly does have at most one stated-time attribute and at most one logged-time attribute; in fact, it has exactly one stated-time attribute, called DURING (which shows when supplier S# was able to supply both part XP# and part YP#), and no logged-time attribute at all.

As a matter of fact, this same query satisfies Conditions *C3* and *C4* as well. Here again are those conditions (now slightly simplified):

C3: Every input or intermediate-result table has at most one valid-time column, at most one transaction-time column, and at least one additional column.

C4: Every valid-time column in every input, output, or intermediate-result table is of exactly the same data type.

Condition *C3* derives from two facts—first, the fact that, again, TSQL2 tables have at most one (hidden) valid-time column and at most one (hidden) transaction-time column; second, the fact that regular SQL tables must have at least one column. Condition *C4* derives, in part, from the fact that TSQL2 makes use of *statement modifiers* to express queries, as we will see, and those modifiers are "global," in the sense that they are meant to apply uniformly to every table involved in the query in question. (We say "meant to" here advisedly; whether they actually do so is another matter. We will return to this point later.)

---

7. In fact Condition *C4* applies to transaction-time columns as well, but transaction times in TSQL2 are always of a data type that is chosen by the DBMS.

To revert to the **Tutorial D** example:

- (Condition *C3*) The relations denoted by SP_DURING, T1, and T2 each have exactly one stated-time attribute (called DURING in every case), as does the final result relation. In the case of SP_DURING, for example, attribute DURING shows when supplier S# was able to supply part P#; in the case of the final result, it shows when supplier S# was able to supply both part XP# and part YP#. Furthermore, the relations denoted by SP_DURING, T1, and T2 each have at least one additional attribute and no logged-time attribute at all.

- (Condition *C4*) Attribute DURING is clearly of the same type in every case: namely, type INTERVAL_DATE.

Back now to Condition *C1*. Here by contrast is a **Tutorial D** query that does *not* satisfy that condition, *mutatis mutandis:*

```
WITH ( SP_DURING RENAME ( P# AS XP#,
                          DURING AS XDURING ) ) AS T1 ,
     ( SP_DURING RENAME ( P# AS YP#,
                          DURING AS YDURING ) ) AS T2 ,
     ( T1 JOIN T2 ) AS T3 :
T3 WHERE XDURING OVERLAPS YDURING
```

This query gives a result with predicate "Supplier S# was able to supply part XP# throughout interval XDURING and part YP# throughout interval YDURING, and intervals XDURING and YDURING overlap." However, it fails to satisfy Condition *C1*, because the relation denoted by T3 and the final result both have two distinct stated-time attributes (in both cases, XDURING shows when supplier S# was able to supply part XP# and YDURING shows when supplier S# was able to supply part YP#). *Note:* In fact, this query also fails to satisfy Condition *C3*. And if we were to add a final step, in which (say) interval YDURING is effectively replaced by an interval expressed in terms of hours instead of days, then it would fail to satisfy Condition *C4* also.

Now let us turn to Condition *C2:*

> *C2:* The result has at least one additional column, over and above any valid- or transaction-time column.

Condition *C2* clearly derives from the same facts as does Condition *C3*. And here is a **Tutorial D** query that fails to satisfy the condition, *mutatis mutandis:*

```
WITH ( SP_DURING { S#, DURING } ) AS T1 ,
     ( USING DURING ◀ S_DURING MINUS T1 ▶ ) AS T2 :
( T2 WHERE S# = S#('S1') ) { DURING }
```

This query gives intervals during which supplier S1 was unable to supply any parts at all. *Note:* Relvar S_DURING shows which suppliers were under contract when.

So much for the four conditions that characterize the "very special case" that, it is claimed, TSQL2 deals with very simply by means of its special "tables with temporal support" (together with certain other features, not yet discussed). Of course, we have not yet shown how queries are formulated in TSQL2 at all (we will come to that later). Nevertheless, some obvious questions suggest themselves right away:

- How often do we need to formulate queries that do not fit the profile described above? Quite frequently, we believe.

- Even if most queries do fit that profile, is the claimed simplification worth all of the accompanying complexity?—in particular, is it worth jettisoning the relational model for? We do not believe it is.

- And in any case, do the simplifications actually work? We believe not (see later).

Temporal Upward Compatibility

In the previous section, we discussed what we called "the central idea" behind the TSQL2 language. However, the design of the language was also strongly motivated by another important idea (related to that previous one) called **temporal upward compatibility**. That idea can be described in outline as follows:

- Suppose we have some nontemporal database *D*, together with a set of applications that run against the database.

- Suppose we now want *D* to evolve to include some temporal support.

- Then it would be nice if we could just "add" that temporal support in such a way that those existing applications can continue to run correctly and unchanged against that temporal version of *D*.

If we meet this goal, then we say we have achieved *temporal upward compatibility* (hereinafter abbreviated, occasionally, to just TUC).

By way of example, suppose the nontemporal database shown in Figure 28-3 is somehow converted into a fully temporal counterpart, such that all of the information in that database at the time of conversion is retained but is now timestamped in some manner that would allow all of the information shown in Figure 28-4 to be recorded. *Note:* We very deliberately show the fully temporal counterpart in Figure 28-4 in proper relational form, in order to simplify certain subsequent explanations that we need to make. In TSQL2, of course, the DURING attributes would be replaced by unnamed hidden columns, the resulting tables would be named just S and SP, not S_DURING and SP_DURING, and they would not in fact be proper relations at all.

S	S#		SP	S#	P#
	S1			S1	P1
	S2			S1	P2
	S3			S1	P3
	S4			S1	P4
	S5			S1	P5
				S1	P6
				S2	P1
				S2	P2
				S3	P2
				S4	P2
				S4	P4
				S4	P5

Figure 28-3. *A nontemporal database*

S_DURING

S#	DURING
S1	[d04:d10]
S2	[d02:d04]
S2	[d07:d10]
S3	[d03:d10]
S4	[d04:d10]
S5	[d02:d10]

SP_DURING

S#	P#	DURING
S1	P1	[d04:d10]
S1	P2	[d05:d10]
S1	P3	[d09:d10]
S1	P4	[d05:d10]
S1	P5	[d04:d10]
S1	P6	[d06:d10]
S2	P1	[d02:d04]
S2	P1	[d08:d10]
S2	P2	[d03:d03]
S2	P2	[d09:d10]
S3	P2	[d08:d10]
S4	P2	[d06:d09]
S4	P4	[d04:d08]
S4	P5	[d05:d10]

Figure 28-4. *A temporal counterpart of Figure 28-3*

Then the conversion to temporal form, however it is carried out, is said to *achieve temporal upward compatibility* if and only if every operation that applied to the database before the conversion:

a. Still applies after the conversion, and

b. Has the same effect as before (apart, possibly, from effects that might become noticeable only by subsequent use of new operators that become available as a result of the conversion).

In order to illustrate this notion, suppose the temporal conversion has indeed been carried out, somehow; suppose further that the converted form of relvar SP is then updated in such a way that it now represents, somehow, exactly the information depicted in Figure 28-4; and consider the effect of evaluating the following simple **Tutorial D** expression:

```
SP
```

Clearly, there are just two possibilities: Either the result is exactly as shown as the value of relvar SP in Figure 28-3—not relvar SP_DURING in Figure 28-4!—or temporal upward compatibility has not been achieved.

By way of a second example, suppose we perform the following DELETE on the temporal version of relvar SP (which we again assume represents the information shown as the value of relvar SP_DURING in Figure 28-4):

```
DELETE SP WHERE S# = S#('S3') AND P# - P#('P2') ;
```

After this DELETE, if TUC is to be achieved, then the result of evaluating the expression

```
SP { S# }
```

on day 10 must not include supplier S3, because (as Figure 28-3 shows) part P2 was the only part supplier S3 was currently—i.e., on day 10—able to supply before the DELETE. By contrast, suppose we have some way, after the temporal conversion, of expressing the query "Who was able to supply some part on day 9?" Then the result of that query on day 10 *must* include supplier S3. (In other words, the effect of the DELETE might be regarded, loosely, as replacing the value [*d08:d10*] of "attribute" DURING in the "tuple" for supplier S3 and part P2 by the value [*d08:d09*]. Remember, however, that in TSQL2 we cannot really explain the effect of the DELETE in this way, because in TSQL2 "relvar" SP does not really include a DURING "attribute," and "tuples" in that "relvar" thus do not really include a DURING component.)

More on terminology: The previous paragraph made use of the term "currently." Unfortunately, we now have to say that we do not find the meaning of that term very clear (in a TSQL2 context, that is), for reasons we now explain:

- Observe first of all that there seems to be a tacit assumption pervading TSQL2 to the effect that a temporal database will contain "historical relvars only" (to use the terminology of reference [6])—there is no suggestion that horizontal decomposition should be performed (yielding separate current and historical relvars), as in our own preferred approach. (Our examples in this chapter are in line with this assumption; in particular, note the appearance of the *d99* "end-of-time markers" in the hidden valid-time column in Figure 28-1.) Thus, whatever *current* information the TSQL2 database contains will in fact be bundled in with those "historical relvars."

- Following on from the previous point: There is no suggestion that vertical decomposition should be performed, either. As a consequence, TSQL2 tables will typically not be in sixth normal form, 6NF [6]. Indeed, the recommended TSQL2 approach of simply "adding temporal support" to an existing nontemporal table—see later in this chapter for further discussion—virtually guarantees that most TSQL2 tables will not be in 6NF. Of course, it is a large part of the point of TUC that it should be possible just to "add temporal support" to an existing table, but then the consequences of having to deal with non6NF tables must be faced up to. The TSQL2 literature has little or nothing to say on this issue.

- Now, the TSQL2 literature frequently refers to the conceptual representation of a temporal database as a *time series*—in other words, as a chronologically ordered sequence of entries, in which each entry is the value or "state" of the database at a particular point in time. However, the last or most recent entry in that time series is then typically referred to as *the current state*—a fact that, it might be argued, tends to suggest that beliefs about the future, such as the belief that a certain supplier's contract will terminate on some specific future date, cannot be expressed using the "temporal support" of "tables with temporal support" (?).

- More to the point: While the time-series notion might be conceptually agreeable (since it is clear that one possible representation of that time series is one involving intervals), surely the TSQL2 specification should state exactly which of those intervals are considered to contain the current time. But it does not.

- Indeed, the actual time referred to by the phrase "the current time" varies over time (of course!). So, if S is the set of all intervals that are considered to contain the current time, does S itself vary over time? If so, then many serious questions arise (some of which are discussed in reference [6]).

In connection with the foregoing, it is possibly relevant to note that reference [13] proposed the following definition for inclusion in the SQL standard: "The current valid-time state of a table with valid-time support is the valid-time state of that table at valid-time CURRENT_TIMESTAMP" (of course, the value of CURRENT_TIMESTAMP—a niladic built-in function in the SQL standard [5]—certainly does vary with time). By contrast, certain examples in reference [15] seem to assume that any interval i such that END(i) = "the end of time" is one that contains the current time, regardless of the value of BEGIN(i).

Back to temporal upward compatibility. The TUC goal is TSQL2's justification for its special kinds of tables, with their hidden columns. For that goal would clearly not be achieved if (e.g.) converting the original nontemporal relvar SP to a temporal counterpart required the addition of an explicit new column—e.g., via an SQL ALTER TABLE statement, as here:

```
ALTER TABLE SP ADD COLUMN DURING ... ;
```

(Throughout this chapter we follow "direct SQL" [5,8] in using semicolons as SQL statement terminators.)

Why would the TUC goal not be achieved? Because, of course, after execution of the foregoing ALTER TABLE statement, the result of the SQL expression

```
SELECT * FROM SP
```

would include column DURING as well as the S# and P# columns it would have included before the temporal conversion, thereby violating TUC. It follows that the conversion process cannot simply involve the addition of explicit new columns (as indeed we will see in more detail later).

One last point: We have deliberately been somewhat vague as to the nature of the operations for which the TUC concept applies (or is even possible). The fact is, it is not at all clear whether it applies to—for example—all possible data definition operations, or dynamic SQL operations, etc. Here is what reference [15] has to say on the matter:

> **Temporal upward compatibility:** An [SQL:1992] ... query, modification, view, assertion, [or] constraint ... will have the same effect on an associated snapshot database as on the temporal counterpart of the database.

(The expression "snapshot database" as used here simply means a regular nontemporal database.)

Current, Sequenced, and Nonsequenced Operations

Suppose now that the process of converting the database to temporal form, however it has to be done in order to achieve temporal upward compatibility, has in fact been done. Then TSQL2 supports three kinds of operations against such a database, which it calls *current, sequenced,* and *nonsequenced* operations, respectively. Briefly, if we regard the database as a time series once again, then we can characterize the three kinds of operations (loosely) as follows:

- **Current** operations apply just to the most recent entry in that time series. (The term *current* derives from the fact that such operations are intended to apply to current data.)

- **Sequenced** operations apply to all of the entries in that time series.[8] (The term *sequenced* derives from the fact that such operations are intended to apply to the entire "temporal sequence," or in other words "at every point in time.")

- **Nonsequenced** operations apply to some specified subset of the entries in that time series. (It is not clear why such operations are said to be *nonsequenced*. It might or might not help to point out that an operation that is not sequenced is not necessarily nonsequenced; likewise, one that is not nonsequenced is not necessarily sequenced. What is more, some operations are both sequenced and nonsequenced—though it is not possible to have an operation that is both current and sequenced or both current and nonsequenced.)

By way of example, consider the valid-time table shown in Figure 28-5. Recall our assumption that today is day 10. Then—*very* loosely speaking—current operations are performed in terms of just those rows of that table whose hidden valid-time component includes day 10; sequenced operations are performed in terms of all of the rows; and nonsequenced operations

---

8. A slight oversimplification; actually, it is possible to restrict sequenced operations (like nonsequenced operations) to apply to some specified subset of the entries in that time sequence.

are performed in terms of just those rows whose hidden valid-time component includes some day or days specified explicitly when the operator in question is invoked.

S	S#	
	S1	$[d01:d01]$
	S1	$[d05:d06]$
	S2	$[d02:d04]$
	S2	$[d06:d99]$
	S3	$[d05:d99]$
	S4	$[d03:d99]$
	S6	$[d02:d03]$
	S6	$[d06:d09]$

Figure 28-5. *A TSQL2 valid-time table*

Current Operations

Current operations are, of course, precisely those operations that were available before the conversion to temporal form; temporal upward compatibility requires those operations still to be available and to have exactly the same effect as they did before the conversion. A *current query* involves the execution of some current operation of a retrieval nature; a *current modification* involves the execution of some current operation of an updating nature. Of course, current modifications must now have some additional effects "behind the scenes" (as it were), over and above those effects that are directly visible to the user of the current modification in question. For example, consider the following DELETE example again:

```
DELETE FROM SP WHERE S# = S#('S3') AND P# = P#('P2') ;
```

(We have added the keyword FROM in order to make the DELETE into a valid SQL statement. Also, we assume throughout this chapter that expressions of the form S#('S*x*') and P#('P*y*') are valid SQL literals, of types S# and P#, respectively.)

If table SP is a valid-time table, with current value the TSQL2 analog of the SP_DURING value shown in Figure 28-4, then the logical effect of the foregoing DELETE must be to do both of the following:

a. To delete the row for supplier S3 and part P2, as requested (since that row's valid-time component does include day 10, "the current date")

b. To insert a row into "the history portion" of the table for supplier S3 and part P2 with a valid time of [*d08:d09*]

In practice, of course, the deletion and subsequent insertion could probably be combined into a single row replacement.

Sequenced Operations

We turn now to sequenced and nonsequenced operations—sequenced in this subsection and nonsequenced in the next. After the conversion to temporal form has been performed and updates have been applied to the temporal version, the database will include historical as well as current data. Thus, the question arises as to how that historical data can be accessed. Clearly, the answer to this question is going to involve some new operations that were not available before the conversion, and those new operations are, precisely, the sequenced and nonsequenced operations under discussion. *Note:* As usual, we take the term *access* to include both query and modification operations. For reasons of brevity and simplicity, however, we will have little to say in this chapter regarding modifications, either sequenced or nonsequenced.

TSQL2 uses "statement modifiers" to specify both sequenced and nonsequenced operations (the term is a misnomer, actually, since it is not always statements *per se* that such modifiers modify). Those modifiers take the form of prefixes that can be attached to certain statements and certain (table-valued) expressions. We can summarize the available prefixes, and the rules regarding the operand table(s) and the result table, if any, as follows:

Prefix	Operand(s)	Result
none	*any*	*nhc*
VALIDTIME	VT *or* BT	VT
TRANSACTIONTIME	TT *or* BT	TT
VALIDTIME AND TRANSACTIONTIME	BT	BT
NONSEQUENCED VALIDTIME	VT *or* BT	*nhc*
NONSEQUENCED TRANSACTIONTIME	TT *or* BT	*nhc*
VALIDTIME AND NONSEQUENCED TRANSACTIONTIME	BT	VT
NONSEQUENCED VALIDTIME AND TRANSACTIONTIME	BT	TT
NONSEQUENCED VALIDTIME AND NONSEQUENCED TRANSACTIONTIME	BT	*nhc*

Explanation: The abbreviations VT, TT, and BT stand for a valid-time table, a transaction-time table, and a bitemporal table, respectively; the abbreviation *nhc* stands for "no hidden columns" (in other words, the table in question is just a regular SQL table). For example, we can see that if the prefix NONSEQUENCED VALIDTIME is used, then every operand table must be either a valid-time table or a bitemporal table, and the result (if the statement or expression to which the prefix applies in fact returns a result) is a regular table. Note that the result has a hidden valid-time column only if a prefix specifying VALIDTIME (without NONSEQUENCED) is specified, and a hidden transaction-time column only if a prefix specifying TRANSACTIONTIME (without NONSEQUENCED) is specified.

At this point, a couple of minor oddities arise:

- First, the prefix (e.g.) NONSEQUENCED VALIDTIME is regarded in the TSQL2 literature as specifying a *valid-time nonsequenced* operation, not a nonsequenced valid-time operation. Although we find this inversion of the modifiers a trifle illogical, we will conform to it in what follows.

- Second, observe that nonsequenced operations involve the explicit keyword NONSEQUENCED, but sequenced operations do not involve any explicit SEQUENCED counterpart; for example, a *sequenced valid-time* operation is specified by just the prefix VALIDTIME, unadorned.

For simplicity, let us concentrate on sequenced valid-time operations specifically, until further notice. Let X be an expression or statement that is syntactically valid on the nontemporal version of the database. Let every table mentioned in X map to a counterpart with valid-time support in the temporal version of the database. Then VALIDTIME X is an expression or statement that

a. Is syntactically valid on the temporal version of the database, and

b. Is conceptually evaluated against that temporal database *at every point in time.*

Each such conceptual evaluation is performed on a nontemporal database that is derived from the temporal one by considering just those rows whose associated valid times include the applicable point in time. The results of those conceptual evaluations are then conceptually combined by a process analogous to packing to yield the overall result. *Note:* Perhaps we should say rather that the combination process is *somewhat* analogous to packing; as we will see later, that overall result is in fact not precisely defined. But let us ignore this point for now.

By way of illustration, consider first the *current* DELETE example from the subsection above entitled "Current Operations":

```
DELETE FROM SP WHERE S# = S#('S3') AND P# = P#('P2') ;
```

As you will recall, the effect of this DELETE (ignoring the side-effect of "inserting into the historical record") is to delete just the fact that supplier S3 is *currently* able to supply part P2. However, if we prefix the DELETE statement with the modifier VALIDTIME, as here—

```
VALIDTIME
DELETE FROM SP WHERE S# = S#('S3') AND P# = P#('P2') ;
```

—then the effect is now to delete *all* rows showing supplier S3 as able to supply part P2 from the valid-time table SP, no matter what the associated valid times might be. (In terms of the data values in Figure 28-4, the effect is to delete the fact that supplier S3 was able to supply part P2 throughout the interval from day 8 to day 10—but it might delete more than that, if there were any other rows for supplier S3 and part P2.)

Analogously, the TSQL2 expression

```
VALIDTIME
SELECT * FROM SP
```

returns the "real" value of the valid-time table SP, hidden valid-time column and all. Note carefully, however, that that hidden column remains hidden in the result; in fact, a valid-time sequenced query always returns a valid-time table (i.e., a table with a hidden valid-time column and *no* hidden transaction-time column). See the final subsection in this section for a discussion of how such hidden columns can be accessed in that result (or in any other table with temporal support, of course).

Incidentally, observe that the expression SELECT * FROM SP is indeed an expression and not a statement. The foregoing example thus illustrates our earlier claim that "statement modifier" is really a misnomer.

Here now are a couple more examples of valid-time sequenced queries:

```
VALIDTIME                          VALIDTIME
SELECT DISTINCT S# FROM SP         SELECT DISTINCT S# FROM S
                                   EXCEPT
                                   SELECT DISTINCT S# FROM SP
```

(In the first example, we assume table S has valid-time support; in the second, we assume tables S and SP both have valid-time support.) These expressions are TSQL2 formulations for two sample queries—or, rather, TSQL2 counterparts to those queries—that we used as a basis for introducing the temporal database problem in reference [6]:

- Get S#-DURING pairs for suppliers who have been able to supply at least one part during at least one interval of time, where DURING designates a maximal interval during which supplier S# was in fact able to supply at least one part.

- Get S#-DURING pairs for suppliers who have been unable to supply any parts at all during at least one interval of time, where DURING designates a maximal interval during which supplier S# was in fact unable to supply any part at all.

The first expression results in a table showing supplier numbers for suppliers who have ever been able to supply anything, paired in the hidden valid-time column with the maximal intervals during which they have been able to do so. The second expression is analogous. Note carefully, however, that those "maximal intervals" are indeed still represented by hidden columns; if we want to access those hidden columns—as surely we will?—we will have to make use of the operators described in the final subsection of this section (see below). Note too that we are being slightly charitable to TSQL2 here! In fact, the proposals of reference [13] did not explicitly require the result of a query like the ones illustrated above to satisfy any such "maximality" condition. What is more, they did not impose any other requirement in place of such a condition, either; as a consequence, the actual value of an expression such as VALIDTIME SELECT DISTINCT S# FROM SP is not precisely specified (it is not even clear whether the inclusion of the keyword DISTINCT has any effect).

Suppose now that S and SP are tables with *transaction*-time support. Then the prefix TRANSACTIONTIME can be used in place of VALIDTIME in examples like those shown above; the operations in question then become *transaction-time sequenced* operations (transaction-time sequenced *queries* specifically, in all of those examples except the very first). A transaction-time sequenced query returns a transaction-time table (i.e., a table with a hidden transaction-time column and *no* hidden valid-time column).

Finally, suppose S and SP are bitemporal tables. Then the prefix VALIDTIME AND TRANSACTIONTIME can be used, in which case the operations in question become (prosaically enough) *valid-time sequenced and transaction-time sequenced* operations. A valid-time sequenced and transaction-time sequenced query returns a bitemporal table. *Note:* If the result of such a query is indeed automatically packed, it is pertinent to ask whether they are packed on valid time first and then transaction time or the other way around (because the results will be different, in general). The literature does not appear to answer this question.

Nonsequenced Operations

Nonsequenced operations are specified by means of the prefixes NONSEQUENCED VALIDTIME and NONSEQUENCED TRANSACTIONTIME. Furthermore, if the operand tables are bitemporal, then all possible combinations—e.g., (sequenced) VALIDTIME AND NONSEQUENCED TRANSACTIONTIME—are available. Thus, operations on bitemporal tables can be simultaneously sequenced with respect to valid time and nonsequenced with respect to transaction time, or the other way around, or sequenced with respect to both, or nonsequenced with respect to both.

Here is an example of a nonsequenced query:

```
NONSEQUENCED VALIDTIME
SELECT DISTINCT P# FROM SP
```

Table SP must have valid-time support in order for this query to be legal. The result is a table with no hidden valid-time column at all, representing part numbers for all parts we currently believe ever to have been available from any supplier.

Despite the somewhat arcane prefixes, nonsequenced operations are comparatively easy to understand, for here TSQL2 is effectively reverting to regular SQL semantics. Well, almost—there is a glitch![9] The glitch is that "regular semantics" implies that we should be able to reference the hidden columns in the regular way; but such references are impossible, precisely because the columns are hidden. We therefore need some special mechanism in order to access the hidden columns. In TSQL2, that mechanism is provided by the operators VALIDTIME(T) and TRANSACTIONTIME(T)—see the subsection immediately following. *Note:* Orthogonality dictates that these operators be available in connection with current and sequenced operations too, despite the fact that we have introduced them in the context of a discussion of nonsequenced operations specifically. However, the effect of including such operators in such queries is unclear to the present writers.

Accessing the Hidden Columns

Consider the following example (note in particular the VALIDTIME operator invocations):

```
NONSEQUENCED VALIDTIME
SELECT T1.S# AS X#, T2.S# AS Y#,
       BEGIN ( VALIDTIME ( T2 ) ) AS SWITCH_DATE
FROM   S AS T1, S AS T2
WHERE  END ( VALIDTIME ( T1 ) ) = BEGIN ( VALIDTIME ( T2 ) )
```

9. At least, there is according to reference [15], but not (or possibly not) according to reference [13]. See Example 14, later.

This expression returns a table *without* any hidden valid-time column in which each row gives a pair of supplier numbers X# and Y# and a date such that, on that date, supplier X#'s contract terminated and supplier Y#'s contract began (according to our current belief). The expression is the TSQL2 analog of the following **Tutorial D** query (expressed in terms of the database of Figure 28-4):

```
WITH ( ( ( S RENAME ( S# AS X#, DURING AS XD ) )
            JOIN
          ( S RENAME ( S# AS Y#, DURING AS YD ) ) )
       WHERE END ( XD ) = BEGIN ( YD ) ) AS T1 ,
     ( EXTEND T1 ADD ( BEGIN ( YD ) AS SWITCH_DATE ) ) AS T2 :
T2 { X#, Y#, SWITCH_DATE }
```

Of course, the operator invocation VALIDTIME(*T*) is valid in TSQL2 only if the table denoted by *T* has valid-time support; likewise, the operator invocation TRANSACTIONTIME(*T*) is valid only if the table denoted by *T* has transaction-time support. Observe, incidentally, how these operators implicitly rely on the fact that any given TSQL2 table has at most one hidden valid-time column and at most one hidden transaction-time column.

Data Definition Statements

We now consider the effects of the ideas discussed in the foregoing sections on the SQL CREATE TABLE and ALTER TABLE statements.

Valid-Time Tables

There are two ways to create a valid-time base table in TSQL2. The underlying principle in both cases is just to extend a nontemporal counterpart of the table in question by "adding valid-time support," both to that counterpart as such and to the constraints—primary and foreign key constraints in particular—that apply to that counterpart. "Adding valid-time support" can be done either directly in the original CREATE TABLE statement or subsequently by means of appropriate ALTER TABLE statements.

By way of example, consider the following CREATE TABLE statements, which will suffice to create a TSQL2 counterpart of the database of Figure 28-3 (note the text in boldface):

```
CREATE TABLE S ( S# S#,
       VALIDTIME PRIMARY KEY ( S# ) )
       AS VALIDTIME PERIOD ( DATE ) ;

CREATE TABLE SP ( S# S#, P# P#,
       VALIDTIME PRIMARY KEY ( S#, P# ),
       VALIDTIME FOREIGN KEY ( S# ) REFERENCES S )
       AS VALIDTIME PERIOD ( DATE ) ;
```

Explanation:

- The specification AS VALIDTIME ... (in line 3 of the CREATE TABLE for suppliers and line 4 of the CREATE TABLE for shipments) indicates that tables S and SP are tables with valid-time support; i.e., they have hidden valid-time columns. They are not packed on those columns (perhaps because such packing could lead to a violation of temporal upward compatibility, if the AS VALIDTIME ... specification appeared in an ALTER TABLE—rather than CREATE TABLE, as here—and the table in question currently contained any duplicate rows).

- The specification PERIOD (DATE) following AS VALIDTIME gives the data type for the hidden valid-time columns; PERIOD is a "type constructor" (it is the TSQL2 counterpart of our INTERVAL type generator), and DATE is the corresponding point type.[10] *Note:* TSQL2 could not use the keyword INTERVAL here, because the SQL standard already uses that keyword for something else. More to the point, observe that—of course—*any* TSQL2 table, regardless of whether or not it has any kind of "temporal support," can have any number of regular columns of some period type. As noted earlier, TSQL2 regards such columns as containing what it calls *user-defined time* [10].

- The VALIDTIME prefixes on the primary key and foreign key specifications specify that the corresponding constraints are *valid-time sequenced constraints.* Moreover:

  - A VALIDTIME PRIMARY KEY constraint is analogous, somewhat, to a WHEN / THEN constraint as defined in reference [6] (except that we do not believe in the idea of being forced to single out some specific candidate key and make it "primary," and as a matter of fact neither does SQL). It is not clear whether TSQL2 allows a VALIDTIME PRIMARY KEY constraint to coexist with a regular PRIMARY KEY constraint, though it is clear that the existence of a VALIDTIME one makes a regular one more or less redundant.

  - A VALIDTIME FOREIGN KEY constraint is analogous, again somewhat, to a "foreign U_key" constraint as defined in reference [6]. Note that the referenced table—S, in our example—must have valid-time support in order for the VALIDTIME FOREIGN KEY constraint to be valid.

Absence of the VALIDTIME prefix on a primary or foreign key specification, in the presence of AS VALIDTIME, means the corresponding constraint is a *current* one; that is, it applies only to those rows whose valid-time component is considered to contain the current time (speaking rather loosely).

Suppose now, in contrast to the foregoing, that the *non*temporal tables S and SP have already been defined, thus:

---

10. Note that TSQL2 follows its keywnrd PERIOD with the name of the point type in parentheses, whereas we follow our keyword INTERVAL with the name of the point type attached by means of an underscore instead. A related observation is that the TSQL2 analog of what we would express as, e.g., INTERVAL_DATE ([*di:dj*]) is just PERIOD ([*di:dj*]); in other words, TSQL2 assumes the type of the interval— or period, rather—can be inferred from the type of the begin and end points *di* and *dj*. We do not agree with this latter position, for reasons explained in detail in reference [6].

```
CREATE TABLE S ( S# S#,
     PRIMARY KEY ( S# ) ) ;

CREATE TABLE SP ( S# S#, P# P#,
     PRIMARY KEY ( S#, P# ),
     FOREIGN KEY ( S# ) REFERENCES S ) ;
```

Suppose further that we now wish to "add valid-time support" to these tables (remember the goal of temporal upward compatibility). Then the following more or less self-explanatory ALTER TABLE statements will suffice (again, note the text in boldface):

```
ALTER TABLE S ADD VALIDTIME PERIOD ( DATE ) ;
ALTER TABLE S ADD VALIDTIME PRIMARY KEY ( S# ) ;

ALTER TABLE SP ADD VALIDTIME PERIOD ( DATE ) ;
ALTER TABLE SP ADD VALIDTIME PRIMARY KEY ( S#, P# ) ;
ALTER TABLE SP ADD VALIDTIME FOREIGN KEY ( S#) REFERENCES S ;
```

In rows that already exist when the valid-time support is added, the new (hidden) column is set to contain a period of the form $[b:e]$, where b is the time of execution of the ALTER TABLE and e is "the end of time."[11] Whether it is necessary to drop the primary and foreign keys that were defined for the tables before the valid-time support was added is unclear.

Transaction-Time Tables

Creation of transaction-time base tables is similar but not completely analogous to the creation of valid-time base tables:

```
CREATE TABLE S ( S# S#,
     TRANSACTIONTIME PRIMARY KEY ( S# ) )
     AS TRANSACTIONTIME ;

CREATE TABLE SP ( S# S#, P# P#,
     TRANSACTIONTIME PRIMARY KEY ( S#, P# ),
     TRANSACTIONTIME FOREIGN KEY ( S# ) REFERENCES S )
     AS TRANSACTIONTIME ;
```

The AS TRANSACTIONTIME specifications are more or less self-explanatory; observe, however, that no data type is specified, because (as mentioned in a footnote earlier) transaction times in TSQL2 are always of a data type that is chosen by the DBMS. The TRANSACTIONTIME prefixes on the primary and foreign key specifications are analogous to their VALIDTIME counterparts—except that there seems to be no point in having them (although they *are* permitted), because the corresponding *current* constraints must surely imply that these *transaction-time sequenced constraints* are always satisfied. (By definition, transaction times cannot be updated; it therefore follows that constraints that apply to the current state of affairs

---

11. Actually, reference [13] says e is *the immediate predecessor* of "the end of time," but this is surely just a slip, probably arising from confusion over notation (in effect, confusing $[b:e]$ with $[b:e]$—see reference [6]). Reference [15] says it is "the end of time."

must apply equally to the historical record, since everything in that historical record must once have been current.) Also, if the prefix is omitted on a foreign key specification, then the referenced table can be of any kind (not necessarily one with temporal support); in every case, the constraint is then treated as a current constraint rather than a transaction-time sequenced one.

Adding transaction-time support to existing tables via ALTER TABLE is analogous to its valid-time counterpart. In particular, in rows that already exist when the transaction-time support is added, the new (hidden) column is apparently set to the same initial value as it is in the case of adding valid time—i.e., it is set to a period of the form $[b:e]$, where b is the time of execution of the ALTER TABLE and e is "the end of time"—even though neither the b value nor the e value seems to make any sense (the b value is clearly incorrect, and the e value means we have transaction times that refer to the future). We omit further discussion here.

Bitemporal Tables

Finally, here are the CREATE TABLE statements needed to create bitemporal versions of tables S and SP:

```
CREATE TABLE S ( S# S#,
       VALIDTIME AND TRANSACTIONTIME PRIMARY KEY ( S# ) )
       AS VALIDTIME PERIOD ( DATE ) AND TRANSACTIONTIME ;

CREATE TABLE SP ( S# S#, P# P#,
       VALIDTIME AND TRANSACTIONTIME PRIMARY KEY ( S#, P# ),
       VALIDTIME AND TRANSACTIONTIME FOREIGN KEY ( S# )
                                REFERENCES S )
       AS VALIDTIME PERIOD ( DATE ) AND TRANSACTIONTIME ;
```

These statements should once again be self-explanatory.

Adding bitemporal support to existing tables via ALTER TABLE is analogous to its valid-time and transaction-time counterparts. We omit further discussion here.

Statement Modifiers Are Flawed

This brings us to the end of our brief overview of TSQL2 basics. In this section and the next three, we give our reasons for rejecting the TSQL2 approach, and indeed for seriously questioning its very motivation. *Note:* Those reasons are very similar to those that have previously been aired in the international standards and academic research communities, precisely because two of the authors of reference [6] (*viz.,* Darwen and Lorentzos, respectively) have been at the forefront in articulating such objections in those communities.

The goal of the present section is to demonstrate a number of logical problems with the basic idea of statement modifiers. In order to meet that goal, we present a series of simple examples that illustrate those problems. The examples are numbered for purposes of subsequent reference. Here then is the first example (a current query against versions of tables S and SP with—let us assume—valid-time support):[12]

---

12. All of the examples in this section are based on a certain simple combination of a join, a restriction, and a projection. Consideration of examples involving something a little more complicated is left as an exercise.

```
1. SELECT DISTINCT S.S#, SP.P#
   FROM   S, SP
   WHERE  S.S# = SP.S#
   AND    SP.P# = P#('P1')
```

Note: It might be objected that this first example is not a very sensible one, inasmuch as (a) the result of the query will have part number P1 in every row and (b) the DISTINCT cannot possibly have any effect. However, the example is adequate as a basis for illustrating the points we wish to make, and we will stay with it.

It is easy to see that the following reformulation (Example 2) is guaranteed under all circumstances to yield the same result as Example 1:

```
2. SELECT DISTINCT S.S#, T1.P#
   FROM   S, ( SELECT * FROM SP WHERE SP.P# = P#('P1') ) AS T1
   WHERE  S.S# = T1.S#
```

Now consider the TSQL2 valid-time counterpart of Example 1:

```
3. VALIDTIME
   SELECT DISTINCT S.S#, SP.P#
   FROM   S, SP
   WHERE  S.S# = SP.S#
   AND    SP.P# = P#('P1')
```

The obvious question arises as to whether simply adding the VALIDTIME prefix to Example 2 gives an equivalent reformulation, as it did before:

```
4. VALIDTIME
   SELECT DISTINCT S.S#, T1.P#
   FROM   S, ( SELECT * FROM SP WHERE SP.P# = P#('P1') ) AS T1
   WHERE  S.S# = T1.S#
```

The answer to this question is *no!*—in fact, the putative reformulation is syntactically invalid. The reason is that, in the presence of the VALIDTIME modifier, each and every "table reference" in the FROM clause is required to denote a table with valid-time support, and in the example the second such reference in the outer FROM clause does not do so; as you can see, in fact, that second reference involves an expression of the form SELECT * FROM SP WHERE SP.P# = P#('P1'), and that expression lacks the statement modifier that is needed to make it yield a table with valid-time support. In order to obtain the correct desired reformulation, therefore, we must insert the VALIDTIME prefix in more than one place, as here:

```
5. VALIDTIME
   SELECT DISTINCT S.S#, T1.P#
   FROM   S, ( VALIDTIME
                  SELECT * FROM SP WHERE SP.P# = P#('P1') ) AS T1
   WHERE  S.S# = T1.S#
```

Note, by the way, that the foregoing quirk arises (at least in part) because of an existing quirk in SQL: The first table reference in the outer FROM clause (i.e., S), does not require the prefix, simply because a simple table name like S does not constitute a valid query in SQL! If we were to replace it by, for example, the expression SELECT * FROM S (which is a valid query, of course), then we would have to include the prefix as well, as here:

```
6. VALIDTIME
   SELECT DISTINCT T2.S#, T1.P#
   FROM ( VALIDTIME
          SELECT * FROM S ) AS T2,
        ( VALIDTIME
          SELECT * FROM SP WHERE SP.P# = P#('P1') ) AS T1
   WHERE  T2.S# = T1.S#
```

What if the table denoted by a table reference in a FROM clause happens to be a view? Suppose, for example, that view VS is defined as follows:

```
7. CREATE VIEW VS AS
           SELECT * FROM S ;
```

In principle—and in SQL too, normally—a reference to a given view and the expression that defines that view are logically interchangeable. The question therefore arises as to whether we can replace the expression SELECT * FROM S in the outer FROM clause in Example 6 by a reference to VS, as follows:

```
8. VALIDTIME
   SELECT DISTINCT T2.S#, T1.P#
   FROM ( VALIDTIME VS ) AS T2,
        ( VALIDTIME
          SELECT * FROM SP WHERE SP.P# = P#('P1') ) AS T1
   WHERE  T2.S# = T1.S#
```

Again the answer is *no,* and again the replacement gives rise to a syntax error, because VS is not a table with valid-time support (and simply inserting the VALIDTIME prefix does not make it one, either). Instead, we have to place that prefix *inside the view definition:*

```
9. CREATE VIEW VS AS
           VALIDTIME
           SELECT * FROM S ;
```

VS is now a table with valid-time support and a reference to it can appear wherever a reference to S can appear.

A similar observation applies when VS is defined "inline," using a WITH clause:

```
10. WITH VS AS ( SELECT * FROM S )
    VALIDTIME
    SELECT DISTINCT T2.S#, T1.P#
    FROM ( VALIDTIME
           SELECT * FROM SP WHERE SP.P# = P#('P1') ) AS T1,
         VS AS T2
    WHERE  T2.S# = T1.S#
```

This expression is again invalid. However, it can be rescued by placing the VALIDTIME prefix inside the WITH clause:

```
11. WITH VS AS ( VALIDTIME SELECT * FROM S )
    VALIDTIME
    SELECT DISTINCT T2.S#, T1.P#
    FROM ( VALIDTIME
            SELECT * FROM SP WHERE SP.P# = P#('P1') ) AS T1,
            VS AS T2
    WHERE  T2.S# = T1.S#
```

In fact, according to reference [13], in a query that includes a WITH clause, the VALIDTIME prefix cannot be placed at the beginning of the entire expression. Rather, it can only be placed as shown above, between the WITH clause and the main body of the expression.

It follows from all of the foregoing that the TSQL2 claim to the effect that a temporal counterpart of a nontemporal query can be easily obtained by just adding a prefix is not entirely valid and needs to be made more precise. For example, consider the following nontemporal query:

```
12. WITH VS AS ( SELECT * FROM S )
    SELECT DISTINCT T2.S#, T1.P#
    FROM ( SELECT * FROM SP WHERE SP.P# = P#('P1') ) AS T1,
          VS AS T2
    WHERE  T2.S# = T1.S#
```

We cannot obtain a temporal counterpart of this query by just adding a VALIDTIME prefix to the beginning, nor, as we have already seen, can we do so by just adding it in the middle, between the WITH clause and the main body. Rather, we have to add it three times, as shown in Example 11.

Now, all of the examples we have shown so far have made use just of the VALIDTIME prefix and have dealt just with tables with valid-time support. As you would probably expect, however, the whole discussion is applicable in like manner to the TRANSACTIONTIME prefix and tables with transaction-time support. Here, for instance, is a bitemporal counterpart of Example 11 (and here we must assume that S and SP are bitemporal tables):

```
13. WITH VS AS ( VALIDTIME AND TRANSACTIONTIME
                SELECT * FROM S )
    VALIDTIME AND TRANSACTIONTIME
    SELECT DISTINCT T2.S#, T1.P#
    FROM ( VALIDTIME AND TRANSACTIONTIME
        SELECT * FROM SP WHERE SP.P# = P#('P1') ) AS T1,
        VS AS T2
    WHERE  T2.S# = T1.S#
```

However, the whole discussion appears not to be applicable in like manner in connection with prefixes that use the NONSEQUENCED modifier! For example, suppose we take Example 5 and replace both of the VALIDTIME prefixes by the prefix NONSEQUENCED VALIDTIME:

```
14. NONSEQUENCED VALIDTIME
    SELECT DISTINCT S.S#, T1.P#
    FROM   S, ( NONSEQUENCED VALIDTIME
                SELECT * FROM SP WHERE SP.P# = P#('P1') ) AS T1
    WHERE  S.S# = T1.S#
```

This expression is syntactically invalid, because the second table reference in the outer FROM clause denotes a table without temporal support. (In fact, it is not clear exactly what table it does denote; references [13] and [15] contradict each other on the issue. Details of just how they contradict each other are beyond the scope of this chapter, however.)

The net of all of the foregoing is as follows. First, the suppliers table S is (according to our original assumption) a table with valid-time support, from which it follows that in TSQL2 the expression S can appear as a table reference in a FROM clause in an SQL query that has the VALIDTIME prefix. However, the expression SELECT * FROM S yields a result that is not a table with valid-time support, and so that expression cannot appear as a table reference in a FROM clause in such a query. By contrast, the expression VALIDTIME SELECT * FROM S can so appear. But the expression VS, when defined to mean the same as the expression SELECT * FROM S, cannot so appear, and nor can the expression VALIDTIME VS—nor, for that matter, can the expression VALIDTIME SELECT * FROM VS. Taken together, these anomalies show that TSQL2 fails to meet normal expectations of a computer language with respect to construction of expressions from subexpressions and replacement of subexpressions by introduced names.

But there is still more to be said regarding introduced names. All such names we have considered so far have resulted from view definitions and WITH clauses. If we go on to consider introduced names that result from user-defined functions, we encounter even more serious problems, problems that make us conclude that the concept of statement modifiers as manifested in TSQL2 is *fundamentally flawed*. By way of example, consider first the following query (again we assume that tables S and SP have valid-time support):

```
15. VALIDTIME
      SELECT  S.S#
      FROM    S
      WHERE   S.S# NOT IN ( SELECT SP.S# FROM SP )
```

The overall result of this query will obviously depend on whether the VALIDTIME prefix applies to the whole expression, including the parenthesized subexpression following the IN operator, or whether it applies only to the portion of the query *not* included in those parentheses:

a. *(VALIDTIME applies to whole expression)* The result is a valid-time table in which the hidden valid-time column indicates, for each supplier number, a time interval throughout which the supplier in question was unable to supply any parts.

b. *(VALIDTIME applies only to outer portion)* The result is a valid-time table in which the hidden valid-time column indicates, for each supplier number, a time interval throughout which the supplier in question was not among those suppliers who are *currently* able to supply any parts.

It is clear from many examples in the TSQL2 literature that the first of these two interpretations is the one intended. Yet it is difficult to obtain a reading of the expression that is consistent with that interpretation, because the table denoted by the parenthesized subexpression seems, according to our understanding of unprefixed expressions in TSQL2, to give just supplier numbers of suppliers *currently* able to supply some part.[13] Clearly, we must revise that understanding

---

13. What is more, it is our further understanding that that table has no hidden valid-time column; as a consequence, it is not clear how the comparisons implied by the IN operator can be the ones that TSQL2 seems to want, either.

somehow, perhaps by replacing that "currently" by something like "at the relevant point in time."
(We are deferring here to the notion that a TSQL2 sequenced query is conceptually evaluated
at each point in time, with subsequent packing—or, rather, some unspecified variant of
packing—of the resulting conceptual sequence of results.)

Although the foregoing revised understanding is very vague, it can presumably be made
more precise, somehow, and so we have probably not dealt a mortal blow, yet, to the idea of
statement prefixing. But let us see where else this example might lead us. We now consider the
possibility of replacing the expression in the WHERE clause—S.S# NOT IN (SELECT SP.S#
FROM SP)—by an equivalent invocation of a user-defined function. The function in question
could be defined in SQL as follows:

```
16. CREATE FUNCTION UNABLE_TO_SUPPLY_ANYTHING ( S# S# )
           RETURNS BOOLEAN
           RETURN ( S# NOT IN ( SELECT SP.S# FROM SP ) ) ;
```

Given this function, the following expression—

```
17. SELECT S.S#
    FROM   S
    WHERE  UNABLE_TO_SUPPLY_ANYTHING ( S.S# )
```

—is clearly equivalent to this one:

```
18. SELECT S.S#
    FROM   S
    WHERE  S.S# NOT IN ( SELECT SP.S# FROM SP )
```

The natural question to ask now is whether the following expression—

```
19. VALIDTIME
    SELECT S.S#
    FROM   S
    WHERE  UNABLE_TO_SUPPLY_ANYTHING ( S.S# )
```

—is equivalent to this one:

```
20. VALIDTIME
    SELECT S.S#
    FROM   S
    WHERE  S.S# NOT IN ( SELECT SP.S# FROM SP )
```

The answer to this question is far from clear! Indeed, the following excerpt from the
concluding section of reference [1] is perhaps revealing in this connection:

> *Implementing functions ... is another interesting research topic. Specifically, function
> calls are affected by statement modifiers, so that the semantics of a function call will
> depend on whether it is used in a temporal upward-compatible, a sequenced, or a
> nonsequenced context.*

The authors of reference [1] appear to be claiming here that Examples 19 and 20 are equivalent. In that case, we have to ask why, if "function calls are affected by statement modifiers,"

the same is not true of references to view names and names introduced using WITH. But in any case the authors are also clearly admitting that "function calls" in the context of statement modifiers have not been fully researched. We venture to think that anybody attempting to undertake that research is likely to meet with insuperable problems. If the body of the function consists of some highly complex series of statements, including assignments, branches, and exception-handling operations, how is the function to be conceptually evaluated at each point in time other than by *actually* evaluating it at each point in time? *Note:* The matter is made even worse in SQL specifically by the fact that user-defined functions can be coded in programming languages other than SQL, using the same facilities (such as embedded SQL, SQL/CLI, or JDBC) as are available to client application programs.

One last point to close this section: It might be thought that the "U_ operators" of reference [6] suffer from the same problems as TSQL2's statement modifiers, since those operators also involve a prefix that affects the semantics of the expression following that prefix. However, we believe—of course!—that the same criticisms do not apply. The reason is that our prefixes are defined very carefully to affect *only the outermost operator* in the pertinent expression (and just what it is that constitutes that "pertinent expression" is well defined, too, both syntactically and semantically). If that operator is monadic, then it is precisely the single relation operand to that monadic operator that is initially unpacked; if the operator is dyadic, then it is precisely the two relation operands to that dyadic operator that are initially unpacked. In both cases, the regular relational operation is then performed on the unpacked operand(s), and the result is then packed again. In brief: Our USING prefixes can be thought of as *operator* modifiers, not *statement* (or, rather, expression) modifiers.

Consequences of Hidden Columns

If, as we believe, the concept of statement modifiers is irredeemably flawed, then perhaps nothing more needs to be said. As we have seen, however, TSQL2 also involves a radical departure from *The Information Principle.* Just to remind you, that principle states that all information in the database should be represented in one and only one way: namely, by means of relations. (SQL tables are not true relations, of course, but for the sake of the present discussion we can pretend they are; that is, we can overlook for present purposes such matters as duplicate rows, nulls, and left-to-right column ordering. What we want to do is consider the differences between *TSQL2* tables—rather than SQL tables in general—and true relations.)

Now, the uniformity of *structure* provided by adherence to *The Information Principle* carries with it uniformity of *mode of access* and uniformity of *description:* All data in a table is accessed by reference to its columns, using column names for that purpose; also, to study the structure of a table, we have only to examine the description (as recorded in the catalog) of each of its columns.

TSQL2's departure from this uniformity leads to several complications of the kind that the relational model was explicitly designed to avoid. For example, new syntax is needed (as we have seen) for expressing temporal queries and modifications; new syntax is also needed for referencing hidden columns; new features are needed in the catalog in order to describe tables with temporal support; and similar new features are needed in the "SQL descriptor areas" used by generalized applications that support *ad hoc* queries [5,8]. These are not trivial matters, as the discussions of earlier sections in this chapter should have been sufficient to demonstrate.

It is worth taking a moment to elaborate on the implications of hidden columns for generalized applications (the final complication in the list called out in the previous paragraph). Consider the tasks typically performed by such an application. A simple example is the task of saving the result of an arbitrary query Q. So long as Q is well formed, in the sense that every result column has a unique name, then all the application has to do is create an SQL table T, taking its definition from the column names and data types given in the SQL descriptor area for the query, and then execute the SQL statement INSERT INTO T Q. Now consider, by contrast, what the application will have to do if the query Q happens to take one of the forms illustrated by the examples in the previous section. The simple solution that worked so well before will clearly now be very far from adequate.

Lack of Generality

TSQL2's support for tables with temporal support and temporal intervals fails to include support for operations on intervals in general. Of course, it does support some of the operators normally defined for intervals in general—BEGIN, MEETS, OVERLAPS, UNION, and so on (though we have not discussed these operators in this chapter)—but even in the case of temporal intervals it fails to provide any counterpart of the useful shorthands we have described in reference [6] for operations on relations and relvars involving interval attributes. In particular, it has nothing equivalent to the PACK and UNPACK operators,[14] nor to any of the "U_ operators," nor to any of the proposed shorthands for constraints ("U_key" constraints and others) or for updating.

TSQL2 lacks generality in another sense, too. If it is reasonable to use hidden columns for valid times and transaction times, would it not be equally reasonable to use hidden columns for other kinds of data? For example, consider a requirement to record measurements showing variation in soil acidity at various depths [9]. If we can have tables with valid-time support, should we not also be able to have, analogously, tables with valid-depth support, tables with valid-pH support, and perhaps tables with both valid-depth and valid-pH support? In fact, is there any reason to confine such facilities to hidden *interval* columns? Perhaps relvar SP in the nontemporal version of suppliers and shipments could be a table with valid-P# support (having S# as its only regular column), or a table with valid-S# support (having P# as its only regular column). Such observations might raise a smile, but we offer them for serious consideration. The fact is, as soon as we permit the first deviation from *The Information Principle*, we have opened the door—possibly the floodgates—to who knows what further indiscretions to follow.

Incidentally, lest we be accused of exaggeration in the foregoing, we would like to draw your attention to another extract from reference [1]. The authors are discussing "interesting directions for future research":

> *It would also be useful to generalize statement modifiers to dimensions other than time—for example, spatial dimensions in spatial and spatiotemporal databases, the "dimensions" in data warehousing, or the new kinds of multidimensional data models. Providing general solutions that support the specific semantics associated with the new dimensions is an important challenge.*

---

14. ATSQL [1] does have an analog of our PACK operator.

Imprecise Specification

Consider the following example once again:

```
3. VALIDTIME
   SELECT DISTINCT S.S#, SP.P#
   FROM   S, SP
   WHERE  S.S# = SP.S#
   AND    SP.P# = P#('P1')
```

We have already mentioned TSQL2's failure to specify precisely what set of rows constitutes the result of a valid-time or transaction-time query. The response usually given to this
complaint is that if all of the tables in some set of tables are equivalent, in the sense that they
yield the same result when unpacked (or packed) on some interval column, and one table in
that set is agreed to be a correct result for a given query, then any table in that set is equally
correct and can be produced as the result of the query. In other words, if tables S and SP represent precisely the information shown for relvars S and SP in Figure 28-4, then either of the
tables shown in Figure 28-6—as well as literally billions of others[15]—might be produced as the
result of the query shown above as Example 3. (It might help to point out explicitly that the
table on the left-hand side of the figure is packed on the hidden valid-time column.)

S#	P#	
S1	P1	[d04:d10]
S2	P1	[d02:d04]
S2	P1	[d08:d10]

S#	P#	
S1	P1	[d04:d08]
S1	P1	[d06:d07]
S1	P1	[d05:d10]
S1	P1	[d04:d09]
S2	P1	[d02:d03]
S2	P1	[d04:d04]
S2	P1	[d08:d10]

Figure 28-6. *Two possible results for Example 3*

But the foregoing position is surely unacceptable. The various results that are regarded as
equally correct under the given equivalence relationship are distinguishable from one another
in SQL. Even the cardinality, unless it happens to be zero (or possibly one), is not constant over
all of those results! It follows that, in general, TSQL2's temporal queries (and modifications too,
presumably) are *indeterminate*.

That said, the problem can easily be addressed by specifying, for example, some suitably
packed form to be the actual result. Therefore, we do not regard this fault in TSQL2, astonishing

---

15. Actually the upper bound is infinite, since SQL tables can have duplicate rows. Even if we ignore duplicate
rows, however, the number of possible results is still astronomical; in the case at hand, for example,
there are over 137,438,953,472 such possible results—and this figure is just a lower bound. (In case you
are interested, an upper bound for the same example is over a trillion—1,099,511,627,776, to be precise.)

though it is, as in itself militating against the whole approach. We think the other reasons we have given are sufficient to do that.

Concluding Remarks

We have presented a brief overview and analysis of TSQL2 and found much in it to criticize. In fact, we have two broad (and orthogonal) sets of criticisms: one having to do with the overall approach in general, and one having to do with the language's poor fit with SQL specifically (even more specifically, with certain of the features that were added in SQL:1999—for example, triggers, row types, and "typed tables"). In this chapter, we have concentrated on the first of these two sets of criticisms; for a discussion of the second, see references [2], [3], and [4].

By way of conclusion, we repeat in summary form some of our biggest criticisms from the first category.

- *Regarding "the central idea":* Even if we accept for the sake of argument that TSQL2 succeeds in its objective of simplifying the formulation of queries that satisfy Conditions *C1–C4*, it is surely obvious that there are many, many queries that fail to satisfy those conditions.

- *Regarding temporal upward compatibility:* Here we reject the very idea that the goal might be desirable, let alone achievable. In particular, we reject the idea that just "adding temporal support" is a good way to design temporal databases, because (a) it leads to the bundling of current and historical data, and (b) it leads to relvars (tables) that are not in 6NF. Further, we reject the notion that "current operations" should work exactly as they did before, because that notion leads to the notion of hidden columns and (apparently) to the notion of statement modifiers.

- *Regarding statement modifiers:* We have discussed at great length our reasons for believing this concept to be logically flawed. Furthermore, we do not believe it can be fixed.

- *Regarding hidden columns:* We have discussed this issue at considerable length, too. Hidden columns are a logical consequence of the objective of temporal upward compatibility—but they constitute the clearest possible violation of *The Information Principle*, and they lead directly to many of TSQL2's other problems.

References

1. Michael H. Böhlen, Christian S. Jensen, and Richard T. Snodgrass: "Temporal Statement Modifiers," *ACM TODS 25*, No. 4 (December 2000).

2. Hugh Darwen: "Valid Time and Transaction Time Proposals: Language Design Aspects," in reference [7].

3. Hugh Darwen, Mike Sykes, *et al.*: "Concerns about the TSQL2 Approach to Temporal Databases," Kansas City, Mo. (May 1996); ftp://sqlstandards.org/SC32/WG3/Meetings/MCI_1996_05_KansasCity_USA/mci071.ps.

A precursor to reference [4]. As explained in the body of the chapter, a major part of the rationale for TSQL2 was *temporal upward compatibility* (TUC). Briefly, TUC means that it should be possible to convert an existing nontemporal database into a temporal one by just "adding temporal support," and then have existing nontemporal applications still run (and run correctly) against the now temporal database. Among other things, this paper [3] raises questions as to whether TUC is even a sensible goal, and some of the arguments it makes in this connection are worth summarizing here. Consider the following example. Suppose we start with an SQL table EMP, with columns EMP#, DEPT#, and SALARY. Suppose we now "add valid time support" to that table as described in the body of the chapter, so that every existing EMP row is timestamped with the valid-time value (a *period* or interval value) "from now till the end of time." But:

■ The table is not yet telling the truth (as reference [3] puts it), since, in general, existing employees did not join the company or move to their current department or reach their current salary "now." So those valid-time timestamps all need to be updated, somehow.

■ The table is also not yet telling the truth in that it contains rows only for current employees and current department assignments and current salary levels. All of the historical information for previous employees and previous departments and previous salaries needs to be added, somehow.

■ We cannot tell for any given row whether the timestamp shows when the employee moved to the indicated department, or when the employee reached the indicated salary, or perhaps even when the employee joined the company. It is thus likely that the table will need to be vertically decomposed into three separate tables (one each for employment history, department history, and salary history), as explained in reference [6].

■ What would happen if—as is not at all unlikely—table EMP already included columns DATE_OF_JOINING_DEPT and DATE_OF_LAST_INCREASE before the "valid-time support" was added?

■ Even if all of the foregoing issues can be addressed successfully, we are left with tables that represent both history and the current state of affairs. It is thus likely that each such table will need to be split into two, as described in reference [6].

The net effect of the foregoing points (it seems to us) is that

a. Converting a nontemporal database to a temporal counterpart involves—necessarily—much more than just "adding temporal support,"

and hence that, in general,

b. Having existing applications run unchanged after such a conversion is not a very realistic goal.

4. Hugh Darwen, Mike Sykes, *et al.*: "On Proposals for Valid-Time and Transaction-Time Support," Madrid, Spain (January 1997); ftp://sqlstandards.org/SC32/WG3/Meetings/MAD_1997_01_Madrid_ESP/mad146.ps.

   The "U.K. response" to reference [13].

5. C. J. Date and Hugh Darwen: *A Guide to the SQL Standard* (4th edition). Reading, Mass.: Addison-Wesley (1997).

6. C. J. Date, Hugh Darwen, and Nikos A. Lorentzos: *Temporal Data and the Relational Model*. San Francisco, Calif.: Morgan Kaufmann (2003).

   The present chapter was originally prepared as an appendix to this book, though it has been edited to make it stand by itself as far as possible.

7. Opher Etzion, Sushil Jajodia, and Suryanaryan Sripada (eds.): *Temporal Databases: Research and Practice*. New York, N.Y.: Springer-Verlag (1998).

   This book is an anthology giving "the state of the temporal database art" as of about 1997. It is divided into four major parts, as follows:

   a. Temporal Database Infrastructure

   b. Temporal Query Languages

   c. Advanced Applications of Temporal Databases

   d. General Reference

8. International Organization for Standardization (ISO): *Database Language SQL*, Document ISO/IEC 9075:1999. Also available as American National Standards Institute (ANSI) Document ANSI NCITS.135-1999.

9. Nikos A. Lorentzos and Vassiliki J. Kollias: "The Handling of Depth and Time Intervals in Soil Information Systems," *Comp. Geosci. 15*, 3 (1989).

10. Richard Snodgrass and Ilsoo Ahn: "A Taxonomy of Time in Databases," Proc. ACM SIGMOD Int. Conf. on Management of Data, Austin, Texas (May 1985).

    The source of the terms *transaction time, valid time*, and *user-defined time*. *Note:* Transaction time and valid time are discussed at length in reference [6], but "user-defined time" is not. Reference [10] defines this term to mean temporal values and attributes that are "not interpreted by the DBMS"; examples are date of birth, date of last salary increase, or time of arrival. Observe, however, that in the approach to temporal databases espoused and described in reference [6], transaction times and valid times are also— like all other values and attributes!—" not interpreted by the DBMS." While it might make sense to have a term for "times" that are neither transaction times nor valid times, the idea that "user-defined times" are *operationally* different from the others makes sense only if we start by assuming a nonrelational approach to the temporal database problem in the first place.

11. R. T. Snodgrass *et al.*: "TSQL2 Language Specification," *ACM SIGMOD Record 23*, No. 1 (March 1994).

12. Richard T. Snodgrass (ed.): *The TSQL2 Temporal Query Language*. Norwell, Mass.: Kluwer Academic Publishers (1995).

13. Richard T. Snodgrass, Michael H. Böhlen, Christian S. Jensen, and Andreas Steiner: "Adding Valid Time to SQL/Temporal" and "Adding Transaction Time to SQL/Temporal," Madrid, Spain (January 1997); `ftp://sqlstandards.org/SC32/WG3/Meetings/MAD_1997_01_Madrid_ESP/mad146.ps`.

14. Richard T. Snodgrass, Michael H. Böhlen, Christian S. Jensen, and Andreas Steiner: "Transitioning Temporal Support in TSQL2 to SQL3," in reference [7].

15. Richard T. Snodgrass: *Developing Time-Oriented Database Applications in SQL*. San Francisco, Calif.: Morgan Kaufmann (2000).

The following remarks on temporal database design are taken from this reference (we find them interesting inasmuch as they describe an approach that is diametrically opposite to that advocated in reference [6]): "In the approach that we espouse here, conceptual design initially ignores the time-varying nature of the applications. We focus on capturing the *current reality* and temporarily ignore any history that may be useful to capture. This selective amnesia somewhat simplifies what is often a highly complex task of capturing the full semantics ... An added benefit is that existing conceptual design methodologies apply in full ... Only after the full design is complete do we augment the ER [= *entity/relationship*] schema with ... time-varying semantics ... Similarly, logical design proceeds in two stages. First, the nontemporal ER schema is mapped to a nontemporal relational schema, a collection of tables ... In the second stage, each of the [temporal annotations on the otherwise nontemporal ER schema] is applied to the logical schema, modifying the tables or integrity constraints to accommodate that temporal aspect."

■ ■ ■

The Role of the Trade Press in Educating the Professional Community: A Case Study

If you think education is expensive, consider the alternative.

—Anon.

If this book has an overriding theme, it is that the database community in general is in desperate need of more and better education—indeed, it has been so ever since its inception. This appendix, first written in 1993 and substantially revised in 2000, is, sadly, all too relevant to that theme.

Overview

During the summer of 1993, a series of items appeared in the trade paper (or journal) *Computerworld* on the general topic of relational *vs.* object-oriented database management. The chronology of events was as follows.

1. First of all, at the request of Fabian Pascal (who was writing an article for inclusion in a forthcoming special "Object-Oriented Programming" feature issue of *Computerworld*), I wrote a short position paper entitled "Relational *vs.* Object-Oriented: Not an Either/Or Decision" (final draft dated March 12th, 1993). The idea was for that position paper to accompany Fabian's piece, thereby lending additional weight to the arguments he was propounding in his own article. The intent behind my paper (as with most of the technical material I write) was primarily to *educate:* more specifically, to try to introduce some clear thinking into an area where most discussions still seemed to suffer from the "more heat than light" syndrome. The original draft of that paper is included in this appendix as Exhibit A.

2. *Computerworld* chose not to publish my paper as written, but instead published an edited and abbreviated version, with a different title ("A Fruitful Union"). While the editing—which was done without any consultation with myself, I might add—did not significantly change the message of the original draft, it did omit a few key points and it did alter the emphasis in some of what remained. (It also introduced some pretty slipshod writing, but let that pass.) That edited version, which appeared in the June 14th, 1993, issue of *Computerworld*, is included herein as Exhibit B.

3. Two weeks later (June 28th, 1993), *Computerworld's* technical editor Charles Babcock commented on the same subject in his regular *Computerworld* column, under the heading "Relational Backlash." His comments, it seemed to me, were definitely in the "more heat than light" category—a fact I found both sad and rather annoying, given (a) my own position as stated in print, with supporting arguments, in his own newspaper only two weeks previously, and given also (b) the responsibility, as I see it, of writers in influential positions such as Babcock's to do their best to educate their readers instead of pandering to a taste, real or perceived, for controversy. Babcock's article is reproduced as Exhibit C.

4. On June 29th, 1993, in response to Babcock's article, I wrote a letter to the editor of *Computerworld*, which was published in abbreviated form on July 12th, 1993. Exhibit D is the letter as originally written, Exhibit E is the version that was published.

5. The published version of the letter provoked a somewhat shrill response from a reader (Donald Burleson, *Computerworld*, August 2nd, 1993). I leave it to readers of this appendix to note how the omissions from my original paper and from my letter enabled Burleson to make some of the comments he did. Burleson's letter (at least as published—probably his original was edited too) is attached as Exhibit F.

6. I wrote a reply to Burleson's letter and sent it with a cover note to the editor of *Computerworld* (August 2nd, 1993). That letter was never published, nor even acknowledged. See Exhibit G.

7. Subsequently, another response to Babcock's column and to my July 12th letter was published (James Barnett, *Computerworld*, August 23rd, 1993). Comments similar to those under paragraph 5 above apply here also. See Exhibit H.

8. I wrote a reply to Barnett's letter and sent it with a cover note to the editor of *Computerworld* (August 24th, 1993). As with my August 2nd letter, that letter was neither published nor acknowledged. See Exhibit I.

The Saga Continues

The day after I completed the first draft of this account, I opened up the most recent issue of *Computerworld* to find a follow-up column by Charles Babcock on the same topic, entitled "SQL *vs.* Objects" (see Exhibit J). Regrettably, though perhaps unsurprisingly, this new column also fell into the "more heat than light" category. In particular, it included, and commented on, a couple of quotes from my own paper as published (i.e., as reproduced in Exhibit B). As might be expected, the comments were, on the whole, less than favorable. What's more, the first of the two passages quoted had been subtly changed in the published version (I had written "implemented," but the editor had changed it to "implements"—compare Exhibits A and B), and that apparently trivial change made it possible for Babcock to take a very cheap shot at my original claims.

The rest of Babcock's column contained numerous errors and misleading statements. Detailed discussion of those errors *per se* would be beyond the scope of the present appendix; however, I have to say that I find it extraordinary that *Computerworld* should refuse to publish—and publish *verbatim*—the carefully considered opinions of someone who has made a lengthy study of the subject, and at the same time see fit to give someone like Babcock the space to pontificate on a topic on which he clearly displays little real understanding.

Conclusions

What are we to conclude from all of the foregoing? Well, I'm only too well aware that any claim by a writer of shabby treatment at the hands of the media tends to smack of special pleading, and runs the risk of making the claimant appear ridiculous. And I'm also well aware that, in the case under discussion, the letters I wrote were at least as much an attempt at self-defense as they were an attempt to educate; a critic might therefore argue that I'm merely suffering from wounded pride. But reading through the exhibits in their entirety, it's hard to escape the impression that (in the case at hand, at least) *Computerworld* was more interested in controversy for its own sake than it was in the dissemination of truly useful information. Certainly it published more in the way of dissenting opinion—ill-informed, unsubstantiated, and incorrect opinion at that—than it did in the way of reasoned argument or material that was genuinely trying to educate the readership.

I'll leave it to readers of this appendix to judge whether this was an isolated incident or the norm. For my own part, I'd like to continue to believe that there are still some trade publications that take their responsibilities seriously; my criticisms are reserved specifically for those that behave as *Computerworld* did in the case at hand. Be that as it may, here are some of the lessons I've learned from my experience in this particular case:

1. Technical articles and letters intended for publication in the trade press, no matter how carefully argued from a technical standpoint and no matter how carefully written, are likely to be altered for publication by editorial staff who don't understand either the substance or the merits of the material in question (and often have a tin ear to boot).

2. Many aspects of the IT field are not well understood by the professional community at large, and the quality of debate is thus often not very high either. Evidence for both of these claims can readily be found in the case under discussion. This state of affairs is hardly surprising, however (and moreover is unlikely to change), given the apparent lack of interest on the part of the trade press—or certain portions thereof, at least—in trying to improve the situation.

3. I will be very wary in the future of relying on the trade press for enlightenment on any technical subject.

This marks the end of the body of this appendix. Exhibits A–J follow immediately.

Exhibit A

Original draft of "Relational vs. Object-Oriented: Not an Either/Or Decision," by C. J. Date (March 12th, 1993):

Where is database technology headed? Some pundits have predicted the imminent demise of relational, claiming that today's relational systems are just too simplistic for the complex databases we need in the 1990s, and have jumped with both feet on to the object-oriented (OO) bandwagon. "The world is much too complex to be represented in flat relational tables" is a typical claim heard from this camp. On the other hand, relational advocates have been defending their position stoutly, arguing the importance of relational's solid theoretical foundation, and pointing out—with some justice—that in certain respects OO technology represents a giant step backward.

Well, I have some good news: We can have our cake and eat it too! Relational *vs.* OO is not an either/or decision—despite the fact that certain people have a vested interest in presenting it as if it were. The fact is, there are two technologies out there, relational and object-oriented, and we should be looking for ways to marry them together, instead of throwing mud at each other. The advantages and benefits of relational are well known; and object-oriented too has many good features, such as inheritance, that are missing from today's relational products. (It would be wrong not to point out in passing that inheritance in particular was proposed for relational systems as far back as 1976. As so often, there is a significant gap between what the technology is theoretically capable of and what the products actually deliver.)

Mind you, object-oriented has some very bad features too! This is not the place to go into details, but such matters as data integrity, optimization, views, and the catalog all represent areas where the object-oriented community has a good deal of work to do to catch up with relational technology. (Indeed, the foregoing might be too charitable. There are some serious questions as to whether such catching up is even feasible if we discard the solid relational foundation, as some OO people seem to be advocating.)

So when I talk of marrying the technologies together, what I mean is that we should be trying to extend relational systems to incorporate the GOOD features of OO. Obviously, I do not want to do this at the expense of having to incorporate the BAD features as well. And let me stress the point also that I am talking about a marriage of *technologies,* not of *products.* I am not pretending that a clean integration between OO product *X* and relational product *Y* is a simple matter, or even achievable, or even necessarily a good thing.

So how are we to meet this desirable goal? Well, the fundamental construct in OO systems is the **object class,** which is (in general) a user-defined, encapsulated data type of arbitrary internal complexity.[1] *Note:* I use the term "data type" here in the sense in which that term is understood in modern programming languages. In particular, I take it to imply that instances of the data type in question can be manipulated only by certain **operators** whose definitions are also provided by the user. I am NOT referring just to primitive, system-defined (i.e., built-in) data types like INTEGER and CHAR.

What about relational systems? Well, here the fundamental construct—mostly not implemented, unfortunately, in today's relational products—is the **domain.** And a domain is (in general) a user-defined, encapsulated data type of arbitrary internal complexity ... In other

---

1. *Note added in 2000:* This sentence is a little misleading. An object class is just a data type, either user- *or system*-defined. User-defined is the more general case, of course, which is why the original sentence included that "in general" qualifier.

words, a domain and an object class are *the same thing!* In my opinion, therefore, domains are the key to achieving our "desirable goal." A relational system that implemented domains properly would be able to do all of the things that OO advocates claim that OO systems can do and relational systems cannot. Thus, criticisms of relational from OO advocates may well be accurate if they are taken as criticisms of today's products, but they are NOT accurate if they are taken as criticisms of the potential of the technology.

To sum up: Relational vendors should do all in their power to extend their systems to include proper domain support. Indeed, an argument can be made that the whole reason we are getting into this somewhat nonproductive debate on the relative merits of OO and relational is precisely because the relational vendors have failed so far to support the relational model adequately. But this fact should not be seen as an argument for abandoning relational entirely. It would be a great shame to walk away from the experience gained from over 20 years of solid relational research and development.

Exhibit B

Edited version of the paper shown in Exhibit A as published in Computerworld *("A Fruitful Union," by C. J. Date, June 14th, 1993):*

Where is database technology headed? Some pundits have predicted the imminent demise of relational databases. They claim today's relational systems are just too simplistic for the complex databases we need in the 1990s and have jumped with both feet onto the object-oriented bandwagon.

"The world is much too complex to be represented in flat relational tables" is a typical claim heard from this camp. On the other hand, relational advocates have been defending their position stoutly, arguing the importance of relational's solid theoretical foundation and pointing out that in certain respects, object-oriented technology represents a giant step backward.

Well, I have some good news: We can have our cake and eat it, too! The point is to marry the two technologies instead of throwing mud at each other.

When I talk of marrying the technologies, I mean we should try to extend relational systems to incorporate the good features of object orientation and shun the bad. Let me stress that I am talking about a marriage of technologies, not of products. I am not pretending a clean integration between object-oriented product *X* and relational product *Y* is a simple matter—or even achievable or a good thing.

So how are we to meet this desirable goal? By looking for what the two have in common.

The fundamental construct in object-oriented systems is the object class, which is (in general) a user-defined, encapsulated data type of arbitrary internal complexity. (*Note:* I use the term data type here in the sense in which that term is understood in modern programming languages. In particular, it means only certain operators, whose definitions are provided by the users, can manipulate instances of the data type in question. I am not referring just to primitive, system-defined, built-in data types such as Integer and Char.)

In relational systems, the fundamental construct is the domain, which for the most part is not implemented in today's relational products. In general, a domain is a user-defined, encapsulated data type of arbitrary internal complexity—i.e., a domain and an object class are the same.

In my opinion, therefore, domains are the key to achieving our "desirable goal." A relational system that implements domains properly would be able to do all of the things that object-oriented advocates claim that object-oriented systems can do and relational systems cannot. Thus, criticisms of relational from object-oriented advocates may well be accurate if they are taken as criticisms of today's products; however, they are not accurate if they are taken as criticisms of the potential of the technology.

Relational vendors should do everything in their power to extend their systems to include proper domain support. Indeed, you can make an argument that the whole reason we are getting into this debate on the relative merits of object-oriented and relational is precisely because the relational vendors have failed so far to support the relational model adequately. But this fact shouldn't be an argument for abandoning relational entirely. It would be a great shame to walk away from the experience gained from more than 20 years of solid relational research and development.

Exhibit C

Charles Babcock's "Commentary" column from Computerworld *("Relational Backlash," June 28th, 1993):*

You know that what used to be the younger generation isn't so young any more when its leaders start taking shots at the talent coming up behind them. That's what's happening now with some of the proponents of relational databases as they train their sights on object database management systems (ODBMS).

This is strange because at one time, the hoary guardians of hierarchical and Codasyl systems said the same sort of things about relational. John Cullinane, president of the late Cullinet Software, used to tell me, "IBM may ship a lot of copies of DB2 but they're all sitting on the customers' shelves." *Right.* Cullinet was acquired by Computer Associates about a year later.

Once again, you can hear the volume of disparaging comments beginning to pick up: "You don't need object-oriented systems. Relational can do everything they can do … You can store unstructured data in relational tables … Object-oriented results in a loss of data independence, not a gain." And so on.

It is hard for relational advocates, having been on the leading edge for 10 to 12 years, to wake up and find that fashionable opinion has moved on to something else. The temptation is to tell the upstarts they don't know what they're talking about.

At their worst, the relational defenders say ODBMSs represent a step backward. ODBMSs resemble the old Codasyl databases with their dependence on pointers to locate stored objects, but it is hard to see this as a vice if the systems then manage objects effectively.

Object databases answered a real need for C++ and Smalltalk programmers who needed a place to store their persistent data. CAD and CAE users in particular sought to store objects, and object-oriented databases sprang up to serve that purpose.

Whatever their deficiencies, ODBMSs succeed in dealing with objects as objects. They do not need to break them down or flatten them as relational systems do. There are a variety of methods used, but the chief one is to assign each object its own identifier and then use that identifier to locate the object intact.

The nature of this system gives object databases a claim to speedier retrieval because there is no mathematical basis on which to do more sophisticated operations such as joins. Clearly relational systems would retain advantages in dealing with massive amounts of tabular data. But relational advocates are reluctant to give object databases their due.

ODBMSs are built as object-handling systems capable of preserving the characteristics of the objects they store—classes, inheritance and messaging.

Because objects are a combination of data, processes and messages, it is difficult to restrict them to a few simple data types. To store an object, "you have to have the processes inside the database as well as the data," notes James Odell, chief methodologist at Inference Corp. and co-author with James Martin of *Principles of Object-Oriented Analysis and Design*.

Relational systems can store objects, but to do so, they must break them down into components and store them in tables. In an analogy that originated with Esther Dyson, editor of the newsletter "Release 1.0," this is like driving your car home and then disassembling it to put it in the garage. It can always be reassembled again in the morning, but one eventually asks whether this is the most efficient way to park a car.

Relational systems were designed to deal with a few data types within the confines of a strict logic. Object databases were designed to deal with the rich variety of data types in a few limited ways. Relational advocates can't wave a magic wand and make the difference go away.

Exhibit D

There were many, many statements in Babcock's column that I would have liked to refute or at least comment on, but in my letter to Computerworld *I concentrated on what seemed to me to be the most important points. The original (June 29th, 1993) draft of that letter follows:*

Well, I guess I'm a "hoary guardian" of relational technology ... I refer to Charles Babcock's column "Relational Backlash" [CW, June 28]. But the analogy of disassembling your car to park it and reassembling it in the morning is just as hoary—and what's more, it's WRONG. Relational technology does *not* necessarily require complex objects to be broken down into components to be stored in the database (see my article "A Fruitful Union" [CW, June 14]). Let me repeat the point: A relational system that supported **domains** properly would be able to all the things that OO systems can do. Moreover, it would still be a relational system and would enjoy all the usual relational advantages.

Also, the implication of Babcock's column that "OO is to relational as relational was to CODASYL" (paraphrased) is completely false and very misleading. Relational displaced CODASYL because it had a solid theoretical foundation and CODASYL did not—and that foundation led in turn to solid practical benefits. OO does not have a comparable foundation. And yes, relational defenders do say that OO represents a step backward—in some ways (e.g., the CODASYL flavor), though not in others (e.g., inheritance).

To paraphrase Babcock again: Relational technology was designed to deal with *arbitrary* data types (not "a few" data types) within the confines of a strict logic (this latter part is correct). What we want is for current relational systems to be extended to include the good features— but not the bad features!—of OO technology. OO advocates cannot wave a magic wand and make the bad features go away.

Exhibit E

This is the letter from Exhibit D as it actually appeared in print ("Reader Backlash," by C. J. Date, July 12th, 1993):

Well, I guess I'm a "hoary guardian" of relational technology, according to Charles Babcock's column "Relational backlash" [CW, June 28]. But the analogy of disassembling your car to park it and reassembling it in the morning is just as hoary—and what's more, it's *wrong*.

Relational technology does *not* necessarily require complex objects to be broken down into components to be stored in the database (see my article "A Fruitful Union," CW, June 14). A relational system that supported domains properly would be able to all the things that object-oriented systems can do. Moreover, it would still be a relational system and would enjoy all the usual relational advantages.

Also, the implication of Babcock's column that "object orientation is to relational as relational was to Codasyl" is completely false. Relational displaced Codasyl because it had a solid theoretical foundation and Codasyl did not—and that foundation led in turn to solid practical benefits. Object orientation does not have a comparable foundation.

Exhibit F

Letter in Computerworld *from Donald Burleson, Rochester, NY ("Relational Redux [sic],"* *August 2nd, 1993):*

I was very surprised to see C. J. Date's naive response to Charles Babcock's "Relational backlash" [Letters to the editor, CW, July 12].

Mr. Babcock's analogy about disassembling a car every time it is driven is an excellent example of the overhead that relational systems impose on the computer industry. Relational databases have never been known as high-speed engines, and atomic data items that are shared by many logical objects do indeed require overhead.

It is ludicrous for Date to imply that proper "domain" support within a relational database would allow a relational database to do all the things an object-oriented database can do. I have yet to see any relational database that can fully support polymorphism or multiple inheritance. Most important, it is very difficult to "shoehorn" a relational database to support the encapsulation of behaviors.

Contrary to Date's assertion about the similarity of Codasyl [Conference of Data Systems Languages] to object technology, it is very clear he missed the point. Both models use pointers to link data items together, thereby reducing the overhead of reassembling the objects.

Object-oriented databases also share the concept of "currency" with Codasyl databases. Currency allows users to see where they are in the database, and the failure of the relational model to support currency is a major drawback.

Finally, Date alleges that the relational model is built on a sound theoretical foundation. Anyone who has read E. F. Codd's criteria for relational databases knows that attempts to apply mathematical rigor to the relational model fall apart in practice.

Relational databases sacrifice performance to remain flexible, and object technology databases sacrifice flexibility to gain performance. Much of this argument reminds me of the Codasyl bashing that was going on when the first commercial relational databases were introduced.

Exhibit G

Cover note to my letter to the editor of Computerworld *replying to Burleson's letter* *(August 2nd, 1993):*

The attached is submitted for publication in the *Computerworld* "letters to the editor" column. It is a reply to some comments on a previous letter. Since portions of my original letter were omitted from the published version and those omissions distorted my message somewhat, I would appreciate your publishing this reply in its entirety. Thank you.

The letter itself (which was not published) ran as follows:

It was with some reluctance that I ventured to comment (Letters to the Editor, CW, July 12th) on Charles Babcock's "Relational Backlash" column of June 28th, since I strongly suspected that anything I said would be misunderstood. And I was right. Now, I certainly don't want to get into a lengthy debate in your columns, but Donald Burleson's letter (CW, August 2nd) demands a response.

1. First of all, I don't think it's appropriate to characterize someone's opinions as "naive" or "ludicrous" when you manifestly either don't understand them and/or haven't bothered to read them properly.

2. I stand by my claim that a relational DBMS with proper domain support would be able to do all the (good) things an OODBMS can do. Burleson's remark that he has "yet to see any relational [DBMS] that can fully support polymorphism" in no way invalidates that claim, and betrays a lack of clear thinking. Ditto for the remarks about "disassembling a car every time it is driven."

3. I did not assert that CODASYL and OO technology were similar; I asserted that the suggestion that OO would replace relational just as relational replaced CODASYL was false.

4. The claim that relational DBMSs "sacrifice performance to remain flexible" is a hoary old canard. See, e.g., Tandem's NonStop SQL, Teradata's DBC/1012, etc., for some commercial counterexamples.

5. "Attempts to apply mathematical rigor to the relational model fall apart in practice"? Does Mr. Burleson really mean what he seems to be saying here? If so, I don't think he knows what the relational model is.

Exhibit H

Letter in Computerworld *from James R. Barnett, Deerfield, Ill. ("OOP Objections,"*
August 23rd, 1993):

After reading Charles Babcock's article "Relational backlash" [CW, June 28] and C. J. Date's previous article "A fruitful union" [CW, June 14], about the merits of object *vs.* relational DBMS, it is my opinion that neither Mr. Date nor Mr. Babcock is completely correct.

The bottom line is not whether one technology is better, but which technology best supports the requirements of the system being developed.

I do agree with Mr. Date's statement that "relational vendors should do everything within their power to include proper domain support." However, his assertion that this would allow relational systems to do everything object-oriented DBMSs are capable of just isn't true. A domain and an object class are not the same!

True domain support would still not allow the complex data types found in object-oriented systems. It would also not provide a mechanism for defining the valid methods for an object class. It would also not support object class hierarchies, which are the foundation of an object-oriented approach.

Mr. Date's suggestion that relational is the better technology because it has a solid theoretical foundation and object oriented does not is a valid point. Object oriented may not have the same mathematical foundation; however, it's a more natural representation of the way people think and organize objects in the real world.

Exhibit I

Cover note to my letter to the editor of Computerworld *replying to Barnett's letter (August 24th, 1993):*

You saw fit not to print my recent letter responding to some remarks made by Donald Burleson (CW, August 2nd) criticizing—in a most ill-informed and *ad hominem* way—my short article "A Fruitful Union" (CW, June 14th). Please restore my faith in *Computerworld*'s commitment to the dissemination of accurate, timely, and relevant technical commentary by publishing the attached letter in its entirety. Thank you.

The letter itself (which was not published) ran as follows:

With reference to the letter from James Barnett (Letters to the Editor, CW, August 23rd): A domain and an object class are the same. True domain support would allow "the complex data types found in object-oriented systems." It would provide "a mechanism for defining the valid methods for an object class." It would support "object class hierarchies."

It is unfortunate that so few people seem to understand these simple facts. It is not however unexpected, given the low quality of much of the public debate in this area. Mr. Barnett's letter does nothing to improve the quality of that debate.

Exhibit J

Charles Babcock's "Meta View" column from Computerworld *("SQL vs. Objects," September 6th, 1993):*

Object-oriented systems are gaining ground in some progressive IS shops, but their use is hampered by the fact that business data residing in relational database systems is not easily available to them. RDBMSs do not support the manipulation of objects, which means the data must be kept in two places or clumsily transferred in and out of the relational systems.

For several years, relational vendors have been saying not to worry, object support is just around the corner. But as you listen to some relational authorities, their responses on this question start to sound suspicious. Instead of getting a time frame for object support, one tends to get a put-down of the young object-oriented DBMSs.

In the June 14 issue of *Computerworld*, expert [*sic*] C. J. Date stated, "A relational system that implements domains properly would be able to do all the things that object-oriented advocates claim object-oriented systems can do ... ." This statement may be true as far as it goes, but it begs a very simple question: Which relational systems implement domains properly? The answer is, "none using SQL," which covers all the relational systems in commercial use.

Date carried the argument a step further in a July 12 letter to the editor when he said: "Relational technology does not necessarily require complex objects to be broken down into components to be stored in the database."

No, theories about the relational model *don't* require it, but SQL *does*. Which do you suppose database programmers are building their new systems with?

Let's take a look at the SQL problem. In its initial implementation, SQL supported a handful of simple data types on which it could carry out its SELECT, JOIN and other operations. When the standard was expanded by the ANSI X3H2 committee in 1992, more complex data types were added, such as date/time, which could be made up of several pieces of data, all stored in a single field. But date/time is still a far cry from the unpredictable, user-defined mix of data types found in objects.

The closest relational systems get to dealing with objects is the binary large object, also known as a Blob, which sort of sounds like the real thing but is actually a baby step in the right direction. Blobs tend to be images, long text strings, video or voice stored as a uniform data type in a kind of "binary bucket," in the words of Fred Carter, chief architect at Ingres.

Storing and retrieving Blobs is not the same thing as full-fledged support of object-class libraries. The database management system can do little with a Blob except put it away and retrieve it. It usually takes an application to seize the data and reconstruct it into an image, etc.

This limitation will give way as the ANSI X3H2 committee adds object support to the next version of SQL. SQL III may be published in 1995, "but more likely in 1996,"[2] says Jim Melton, a Digital database architect who serves as editor for the committee.

Oracle is playing an active role before X3H2 and is committed to including object support in Oracle8. Company spokesmen estimate Oracle8 will be available in early 1995. Informix, a pioneer in the field, also won't wait for the standard to be published before it adds object management features.

But all of this remains somewhat up in the stratosphere. No one knows for sure when any vendor will have object support or how extensive that support will be. And the ANSI committee must act if support is to be uniform. ANSI panels have been known to fall behind their timetables on less complicated matters than this.

To my mind, the interest in object-oriented programming has caught the relational vendors somewhat unawares. Their systems cannot be replaced willy-nilly by object-oriented database systems, and I do not know of any users contemplating doing so. But then again, some users will have to wait two to three years before an ingredient they need is added to their systems.

Postscript

To say it again, the exchanges described above took place in 1993, but I believe the overall message is just as relevant now as it was then. Note in particular that—as I hope you will agree—subsequent events in the IT field have tended to support the point of view I was trying to express in the paper I originally wrote (Exhibit A). To summarize the current situation:[3]

---

2. *Note added in 2000:* In fact it was 1999, and late 1999 at that—and it would have been much later still, if the decision to publish had been based on technical considerations rather than political ones. From a technical point of view, SQL:1999 was, and still is, very seriously flawed. (This is not just my own opinion. Indeed, the SQL committee was *already* working on a major Technical Corrigendum at the very time the standard was being ratified! That Corrigendum has yet to appear, so whether it will address any of the really fundamental problems is unknown; my own guess is that it probably won't.)

3. "Current" here originally meant 2000, but I believe my assessments are even more valid today (2006).

- Pure object-oriented DBMSs are now mostly seen for what they really were all along: *viz.*, as "DBMSs" that are *specific to some particular application area*, not general-purpose ones (and thus not true DBMSs, as that term is usually understood in the IT community, at all). As such, they might have a useful role to play in certain circumstances, but—to repeat—they aren't true general-purpose DBMSs, and they represent something of a niche market. Certainly they'll never replace relational DBMSs.

- By contrast, "object/relational" DBMSs *are* true general-purpose DBMSs that do provide both relational and object capabilities. As I was saying all along, we really can have our cake and eat it too! And as Hugh Darwen and I have written elsewhere,[4] the idea of integrating relational and object technologies in such a manner is not just another fad, soon to be replaced by some other briefly fashionable idea. *Au contraire*, we believe an object/relational system is in everyone's future.

- Of course, I feel bound to add that (to quote from that same book by Hugh Darwen and myself again), a true "object/relational" DBMS would be nothing more nor less than a true *relational* DBMS—which is to say, a DBMS that supports the relational model, with all that such support entails (in particular, it entails proper *domain* support). The trouble is, the term "relational DBMS" has effectively been usurped by systems that are *SQL* DBMSs merely, so we need a new term ... Hence the "object/relational" terminology.

- Finally, it does need to be said that, unfortunately, the vendors are (once again) getting it wrong! I refer to the fact that every object/relational product on the market—at least, every one I'm aware of—is committing at least one of **The Two Great Blunders**. For details, I refer you once again to the book by Hugh Darwen and myself already mentioned a couple of times above; here I just want to raise the question: *Why* are the vendors getting it wrong? The answer, it seems to me, is because the relational model is so widely misunderstood. Why is it so widely misunderstood? Because of the lack of good education. Why is that good education lacking? ... *Now go back to the beginning of this appendix (starting with the title!) and read it all over again.*

---

4. C. J. Date and Hugh Darwen, *Databases, Types, and the Relational Model: The Third Manifesto,* 3rd edition. Reading, Mass.: Addison-Wesley, 2006.

Index

CPSIA information can be obtained at www.ICGtesting.com
Printed in the USA
LVOW120727090612

285379LV00005B/3/P